International Law and Economics

The world has been experiencing a long period of globalization. At the same time, ever more international law has been created to deal with the many consequences of globalization such as problems of coordination, spillover effects across countries, the protection of foreign direct investment or the prosecution of crimes against humanity. To date, the economic analysis of international law has been lagging behind this development. This series aims at changing this by contributing to the understanding of international law. It strives to be a forum for contributions on all aspects of the economic analysis of international law ranging from the analysis of the genesis of international law, its ratification, its effects on government behavior, the means to monitor compliance to sanctions against actors not complying with the law.

Julia Lemke

The Protection of Community Interests in the International Law of State Responsibility

Insights from Rational Choice Theory

Springer

Julia Lemke
Institute of Law and Economics
University of Hamburg
Hamburg, Germany

ISSN 2364-1851 ISSN 2364-186X (electronic)
International Law and Economics
ISBN 978-3-031-87926-5 ISBN 978-3-031-87927-2 (eBook)
https://doi.org/10.1007/978-3-031-87927-2

This Springer imprint is published by the registered company Springer Nature Switzerland AG.
The registered company address is: Gewerbestrasse 11, 6330 Cham, Switzerland

To my parents

Preface

The international community faces a wide range of global challenges: ensuring international security (affected, for instance, by the armed conflicts in Ukraine or Gaza), protecting the environment (for example, by addressing cross-border pollution, preserving biodiversity, or countering climate change), preventing the spread of diseases, or promoting economic growth and combatting poverty. Global challenges require internationally coordinated action, as national measures alone are often insufficient to tackle cross-border problems. Over time, nation states have developed various international institutions to facilitate the provision of different types of goods on a global scale, such as peace, a clean environment, health, or prosperity, and to ultimately improve global well-being. One key instrument in the global governance framework is international law. Yet, in a decentralised legal order the creation of international legal norms and their enforcement constitute global cooperative challenges in their own right.

In times of growing nationalist movements, it remains an ongoing challenge for sovereign nation states to agree upon and uphold international legal obligations, although the difficulty to cooperate varies depending on the underlying issue. International law developed over time from a bilateral system regulating inter-state relations towards the protection of interests of the international community as a whole. The increasing number of multilateral agreements that address contemporary global challenges, for example in the field of environmental protection, reflect this community interest dimension of international law. Moreover, in the absence of a central law-enforcement power, getting states to comply with their international commitments is another difficulty. Russia's war of aggression against Ukraine is probably the most illustrative recent example of non-compliance with international law. How the adverse effects caused by breaches of international law are remediated matters significantly not only for the injured states but also for the individual victims. In addition, respect for the rule of law and the stability of the international legal order are vital interests of all states in the international community. Questions of state responsibility are thus back at the forefront of the international legal discourse.

International treaties—as the prime source of international law—can be designed in various ways: they can state specific obligations or broadly framed goals, they can foresee exceptions from international commitments in case of extraordinary circumstances, they can provide for strong or weak consequences of non-compliant behaviour, or they can contain on a procedural level a more or less developed dispute settlement system. Alternative design elements facilitate or constrain state behaviour to different degrees. And the way they set incentives for states can influence and even achieve desired state behaviour. The underlying idea of this book is thus not that we need more international law to address the global challenges of our time but effective international law, including on the appropriate remedies. Admittedly, what the 'right' law is, is a highly philosophical question: should it be just and fair, or, as law and economics scholars sometimes hold, at least in the national context, should it be (cost) efficient? These normative principles do not necessarily have to contradict each other, but from a functionalist view the law is optimal when it fulfils its objectives in the best possible way, whatever the objectives may be.

The focus of this book is on one important sub-field of international law, the law on state responsibility. Thus, it does not enquire what the international obligations of states in different substantive areas are, but how international law is effectively protected. The existing principles of state responsibility, i.e. both the customary international law that to a large extent is now reflected in the Articles on the Responsibility of States for Internationally Wrongful Acts (ARSIWA) adopted by the International Law Commission in 2001 and the rules contained in specialised treaty regimes such as the World Trade Agreements, have been widely discussed from a doctrinal perspective. However, there is limited theoretical understanding about whether and when these rules set optimal incentives for state behaviour. In fact, from an economic perspective, the law of state responsibility is a relatively unexplored area of international law. The interest of this book thus does not lie in describing what the conditions are for states to be held responsible for the harm they cause by violating international legal obligations or what consequences derive from such behaviour. In contrast, this book analyses whether and under what conditions the existing state responsibility rules are effectively fulfilling their different objectives, and by addressing shortcomings it will also suggest improvements for their interpretation and application. On a practical level, these theoretical insights might therefore offer guidance for international treaty design and for adjudicators in interstate disputes involving questions of responsibility.

Against this background, this book will take the ARSIWA as a starting point of the analysis. More than twenty years after their adoption, the international legal order has evolved further away from the traditional bilateralist model to a multilateral one, centred around the notion of community interest protection and the quest to address global challenges. The law on state responsibility, as reflected in the ARSIWA, already mirrors these developments. It contains, on the one hand, fundamental principles of dispute resolution in the bilateral context deeply enshrined in customary international law, broadly understood as the private dimension, where sovereign states interact to reconcile opposed national interests or reciprocally exchange mutual benefits. On the other hand, it includes attempts to contribute progressively to the further development of international law, in particular with regard to the so-called public dimension of international, where states cooperate to address global challenges, such as the preservation of common resources or the protection of fundamental norms of the international community (later to be defined as global public goods). In this sense, the law on state responsibility is a legal regime *sui generis*, which builds conceptually in large parts on principles of domestic liability law governing private relations, yet without distinguishing clearly between scenarios similar to contractual liability, on the one hand, and tort law, on the other. It also includes rather novel elements that are unique to the decentralised international legal order and reflect the community interest dimension (for instance, the consequences for breach of peremptory norms of international law and the specific provisions for the invocation and enforcement of state responsibility by non-directly injured third states).

The ARSIWA lack, however, a comprehensive theoretical underpinning that carefully distinguishes according to the underlying characteristics of different global cooperative challenges in both dimensions of international law. This is not to say that the law is inadequate in its entirety, but rather a pledge to go beyond the 'one-size-fits-all' approach to a more refined and systematic one. In this book, a social science approach, namely the economic analysis of (international) law and, more specifically, the method of rational choice theory, is used to analyse the incentive structures of legal norms, in this case the ARSIWA. Specifically, this book encompasses an impact analysis of the conditions for state responsibility (i.e. the standards of responsibility), the excuses and justifications for breaches of international obligations, the consequences of internationally wrongful acts (in other words, the remedies), and the implementation of state responsibility by way of countermeasures. It will enquire, in particular, how each of these aspects of state responsibility operates in the private and the public dimension of international law. The ambition is to conclude whether there are economic rationales for the fundamental customary principles of state responsibility and to make suggestions for the interpretation and future development of responsibility rules where issues were deliberately left open in the ARSIWA or consist in progressive development of international law. Ultimately, this book thus seeks to contribute to a better theoretical understanding of community interest protection in the international law of state responsibility.

Hamburg, Germany Julia Lemke

Acknowledgements

This book, which is based on my doctoral thesis, would not exist without the inspiration, advice, and encouragement of my supervisor Anne van Aaken. I owe her deepest gratitude for pointing me towards this research gap in the international law of state responsibility, helping me to bring legal and economic thinking together, providing extremely valuable feedback on earlier drafts by coupling constructive critique with kindest words of encouragement, and showing enormous patience over the many years of this research project.

Equally, I wish to thank my second supervisor Stefan Voigt for his comments on my early works and for offering me the productive research environment of the graduate school 'The Economics of the Internationalisation of the Law' at the Institute of Law and Economics in Hamburg. As part of the graduate school, the work on my doctoral thesis and my research stay abroad were funded by the German Research Foundation (DFG).

Furthermore, I want to thank Andrew Guzman for sponsoring my research stay at UC Berkeley School of Law. Among the professors who have commented on earlier versions of my thesis, I profited especially from the advice of Rachel Brewster and Nienke Grossman. André Nollkaemper provided helpful feedback during the thesis defence.

I also wish to thank my fellow doctoral students at the Institute of Law and Economics in Hamburg, at Berkeley Law, and at the Staatsbibliothek zu Berlin for useful comments on early drafts, the fruitful discussions, and the practical research advice across disciplines. I am particularly grateful to my graduate school colleagues and friends Agnes Brender and Katharina Pfaff.

Last but not least, I am thankful to my sister and brother-in-law Annika and Sven Lorenzen for providing me a home during my time in Hamburg. I also owe deepest gratitude to my dearest friend and husband Hanno Stremmel for his patience, encouragement, and infinite support. Above all, however, I am grateful to my parents, Rita and Erwin Lemke, to whom I dedicate this work for their tremendous support throughout my entire studies.

Contents

About the Author

Julia Lemke is a member of the cabinet of the European Commission Executive Vice-President for a Clean, Just and Competitive Transition, Teresa Ribera. Before this, she was a member of the cabinet of the European Commissioner for Economy, Paolo Gentiloni, and held several senior advisor positions in international and European affairs at the German Federal Ministry of Finance and the French Treasury. She completed her Doctorate in Law at the University of Hamburg, Germany, and obtained the First and Second State Examination in Law in Berlin, Germany. She also holds law degrees from the University of Paris X, Nanterre, France, and the London School of Economics and Political Science, United Kingdom, and was a visiting researcher at the University of California, Berkeley, USA.

List of Abbreviations

AJIL	American Journal of International Law
ARSIWA	Articles on the Responsibility of States for Internationally Wrongful Acts
ASEAN	Association of Southeast Asian Nations
BEPS	Base Erosion and Profit Shifting
BGB	*Bürgerliches Gesetzbuch* (German Civil Code)
BIT	Bilateral Investment Treaty
CETA	Comprehensive Economic and Trade Agreement
CIL	Customary International Law
CITES	Convention on International Trade in Endangered Species of Wild Fauna and Flora
CPR	Common Pool Resource
DSU	Understanding on Rules and Procedures Governing the Settlement of Disputes
ECHR	European Convention on Human Rights
ECtHR	European Court of Human Rights
EEA	European Economic Area
EJIL	European Journal of International Law
EU	European Union
FATF	Financial Action Task Force
FTA	Free Trade Agreement
GDP	Gross Domestic Product
GG	*Grundgesetz* (German Basic Law)
GPG	Global Public Good
GSP	Generalized System of Preferences
G7	Group of Seven
G20	Group of Twenty
ICJ	International Court of Justice
ICSID	International Centre for Settlement of Investment Disputes
IEL	International Economic Law
IHL	International Humanitarian Law

IIA	International Investment Agreement
IIL	International Investment Law
ILC	International Law Commission
ILM	International Legal Materials
ITLOS	International Tribunal for the Law of the Sea
KP	Kimberley Process
KPCS	Kimberley Process Certification Scheme
Mercosur	Mercado Común del Sur
MFN	Most-Favoured Nation clause
NATO	North Atlantic Treaty Organization
NGOs	Non-Governmental Organisations
NT	National Treatment clause
OECD	Organisation for Economic Cooperation and Development
PCIJ	Permanent Court of International Justice
RIAA	Reports of International Arbitral Awards
StGB	*Strafgesetzbuch* (German Criminal Code)
StVG	*Straßenverkehrsgesetz* (German Traffic Law)
UN	United Nations
UNCIO	United Nations Conference on International Organization
UNCITRAL	United Nations Commission on International Trade Law
UNCLOS	United Nations Convention on the Law of the Sea
UNESCO	United Nations Educational, Scientific and Cultural Organization
UNTS	United Nations Treaty Series
VCLT	Vienna Convention on the Law of Treaties
WHO	World Health Organization
WTO	World Trade Organization

List of Figures

List of Tables

Part I
Introductory Part

Chapter 1
Introduction: A Rational Choice Analysis of International State Responsibility

This introductory chapter will set out the framework for the subsequent analysis. It will firstly circumscribe the concrete research topic by defining the legal status and the main characteristics of state responsibility in public international law. Secondly, it will clarify the research objective of this book, which is to develop an economic theory of how the international law of state responsibility accounts for and could better ensure the protection of community interests. Subsequently, rational choice theory will be presented as the concrete research method to reach this objective and its different assumptions, such as the state as a unitary and rational actor, and its application to international law will be outlined and justified. The last section presents the research question and offers an overview of the book.

1.1 State Responsibility in Public International Law

The concept of responsibility can be understood differently in public international law. André Nollkaemper presents five meanings of responsibility in international law: firstly, responsibility as a description of a mere causal relationship between a situation and the action of a legal person (e.g. states being responsible for climate change because it was caused by their politics); secondly, responsibility as a legal or moral duty to deal with something (e.g. the principle in international law of the "responsibility to protect"); thirdly, responsibility as a synonym for a legal obligation (e.g. the responsibility of states to ensure that they do not cause significant transboundary harm); fourthly, responsibility as answerability for past events (e.g. states being called to account for their conduct and made to respond to moral or legal charges); and fifthly, responsibility as the connection between a wrong and its consequences to right the wrong (e.g. a state committing an act in breach of an

J. Lemke, *The Protection of Community Interests in the International Law of State Responsibility*, International Law and Economics,
https://doi.org/10.1007/978-3-031-87927-2_1

international obligation and the subsequent obligation to provide remedies).[1] It is the last understanding of responsibility, "[t]he idea that international law requires that a breach is undone and reparation is provided", that "has become a central structuring principle of the international legal system", if not of legal systems generally.[2]

The analysis in this book remains within the framework of this last concept of state responsibility in international law, that is the characteristics of states as the central actors and breach of international obligations as the relevant wrongdoing for which remedies need to be provided, even if other meanings of responsibility may also briefly be touched upon.[3]

Legal Status of the Articles on the Responsibility of States for Internationally Wrongful Acts

This book focuses on the international law concerning the responsibility of states for internationally wrongful acts, taking the codification by the International Law Commission (ILC) as a starting point. In 2001, the ILC finalised one of its major works on formulating the law of international relations, namely the Articles on the Responsibility of States for Internationally Wrongful Acts (ARSIWA).[4] Together

[1] André Nollkaemper, "Responsibility," in *Concepts for International Law: Contributions to Disciplinary Thought*, ed. Jean d'Aspremont and Sahib Singh (Cheltenham, UK: Edward Elgar, 2019), 760.

[2] Ibid., 761. Alain Pellet famously noted that responsibility is the "necessary corollary of law" and thus "[n]o responsibility, no (international) law." Alain Pellet, "The Definition of Responsibility in International Law," in *The Law of International Responsibility*, ed. James Crawford, Alain Pellet, and Simon Olleson (Oxford: Oxford University Press, 2010), 4.

[3] The third concept of responsibility as a synonym for a legal obligation is reflected in the international rules on liability for causing transboundary harm and will be discussed in Chap. 4 on the conditions for state responsibility and different responsibility standards. The second understanding of responsibility to take certain actions, in particular, to protect people from mass atrocities and serious human rights violations, may become relevant when discussing circumstances precluding wrongfulness, obligations of all states in response to serious breaches of peremptory international norms, and the right of non-directly injured third states to take countermeasures (Chaps. 5 to 7). The first meaning of responsibility relates to the problem of establishing a causal link between injuries caused by climate change and (wrongful) state behaviour and will be discussed in Chap. 6 on remedies in international law. The fourth understanding of responsibility as answerability for past events relates to the concept of accountability in international law, which is much broader in scope, covering not only different actors and addresses beyond the nation state, but also various kinds of conduct deriving from the exercise of power and authority, which do not necessarily have to amount to the breach of an international legal obligation (e.g. non-compliance with non-binding commitments). On the distinction between "responsibility as answerability" and "responsibility as liability", see further James Crawford and Jeremy Watkins, "International Responsibility," in *The Philosophy of International Law*, ed. Samantha Besson and John Tasioulas (Oxford: Oxford University Press, 2010), 283–284. On accountability in international law, and the law of state responsibility in particular, see Deirdre Curtin and André Nollkaemper, "Conceptualizing Accountability in International and European Law," *Netherlands Yearbook of International Law* 36 (2005): 3–20; Jutta Brunnée, "International Legal Accountability through the Lens of the Law of State Responsibility," *Netherlands Yearbook of International Law* 36 (2005): 21–56.

[4] United Nations International Law Commission, „Draft Articles on Responsibility of States for Internationally Wrongful Acts," in *Report of the Commission to the General Assembly on the Work*

with the accompanying commentaries (hereinafter: the ARSIWA Commentaries),[5] the ARSIWA form an important part of the law of international responsibility, which encompasses a broad range of issues, including principles and rules on the responsibility of international organisations, diplomatic protection, and the liability of states for injurious consequences arising out of acts not prohibited by international law.[6] The United Nations (UN) General Assembly in its resolution 56/83 took note of the ARSIWA and commended them to the attention of member state governments "without prejudice to the question of their future adoption or other appropriate action".[7] The ILC proposed this compromise approach as there was no consensus among the members of the Commission as to whether the ARSIWA were to be considered evidence of international law (that is, "judicial decisions and the teachings of the most highly qualified publicists of the various nations, as subsidiary means for the determination of rules of law" according to Article 38 (1) (d) of the Statute of the International Court of Justice (ICJ)[8]) or whether they required the adoption as an international codification convention as a source of law in its own right (Article 38 (1) (a) ICJ Statute).[9] As of today, no decision on the adoption of a codification treaty or another final form has been taken by the General Assembly,[10] and this compromise approach of the ILC has subsequently launched a debate among legal scholars on its general implications for the codification of international law.[11] Despite not being formally binding, the ARSIWA contribute, however, to the

---

of its Fifty-Third Session, 2001 (UN Doc. A/56/10), in *Yearbook of the International Law Commission*, 2001, Volume II, Part Two (UN Doc. A/CN.4/SER.A/2001/Add.1 (Part 2)).

[5] United Nations International Law Commission, „Commentaries to the Draft Articles on Responsibility of States for Internationally Wrongful Acts," in *Report of the Commission to the General Assembly on the Work of its Fifty-Third Session*, 2001 (UN Doc. A/56/10), in *Yearbook of the International Law Commission*, 2001, Volume II, Part Two (UN Doc. A/CN.4/SER.A/2001/Add.1 (Part 2)).

[6] For an overview of the work of the ILC in general and on the law of international relations in particular, see http://legal.un.org/ilc/summaries/summaries.shtml. An analytical guide to the work of the ILC on state responsibility with a summary and references to all texts and instruments is available here: https://legal.un.org/ilc/guide/9_6.shtml

[7] United Nations General Assembly, Resolution 56/83, *Responsibility of States for Internationally Wrongful Acts*, 12 December 2001 (UN Doc. A/RES/56/83).

[8] Statute of the International Court of Justice (ICJ Statute) (concluded 26 June 1945, entered into force 24 October 1945) 15 *UNCIO* 355.

[9] James Crawford, *State Responsibility: the General Part*, first paperback ed. (Cambridge: Cambridge University Press, 2014), 42. For further details, see also Pellet, "The ILC's Articles on State Responsibility for Internationally Wrongful Acts and Related Texts," in *The Law of International Responsibility*, ed. Crawford, Pellet, and Olleson, 86–87.

[10] On the current state of the debate about concluding a convention on state responsibility, see Arman Sarvarian, "The Ossified Debate on a UN Convention on State Responsibility," *International and Comparative Law Quarterly* 70, no. 3 (2021): 769–798.

[11] On the characterisation of this trend as "codification light", see Santiago Villalpando, "Codification Light: A New Trend in the Codification of International Law at the United Nations," *VIII Anuário Brasileiro de Direito Internacional* 2, no. 15 (2013): 117–155. On the paradox that the ARSIWA "could have more influence as an ILC text than as a multilateral treaty," see David D. Caron, "The ILC Articles on State Responsibility: The Paradoxical Relationship between Form

formation of the international law on state responsibility through their application by international courts and tribunals[12] as well as through the vast amount of scholarship accompanying the work of the ILC and following the adoption of the ARSIWA (Article 38 (1) (d) ICJ Statute).[13]

When analysing the law of state responsibility, as reflected in the ARSIWA, it is therefore important to clarify the exact legal status of the individual provisions under scrutiny.[14] In fact, many of the provisions in the ARSIWA are in terms of their legal status widely considered by international courts and scholars to be "an accurate codification of the customary international law of state responsibility",[15] thus as evidence of a general practice accepted as law (Article 38 (1) (b) ICJ Statute). These are, at least in principle, but not necessarily in their exact wording, for instance, the traditional circumstances precluding wrongfulness such as necessity or *force majeure*, the obligations to put an end to acts in breach of international law and to provide full reparation of injury caused by a wrongful act, or countermeasures as a reciprocal implementation tool.[16] Other provisions, however, for example on the consequences arising for all states in the case of serious breaches of *jus cogens* norms or on the possibility for non-directly injured third states to invoke

and Authority," *American Journal of International Law* 96, no. 4 (2002): 857–873. More generally on the authority of codification conventions and ILC draft articles (denominated "non-legislative codifications") as reflections of customary international law, see Fernando Lusa Bordin, "Reflections of Customary International Law: the Authority of Codification Conventions and ILC Draft Articles in International Law," *International and Comparative Law Quarterly* 63, no. 3 (2014): 535–567.

[12] For an extensive overview of international judicial decisions that refer to the ARSIWA, see United Nations Secretary-General, „Responsibility of States for Internationally Wrongful Acts: Compilation of Decisions of International Courts, Tribunals and other Bodies," in *Reports to the General Assembly*, Sixty-Second Session, 2007 (UN Doc. A/62/62 and A/62/62/Add.1), Sixty-Fifth Session, 2010 (UN Doc. A/65/76), Sixty-Eighth Session, 2013 (UN Doc. A/68/72), Seventy-First Session, 2016 (UN Doc. A/71/80), Seventy-Fourth Session, 2019 (UN Doc. A/74/83), and Seventy-Seventh Session, 2022 (UN Doc. A/77/74).

[13] See, for instance, the symposium "State Responsibility" in the *European Journal of International Law* 10, no. 2 (1999); the symposium "Assessing the Work of the International Law Commission on State Responsibility" in the *European Journal of International Law* 13, no. 5 (2002); as well as the symposium "The ILC's State Responsibility Articles" in the *American Journal of International Law* 96, no. 4 (2002).

[14] The ARSIWA Commentaries state clearly in para. 1, that "[t]hese articles seek to formulate, *by way of codification and progressive development*, the basic rules of international law concerning the responsibility of States for their internationally wrongful acts." Emphasis added.

[15] Crawford, *State Responsibility: the General Part*, 43.

[16] Another example are the rules of attribution of conduct to the state, regarding to which the ICJ held that "[t]his is the state of customary international law, as reflected in the ILC Articles on State Responsibility." *Application of the Convention on the Prevention and Punishment of the Crime of Genocide (Bosnia and Herzegovina v. Serbia and Montenegro)*, Judgment, 26 February 2007, ICJ Reports 2007, p. 43, pp. 208–209, para. 401.

responsibility for breaches of *erga omnes* and *erga omnes partes* obligations,[17] constitute rather progressive development of the rules on state responsibility. Moreover, the ARSIWA do not necessarily solve conclusively all issues of state responsibility. Certain key aspects were left open by the ILC, for instance, regarding the adequate standard of attribution of acts by private individuals to the state, the exact allocation of responsibility between several responsible states, or the extent to which non-directly injured third states may have recourse to countermeasures. This hybrid legal status of and the unsettled issues within the ARSIWA can be explained as being the result of practical considerations and ultimately the necessity to find a compromise solution and strike a balance within the ILC to finalise the project after more than 40 years of work. This should not diminish the fact that due to their wide support and important role in state practice, the ARSIWA can, at least to a certain extent, be considered a successful example of restating existing international custom, and for the rest a key reference document for the further development of the international law of state responsibility.

It is precisely in this regard, that this book seeks to contribute with its economic analysis, namely by offering justifications for fundamental principles of state responsibility reflecting customary international law, making different or more refined suggestions when rules constitute progressive development of international law, and proposing solutions when issues have deliberately been left open. The exact legal status of each provision under scrutiny will therefore be determined throughout the analysis in the respective sections.

Characteristics of State Responsibility in Public International Law

The law of state responsibility is now commonly understood as the rules in public international law that determine the conditions, consequences, and the implementation of international responsibility with regard to states.[18]

These rules build on the concept of an internationally wrongful act of a state, which entails the international responsibility of that state,[19] as detailed in Part one of the ARSIWA. There is an internationally wrongful act of a state when conduct consisting of an action or omission (a) is attributable to the state under international law, and (b) constitutes a breach of an international obligation of that state.[20] According to Article 12 ARSIWA, there is a breach of an international obligation by a state when an act of that state is not in conformity with what is required of it by that obligation, regardless of its origin or character. Damage to a state is thus not required as a condition, which is why the current law of international state

[17] For definitions of the concepts of *jus cogens* norms and *erga omnes (partes)* obligations, see Sect. 3.3.

[18] See generally, Pellet, "The Definition of Responsibility in International Law," in *The Law of International Responsibility*, ed. Crawford, Pellet, and Olleson, 3–16.

[19] Article 1 ARSIWA.

[20] Article 2 ARSIWA. On attribution of conduct to a state, see Part one, Chap. II ARSIWA. On breach of an international obligation, see Part one, Chap. III ARSIWA. On responsibility of a state in connection with the act of another state, see Part one, Chap. IV ARSIWA.

responsibility has "passed from a purely inter-subjective conception of responsibility, with decidedly 'civil' or 'private law' overtones, to a more 'objective' approach".[21] Furthermore, certain extraordinary circumstances may preclude wrongfulness of a state act, and thus exempt a state from international responsibility.[22] Invocation of these six circumstances—consent, self-defence, countermeasures, *force majeure*, distress, and necessity—is, however, precluded in the case of an obligation arising under a peremptory norm of general international law (Article 26 ARSIWA) and without prejudice to the question of compensation for any material loss caused by the act in question (Article 27 lit. b) ARSIWA).

According to the ARSIWA Commentaries, "the term 'international responsibility' covers the new legal relations which arise under international law by reason of the internationally wrongful act of a state".[23] Thus, once the conditions for the international responsibility of a state are fulfilled, certain legal consequences follow which constitute the content of the international responsibility of that state, as detailed in Part two of the ARSIWA. In particular, the responsible state is under an obligation to cease that act, if it is continuing, and to offer appropriate assurances and guarantees of non-repetition, if circumstances so require,[24] as well as to make full reparation for the injury caused by the internationally wrongful act.[25] Serious breaches of obligations arising under peremptory norms of general international law entail particular consequences for all other states, namely to cooperate to bring such situation to an end as well as not to recognise as lawful nor render aid or assistance in maintaining such situation.[26]

In Part three, the ARSIWA contain provisions on the implementation of the international responsibility of a state, in particular on the invocation of responsibility,[27] both by injured states and non-directly injured third states,[28] as well as on the use of countermeasures against a state which is responsible for an internationally wrongful act in order to induce that state to comply with its obligations under Part two.[29]

In sum, the law of state responsibility, as reflected in the ARSIWA, determines in general terms the conditions, exceptions, consequences, and possibilities of implementation of state responsibility. In particular, the ARSIWA set out the so-called

[21] Pellet, "The Definition of Responsibility in International Law," in *The Law of International Responsibility*, ed. Crawford, Pellet, and Olleson, 9.

[22] Part one, Chap. V ARSIWA.

[23] ARSIWA Commentaries, Article 1, para. 1.

[24] Article 30 ARSIWA.

[25] Article 31 ARSIWA. Reparation for injury can take the forms of restitution, compensation or satisfaction, see Part two, Chap. II ARSIWA.

[26] Part two, Chap. III ARSIWA.

[27] Part three, Chap. I ARSIWA.

[28] Articles 42 and 48 ARSIWA.

[29] Part three, Chap. II ARSIWA.

secondary rules of state responsibility,[30] which are applicable independent from the nature and the content of the primary international obligation breached by a state. The general law of state responsibility is thus applicable to all subject areas of inter-state relations, independent to the source of the international obligation and to the extent that they are not governed by special treaty regimes with their own rules on responsibility.[31] Depending on the degree to which special treaty regimes conclusively address issues of state responsibility (e.g. in international trade, investment or human rights law), the general law of state responsibility therefore plays a complementary role or, as the ARSIWA Commentaries put it, "operate in a residual way".[32]

The most important point to note from this very brief overview of the ARSIWA is that the international law of state responsibility exhibits on all three levels characteristics from the "bilateralist" and the "communitarian" considerations of general international law.[33] The law of state responsibility governs, on the one hand, the bilateral relations between sovereign states to reconcile their respective national interests. For instance, when a state violates the territorial integrity of a neighbouring state, the victim state may claim compensation for the harm caused to its citizens and take countermeasures if the responsible state refuses to provide reparation. On the other hand, the international law of state responsibility is also concerned with the protection of interests of the international community, even if this is not mentioned expressly in the ARSIWA.[34] For example, when a state breaches an obligation that is deemed fundamental for the international community as a whole (e.g. the commission of an act of aggression or genocide), the ARSIWA foresee that a non-directly injured third state can invoke the responsibility of the wrongdoing state and, eventually, take countermeasures to induce the responsible state to comply with its obligations of cessation and reparation owed to the victim state.[35] Understanding the extent to which the international law of state responsibility can contribute to the effectuation of the protection of community interests in modern international law will be the core objective of this book.

[30] ARSIWA Commentaries, para. 1.

[31] Article 55 ARSIWA qualifies the ARSIWA as a *lex generalis*, which is inapplicable where and to the extent that the conditions, content or implementation of the international responsibility of a state is governed by special rules of international law. Other general provisions are included in Part four of the ARSIWA.

[32] ARSIWA Commentaries, Article 55, para. 2.

[33] See, amongst others, Bruno Simma, "From Bilateralism to Community Interest in International Law," *Collected Courses of the Hague Academy of International Law* 250, no. 2 (1994): 217–384.

[34] See, for instance, Santiago Villalpando, *L'émergence de la communauté internationale dans la responsabilité des Etats* (Paris: Presses universitaires de France, 2005); James R. Crawford, "Responsibility to the International Community as a Whole," *Indiana Journal of Global Legal Studies* 8, no. 2 (2001): 303–322.

[35] A recent example is the invocation by Gambia of state responsibility for the alleged commission of genocide of the Rohingya people by Myanmar, see *Application of the Convention on the Prevention and Punishment of the Crime of Genocide (The Gambia v. Myanmar)*, Order (Provisional Measures), 23 January 2020, ICJ Reports 2020, p. 3. See also, *Application of the Convention on the Prevention and Punishment of the Crime of Genocide in the Gaza Strip (South Africa v. Israel)*, Order (Provisional Measures), 26 January 2024, ICJ Reports 2024, p. 1

1.2 An Economic Understanding of Community Interest Protection in the International Law of State Responsibility

Since the adoption of the ARSIWA in 2001, the international law of state responsibility, as a core sub-field of public international law, has received considerable attention in the legal literature.[36] In recent years, the focus of scholarly work on international responsibility moved towards enquiring its role in an increasingly interdependent and heterogeneous international legal order, where oftentimes multiple actors, of both public and private nature, interact.[37] These developments raise fundamental questions of attribution of conduct of non-state actors to the state and of allocation of responsibility among several states and/or international organisations, including the apportionment of reparations for injuries to third parties.[38] The twentieth anniversary of the adoption of the ARSIWA marked another occasion "to take stock on where we are, and to think ahead to the challenges of the next few decades and the extent to which the ILC Articles can cater to them and where they will fall short".[39]

More than 20 years later, these are indeed the key points to raise, and this book aims to contribute exactly to this debate on the capability of the current law of state responsibility to address effectively current and future global challenges. The

---

[36] For a comprehensive overview of the law of state responsibility, as reflected in the ARSIWA, and its application in contemporary international practice, see, amongst many others, the works of James Crawford, the former ILC Special Rapporteur on State Responsibility (1997–2001): James Crawford, *The International Law Commission's Articles on State Responsibility: Introduction, Text, and Commentaries* (Cambridge: Cambridge University Press, 2002); Crawford, *State Responsibility: the General Part*. For detailed discussions of the broad range of issues surrounding the international law of state responsibility, see the numerous contributions to the main commentary on the law of international responsibility in James Crawford, Alain Pellet, and Simon Olleson, eds., *The Law of International Responsibility* (Oxford: Oxford University Press, 2010).

[37] For the analytical framework, which will also partially, as regards the distinction between a private and public dimension of the international law of state responsibility, form the basis of the normative framework in this book, see André Nollkaemper and Dov Jacobs, "Shared Responsibility in International Law: A Conceptual Framework," *Michigan Journal of International Law* 34, no. 2 (2013): 359–438.

[38] See, in particular, André Nollkaemper and Ilias Plakokefalos, eds., *Principles of Shared Responsibility in International Law: An Appraisal of the State of the Art* (Cambridge: Cambridge University Press, 2014); André Nollkaemper and Dov Jacobs, eds., *Distribution of Responsibilities in International Law* (Cambridge: Cambridge University Press, 2015); André Nollkaemper and Ilias Plakokefalos, eds., *The Practice of Shared Responsibility in International Law* (Cambridge: Cambridge University Press, 2017). These insights resulted in the proposal of guiding principles on shared responsibility in international law, see André Nollkaemper et al., "Guiding Principles on Shared Responsibility in International Law," *European Journal of International Law* 31, no. 1 (2020): 15–72.

[39] Federica I. Paddeu and Christian J. Tams, "The ILC Articles at 20: Introduction to the Symposium," *EJIL: Talk!* (Blog of the European Journal of International Law), 2 August, 2021, https://www.ejiltalk.org/the-ilc-articles-at-20-introduction-to-the-symposium/

problem is that these are essentially social science questions, and that the methodological toolbox of lawyers, focusing on the interpretation and the application of the law in concrete cases, is inadequate to address questions regarding the problem-solving capacity of law in a systematic way and risks to rely too easily on intuitive rather than socio-scientific arguments.[40] For instance, if one aims to make a statement about the impact of the ARSIWA, it is certainly important but not sufficient to refer to the wide reception of the articles in international judicial decisions and their application across different fields of international law ranging from international humanitarian and human rights law over environmental law to trade or investment law. This is because these insights tell us little about the causal effect of the different rules on state behaviour. This book therefore differs from previous legal research in that it only briefly summarises what the relevant rules in the ARSIWA and their legal status are and then takes, in addition to this traditional internal perspective, an external point of view on state responsibility in international law.[41] The social-scientific approach followed here consists in an economic analysis of the international law of state responsibility, more precisely, in the application of rational choice theory in order to better understand the role state responsibility rules can play in addressing global challenges.[42] This book can draw on extensive existing research in the economic analysis of international law, on the one hand, and of domestic liability law (in both contracts and tort), on the other hand. It thereby fills a research gap as the international law of state responsibility is, from an economic perspective, a relatively unexplored area of international law.

In the economic analysis of international law, global challenges can be differentiated based on theoretical problem structures rather than different fields of international law, and are usually modelled in game-theoretic terms, mostly in the form of a prisoner's dilemma representing a specific type of collective action problems.[43] For

[40] Social science methodology provides, amongst others, the tools to theoretically explain the effect of legal rules on state behaviour and to empirically test hypotheses (usually about causal relationships) regarding actual state practice. On social science methodology generally, see John Gerring, *Social Science Methodology: A Unified Framework*, second ed. (Cambridge: Cambridge University Press, 2012).

[41] On the methodological clarifications for the economic analysis of international law, including the difference between the sociological (or economic) and the doctrinal perspective, see Anne van Aaken, "Opportunities for and Limits to an Economic Analysis of International Law," *Transnational Corporations Review* 3, no. 1 (2011): 28–31; Anne van Aaken and Joel P. Trachtman, "Political Economy of International Law: Towards a Holistic Model of State Behavior," in *The Political Economy of International Law: A European Perspective*, ed. Alberta Fabbricotti (Cheltenham, UK: Edward Elgar, 2016), 11–16. On the theoretical foundations of economic analysis in law more generally, see Anne van Aaken, *"Rational Choice" in der Rechtswissenschaft: Zum Stellenwert der ökonomischen Theorie im Recht* (Baden-Baden: Nomos, 2003).

[42] For an overview of rational choice theory in international law, see Anne van Aaken, "Rational Choice Theory," ed. Anthony Carty, *Oxford Bibliographies in International Law* (Oxford Bibliographies Online: Oxford University Press, 2021), Article last modified on 30 November 2015, https://doi.org/10.1093/OBO/9780199796953-0051

[43] Game theory is a common methodological approach in the social sciences (and increasingly used in international law and economics) to analyse strategic interactions between two or more actors by

instance, the protection of cultural heritage or natural resources are both characterised by the same problem structure which consists in the preservation of "common pool resources", with the consequence that incentive structures created by legal rules to address the underlying cooperation problem should be similar.[44] International obligations protecting fundamental values of the international community, such as the prohibition of genocide or other mass atrocities, are often characterised as protecting "global public goods".[45] The overarching legal concept to describe these global challenges is, as mentioned previously, the idea of community interest protection, as opposed to the traditional bilateralist dimension of international law. Also in the bilateralist dimension, states interact to address cooperative challenges, for instance, the protection of their territory against foreign invasion or cross-border pollution, or they cooperate to mutually further economic gains and exchange trading benefits, later to be described as "private goods" or "club goods" constellations respectively. For an assessment of the problem-solving capacity of the international law of state responsibility it is thus crucial to understand, as a first step, the meaning of community interests in general international law and the extent to which it is congruent with economic concepts of goods at the international level, notably global public goods (GPGs) and common pool resources (CPRs). This constitutes the main objective of Chap. 2 in this introductory part, which will outline in detail the cooperation problems underlying primary obligations across subject areas of international law. A particular focus here will also be on the subsequent global challenge, namely the cooperation problem to provide enforcement of compliance in a decentralised international legal order. It is important to distinguish between, on the one hand, first-order cooperation problems, that is the creation of international legal obligations addressing global challenges and the decision to comply with them, and, on the other hand, second-order cooperation problems, which relate to the decision to enforce compliance with international obligations

---

modelling the underlying problem structure of the interaction with games. Interactions are strategic when the decision of one actor depends on the actions of another. This approach allows for comparing the outcomes of a game ("solution structure") under different conditions, e.g. alternative given institutions or legal rules as rules of the game. For an introduction to game theory and its application in the social sciences, see Prajit K. Dutta, *Strategies and Games: Theory and Practice* (Cambridge, MA: MIT Press, 1999); James D. Morrow, *Game Theory for Political Scientists* (Princeton: Princeton University Press, 1994).

[44] Generalisation is one advantage of rational choice theory because abstract concepts and models transcend substantive problems and facilitate the transfer of insights from domestic politics to international relations, and from international relations to international law. See specifically on this point, but also generally on the rational choice approach in international relations, Duncan Snidal, "Rational Choice and International Relations," in *Handbook of International Relations*, ed. Walter Carlsnaes, Thomas Risse, and Beth A. Simmons, second ed. (London: SAGE, 2013), 89.

[45] For an analysis of the concepts global public goods, global commons, and fundamental values as theoretical tools reflecting the protection of the general interests of the international community, see the different contributions in Massimo Iovane et al., eds., *The Protection of General Interests in Contemporary International Law: A Theoretical and Empirical Inquiry* (Oxford: Oxford University Press, 2021).

either individually or collectively, as the effectiveness of addressing the first type of problems ultimately depends on the effectiveness of the latter, in particular in the community interest dimension.

The international law of state responsibility needs to be understood in this context, because it is linked to the existence, content, and design of primary obligations, includes remedies for wrongful acts which depend on effective enforcement, and provides with countermeasures a specific implementation tool to enforce compliance with these secondary obligations. The ARSIWA have been described as a set of secondary rules which are applicable independent of the subject area regulated by primary obligations. This dichotomy between primary and secondary rules lacks, however, a sound conceptual basis, as, for instance, the determination of a wrongful action or omission and, to a certain extent, the application of circumstances precluding wrongfulness can hardly be separated from the content of the primary obligation in question.[46] An economic perspective on the international law of state responsibility requires to take into account the context in which they operate and it is thus suggested here to analyse these general rules with regard to the different cooperative challenges underlying "bilateral" or "community interest" obligations.[47] To put it differently, if the "main role [of the ARSIWA] is to supply categories and structures",[48] it is essential to understand how these articulate with the structures of general international law characterised by their underlying cooperation problems. Theoretical insights on the general law of state responsibility, as reflected in the ARSIWA, might then explain, amongst others, why responsibility rules are similar or deviate in specialised treaty regimes in certain issue areas, for instance, in the case of international investment law treaties or human rights conventions, and in which circumstances special rules of responsibility might be preferable to the general regime.[49] The research objective of this book is therefore to assess the extent to

[46] On the distinction between primary and secondary rules, see Eric David, "Primary and Secondary Rules," in *The Law of International Responsibility*, ed. James Crawford, Alain Pellet, and Simon Olleson (Oxford: Oxford University Press, 2010), 27–33. For a reconsideration of this distinction due to their mutual connection, in particular in the analysis of multi-actor constellations, see, with further references, Nollkaemper and Jacobs, "Shared Responsibility in International Law: A Conceptual Framework," 408–412.

[47] The notion of secondary obligations will, however, be used when referring to the different remedies (or the content of state responsibility).

[48] Federica I. Paddeu and Christian J. Tams, "Dithering, Trickling down, and Encoding: Concluding Thoughts on the 'ILC Articles at 20' Symposium," *EJIL: Talk!* (Blog of the European Journal of International Law), 9 August, 2021, https://www.ejiltalk.org/dithering-trickling-down-and-encoding-concluding-thoughts-on-the-ilc-articles-at-20-symposium/

[49] The *lex specialis* principle contained in Article 55 ARSIWA is intensely debated and linked to the issue of fragmentation in the international legal order. On the important role of the general law of state responsibility compared to special or self-contained regimes, see Bruno Simma and Dirk Pulkowski, "*Leges Speciales* and Self-Contained Regimes," in *The Law of International Responsibility*, ed. James Crawford, Alain Pellet, and Simon Olleson (Oxford: Oxford University Press, 2010), 139–163. On the varying importance of the general framework across areas of international law and the growing role of specialised regimes, see Katja Creutz, *State Responsibility in the International Legal Order: A Critical Appraisal* (Cambridge: Cambridge University Press, 2020).

which the international law of state responsibility can contribute to addressing global challenges or their underlying cooperation problems by effectuating different types of international obligations in primary law. Such an impact analysis of international state responsibility requires as a preliminary step to set out a normative framework. This will be the objective of Chap. 3 in this introductory part, which will differentiate between the "bilateral" and the "communitarian" approach in international law, and distinguish between a "private" and a "public" dimension which is also reflected in the law of international state responsibility.[50] In the private dimension, the analysis of state responsibility can build on the insights from the economic analysis of domestic liability law (in both contracts and tort), due to similar problem constellations, and on theories of bilateral enforcement of international law. In the public dimension, responsibility rules relate to the protection of community interest obligations, represented, for instance, by global public good constellations, and rely on collective enforcement mechanisms in the case of non-compliance with *jus cogens* norms and *erga omnes (partes)* obligations. From a normative perspective, an economic analysis of the international law of state responsibility is therefore by no means restricted to an evaluation of the efficiency of its rules,[51] but rather enquires how international obligations with different underlying problem structures can be optimally protected in a decentralised legal order. In this regard, this book builds to a large extent on the integrated approach developed by Joost Pauwelyn in his book on the optimal protection of entitlements in international law, in particular by referring to the notion of inalienable entitlements and differentiating between liability rules and property protection as a framework for the analysis of remedies.[52] In addition, this book focuses more specifically on the effectiveness of the different rules of state responsibility, as reflected in the ARSIWA, in different problem constellations, for instance, amongst other goals, on their capability to increase compliance with primary international obligations.

Questions of attribution of conduct and allocation between multiple responsible actors will, however, be left out, not only because these issues have already been intensively discussed, including from a social-scientific perspective,[53] but because

---

[50] See Nollkaemper and Jacobs, "Shared Responsibility in International Law: A Conceptual Framework," 398–408.

[51] On the limited importance of efficiency as a normative criterion in the economic analysis of public international law, see van Aaken, "Opportunities for and Limits to an Economic Analysis of International Law," 29.

[52] Joost Pauwelyn, *Optimal Protection of International Law: Navigating between European Absolutism and American Voluntarism* (Cambridge: Cambridge University Press, 2008). For a presentation of this analytical framework, see Sect. 6.1.

[53] On the attribution of conduct of individuals and other non-state actors to the state, see Eric A. Posner and Alan O. Sykes, "An Economic Analysis of State and Individual Responsibility under International Law," *American Law and Economics Review* 9, no. 1 (2007): 72–134; Bulbul Khaitan, "Alternative to the Existing Rule of Attribution for Use of Force by Non-State Actors in an Armed Conflict," *Journal of Conflict and Security Law* 26, no. 1 (2020): 41–78. On the allocation of responsibilities between multiple actors, see Lewis A. Kornhauser, "Incentives, Compensation, and Irreparable Harm," in *Distribution of Responsibilities in International Law*, ed. André Nollkaemper

they add too much complexity to the analytical framework. The idea here is not to account for the complexities of the international legal order, but reduce the complexity of real-world challenges to inter-state cooperation problems in order to provide clear hypotheses about the incentive structures in the law of state responsibility. This does not mean that the analysis cannot be broadened in that direction at a later stage, but the focus here will be on a stock-taking exercise and an assessment of the problem-solving capacity of the international law of state responsibility, as reflected in the ARSIWA, with a particular focus on the protection of community interests. In this regard, this book will further develop the selective previous social-scientific research on different aspects of the law of state responsibility, for instance, on the design of international rules, the necessity excuse or remedies to a comprehensive theoretical understanding of the law of state responsibility in both the private and public dimension of international law.

To be more precise, an economic analysis of the international law of state responsibility means in terms of methodology, that one can analyse its rules as *explanandum* (dependent variable) or *explanans* (independent variable): one can enquire either the causes or the consequences of these rules, i.e. either the determinants that lead to these existing rules of state responsibility or the incentive effects of these rules on state behaviour respectively.[54] In light of the research objective outlined above, this book focuses on how the ARSIWA set incentives for state behaviour (the international law of state responsibility as *explanans*). This consequentialist view is different from the legal perspective that would analyse, amongst others, whether states complied with certain rules, i.e. whether their behaviour was identical with what the rule required them to do, and if not what consequences follow from such a breach. The analysis of the law of state responsibility conducted in this book is not backward-looking—the classical lawyer's perspective—on how to correct an injustice that has been done by breaching international obligations. These rules of state responsibility are analysed regarding their extent to shape the behaviour of states as law-takers, and thus in a forward-looking way, for instance, how they affect a state's compliance or enforcement decision. To give a concrete example, an internationally wrongful act may under certain conditions give rise to an obligation to provide compensation for damage to the injured state (*ex post* perspective), but such a legal duty, if coupled with adequate enforcement, may create costs and thus, by backward induction, deter breach of the international obligation in the first place (*ex ante* perspective). How actors respond to changing conditions can be

---

and Dov Jacobs (Cambridge: Cambridge University Press, 2015), 120–152; Anne van Aaken, "Shared Responsibility in International Law: A Political Economy Analysis," in *Distribution of Responsibilities in International Law*, ed. André Nollkaemper and Dov Jacobs (Cambridge: Cambridge University Press, 2015), 153–191.

[54] On the distinction between *explanans* and *explanandum* in the analysis of public international law, see van Aaken, "Opportunities for and Limits to an Economic Analysis of International Law," 29.

explained with decision theory.[55] This methodological approach forms the basis of microeconomic theory and allows for analysing the effects of norms on individual behaviour and is widely used in the economic analysis of different fields of domestic law, especially in contract and tort law.[56] The following section on rational choice theory will explain how this approach can be applied to the analysis of state behaviour and how it operates in detail. It suffices to say here, that legal rules can constrain or facilitate state behaviour, because they make the consequences of certain actions or omissions more or less costly.[57] Alternative rules of state responsibility therefore set different incentives for states, and so depending on their design they vary in the way they can influence and ultimately achieve desired state behaviour. Conversely, the same rules of state responsibility can lead to behavioural outcomes that are optimal with regard to certain underlying problem structures but not with regard to others.[58]

Therefore, this book will consist in its main part in a positive analysis (in the social science sense) of selective aspects of the international law of state responsibility, as reflected in the ARSIWA, namely the conditions (or responsibility standards), the exceptions (i.e. circumstances precluding wrongfulness), remedies (i.e. secondary obligations), and countermeasures as an implementation tool.[59] This means, that the incentive structures of different rules will be analysed and the expected state behaviour compared against the objectives of state responsibility defined in Chap. 3, which distinguishes between the role of state responsibility in the private and public dimension of the international legal order, and thus the different problem structures underlying primary obligations in international law. In this regard, this book will also discuss the few existing contributions analysing from an economic perspective different aspects of the law of state responsibility, in

[55] For an introduction to decision theory, see Martin Peterson, *An Introduction to Decision Theory* (Cambridge: Cambridge University Press, 2009).

[56] For a brief explanation of microeconomic theory, see Robert Cooter and Thomas Ulen, *Law & Economics*, sixth international ed. (Boston, MA: Pearson, 2012), 11–54. For a comprehensive overview, see Robert S. Pindyck and Daniel L. Rubinfeld, *Microeconomics*, ninth global ed. (Harlow, UK: Pearson, 2018).

[57] "The rational choice approach to law assumes that law acts as a constraint, making certain behavior more or less costly. It also assumes that law does not only constrain behavior but also enables and facilitates behavior that makes actors better off—marriage laws, for example, enable marriage, contract law facilitates market exchange by reducing transaction costs, and international law facilitates cooperation between states." van Aaken, "Rational Choice Theory."

[58] On the link between knowledge about the causes and effects of public international law and the ability to explain or prescribe specific rules or procedures depending on the underlying problem structures, see van Aaken, "Opportunities for and Limits to an Economic Analysis of International Law," 29.

[59] On the distinction between positive explanation (as opposed to legal positivism) and the normative perspective in the economic analysis of public international law, see van Aaken and Trachtman, "Political Economy of International Law: Towards a Holistic Model of State Behavior," in *The Political Economy of International Law: A European Perspective*, ed. Fabbricotti, 12.

particular on remedies,[60] and put them in a broader context. The aim of this exercise is to provide justifications for current rules and to suggest solutions in the form of different or more refined rules for aspects that have been left open at the time of the adoption of the ARISWA (normative conclusions). A particular focus will be on the specific provisions in the ARSIWA which relate to community interest protection and which are, in terms of their legal status, largely progressive development of international law. On a practical level, these theoretical insights on the behavioural consequences of the law of state responsibility might offer guidance for states and adjudicators in international disputes involving questions of state responsibility (for instance, when relying on teleological interpretation or applying the proportionality principle).[61] In addition to contributing to the legal literature on state responsibility, these theoretical insights on "only half of a causal cycle" can also inform the literature on the rational design of treaties, as states are expected to take into account the consequences of international obligations when entering into cooperative engagements (international law as *explanandum*).[62]

Briefly summarised, this book consists in an economic analysis of the international law of state responsibility, as reflected in the ARSIWA, and aims to contribute with this external view to a better theoretical understanding of the functioning of these rules in the international legal order. In particular, the objective of this book is to understand the extent to which the international law of state responsibility with its attempts to account for the protection of community interests can effectively contribute to addressing global challenges, which are expressed as cooperation problems underlying different types of international obligations in primary law.

1.3 The Rational Choice Approach in International Law

Decision and game theory rely on simplifying assumptions regarding the relevant actors and their preferences in order to explain and predict their behaviour. States in international relations can, for instance, be assumed to be unitary actors, thus

[60] Pauwelyn, *Optimal Protection of International Law: Navigating between European Absolutism and American Voluntarism*; Rachel Brewster, "Pricing Compliance: When Formal Remedies Displace Reputational Sanctions," *Harvard International Law Journal* 54, no. 2 (2013): 259–314; Eric A. Posner and Alan O. Sykes, *Economic Foundations of International Law* (Cambridge, MA: Belknap Press of Harvard University Press, 2013), chap. 9.

[61] On the contribution of consequentialist arguments to the interpretation of (international) law, see van Aaken, "Opportunities for and Limits to an Economic Analysis of International Law," 29–30.

[62] On this holistic model of state behaviour for the analysis of the whole cycle of international law, see van Aaken and Trachtman, "Political Economy of International Law: Towards a Holistic Model of State Behavior," in *The Political Economy of International Law: A European Perspective*, ed. Fabbricotti, 13. On the rational design literature, see Barbara Koremenos, Charles Lipson, and Duncan Snidal, "The Rational Design of International Institutions," *International Organization* 55, no. 4 (2001): 761–799; Barbara Koremenos, *The Continent of International Law: Explaining Agreement Design* (Cambridge: Cambridge University Press, 2016).

abstracting from individual or group behaviour which constitutes real state behaviour. Like market actors (i.e. individuals, households, and firms) or politicians in the domestic context, states in the international context can furthermore be assumed to take rational decisions.[63] Rational choice theory builds on the basic assumption that states are rational actors, and is now a well-acknowledged research approach in the fields of international relations and international law and economics.[64] However, these assumptions about how states take decisions and behave strategically have always to be justified against the background of the research objective.[65] There are multiple critiques and refinements of the rational choice method chosen here and these related or alternative approaches can be very fruitful in the analysis of other aspects of international law beyond state responsibility.[66] The challenge, as for every social science theory, is to find the right balance between, on the one hand, the

[63]Rational choice theory plays an important role in economics and political science in general and has later also been used for the analysis of state behaviour in the specific field of international relations.

[64]International relations scholars advocated first for the application of rationalist assumptions to explain international law, see Kenneth W. Abbott, "Modern International Relations Theory: A Prospectus for International Lawyers," *Yale Journal of International Law* 14, no. 2 (1989): 335–411; Anne-Marie Slaughter, Andrew S. Tulumello, and Stepan Wood, "International Law and International Relations Theory: A New Generation of Interdisciplinary Scholarship," *American Journal of International Law* 92, no. 3 (1998): 367–397; Anne-Marie Slaughter, "International Law and International Relations," *Collected Courses of the Hague Academy of International Law* 285, no. 1 (2000): 9–249; Robert O. Keohane, "Rational Choice Theory and International Law: Insights and Limitations," *Journal of Legal Studies* 31, no. S1 (2002): S307-S319. The first economic theories on the emergence of and compliance with customary international law and international agreements as well as on the formation of and accession to international organisations include: Jeffrey L. Dunoff and Joel P. Trachtman, "Economic Analysis of International Law," *Yale Journal of International Law* 24, no. 1 (1999): 1–59; Alan O. Sykes, "The Economics of Public International Law," *John M. Olin Program in Law and Economics Working Paper*, no. 216 (2004), https://chicagounbound.uchicago.edu/law_and_economics/515/; George Norman and Joel P. Trachtman, "The Customary International Law Game," *American Journal of International Law* 99, no. 3 (2005): 541–580; Jack L. Goldsmith and Eric A. Posner, *The Limits of International Law* (Oxford: Oxford University Press, 2005); Andrew T. Guzman, *How International Law Works: A Rational Choice Theory* (Oxford: Oxford University Press, 2008); Joel P. Trachtman, *The Economic Structure of International Law* (Cambridge, MA: Harvard University Press, 2008). For a collection of the main early contributions to the economic analysis of international law, see Eric A. Posner, ed., *Economics of Public International Law* (Cheltenham, UK: Edward Elgar, 2010). For an overview of the application of economic methodology to different subject areas of public international law, see Posner and Sykes, *Economic Foundations of International Law*.

[65]Difficulties associated with rational choice theory are then rather internal to the rationalist framework and lie in the specifics of its application in the context of international law. Anne van Aaken, "To Do Away with International Law? Some Limits to 'The Limits of International Law'," *European Journal of International Law* 17, no. 1 (2006): 291.

[66]Duncan Snidal defines rational choice theory in general terms "as a methodological approach that explains both individual and collective (social) outcomes in terms of *individual goal-seeking under constraints*," while acknowledging that there are multiple possible ways to fill this broad conception with content. Snidal, "Rational Choice and International Relations," in *Handbook of International Relations*, ed. Carlsnaes, Risse, and Simmons, 87.

adequate level of abstraction to explore the incentive structures of international legal rules (and to have generalisable conclusions that expand across subject areas) and, on the other hand, the necessary proximity to reality by building as close as possible on actual and observable state behaviour in order to reach conclusions which are of value to real-world problems. This section will therefore briefly explain and justify the different elements of the applied research method.[67]

The State as a Unitary Actor

Selecting workable assumptions about how states make decisions and what preferences they may have, presupposes a clear identification of the state as the relevant actor in those interactions that are governed by the law of state responsibility. Following the institutionalist tradition in international relations theory, states will be assumed to be unitary entities and the primary actors on the international scene with their own preferences in international relations and international law.[68]

The unitary actor assumption is traditionally criticised by economists for contradicting the foundation of rational choice theory, namely methodological individualism. As an economic decision theory, the rational choice approach is based on the assumption that the actors making choices are individuals.[69] In order to explain larger-scale social phenomena, rational choice aims to understand the behaviour of human beings and thus considers the individual as the relevant unit of analysis.[70] The state, however, is an abstract legal entity, which cannot act itself, but only through individual persons endowed with some form of authority, i.e. public officials.[71] The problem is that these individuals acting on behalf of the state have their own preferences, which might differ from the state's interest. Moreover, it is questionable whether a group or society of individual citizens with heterogeneous preferences can actually produce a coherent state preference in the sense of a national

[67] The model followed here is largely identical with the one explained and subsequently applied by Andrew T. Guzman. See Guzman, *How International Law Works: A Rational Choice Theory*, 15–22.

[68] Ibid., 19. The unitary actor assumption is also employed in the realist tradition of international relations, see Richard H. Steinberg, "Wanted—Dead or Alive: Realism in International Law," in *Interdisciplinary Perspectives on International Law and International Relations: The State of the Art*, ed. Jeffrey L. Dunoff and Mark A. Pollack (Cambridge: Cambridge University Press, 2013), 148–149.

[69] It shall be noted that behavioural studies of corporate actors are not unknown to microeconomics, as it includes theories on the behaviour of firms, which are treated as unitary profit maximising entities.

[70] Andrew H. Kydd, "Methodological Individualism and Rational Choice," in *The Oxford Handbook of International Relations*, ed. Christian Reus-Smit and Duncan Snidal (Oxford: Oxford University Press, 2008), 427. Referring to Max Weber for the origins of methodological individualism. Max Weber, *Economy and Society: An Outline of Interpretive Sociology*, ed. Guenther Roth and Claus Wittich (Berkeley: University of California Press, 1968; repr., 1978), 4–15.

[71] Malcolm N. Shaw, *International Law*, seventh ed. (Cambridge: Cambridge University Press, 2014), 572.

interest in international relations.[72] One possibility to address the critique of methodological individualism would be to frame a state's preferences in terms of the preferences of the national leader.[73] Modelling the state as a unitary actor seems particularly appealing in the case of autocracies, where the state's and the dictator's preferences are more or less aligned.[74] In the case of democracies, however, it is far less convincing that the preferences of an elected political leader, even in the case of a single powerful head of state or government, transmit directly and uniquely into the state's preferences.[75]

In this regard, public choice theory (in economics) and liberal theory (in international relations) offer an alternative approach to respect methodological individualism.[76] They turn away from the unitary actor assumption at the state level and include domestic politics into the model of state preference formation.[77] Liberalism (and public choice) opens "the black box of the state" and assumes that the state's interests on the international stage are informed by the interplay of domestic actors.[78] In the words of Robert D. Putnam, state behaviour on the international level can be explained as the result of a "two-level game".[79] However, many of the domestic actors in such models, e.g. "the legislature" or "the electorate", are not

---

[72] Kydd, "Methodological Individualism and Rational Choice," in *The Oxford Handbook of International Relations*, ed. Reus-Smit and Snidal, 428. With reference to Kenneth J. Arrow, *Social Choice and Individual Values*, second ed. (New Haven: Yale University Press, 1970).

[73] Kydd, "Methodological Individualism and Rational Choice," in *The Oxford Handbook of International Relations*, ed. Reus-Smit and Snidal, 428. Referring to Bruce Bueno de Mesquita who argues that decisions about war and peace are made by a single strong leader. Bruce Bueno de Mesquita, *The War Trap* (New Haven: Yale University Press, 1981), 27–29.

[74] Kydd, "Methodological Individualism and Rational Choice," in *The Oxford Handbook of International Relations*, ed. Reus-Smit and Snidal, 428.

[75] Ibid.

[76] On the public choice approach in international law, see, in particular, Joel P. Trachtman, "International Law and Domestic Political Coalitions: The Grand Theory of Compliance with International Law," *Chicago Journal of International Law* 11, no. 1 (2010): 127–158. Andrew Moravcsik defines liberal theories of international relations as focusing "on the demands of individuals and social groups, and their relative power in society, as fundamental forces driving state policy." Andrew Moravcsik, "Liberal Theories of International Law," in *Interdisciplinary Perspectives on International Law and International Relations: The State of the Art*, ed. Jeffrey L. Dunoff and Mark A. Pollack (Cambridge: Cambridge University Press, 2013), 83. On the beginning of liberal theories, see, in particular, Andrew Moravcsik, "Taking Preferences Seriously: A Liberal Theory of International Politics," *International Organization* 51, no. 4 (1997): 513–553.

[77] Without naming explicitly public choice and liberalism, Kydd, "Methodological Individualism and Rational Choice," in *The Oxford Handbook of International Relations*, ed. Reus-Smit and Snidal, 428.

[78] Guzman, *How International Law Works: A Rational Choice Theory*, 18–21.

[79] Robert D. Putnam argues that a state's negotiating behaviour reflects simultaneously the imperatives of a domestic political game and an international game. Robert D. Putnam, "Diplomacy and Domestic Politics: The Logic of Two-Level Games," *International Organization* 42, no. 3 (1988): 427–460.

unitary themselves and thus methodological individualism in its strict sense is not satisfied either.[80]

Public choice and liberalism may allow for more accurate descriptive accounts of state preference formation, but compared to the institutionalist approach they are difficult tools for generating strong predictions about state behaviour.[81] The advantage is that both approaches are not irreconcilable with institutionalism as they can serve as input for the unitary actor assumption: the domestic bargaining process can be considered as producing a policy outcome, which the state as a unitary rational actor subsequently defends on the international level.[82] Hence, the institutionalist model simply reduces the complexity of the domestic influence factors by transforming the formation of state interests to a one-level game.

Liberalism takes the sub-state actor perspective even one step further and looks not only at how various domestic actors (e.g. public officials, interest groups) influence or generate the state's preferences on a vertical level but also at how they interact on a horizontal level with their counterparts in the international sphere.[83] Anne-Marie Slaughter prominently described this "new world order" of the "disaggregated state", where informal networks of government officials engage in international legal governance.[84] Yet, the fact that the international legal order moved from, to use again her words, a "billiard ball world" to a "Lego world" does not diminish the necessity to enquire first the former world with the state as the primary actor in international relations and international law and discuss the latter in the context of accountability.[85]

Which approach offers the best tools to predict state behaviour ultimately depends on the selected research topic and objective, which consists here in establishing hypotheses on how state responsibility rules influence state behaviour in different problem constellations. Considering the state as the relevant unit of analysis is consistent with the traditional post-Westphalian legal doctrine in international law,[86] in particular in the international law of state responsibility.[87] These

[80] Kydd, "Methodological Individualism and Rational Choice," in *The Oxford Handbook of International Relations*, ed. Reus-Smit and Snidal, 428.

[81] Admittedly, one advantage of relaxing the unitary actor assumption is that such an approach can account for the fact that international legal rules may affect domestic actors differently.

[82] Guzman, *How International Law Works: A Rational Choice Theory*, 21.

[83] Ibid., 19, 21.

[84] Anne-Marie Slaughter, *A New World Order* (Princeton: Princeton University Press, 2004).

[85] Anne-Marie Slaughter, "Remarks, The Big Picture: Beyond Hot Spots & Crises in Our Interconnected World," *Penn State Journal of Law & International Affairs* 1, no. 2 (2012): 286–302. See also Sect. 1.1.

[86] According to Steinberg, "[…] for realists, the state remains the central actor in international law […], as it is for legal positivists." Steinberg, "Wanted—Dead or Alive: Realism in International Law," in *Interdisciplinary Perspectives on International Law and International Relations: The State of the Art*, ed. Dunoff and Pollack, 149.

[87] International state responsibility falls on the state as a corporate legal person (and legal entity in its own right), not on individual persons within the state.

rules are only applicable in relations among equally sovereign states with the ability of the nation-state to "engage its own responsibility and invoke the consequences of the responsibility of others".[88] When "responsibility lies at the heart of the concept of sovereignty" and "has a central role in understanding and defining the meaning of the statehood in an interstate system",[89] it seems particularly inadequate to disaggregate the state when conducting an economic analysis of its rules. Naturally, the law of state responsibility also deals with the question of attribution of conduct of non-state actors to the state.[90] These issues will, however, as mentioned earlier, be excluded from the analysis due to their complexity, and individual conduct is assumed to be automatically attributed to the state. The analysis will focus on the interactions among states playing one-level games: the responsible state, the injured state invoking responsibility on behalf of its citizens based on the principle of diplomatic protection, and non-directly injured third states that may under certain conditions also be entitled to invoke state responsibility.[91] For this purpose, the assumption that states are unitary actors and the principal actor in international relations (i.e. states are acting themselves, according to their own preferences, and interacting only with other states), as used in the institutionalist (and realist) tradition, is considered to be the most promising tool for generating strong predictions about state behaviour.

The State as a Rational Actor

Following the institutionalist (and realist) tradition in international relations theory, states will also be assumed to be rational actors pursuing their self-interest. Thus, the second assumption of the model used to analyse and predict state behaviour is rationality. This assumption regarding the decision-making style presupposes that states are able to identify their self-interest and to act accordingly.[92] Their self-interest is to maximise the realisation of their goals, i.e. their preferences, under the circumstances they are facing (e.g. legal constraints).[93]

A frequent criticism of the rationality assumption in economic analysis, including the economic analysis of law, can be summarised under the term "bounded rationality", which refers "to the varying kinds of cognitive limitations in the way that many or most people make decisions, evaluate options, and deal with uncertainty,

[88] Pellet, "The Definition of Responsibility in International Law," in *The Law of International Responsibility*, ed. Crawford, Pellet, and Olleson, 4.

[89] Nollkaemper, "Responsibility," in *Concepts for International Law: Contributions to Disciplinary Thought*, ed. d'Aspremont and Singh, 766.

[90] For an economic analysis of the question of attribution using contract theory, see Posner and Sykes, "An Economic Analysis of State and Individual Responsibility under International Law," 72–134; Posner and Sykes, *Economic Foundations of International Law*, chap. 8.

[91] This relates, in particular, to constellations where the individuals suffering harm are the citizens of the responsible state, as usually in the case of human rights violations.

[92] Guzman, *How International Law Works: A Rational Choice Theory*, 17.

[93] van Aaken, "Rational Choice Theory."

relative to the 'rational utility maximizer' [...]".[94] Behavioural economists explain these deviations from predicted behaviour, that is "imperfectly rational" or "irrational" decision-making, with psychological insights and offer refined models for the prediction of human behaviour, for instance, by building in biases.[95]

Naturally, this criticism of the deviation of actual decision-making from the rationality assumption regards not only individual behaviour but also the behaviour of states, even if they are assumed to be unitary. State actions might diverge from theoretical predictions for multiple reasons, and thus adapting the rationality assumption is, in principle, also possible with regard to the state. Psychological insights have, in fact, increasingly been used to analyse decision-making not only in international relations,[96] but also in international law.[97] However, the adequacy of the rationality assumption depends not on how well it describes actual state behaviour but on how powerful it is in explaining and predicting behaviour and whether it is more successful than alternative models. Rationality persuades by its simplicity in predicting behaviour in complex settings and by deriving testable hypotheses, which can subsequently be contrasted with actual behaviour or psychological insights. In fact, many deviations from predicted behaviour can only be properly understood against a rationalist baseline.[98] This is especially true in the area of state

---

[94] Brian Bix, *A Dictionary of Legal Theory* (Oxford: Oxford University Press, 2004), s.v. "bounded rationality". Daniel Kahneman and Amos Tversky developed an alternative model for decision-making under risk, called prospect theory, which essentially argues that people's attitude toward risk depends on how the problem is framed. Daniel Kahneman and Amos Tversky, "Prospect Theory: An Analysis of Decision under Risk," *Econometrica* 47, no. 2 (1979): 263–291. On an application of prospect theory to international relations, see Rose McDermott, *Risk-Taking in International Politics: Prospect Theory in American Foreign Policy* (Ann Arbor: University of Michigan Press, 1998).

[95] With regard to the economic analysis of tort law, one example would be to account for the "hindsight bias", i.e. the finding that the probability of an accident is perceived higher after the accident has occurred, which has consequences for the determination of the efficient level of precaution. For an overview of the application of behavioural insights to the analysis of law, see Eyal Zamir and Doron Teichman, *Behavioral Law and Economics* (New York: Oxford University Press, 2018).

[96] See, amongst others, Rose McDermott, *Political Psychology in International Relations* (Ann Arbor: University of Michigan Press, 2004); James W. Davis, *Psychology, Strategy and Conflict: Perceptions of Insecurity in International Relations* (London: Routledge, 2013). On the state of the art in using behavioural insights in international relations, see James W. Davis and Rose McDermott, "The Past, Present, and Future of Behavioral IR," *International Organization* 75, no. 1 (2021): 147–177.

[97] See, in particular, Anne van Aaken, "Behavioral International Law and Economics," *Harvard International Law Journal* 55, no. 2 (2014): 421–481; Tomer Broude, "Behavioral International Law," *University of Pennsylvania Law Review* 163, no. 4 (2015): 1099–1157. See also, including the different contributions to the symposium on the psychology of international law, Anne van Aaken and Tomer Broude, "The Psychology of International Law: An Introduction," *European Journal of International Law* 30, no. 4 (2019): 1225–1236.

[98] Snidal, "Rational Choice and International Relations," in *Handbook of International Relations*, ed. Carlsnaes, Risse, and Simmons, 94; Kydd, "Methodological Individualism and Rational Choice," in *The Oxford Handbook of International Relations*, ed. Reus-Smit and Snidal, 437–438.

responsibility, which is, from an economic perspective, a relatively unexplored area of international law, even if few exceptions exist which build on the behavioural insights regarding rewards or sanctions.[99] This is why the assumption of rationality needs to be seen as the starting point, and the predictions of state behaviour may and should at some point in the future be further refined with the insights gained in behavioural (international) law and economics.

Going more into detail of the rationality assumption, I assume the state's self-interest as a function of given and fixed preferences.[100] This means that state preferences are exogenous and remain stable in the short run.[101] This assumption is challenged by constructivism, another theory of international relations.[102] Constructivists posit that state preferences are endogenous to the state, in the sense that the state's beliefs are continuously influenced by international institutions and laws.[103] Contrary to institutionalism (and realism), they regard international institutions and rules not as structures created and controlled by rational states, but accord them an independent role on the international stage that can influence the attitudes of states.[104] Consequently, international law itself has the potential to affect not only a state's payoffs but to alter state preferences.[105] Constructivism thus offers not only a plausible description of how international law exerts an influence on preference formation but also allows to account for change in preferences over time. This is

[99] See, respectively, Anne van Aaken and Betül Simsek, "Rewarding in International Law," *American Journal of International Law* 115, no. 2 (2021): 195–241; Alexandra Hofer, "The Efficacy of Targeted Sanctions in Enforcing Compliance with International Law," *AJIL Unbound* 113 (2019): 163–168.

[100] Guzman, *How International Law Works: A Rational Choice Theory*, 17, 21. See also van Aaken, "Opportunities for and Limits to an Economic Analysis of International Law," 44; van Aaken, "Rational Choice Theory."

[101] Guzman, *How International Law Works: A Rational Choice Theory*, 17, 21.

[102] See, in particular, Friedrich V. Kratochwil, *Rules, Norms, and Decisions: On the Conditions of Practical and Legal Reasoning in International Relations and Domestic Affairs* (Cambridge: Cambridge University Press, 1989); Alexander Wendt, *Social Theory of International Politics* (Cambridge: Cambridge University Press, 1999); James D. Fearon and Alexander Wendt, "Rationalism v. Constructivism: A Skeptical View," in *Handbook of International Relations*, ed. Walter Carlsnaes, Thomas Risse, and Beth A. Simmons (London: SAGE, 2002), 52–72. For an overview of constructivist theories, see Emanuel Adler, "Constructivism in International Relations: Sources, Contributions, and Debates," in *Handbook of International Relations*, ed. Walter Carlsnaes, Thomas Risse, and Beth A. Simmons, second ed. (London: SAGE, 2013), 112–145; Jutta Brunnée and Stephen J. Toope, "Constructivism and International Law," in *Interdisciplinary Perspectives on International Law and International Relations: The State of the Art*, ed. Jeffrey L. Dunoff and Mark A. Pollack (Cambridge: Cambridge University Press, 2013), 119–145.

[103] Constructivism is based on the idea that "[t]he identities and preferences of the actors are said to result from socialization by groups to which they belong." Kydd, "Methodological Individualism and Rational Choice," in *The Oxford Handbook of International Relations*, ed. Reus-Smit and Snidal, 436.

[104] Guzman, *How International Law Works: A Rational Choice Theory*, 19.

[105] Ibid., 19–20. See also Snidal, "Rational Choice and International Relations," in *Handbook of International Relations*, ed. Carlsnaes, Risse, and Simmons, 99.

because states are assumed to update their normative beliefs when international norms change.[106] The assumption that state preferences can shift over time can then explain why states change international laws or increase their compliance rate.[107] The constructivist perspective has a strong descriptive force, especially in areas that are more value driven and difficult to explain in terms of state payoffs only (e.g. international human rights law).[108]

In the international relations literature, there are efforts to integrate this strand of scholarship with the rational choice approach. Kenneth Abbott and Duncan Snidal have established a model that explains the interplay of values and interests in the creation and modification of international law, showing that both approaches are rather complementary than mutually exclusive.[109] However, the fact that constructivism (even when combined with rational choice) has more flexible assumptions that allow for a more accurate description of state behaviour, makes it also more difficult to generate generalisable and traceable predictions of state behaviour.[110] Constructivism can play an important role in explaining the changes in state behaviour and in international law over relatively long periods of time (e.g. the increase in human rights treaties).[111] The research objective of this book is, however, to enquire the immediate causal link between different responsibility norms and state behaviour (e.g. in terms of a state's compliance or enforcement decision) across areas of international law. Determining how a change in the law leads to a change in the state's payoffs requires to hold the preferences constant.[112] This does not mean that

[106] Guzman, *How International Law Works: A Rational Choice Theory*, 20.

[107] Kydd, "Methodological Individualism and Rational Choice," in *The Oxford Handbook of International Relations*, ed. Reus-Smit and Snidal, 437. For a model of international normative change following changes in normative beliefs and thus rejecting the rationality assumption, see Martha Finnemore and Kathryn Sikkink, "International Norm Dynamics and Political Change," *International Organization* 52, no. 4 (1998): 887–917.

[108] Ellen L. Lutz and Kathryn Sikkink argue that a broad regional norm shift has led to increased regional and international consensus with respect to an interconnected bundle of human rights norms which are reinforced by diverse legal and political enforcement mechanisms that help to implement and ensure compliance with them. Ellen L. Lutz and Kathryn Sikkink, "International Human Rights Law and Practice in Latin America," *International Organization* 54, no. 3 (2000): 633–659.

[109] Kenneth W. Abbott and Duncan Snidal, "Values and Interests: International Legalization in the Fight against Corruption," *Journal of Legal Studies* 31, no. S1 (2002): S141-S177; Kenneth W. Abbott and Duncan Snidal, "Law, Legalization, and Politics: An Agenda for the Next Generation of IL/IR Scholars," in *Interdisciplinary Perspectives on International Law and International Relations: The State of the Art*, ed. Jeffrey L. Dunoff and Mark A. Pollack (Cambridge: Cambridge University Press, 2013), 33–56.

[110] Guzman, *How International Law Works: A Rational Choice Theory*, 20.

[111] Ibid.

[112] "[...] only if one variable is held constant (the preferences) is it possible to test the hypothesis of the consequences for actors' behavior when there is a change in the restrictions (law) that actors face. If both variables were allowed to vary, it would be impossible to say why a change in behavior occurs." van Aaken, "Opportunities for and Limits to an Economic Analysis of International Law," 44.

value considerations (e.g. concerns for citizens of other states) are completely absent from the rational choice model based on self-interested states followed here.[113] They are actually crucial to understand why rational states have an interest in other states complying with international human rights obligations which predominantly protect the rights of individuals against their own government. This issue of value considerations is, however, a matter of the content of state preferences. Hence, I assume state preferences to be given and stable in the short run, and thus leave out aspects regarding the formation and change of preferences, as this approach is more promising to achieve the research objective, namely to understand the effectiveness of the rules of international state responsibility.

Determination of State Preferences: Maximisation of Absolute Gains
The institutionalist and realist tradition in international relations theory diverge in how they determine the maximisation of the state's self-interest. Institutionalism, which will be followed here, understands a state's self-interest as the maximisation of its goals in absolute terms, meaning that a state wants to obtain more compared to its situation *ex ante*. This approach contrasts with the realist tradition that views political survival as the primary goal of every state and considers the state's self-interest to be the maximisation of relative gains, in other words to obtain more compared to the gains or losses of other states.[114]

In more detail, realist theories consider the state as the central actor within an anarchic international system where states interact in their own national interest in pursuit of either power (classical and offensive realism) or security (defensive realism).[115] Structural realism, as the most recent realist theory,[116] is based on the assumption that states have divergent interests and models state interactions as zero-

[113] State preferences in the rational choice model can include beyond material interests also other-regarding interests, such as normative or ideational goals, see Snidal, "Rational Choice and International Relations," in *Handbook of International Relations*, ed. Carlsnaes, Risse, and Simmons, 87; Steinberg, "Wanted—Dead or Alive: Realism in International Law," in *Interdisciplinary Perspectives on International Law and International Relations: The State of the Art*, ed. Dunoff and Pollack, 149.

[114] On the distinction between institutionalism and realism, see Guzman, *How International Law Works: A Rational Choice Theory*, 18.

[115] Jonathan Cristol, "Realism," ed. Patrick James, *Oxford Bibliographies in International Relations* (Oxford Bibliographies Online: Oxford University Press, 2021), Article last modified on 27 June 2017, https://doi.org/10.1093/OBO/9780199743292-0042. For modern realism, see in particular Hans J. Morgenthau, *Politics among Nations: The Struggle for Power and Peace* (New York: Alfred A. Knopf, 1948); Kenneth N. Waltz, *Theory of International Politics* (New York: McGraw-Hill, 1979); John J. Mearsheimer, *The Tragedy of Great Power Politics* (New York: Norton, 2001).

[116] As opposed to traditional realism represented by Hans J. Morgenthau, which used additional "non-realist" factors, such as normative interests, to explain international law, see Steinberg, "Wanted—Dead or Alive: Realism in International Law," in *Interdisciplinary Perspectives on International Law and International Relations: The State of the Art*, ed. Dunoff and Pollack, 150–152.

sum games,[117] in which states focus on relative gains for survival, i.e. on doing better at the expense of other states.[118] Hence, when states come together on the international scene, material power, for example in the form of trade or bargaining power, plays an important role in shaping the substance and structure of international law.[119] Realists claim, for instance, that powerful states will not comply with international law if it contradicts their long-term interests.[120] This centrality of power as an assumption has thus led to scepticism about achieving meaningful cooperation in international politics (in particular, in the form of international law), and consequently about the effect of international law on state behaviour.[121]

Institutionalism, in contrast, is less sceptical about international cooperation.[122] It posits that states seek to realise absolute gains, and thus to improve their situation regardless of the comparative advantage over other states. This does not mean that institutionalism is favouring cooperation per se, but that, on the contrary, "states will only cooperate when doing so increases their own payoffs".[123] There will be

---

[117] In game theory, zero-sum games describe "a game or situation where the participants' collective losses and gains add up to zero. The term is often used more loosely to indicate a situation [...] where one party can win only if another party loses (as contrasted to a co-operative situation where all parties could end up gaining)." Bix, *A Dictionary of Legal Theory*, s.v. "zero sum game".

[118] Steinberg, "Wanted—Dead or Alive: Realism in International Law," in *Interdisciplinary Perspectives on International Law and International Relations: The State of the Art*, ed. Dunoff and Pollack, 149. Structural realism has been constructed by Kenneth N. Waltz and applied to international regimes by Stephen D. Krasner. Stephen D. Krasner, "Structural Causes and Regime Consequences: Regimes as Intervening Variables," in *International Regimes*, ed. Stephen D. Krasner (Ithaca, NY: Cornell University Press, 1983), 1–22.

[119] Steinberg, "Wanted—Dead or Alive: Realism in International Law," in *Interdisciplinary Perspectives on International Law and International Relations: The State of the Art*, ed. Dunoff and Pollack, 149, 150.

[120] Ibid., 150.

[121] See in this regard, especially Goldsmith and Posner, *The Limits of International Law*. Although not explicitly realists, their approach and scepticism about international law resembles realism.

[122] For institutionalism, see, in particular, Robert O. Keohane, *After Hegemony: Cooperation and Discord in the World Political Economy* (Princeton: Princeton University Press, 1984); Robert Axelrod, *The Evolution of Cooperation* (New York: Basic Books, 1984); Kenneth A. Oye, "Explaining Cooperation under Anarchy: Hypotheses and Strategies," in *Cooperation under Anarchy*, ed. Kenneth A. Oye (Princeton: Princeton University Press, 1986), 1–24; Robert Axelrod and Robert O. Keohane, "Achieving Cooperation under Anarchy: Strategies and Institutions," *World Politics* 38, no. 1 (1985): 226–254. Rational design theory, which aims to explain why states have created international institutions such as treaties in particular forms (e.g. membership, scope, flexibility provisions, centralised adjudication), is also rooted in the institutionalist tradition. See, in particular, Koremenos, Lipson, and Snidal, "The Rational Design of International Institutions," 761–799; Koremenos, *The Continent of International Law: Explaining Agreement Design*. For an overview of institutionalism in international law, see Barbara Koremenos, "Institutionalism and International Law," in *Interdisciplinary Perspectives on International Law and International Relations: The State of the Art*, ed. Jeffrey L. Dunoff and Mark A. Pollack (Cambridge: Cambridge University Press, 2013), 59–82.

[123] Guzman even argues that "the [rational choice] assumptions are basically hostile to cooperation." Guzman, *How International Law Works: A Rational Choice Theory*, 17.

instances where both (or several) states see the possibility to realise absolute gains from cooperation, and thus, for institutionalists, cooperation can rather be framed as a positive-sum game than a zero-sum game.[124]

Institutionalism is less concerned with the centrality of power as realism is as a political scientific approach,[125] but is rooted in economics, which makes it more suitable for the impact analysis of international legal rules, which draws on insights from the economic analysis of law in the domestic context. Moreover, the realist assumption with survival as the ultimate concern of states might be inappropriate in many issue areas regulated by international law today.[126] In addition, international relations and legal scholars in the institutionalist tradition have established convincing accounts about why states comply with international law and how these rules are enforced, which makes it questionable whether one should assume an anarchic world without any mechanisms of law enforcement, as in the realist tradition.[127]

Moreover, the two theories are not mutually exclusive as may appear at first sight. Institutionalism is not ignorant of the fact that relative gains and losses as well as interests of power can play a role in cooperation. For instance, a military alliance agreement between two or several states can, although offering absolute gains for all parties to the agreement, be concluded with the aim to maintain relative gains over states outside the agreement.[128] In addition, institutionalism can integrate realist accounts through distribution problems and power asymmetries among states. Relative gains and losses can occur when two states with divergent bargaining power divide the cooperative surplus of a mutually beneficial agreement.[129] Power asymmetries may also play a role with respect to the decentralised enforcement of international law, as only powerful or rich states might be able to afford retaliatory measures over a long period of time.[130] All this does not mean that the accumulation of relative power is the ultimate interest of states, only that it can play a role in constellations where states seek to further their absolute gains through cooperation.

---

[124] Koremenos, "Institutionalism and International Law," in *Interdisciplinary Perspectives on International Law and International Relations: The State of the Art*, ed. Dunoff and Pollack, 59.

[125] According to Steinberg, "whereas liberal and constructivist theories import sociological concepts and processes to explain international law, and rationalist institutionalism is built on the back of economics, realism is—by virtue of the centrality of power—the most distinctly political of contemporary approaches to international law." Steinberg, "Wanted—Dead or Alive: Realism in International Law," in *Interdisciplinary Perspectives on International Law and International Relations: The State of the Art*, ed. Dunoff and Pollack, 150.

[126] Guzman, *How International Law Works: A Rational Choice Theory*, 18.

[127] For these enforcement mechanisms in international law, see Sect. 2.4.

[128] Cooperation can thus be successful even under realist assumptions, see Guzman, *How International Law Works: A Rational Choice Theory*, 18. The same argument can be made for trade agreements, which offer benefits for all participating states, but are (also) concluded with the aim to maintain a competitive advantage over outsiders.

[129] Ibid.

[130] See Chap. 7 on countermeasures in international law.

A last crucial question is what states seek to maximise in absolute terms. At the core of the rationality assumption lies the idea that each economic actor maximises something: for instance, consumers maximise utility (that is, happiness or satisfaction), firms maximise profits, politicians maximise votes, and bureaucracies maximise revenues.[131] The determination of state preferences is an equally challenging endeavour, as they consist, in reality, of many different aspects.

Building upon the unitary actor assumption, states are in this analysis assumed to behave in the international arena much like private or market actors in the domestic context. This means that their characteristic as a public entity in the internal dimension does not play a role in pure inter-state relations. To the contrary, states interact as abstract entities on the international level in the formation and application of international law, and it is only in this regard that they have interests. From this perspective, state preferences are then assumed to resemble the preferences of firms or consumers rather than bureaucracies or politicians.[132]

Maximisation of absolute gains means, first and foremost, that states seek to maximise their own payoffs (i.e. expected utility) in the sense that they are better, or at least not worse, off than before. The state's set of preferences can consist in different types of goals, monetary or non-monetary.[133] A starting point for the identification of state preferences derives from the concept of the sovereign equality of states and thus the idea that states want to use their territory and the resources to which they are entitled in a way to derive the most benefits from them, and without interference from other states. An analogy to domestic property law can be drawn here and this conception of legal entitlements of states is also the underlying theme of Pauwelyn's analysis of the optimal protection of international law.[134] The mere existence or survival of the state, as the ultimate state interest in the realist tradition, is one example for a fundamental state goal.[135] Another state interest can be to enhance the state's welfare in terms of economic gains, for example, by obtaining benefits from free trade.[136] State preferences can also consist in various other national interests such as the health of the own population or the protection of natural resources. Another way to express state preferences, grounded in the

---

[131] Cooter and Ulen, *Law & Economics*, 12.

[132] On the analogy between firms and states, see Robert E. Scott and Paul B. Stephan, *The Limits of Leviathan: Contract Theory and the Enforcement of International Law* (Cambridge: Cambridge University Press, 2006), 29–58.

[133] "These [preferences] are not confined to monetary goals but can represent (for states) security, (economic) power, providing public goods, or not harming the environment." van Aaken, "Rational Choice Theory."

[134] Pauwelyn, *Optimal Protection of International Law: Navigating between European Absolutism and American Voluntarism.*

[135] For an overview of possible state interests, while refraining from any particular commitment as to their content other than the survival of the state, see Steinberg, "Wanted—Dead or Alive: Realism in International Law," in *Interdisciplinary Perspectives on International Law and International Relations: The State of the Art*, ed. Dunoff and Pollack, 149.

[136] Ibid.

constructivist tradition, is to assume that states seek to maximise their status in terms of both material and non-material interests, such as reputational improvements or the mere perception of being a valued member of a reference group.[137]

The fact that the state's self-interest is rather "private" or "national" in nature, does not exclude that states also pursue other-regarding or community interests, usually because they are the precondition for furthering their own interests. These can be material goals such as security and stability at the international level as a precondition for economic growth or the preservation of biodiversity and the fight against climate change because adverse effects threaten the population or ultimately even the mere survival of the state. Community interests can also be non-material such as respect for the international rule of law (e.g. as a precondition for international trade) or normative goals such as peace, democracy, or human rights protection around the globe.[138] The crucial point here is that states profit from these ideational goals and thus integrate them in their set of self-interested preferences. Whether states are able to achieve all these goals will be the key issue of Chap. 2, which outlines the cooperation challenges states are facing in international relations.

In conclusion, state preferences are multiple and different in kind. While it will be possible to define state interests in specific issue areas, for example in international trade law, in more concrete terms, it will be difficult, if not impossible, to do so when analysing rules of general international law across subject areas. A certain level of abstraction regarding the content of state preferences is thus appropriate when analysing the law of international state responsibility from an economic perspective. Since such an economic analysis requires comparing the costs and benefits of state decisions, it will only be assumed that states seek to maximise their material and non-material interests in terms of absolute gains (i.e. being better or at least not worse off than before), as in the institutionalist tradition. Considering the research objective, this simplicity has the advantage of making the model workable to explain how state responsibility rules set incentives for states.

On the Application of Rational Choice Theory

To sum up, this analysis follows the institutionalist tradition and assumes states to be unitary rational actors, which are able to identify and act according to their self-interest. Their self-interest is a function of exogenous and fixed preferences, which means that state preferences are given and remain stable in the short run. States are then assumed to maximise the realisation of their goals, i.e. their set of preferences, in terms of absolute gains in order to be better, or at least not worse, off than before.

---

[137] Ian Johnstone, "Status as a Reward," *AJIL Unbound* 115 (2021): 226–231. Referring in particular to Alastair Iain Johnston, "Treating International Institutions as Social Environments," *International Studies Quarterly* 45, no. 4 (2001): 487–515.

[138] Steinberg, "Wanted—Dead or Alive: Realism in International Law," in *Interdisciplinary Perspectives on International Law and International Relations: The State of the Art*, ed. Dunoff and Pollack, 149.

In rational choice theory, behaviour is a function of preferences and other exogenous factors, also termed as restrictions or constraints, for instance, the law.[139] In this book, state behaviour (B_S) can therefore be modelled as a function of state preferences (P_S) and the international legal rule deriving from the law of state responsibility (L_{SR}):

$$B_S = f\ (P_S, L_{SR})$$

An exogenous change in the independent variable of the equation (i.e. the legal rule), while state preferences stay fixed, will result in an endogenous change in the dependent variable (i.e. the behavioural outcome).[140] In other words, '[i]f behaviour is a function of preferences and restrictions (law), then, on the basis of given preferences, a change in behaviour is attributed to a change in law. If the law changes, the expected utility of the behaviour will also change, at least if the law is effective".[141] The role of law in the rational choice approach is then to make certain behaviour more or less costly, that is, to constrain behaviour in a way that it makes actors worse off or to facilitate behaviour in that it makes actors better off.[142] Based on the assumptions that states are unitary rational actors maximising their gains in absolute terms, we can thus explain how international rules of state responsibility affect the behavioural outcome ceteris paribus ("all other things equal") and thus predict and compare the behavioural responses of states to changes in the law.

In the area of state responsibility, one significant behavioural outcome to analyse is the compliance decision of a state from an *ex ante* perspective, that is whether a rule of state responsibility, for instance, the obligation to provide reparation for injury, by backward induction sets incentives for the state not to breach an international obligation in the first place. This is not about stating whether states comply with what a primary obligation requires them to do, but about the effectiveness of state responsibility, that is whether a certain legal rule has the potential to increase the compliance rate.[143] The compliance decision of a state will become relevant at different stages of the analysis, for instance, when considering whether or not to comply with a primary obligation in international law, whether or not to invoke a

[139] van Aaken, "To Do Away with International Law? Some Limits to 'The Limits of International Law'," 292–293.

[140] On the operation of rational choice as a causal theory, see also Snidal, "Rational Choice and International Relations," in *Handbook of International Relations*, ed. Carlsnaes, Risse, and Simmons, 89.

[141] van Aaken, "To Do Away with International Law? Some Limits to 'The Limits of International Law'," 293.

[142] van Aaken, "Rational Choice Theory."

[143] On compliance and effectiveness as related but different concepts, see extensively Andrew T. Guzman, "A Compliance-Based Theory of International Law," *California Law Review* 90, no. 6 (2002): 1823–1887. See also, Guzman, *How International Law Works: A Rational Choice Theory*, 22–23.

circumstance precluding wrongfulness (which is not "non-compliance" strictly speaking, but nonetheless a justified deviation from the behaviour required by the primary obligation), whether or not to comply with a secondary obligation (e.g. to cease the wrongful act or provide reparation), and, lastly, whether or not to enforce compliance with these secondary obligations (that is, countermeasures as a temporary exemption from compliance). Every time, a rational state considers in the decision-making process the expected benefits and costs of each alternative (i.e. compliance versus non-compliance). Cost and benefit factors will vary depending on the decision under scrutiny, but in general terms, the compliance decision can be modelled as an expected utility function, where the expected utility equals the sum of the value of each possible outcome (benefit and cost factors) to the state, each of them multiplied by the probability of that outcome occurring.[144] In a binary decision between compliance and non-compliance, rational states would compare the payoffs of each alternative with their set of preferences and thus choose the behaviour which maximises their gains in absolute terms. This book seeks to explain the role of one particular cost factor which has the potential to alter a state's payoffs (or expected utility), namely an international legal rule deriving from the law of state responsibility, and the probability of that rule being enforced.[145] Therefore, it will be assumed that a state will violate an international obligation if the expected benefits of the act (B_V) for the wrongdoing state outweigh the associated costs of non-compliance (C_V). It will further be assumed, for simplicity reasons, that the expected costs of the violation of an international obligation (C_V) equal the costs imposed by the responsibility rule (L_{SR}) times the probability (p) of being held responsible, that is enforcement of that rule being effective:

$$B_V > C_V; \textit{whereas}$$

$$C_V = p(L_{SR})$$

Admittedly, this approach cannot tell us whether a responsibility rule, such as a compensation requirement, will shift the decision of the state toward compliance, but it allows to compare the costs of alternative legal rules, and thus their relative impact on the compliance rate, that is whether compliance is more or less likely. The first advantage of this approach is thus to illuminate the incentive structures of the law of state responsibility, that is to explain how (and not why) its rules affect state

[144]On the concept of expected utility, see Daniel E. Palmer, "Expected Utility," *Encyclopaedia Britannica*, https://www.britannica.com/topic/expected-utility, Article last modified on 18 May 2016.

[145]To express this argument in the words of Guzman, "[e]ven if one assumes that the rules of state responsibility have an effect on states, it remains to be explained why this is so. In trying to understand why a state might comply with an international obligation, it makes no sense to turn to a rule of international law that says a failure to comply generates an obligation to make reparation. If there is nothing else to encourage compliance with the initial obligation, then the rule requiring reparations will be similarly impotent." Guzman, *How International Law Works: A Rational Choice Theory*, 55.

behaviour and to compare the outcome with the goals of state responsibility, which will be outlined in detail in Chap. 3, with compliance being only one of them. The second advantage relates to the analysis of the functioning of the law of state responsibility in different problem constellations. On the one hand, the problem structures underlying primary obligations across subject areas of international law, that is the first-order cooperation problems, determine whether the benefits and the costs of compliance or non-compliance are fully internalised by the responsible state or the injured state, or whether they also fall partly on all other states in the international community. On the other hand, a given legal rule will set different incentives depending on the probability of enforcement being effective. Taking into account differences in the underlying problem constellation, illustrated by variations in the variable p, thus allows for a better understanding of the role of second-order cooperation problems. All these issues will be explained in detail in Chap. 2, but it suffices to say here, that there is a link between second-order and first-order cooperation problems, and that the likelihood of enforcement being effective depends significantly on whether the dispute can be situated in the private or public dimension of international law, that is whether enforcement can be provided individually or whether it depends on collective action.

Rational choice theory therefore proves to be the most adequate research approach to explain the different rules of state responsibility and suggest modifications, in particular with regard to problem constellations relating to the protection of community interests in international law. Finding the most appropriate assumptions for a given research objective requires always a trade-off between, on the one hand, the broadness of the scope of the analysis, and, on the other hand, the specification of the model. Surely, the chosen rational choice model is leaving out important aspects such as domestic processes of preference formation or changes in preferences, which might limit its ability to reflect important aspects of state behaviour in international relations. However, the simplicity of the model has the benefit of allowing to analyse more rigorously one sub-field of general international law, the rules of state responsibility. Holding as many factors as possible constant allows for deriving stronger theoretical hypotheses about the behavioural effects of the international rules of state responsibility. The chosen assumptions were selected with the purpose to establish a rationalist baseline for a broad and barely analysed set of rules, and insights from alternative approaches should be applied at a future point to see if state behaviour approximates or deviates from the predictions made.

1.4 Research Question and Overview of the Book

This book seeks to contribute to the legal debate on the capability of the current international law of state responsibility, that is the set of rules reflected in the ARSIWA, to effectively address global challenges. Yet, the research objective is not to map out how the different rules of the international law of state responsibility account for the protection of community interests, as this has been done extensively in the legal literature, notably with regard to the consequences in case of breach of *jus cogens* or *erga omnes (partes)* obligations.[146] This book differs fundamentally in terms of the research method, namely in that it proceeds by positively and qualitatively analysing the incentive structures of the international law of state responsibility based on the assumption that states are unitary rational actors aiming to maximise their payoffs in absolute terms. This approach allows for a better theoretical understanding of how the rules of state responsibility affect the behaviour of self-interested states against the background of the cooperation challenges underlying primary obligations in international law, and thus independent of the respective subject area, and those stemming from the issue of decentralised enforcement. This book thus seeks to answer the following research question:

> To what extent does the international law of state responsibility, as reflected in the ARSIWA, set adequate incentives for states as unitary rational actors to respond to the underlying cooperation challenges?

In addition, depending on the results regarding the economic justification of the current rules, this book aims to offer normative proposals on how they may be improved, in particular in terms of how the international law of state responsibility could set better incentives for the protection of community interests, and thus contribute to the progressive development of international law in this area.

This book will analyse in its second part the four main aspects of international state responsibility, the conditions,[147] the exemptions,[148] the legal consequences,[149] and their enforcement with countermeasures.[150] It will exclude, as indicated above, issues of attribution of conduct to the state due to the unitary actor assumption,[151] as well as issues of responsibility of a state in connection with the act of another state,[152] and issues related to the plurality of responsible states.[153] It will dedicate specific attention to the most controversial and unresolved issues and thus aims to contribute to existing debates in the legal literature with recourse to rational choice theory.

---

[146] See, amongst others, Christian J. Tams, *Enforcing Obligations Erga Omnes in International Law* (Cambridge: Cambridge University Press, 2005); Elena Katselli Proukaki, *The Problem of Enforcement in International Law: Countermeasures, the Non-Injured State and the Idea of International Community* (London: Routledge, 2010).

[147] Part one, Chaps. I and III ARSIWA.

[148] Part one, Chap. V ARSIWA.

[149] Part two ARSIWA.

[150] Part three ARSIWA.

[151] Part one, Chap. II ARSIWA.

[152] Part one, Chap. IV ARSIWA.

[153] Article 47 ARSIWA. This analysis focuses on a single responsible actor for reasons of simplicity of the model. For an economic analysis of the provision to understand under which form of shared responsibility states are more likely to cooperate in the first place, see van Aaken, "Shared Responsibility in International Law: A Political Economy Analysis," in *Distribution of Responsibilities in International Law*, ed. Nollkaemper and Jacobs, 153–191.

Against this background, the book is structured as follows: Chapter 2 outlines the research area of this book in that it defines, on the one hand, the concept of community interests in international law and presents, on the other hand, the current state of knowledge in international law and economics on the role of international law in addressing different types of global challenges. Based on these two threads of thought, it develops the theoretical framework for the subsequent analysis, and outlines, firstly, the cooperation challenges underlying different types of primary obligations in international law (including the degree of congruence with community interest obligations), and secondly, the compliance mechanisms in the international legal order which rely on decentralised self-enforcement by states. Chapter 3 outlines the normative framework of the analysis and discusses the objectives of state responsibility in international law. In this regard, it distinguishes between the private and public dimension of international state responsibility and draws, where appropriate in terms of the underlying problem structure, on insights from economic theories of responsibility in the domestic context, notably tort and contract law. It also situates the specific provisions in the ARSIWA on the invocation and enforcement of state responsibility in the context of the general theories about compliance with international law, and analyses in particular the degree of congruence between the concepts of *jus cogens* norms and *erga omnes (partes)* obligations with the economic concept of global public goods. Chapter 4 analyses the conditions for state responsibility with a particular focus on the implications of objective responsibility as the main responsibility standard in international law, namely the interplay between the design of primary obligations and the effectiveness of enforcement of state responsibility. In this context, the concept of liability for lawful acts, that is, obligations of compensation for harm resulting from hazardous activities not prohibited by international law, as an alternative cost allocation mechanism is also briefly discussed. Chapter 5 looks at exemptions from state responsibility and provides an in-depth analysis of how the different circumstances precluding wrongfulness in international law, in particular the necessity excuse, integrate the protection of community interests in their incentive structures, by focusing in particular on the question of cost allocation following the invocation of the different defences. Chapter 6 examines the extent to which the different consequences of an internationally wrongful act in the law of state responsibility, and thus the default rules on remedies in public international law, take into account in their allocation of duties and costs the protection of community interests in international law. Chapter 7 enquires countermeasures as a circumstance precluding wrongfulness and a tool for implementing state responsibility by analysing the incentive structures with regard to the decision to have recourse to countermeasures in response to an internationally wrongful act, especially in reaction to violations of *erga omnes (partes)* obligations and thus the unsettled issue whether non-directly injured third states are limited in their enforcement efforts to lawful measures. Chapter 8 concludes on the functioning of the international law of state responsibility and the extent to which it effectively contributes to the protection of community interests in international law.

Chapter 2
The Protection of Community Interests in International Law and Economics

This chapter outlines the broader research context of this book, namely the capability of international law in addressing global challenges, or, in legal terms, in protecting interests of the international community, and the contribution of economic analysis in this regard. It begins with taking a legal perspective and presents the concept of community interests in international law. In order to gain a more systematic understanding of global challenges, this chapter then outlines the economic concepts of private goods, public goods, and mixed goods, as applied in economics and international relations theories, as well as their respective underlying cooperation problems. It explains in particular the collective action problems underlying the provision of global public goods (GPGs) and the protection of common pool resources (CPRs) and describes the role of international law in addressing them. In a third step, it brings the two threads together and analyses the extent to which the legal concept of community interests in international law is congruent with the different economic categories of goods, and illustrates the (in-)congruence across areas of international law. Building on these insights regarding first-order cooperation problems, the fourth section explains in more detail the implications of the main characteristic of the international legal order, namely decentralised law enforcement, for the effective protection of community interests and outlines their underlying second-order cooperation problems. The last section concludes.

2.1 The Concept of Community Interests in International Law

In the traditional Westphalian order, international law, including state responsibility, has served to regulate bilateral relations between equal sovereign nation states with the objective to reconcile or further their respective national interests. Obligations governing such bilateral relations usually derive from bilateral norms, such as

J. Lemke, *The Protection of Community Interests in the International Law of State Responsibility*, International Law and Economics,
https://doi.org/10.1007/978-3-031-87927-2_2

bilateral treaties, but they can also be based on multilateral norms, such as multilateral treaties or custom, to the extent that they are reflecting bundles of bilateral relationships between states. A classic example is the customary international law and multilateral international agreement regulating the fundamental principles of diplomatic relations between individual states.[1] Over the years, in particular after the Second World War, international law developed significantly, inspired by concepts of natural law, and increasingly includes references to the protection of community interests. In the international legal discourse these are also referred to as common or collective interests, common concerns, or common values.[2] Early writings on the subject consider a universal community interest, "a consensus according to which respect for certain fundamental values is not to be left to the free disposition of [s] tates individually or *inter se* but is recognized and sanctioned by international law as a matter of concern to all [s]tates".[3] In his famous quote, ICJ Vice-President Weeramantry extends the notion in his separate opinion beyond common values to community interests more generally, including environmental concerns: "We have entered an era of international law in which international law subserves not only the interests of individual [s]tates, but looks beyond them and their parochial concerns to the greater interests of humanity and planetary welfare".[4] Today, the concept of community interests is understood in an even wider sense. According to Isabel Feichtner, it refers not only to "interests held by the international community as a whole", but also denotes "community interests shared on a non-universal level and protected by law which only binds groups of [s]tates".[5] Moreover, "the group of community interest norms encompasses norms which are deemed so fundamental as to be beyond the free disposition of [s]tates, but also norms of a lesser status" as long as they are protecting "values and interests which are shared across borders and transcend national interests in reciprocal exchanges of benefits between [s]tates".[6]

[1]Vienna Convention on Diplomatic Relations (concluded 18 April 1961, entered into force 24 April 1964) 500 *UNTS* 95.

[2]Isabel Feichtner, "Community Interest," ed. Anne Peters and Rüdiger Wolfrum, *Max Planck Encyclopedia of Public International Law* (Oxford Public International Law: Oxford University Press, 2021), http://opil.ouplaw.com, Article last updated in February 2007, para. 1.

[3]Simma, "From Bilateralism to Community Interest in International Law," 233.

[4]*Gabčíkovo-Nagymaros Project (Hungary v. Slovakia)*, Judgment, 25 September 1997, ICJ Reports 1997, p. 7, p. 118.

[5]Feichtner, "Community Interest," para. 4.

[6]Ibid. Along the same lines, Samantha Besson affirms that community interest norms are not necessarily congruent with the principles of generality, universality, hierarchy, and constitutionality of international law. That is, community interests do not automatically derive from multilateral sources of international law (as they can provide for bundles of bilateral obligations), are not automatically universal in terms of territorial scope (e.g. regional agreements), are not automatically protected by peremptory norms (see Chap. 3 on the distinction between *jus cogens* norms and *erga omnes* duties), and do not (yet) confirm a constitutional dimension of international law (see Chap. 3 on the coexistence of a private and public dimension in international law, the latter not being equivalent to a national constitutional order). See Samantha Besson, "Community Interests in International Law: Whose Interests Are They and How Should We Best Identify Them?," in

According to Samantha Besson, "[t]he recognition and protection of certain community interests in the normative content and structure of contemporary international law are well established".[7]

For the purpose of a recent comprehensive study of community interests across international law,[8] Eyal Benvenisti and Georg Nolte understand the term "community interests" in a broad sense in order to explore "the extent to which states owe duties toward those who are affected by their actions and omissions", or, in other words, "the extent to which contemporary international law expects states [...] to take into account the interests of others, namely third states or their citizens" or "of the persons under their jurisdiction or control".[9] They argue that '[t]he relevant 'community' may thus extend beyond the 'international community of states' and may also cover individuals and groups whose interests, for various reasons, were not fully considered at the negotiation table or in policymaking bodies".[10] The international community can also refer to "humanity at large, as reflected in the concept of crimes against humanity".[11] Community interest obligations can then derive either from agreements on the protection of individuals or collective interests in different areas of international law (e.g. international human rights law, international humanitarian law, international refugee law, international environmental law) or from treaties or other rules and principles of international law that recognise and seek to

---

Community Interests across International Law, ed. Eyal Benvenisti and Georg Nolte (Oxford: Oxford University Press, 2018), 43–44.

[7] Besson, "Community Interests in International Law: Whose Interests Are They and How Should We Best Identify Them?," in *Community Interests across International Law*, ed. Benvenisti and Nolte, 36. With reference to Simma, "From Bilateralism to Community Interest in International Law," 217–384; Giorgio Gaja, "The Protection of General Interests in the International Community," *Collected Courses of the Hague Academy of International Law* 364, no. 1 (2012): 9–185; Ulrich Fastenrath et al., eds., *From Bilateralism to Community Interest: Essays in Honour of Bruno Simma* (Oxford: Oxford University Press, 2011); Wolfgang Benedek et al., eds., *The Common Interest in International Law* (Cambridge, UK: Intersentia, 2014).

[8] Eyal Benvenisti and Georg Nolte, eds., *Community Interests across International Law* (Oxford: Oxford University Press, 2018).

[9] Eyal Benvenisti and Georg Nolte, "Community Interests across International Law: Introduction," in *Community Interests across International Law*, ed. Eyal Benvenisti and Georg Nolte (Oxford: Oxford University Press, 2018), 3–5. See also Eyal Benvenisti, "Sovereigns as Trustees of Humanity: On the Accountability of States to Foreign Stakeholders," *American Journal of International Law* 107, no. 2 (2013): 295–333.

[10] Benvenisti and Nolte, "Community Interests across International Law: Introduction," in *Community Interests across International Law*, ed. Benvenisti and Nolte, 5. With reference to Dino Kritsiotis, "Imagining the International Community," *European Journal of International Law* 13, no. 4 (2002): 961–992. On the term 'international community of states', see also Bruno Simma and Andreas L. Paulus, "The 'International Community': Facing the Challenge of Globalization," *European Journal of International Law* 9, no. 2 (1998): 266–277; Santiago Villalpando, "The Legal Dimension of the International Community: How Community Interests Are Protected in International Law," *European Journal of International Law* 21, no. 2 (2010): 387–419.

[11] Benvenisti and Nolte, "Community Interests across International Law: Introduction," in *Community Interests across International Law*, ed. Benvenisti and Nolte, 5.

promote interests of the international community (e.g. "the common heritage of mankind", or the concept of *jus cogens* norms).[12] In an even broader sense, they consider also "the existence of open and inclusive venues for deliberating such questions" as well as institutions facilitating collective action to achieve them as a community interest.[13]

Despite the rise of community interest norms, contemporary international law relies on "[t]he primacy of [inter-state] consent as the source of international legal duties", which "originates in a view of international law as being principally focused on states respecting each other's sovereignty, ensuring that *pacta sunt servanda*, and respecting general practices that are accepted by them as law".[14] Yet, international law based on consent does not exclude international legal rules serving community interests, because states either explicitly agree to them or accept them as law.[15] Besson argues that states "can pursue both individual interests and collective ones and that the latter can include domestic collective interests as well as global ones".[16] In that way, "a consent-based and a community interest-oriented international law" complement each other, as "elements of one or the other paradigm coexist and interact in different fields of international law".[17] The challenge is "to accommodate community interests in a system that contains strong structural elements for the protection of self-interest".[18] In other words, in an international system where the functions of law-making and law enforcement, in the absence of a centralised institution, are exercised predominantly by equally sovereign states, the challenge arises to achieve community interest protection (and address global challenges) by cooperation among self-interested states.

---

[12] Ibid., 4. Besson identifies five types of normative instantiations of community interests in contemporary international law, that may also overlap: (i) community interests as the *object* of certain norms or regimes (e.g. in different areas of international law or third-party countermeasures in state responsibility law), (ii) community interests protected by different *types* of norms (i.e. duties, rights, and/or principles), (iii) community interests protected through substantive and/or procedural *structural features* of international norms (e.g. *erga omnes* duties, peremptory character of *jus cogens* norms, and third-party enforcement mechanisms), (iv) community interests reflected in the multilateral *sources* of international law (e.g. multilateral treaties, customary international law, and general principles of international law), and (v) community interests as *aims* or *purposes* of certain norms or regimes (e.g. internal normative conflicts in multipurpose regimes). Besson, "Community Interests in International Law: Whose Interests Are They and How Should We Best Identify Them?," in *Community Interests across International Law*, ed. Benvenisti and Nolte, 41–43.

[13] Benvenisti and Nolte, "Community Interests across International Law: Introduction," in *Community Interests across International Law*, ed. Benvenisti and Nolte, 6.

[14] Ibid., 3.

[15] Ibid., 4.

[16] Besson, "Community Interests in International Law: Whose Interests Are They and How Should We Best Identify Them?," in *Community Interests across International Law*, ed. Benvenisti and Nolte, 37.

[17] Benvenisti and Nolte, "Community Interests across International Law: Introduction," in *Community Interests across International Law*, ed. Benvenisti and Nolte, 4.

[18] Ibid., 8.

2.2 Taxonomy of Goods on the International Level and Underlying Collective Action Problems

International cooperation problems relating to global challenges (and the protection of community interests) are often framed with the analytic concept of global public goods (GPGs). Building on the classical economic theory of goods, global public goods theory originated in the international relations literature, notably in the field of development studies.[19] The following explanations of the different concepts of goods therefore build predominantly on the work of Inge Kaul.[20]

J. Samuel Barkin and Yuliya Rashchupkina observe that GPGs are often understood in the international relations and international law literature in a broad way, namely "as those public goods that are associated with global issues", such as "environment, trade, financial stability, health care, poverty reduction, and culture preservation across states' borders".[21] But from an economic perspective further refinement is needed. According to Inge Kaul, Isabelle Grunberg, and Marc A. Stern, GPGs must meet two criteria: firstly, as all public goods,[22] "their benefits have strong qualities of publicness—that is, they are marked by nonrivalry in consumption and nonexcludability", and, secondly, as a global public good, "their benefits are quasi universal in terms of countries (covering more than one group of countries),

[19] See, in particular, Todd Sandler, *Global Challenges: An Approach to Environmental, Political, and Economic Problems* (Cambridge: Cambridge University Press, 1997); Inge Kaul, Isabelle Grunberg, and Marc A. Stern, eds., *Global Public Goods: International Cooperation in the 21st Century* (New York: Oxford University Press, 1999); Marco Ferroni and Ashoka Mody, eds., *International Public Goods: Incentives, Measurement, and Financing* (Boston, MA: Springer, 2002); Inge Kaul et al., eds., *Providing Global Public Goods: Managing Globalization* (New York: Oxford University Press, 2003); Todd Sandler, *Global Collective Action* (Cambridge: Cambridge University Press, 2004); Inge Kaul and Pedro Conceição, eds., *The New Public Finance: Responding to Global Challenges* (New York: Oxford University Press, 2006); International Task Force on Global Public Goods, *Meeting Global Challenges: International Cooperation in the National Interest*, Final Report, Stockholm, Sweden (2006), https://ycsg.yale.edu/sites/default/files/files/meeting_global_challenges_global_public_goods.pdf; Scott Barrett, *Why Cooperate? The Incentive to Supply Global Public Goods* (Oxford: Oxford University Press, 2007); Eric Brousseau, Tom Dedeurwaerdere, and Bernd Siebenhüner, eds., *Reflexive Governance for Global Public Goods* (Cambridge, MA: MIT Press, 2012); Inge Kaul, ed., *Global Public Goods* (Cheltenham, UK: Edward Elgar, 2016).

[20] See, in particular, Inge Kaul, Isabelle Grunberg, and Marc A. Stern, "Defining Global Public Goods," in *Global Public Goods: International Cooperation in the 21st Century*, ed. Inge Kaul, Isabelle Grunberg, and Marc A. Stern (New York: Oxford University Press, 1999), 2–19.

[21] J. Samuel Barkin and Yuliya Rashchupkina, "Public Goods, Common Pool Resources, and International Law," *American Journal of International Law* 111, no. 2 (2017): 377–378.

[22] Fundamental works on public goods include: Paul A. Samuelson, "The Pure Theory of Public Expenditure," *Review of Economics and Statistics* 36, no. 4 (1954): 387–389; Richard A. Musgrave and Alan T. Peacock, eds., *Classics in the Theory of Public Finance* (London: Macmillan, 1958); Richard A. Musgrave, *The Theory of Public Finance: A Study in Public Economy* (New York: McGraw-Hill, 1959); James M. Buchanan, *The Demand and Supply of Public Goods* (Chicago: Rand McNally, 1968).

people (accruing to several, preferably all, population groups), and generations (extending to both current and future generations, or at least meeting the needs of current generations without foreclosing development options for future generations)".[23] As much as the characteristics of "publicness and privateness are in most cases not innate properties of a good but social constructs", globalness of a public good in most cases, too, "can be viewed [...] as a policy choice".[24] Thus, while some GPGs "are by nature global and public", such as sunlight, others "have changed their properties from, for example, being national (including local) public goods to being GPGs", such as international peace and security.[25] Globalness, meaning "the fact that the benefits and costs of some goods have nearly universal coverage" and can "potentially [or *de facto*] affect anyone anywhere", refers thus in terms of consumption or provision to the property of geographical coverage of a certain public good.[26] Therefore, "[t]ogether with regional public goods, GPGs constitute the category of transnational public goods".[27]

On the opposite side of the spectrum are then private goods in the international context. As all private goods they are marked by rivalry in consumption[28] and excludability, while being restricted in terms of geographical coverage to one country. Examples for such private goods are the natural resources on the territory of one state delimitated by the national borders as an international legal construct.[29] Similarly, ocean resources between the coastal baseline and 200 nautical miles were non-excludable until states recognised exclusive economic zones (EEZ) in the United Nations Convention on the Law of the Sea (UNCLOS).[30] These resources thus "became excludable [by international law], and remain so in principle even if many states do not have the physical capability to enforce that exclusion in practice".[31] To put it more generally, private goods on the international level can be

[23] Kaul, Grunberg, and Stern, "Defining Global Public Goods," in *Global Public Goods: International Cooperation in the 21st Century*, ed. Kaul, Grunberg, and Stern, 2–3.

[24] Inge Kaul, "Global Public Goods: Explaining Their Underprovision," *Journal of International Economic Law* 15, no. 3 (2012): 731–732.

[25] Ibid., 732.

[26] Ibid., 731–732.

[27] Ibid. An example for regional public goods are European public goods that are provided by the Member States of the European Union.

[28] Rivalry in consumption means that, once consumed, the good cannot be enjoyed by others (e.g. firewood). Kaul, Grunberg, and Stern, "Defining Global Public Goods," in *Global Public Goods: International Cooperation in the 21st Century*, ed. Kaul, Grunberg, and Stern, 3.

[29] It should be noted here that legal clarity about national borders is a global public good. See, Barkin and Rashchupkina, "Public Goods, Common Pool Resources, and International Law," 379.

[30] Article 55, United Nations Convention on the Law of the Sea (UNCLOS) (concluded 10 December 1982, entered into force 16 November 1994) 1833 *UNTS* 397.

[31] Barkin and Rashchupkina, "Public Goods, Common Pool Resources, and International Law," 379.

deduced from the concept of property rights,[32] basically covering all kinds of activities that aim at the protection of the national sovereign territory or use of natural resources,[33] reaching from national security to the national economy.[34]

Only few goods, however, are purely public or purely private in nature, most goods rather possess mixed benefits.[35] Impure public goods are goods that only meet one of the two defining criteria of public goods.[36] There are essentially two categories of mixed goods.[37] The first type are club goods, which are goods that are non-rivalrous in consumption but excludable.[38] Excludability as a characteristic is different in kind from rivalness in consumption "in that it is, to a significant extent, a legal construct rather than inherent in the good", and can therefore be changed by law.[39] In the domestic context, club goods often consist in networks and are mostly non-rivalrous inside the club, for instance, a radio broadcast which has been made excludable to certain users or regional infrastructure.[40] An example of a club good at the international level is the international trade regime.[41] States entering into a trading relationship create mutual benefits, for instance, in the form of tariff reductions, which are non-rivalrous within and limited to the members of the club. The second category of mixed goods are common pool resources (CPRs), which are goods that are non-excludable but rivalrous in consumption.[42] Like GPGs, these are

[32] Pauwelyn builds his analysis on a similar understanding, namely the idea of legal entitlements and their protection in international law. Pauwelyn, *Optimal Protection of International Law: Navigating between European Absolutism and American Voluntarism*.

[33] Joel P. Trachtman cites two examples of legal rules that might provide a default allocation of property rights in international law: the right of territorial sovereignty and the sic *utere tuo ut alienum non laedas* principle of international environmental law: use your own property (territory) in such a manner as not to injure that of another (state). Joel P. Trachtman, "Ex Ante and Ex Post Allocation of International Legal Responsibility," in *Distribution of Responsibilities in International Law*, ed. André Nollkaemper and Dov Jacobs (Cambridge: Cambridge University Press, 2015), 89.

[34] It should be noted that private goods on the international level can well be public goods or common pool resources on the national level, for instance, national security or national resources.

[35] Kaul, Grunberg, and Stern, "Defining Global Public Goods," in *Global Public Goods: International Cooperation in the 21st Century*, ed. Kaul, Grunberg, and Stern, 4.

[36] Impure public goods are also goods that only partly meet one or both of the defining criteria. Ibid.

[37] Ibid., 5.

[38] Ibid. On club goods, see in particular James M. Buchanan, "An Economic Theory of Clubs," *Economica* 32, no. 125 (1965): 1–14; Richard Cornes and Todd Sandler, *The Theory of Externalities, Public Goods and Club Goods* (Cambridge: Cambridge University Press, 1985).

[39] Barkin and Rashchupkina, "Public Goods, Common Pool Resources, and International Law," 379.

[40] Kaul, Grunberg, and Stern, "Defining Global Public Goods," in *Global Public Goods: International Cooperation in the 21st Century*, ed. Kaul, Grunberg, and Stern, 5; Barkin and Rashchupkina, "Public Goods, Common Pool Resources, and International Law," 379.

[41] Barkin and Rashchupkina, "Public Goods, Common Pool Resources, and International Law," 380.

[42] Kaul, Grunberg, and Stern, "Defining Global Public Goods," in *Global Public Goods: International Cooperation in the 21st Century*, ed. Kaul, Grunberg, and Stern, 5. On common pool

accessible to all, but due to their physical characteristics they are subject to congestion or depletion.[43] Examples for CPRs on the international level are fish stocks in the high seas or the atmosphere, because unrestricted pollution can change its gas composition and contribute to global warming.

Other mixed goods can be both rival and non-rival at the same time.[44] Certain non-excludable goods, usually natural or cultural resources, have characteristics of CPRs when the good is consumed, and public goods characteristics when they have an existence value, in the sense that people derive value from the knowledge that the good exists, even without using the good.[45] Biodiversity or the preservation of monuments and art, for example, are public goods subsidised by the polity because their existence or their enjoyment is highly valued by the community.[46] Yet, at the same time, these non-use value goods face the risk of irreversible destruction. A similar example is the protection of human rights, which has characteristics of a normative public good to the extent that people derive value from the knowledge that fundamental rights norms exist and are effectively enforced in a community.[47]

In sum, all types of goods need to be understood as lying on a spectrum with pure private and pure (global) public goods at the extreme ends.[48] Goods are in most cases not inherently private or public, but this characteristic is usually a social construct or the result of a policy choice.[49] It is therefore important to differentiate clearly

resources, see in particular Garrett Hardin, "The Tragedy of the Commons," *Science* 162, no. 3859 (1968): 1243–1248; Per Magnus Wijkman, "Managing the Global Commons," *International Organization* 36, no. 3 (1982): 511–535; Carlo Carraro and Domenico Siniscalco, eds., *New Directions in the Economic Theory of the Environment* (New York: Cambridge University Press, 1997); Partha Dasgupta, Karl-Göran Mäler, and Alessandro Vercelli, eds., *The Economics of Transnational Commons* (Oxford: Oxford University Press, 1997).

[43] Barkin and Rashchupkina, "Public Goods, Common Pool Resources, and International Law," 379.

[44] Ibid.

[45] Kaul, Grunberg, and Stern, "Defining Global Public Goods," in *Global Public Goods: International Cooperation in the 21st Century*, ed. Kaul, Grunberg, and Stern, 5; Barkin and Rashchupkina, "Public Goods, Common Pool Resources, and International Law," 379.

[46] Kaul, Grunberg, and Stern, "Defining Global Public Goods," in *Global Public Goods: International Cooperation in the 21st Century*, ed. Kaul, Grunberg, and Stern, 5. Referring on the valuation of public goods, for instance, to John B. Loomis, "How Large Is the Extent of the Market for Public Goods: Evidence from a Nationwide Contingent Valuation Survey," *Applied Economics* 28, no. 7 (1996): 779–782.

[47] For human rights protection as a normative public good, see, for instance, Paulo Pinto de Albuquerque and Anne van Aaken, "Punitive Damages in Strasbourg," in *The European Convention on Human Rights and General International Law*, ed. Anne van Aaken and Iulia Motoc (Oxford: Oxford University Press, 2018), 247.

[48] Kaul, Grunberg, and Stern, "Defining Global Public Goods," in *Global Public Goods: International Cooperation in the 21st Century*, ed. Kaul, Grunberg, and Stern, 4. See also Inge Kaul, Donald Blondin, and Neva Nahtigal, "Understanding Global Public Goods: Where We Are and Where to Next," in *Global Public Goods*, ed. Inge Kaul (Cheltenham, UK: Edward Elgar, 2016), xv.

[49] Kaul, "Global Public Goods: Explaining Their Underprovision," 731.

	Rivalrous	Non-rivalrous
Excludable	**Private goods** (e.g. natural resources within national borders, ocean resources in the EEZ)	**Club goods** (e.g. international trade rules)
Non-excludable	**Common pool resources** (e.g. fish stocks in the high seas, atmosphere as a pollution sink)	**Global public goods** (e.g. international peace and security, non-use value goods, human rights as normative public goods)

Fig. 2.1 Taxonomy of goods on the international level

"between the potential and *de facto* publicness of a good".[50] Generally, while the property of rivalry in consumption as a physical characteristic of a good is fixed, changing the property of excludability, for instance, by (international) law, leads to a change in the character of the good.[51] Mechanisms of exclusion for a public good create a club good and mechanisms of exclusion for a common pool resource create a private good.[52] A dichotomous reading of the two properties (i.e. rivalness and excludability) thus yields four ideal types of goods, and not mere two categories of goods, private and (global) public goods.[53]

The characteristics of these four ideal types of goods at the international level are summarised with respective examples in Fig. 2.1. For an economic analysis, this taxonomy is preferable to a broad and simplified definition of GPGs, including impure public goods or mixed goods, as often used in the international relations and international law literature.[54]

The different characteristics of these four types of goods have implications for their way of provision and/or their continued existence. On the domestic level, private goods are provided by the market where supply and demand reach an equilibrium through the price mechanism and resource allocation in theory is

[50] Ibid.

[51] Barkin and Rashchupkina, "Public Goods, Common Pool Resources, and International Law," 378, 387.

[52] Ibid., 387.

[53] Ibid., 379.

[54] For an even more refined definition of different types of goods on the public-private continuum, see Kaul, Blondin, and Nahtigal, "Understanding Global Public Goods: Where We Are and Where to Next," in *Global Public Goods*, ed. Kaul, xvi.

optimal.[55] However, markets are rarely perfect and the provision and/or consumption of different types of goods can lead to side-effects due to market failures and collective action problems. In the international context these are often described more broadly as global challenges or cooperation problems.[56]

Classical economy theory knows the concept of externalities, which can be defined as "*indirect* effects of consumption or production activity, that is, effects on agents other than the originator of such activity which do not work through the price system. In a private competitive economy, equilibria will not be in general Pareto-optimal since they will reflect only *private* (direct) effects and not *social* (direct plus indirect) effects of economic activity".[57] "Because externalities are not accounted for in the costs and prices of the free market, market agents will receive the wrong signals and allocate resources toward bad externalities and away from good externalities".[58] In other words, "externalities are by-products of certain activities—spillovers into the public sphere", and can take the form of indirect costs or benefits.[59] For example, by releasing pollutants free of charge into a river a factory may cause harm to nature and human beings. Publishing medical or pharmaceutical knowledge, by contrast, can benefit human beings worldwide. The provision or consumption of a good can consist either in an activity with negative utility to third parties, thus creating negative externalities ("public bad"), or in an activity with positive utility to third parties, thus creating positive externalities ("public good").[60]

The fact that certain activities have a positive utility to third parties sets strong incentives for actors other than the originator of such activity to enjoy the benefits of public goods without contributing with own resources to their provision.[61] This

---

[55] Kaul, Grunberg, and Stern, "Defining Global Public Goods," in *Global Public Goods: International Cooperation in the 21st Century*, ed. Kaul, Grunberg, and Stern, 3.

[56] For an early comparison between market failures and collective action problems in the domestic context and global challenges and cooperation problems on the international level, see in particular Sandler, *Global Challenges: An Approach to Environmental, Political, and Economic Problems.*

[57] J. J. Laffont, "Externalities," *The New Palgrave Dictionary of Economics* (London: Palgrave Macmillan), Article last modified on 13 March 2017, https://doi.org/10.1057/978-1-349-95121-5_126-2. Pareto-optimality is "a concept of efficiency used in the social sciences, including economics and political science, named for the Italian sociologist Vilfredo Pareto. A state of affairs is Pareto-optimal (or Pareto-efficient) if and only if there is no alternative state that would make some people better off without making anyone worse off." Sean Ingham, "Pareto-Optimality," *Encyclopaedia Britannica*, https://www.britannica.com/topic/Pareto-optimality, Article last modified on 28 November 2019.

[58] Erik Bækkeskov, "Market Failure," *Encyclopaedia Britannica*, https://www.britannica.com/topic/market-failure, Article last modified on 1 October 2019.

[59] Kaul, Grunberg, and Stern, "Defining Global Public Goods," in *Global Public Goods: International Cooperation in the 21st Century*, ed. Kaul, Grunberg, and Stern, 5.

[60] Ibid., 6.

[61] Ibid.

phenomenon is the so-called free-rider problem.[62] The problem consists in the signal that is sent to potential suppliers which fear that they will have to bear all the costs of provision, thus deciding not to provide the good.[63] With regard to public goods, the free-rider problem ultimately leads to the result that cooperation fails and the good is not provided at all.[64] In game theory, this collective action problem is often described with the so-called prisoner's dilemma. It illustrates many real-life situations, including in international relations, "in which two or more parties face similar incentives to 'defect' from cooperation unless mechanisms are established to facilitate communication [or information exchange] and build trust".[65] The prisoner's dilemma not only illustrates the challenge to provide public goods by market actors, but also why markets fail to preserve CPRs.[66] Like public goods, they are non-excludable so that everyone can profit from the benefits of the good. Yet, they are rival in consumption which is why free-riding leads to over-consumption and ultimately to their extinction (e.g. fish stocks). This dilemma is the so-called tragedy of the commons.[67]

In the national context, the solution to market failures and collective action problems consists often in an intervention by the state.[68] For instance, in the case of river pollution, negative externalities of a factory's activities can be limited, for instance, by prohibiting or regulating the emissions and/or by creating an obligation to compensate victims for the harm caused, thus inducing the polluter to internalise the costs of its actions on third parties.[69] The publication of medical or pharmaceutical knowledge can be encouraged by establishing property rights, for example via patents, thus allowing researchers, at least for a certain time, to fully internalise the benefits from producing and selling the medical or pharmaceutical product. Furthermore, the state can improve the conditions for public good provision by setting norms and standards, thus facilitating cooperation among market actors, or by providing tax incentives.[70] In the last resort, the state can decide to provide public goods itself through its institutions and financed by the tax payer, which is common practice for public goods supply at the national level such as law and order (via the

[62] See, in particular, Mancur Olson, *The Logic of Collective Action: Public Goods and the Theory of Groups* (Cambridge, MA: Harvard University Press, 1965).

[63] Kaul, Grunberg, and Stern, "Defining Global Public Goods," in *Global Public Goods: International Cooperation in the 21st Century*, ed. Kaul, Grunberg, and Stern, 6–7.

[64] Ibid.

[65] Ibid., 7–8. There are also other games representing situations in international relations, such as assurance games, which will be explained further below.

[66] Bix, *A Dictionary of Legal Theory*, s.v. "prisoner's dilemma".

[67] See, in particular, Hardin, "The Tragedy of the Commons," 1243–1248.

[68] Kaul, Grunberg, and Stern, "Defining Global Public Goods," in *Global Public Goods: International Cooperation in the 21st Century*, ed. Kaul, Grunberg, and Stern, 8.

[69] On the allocation of social costs, see, in particular, R. H. Coase, "The Problem of Social Cost," *Journal of Law and Economics* 3 (1960): 1–44.

[70] Kaul, Grunberg, and Stern, "Defining Global Public Goods," in *Global Public Goods: International Cooperation in the 21st Century*, ed. Kaul, Grunberg, and Stern, 8.

police and the justice system). Hence, the monopoly of power of the state to create institutions, adopt and enforce policies, laws (for instance, through the imposition of fines), and even private contracts (in order to facilitate transactions) allows for the correction of market failures and the production of socially optimal outcomes through governance at the central level.[71]

These market failures and collective action problems can be transferred to the international level with the major difference that in the international context, there is no central coercive power or institution comparable to the state on the national level. Thus, all goods need in principle to be provided and preserved by states themselves, independently or by cooperating with each other.[72] The primary cooperation problem related to private goods is not their provision, but their protection from outside interference (negative externalities). In an ever more interconnected world, activities in one country (e.g. industrial production) may cause negative externalities to other states who must bear the costs of these activities.[73] This can, for instance, include cross-border environmental issues that are strongly directional, involving river or air pollution that is carried downstream or downwind across borders. But examples can also be found beyond the context of cross-border pollution and relate to basically all kinds of disputes over the territorial integrity of sovereign states, including the illegal exploitation of natural resources belonging to other states. States thus need to cooperate to create international mechanisms (similar to property or tort law in the domestic context) that induce states to internalise the social costs of activities with negative cross-border impact.[74] It is especially in these contexts that the international law of state responsibility has an important role to play. Another type of international cooperation problem relates to the creation of property rights in the first place by mechanisms of exclusion. The prime example is that of intellectual property rights protection, as patents can make the benefits of public knowledge, at least for a limited period of time, excludable to the patent owner.[75] But also CPRs, when made excludable, become private goods, and thus allow the state to internalise all the benefits of the privatised good and increase the incentive for states to manage the

[71] Ibid.

[72] For an explanation of collective action problems in international law distinguishing between public goods and common pool resources from a rationalist perspective, see Barkin and Rashchupkina, "Public Goods, Common Pool Resources, and International Law," 376–394. For behavioural aspects of the international law of GPGs and CPRs, see Anne van Aaken, "Behavioral Aspects of the International Law of Global Public Goods and Common Pool Resources," *American Journal of International Law* 112, no. 1 (2018): 67–79.

[73] Sandler, *Global Challenges: An Approach to Environmental, Political, and Economic Problems*, 9–10.

[74] Ibid.

[75] See, for instance, Agreement on Trade-Related Aspects of Intellectual Property Rights, Annex 1C of the Agreement Establishing the World Trade Organization (WTO Agreement) (concluded at Marrakesh on 15 April 1994, entered into force 1 January 1995) 33 *ILM* 1197.

resource well.[76] However, it has to be kept in mind that their characteristic of rivalness does not exclude the risk of extinction by over-consumption and that privatisation is by no means the only policy instrument to preserve CPRs (e.g. shared management by determining quotas or prohibitions).

When states cooperate to form a club, problems relate less to free-riding on the participation of other states, but rather to the details of the rules of the club and the internal distribution of benefits among club members.[77] The benefits of membership can then be used to obtain an agreement to the rules from potential new members, while the threat of exclusion from the club can be used to punish members breaching the rules.[78] This explains also why club good constellations are often found in international law in subject areas beyond trade law. International regimes relating to GPGs or CPRs may be linked to trading benefits, exclusion from which may serve as a tool to enforce compliance.[79]

GPGs and CPRs are similar as they are marked by the non-excludability of their benefits, which affect all states and thus generate classic collective action problems of free-riding. They differ, however, in their focus of international cooperation.[80] As rivalrous goods, CPRs face the challenge of (over-)consumption, the so-called tragedy of the commons, as common resources are given by nature (or in the case of cultural heritage are unique creations of humankind) and cannot be reproduced in the case of extinction or destruction.[81] The focus of international cooperation thus needs to lie on non-consumption or preservation of the global commons. Prime examples are the protection of the high seas, the atmosphere or the ozone layer from pollution, the protection of biodiversity and endangered species from extinction, the protection of fish stocks from overfishing or the protection of seabed mineral deposits from deep seabed mining. CPR mechanisms in international law to counter, for instance, ozone depletion or climate change, are thus about prohibitions or limitations of emissions, fishing, hunting, trading, or other harmful activities. The problem of international cooperation is that free-riders can act as spoilers of

[76] Barkin and Rashchupkina, "Public Goods, Common Pool Resources, and International Law," 387. With reference to Edella Schlager and Elinor Ostrom, "Property-Rights Regimes and Natural Resources: A Conceptual Analysis," *Land Economics* 68, no. 3 (1992): 249–262.

[77] Barkin and Rashchupkina, "Public Goods, Common Pool Resources, and International Law," 379–380. With further references.

[78] Ibid., 388.

[79] On enforcement of international law, in particular compliance with GPG obligations, by mechanisms of exclusion from trading regimes (i.e. outcasting), see Sect. 2.4.

[80] J. Samuel Barkin and Yuliya Rashchupkina clearly point out that there can be, in many cases, a difference between the proximate good in question and the proximate focus of international cooperation. Barkin and Rashchupkina, "Public Goods, Common Pool Resources, and International Law," 382.

[81] Ibid., 383–384. On cultural commons, with reference to Francesco Francioni, "Public and Private in the International Protection of Global Cultural Goods," *European Journal of International Law* 23, no. 3 (2012): 719–730.

cooperation through consumption and thus partially or fully undermine cooperation.[82] One problem is that the free-riders frustrating international cooperation over CPRs are likely to be those states that have the greatest ability to use up the resource (for instance, the largest emitters of carbon dioxide with regard to climate change mitigation).[83] CPR mechanisms must therefore focus on discouraging those states most able to consume and on inducing them to participate for legal mechanisms to be effective.[84] However, those potential free-riders are likely to have the greatest say in matters regarding the content of the law regulating the CPR and regarding the distribution of the resource.[85] Consequently, effective cooperation is often only spurred by the threat of an imminent disaster or an actual catastrophe.[86] The Montreal Protocol on Substances that Deplete the Ozone Layer is a positive example in that regard,[87] although its success is also due to other factors, such as enforcement by way of exclusion from trading benefits.[88]

The problem of GPGs as non-rivalrous goods, by contrast, lies in their provision, at least in cases where the GPG needs to be provided by states in a decentralised legal order (e.g. international peace).[89] In such a prisoner's dilemma situation, two or more states face strong incentives to defect from cooperation (for example, defence cooperation aiming at maintaining international peace) and to free-ride on the provision of the GPG by others. GPGs face the risk that cooperation ultimately fails and the good is not provided at all. Many aspects in international cooperation have GPG characteristics, which are marked primarily by the non-excludability of benefits. These can relate to the primary object of the international treaty (i.e. the provision of a certain GPG such as international peace or global health), to financing arrangements aiming to facilitate participation in the provision of the GPG or the preservation of a CPR (e.g. climate financing)[90] or enforcement mechanisms such as sanctions.[91] Insights about different ways of providing GPGs are therefore crucial to understand many institutions in international law.

---

[82] Barkin and Rashchupkina, "Public Goods, Common Pool Resources, and International Law," 385.

[83] Ibid.

[84] Ibid.

[85] Ibid.

[86] Kaul, Grunberg, and Stern, "Defining Global Public Goods," in *Global Public Goods: International Cooperation in the 21st Century*, ed. Kaul, Grunberg, and Stern, 8–9.

[87] Montreal Protocol on Substances that Deplete the Ozone Layer (Montreal Protocol) (concluded 16 September 1987, entered into force 1 January 1989) 1522 *UNTS* 28.

[88] Such enforcement mechanisms are also used in the Convention on International Trade in Endangered Species of Wild Fauna and Flora (CITES) (concluded 3 March 1973, entered into force 1 July 1975) 993 *UNTS* 243.

[89] For GPGs created by nature (e.g. sunlight), there is no cooperation problem as consumption of the good by one state does not diminish its availability for others.

[90] On financing of global public goods, see, in particular, Kaul and Conceição, *The New Public Finance: Responding to Global Challenges*.

[91] On public good characteristics of enforcement mechanisms, see Sect. 2.4.

The conditions for the provision of GPGs can, however, be more or less favourable depending on the type of the public good, and thus lead to a different prognosis regarding the success of a collective response to a certain global challenge.[92] The issue of provision relates to another property of public goods, beyond non-excludability and non-rivalness, namely "how individual contributions influence the total quantity of the public good that is available for consumption", the so-called aggregation technology.[93] Jack Hirshleifer developed the argument that one needs to distinguish between different types of public goods, each having a different problem structure in terms of provision: in addition to the standard summation formula, there are the weakest-link and the best-shot rule.[94] Scott Barrett offered an illustrative overview of these three different types of public goods in the international context,[95] while Todd Sandler provided the game-theoretical underpinning of their respective ways of provision.[96]

The first type of goods are weakest-link GPGs, whose supply depends on the weakest individual effort.[97] The weakest-link aggregator entails that the quantity of the GPG provided, and thus available for consumption, equals the smallest contribution with the consequence that a single non-cooperator can undermine the collective efforts of other states.[98] Common examples are the eradication of diseases, the maintenance of trade boycotts, the elimination of terrorist safe havens, the fight against money laundering, or the non-proliferation of nuclear weapons.[99] Weakest-link GPGs face the challenge that they require, in principle, universal participation for effective provision.[100] In many instances, the underlying game will foremost be a coordination game,[101] and more specifically, an assurance game. States have an incentive to participate in the provision of the GPG once assured that all other

---

[92]Todd Sandler, "Strategic Aspects of Difficult Global Challenges," *Global Policy* 7, Supplement 1 (2016): 34.

[93]Ibid., 35.

[94]Jack Hirshleifer, "From Weakest-Link to Best-Shot: The Voluntary Provision of Public Goods," *Public Choice* 41, no. 3 (1983): 371–386.

[95]Barrett, *Why Cooperate? The Incentive to Supply Global Public Goods.*

[96]Sandler, *Global Challenges: An Approach to Environmental, Political, and Economic Problems*; Sandler, *Global Collective Action*; Todd Sandler, "Overcoming Global and Regional Collective Action Impediments," *Global Policy* 1, no. 1 (2010): 40–50; Sandler, "Strategic Aspects of Difficult Global Challenges," 33–44.

[97]Barrett, *Why Cooperate? The Incentive to Supply Global Public Goods*, 3–5.

[98]Sandler, "Strategic Aspects of Difficult Global Challenges," 35.

[99]Further examples of weakest-link GPGs involve eliminating the dispersion of invasive species, monitoring environmental degradation, stopping the spread of computer viruses, or preserving an endangered species. Ibid., 33–35. Hence, some examples relate to the provision of pure GPGs while others relate to the preservation of CPRs.

[100]Barrett, *Why Cooperate? The Incentive to Supply Global Public Goods*, 3.

[101]Ibid., 3–5, 200. In coordination games, "the largest (joint or individual) pay-offs to the players would come from their co-ordinating their behaviour. Because players have difficulty anticipating other players' strategies, co-ordination is hard to achieve." Bix, *A Dictionary of Legal Theory*, s.v. "co-ordination games".

countries participate as well,[102] provided they have the capacity to participate and have more to gain from the provision of the GPG than from the active frustration of these efforts. Thus, in some cases financing and cost-sharing arrangements may be needed,[103] thus transforming the underlying game from that of assurance to a prisoner's dilemma.[104]

The provision of summation GPGs, or aggregate-effort GPGs, only yields benefits once the total contributions of states exceed some threshold level.[105] Examples for a threshold aggregator are the mitigation of global climate change, the protection of the ozone layer, species preservation requiring a threshold habitat size, or (supposing a transnational dimension) collective efforts to extinguish a forest fire.[106] Summation GPGs differ from weakest-link GPGs in that contributions by one state benefit all other states without the need to match contribution levels, and thus generally abide by a prisoner's dilemma.[107] The underlying game of aggregate-effort GPGs will therefore often correspond to a cooperation game, where assurances for participation may have the opposite effect and rather encourage free-riding.[108] Free-riding is aggravated in the presence of other factors such as consequences of inaction materialising in the far future, uncertainty about the extent of the negative consequences, individual states contributing differently to the harm, or states being affected to different degrees (for instance, in the case of climate change mitigation).[109] Provision of aggregate-effort GPGs can, however, be successful when the circumstances are favourable (as they have been, for instance, in the case of the protection of the ozone layer).[110] Aggregate-effort and weakest-link GPGs can face similar challenges, namely uncertainty about the cooperative intent of other states and coordination of efforts among many states, especially when a minimal-sized coalition is needed.[111] The success of partial cooperation of a group of states can be

---

[102] Barrett, *Why Cooperate? The Incentive to Supply Global Public Goods*, 3–5.

[103] Ibid., 20.

[104] Sandler, "Strategic Aspects of Difficult Global Challenges," 33, 36, 42. With reference to Simon Vicary, "Transfers and the Weakest-Link: An Extension of Hirshleifer's Analysis," *Journal of Public Economics* 43, no. 3 (1990): 375–394; Simon Vicary and Todd Sandler, "Weakest-Link Public Goods: Giving in-Kind or Transferring Money," *European Economic Review* 46, no. 8 (2002): 1501–1520.

[105] Sandler, "Strategic Aspects of Difficult Global Challenges," 35.

[106] Ibid.; Barrett, *Why Cooperate? The Incentive to Supply Global Public Goods*, 5–7.

[107] Sandler, "Strategic Aspects of Difficult Global Challenges," 35–36, 41.

[108] Barrett, *Why Cooperate? The Incentive to Supply Global Public Goods*, 5–7.

[109] Ibid.

[110] Ibid.

[111] Sandler, "Strategic Aspects of Difficult Global Challenges," 35, 42. Like Barkin and Rashchupkina, I will refer to such a minimal-sized coalition as a *k-group*, for the purpose of GPG provision usually consisting of the biggest and richest countries. Barkin and Rashchupkina, "Public Goods, Common Pool Resources, and International Law." The term *k-group* is traditionally used in the relevant economics and political science literature, see, for instance, Duncan Snidal, "The Limits of Hegemonic Stability Theory," *International Organization* 39, no. 4 (1985): 599.

frustrated when non-cooperating countries have the capacity and motivation to more than offset the achievements of the cooperating states.[112] International institutions can facilitate coordination by correlating the level of individual contributions (e.g. the permitted emissions level),[113] and cooperation among states by determining financial contributions (e.g. climate finance).[114]

The third type of goods are best-shot GPGs, whose level of provision is determined by the largest contribution.[115] Best-shot GPGs are in the literature also referred to as single best-effort GPGs meaning that provision of the good depends on the best individual or collective effort.[116] Examples for a best-shot aggregator are peacekeeping efforts (e.g. the neutralisation of a transnational terrorist group) or the production of knowledge (e.g. the development of a vaccine or cure against an infectious disease).[117] Theoretically, best-shot GPGs are the easiest to supply as their provision requires only a single sufficient contribution, usually by a large country with the necessary means, but at the same time the stakes need to be high enough for the state to be motivated to provide the good despite the risk of free-riding by other states (e.g. an existential threat affecting all countries).[118] In many cases, the contribution to a best-shot GPG must surpass a threshold before the good is supplied, but unlike aggregate-effort GPGs individual contributions to a best-shot GPG are not cumulative, as it is the greatest effort that stands the best chance of accomplishing the task.[119] States thus need to coordinate their actions, so that efforts for provision are not duplicated.[120] The underlying game is a coordination game, but for which only one state needs to act since the actions of other countries are redundant once the good is provided.[121] In many cases, international cooperation through international institutions will therefore be needed in order to determine the necessary action to be taken and how to share the costs of provision.[122]

In sum, the prognosis for GPG provision is less pessimistic as the success of a collective response to a certain global challenge depends on the actual underlying game and the individual contribution of states to the quantity of the good provided. For all three types of GPGs, one needs to clearly determine whether the underlying game is one of coordination (for instance, the determination of individual

---

112 Sandler, "Strategic Aspects of Difficult Global Challenges," 40–43.

113 Ibid., 42. With reference to Daniel G. Arce M. and Todd Sandler, "Transnational Public Goods: Strategies and Institutions," *European Journal of Political Economy* 17, no. 3 (2001): 493–516.

114 Barrett, *Why Cooperate? The Incentive to Supply Global Public Goods*, 20.

115 Sandler, "Strategic Aspects of Difficult Global Challenges," 35.

116 Barrett, *Why Cooperate? The Incentive to Supply Global Public Goods*, 2–3.

117 Sandler, "Strategic Aspects of Difficult Global Challenges," 35, 42.

118 Barrett, *Why Cooperate? The Incentive to Supply Global Public Goods*, 2–3.

119 Sandler, "Strategic Aspects of Difficult Global Challenges," 35.

120 Ibid.

121 Ibid. With reference to Todd Sandler, *Collective Action: Theory and Applications* (Ann Arbor: University of Michigan Press, 1992).

122 Barrett, *Why Cooperate? The Incentive to Supply Global Public Goods*, 20.

contribution levels) or cooperation (for instance, the issue of financing), as they create different incentives for provision. GPGs which require that states agree on a certain global standard, for instance, universally accepted time zones, depend on states doing the same thing and are thus relatively easy to supply through coordination.[123] In coordination games, international norms set standards (e.g. regulation of air travel) and thus serve as a focal point for the coordination of state behaviour.[124] Agreement on a common standard does not require financing or cost-sharing, only a certain threshold level of participating countries, but once states have chosen a common standard, no country has an incentive to deviate from the legal norm which is largely self-enforcing.[125] International institutions for provision can therefore be treaties, but also other forms of non-binding international law (e.g. resolutions or soft law).[126] This is different for those GPGs which require that states agree to abstain from a certain behaviour, for instance, norms prohibiting the use or proliferation of nuclear weapons.[127] Effective supply of the good depends on continuous provision through mutual restraint and compliance is comparatively challenging to sustain.[128] Those GPGs which require an active contribution of a large number of states are probably the most challenging to supply, in particular when they require financing and cost-sharing.[129] Issues of financing and burden sharing are thus important elements of all international agreements addressing GPGs, which is not surprising given that international law has from an economic perspective, amongst others, a cost allocation function. Cost allocation also plays a significant role in the economic analysis of the law of state responsibility, which includes compensation requirements, for instance, in the case of the invocation of exemptions or as reparation of damage caused by an internationally wrongful act.

To conclude, from an economic perspective, the role of international institutions and international law is to set incentives for overcoming the collective action problems underlying different global challenges. Alongside informal global governance mechanisms (e.g. non-binding declarations), international law serves as a more formalised policy tool to overcome cooperative challenges. The tools with which international law can facilitate cooperation among states consist in various legal instruments: states can create international obligations that determine the level of supply of GPGs (e.g. norms of human rights protection), they can adopt international agreements that set common standards to better coordinate their efforts in fighting the extinction of common resources, they can create clubs to facilitate the mutual exchange of benefits and exclude non-members, they can allocate property

[123] Ibid., 9, 20.

[124] Guzman, *How International Law Works: A Rational Choice Theory*, 25–29.

[125] Barrett, *Why Cooperate? The Incentive to Supply Global Public Goods*, 9, 20. See also Sect. 2.4 on enforcement mechanisms in international law.

[126] Ibid., 20.

[127] Ibid., 9, 20.

[128] Ibid.

[129] Ibid., 7–9.

rights by mechanisms of privatisation (e.g. the creation of patents or national borders), adopt compensation requirements to mitigate the consequences of negative externalities like cross-border pollution, and so on. As will be further outlined in Chap. 3 on the normative framework of this book, the international law of state responsibility is one such tool of international law that serves multiple objectives depending on the underlying cooperation problem.

2.3 An Economic Perspective on Community Interest Protection in International Law

This section brings the two threads of international law and economic theory together by taking an economic perspective on the protection of community interests in international law. It will examine existing community interest norms from the perspective of economic goods theory and explain and exemplify their degree of congruence across areas of international law. The idea is to gain a more systematic understanding of different types of primary obligations based on their content and objectives. This will set the ground for the subsequent analysis of the problem-solving capacity of state responsibility rules with regard to different global challenges, in particular the provision of GPGs, and thus independent from the concrete issue area of the primary obligation in question.[130]

The terms GPGs and community interests are often used interchangeably in the legal literature for issues of common concern, transcending the self-interest of sovereign nation states.[131] If one understands community interests in a broad sense, covering all kinds of other-regarding interests beyond the particular interests of nation states, it becomes clear why this is tempting, given that GPGs are also often

---

[130] It shall be noted that the effectiveness of the secondary law of state responsibility in addressing global challenges depends inherently on the existence and ambition of primary international obligations, and that the creation of community interest norms in the decentralised international legal order is a cooperative challenge in its own right. On the role of consent- or consensus-based decision-making in international law for the provision of global public goods, see for a critical account Nico Krisch, "The Decay of Consent: International Law in an Age of Global Public Goods," *American Journal of International Law* 108, no. 1 (2014): 1–40. For moving towards greater support for non-consensual soft law in order to overcome the consent problem, see Andrew T. Guzman, "Against Consent," *Virginia Journal of International Law* 52, no. 4 (2012): 747–790. However, failure to address global challenges through cooperation between states may have many reasons and need not be traced back uniquely to the principle of consent-based law-making, as international law can also serve to induce cooperation between states. For such a more optimistic view on international law, see Anne van Aaken, "Is International Law Conducive to Preventing Looming Disasters?," *Global Policy* 7, Supplement 1 (2016): 81–96.

[131] For the most recent theoretical analysis of community interest protection building on the concepts of global public goods, global commons, and fundamental values, see the different contributions in Iovane et al., *The Protection of General Interests in Contemporary International Law: A Theoretical and Empirical Inquiry*.

understood broadly in the legal and international relations literature. However, community interests and GPGs are conceptually not the same, both concepts simply allow us to look on the same issue of global challenges from a different angle. As outlined before, from an economic perspective, international law aims to facilitate the provision of GPGs (or to address other cooperation problems underlying different goods) by self-interested states. This is conceptually different from a normative understanding of international law reflecting the interests of the international community as a whole or of third states (and people under their jurisdiction) more generally.[132] From a legal perspective, states are presumed to pursue both individual and community interests.[133] In contrast, based on the rational choice model followed here,[134] states are assumed to act only in their self-interest. This does not exclude the provision of GPGs (or the preservation of CPRs), but states would only cooperate unless it is also in their self-interest, that is when the benefits of providing the good outweigh the costs, notwithstanding that others can also benefit from the good without having contributed or having contributed less. However, both approaches overlap in the sense that the law protecting a community interest can at the same time be the legal instrument designed to further the provision of GPGs by self-interested states.

Keeping these conceptual differences in mind, one can still sketch out the extent to which community interest norms and different types of goods relate to the same global challenge. When GPGs are understood in pure economic terms, that is with regard to their main characteristics of non-excludability and nonrivalry, the concept is only congruent with community interests to a certain extent. International obligations reflecting community interests that aim to protect interests of the international community as a whole (e.g. "the common heritage of mankind", or the concept of *jus cogens*)[135] overlap with international legal rules facilitating the provision of GPGs (e.g. international peace and security, enjoyment of a common cultural or natural resource per se, the international legal order as such[136]) to the extent that these goods potentially benefit everyone everywhere around the world and that their consumption does not prevent others from profiting from the same good. As indicated earlier,

---

[132] This understanding relates to the broad definition of community interests outlined in Sect. 2.1, stemming from Benvenisti and Nolte, "Community Interests across International Law: Introduction," in *Community Interests across International Law*, ed. Benvenisti and Nolte, 3–5.

[133] Besson, "Community Interests in International Law: Whose Interests Are They and How Should We Best Identify Them?," in *Community Interests across International Law*, ed. Benvenisti and Nolte, 37.

[134] See Sect. 1.3 on the rational choice approach in international law.

[135] Benvenisti and Nolte, "Community Interests across International Law: Introduction," in *Community Interests across International Law*, ed. Benvenisti and Nolte, 4. On the degree of congruence between *jus cogens* and *erga omnes (partes)* norms with different types of goods, see Chap. 3 on the objectives of the international law of state responsibility.

[136] Legal clarity about national borders is a GPG, but the delimitation of national territories constitutes an act of privatising, the national territory being a private good. Thus, not every international agreement or obligation is itself a GPG, because that depends on the underlying cooperation problem.

common values can be translated into GPGs to the extent that all states derive value from their existence (the so-called non-use value goods).[137] This holds also true for the protection of human rights, which has characteristics of a normative public good to the extent that people derive value from the knowledge that fundamental rights norms exist and are effectively enforced in the international community.[138] Non-use value GPGs or normative GPGs then cover international obligations reflecting community interests that aim to protect interests of other states including the people under their jurisdiction. Community interests also denote interests shared on a non-universal level and protected by international agreements binding only groups of states.[139] This dimension of community interests corresponds to the concept of transnational or regional public goods, thus public goods on the international scene that are in terms of their geographical reach less than global. International treaties that serve as mechanisms to provide GPGs can have different forms of participation, from almost all states being part of the agreement (e.g. the treaty establishing the UN[140]) to only a critical *k-group* (e.g. bilateral arms control treaties) to provide the GPG of international peace and security. The European Convention on Human Rights (ECHR), concluded among members of the Council of Europe, constitutes an example of an agreement serving the provision of a regional public good, namely human rights protection.[141] Lastly, to the extent that the consumption of certain goods leads to their extinction (e.g. common natural or cultural resources), the concept of community interests overlaps with CPRs. Hence, both GPG and CPR obligations reflect community interest norms in the public dimension of international law.[142]

On the opposite side of community interest norms are international obligations covering bilateral relations with the aim to serve exclusively the protection of mutual self-interests (e.g. defence of national borders, protection of territorial waters, protection of foreign investments). These can be considered private goods obligations, as the object is characterised by rivalry in consumption and excludability of benefits (building on the notion of property rights transferred to states). I therefore consider them belonging to the private dimension of international law, where self-interested states cooperate to resolve disputes over negative externalities (similar to tort law in the domestic context).[143] In the private dimension, self-interested states

[137] On the definition of non-use value goods, see Sect. 2.2.

[138] For human rights protection as a normative public good, see, for instance, Pinto de Albuquerque and van Aaken, "Punitive Damages in Strasbourg," in *The European Convention on Human Rights and General International Law*, ed. van Aaken and Motoc, 247.

[139] Feichtner, "Community Interest," para. 4.

[140] Charter of the United Nations (UN Charter) (concluded 26 June 1945, entered into force 24 October 1945, as amended 24 September 1973) 892 *UNTS* 119.

[141] European Convention for the Protection of Human Rights and Fundamental Freedoms (ECHR) (concluded 4 November 1950, entered into force 3 September 1953) 213 *UNTS* 221.

[142] See Chap. 3 on the private and public dimensions of the international law of state responsibility.

[143] International legal rules then address negative externalities emanating from a state acting in its self-interest or from a club of states (i.e. spillovers outside the club).

can also cooperate to further their mutual self-interest in terms of economic gains by forming a club (similar to contract law in the domestic context). International obligations with the object to promote only the mutual interests of a certain community or group of states, while excluding outsiders from such non-rival benefits, exist, for instance, in international trade law. However, club goods (as mixed goods) are particular in that regard as the formation of a club can serve multiple objectives ranging from the provision of GPGs (e.g. human rights protection) to the reduction of trade barriers. Because it is possible to exclude outsiders from certain benefits of cooperation (i.e. trading benefits), clubs are a forceful compliance mechanism.[144] It is important to bear in mind that one single regime can serve multiple purposes. For example, the European Union (EU) facilitates the provision of European and global public goods (e.g. climate policies having potentially worldwide benefits) but also constitutes a club regarding the internal market rules and the common trade policy. The character of an international agreement thus depends on the specific objectives and obligations as well as the underlying enforcement mechanisms.

In a nutshell, from an economic perspective, states always act in their self-interest and face in a decentralised international legal order different cooperative challenges that belong rather to one or the other dimension of international law. The dividing line between the private and the public dimension does not relate to states acting either in the self-interest or the interest of the community at large, but to the characteristic of excludability of benefits vis-à-vis third parties. Community interests in the public dimension of international law encompass GPGs and CPRs, while the private dimension of international law relates to the creation of economic gains or deals with the problem of externalities emanating from private goods.

This degree of congruence between community interests and different types of goods at the international level can be illustrated with a few examples. Firstly, community interests are protected to a certain extent in the international law regulating the use of force.[145] I argue that one needs to understand the general prohibition of the use of force laid down in Article 2(4) UN Charter as an obligation aiming to ensure the GPG of international peace and security by way of mutual restraint. That states have under certain conditions outlined in Chapter VII of the UN Charter (e.g. a mandate from the UN Security Council) the exceptional right to the use of force points in the same direction. This is because international norms regulating interventions for the protection against egregious breaches of common interests of humankind (e.g. acts of aggression, genocide, or crimes against humanity) can equally be considered as aiming to facilitate the provision of the GPG of international peace and security or the protection of fundamental human rights norms as an explicit derogation from the prohibition of the use of force lowers the costs of such interventions. However, states having recourse to the use of force as a matter of

[144] On compliance mechanisms, see Sect. 2.4.

[145] See, for instance, Enzo Cannizzaro, "Common Interests of Humankind and the International Regulation of the Use of Force," in *Community Interests across International Law*, ed. Eyal Benvenisti and Georg Nolte (Oxford: Oxford University Press, 2018), 417–429.

individual self-defence against an armed attack of another state (Article 51 UN Charter) are rather acting in the aim of protecting national interests, which relates to a private goods scenario (e.g. non-interference in national affairs protection of national sovereignty).[146] As regards the *ius in bello*, international humanitarian law (IHL) lays down community rights and obligations of the parties to an international armed conflict as well as of third parties to such conflict.[147] This body of law is grounded at its origin on reciprocal bilateral relations between states with the mutual self-interest in making warfare more humanitarian. Yet, to the extent that IHL expects parties to take into account interests of the community as a whole when conducting hostilities (e.g. the prohibition of war crimes) and even creates third-party obligations (see Common Article 1 of the Geneva Conventions: "to ensure respect for the present Convention in all circumstances"[148]), I argue that it reflects the protection of GPGs. The benefits of these obligations are non-rival and non-excludable beyond the fate of individual victims as people anywhere in the world derive value from the assurance that fundamental community norms (such as the protection of civilians during military conflicts) are respected even in times of warfare. To the extent that IHL creates third-party rights (for instance, in terms of compensation for individual harm) it addresses the impact of an armed conflict on states and the people under its jurisdiction, thus addressing in my opinion negative externalities (cross-border effects) resulting from an armed conflict.

Secondly, most international law regulating natural resources can intuitively be thought of as serving the protection of community interests. However. international rules addressing different common resource issues are not automatically directly addressing CPR problems. As for the law of the sea, for example, the legal concept "common heritage of mankind" reflects the need to protect natural resources (e.g. by regulating deep seabed mining) from extinction, a classic CPR mechanism.[149] By

---

[146]This principle is also reflected in the justification of self-defence in Article 21 ARSIWA, which requires as a condition a lawful measure taken in conformity with the UN Charter and leads to an exemption from state responsibility. The underlying cooperation problem of collective self-defence, that is a scenario where one state is permitted to use force in response to an armed attack against another state, provided that the victim state of an armed attack requests assistance, is equally not to provide a GPG, but primarily to assist each other in the defence of national state interests, notably the interest in survival. See Sect. 5.3.2.2 on self-defence.

[147]For more details, see Janina Dill, "'The Rights and Obligations of Parties to International Armed Conflicts': From Bilateralism but Not Towards Community Interest?," in *Community Interests across International Law*, ed. Eyal Benvenisti and Georg Nolte (Oxford: Oxford University Press, 2018), 430–447; Heike Krieger, "Rights and Obligations of Third Parties in Armed Conflicts," in *Community Interests across International Law*, ed. Eyal Benvenisti and Georg Nolte (Oxford: Oxford University Press, 2018), 448–467.

[148]See, for instance, Geneva Convention for the Amelioration of the Condition of the Wounded and Sick in Armed Forces in the Field (Geneva Convention I) (concluded 12 August 1949, entered into force 21 October 1950) 75 *UNTS* 31.

[149]Articles 136, 137 of the United Nations Convention on the Law of the Sea (UNCLOS). For more details on this issue, see Surabhi Ranganathan, "The Law of the Sea and Natural Resources," in *Community Interests across International Law*, ed. Eyal Benvenisti and Georg Nolte (Oxford: Oxford University Press, 2018), 121–135.

contrast, the creation of EEZ within the same issue area, transforms the CPR by way of exclusion in a private good issue, as seabed mining comes under the jurisdiction of nation states.[150] Similarly, international environmental law, while being an area predominantly aiming to serve the common interest (e.g. addressing biodiversity loss[151]), contains different dimensions when examined through the lens of economic goods theory. Regarding climate change law,[152] rules aiming to protect the atmosphere from further pollution, thus preventing over-consumption, constitute a CPR mechanism relying on aggregate efforts but the enjoyment of the climate is a GPG. The scenario of environmental pollution stemming from industrial activity in a transboundary context is addressed by international law with mechanisms mitigating negative externalities such as the harm prevention rule and the due diligence standard.[153] International law regulating another common resource namely cultural goods can also be considered a CPR mechanism, as adding a cultural heritage site (the enjoyment of which would be a GPG) to the list of world culture heritage aims to serve its preservation from extinction in the common interest.[154] Cross-border disputes about ownership, trade, or destruction of cultural heritage would relate to private good scenarios.

Thirdly, international economic law does not only reflect the mutual promotion of national interests, but may also integrate community interests to a certain extent. Christian Tietje and Andrej Lang argue that the law of the World Trade Organization (WTO)[155] aims to protect "the community interest of promoting an essentially rules-based and fair world market" as well as "trade-conducive structures that enable and further global economic activity for the purpose of generating overall welfare".[156]

[150]Part V of the United Nations Convention on the Law of the Sea (UNCLOS).

[151]See, for instance, the Convention on Wetlands of International Importance Especially as Waterfowl Habitat (Ramsar Convention) (concluded 2 February 1971, entered into force 21 December 1975) 996 *UNTS* 245.

[152]See, in particular, Paris Agreement (concluded 12 December 2015, entered into force 4 November 2016) 55 *ILM* 743.

[153]For more details on this issue, see Jutta Brunnée, "International Environmental Law and Community Interests: Procedural Aspects," in *Community Interests across International Law*, ed. Eyal Benvenisti and Georg Nolte (Oxford: Oxford University Press, 2018), 151–175. The harm prevention rule and the due diligence standard will be further discussed in Chap. 4 on conditions for state responsibility and responsibility standards.

[154]UNESCO Convention for the Protection of the World Cultural and Natural Heritage (concluded 16 November 1972, entered into force 7 December 1975) 1037 *UNTS* 151. See for more details on this issue, Lorenzo Casini, "Cultural Sites between Nationhood and Mankind," in *Community Interests across International Law*, ed. Eyal Benvenisti and Georg Nolte (Oxford: Oxford University Press, 2018), 176–187.

[155]Agreement Establishing the World Trade Organization (WTO Agreement) (concluded at Marrakesh on 15 April 1994, entered into force 1 January 1995) 33 *ILM* 1144.

[156]Christian Tietje and Andrej Lang, "Community Interests in World Trade Law," in *Community Interests across International Law*, ed. Eyal Benvenisti and Georg Nolte (Oxford: Oxford University Press, 2018), 220. See also Christian Tietje and Andrej Lang, "Community Interests in World Trade Law," *Beiträge zum Transnationalen Wirtschaftsrecht* Heft 141 (Dezember 2016).

While this line of argumentation seems to interpret world trade as a GPG (as much as the existence of an international legal order as such), I argue that trade rules in their underlying logic need to be understood primarily as rules creating and governing a club. The WTO does not have universal membership and should in terms of its structure rather be compared with other free-trade regimes, notably regional free-trade agreements. The foundational principles of WTO law are the most-favoured nation (MFN) and the national treatment (NT) clauses aiming at protecting the equality of competitive conditions between WTO members.[157] These principles point towards the main characteristics of a club good mechanism, limiting the non-rival benefits of the club to its members by way of exclusion, while trying to limit distributional concerns within the club. Consequently, disputes over trade rules usually arise between individual members of the club, which means that enforcement of trade rules is still based on reciprocity. The same logic applies with every step of deeper economic integration, from a customs union (e.g. Andean Community or European Union Customs Union) over a common market (e.g. ASEAN or European Economic Area) to an economic union (e.g. EU or Mercosur). The latter are characterised by common policies on product regulation, free movement of goods, services, capital and labour, as well as a common external trade policy. To put it more generally, the deeper the economic integration of the members of a club, the more benefits are to be distributed among its members, while non-members are excluded from their enjoyment.

Regarding international investment law (IIL), international investment agreements (IIAs) can be considered mixed goods. In their original form as bilateral investment treaties (BITs) they are private goods where the contracting parties exchange mutual benefits: while the investor host state benefits economically from attracting foreign investments, the investor home state benefits from a framework of legal review protecting its investors (e.g. their property) against illegal national regulations and laws and misconduct of administrative entities.[158] The characterisation of private goods holds also for multilateral treaty regimes such as the Comprehensive Economic and Trade Agreement (CETA), to the extent that they contain an investment promotion and protection component, in this example between the EU

[157] Tietje and Lang, "Community Interests in World Trade Law," in *Community Interests across International Law*, ed. Benvenisti and Nolte, 220. Both principles are laid down in several WTO agreements, the most-favoured nation clause, for instance, in Article I of the GATT and Article II of the GATS, the national treatment clause in Article III of the GATT and Article XVII of the GATS. See, respectively, Multilateral Agreements on Trade in Goods, General Agreement on Tariffs and Trade (GATT), Annex 1A of the Agreement Establishing the World Trade Organization (WTO Agreement) (concluded at Marrakesh on 15 April 1994, entered into force 1 January 1995) 33 *ILM* 1154; General Agreement on Trade in Services (GATS), Annex 1B of the Agreement Establishing the World Trade Organization (WTO Agreement) (concluded at Marrakesh on 15 April 1994, entered into force 1 January 1995) 33 *ILM* 1168.

[158] On the framework of legal review in international investment law, see in particular Anne van Aaken, "Primary and Secondary Remedies in Investment Arbitration and State Liability: A Functional and Comparative View," in *International Investment Law and Comparative Public Law*, ed. Stephan Schill (Oxford: Oxford University Press 2010), 721–722.

and Canada. But as they grant the investment promotion and protection benefits (like the non-rival benefits of the free-trade component) to all parties of the treaty regime, multilateral investment treaties can in terms of their underlying logic also be conceived as club goods. Almost any international investment agreement contains MFN clauses based on which investors can invoke a more favourable substantive treatment included in investment treaties the host state has concluded with third countries, which is why Stephan Schill views MFN clauses as bilateral commitments to multilateralism.[159] From this angle, IIAs contain also a club goods dimension to the extent that benefits granted to investors of one state in a mutual agreement are extended to investors of third parties. Stephan Schill and Vladislav Djanic argue, however, further that IIL even has a community interest dimension, because it is part of the legal infrastructure necessary for the functioning of the global economy and aims at supporting economic growth, thus furthering economic and noneconomic community interests, including sustainable development.[160] Taken all IIAs together one could certainly think of the GPG of an international legal order in the field of economic relations. In an interlinked global economy with multiple bilateral and multilateral investment treaties, these create a certain rule-based global market which eventually facilitates positive spillovers in terms of economic growth and welfare. Yet, I would not go so far as to characterise individual investment treaties as GPG treaties. Even if sustainable development goals are now enshrined in the preambles or provisions of a new generation of IIAs, this does not change their underlying nature as private or club goods treaties, furthering certainly the economic, and eventually sustainable, development in the investor host country, but only to a limited extent worldwide which would accord them GPG characteristics (mostly as normative or non-use value goods).

Another issue is how different areas of international economic law try to alleviate the negative externalities deriving from cross-border economic activities. To a certain degree, investment as well as trade regimes integrate mechanisms to mitigate conflicts by balancing noneconomic community interests such as environmental protection, labour standards, public health or human rights against trade and investment objectives.[161] As we will see further below, the necessity excuse in the international law of state responsibility constitutes one such mechanism to

---

[159] Stephan W. Schill, "MFN Clauses as Bilateral Commitments to Multilateralism: A Reply to Simon Batifort and J. Benton Heath," *American Journal of International Law* 111, no. 4 (2017): 914. For a more detailed analysis on why international investment law constitutes a multilateral regime built on bilateral treaties, see Stephan W. Schill, *The Multilateralization of International Investment Law* (Cambridge: Cambridge University Press, 2009).

[160] Stephan Schill and Vladislav Djanic, "International Investment Law and Community Interests," in *Community Interests across International Law*, ed. Eyal Benvenisti and Georg Nolte (Oxford: Oxford University Press, 2018), 248.

[161] See Tietje and Lang, "Community Interests in World Trade Law," in *Community Interests across International Law*, ed. Benvenisti and Nolte, 191–220; Schill and Djanic, "International Investment Law and Community Interests," in *Community Interests across International Law*, ed. Benvenisti and Nolte, 221–248.

accommodate conflicting interests more generally (beyond international economic relations).[162] One might also have to think about the negative effects of an economic club that sets its own standards to regulate market access, for instance, in terms of global poverty and economic inequalities, on the outsiders but also as a distributional issue within the club and how international economic law can mitigate these conflicts.[163]

Fourthly, international law addresses to a certain extent extraterritorial effects of state actions or of activities under state authority and protects in this regard community interests. This can be best explained with regard to international human rights law, which has primarily an internal dimension, because it contains obligations relating to the treatment by the state of its own citizens. These obligations are difficult to grasp from an economic perspective. They are not entirely a "private" matter of the state (contrary to fundamental rights obligations under constitutional law) but constitute promises of a state towards other states in the international community. These obligations relate therefore to the protection of interests of the international community, as people everywhere derive value from the knowledge that other states protect the fundamental rights of their citizens in accordance with international standards (human rights as a non-use value good or a normative public good).[164] This is even more evident regarding fundamental human rights obligations of *jus cogens* character (e.g. prohibition of slavery or torture).[165] From a legal perspective, international human rights obligations are *erga omnes* norms, that is obligations that are owed to the international community as a whole in which all states have an interest in compliance.[166] From a rational choice perspective, the behaviour of other states in their internal dimension is irrelevant, which is why there exists no prisoner's dilemma in the provision of the GPG of human rights protection as such, but only in the enforcement dimension of international state responsibility in the form of a sanctioners' dilemma.[167] These GPG characteristics explain why respect of human rights obligations is difficult to enforce by other states and why

---

[162] See Chap. 5 on exemptions from state responsibility.

[163] See for more details on this issue Ralph Wilde, "Socioeconomic Rights, Extraterritorially," in *Community Interests across International Law*, ed. Eyal Benvenisti and Georg Nolte (Oxford: Oxford University Press, 2018), 381–395.

[164] For human rights protection as a normative public good, see, for instance, Pinto de Albuquerque and van Aaken, "Punitive Damages in Strasbourg," in *The European Convention on Human Rights and General International Law*, ed. van Aaken and Motoc, 247.

[165] On the definition of *jus cogens* obligations and the congruence with GPGs, see Sect. 3.3.2.

[166] On the definition of *erga omnes* and *erga omnes partes* obligations and the congruence with the concept of GPGs, see Sect. 3.3.3.

[167] Anne van Aaken, "Die Befolgung des Völkerrechts zwischen Rationalismus, Konstruktivismus und Verhaltensökonomik," in *Warum befolgen wir Recht? Rechtsverbindlichkeit und Rechtsbefolgung in interdisziplinärer Perspektive*, ed. Patrick Hilbert and Jochen Rauber (Tübingen: Mohr Siebeck, 2019), 141. On the enforcement of international human rights obligations, including on the sanctioners' dilemma, see Sect. 2.4.

international human rights agreements are in many instances accompanied by individual complaint mechanisms.[168]

The reasoning is different when international human rights law has a cross-border dimension, as in the case of foreigner protection within the state's jurisdiction or the exercise of state authority outside its jurisdiction (extraterritoriality). I would translate these cross-border scenarios where sovereign states transgress their allocated spheres of jurisdiction as a constellation where "property rights" of other states (including people under their jurisdiction) are infringed by negative externalities emanating by activities of that state or private actors under their jurisdiction (by way of interference in internal affairs). International human rights obligations, even if they benefit subjectively individuals that suffered the harm, then serve to mitigate the negative spillovers between different spheres of jurisdiction. But also in this external dimension, international human rights law maintains its characteristics as a normative public good protecting the objective interests of the international community and can thus be considered an instrument protecting GPGs. The difference to human rights violations with a pure internal dimension is that there are victim states which may be more willing to bear the costs of enforcing compliance.

This overview served to illustrate the conceptual differences and the degree of congruence between community interests as a legal concept (broadly understood as other-regarding interests as opposed to national self-interests) and the economic concept of goods, where four ideal types represent different collective action problems for self-interested states. What the legal literature understands as a community interest constitutes from an economic perspective rather the challenge for self-interested states to provide GPGs and preserve CPRs characterised by the non-excludability of their benefits (in the public dimension of international law), whereas the reconciliation of opposing interests or the furthering of mutual interests in the private dimension of international law can in economic terms be translated into cooperative challenges related to private goods or club goods.

Therefore, I argue firstly that a stricter differentiation is needed within each issue area following the typology of goods at the international level, and not to equate community interests in a certain issue area too easily with GPGs as opposed to private goods. Secondly, when assessing legal rules in terms of their potential to address global challenges it is paramount to look at the underlying cooperation

---

[168] The number of inter-state complaints in human rights matters is, in fact, very low. For exceptions in the framework of the Council of Europe, see *Austria v. Italy*, Decision on admissibility, 11 January 1961, European Commission of Human Rights (Application No. 788/60). More recent examples are the pending cases at the European Court of Human Rights brought by Ukraine against the Russian Federation, most recently the allegations of an ongoing administrative practice consisting of state-authorised targeted assassination operations against perceived opponents of the Russian Federation in Russia and on the territory of other states (Application No. 10691/21). At the ICJ, a recent example is the invocation by Gambia as an African state of alleged genocide of the Rohingya by Myanmar, see *Application of the Convention on the Prevention and Punishment of the Crime of Genocide (The Gambia v. Myanmar)*, Order (Provisional Measures). See also, *Application of the Convention on the Prevention and Punishment of the Crime of Genocide in the Gaza Strip (South Africa v. Israel)*, Order (Provisional Measures).

problem addressed by an international obligation, and not whether state or community interests are protected. As these four different ideal types of goods and their underlying collective action problems are independent of the issue area, the idea is that the statements made in the analysis in the main part of this book hold true for the same cooperation problems across different subject areas of international law.

2.4 Enforcement of International Law and Mechanisms of Compliance

The effectiveness of international law in addressing global challenges requires not only adequate primary and secondary obligations, but it also depends on effective monitoring and enforcement mechanisms. A given international legal rule will set different incentives depending on the probability of enforcement being effective.[169] Unlike in the domestic context, where the enforcement function is exercised by executive organs, which have the power to impose costs and ultimately physical force on those that do not abide by the rules, international law is enforced by states as legal subjects themselves, either individually or collectively (private or first-party enforcement versus public or third-party enforcement).[170] This section will explain the so-called first-order and second-order cooperation problems in international law, that is, issues of compliance with primary and secondary obligations as well as enforcement thereof.[171] They relate to the different cooperative challenges for

[169] This probability is reflected in the variable p in the basic equation introduced in the previous chapter (Sect. 1.3), $C_V = p(L_{SR})$, according to which the costs of the violation of an international obligation equal the probability of the legal rule of state responsibility being effectively enforced.

[170] On the domestic level, a sanction (e.g. fine) can be enforced under different institutional arrangements, namely by public agencies and/or private parties (i.e. the victims of the violation). A. Mitchell Polinsky, "Private versus Public Enforcement of Fines," *Journal of Legal Studies* 9, no. 1 (1980): 105–127. Yet, even behind private enforcement, for instance a creditor suing a debtor, stand in domestic legal systems ultimately state organs threatening or exercising physical force, for instance a court order and subsequently the police permitting creditors to seize property from debtors. On the international level, state responsibility is in principle invoked by states against states on behalf of the person injured (Article 42 ARSIWA), thus via the so-called mechanism of diplomatic protection, see United Nations International Law Commission, „Draft Articles on Diplomatic Protection,"in *Report of the Commission to the General Assembly on the Work of its Fifty-Eighth Session*, 2006 (UN Doc. A/61/10). However, non-state actors have in certain subject areas standing to claim violation of their rights, for instance, individuals in (regional) human rights litigation and companies in international investment disputes. Yet, enforcement of judgments and awards of international courts and tribunals still relies on decentralised enforcement mechanisms of states themselves (that is, either by injured states or third states). This distinction between private and public enforcement in the national context and the use of these terms in international law will be further discussed in Chap. 3.

[171] For an overview of the compliance literature, including institutionalist, constructivist, and behavioural approaches, see Benedict Kingsbury, "The Concept of Compliance as a Function of Competing Conceptions of International Law," *Michigan Journal of International Law* 19, no.

rational self-interested states to comply with international law as well as to enforce international law in the decentralised legal order. The effectiveness of enforcement may vary depending on the underlying problem constellation, in particular whether it has GPG characteristics. These insights are relevant for the analysis of state responsibility law in the main part of this book as they explain the probability of enforcement being effective and thus setting incentives for compliance with the primary obligation in question (i.e. avoiding state responsibility).

Following the institutionalist tradition, we will see that international law relies on different enforcement mechanisms than law in the domestic context. Institutionalists argue that whether states comply with international norms depends on the underlying problem structures. In coordination games, the compliance level is high, since no state has an interest to defect once a common standard has been agreed.[172] As deviant behaviour is costly by nature, there is no problem to effectuate such international norms, and cooperation is achieved without specific enforcement requirements. In cooperation games, enforcement of international norms is much more difficult. In prisoner's dilemma constellations, a state may be better off not complying with the international rule, for instance, in GPG and CPR scenarios. From a rationalist view, states comply with international law when the benefits of compliance are higher than the costs of compliance, which include the forgone benefits from non-compliance.[173] Institutionalists explain compliance with essentially three enforcement mechanisms: retaliation, reciprocity, and reputation.[174] These can be understood as three different cost (or benefit) factors that rational self-interested states take into account in their decision whether to comply with international law.

2 (1998): 345–372; Beth A. Simmons, "Compliance with International Agreements," *Annual Review of Political Science* 1, no. 1 (1998): 75–93; Beth A. Simmons, "Treaty Compliance and Violation," *Annual Review of Political Science* 13, no. 1 (2010): 273–296; Jana von Stein, "The Engines of Compliance," in *Interdisciplinary Perspectives on International Law and International Relations: The State of the Art*, ed. Jeffrey L. Dunoff and Mark A. Pollack (Cambridge: Cambridge University Press, 2013), 477–501; Ingrid Wuerth, "Compliance," in *Concepts for International Law: Contributions to Disciplinary Thought*, ed. Jean d'Aspremont and Sahib Singh (Cheltenham, UK: Edward Elgar, 2019), 117–126; van Aaken, "Die Befolgung des Völkerrechts zwischen Rationalismus, Konstruktivismus und Verhaltensökonomik," in *Warum befolgen wir Recht? Rechtsverbindlichkeit und Rechtsbefolgung in interdisziplinärer Perspektive*, ed. Hilbert and Rauber, 135–160.

172 Guzman, *How International Law Works: A Rational Choice Theory*, 25–29.

173 Or, vice versa, and as outlined in Sect. 1.3, a state will be assumed to violate an international obligation if the expected benefits of the act (B_V) for the wrongdoing state outweigh the associated costs of non-compliance (C_V), that is $B_V > C_V$.

174 Guzman summarised these mechanisms as "the three Rs of compliance", see Guzman, *How International Law Works: A Rational Choice Theory*, 33–34. For von Stein, these three mechanisms are (alongside domestic institutions and politics) the main instrumentalist "engines of compliance". von Stein, "The Engines of Compliance," in *Interdisciplinary Perspectives on International Law and International Relations: The State of the Art*, ed. Dunoff and Pollack, 477–501.

To these, one can add outcasting and, more recently, rewarding, which further refine and elaborate the three "classical" enforcement mechanisms.[175]

Retaliation Retaliation relates to the use of sanctioning mechanisms, that is coercive measures by one or more states against the state in breach of an international obligation (e.g. retorsions and countermeasures,[176] such as economic, diplomatic, or military sanctions, outside the treaty regime in question).[177] Retaliatory actions increase the costs of non-compliance for the violating state, but their main characteristic is that they are also costly to the retaliating state.[178] The main problem of sanctions as a tool to enforce international law is therefore that retaliating states need to be willing to accept the associated enforcement costs.[179] States are only expected to take retaliatory actions when the benefits of sanctioning the breach exceed the related costs.[180] States immediately affected by a breach of international law are likely to derive most benefits from retaliation, if the sanctions succeed in forcing the violating state to return to legality (private or first-party enforcement). It becomes more complicated when more states are involved in providing enforcement (public or third-party enforcement).[181] In such a scenario, each state has incentives to wait until another state incurs the costs of sanctioning and thus to free-ride on the enforcement efforts of other states (the "sanctioners' dilemma").[182] Enforcement of international law constitutes therefore another collective action problem, a so-called second-order enforcement problem, and is in itself a global public good. In such a prisoners' dilemma situation, enforcement will usually be provided by a single powerful state (or group of states, a *k-group*), when the share of the benefits it

[175] Following the distinction made by Alexander Thompson, the focus here is on "horizontal" mechanisms of enforcement, where states target other states, thus leaving aside domestic avenues of international law enforcement, see Alexander Thompson, "Coercive Enforcement of International Law," in *Interdisciplinary Perspectives on International Law and International Relations: The State of the Art*, ed. Jeffrey L. Dunoff and Mark A. Pollack (Cambridge: Cambridge University Press, 2013), 503. For an overview of "vertical" mechanisms of enforcement through domestic institutions and politics, see Joel P. Trachtman, "Open Economy Law," in *Interdisciplinary Perspectives on International Law and International Relations: The State of the Art*, ed. Jeffrey L. Dunoff and Mark A. Pollack (Cambridge: Cambridge University Press, 2013), 544–567.

[176] On the definitions of retorsions (i.e. unfriendly but lawful measures) and countermeasures (i.e. pacific unilateral and intrinsically unlawful measures), see Chap. 7.

[177] Guzman, *How International Law Works: A Rational Choice Theory*, 32, 34.

[178] Ibid.

[179] van Aaken, "Die Befolgung des Völkerrechts zwischen Rationalismus, Konstruktivismus und Verhaltensökonomik," in *Warum befolgen wir Recht? Rechtsverbindlichkeit und Rechtsbefolgung in interdisziplinärer Perspektive*, ed. Hilbert and Rauber, 141.

[180] Ibid.

[181] For a more detailed explanation of private and public enforcement, see Chap. 3

[182] Alexander Thompson, "The Rational Enforcement of International Law: Solving the Sanctioners' Dilemma," *International Theory* 1, no. 2 (2009): 307–321.

can obtain exceeds the cost of providing the good.[183] Going more into detail of the nature of the benefits of law enforcement, Andrew T. Guzman argues that retaliating states accept the associated costs, because, if the violation is ongoing, sanctions provide an incentive for the violating state to come into compliance, and if successful, the retaliatory actions will enhance the state's reputation as one that punishes states violating their international engagements, thus deterring the violating state as well as third states from breaching international law in the future.[184] At the same time, he argues, the costs of retaliatory actions are often prohibitively high, so that the threat of sanctions is not credible, in particular in multilateral settings.[185] Alexander Thompson offers a more sophisticated argument on the conditions under which we might expect enforcement to be effective, that is, on when the sanctioners' dilemma can be overcome. He argues that states also need to take into account the potential political costs of sanctions, because other states of the international community (beyond the state which is targeted of the sanctions) may interpret the coercive act as an aggressive pursuit of selfish goals and not as a form of sincere enforcement in defence of international legal rules.[186] According to him, enforcement is most likely to be effective when the material and political costs of sanctioning are low, which is usually the case when a sanctioning state is much more powerful than the non-compliant state, thus rendering the material costs insignificant, and when the violation is egregious and obvious, thus making international support unproblematic.[187] He concludes that international institutions play an important role in inducing compliant behaviour by reducing the material costs (through burden sharing) and the political costs incurred by a sanctioning state (e.g. monitoring mechanisms).[188]

[183]With relation to the existence and maintenance of free-trade regimes, see Duncan Snidal in his discussion of hegemonic stability theory: "This outcome will be most likely when some single state, the hegemonic power, is sufficiently large relative to all others that it will capture a share of the benefit of the public good larger than the entire cost of providing it." Snidal, "The Limits of Hegemonic Stability Theory," 581.

[184]Guzman, *How International Law Works: A Rational Choice Theory*, 46–48. Thompson argues that states contemplating about taking sanctions consider also the long-term benefits supplied by the relevant treaty regime, not just the immediate benefits of compliance in a given case, see Thompson, "The Rational Enforcement of International Law: Solving the Sanctioners' Dilemma," 315.

[185]Guzman, *How International Law Works: A Rational Choice Theory*, 66–68, 138.

[186]Thompson, "The Rational Enforcement of International Law: Solving the Sanctioners' Dilemma," 311–312.

[187]Ibid., 317.

[188]Ibid., 309, 317–318. For more details on institutional setting and design as important factors for managing decentralised enforcement, see Thompson, "Coercive Enforcement of International Law," in *Interdisciplinary Perspectives on International Law and International Relations: The State of the Art*, ed. Dunoff and Pollack, 506–510.

Reciprocity The second mechanism, reciprocity, derives from a key principle in international law[189] and international relations.[190] As a compliance mechanism, it relates to states responding to a violation by withdrawing their own compliance with an international agreement, which is—unlike retaliatory action—not costly, as the reciprocating state merely adjusts its behaviour in light of these new circumstances.[191] The classic example would be Article 60 of the Vienna Convention on the Law of Treaties (VCLT), which foresees the termination or suspension of the operation of a treaty as a consequence of a material breach (e.g. breach of an essential treaty provision).[192] Also countermeasures as an enforcement tool rely on reciprocity, at least to the extent that they operate within the same treaty regime and concern obligations that are similar in-kind to the obligation violated in the first place. Reciprocity can serve as a powerful compliance-enhancing tool as the credible threat of non-performance can be enough to induce compliance by the other party, as long as both parties have more to gain from ongoing cooperation than from immediate defection.[193] In other words, the "shadow of the future"[194] needs to be sufficiently long, that is the costs of the entire treaty regime breaking down.[195] Reciprocity implies that non-compliance is sanctioned by the parties to an international treaty themselves, which is why such self-enforced agreements do not require enforcement through external mechanisms or third parties.[196] Reciprocal treaties, in particular bilateral treaties,[197] are thus inherently self-enforced, under the condition

[189] Oscar Schachter, *International Law in Theory and Practice* (Dordrecht: Martinus Nijhoff Publishers, 1991). For an overview of the principle of reciprocity in international law, see Bruno Simma, "Reciprocity," ed. Anne Peters and Rüdiger Wolfrum, *Max Planck Encyclopedia of Public International Law* (Oxford Public International Law: Oxford University Press, 2021), http://opil.ouplaw.com, Article last updated in April 2008.

[190] Robert O. Keohane, "Reciprocity in International Relations," *International Organization* 40, no. 1 (1986): 1–27.

[191] Guzman, *How International Law Works: A Rational Choice Theory*, 33.

[192] Vienna Convention on the Law of Treaties (VCLT) (concluded 23 May 1969, entered into force 27 January 1980) 1155 *UNTS* 331.

[193] Guzman, *How International Law Works: A Rational Choice Theory*, 42–43. From a game-theoretic perspective, see Axelrod, *The Evolution of Cooperation*; Francesco Parisi and Nita Ghei, "The Role of Reciprocity in International Law," *Cornell International Law Journal* 36, no. 1 (2003–2004): 93–124.

[194] Robert Axelrod understood the "shadow of the future" as the effects of present actions on others' future behaviour. Based on the assumption that players meet again, the future can cast a shadow back upon the present and thereby affect the current strategic situation. Axelrod, *The Evolution of Cooperation*, 12.

[195] Effectuating international law through reciprocity requires that the parties have an ongoing interest in the validity of a rule, see van Aaken, "Die Befolgung des Völkerrechts zwischen Rationalismus, Konstruktivismus und Verhaltensökonomik," in *Warum befolgen wir Recht? Rechtsverbindlichkeit und Rechtsbefolgung in interdisziplinärer Perspektive*, ed. Hilbert and Rauber, 142.

[196] Ibid.

[197] Reciprocal treaties include multilateral treaties which consist in bundles of bilateral obligations, such as in international trade law.

that non-compliance by the reciprocating state is costly for the violating state.[198] Non-reciprocal treaties, often in a multilateral context, cannot be self-enforced through reciprocal non-compliance.[199] In GPG constellations (and CPR scenarios for that matter), reciprocal non-compliance is ineffective, because the violating state cannot be excluded from the benefits of the agreement and therefore incurs no significant cost as a consequence of its breach.[200] For member states of a human rights agreement, it would neither be credible nor legal to respond to a serious breach of human rights obligations by suspending its own compliant behaviour.[201] Article 60 (5) VCLT prohibits expressly the termination or suspension of the operation of treaties of a humanitarian character as a consequences of a material breach. Non-reciprocal treaties require thus other enforcement mechanisms, for instance, linkage with other reciprocal treaties in a way that reciprocity can play a role as an enforcement mechanism.[202] Issue linkage is in fact a common tool to ensure compliance in GPG and CPR constellations, for example by excluding the violating state from the benefits of trade agreements (negative inducements),[203] or conversely by offering a reward such as trade concessions in case of compliance (positive inducements).

---

[198] In addition, non-compliant behaviour needs to be detected, which is more difficult when the ultimate addressees of the norm are not states, but individuals or firms. Van Aaken, "Die Befolgung des Völkerrechts zwischen Rationalismus, Konstruktivismus und Verhaltensökonomik," in *Warum befolgen wir Recht? Rechtsverbindlichkeit und Rechtsbefolgung in interdisziplinärer Perspektive*, ed. Hilbert and Rauber, 142–143. If it is not clear whether a violation has happened, reciprocity bears the risk of setting off "spirals" of non-compliance. Von Stein, "The Engines of Compliance," in *Interdisciplinary Perspectives on International Law and International Relations: The State of the Art*, ed. Dunoff and Pollack, 480–481.

[199] van Aaken, "Die Befolgung des Völkerrechts zwischen Rationalismus, Konstruktivismus und Verhaltensökonomik," in *Warum befolgen wir Recht? Rechtsverbindlichkeit und Rechtsbefolgung in interdisziplinärer Perspektive*, ed. Hilbert and Rauber, 143.

[200] Thompson, "The Rational Enforcement of International Law: Solving the Sanctioners' Dilemma," 309; von Stein, "The Engines of Compliance," in *Interdisciplinary Perspectives on International Law and International Relations: The State of the Art*, ed. Dunoff and Pollack, 481.

[201] Guzman, *How International Law Works: A Rational Choice Theory*, 45. On the questions of why states comply with international human rights treaties and on why they commit to them in the first place, see Oona A. Hathaway, "Do Human Rights Treaties Make a Difference?," *The Yale Law Journal* 111, no. 8 (2002): 1935–2042; Oona A. Hathaway, "Why Do Countries Commit to Human Rights Treaties?," *The Journal of Conflict Resolution* 51, no. 4 (2007): 588–621.

[202] van Aaken, "Die Befolgung des Völkerrechts zwischen Rationalismus, Konstruktivismus und Verhaltensökonomik," in *Warum befolgen wir Recht? Rechtsverbindlichkeit und Rechtsbefolgung in interdisziplinärer Perspektive*, ed. Hilbert and Rauber, 143. However, other authors consider issue linkage rather as a retaliatory mechanism, because reciprocity is about responding to a certain behaviour with the same behaviour. Von Stein, "The Engines of Compliance," in *Interdisciplinary Perspectives on International Law and International Relations: The State of the Art*, ed. Dunoff and Pollack, 479.

[203] Emilie M. Hafner-Burton argues that states can "force" others to comply with international human rights obligations by explicitly linking them to trade concessions. Emilie M. Hafner-Burton, "Trading Human Rights: How Preferential Trade Agreements Influence Government Repression," *International Organization* 59, no. 3 (2005): 593–629; Emilie M. Hafner-Burton, *Forced to*

Reputation A third mechanism for enforcement of international law is state reputation.[204] Based on the assumption of the repeated nature of interactions between states,[205] Guzman defines a state's reputation for compliance with legal obligations as consisting "of judgments about the state's past behaviour and predictions made about future compliance based on that behaviour".[206] He further explains that reputational sanctions relate to the cost imposed on a state regarding future cooperation when its reputation for compliance is damaged.[207] Once a state is no longer considered as a cooperative partner as a consequence of non-compliant behaviour in the past, other states could be induced not to cooperate with this state in the future.[208] Reputation as a compliance mechanism thus builds on the assumption that states anticipate the denial of future cooperation in case of non-compliance and take this threat into account as a cost factor in the case of defection.[209] When the benefits from future cooperation with other states are large enough and the probability of reputational sanctions is sufficiently high, states will comply with the international rule even if it is in their short-term interest to defect.[210] The size of the reputational loss depends on the seriousness of a breach of international law, and the importance of the norm (for instance, *jus cogens* norms).[211] Reputation as a compliance mechanism can complement retaliation and reciprocity or work alone, when these enforcement mechanisms reach their limits, for instance, in enforcing human rights treaties. Whether non-compliance in one area of international law affects a state's reputation

Be Good: Why Trade Agreements Boost Human Rights (Ithaca, NY: Cornell University Press, 2009).

[204] On reputation as a compliance mechanism, see in particular Beth A. Simmons, "International Law and State Behavior: Commitment and Compliance in International Monetary Affairs," *American Political Science Review* 94, no. 4 (2000): 819–835; George W. Downs and Michael A. Jones, "Reputation, Compliance, and International Law," *Journal of Legal Studies* 31, no. S1 (2002): 95–114; Guzman, *How International Law Works: A Rational Choice Theory*, 71–117; Rachel Brewster, "Unpacking the State's Reputation," *Harvard International Law Journal* 50, no. 2 (2009): 231–269. For a general overview of reputation in international relations and international legal theory, see Rachel Brewster, "Reputation in International Relations and International Law Theory," in *Interdisciplinary Perspectives on International Law and International Relations: The State of the Art*, ed. Jeffrey L. Dunoff and Mark A. Pollack (Cambridge: Cambridge University Press, 2013), 524–543.

[205] State interactions in public international law are usually modeled as repeated games, because states do normally not disappear from the international scene.

[206] Guzman, *How International Law Works: A Rational Choice Theory*, 33.

[207] Ibid.

[208] van Aaken, "Die Befolgung des Völkerrechts zwischen Rationalismus, Konstruktivismus und Verhaltensökonomik," in *Warum befolgen wir Recht? Rechtsverbindlichkeit und Rechtsbefolgung in interdisziplinärer Perspektive*, ed. Hilbert and Rauber, 143.

[209] Ibid.

[210] Ibid.

[211] Ibid.

in another issue area, remains an open question.[212] Guzman argues that state reputation is comprehensive, meaning that a breach of international law in one field (for instance, international environmental law) can damage a state's reputation for compliance generally, so that the state may lose possibilities of future cooperation in other areas of international law (for instance, trade law).[213] Others have argued for a limited effect of reputational sanctions, as reputations are "compartmentalised"[214] to specific areas of international law.[215] Breach in one field of international law (e.g. human rights law) would thus not impede on the willingness of other states to cooperate in another field of international law (e.g. international security).[216] Furthermore, a state's reputation may vary depending on the regime type or, even with regard to democracies, simply change when governments change, so that over long periods of time reputational loss may not necessarily relate to the state, but to the administration in power.[217] As reputation depends on perception, it may also vary from one counter-party to another, thus cumulating in multiple reputations for one state.[218]

As the previous two mechanisms, reputation finds several limits: firstly, between states which barely cooperate which each other; secondly, with regard to states which have little interest in international cooperation (for instance, because they are aggressive types and do not anticipate relying on credible promises in the future,[219] or they are pariah states which already have such a poor reputation for non-compliance that they have little to lose by degrading it further[220]); thirdly, regarding states seeking a reputation as a "tough" state which protects its interests

[212] For an overview of this debate, see von Stein, "The Engines of Compliance," in *Interdisciplinary Perspectives on International Law and International Relations: The State of the Art*, ed. Dunoff and Pollack, 481–482.

[213] Guzman, *How International Law Works: A Rational Choice Theory*, 100–106.

[214] "Governments have, however, a remarkable ability to compartmentalize their reputations. A government is able to distinguish between a category of cases in which it routinely respects its legal obligations from other categories in which respecting its legal obligations may be a problem. It thus develops highly specialized reputations." Roger Fisher, *Improving Compliance with International Law* (Charlottesville: University Press of Virginia, 1981), 130.

[215] Downs and Jones, "Reputation, Compliance, and International Law," 95–114.

[216] van Aaken, "Die Befolgung des Völkerrechts zwischen Rationalismus, Konstruktivismus und Verhaltensökonomik," in *Warum befolgen wir Recht? Rechtsverbindlichkeit und Rechtsbefolgung in interdisziplinärer Perspektive*, ed. Hilbert and Rauber, 143–144.

[217] Guzman, *How International Law Works: A Rational Choice Theory*, 106; Brewster, "Reputation in International Relations and International Law Theory," in *Interdisciplinary Perspectives on International Law and International Relations: The State of the Art*, ed. Dunoff and Pollack, 534–536; Posner and Sykes, *Economic Foundations of International Law*, 33.

[218] Guzman, *How International Law Works: A Rational Choice Theory*, 107–108. See, in particular, Jonathan Mercer, *Reputation and International Politics* (Ithaca, NY: Cornell University Press, 1996).

[219] Guzman, *How International Law Works: A Rational Choice Theory*, 111–112.

[220] Ibid., 81.

and allies irrespective of international legal rules.[221] Moreover, reputation faces the same collective action problem than coercive enforcement, as states need to overcome the sanctioners' dilemma in order to reach a collective response in the sense that they all deny future cooperation. Information plays a crucial role in this regard.[222] As for the other enforcement mechanisms, for reputational sanctions to be effective, non-compliant behaviour needs to be detected and legally qualified as breach of international legal rules.[223] International institutions can facilitate enforcement by reducing uncertainty when they provide for an authoritative decision-making body whose judgments, opinions, reports, or views on the existence of a breach of international law bears a higher reputational risk as the assessment by the self-interested state parties involved in a dispute.[224]

Outcasting To these three "classical" enforcement mechanisms, one can add outcasting as a fourth one.[225] Oona Hathaway and Scott J. Shapiro argue that international law is predominantly enforced through outcasting, which consists in "denying the disobedient the benefits of social cooperation and membership".[226]

Outcasting overlaps to a large extent with retaliation (as a penalty) and reciprocity (as a form of collective withdrawal of promises).[227] However, as a stand-alone mechanism, outcasting operates effectively in three regards. This is, firstly, the

[221] van Aaken, "Die Befolgung des Völkerrechts zwischen Rationalismus, Konstruktivismus und Verhaltensökonomik," in *Warum befolgen wir Recht? Rechtsverbindlichkeit und Rechtsbefolgung in interdisziplinärer Perspektive*, ed. Hilbert and Rauber, 144. Guzman, *How International Law Works: A Rational Choice Theory*, 115. On conflicting reputational incentives, notably on states which may value reputations for toughness over reputations for compliance with commitments, see Robert O. Keohane, "International Relations and International Law: Two Optics," *Harvard International Law Journal* 38, no. 2 (1997): 497.

[222] Guzman, *How International Law Works: A Rational Choice Theory*, 91–100.

[223] van Aaken, "Die Befolgung des Völkerrechts zwischen Rationalismus, Konstruktivismus und Verhaltensökonomik," in *Warum befolgen wir Recht? Rechtsverbindlichkeit und Rechtsbefolgung in interdisziplinärer Perspektive*, ed. Hilbert and Rauber, 144.

[224] Authoritative decision-making bodies (e.g. international courts, independent committees) are often accompanied by monitoring mechanisms and reporting duties. In addition, non-state actors, in particular NGOs, play a substantial role in detecting and announcing violations of international legal rules, predominantly in the fields of human rights and environmental law. Ibid.

[225] Oona Hathaway and Scott J. Shapiro, "Outcasting: Enforcement in Domestic and International Law," *The Yale Law Journal* 121, no. 2 (2011): 252–349.

[226] Ibid., 258.

[227] Outcasting as an enforcement mechanism should not be confounded with "shaming" as an enforcement tool, which is much smaller in scope. Shaming describes ways in which non-compliant states are publicly singled out in order to discourage lawbreaking behaviour, in particular in the area of human rights law. See, in particular, Hathaway, "Do Human Rights Treaties Make a Difference?," 1935–2042; Oona A. Hathaway, "The Cost of Commitment," *Stanford Law Review* 55, no. 5 (2003): 1821–1862; Hathaway, "Why Do Countries Commit to Human Rights Treaties?," 588–621; Emilie M. Hafner-Burton, "Sticks and Stones: Naming and Shaming the Human Rights Enforcement Problem," *International Organization* 62, no. 4 (2008): 689–716. Along the same vein, outcasting also overlaps with reputation as an enforcement mechanism. Being an outcast may

case in the form of "internal outcasting", that is the temporary suspension of membership rights for non-compliant member states in international treaty regimes.[228] Secondly, outcasting in the form of "cross-countermeasures" differs from reciprocity in that it consists in the withdrawal of non-in-kind benefits and from retaliation in that this mechanism operates within a given treaty framework and is not costly for the enforcing state.[229] Outcasting has proven to be a comparably effective and cheap sanctioning mechanism with regard to the enforcement of GPG and CPR obligations (e.g. human rights and environmental agreements).[230] The creation of institutions which transform GPGs or CPRs into club goods has the consequence that these goods become excludable; the sanction in the case of non-compliance then consists in exclusion from the club, usually by withdrawing trading benefits.[231] This form of outcasting mechanism is included, for instance, in the Council of Europe (in case of breach of the ECHR), in the Montreal Protocol on Substances that Deplete the Ozone Layer, and the Convention on International Trade in Endangered Species of Wild Fauna and Flora (CITES).[232] Thirdly, outcasting can be made even more effective by including private market actors as enforcers.[233] Market mechanisms make use of different incentive structures, for instance, regulatory network externalities or consumer preferences, in order to enforce compliance with international obligations regulating GPGs or CPRs, as it is in the self-interest of the state to comply with the rules of the club, even if the ultimate addressee of the norm is not a private actor (e.g. private market actors lobbying governments or monitoring compliance of states).[234] It is important to keep these market

---

increase a state's reputation for non-compliance, thus increasing the costs for future cooperation, as other states may favour cooperation with other insiders over cooperation with outsiders of the club.

[228] The revocation of voting rights or the exclusion from participation in treaty bodies are internal sanction mechanisms which are found in international organisations, such as the WHO, and many regional organisations (e.g. the EU, the Council of Europe, the Organization of American States, or the African Union). Hathaway and Shapiro, "Outcasting: Enforcement in Domestic and International Law," 302, 305–306.

[229] Related or unrelated "cross-countermeasures" are most likely to be adjudicated and to be found in contexts in which it is illegal, impossible, or excessively costly for states to retaliate for lawbreaking behaviour by withdrawing in-kind benefits (e.g. reciprocal non-compliance in the case of international human rights violations). Ibid., 314–316, 320–322, 324.

[230] van Aaken, "Die Befolgung des Völkerrechts zwischen Rationalismus, Konstruktivismus und Verhaltensökonomik," in *Warum befolgen wir Recht? Rechtsverbindlichkeit und Rechtsbefolgung in interdisziplinärer Perspektive*, ed. Hilbert and Rauber, 158.

[231] On club good mechanisms in economics and in international law, see Sects. 2.2 and 2.3.

[232] Hathaway and Shapiro, "Outcasting: Enforcement in Domestic and International Law," 316–317, 320–322, 337–339.

[233] We thus extend for a second the model on the level of enforcement to a two-level game. For more details on how market mechanisms can effectuate public international law, see Anne van Aaken, "Effectuating Public International Law through Market Mechanisms?," *Journal of Institutional and Theoretical Economics (JITE)/Zeitschrift für die gesamte Staatswissenschaft* 165, no. 1 (2009): 33–57.

[234] See further with a focus on effectuating international law of global public goods, Anne van Aaken, "Trust, Verify, or Incentivize? Effectuating Public International Law Regulating Public

mechanisms in mind, because they explain to a large extent why self-interested states in a one-level game comply with international law (for instance, in order to avoid that their economic operators lose global market shares). Examples in international soft law are the Financial Action Task Force (FATF), which relies on participating private banks in the fight against money laundering and terrorism financing,[235] and the Kimberly Process, in which governments, industry, and civil society participate in removing conflict diamonds from the global supply chain.[236]

At the same time, the effectiveness of outcasting mechanisms has certain limits: it relies heavily on the existence of private cooperative benefits and a large number of participants to increase the cost of exclusion, in particular as the act of outcasting itself is in contradiction with the very cooperation it aims to achieve.[237] Moreover, outcasting favours powerful over weak states, in the sense that the more a state contributes to the collective benefits shared by all the members of a particular legal regime, the harder it is for the other member states to discipline that member through outcasting (especially first-party outcasting).[238]

Rewarding Since the three "classical" enforcement mechanisms and outcasting as a further refinement focus primarily on negative incentives, Anne van Aaken and Betül Simsek argue in favour of making greater use of rewarding as a fifth compliance mechanism in international law.[239] As opposed to penalties, they understand rewards as "transfers of positively valued material or immaterial goods, such as opportunities for and benefits of cooperation, money, technology, or social approval/ good reputation" measured as "improvements in a target's value position relative to a

Goods through Market Mechanisms," *Proceedings of the Annual Meeting (American Society of International Law)* 104 (2010): 153–156.

[235]The Financial Action Task Force (FATF) is an intergovernmental body which sets international standards that aim to prevent global money laundering and terrorist financing. As a policy-making body, the FATF works to generate the necessary political will to bring about national legislative and regulatory reforms in these areas. See https://www.fatf-gafi.org

[236]The Kimberley Process (KP) is a multilateral trade regime established in 2003 with the goal of preventing the flow of conflict diamonds. The core of this regime is the Kimberley Process Certification Scheme (KPCS) under which states implement safeguards on shipments of rough diamonds and certify them as "conflict free". See https://www.kimberleyprocess.com

[237]As for reputation, outcasting is ineffective when states have little interest in international cooperation as "it is impossible to further outcast a voluntary outcast". Hathaway and Shapiro, "Outcasting: Enforcement in Domestic and International Law," 339–341. Effective outcasting rather requires that group membership goes in hand with economies of scale and that, as for the other enforcement mechanisms, non-compliant behaviour is observable in order to serve as a basis for exclusion. Van Aaken, "Die Befolgung des Völkerrechts zwischen Rationalismus, Konstruktivismus und Verhaltensökonomik," in *Warum befolgen wir Recht? Rechtsverbindlichkeit und Rechtsbefolgung in interdisziplinärer Perspektive*, ed. Hilbert and Rauber, 158.

[238]Hathaway and Shapiro, "Outcasting: Enforcement in Domestic and International Law," 341–342.

[239]van Aaken and Simsek, "Rewarding in International Law," 195–241.

baseline of expectations".[240] They present a typology which distinguishes between, on the one hand, internal and external rewards (i.e. depending on whether the benefits from cooperation stem from the treaty in question or from a bargain outside this so-called base treaty) and, on the other hand, entry and compliance rewards (i.e. depending on the time when the benefit accrues, thus when the state enters the commitment or complies with it).[241] Internal and external compliance rewards also differ in terms of their predictability and flexibility, with internal rewards operating within the treaty (e.g. redemption after previous exclusion, financial assistance)[242] being more predictable and less flexible, whereas external rewards (e.g. side-payments, technical assistance promoting objectives outside the treaty, linkage with other treaties or benefits,[243] or positive reputation for compliance[244]) are more flexible but less predictable.[245] External rewards can become necessary when the benefits of entering or complying with a treaty (internal rewards) are insufficient incentives for accession or compliance, often in GPG and CPR constellations, which is why these types of treaty regimes (e.g. in multilateral environmental, disarmament or human rights agreements) often combine different types of rewards.[246] This is in particular the case when the other four enforcement mechanisms reach their limits, because retaliation or negative reputation are unlikely to induce compliance in the case of incapacity (e.g. lack of financial, administrative, or

[240] Ibid., 196. With reference, amongst others, to Peter M. Blau, *Exchange and Power in Social Life* (New York: Wiley, 1964); David A. Baldwin, "The Power of Positive Sanctions," *World Politics* 24, no. 1 (1971): 19–38.

[241] van Aaken and Simsek, "Rewarding in International Law," 196–197, 203–206. Entry rewards can be either the cooperative benefits of the treaty in question such as the exchange of goods or the provision of GPGs (internal rewards) or side payments, trade concessions and positive reputation for normative commitments outside the base treaty (external rewards). For the purpose of this book, which focuses on state responsibility rules and the role compliance mechanisms play in this regard, entry rewards will be disregarded.

[242] For instance, the Montreal Protocol on Substances that Deplete the Ozone Layer includes both the possibility of redemption in response to outcasting from the trading privileges and, in Article 10, a multilateral fund in order to assist developing countries.

[243] A frequently employed mechanism would be the external reward of trading benefits in case of compliance with a base treaty, for instance, the reduction of existing barriers to trade as unilateral and voluntary measures under the WTO's Generalized System of Preferences (GSP).

[244] The external reward consists here in naming and praising compliant practices, for instance, in annual reports, as the opposite side of naming and shaming, in particular in the area of international human rights law. On "shaming", see footnote 227. On "praising", see Margarita H. Petrova, "Naming and Praising in Humanitarian Norm Development," *World Politics* 71, no. 3 (2019): 586–630.

[245] van Aaken and Simsek, "Rewarding in International Law," 204, 206. For a more detailed illustration of rewarding, see ibid., 206–218.

[246] Ibid., 205–206. International agreements with the objective of fighting climate change (e.g. the Paris Agreement) are the prime example, as they contain commitments from advanced economies to provide technical and financial assistance in the adaptation efforts of emerging economies and developing countries as well as to make financial contributions to multilateral funds with the objective to mitigate harm for those countries most affected by climate change.

technological resources) and negative reciprocity and complete outcasting are undesirable in (global) public goods treaties.[247]

The rationale for rewarding in international law is that cooperation can be encouraged through rewards offered by one party (i.e. the rewarding or enforcing state) to offset the benefits that the other country (i.e. the rewarded or target state) draws from non-compliance.[248] In contrast to penalising enforcement mechanisms, such as retaliation or outcasting, which focus on how the costs of non-compliance can be increased, rewarding mechanisms consist in positive inducements and consider ways to increase the benefits of compliance.[249] Rewarding, like other compliance mechanisms, has also its limitations. First, rewards may not be as costly as retaliatory sanctions, but they nonetheless require sufficient resources of the rewarding state or states, especially if rewards are tangible (e.g. financial assistance) or have to be paid to a large number of states.[250] Another related problem that arises—similar to the sanctioners' dilemma in the case of retaliation—is that states may want to free-ride on the contributions of others to the reward (i.e. the rewarders' dilemma having public good characteristics), but this effect can be mitigated if the benefits from rewarding outweigh the costs (e.g. the public good of the base treaty being provided) or if rewarding generates a positive reputation at the enforcement level.[251] Second, rewards can cause moral hazard[252] at the compliance stage because states may want to present themselves in need of assistance in order to receive a reward,[253] but there are means for rewarding states to address this problem for instance, through burden sharing (e.g. co-financed programmes), shifting the burden of proof to the target state, or combing the reward with a previous sanction (e.g. redemption).[254] Thirdly, rewarding, in particular economic aid, may crowd-out the receiving state's own motivation to comply with international law, but the

[247] Ibid., 207–208, 217–218. With reference to Anu Bradford and Omri Ben-Shahar, "Efficient Enforcement in International Law," *Chicago Journal of International Law* 12, no. 2 (2012): 383–384.

[248] In the words of van Aaken and Simsek, "compliance can be achieved if a reward outweighs the benefits from breaching international law." van Aaken and Simsek, "Rewarding in International Law," 197.

[249] Van Aaken and Simsek draw on rationalist and psychological approaches to argue that rewards can produce better results than penalties, both on efficiency grounds (Pareto-optimality) and psychological grounds (behavioural differences). Ibid., 197–198, 218–235.

[250] Ibid., 221.

[251] Ibid., 222–223, 225–226.

[252] Moral hazard is a term from economic analysis, originally related to the problem that "insurance coverage may increase the likelihood of an accident, because the insured has less incentive to take precautions", which describes in modern usage "any circumstance where an actor maximizes his or her own utility, and where this may cause harm to the interests of others, but the actor does not bear the costs". Bix, *A Dictionary of Legal Theory*, s.v. "moral hazard".

[253] Bradford and Ben-Shahar, "Efficient Enforcement in International Law," 423–424.

[254] van Aaken and Simsek, "Rewarding in International Law," 236–237.

opposite effect (i.e. crowding-in) may exist with intangible rewards such as praising or even tangible rewards such as readmission to a club.[255]

In sum, as a positive inducement, rewarding overlaps to a certain extent with other "classical" compliance mechanisms: as positive reputation (e.g. praising), positive reciprocity (e.g. issue linkage), and redemption after outcasting. In addition, rewarding, for instance, in the form of side-payments, presents the opposite side of the coin with regard to costly retaliatory sanctions. Rewarding in its different forms thus constitutes an important compliance mechanism and can replace or complement the "classical" penalising mechanisms when they reach their limits, in particular in GPG and CPR constellations.

The Facilitating Role of International Judicial Institutions A common theme throughout the "classical" compliance mechanisms (and outcasting) is the facilitating role of adjudication in the decentralised international legal system.[256] There is no universal judiciary in international relations, although international courts and tribunals exist in some subject areas or treaty regimes, but they also depend on whether states have accepted jurisdiction over a single dispute or kind of disputes.[257] Yet, their role is not equivalent to the role of courts in the domestic legal order, where judgments (e.g. obligations to pay damages for breach of contract) are enforced with the help of the coercive power of the state, for instance, by seizing assets or arresting responsible actors.[258] Where international courts exist, their decisions still depend on the decentralised enforcement mechanisms outlined above (including rewards for compliance with court decisions).

International courts and tribunals, or other types of authoritative decision-making bodies within international legal regimes (e.g. human rights monitoring committees), rather serve predominantly as mechanisms to disseminate information to the international community.[259] In essence, they provide clarification of ambiguous legal rules, identify non-compliant behaviour, and supply information on the motivations

[255] Ibid., 237–238.

[256] On the role of courts in international law, in particular on their impact on compliance, see Karen J. Alter, "Do International Courts Enhance Compliance with International Law?," *Review of Asian and Pacific Studies* 25 (2003): 51–78; Karen J. Alter, "Agents or Trustees? International Courts in Their Political Context," *European Journal of International Relations* 14, no. 1 (2008): 33–63. It shall be noted that international law is also enforced through national courts, but as for other domestic institutions this aspect will be disregarded here as a compliance mechanism, see above footnote 175. Specifically on the role of national courts in international law-making and enforcement, see Anthea Roberts, "Comparative International Law? The Role of National Courts in Creating and Enforcing International Law," *International and Comparative Law Quarterly* 60, no. 1 (2011): 57–92.

[257] Thompson concludes that the proliferation of international courts does not automatically entail a more hierarchical or rule-oriented enforcement regime for international law, for instance, due to conflicting interpretations and possibilities of forum shopping, see Thompson, "Coercive Enforcement of International Law," in *Interdisciplinary Perspectives on International Law and International Relations: The State of the Art*, ed. Dunoff and Pollack, 504–505.

[258] Guzman, *How International Law Works: A Rational Choice Theory*, 49, 51.

[259] Ibid., 51. See also Trachtman, *The Economic Structure of International Law*, 210.

of states that interact within them.[260] Therefore, the role of international courts is assumed here to be predominantly one of fact-finding and law-finding, thus to reduce uncertainty through their rulings, which helps the parties to settle the dispute and to render the above-mentioned enforcement mechanisms more effective.[261] First, by imposing procedural conditions, increasing public scrutiny, and delaying retaliatory action, they can reduce the political cost of sanctioning by signalling to the international community that the sanctioning state is sincerely acting in defence of international rules, thus limiting the risk of abusive sanctions and the escalation of disputes.[262] Consequently, as retaliatory sanctions become more likely, for instance, in the case of expressive authorisation as in WTO law, adjudicatory mechanisms encourage states to comply with their legal commitments by increasing the costs of violation.[263] Second, by clarifying whether a state has violated international law, adjudication can facilitate reciprocal non-compliance as it becomes less likely that the cooperative regime breaks down due to "spirals of non-compliance".[264] Third, by providing information about non-compliant behaviour to the parties of the dispute and to third parties, adjudication increases the reputational costs of violating international obligations as other states are likely to update their beliefs about a state's willingness to comply with its international commitments.[265] Fourth, adjudication can effectuate outcasting mechanisms and induce compliance in particular in the case of non-in-kind and non-proportionate sanctions as well as in cases of third-party involvement. Fifth, authoritative decision-making bodies within international legal regimes (e.g. human rights monitoring committees) could also play a more prominent role in rewarding compliant behaviour, for instance, by praising good practices in their concluding observations.[266] Lastly, how effective international courts can promote compliance depends not only on whether they serve as a dispute settlement mechanism or as a facilitator for state sanctions, but also on the degree of

[260] Thompson, "The Rational Enforcement of International Law: Solving the Sanctioners' Dilemma," 317.

[261] Guzman, *How International Law Works: A Rational Choice Theory*, 51–54. For more details on the functions of international tribunals from a rational choice perspective, see Andrew T. Guzman, "International Tribunals: A Rational Choice Analysis," *University of Pennsylvania Law Review* 157, no. 1 (2008): 171–235.

[262] Thompson, "The Rational Enforcement of International Law: Solving the Sanctioners' Dilemma," 317.

[263] Guzman, *How International Law Works: A Rational Choice Theory*, 52–54. For an economic analysis of the dispute resolution system in the World Trade Organization which arbitrates the magnitude of the authorised sanctions, see Warren F. Schwartz and Alan O. Sykes, "The Economic Structure of Renegotiation and Dispute Resolution in the World Trade Organization," *Journal of Legal Studies* 31, no. S1 (2002): S179-S204.

[264] On the term "spirals of non-compliance", see above footnote 198.

[265] Guzman, *How International Law Works: A Rational Choice Theory*, 52, 54.

[266] van Aaken and Simsek, "Rewarding in International Law," 214–215.

independence, the concrete design elements and ultimately on the specific context in which it operates.[267]

In addition to their dispute resolution role, international courts and tribunals also serve to some extent to clarify or even establish substantive rules of international law.[268] As focal point for coordinating the behaviour of states, they are uniquely situated to take community interests into consideration as well as to develop and promote community obligations.[269] This role may be one factor why states are at times reluctant to include adjudicatory mechanisms in their agreements or to consent to universal jurisdiction.[270] Moreover, even though also the international procedural law has evolved to some extent following the recognition of community interests, international adjudication rests structurally a bilateral system of dispute settlement,[271] in particular because other states than those directly affected by a breach of a community interest obligation often do not have standing.[272] Nollkaemper concludes that "international adjudication plays a marginal role in the protection of global public goods", and that "energy should be equally spent in thinking about other decentralized approaches" of enforcement.[273]

Thus, for the purpose of this book, international courts and tribunals will be understood as mechanisms to promote GPGs and CPRs through substantive rules and, from a procedural perspective, as information-disseminating devices to facilitate third-party enforcement as a global public good.[274]

---

[267] Guzman, *How International Law Works: A Rational Choice Theory*, 52–54. For a comprehensive theoretical and empirical assessment of the effectiveness of international courts, see Yuval Shany, *Assessing the Effectiveness of International Courts* (Oxford: Oxford University Press, 2014).

[268] Guzman, *How International Law Works: A Rational Choice Theory*, 54. See also Trachtman, *The Economic Structure of International Law*, 210.

[269] Eyal Benvenisti, "Community Interests in International Adjudication," in *Community Interests across International Law*, ed. Eyal Benvenisti and Georg Nolte (Oxford: Oxford University Press, 2018), 71.

[270] Guzman, *How International Law Works: A Rational Choice Theory*, 54.

[271] Markus Benzing, "Community Interests in the Procedure of International Courts and Tribunals," *Law and Practice of International Courts and Tribunals* 5, no. 3 (2006): 369–408.

[272] Article 62 of the ICJ Statute foresees, other than for the parties of the dispute, only the possibility of intervention for states having a legal interest which may be affected by the decision in the case.

[273] André Nollkaemper, "International Adjudication of Global Public Goods: The Intersection of Substance and Procedure," *European Journal of International Law* 23, no. 3 (2012): 791. He acknowledges, however, recent promising examples for the protection of global public goods via international adjudication. See, for instance, *Whaling in the Antarctic (Australia v. Japan: New Zealand Intervening)*, Judgment, 31 March 2014, ICJ Reports 2014, p. 226.

[274] On whether international adjudication might constitute a global public good in itself or a mechanism that produces such goods, see Joshua Paine, "International Adjudication as a Global Public Good?," *European Journal of International Law* 29, no. 4 (2019): 1223–1249.

2.5 Conclusion on the Protection of Community Interests in International Law and Economics

The characteristics of the international legal order—the fact that both law-making and law enforcement rely on states themselves—favours state behaviour that consists in protecting and furthering their own interests. The challenge for states is to nonetheless accommodate and achieve community interests through cooperation.[275] This relates, on the one hand, to first-order cooperation problems (in particular, to the collective action problems underlying the provision of GPGs and the protection of CPRs), which consist in both the commitment to primary international legal obligations as well as compliance with such obligations and connected secondary obligations. First-order free-riders are then those that either do not contribute to the provision of the GPG (or the preservation of the CPR), thus spoiling by non-participation in a legal regime, or those that do not comply with the international obligations they have agreed upon, thus spoiling by non-compliance. On the other hand, the challenge for states is to overcome second-order cooperation problems, to the extent that enforcement also constitutes a GPG. Second-order free-riders are then those that free-ride on the enforcement efforts of other states.

Against this background, it is possible to analyse, firstly, the behaviour of states towards international state responsibility rules (that is, their compliance or enforcement decisions) with recourse to rational choice theory as used in international relations theory and international law and economics. Secondly, the structural elements of the international legal order justify recourse to economic theory to explain the often limited incentives for states to adequately address cooperative challenges on the global level, including in the law of state responsibility. Thirdly, depending on the underlying cooperation problem, the objectives of state responsibility rules may differ along the private and the public dimension of international law. This last issue will be dealt with in the following Chap. 3, which sets out the normative framework of the analysis in this book.

[275] Benvenisti and Nolte, "Community Interests across International Law: Introduction," in *Community Interests across International Law*, ed. Benvenisti and Nolte, 8.

Chapter 3
The Normative Framework: Objectives of State Responsibility in International Law

The ARSIWA do not explicitly define the goals of the state responsibility regime. This chapter therefore outlines the objectives of the international law of state responsibility which can be derived from the different provisions of the ARSIWA along the private and the public dimensions of international law and explains how they differ depending on the underlying cooperation problem. These insights will serve as the normative framework for the subsequent economic analysis of the international law of state responsibility.

3.1 The Private and Public Dimensions of the International Law of State Responsibility

The international law of state responsibility is uniquely designed for the international legal order, or, in the words of Alain Pellet, international responsibility is "simply international".[1] It consists in a set of second-order transversal rules that are applicable across all areas of international law and that form a "single, unitary system".[2] International responsibility has also been ascribed an independent normative content, in the sense that the concept "is not just a neutral connector between a breach [of an international obligation] and the legal consequences of such a breach, but entails certain normative choices [...]".[3] These choices relate to questions of what

[1] Pellet, "The Definition of Responsibility in International Law," in *The Law of International Responsibility*, ed. Crawford, Pellet, and Olleson, 3.

[2] André Nollkaemper and Dov Jacobs also refer to this as the "unity of international responsibility." Nollkaemper and Jacobs, "Shared Responsibility in International Law: A Conceptual Framework," 399.

[3] Nollkaemper, "Responsibility," in *Concepts for International Law: Contributions to Disciplinary Thought*, ed. d'Aspremont and Singh, 764.

J. Lemke, *The Protection of Community Interests in the International Law of State Responsibility*, International Law and Economics,
https://doi.org/10.1007/978-3-031-87927-2_3

types of conduct engage responsibility while others are exempted from responsibility, what legal consequences follow from such a breach and, lastly, how and by whom these consequences can be enforced.[4] Ultimately, "[s]uch choices constitute dividing lines between legality and illegality [of state actions], which may be quite different from the dividing lines formulated by primary rules of international law".[5] In the main part of this book, these choices are evaluated against the objectives of state responsibility in international law.

The fact that "[i]nternational responsibility has a distinct and autonomous normative dimension",[6] does not mean that it does not share substantial characteristics with the concept of liability in domestic law.[7] To a certain extent, it can thus be helpful to draw on normative concepts of liability in the domestic legal order,[8] while keeping in mind the context of an international legal order *sui generis*. As outlined in the previous chapter, the international legal order developed from a traditional inter-state or bilateral system towards integrating public features such as the protection of community interests. And as the structure of international law changes in the face of the challenges of globalisation, the structure of state responsibility as one essential element of international law also changes.[9] While state responsibility has traditionally served the interests of individual sovereign nation states, it can be said that modern international state responsibility law also has a distinct public dimension.[10]

[4]Ibid., 764–765.

[5]Ibid., 765.

[6]Ibid., 764.

[7]It shall be noted that in international law 'responsibility' and 'liability' are different concepts, as the latter relates to harmful consequences of acts not prohibited by international law. Both concepts and their respective conditions will be discussed in Chap. 4.

[8]Liam Murphy states that "[t]here is no theory of international responsibility without a theory of domestic responsibility, and vice versa." Liam Murphy, "International Responsibility," in *The Philosophy of International Law*, ed. Samantha Besson and John Tasioulas (Oxford: Oxford University Press, 2010), 299.

[9]Nollkaemper, "Responsibility," in *Concepts for International Law: Contributions to Disciplinary Thought*, ed. d'Aspremont and Singh, 771–772.

[10]Ibid., 769–770. On why the unity of the law of international responsibility is difficult to maintain against the background of the process of constitutionalisation of international law, see further André Nollkaemper, "Constitutionalization and the Unity of the Law of International Responsibility," *Indiana Journal of Global Legal Studies* 16, no. 2 (2009): 535–563. On the articulation of the bilateral and community interest dimensions in the international law of state responsibility, see also Georg Nolte, "From Dionisio Anzilotti to Roberto Ago: The Classical International Law of State Responsibility and the Traditional Primacy of a Bilateral Conception of Inter-State Relations," *European Journal of International Law* 13, no. 5 (2002): 1083–1098; Martti Koskenniemi, "Doctrines of State Responsibility," in *The Law of International Responsibility*, ed. James Crawford, Alain Pellet, and Simon Olleson (Oxford: Oxford University Press, 2010), 47–50. For a more recent discussion, see Martins Paparinskis, "The Once and Future Law of State Responsibility," *American Journal of International Law* 114, no. 4 (2020): 618–626.

Both dimensions are not mutually exclusive, and, in fact, notions of private and public law can be found throughout the international law of state responsibility.[11]

The modern law of state responsibility (as laid down in the ARSIWA) is objective in nature, in the sense that responsibility does not require damage to a state as a condition.[12] Responsibility thus follows from illegal conduct, not a harmful result, which bears similarities to administrative law (e.g. regulation of activities causing pollution). The international obligation that has been breached by a state can be an obligation serving only the mutual interests of nation states or a third-party obligation serving community interests. In the private dimension, responsibility shares dominant features with liability in domestic law to the extent that individual states suffer a legal injury caused by infringements of the law protecting their subjective rights by other states. In the public dimension, responsibility protects the international legal order as such against state acts that violate community interests in international law. Moreover, some international obligations that are considered peremptory norms of general international law are so fundamental to the international community that breach cannot be excused (*jus cogens* norms),[13] a provision which hints at a certain hierarchy of norms in international law.

As regards the legal consequences of state responsibility, the private dimension relates to the right of injured states to seek reparation for a damage occurred, and thus the concrete harmful consequences of the illegal act.[14] In the public dimension, the secondary obligations of continued performance and cessation/non-repetition rather pursue the objective of returning to a state of legality.[15]

In terms of implementation of responsibility, in the private dimension, it remains the prerogative of the injured state to invoke responsibility and to induce the responsible state to comply with the reparation and cessation requirement by having recourse to countermeasures.[16] Basing responsibility on illegality rather than injury also has consequences in multilateral contexts, where international obligations protect the collective interests of the parties or of the international community as a whole (*erga omnes* or *erga omnes partes* norms). In this public dimension, the law of state responsibility allows all non-directly injured third states to invoke the responsibility of the state violating these obligations, without having suffered an injury.[17] In addition, these states may have recourse to countermeasures to ensure cessation of

---

[11] For a detailed outline of the private and public law dimensions of international responsibility and the need to move away from the unity of the law of international responsibility to a more differentiated approach, see Nollkaemper and Jacobs, "Shared Responsibility in International Law: A Conceptual Framework," 398–408.

[12] The only conditions for an internationally wrongful act being attribution of conduct to the state and breach of an international obligation (Articles 1, 2 ARSIWA).

[13] Article 26 ARSIWA.

[14] Article 31 ARSIWA.

[15] Articles 29, 30 ARSIWA.

[16] Articles 42, 49–53 ARSIWA.

[17] Article 48 ARSIWA.

the breach and reparation in the interest of the injured state.[18] Furthermore, in cases of serious breaches of peremptory norms of general international law, all states in the international community are under an obligation to cooperate to bring to an end the situation created by the breach and to neither recognise nor render aid or assistance to the maintenance of such a situation, obligations that aim at the protection of the international legal order as such.[19]

This brief overview shows that the protection of community interests is also enshrined in the modern international law of state responsibility. Some even say that "a community interest can be identified for almost every such rule [on state responsibility]".[20] Yet, that would be equivalent to saying the entire set of rules of state responsibility is a global public good, like the international order as such. Instead, most rules are uniformly applicable to both constellations of conciliation of national state interests and those related to the protection of community interests. Other rules specifically relate to the protection of community interests with the recognition of a special regime for breach of peremptory norms of general international law and *erga omnes (partes)* obligations.[21] In the typical constellations of state responsibility relating to the private dimension, that is the invocation of responsibility by an injured state for breach of its rights, rules of state responsibility continue to play a central role in international law, in particular in the practice of international courts and tribunals.[22] The constellations, which connect the concept of responsibility to the international community, expose the same weaknesses of the public dimension of the international legal order, notably regarding the provision of global public goods (GPGs), including collective enforcement in decentralised inter-state system.[23] Both constellations need to be borne in mind when sketching out the objectives of state responsibility in international law, first in the private, then in the public dimension.

---

[18] Article 54 ARSIWA.

[19] Articles 40, 41 ARSIWA.

[20] Georg Nolte, "The International Law Commission and Community Interests," in *Community Interests across International Law*, ed. Eyal Benvenisti and Georg Nolte (Oxford: Oxford University Press, 2018), 105.

[21] See Articles 26, 40–41, 48 and 54 ARSIWA.

[22] Nollkaemper, "Responsibility," in *Concepts for International Law: Contributions to Disciplinary Thought*, ed. d'Aspremont and Singh, 771–772. On the bilateral nature of procedural rules in international adjudication, see also Sect. 2.4.

[23] Ibid., 770.

3.2 Objectives of State Responsibility in the Private Dimension of International Law

In the private law dimension, the responsibility regime in international law contains similarities to liability rules that determine the conditions and consequences of a breach of law in the domestic context. In fact, many principles that are common in domestic liability law, both contractual and delictual, are reflected in the international law of state responsibility, for instance, the concepts of causation,[24] contribution to the injury,[25] negligence,[26] exceptions,[27] and the obligation of reparation.[28] Law and economics research has produced valuable insights about how liability rules in both contract and tort law shape individual behaviour.[29] Hence, when analysing the international law of state responsibility with recourse to rational choice theory, this book can draw on many of these insights from the economic analysis of domestic liability law, while taking into account the particularities of the international legal order. As this section will show, economic theories of responsibility, i.e. liability in both domestic tort and contract law, can explain to a large extent the objectives of international state responsibility in the private law dimension. The aims and problems of domestic liability law differ, however, at least to a certain extent, between contractual liability law and tort law. Similarly, within the private dimension of international law one can distinguish scenarios which are closer to tort scenarios and others closer to contractual liability scenarios. Lastly, as much as contractual and delictual liability are invoked by the victims of a breach of their subjective rights, responsibility in the private dimension is invoked and enforced by injured states themselves. These three aspects will be considered in turn.

[24] Article 31 ARSIWA.

[25] Article 39 ARSIWA.

[26] Article 39 ARSIWA.

[27] Articles 20–25 ARSIWA.

[28] Article 31 ARSIWA.

[29] For a general overview of economic analysis of law, and private law in particular, see Avery Wiener Katz, ed., *Foundations of the Economic Approach to Law* (New York: Oxford University Press, 1998); Steven Shavell, *Foundations of Economic Analysis of Law* (Cambridge, MA: Belknap Press of Harvard University Press, 2004); Hans-Bernd Schäfer and Claus Ott, *The Economic Analysis of Civil Law* (Cheltenham, UK: Edward Elgar, 2004); A. Mitchell Polinsky and Steven Shavell, eds., *Handbook of Law and Economics*, 2 vols. (Amsterdam: North-Holland, 2007); Gerrit De Geest, ed., *Encyclopedia of Law and Economics*, 2nd ed., 12 vols. (Cheltenham, UK: Edward Elgar, 2012); Cooter and Ulen, *Law & Economics*; Richard A. Posner, *Economic Analysis of Law*, 9th ed. (New York: Wolters Kluwer, 2014); Anthony W. Dnes, *Principles of Law and Economics*, 3rd ed. (Cheltenham, UK: Edward Elgar, 2018); A. Mitchell Polinsky, *An Introduction to Law and Economics*, 5th ed. (New York: Wolters Kluwer, 2019).

3.2.1 *Insights from Economic Theories of Tort*

Traditional inter-state relationships within the private dimension of international law relate, for instance, to "the delimitation of sovereign spheres of influence or the reconciliation of opposed national interests".[30] Disputes between states can, for instance, arise over the illegal pollution of natural resources on foreign territories or of ocean resources in a foreign EEZ. They can also relate to the destruction of foreign property or the infliction of harm on foreigners, both abroad and within the state's territory. In the latter case, disputes can also follow more specifically from the violation of consular and diplomatic obligations.[31] These scenarios have in common the extraterritorial effect of state actions. From an economic perspective, one can translate them to private goods constellations, because they relate to goods that are excludable and rival in consumption (derived from the notion of property rights in the domestic context). As we have seen above, the underlying cooperation problem is how to deal with negative externalities. This cooperation problem on the international level lies at the core of tort law, and should thus be analysed primarily through the lens of economic theories of tort law.[32]

Instrumental theories of law understand legal rules as a tool for solving a social problem or the realisation of social ends, typically, in the economic analysis of tort law, the allocation of accident costs.[33] How costs should be allocated depends on the goals that ought to be achieved by tort law, namely fairness or utility/welfare.[34] Building on the Coase theorem,[35] economists view a role for tort law, when the costs

[30] Feichtner, "Community Interest," para. 2.

[31] Vienna Convention on Diplomatic Relations; Vienna Convention on Consular Relations (concluded 24 April 1963, entered into force 19 March 1967) 596 *UNTS* 261. It shall, however, already be noted here that these obligations also have a public dimension to the extent that they protect the functioning of diplomatic and consular relations as an essential element of the international legal order. See Sect. 3.3 on the implications of this public dimension for the issue of enforcement.

[32] On the determination of goals of the responsibility regime in international law drawing mainly on theories of tort, see also van Aaken, "Shared Responsibility in International Law: A Political Economy Analysis," in *Distribution of Responsibilities in International Law*, ed. Nollkaemper and Jacobs, 158–161.

[33] Jules Coleman, Scott Hershovitz, and Gabriel Mendlow, "Theories of the Common Law of Torts," ed. Edward N. Zalta, *The Stanford Encyclopedia of Philosophy*, http://plato.stanford.edu/archives/fall2010/entries/tort-theories/, Article last revised on 17 December 2015, Section 1.3.2.

[34] In legal theory, bodies of law are justified or explained with reference to one of two fundamental value systems: fairness *versus* utility or welfare. See, in particular, George P. Fletcher, "Fairness and Utility in Tort Theory," *Harvard Law Review* 85, no. 3 (1972): 537–573; Louis Kaplow and Steven Shavell, *Fairness versus Welfare* (Cambridge, MA: Harvard University Press, 2002).

[35] Coase, "The Problem of Social Cost," 1–44. "Today, [the Coase Theorem] is generally regarded as having two dimensions: the positive and the normative. The original formulation of the Coase Theorem, describing the optimal allocation of rights given free exchange without transaction costs, is the "positive" claim. The normative component is composed of a number of corollaries, which may be derived from the Positive Coase Theorem. In the real world, bargaining is never costless, and indeed actual exchange costs, strategic behavior, and non-rational judgment may sometimes create substantial impediments to desirable exchanges." Richard A. Posner and Francesco Parisi,

of bargaining are so high that individual actors do not fully internalise the costs of the externalities generated by their activities,[36] thus producing inefficient outcomes.[37] The principal claim of economic analysts, developed by Guido Calabresi, is that the aim of tort law should be to minimise the sum of the costs of accidents and the costs of avoiding them.[38] Economic analysis of tort then enquires what substantive liability rules have the greatest impact on reducing the incidence of accidents at the lowest cost, that is, optimal deterrence.[39] According to these theorists, tort liability rules should set incentives for efficient levels of precaution and activity. For instance, under the condition of perfect compensation of the harm caused by the tortfeasor, the rule of strict liability and the negligence rule (with the legal standard equal to the efficient level of care) both set optimal incentives for an efficient level of precaution.[40] This holds also true for the efficient level of activity, as "the ultimate bearer of harm internalizes the benefits of any of his or her actions that reduce the probability or severity of accidents, including more precaution and less activity".[41] Cost allocation, however, does not necessarily have to be efficient, as would be the allocation to those activities that can avoid the accident at the least cost (i.e. to the cheapest cost avoider).[42] Responsibility rules can also allocate costs fairly, for instance, to the party that caused the harm in order to compensate the victim of the tort.[43] The idea rooted in corrective justice is that the victim should be relieved of the burden of the damage by way of transferring the costs of the accident to the wrongdoing party.[44] Yet, when a liability rule assigns the costs of an accident to the injurer as a matter of moral responsibility, it is setting incentives, which can but may not always be efficient from a social welfare perspective.[45]

In sum, when transferring insights from tort theory to comparable scenarios on the international level, state responsibility rules can be understood as having the

---

Law and Economics: Elgar Research Reviews in Economics (Elgaronline: Edward Elgar, 2016), Section 5.

[36] Furthermore, "[b]argaining costs are the costs of negotiating and enforcing agreements, and are a form of transaction costs, which are best defined as the costs of establishing and enforcing economic property rights – the de facto entitlements to make use of resources." Dnes, *Principles of Law and Economics*, 61.

[37] Or, as Robert Cooter and Thomas Ulen put it: "The economic essence of tort law is its use of liability to internalize externalities created by high transaction costs." Cooter and Ulen, *Law & Economics*, 190.

[38] Guido Calabresi, *The Costs of Accidents: A Legal and Economic Analysis* (New Haven: Yale University Press, 1970).

[39] Coleman, Hershovitz, and Mendlow, "Theories of the Common Law of Torts," Section 2.

[40] Cooter and Ulen, *Law & Economics*, 203, 206.

[41] Ibid., 212. On this discussion, see, in particular, Steven Shavell, "Strict Liability versus Negligence," *Journal of Legal Studies* 9, no. 1 (1980): 1–25.

[42] Dnes, *Principles of Law and Economics*, 183–184.

[43] Coleman, Hershovitz, and Mendlow, "Theories of the Common Law of Torts," Section 1.3.2.

[44] Ibid., Section 3.1.1.

[45] Bix, *A Dictionary of Legal Theory*, s.v. "tort law".

function of cost allocation between the responsible and the injured state. They pursue the objectives of prevention of harmful outcomes, that is (optimal) deterrence, and (just) compensation for harm.[46] Furthermore, these insights from economic theories of tort law will be relevant at different stages of the analysis of the state responsibility regime.[47] Firstly, insights from the economic analysis of different responsibility rules (i.e. strict liability *versus* negligence) and the appropriate level of care can inform the comparison of the concepts of "liability" (i.e. for harmful consequences of acts not prohibited by international law) and "responsibility" in international law, and, regarding the latter more specifically, the discussion on the incentive effects of primary obligations depending on their concrete responsibility standard (e.g. notions of fault or due diligence).[48] Secondly, the goal of optimal deterrence (or idea of efficient levels of precaution) can explain the different exemptions from tortious liability, in particular when avoiding the accident is materially impossible (e.g. *force majeure*) or would cause harm to an overriding private or public interest (i.e. private or public necessity). An economic analysis of the different circumstances precluding wrongfulness in the international law of state responsibility, in particular the necessity excuse, can therefore draw on these insights, notably with regard to the issue of cost allocation following their invocation in order to prevent moral hazard.[49] Thirdly, insights from the economic analysis of tort law can inform the discussion on different types of remedies in the law of state responsibility,[50] and on the appropriate level of compensation, including questions of contribution to the injury (i.e. incentives for potential victim states to mitigate losses) and punitive damages.[51]

---

[46] On this conclusion, including securing international cooperation as a third goal, see van Aaken, "Shared Responsibility in International Law: A Political Economy Analysis," in *Distribution of Responsibilities in International Law*, ed. Nollkaemper and Jacobs, 158–161. On this conclusion in the context of climate change law, see Michael G. Faure and André Nollkaemper, "International Liability as an Instrument to Prevent and Compensate for Climate Change," *Stanford Journal of International Law* 43 A (2007): 123–179.

[47] For further insights of economic analysis of tort law, see, for instance, Steven Shavell, *Economic Analysis of Accident Law* (Cambridge, MA: Harvard University Press, 1987); William M. Landes and Richard A. Posner, *The Economic Structure of Tort Law* (Cambridge, MA: Harvard University Press, 1987); Alan O. Sykes, ed., *Economics of Tort Law*, 2 vols. (Cheltenham, UK: Edward Elgar, 2007); Jennifer Arlen, ed., *Research Handbook on the Economics of Torts* (Cheltenham, UK: Edward Elgar, 2013).

[48] See Chap. 4.

[49] See Chap. 5.

[50] The most important contribution in this regard stems from Guido Calabresi and A. Douglas Melamed, who developed an integrated framework of entitlements being protected by property rules, liability rules, or inalienability rules and demonstrated that a liability rule may be preferable in the presence of high transaction costs. Guido Calabresi and A. Douglas Melamed, "Property Rules, Liability Rules, and Inalienability: One View of the Cathedral," *Harvard Law Review* 85, no. 6 (1972): 1089–1128. See also Louis Kaplow and Steven Shavell, "Property Rules versus Liability Rules: An Economic Analysis," *Harvard Law Review* 109, no. 4 (1996): 713–790.

[51] See Chap. 6.

3.2.2 Insights from Economic Contract Theory

Traditional inter-state relationships within the private dimension of international law can also relate to "the reciprocal exchange of benefits between sovereign [s]tates".[52] A classic example for the mutual exchange of benefits would be economic relations between states, for instance, in the area of trade law, when states agree on the mutual reduction or abolition of tariffs. From an economic perspective, these scenarios represent club goods constellations, because they relate to goods that are excludable but non-rival in consumption.[53] From a legal perspective, these relationships demonstrate structural similarities with contractual relations on the domestic level. Contract law deals with the enforcement of promises, agreements, and exchanges in voluntary relationships, and thus raises questions about, amongst others, enforcing only some agreements and not others (e.g. performance excuses), and the role of contractual remedies (e.g. reliance *versus* expectation damages).[54] Hence, these cooperation problems on the international level can be analysed through the lens of economic theories of contract law. But even beyond these specific "breach of contract"-like constellations which are transferrable to questions of responsibility on the international level, contract theory lends itself to a better understanding of international law more generally, as treaties are the predominant source of international law,[55] and can thus explain, amongst others, why certain primary obligations for compensation (e.g. strict liability regimes) exist.[56]

Economic contract theory[57] understands enforceable contracts as "a mechanism for achieving compliance with cooperative goals that are supposed to benefit the collective interest (maximising the joint surplus) of parties whose particular interests may diverge at a given time".[58] It analyses from an *ex ante* perspective why and when actors enter into which contractual arrangements, thus acknowledging the importance of consent as well as the participation constraint of parties, a game-theoretic term to express that parties enter into a contract only if it leaves all participating parties at least as well off as they would have been if they had not

---

[52] Feichtner, "Community Interest," para. 2.

[53] The benefits of a club are excludable regarding outsiders of the club. Contract theory then applies to the relations between the club members whereas tort theory applies to spillovers on outsiders of the club.

[54] Bix, *A Dictionary of Legal Theory*, s.v. "contract law". See further, Charles J. Goetz and Robert E. Scott, "Enforcing Promises: An Examination of the Basis of Contract," *Yale Law Journal* 89, no. 7 (1980): 1261–1322.

[55] van Aaken, "Rational Choice Theory." On the application of contract theory to general international law, with a focus on the question of enforcement, see Scott and Stephan, *The Limits of Leviathan: Contract Theory and the Enforcement of International Law*.

[56] See Chap. 4.

[57] See generally Patrick Bolton and M. Dewatripont, *Contract Theory* (Cambridge, MA: MIT Press, 2005).

[58] van Aaken, "Rational Choice Theory."

participated.[59] Unlike economic tort theories which deal with optimal deterrence, economic contract theory is concerned with optimal contracting.[60] Since contracts are incomplete,[61] contract theory deals with the question of how to account for unforeseen circumstances and the distribution of risks in a contract.[62] Generally, "[c] ontract theory distinguishes between uncertainty about the future (unforeseeability), uncertainty about the actions of the others players (asymmetrical information) and uncertainty about the meaning and scope of the contractual provisions (i.e. textual ambiguity and legal indeterminateness)".[63] Out of these three, information asymmetries between the contractual parties constitute the biggest challenge, as both parties have private information about themselves that the other party does not have, thus bearing the risk for opportunistic behaviour (such as adverse selection or moral hazard).[64] In particular in the context of contractual liability and enforcement of contracts, another problem of asymmetrical information has occupied contractual theorists, "namely, that some states of the world are not verifiable to a court, even though they may be observable to both the parties".[65] Against the background of these uncertainties, a balance needs to be found in contracting between *ex ante* credible commitments and *ex post* flexibility "with the following goals of the contract in mind: securing a high level of cooperation *ex ante*, distinction between (desired) flexibility in relation to new circumstances on the one hand and cases of purely opportunistic breach of the contract *ex post* on the other and adequate compensation for the victim".[66] Economic contract theory also focuses on when and which remedies are available, and considers whether they give parties the optimal

[59] Anne van Aaken, "International Investment Law between Commitment and Flexibility: A Contract Theory Analysis," *Journal of International Economic Law* 12, no. 2 (2009): 9.

[60] Ibid.

[61] For the economic concept of incomplete contracts, see, in particular, Jean Tirole, "Incomplete Contracts: Where Do We Stand?," *Econometrica* 67, no. 4 (1999): 741–781; Oliver Hart and John Moore, "Foundations of Incomplete Contracts," *Review of Economic Studies* 66, no. 1 (1999): 115–138. For an overview of incomplete contracting in the economic analysis of law, see Robert E. Scott, "The Law and Economics of Incomplete Contracts," *Annual Review of Law and Social Science* 2, no. 1 (2006): 279–297.

[62] van Aaken, "Rational Choice Theory." See also, Schäfer and Ott, *The Economic Analysis of Civil Law*, 273–274.

[63] van Aaken, "International Investment Law between Commitment and Flexibility: A Contract Theory Analysis," 10.

[64] Ibid. "Adverse selection, also called antiselection, term used in economics and insurance to describe a market process in which buyers or sellers of a product or service are able to use their private knowledge of the risk factors involved in the transaction to maximize their outcomes, at the expense of the other parties to the transaction." Carmen M. Alston, "Adverse Selection," *Encyclopaedia Britannica*, https://www.britannica.com/topic/expected-utility, Article last modified on 20 May 2016. On moral hazard, see footnote 252 in Chap. 2.

[65] Robert E. Scott and George G. Triantis, "Incomplete Contracts and the Theory of Contract Design," *Case Western Reserve Law Review* 56, no. 1 (2005): 191.

[66] van Aaken, "International Investment Law between Commitment and Flexibility: A Contract Theory Analysis," 11.

incentives to act in accordance with the purposes ascribed to contract law.[67] The economic function of contract remedies can then be described as "alter[ing] the incentives facing the party who regrets entering into the contract, which will directly affect the probability of performance and indirectly affect the number and type of contracts people make, the level of detail with which they identify their mutual obligations, the allocation of risks between the parties, the amount they invest in anticipation of performance once a contract is made, the precautions they take against the possibility of breach, and the precautions they take against the possibility of a regret contingency".[68] Since entering into an agreement and transferring the costs after a breach has occurred also creates transactions costs (e.g. for determining which and how damages should be compensated), their reduction, in application of the Coase theorem, can be considered another way of expressing the functions of contract law and contractual remedies.[69]

In sum, when applying the contract theory perspective to the international level, state responsibility can also be understood as having a cost allocation function while pursuing the following objectives: facilitation of entering into cooperative agreements (e.g. by reducing transaction costs), flexibility regarding unforeseen circumstances (i.e. allocation of risks), prevention of breach of agreements (i.e. inducing compliance), and compensation in case of breach. Insights from the economic analysis of contract law can consequently serve useful on all levels of the subsequent analysis in the following chapters,[70] from the analysis of the implications of the design of primary international obligations (i.e. in terms of *ex ante* defined precise rules or vague standards giving discretion for interpretation by judicial institutions),

---

[67] Bix, *A Dictionary of Legal Theory*, s.v. "contract law". According to Steven Shavell, damage measures (i.e. rules determining that and how much compensation needs to be paid by the defaulting party) set incentives for parties to behave as they would have under a fully specified contract. Steven Shavell, "Damage Measures for Breach of Contract," *Bell Journal of Economics* 11, no. 2 (1980): 466–490. For 'welfarist' theories, efficiency can be the guiding normative value for contract law, as reflected in the concept of efficient breach. See, in particular, Eric A. Posner, "Contract Theory," in *The Blackwell Guide to the Philosophy of Law and Legal Theory*, ed. Martin P. Golding and William A. Edmundson (Malden, MA: Blackwell, 2005), 138–147. With respect to contract law, the normative criterion of efficiency is relatively uncontroversial, but there exist, of course, alternative criteria for evaluating these legal rules. Posner and Parisi, *Law and Economics: Elgar Research Reviews in Economics*, Section 6.

[68] Paul G. Mahoney, "Contract Remedies: General," in *Encyclopedia of Law and Economics*, ed. Boudewijn Bouckaert and Gerrit de Geest (Cheltenham, UK: Edward Elgar, 2000), 118.

[69] Coase, "The Problem of Social Cost," 1–44. See, for instance, Cooter and Ulen, *Law & Economics*, 91–92.

[70] For further insights of economic analysis of contract law, see, for instance, Douglas G. Baird, ed., *Economics of Contract Law* (Cheltenham, UK: Edward Elgar, 2007). On the distinction between rules and standards, see, in particular, Louis Kaplow, "Rules versus Standards: An Economic Analysis," *Duke Law Journal* 42, no. 3 (1992): 557–629. On default rules, see, in particular, Richard A. Posner and Andrew M. Rosenfield, "Impossibility and Related Doctrines in Contract Law: An Economic Analysis," *Journal of Legal Studies* 6, no. 1 (1977): 83–118. On the remedies of compensation *versus* specific performance, see, in particular, Alan Schwartz, "The Case for Specific Performance," *Yale Law Journal* 89, no. 2 (1979): 271–306.

over circumstances precluding wrongfulness as flexibility provisions while safeguarding against opportunistic breach, to the analysis of remedies in international law, in particular compensation of damage to an injured state.

3.2.3 Private Enforcement of International State Responsibility

The transfer of insights from economic theories of tort and contract to the international level is not only helpful regarding the substance of responsibility rules. It can also explain enforcement in the private dimension of international state responsibility. On the domestic level, one can distinguish between private and public enforcement.[71] Tort law and contractual liability law, for instance, are usually enforced *via* litigation by the victim of a violation. In other areas of domestic law which regulate individual behaviour, such as criminal law, antitrust law, anti-pollution, or consumer product safety regulation, public agencies play an exclusive or additional role in enforcing such rules (e.g. by imposing fines or prohibiting products). While private and public enforcement mechanisms differ regarding who is bringing a legal claim, they have in common their dependence on adjudicatory mechanisms and ultimate coercive enforcement by state organs.[72]

As in domestic law, one needs to clearly distinguish in international law between the content of legal rules and their enforcement. On the international level, this distinction takes the form of first-order cooperation problems, which can relate to all four types of goods (thus including also breach of common pool resource (CPR) and GPG obligations), and the second-order cooperation problem of enforcement among states. Even if international law relies on decentralised self-enforcement mechanisms (in contrast to centralised law enforcement on the domestic level), one can equally distinguish between private and public enforcement mechanisms. The international law of state responsibility thus differs between enforcement by injured states (i.e. private, bilateral, or first-party enforcement) and enforcement by non-directly injured states (i.e. public, collective, or third-party enforcement).[73] While private

[71] See, in particular, Polinsky, "Private versus Public Enforcement of Fines," 105–127.

[72] Domestic legal systems may also contain non-coercive enforcement mechanisms. Contracts, for instance, may also be enforced by informal mechanisms, such as reputation or reciprocity. Scott, "The Law and Economics of Incomplete Contracts," 279–297. Jack Goldsmith and Daryl Levinson argue that public law, constitutional law, and public international law share the inability to coerce the compliance of powerful political actors, due to the lack of an "external" enforcement mechanism that states provide for ordinary domestic law. Jack Goldsmith and Daryl Levinson, "Law for States: International Law, Constitutional Law, Public Law," *Harvard Law Review* 122, no. 7 (2009): 1840–1842.

[73] The way private and public enforcement in international law are understood should not be confounded with the distinction between enforcement by private actors (that is, individuals or firms) and public actors (that is, the state on behalf of the injured individual or firm). Alan O. Sykes,

enforcement endows injured states with certain prerogatives to defend their subjective rights, public enforcement relates to non-directly injured states having an interest in the respect of fundamental rules of international law. Both mechanisms are not mutually exclusive, they can operate independent from each other or be combined. In addition, they are usually linked to the character of the underlying obligation, with bilateral enforcement in private and club good constellations and collective enforcement in GPG and CPR constellations. However, compliance with GPG and CPR obligations can also be enforced with private enforcement mechanisms, but this requires prior transformation into private or club good constellations.

However, the fact that on the domestic level both private and public enforcement are ultimately backed up by coercive powers of state organs means that insights on which form is preferable to the other and under which circumstances are not transferable as such to the international level, where compliance with international obligations relies on decentralised self-enforcement by states. With regard to the domestic context, A. Mitchell Polinsky concludes "that any of the methods of enforcement may be socially preferable, depending on the costs of each method as well as on the magnitude of the external damage".[74] He argues, more precisely, that private enforcement leads in a wide range of circumstances to less enforcement than public enforcement, especially when the external damage from the violation is large.[75] In parallel, public enforcement is socially preferable to private enforcement in many circumstances, especially when the external damage from the violation is large, even when public enforcement is much more costly.[76] Polinsky argues that the advantages of public enforcement, notably deterrence of potential violators due to a high probability of enforcement, will exceed the disadvantages of higher enforcement costs (which private parties are not willing to bear when they exceed the immediate fine revenue).[77] Yet, these conclusions rest on the assumption that public enforcement as a public good can be easily provided by the state even in the case of high enforcement costs, as centralised enforcement does not suffer from a free-rider problem. In international law, public enforcement (that is, collective or third-party enforcement) constitutes a sanctioners' dilemma with the consequence that the

---

for instance, uses these terms with regard to the analysis of international economic law in the latter sense as he distinguishes between private enforcement of international investment agreements and public enforcement of international trade agreements. Alan O. Sykes, "Public versus Private Enforcement of International Economic Law: Standing and Remedy," *Journal of Legal Studies* 34, no. 2 (2005): 631–666.

[74] Polinsky, "Private versus Public Enforcement of Fines," 108.

[75] Ibid., 107.

[76] Ibid.

[77] Ibid. Along the same vein, Polinsky and Shavell discuss the optimal tradeoff between the probability of enforcement and the magnitude of the fine. A. Mitchell Polinsky and Steven Shavell, "The Optimal Tradeoff between the Probability and Magnitude of Fines," *American Economic Review* 69, no. 5 (1979): 880–891. In cases where the probability of enforcement is less than one, the deterrence effect of a legal rule can be upheld by increasing the magnitude of the fine (e.g. punitive damages). See further, A. Mitchell Polinsky and Steven Shavell, "Punitive Damages: An Economic Analysis," *Harvard Law Review* 111, no. 4 (1998): 869–962.

probability of enforcement and thus the deterrence effect are rather low, as enforcement is in many circumstances prohibitively costly and likely not to take place. On the international level, it is often private enforcement mechanisms which are most effective, especially when it comes to effectuate GPG and CPR obligations. It is thus important to enquire carefully the costs and benefits of an enforcement decision, as they vary between the national and the international context and depending on the underlying circumstances.

Following the distinction between private and public enforcement in international law, this section takes a closer look at private enforcement as foreseen in the law of state responsibility.[78] In the private dimension of the international law of state responsibility, the injured state is, firstly, entitled to invoke the responsibility of the responsible state (Article 42 ARSIWA).[79] A state is qualified as injured if the obligation breached is owed to that state individually, but it can also be owed to a group of states including that state or the international community as a whole, under the condition that the breach of the obligation either specifically affects that state or radically changes the position of all other states with respect to the further performance of the obligation. Thus, state responsibility can be invoked bilaterally independent of the type of the obligation breached and the underlying first-order cooperation problem, provided that the state is somehow injured by that breach. Secondly, injured states are entitled to implement state responsibility by having recourse to countermeasures (Articles 49 ARSIWA) in order to induce the responsible state to comply with the secondary obligations that follow an internationally wrongful act. Countermeasures in the private enforcement dimension of international law thus serve to induce compliance with, on the one hand, the obligation to provide reparation for injury (in particular, compensation for damage), and, on the other hand, the obligation to cease and not to repeat the wrongful act (i.e. return to compliance with the primary obligation). The international law of state responsibility thus sets the legal framework for countermeasures. The ARSIWA outline the conditions, in particular the objects and limits (Part three, Chapter II, Articles 49-53 ARSIWA), and the consequences, as wrongfulness of the act not in

---

[78] This section looks at private enforcement in international law, while public enforcement will be dealt with in Sect. 3.3 on the objectives of state responsibility in the public dimension of international law.

[79] Article 42 ARSIWA reads as follows: "A State is entitled as an injured State to invoke the responsibility of another State if the obligation breached is owed to:

(a) that State individually; or
(b) a group of States including that State, or the international community as a whole, and the breach of the obligation:
    (i) specially affects that State; or
    (ii) is of such a character as radically to change the position of all the other States to which the obligation is owed with respect to the further performance of the obligation." On the notion of injury with relation to states, see further Giorgio Gaja, "The Concept of an Injured State," in *The Law of International Responsibility*, ed. James Crawford, Alain Pellet, and Simon Olleson (Oxford: Oxford University Press, 2010), 941–947.

conformity with an international act is precluded (Article 22 ARSIWA). In other words, a state that does not comply with the requirements for countermeasures is itself in breach of international law.

From an economic perspective, first-party countermeasures as a specific enforcement tool rely on two of the general compliance mechanisms in international law,[80] to the extent that they are driven by the injured state or states. Depending on the concrete measure, first-party countermeasures either consist in reciprocal non-compliance or, to the extent that they are costly to the retaliating state, constitute retaliatory actions. Countermeasures rely on reciprocity, at least to the extent that they are enacted by the parties to an international agreement themselves and concern obligations that are similar in-kind to the obligation violated in the first place. Countermeasures operating outside the base treaty are retaliatory actions to the extent that they create material and political costs for the sanctioning state.

First-party countermeasures can in principle serve to effectuate all four types of international obligations. This is intuitive for private or club good constellations, where the obligation breached is owed to the injured state individually and where parallels to tort and contractual liability respectively have been sufficiently demonstrated.[81] In a private goods scenario, for instance, when a ship belonging to one state dumps oil in the territorial waters of another state, the latter may seize the ship as a countermeasure until the state responsible for the pollution has paid compensation for the harm caused.[82] Other examples are violations of the obligations contained in multilateral extradition treaties or in the conventions on diplomatic and consular relations.[83] In a club goods scenario, a state may respond to a raise in tariffs with retaliatory trade sanctions as a countermeasure.

For GPG and CPR constellations establishing an individual injury is less evident, because free-riding in the form of non-compliance principally affects all states to a certain extent. According to Article 42 lit. b) ARSIWA, in order to invoke responsibility, the obligation breached can also be owed to a group of states including that state or the international community as a whole. However, a state is only qualified as injured state if the breach of such a collective obligation either (i) specifically affects that state or (ii) radically changes the position of all other states with respect to the further performance of the obligation. Injury thus requires more than a mere legal interest in compliance. Firstly, a state can be considered specifically affected by a breach, and thus as injured state, when the wrongful act has particular adverse effects on that state, even in cases where the legal effects of that act extend by implication to the whole group of states bound by the obligation or to the international community

[80] See Sect. 2.4 on the different enforcement mechanisms in international law.

[81] Article 42 lit. a) ARSIWA.

[82] See further, ARSIWA Commentaries, Article 42, paras. 6–10.

[83] Gaja, "The Concept of an Injured State," in *The Law of International Responsibility*, ed. Crawford, Pellet, and Olleson, 942–944.

as a whole.[84] For instance, the dumping of oil in the high seas in breach of Article 194 UNCLOS may particularly impact one or several states whose coastlines may be polluted or whose fishing industry may break down. In such cases, the coastal states may be considered as injured by the breach of the CPR obligation, and thus as entitled to have recourse to first-party countermeasures (provided that all other requirements are fulfilled), independent of the legal interest of the other state parties in compliance with the treaty obligations and ultimately in the preservation of the natural resource, here the maritime environment. The latter states may from an enforcement perspective considered non-directly injured third states.[85] Taking as another example a GPG constellation, for instance, the case of an armed attack, where the author is in breach of the obligation prohibiting the recourse to the use of force, and the state specially affected by such an aggressive act may be considered as injured state and have recourse to first-party countermeasures, usually non-in-kind or cross-countermeasures (for instance, economic sanctions). Such a situation also has a private goods dimension, as the state author of the armed attack also violates the obligation to respect the territorial integrity owed to the victim state. Thus, what both CPR and GPG constellations have in common is that while all (participating) states are concerned by non-compliant behaviour, first-party enforcement measures require a certain private goods dimension, namely that the state having recourse to countermeasures is specifically affected by such a breach (in economic terms, bearing a large part of the costs of the negative externality). Private enforcement in CPR and GPG constellations thus does not serve to ensure compliance generally, but rather to defend the subjective rights of injured states (usually their demand for compensation or restitution). Secondly, a state can also be injured when the breach of a collective obligation affects *per se* every other state to which the obligation is owed.[86] Examples of such interdependent (or integral) obligations include disarmament treaties, nuclear-free zone treaties, or any other treaty where each party's performance is effectively conditioned upon and requires the performance of each of the other parties (e.g. Antarctic Treaty).[87] In these particular treaty regimes, all states are individually entitled to react to a breach (even when they are not specifically affected in terms of having suffered a particular damage), as they are all equally affected and may have a strong interest in cessation and in other aspects of reparation, in particular restitution. In these limited cases, all treaty parties may, as injured states, have recourse to first-party countermeasures.

[84] Article 42 lit. b) (i) ARSIWA. ARSIWA Commentaries, Article 42, para. 12, and Article 48, para. 10. See further ibid., 946–947.

[85] The same applies for obligations aiming to mitigate climate change, as those states that are specifically affected, for instance, by extreme weather phenomena such as droughts or floods may not be able to establish causation between the breach of an CPR obligation and the harm suffered. In terms of the law of state responsibility, they cannot be considered as injured states, but may rely on their legal interest in compliance and act as third parties to effectuate the CPR regime.

[86] Article 42 lit. b) (ii) ARSIWA.

[87] ARSIWA Commentaries, Article 42, paras. 13–15. See further, Gaja, "The Concept of an Injured State," in *The Law of International Responsibility*, ed. Crawford, Pellet, and Olleson, 944–946.

We have seen in the previous chapter that private enforcement mechanisms may also complement third-party enforcement measures by states with a legal interest in compliance. Since third-party countermeasures are confronted with the sanctioners' dilemma, there exists another way to effectuate GPG and CPR obligations, namely by transforming them into club goods, and relying on first-party non-in-kind or cross-countermeasures (for example, exclusion from trading benefits).[88]

To sum up, first-party countermeasures, like all enforcement mechanisms, aim to deter violations by increasing the costs of non-compliance for the responsible state while at the same time seeking to uphold future cooperation. Their effectiveness requires that the wrongdoing state accepts countermeasures as justified (for instance, because they fulfil the proportionality requirement), otherwise they bear the risk that cooperation breaks down following "spirals of non-compliance". Such a breakdown becomes less likely when the "shadow of the future" is long (and thus the prospects from future cooperation are large) enough. In addition, as a private enforcement tool (and thus opposed to public enforcement which will be discussed further below), first-party countermeasures in the private dimension of the law of state responsibility serve the defence of subjective rights of injured states, in particular in order to enforce compliance in private goods and club goods constellations. However, to the extent that breach of an agreement aiming to provide GPGs or preserve CPRs has a private goods dimension (and thus specifically affects an injured state) or the agreement includes a club goods dimension, first-party countermeasures also serve to effectuate these agreements by denying the responsible state certain cooperative non-in-kind benefits.

3.3 Objectives of State Responsibility in the Public Dimension of International Law

The ARSIWA refer explicitly to two doctrinal concepts rooted in the notion of community interests: firstly, peremptory norms of general international law, also known as *jus cogens* norms, and, secondly, obligations *erga omnes* and *erga omnes partes*. The public dimension of the international law of state responsibility, however, extends beyond these two specific legal concepts and is reflected on different levels of the law of state responsibility. Community interests in the law of state responsibility can thus be understood in a larger sense.

---

[88] See Sect. 2.4.

3.3.1 Insights from the International Law of GPGs and CPRs

Due to the particularities of the international legal order, the responsibility regime in the public dimension of international law cannot derive its objectives easily from domestic liability law (in particular, tort and contractual liability) as it was possible in the private dimension, not even from domestic state liability law. Domestic state liability law shares the principal elements of tort law, with the major difference that the actor is public, and that responsibility is not borne by the individual state agent but transferred to the state. This is similar in international law. Yet, this book does not enquire the relations between public actors and individual victims but between equal sovereign nation states that are assumed to be unitary rational actors, and thus interact with each other similar to private actors in the domestic context.

What characterises the public dimension, is thus not the quality of the actor, but the substance of the responsibility rules. While on the domestic level, negative externalities from individual behaviour (e.g. pollution) are either mitigated *via* tort liability (among private actors) or *via* public regulation (that is, the state prohibiting or otherwise regulating certain harmful activities),[89] absent a central regulator, insights on the latter option are not easily transferable to the international level. Administrative tasks on the global level such as the management of shared resources are performed by states which cooperate in a decentralised manner, thus facing collective action problems. We have seen that the public dimension of international law encompasses the protection of the community interests, and relates to GPG and CPR obligations by addressing their underlying cooperation challenges.[90] As regards CPRs, disputes between states can, for instance, arise over the pollution of natural resources such as the atmosphere due to the adverse effects of climate change, the extinction of fish stocks in the high seas, or the destruction of cultural heritage. Inter-state disputes over GPGs, for instance, relate to the use of force or the commission of war crimes, thus typically within the area of international peace and security, or to violations of international human rights obligations. These scenarios have in common that state actions relate to violations of international obligations protecting goods that are in the public domain, and where the adverse effects of the breach are non-excludable (i.e. GPG characteristics), and, in the case of CPRs, relate to resources that are also rival in consumption. The underlying cooperation problem for both constellations is how to overcome the collective action problem of free-riding on the provision or non-consumption efforts of other states, as the benefits of a breach are fully internalised by the wrongdoing state but the costs are distributed

---

[89] On an economic perspective on how the two modes liability and safety regulation are employed on the domestic level in order to alleviate risks, see Steven Shavell, "Liability for Harm versus Regulation of Safety," *Journal of Legal Studies* 13, no. 2 (1984): 357–374.

[90] See Sect. 2.3 on the economic understanding of community interests in international law.

among all other participating states. Objectives of state responsibility in the public dimension can thus be derived from the international law of GPGs and CPRs.[91]

State responsibility norms in the public dimension of international law deal with the conditions for and the doctrinal consequences of breach of international obligations regulating GPGs and CPRs. The concrete objectives of international state responsibility thus depend on the relevant issue: the responsibility standard, the possible excuses from breach and the level of remedies. Firstly, regarding the responsibility standard, state responsibility has been conceived as objective responsibility, that is requiring for the commission of an internationally wrongful act only breach of an international obligation (and attribution of the conduct to the state) but not the causation of harm. A state can be responsible for breach whatever the type or content of the international obligation, which can thus also consist in a GPG or CPR obligation.[92] This bears similarities with administrative law, where citizens, even without causing a concrete harm, can be required by the state to abstain from illegal behaviour (e.g. regulation of therapeutic goods and environmental law such as regulation of water resources).[93] Surely, the essence of administrative law is to ensure that public authorities abide by the rule of law in their relation towards private citizens, thus governing, for instance, proceedings of individuals against the imposition of a fine (i.e. administrative procedure law).[94] In specific subject areas, however, it relates in the first place to the administration of public services (that is, public goods and common resources on the national level), as the state sets and enforces compliance with regulatory standards against its citizens (e.g. command and control regulation).[95] This task falls on the international level on states cooperating with each other (notwithstanding the role of international organisations). The underlying idea in international law is to uphold respect for the international legal order as such and to ensure that states can be held responsible for legal injuries to the international community. Regarding GPG and CPR constellations in primary law, the challenge in terms of responsibility is often to attribute a concrete harm to the behaviour of a responsible state (for instance, in international human rights law when the breach has a purely internal dimension or in international climate change

---

[91] Van Aaken first brought forward the idea that cooperation of states, especially in public goods constellations, constitutes an independent goal of the responsibility regime, see van Aaken, "Shared Responsibility in International Law: A Political Economy Analysis," in *Distribution of Responsibilities in International Law*, ed. Nollkaemper and Jacobs, 158–161.

[92] See Chap. 4 on the conditions for international state responsibility.

[93] For example, in substantive administrative law, a state can impose a fine for crossing a red light, even if a driver has not caused harm to another person. On this conclusion and example, see van Aaken, "Shared Responsibility in International Law: A Political Economy Analysis," in *Distribution of Responsibilities in International Law*, ed. Nollkaemper and Jacobs, 161.

[94] Such scenarios which are governed on the domestic level by rules of administrative procedure relate on the international level to cases where states defend themselves against public or third-party enforcement measures which they deem abusive.

[95] On the definition of regulation, see Robert Baldwin, Martin Cave, and Martin Lodge, *Understanding Regulation: Theory, Strategy, and Practice*, 2nd ed. (Oxford: Oxford University Press, 2012), 2–3.

law, where causation to a specific event such as a flood is difficult to establish), and responsibility is therefore based on illegality (e.g. exceedance of permitted greenhouse gas emissions levels) rather than injury. State responsibility has then in the public dimension, in particular, the objective to induce compliance with GPG and CPR obligations by setting incentives for compliance (or at least not further disincentivising compliance), which in the case of CPRs ultimately serves to mitigate the harm to common resources. Furthermore, it needs to be borne in mind that also the international legal order as such constitutes a GPG, which is also captured by the concept of objective responsibility based on the notion of illegality, and that even breach of international obligations in purely private scenarios (e.g. in investment or trade law) cannot be thought of in isolation from their impact on the international community as a whole, thus rejecting the notion of efficient breach of international obligations (i.e. efficiency as a normative guiding principle in the international law of state responsibility).[96]

Secondly, regarding possible excuses from breach of international obligations, references can be made to domestic law and the principle of necessity, which can excuse harm caused because the action served the protection of a higher interest. In tort law, such excuses can take the form of either private necessity, if the actor protects its own interest, or, public necessity, if the act relates to the protection of a common interest (e.g. the destruction of alien property to safe one's life or the life of others). On the international level, under certain circumstances, it may also be possible for states to breach their international obligations, on the one hand, in order to protect a pure national interest such as national security in defending its own territory (private necessity), or, on the other hand, to protect an interest of the international community (e.g. destruction of a foreign vessel to stop pollution of the high seas). Even if the invocation of private necessity, in particular in the form of economic necessity, is more common in practice, public necessity may occur in constellations where the obligation breached is private in nature (e.g. a private of club goods obligation, such as in investment or trade law) and the interest protected is from a global perspective public in nature (i.e. relating to a GPG or CPR).[97] Necessity in the law of state responsibility (Article 25 ARSIWA) is a provision that allows for weighing of competing interests and for taking into account the protection of community interests. The public dimension of the international law of state responsibility thus also includes the objectives to allow for a certain degree of flexibility, and to allocate the costs (see Article 27 lit. b) ARSIWA) between the injured state, the state acting in necessity, and the international community with a view to ensure the provision of GPGs and the protection of CPRs.

Thirdly, regarding the level of remedies, state responsibility in the public dimension follows a primary objective of inducing compliance. The emphasis of the

[96] On the use of the concept of efficient breach in the international law of state responsibility, see, in particular, Posner and Sykes, *Economic Foundations of International Law*, 127.

[97] On a rational choice analysis of the necessity excuse, in particular the concept of public necessity, see Sect. 5.2.

different available remedies lies on returning to legality by introducing a secondary obligation to cease the act in breach of a community interest obligation and to give assurances not to repeat the illegal act in the future, independent of whether the illegal act caused an injury. In addition, in constellations where there is an overlap between a private goods and a GPG/CPR scenario, that is, when a community interest obligation is violated but one state is specifically affected (for instance, breach of an international human rights obligation with a cross-border dimension, or pollution of the high seas specifically affecting a coastal state), reparation of injury is another available remedy, but may only be requested in the interest of the injured state.[98] That reparation of injury can also take the forms of restitution or satisfaction, and is not limited to compensation, hints to the fact that remedies in the public dimension are not limited to a mere cost allocation function. Invocation of these remedies on behalf on the injured states means that compliance with these secondary obligations as well as discouraging breach of primary obligations in the first place, are also important objectives of the law of state responsibility in the public dimension.[99]

When applying economic goods theory to the international level, substantive rules of state responsibility can be understood as pursuing the following objectives: preventing and ending breach of community interest obligations (i.e. inducing compliance with obligations serving GPG provision and CPR protection) and ensuring flexibility regarding circumstances that require the protection of a community interest (i.e. public necessity), while allocating the associated costs between the injured state, the responsible or excused state and the international community as a whole.

3.3.2 *A Hierarchy of International Norms: The Role of* Jus Cogens *Obligations in the Law of State Responsibility*

In order to further examine the objectives of state responsibility in the public dimension, it is necessary to assess in detail the role of peremptory norms of general international law, as one doctrinal concept flowing from the notion of community interests in international law.[100] Two distinct parts of the ARSIWA refer to these types of norms, in the international legal literature also referred to as *jus cogens* norms. Article 26 ARSIWA provides that peremptory norms need to be complied

---

[98] If a GPG or CPR obligation is breached, but causation of harm cannot be established, the obligations of cessation and assurances of non-repetition remain the only available remedies for states in the international community.

[99] On remedies, see Chap. 6.

[100] On the current work of the International Law Commission on peremptory norms of general international law (*jus cogens*), see http://legal.un.org/ilc/summaries/1_14.shtml. For a comprehensive overview of the concept of peremptory norms, see Alexander Orakhelashvili, *Peremptory Norms in International Law* (Oxford: Oxford University Press, 2006).

with under any circumstances, and that states thus cannot invoke the six circumstances precluding wrongfulness of a state act to excuse or justify breach of a *jus cogens* norm.[101] Articles 40 and 41 ARSIWA provide for specific obligations of third states in case of serious breaches of obligations under peremptory norms of general international law, namely the obligation to cooperate to bring to an end through lawful means any serious breach of *jus cogens* norms as well as the obligations neither to recognise as lawful nor to render aid or assistance in maintaining such situation.[102]

Community interests norms can vary in their degree of importance.[103] Peremptory norms of general international law constitute one doctrinal expression for international legal norms that are of fundamental importance and are considered superior in the hierarchy of international legal norms.[104] Public international law reflects the distinction between *ius strictum* and *ius dispositivum*, which is known from many legal systems based on Roman law and means that "[w]hile parties may disregard rules of *ius dispositivum* in their contractual relationships, their legal acts must comply with the *ius strictum*, otherwise they are void or at least not completely valid".[105] In international law, norms that have been attributed *jus cogens* status are excluded from the free disposition of states.[106] The VCLT defines a peremptory norm of general international law as "a norm accepted and recognized by the international community of [s]tates as a whole as a norm from which no derogation is permitted and which can be modified only by a subsequent norm of general international law having the same character".[107] The doctrinal consequence foreseen in the law of treaties in case of conflict with a *jus cogens* norm is the invalidity of an international treaty, either at the time of its conclusion or when a new peremptory

---

[101] Article 26 ARSIWA reads: "Nothing in this chapter precludes the wrongfulness of any act of a State which is not in conformity with an obligation arising under a peremptory norm of general international law." For an analysis of this provision, see Chap. 5.

[102] Article 40 ARSIWA on the application of Part two, Chap. III reads: "1. This chapter applies to the international responsibility which is entailed by a serious breach by a State of an obligation arising under a peremptory norm of general international law. 2. A breach of such an obligation is serious if it involves a gross or systematic failure by the responsible State to fulfil the obligation." Article 41 ARSIWA on the particular consequences of a serious breach of an obligation under this chapter reads: "1. States shall cooperate to bring to an end through lawful means any serious breach within the meaning of article 40. 2. No State shall recognize as lawful a situation created by a serious breach within the meaning of article 40, nor render aid or assistance in maintaining that situation. 3. This article is without prejudice to the other consequences referred to in this part and to such further consequences that a breach to which this chapter applies may entail under international law." For an analysis of these specific consequences, see Sect. 6.4.

[103] Feichtner, "Community Interest," para. 40.

[104] Ibid., para. 41.

[105] Jochen A. Frowein, "Ius Cogens," ed. Anne Peters and Rüdiger Wolfrum, *Max Planck Encyclopedia of Public International Law* (Oxford Public International Law: Oxford University Press, 2021), http://opil.ouplaw.com, Article last updated in March 2013, para. 1.

[106] Feichtner, "Community Interest," para. 41.

[107] Article 53 Vienna Convention on the Law of Treaties (VCLT).

norm of general international law emerges.[108] This idea is also reflected in the law of state responsibility, which excludes in Article 26 ARSIWA exemptions from breaches of *jus cogens* obligations.[109]

While the existence of the concept of *jus cogens* norms in terms of their status and the doctrinal consequences outlined above are now widely recognised by state practice, codified treaty law and international case law,[110] other aspects remain disputed. Firstly, the substantive rules having been accorded the legal character of *jus cogens* have not been conclusively determined. This is why both the law of treaties and the law of state responsibility refrain from giving examples and only offer an abstract definition of the concept of peremptory norms of general international law. Relatively few peremptory norms have been recognised as such, but various courts and tribunals have affirmed the idea of *jus cogens* norms in contexts beyond the validity of treaties.[111] Those peremptory norms that are undisputedly accepted include the prohibitions of aggression, genocide, slavery, apartheid and racial discrimination, crimes against humanity, torture, and the right to self-determination.[112] Other recognised peremptory norms include the basic rules of IHL

---

[108] Articles 53 and 64 VCLT.

[109] ARSIWA Commentary, Article 26, paras. 1, 4.

[110] For an overview of the historical evolution of the concept of *jus cogens* and the legal nature of *jus cogens*, see United Nations International Law Commission, *First Report on Jus Cogens by Special Rapporteur Dire Tladi*, Sixty-Eighth Session, 2016 (UN Doc. A/CN.4/693).

[111] ARSIWA Commentary, Article 26, para. 5. For an implicit reference to the existence of *jus cogens* norms, while confusingly referring to obligations *erga omnes*, see *Barcelona Traction, Light and Power Company, Limited (Belgium v. Spain) (New Application: 1962)*, Judgment (Second Phase), 5 February 1970, ICJ Reports 1970, p. 3, p. 32, paras. 33–34. See also *East Timor (Portugal v. Australia)*, Judgment, 30 June 1995, ICJ Reports 1995, p. 90, p. 102, para. 29. *Legality of the Threat or Use of Nuclear Weapons*, Advisory Opinion, 8 July 1996, ICJ Reports 1996, p. 226, pp. 257–258, paras. 79–83. *Application of the Convention on the Prevention and Punishment of the Crime of Genocide (Bosnia and Herzegovina v. Yugoslavia)*, Judgment (Preliminary Objections), 11 July 1996, ICJ Reports 1996, p. 595, pp. 615–616, paras. 31–32. Further references to *jus cogens* in cases of the ICJ include: *Application of the Convention on the Prevention and Punishment of the Crime of Genocide (Bosnia and Herzegovina v. Serbia and Montenegro)*, Judgment, pp. 110–111, para. 161. *Accordance with International Law of the Unilateral Declaration of Independence in Respect of Kosovo*, Advisory Opinion, 22 July 2010, ICJ Reports 2010, p. 403, pp. 437–438, para. 81. *Jurisdictional Immunities of the State (Germany v. Italy: Greece Intervening)*, Judgment, 3 February 2012, ICJ Reports 2012, p. 99, pp. 140–142, paras. 92–97. *Application of the Convention on the Prevention and Punishment of the Crime of Genocide (Croatia v. Serbia)*, Judgment, 3 February 2015, ICJ Reports 2015, p. 3, pp. 46–47, paras. 87–88.

[112] ARSIWA Commentary, Article 26, para. 5. For the prohibition of aggression or the use of force, see *Military and Paramilitary Activities in and against Nicaragua (Nicaragua v. United States of America)*, Judgment (Merits), 27 June 1986, ICJ Reports 1986, p. 14, pp. 100–101, para. 190. For the prohibition of genocide, see, for example, *Application of the Convention on the Prevention and Punishment of the Crime of Genocide (Bosnia and Herzegovina v. Yugoslavia (Serbia and Montenegro))*, Order (Provisional Measures), 13 September 1993, ICJ Reports 1993, p. 325, pp. 439–440. See also *Application of the Convention on the Prevention and Punishment of the Crime of Genocide (Bosnia and Herzegovina v. Yugoslavia)*, Order (Counter-Claims), 17 December 1997, ICJ Reports 1997, p. 243. See also *Armed Activities on the Territory of the Congo*

applicable in armed conflict.[113] It should be noted that this list of examples is not exhaustive.[114] It derives from Article 64 VCLT that new peremptory norms of general international law can emerge under the condition that they are accepted and recognised by the international community of states as a whole. For the economic analysis of state responsibility in this book, it is not necessary to determine conclusively which norms have been accorded *jus cogens* status,[115] but sufficient to refer to the legal characteristics of *jus cogens* norms.[116]

Secondly, the legal consequences—other than invalidity of a treaty and non-applicability of circumstances precluding wrongfulness—of a breach of an international obligation with *jus cogens* status in the regime of state responsibility have been intensively debated. Initially, the ILC acknowledged in its first project of Draft Articles that there was a need to distinguish in the law on state responsibility between "international crimes of states" and all other cases of internationally wrongful acts ("international delicts").[117] Yet, in contrast to the international

---

(Democratic Republic of the Congo v. Rwanda) (New Application: 2002) Judgment (Jurisdiction of the Court and Admissibility of the Application), 3 February 2006, ICJ Reports 2006, p. 6, pp. 31–32, para. 64. For the prohibition of torture, see, in particular, Articles 1 and 2 of the Convention against Torture and other Cruel, Inhuman or Degrading Treatment or Punishment (Torture Convention) (concluded 10 December 1984, entered into force 26 June 1987) 1465 *UNTS* 85. See also *Questions Relating to the Obligation to Prosecute or Extradite (Belgium v. Senegal)*, Judgment, 20 July 2012, ICJ Reports 2012, p. 422, p. 457, para. 99. For the right to self-determination, see the fifth principle of United Nations General Assembly, Resolution 2625 (XXV), *Declaration on Principles of International Law Concerning Friendly Relations and Cooperation among States in Accordance with the Charter of the United Nations*, 24 October 1970 (UN Doc. A/8082). See also *East Timor (Portugal v. Australia)*, Judgment, p. 102, para. 29. See also *Legal Consequences of the Construction of a Wall in the Occupied Palestinian Territory*, Advisory Opinion, 9 July 2004, ICJ Reports 2004, p. 136, pp. 199–200, paras. 157–159.

[113] ARSIWA Commentaries, Article 40, paras. 4–5. See also the examples of peremptory norms given by the ILC in its commentary to what became Article 53 of the 1969 Vienna Convention (then Article 50 of the Draft Articles), United Nations International Law Commission, „Draft Articles on the Law of Treaties with Commentaries," *in Report of the Commission to the General Assembly on the Work of its Eighteenth Session*, 1966 (UN Doc. A/21/9), in *Yearbook of the International Law Commission*, 1966, Volume II (UN Doc. A/CN.4/SER.A/1966/Add.1). For the peremptory character of the basic rules of international humanitarian law, see *Legality of the Threat or Use of Nuclear Weapons*, Advisory Opinion, pp. 257–258, paras. 79–83. See also *Legal Consequences of the Construction of a Wall in the Occupied Palestinian Territory*, Advisory Opinion, pp. 199–200, paras. 157–159.

[114] ARSIWA Commentaries, Article 40, para. 6.

[115] For an extensive overview and a proposal of a non-exhaustive list of peremptory norms of general international law (*jus cogens*), see United Nations International Law Commission, *Fourth Report on Peremptory Norms of General International Law (Jus Cogens) by Special Rapporteur Dire Tladi*, Seventy-First Session, 2019 (UN Doc. A/CN.4/727).

[116] On criteria for *jus cogens*, see further United Nations International Law Commission, *Second Report on Jus Cogens by Special Rapporteur Dire Tladi*, Sixty-Ninth Session, 2017 (UN Doc. A/CN.4/706).

[117] Commentary to Article 19 of the Draft Articles, see United Nations International Law Commission, „Draft Articles on State Responsibility," in *Report of the Commission to the General Assembly on the Work of its Twenty-Eighth Session*, 1976 (UN Doc. A/31/10), in *Yearbook of the*

criminal liability of individuals, there has been no development of penal consequences for states in case of breaches of peremptory norms.[118] For instance, punitive damages are not recognised in the international law of state responsibility, even in the case of serious breaches of *jus cogens* obligations.[119] Consequently, the ARSIWA in their current form do not maintain the distinction between state "crimes" and "delicts" regarding the concept of an internationally wrongful act underlying Part one of the ARSIWA.[120] Nonetheless, the ARSIWA reflect that certain violations of peremptory norms of general international law entail particular consequences in terms of state responsibility.[121] As outlined in Articles 40 and 41 ARSIWA, serious breaches of obligations arising under *jus cogens* norms can attract additional consequences, not only for the responsible state but in particular for all other states, and are (with the exception of the obligation of non-recognition) an expression of the progressive development of international law.[122] The consequences of a breach of peremptory norms are thus, in addition to the small number of obligations to which they apply, further limited to the extent that the breach itself should have been "serious", which "signifies that a certain order of magnitude of violation is necessary".[123] According to Article 40 (2) ARSIWA, a breach of such an obligation is serious, if it involves a gross or systematic failure by the responsible state to fulfil the obligation.[124] While a "systematic" violation would have to be

International Law Commission, 1976, Volume II, Part Two (UN Doc. A/CN.4/SER.A/1976/Add.1 (Part 2)).

[118] ARSIWA Commentaries, Part two, Chap. III, para 5. See also James Crawford, "International Crimes of States," in *The Law of International Responsibility*, ed. James Crawford, Alain Pellet, and Simon Olleson (Oxford: Oxford University Press, 2010), 405–414. See also the extensive discussion by Nina H.B. Jørgensen, arguing that the concept of state responsibility for international crimes is emerging as customary international law. Nina H.B. Jørgensen, *The Responsibility of States for International Crimes* (Oxford: Oxford University Press, 2000).

[119] ARSIWA Commentaries, Part two, Chap. III, para 5. According to Article 34 ARSIWA, the function of damages is essentially compensatory. However, punitive damages have been used implicitly by the European Court of Human Rights, are not necessarily prohibited in European and international law, and rely on a social science rationale, namely to effectuate international law. See Pinto de Albuquerque and van Aaken, "Punitive Damages in Strasbourg," in *The European Convention on Human Rights and General International Law*, ed. van Aaken and Motoc, 230–247. On an economic perspective on punitive damages in the international law of state responsibility, see Sect. 6.3.2.2.

[120] ARSIWA Commentaries, Part two, Chap. III, para. 7.

[121] ARSIWA Commentaries, Part two, Chap. III, para. 7. On why there has been no substantial change between the concept of "international crimes" in the Draft Articles and the provisions on *jus cogens* norms in the ARSIWA, see Eric Wyler, "From 'State Crime' to Responsibility for 'Serious Breaches of Obligations under Peremptory Norms of General International Law'," *European Journal of International Law* 13, no. 5 (2002): 1147–1160.

[122] Crawford, "International Crimes of States," in *The Law of International Responsibility*, ed. Crawford, Pellet, and Olleson, 410.

[123] ARSIWA Commentaries, Article 40, para. 7.

[124] On the characteristic of seriousness of the breach of a *jus cogens* norm, questioning whether this limitation is necessary, see further Paola Gaeta, "The Character of the Breach," in *The Law of*

carried out in an organised and deliberate way, the term "gross" refers to the intensity of the violation or its effects, and serious breaches will usually fulfil both characteristics.[125] This limit in scope emphasises the exceptional nature of the additional consequences accorded to serious breaches of peremptory norms in the law of state responsibility.[126] Chapters 6 and 7 will analyse in detail whether the incentives these provisions are setting for states are adequate in order to end breaches of this kind and gravity or even discourage them in the first place.

What matters for the subsequent analysis is the answer to the question to what extent the concept of *jus cogens* or peremptory norms of general international law is congruent with the concept of GPGs. One way to respond to this question is to look at the cooperation challenges (i.e. provision of GPGs, preservation of CPRs, and mitigating negative externalities) underlying the respective primary obligation in international law, which has been accorded *jus cogens* status. The reason is that a different status of an international norm in terms of its hierarchy does not change the underlying characteristic of the individual obligation. In terms of their content, the peremptory norms outlined above basically fall into two groups: on the one hand, obligations stemming from the law of armed conflict (*jus ad bellum*), including violations of the right to self-determination through the acquisition of territory, and IHL (*jus in bello*); on the other hand, fundamental human rights norms, breach of which mostly even engages individual responsibility under international criminal law.[127] To put it more generally, peremptory norms in general international law stem from "those substantive rules of conduct that prohibit what has come to be seen as intolerable because of the threat it presents to the survival of [s]tates and their peoples and the most basic human values".[128] The objective of most obligations with *jus cogens* status is thus the protection of the basic rights of the human person.[129] Feichtner concludes that "[a]ll of them can be conceptualized as norms protecting a common good (peace) or common values (certain fundamental human rights or group rights) and thus as community interest norms".[130] In economic terms,

---

International Responsibility, ed. James Crawford, Alain Pellet, and Simon Olleson (Oxford: Oxford University Press, 2010), 421–426.

[125] It should be noted that some peremptory norms (e.g. prohibitions of aggression and genocide) require by definition an intentional violation on a large scale. See ARSIWA Commentaries, Article 40, para. 8.

[126] However, Article 41 (3) ARSIWA leaves open the possibility for further consequences in international law. On the consequences and legal effects of peremptory norms of general international, see also United Nations International Law Commission, *Third Report on Peremptory Norms of General International Law (Jus Cogens) by Special Rapporteur Dire Tladi*, Seventieth Session, 2018 (UN Doc. A/CN.4/714).

[127] To recall them: prohibitions of aggression, genocide, slavery, apartheid and racial discrimination, crimes against humanity, torture, the right to self-determination, and the basic rules of international humanitarian law in armed conflict.

[128] ARSIWA Commentaries, Article 40, para 3.

[129] *Barcelona Traction, Light and Power Company, Limited (Belgium v. Spain) (New Application: 1962)*, Judgment (Second Phase), p. 32, para. 34. See also Frowein, "Ius Cogens," para. 8.

[130] Feichtner, "Community Interest," para. 41.

independent of whether the fundamental obligations stemming from IHL or human rights law relate to facts with a purely internal dimension or to a cross-border scenario, their underlying cooperative challenge constitutes the provision of GPGs, that is international peace and security or global human rights protection as a non-use value GPG,[131] notably due to their universal applicability in terms of scope.[132] This relation between *jus cogens* norms and GPG obligations is however not automatic, as new peremptory norms can emerge over time. For instance, in its first project of Draft Articles, the ILC foresaw in its definition of 'international crimes of states' in Article 19 different examples, one of them being "a serious breach of an international obligation of essential importance for the safeguarding and preservation of the human environment, such as those prohibiting massive pollution of the atmosphere or of the seas".[133] This Article has not been retained in the ARSIWA, only the concept of *jus cogens* norms without citing concrete examples. This aspect demonstrates that the protection of the environment and in particular the prohibition of pollution of the atmosphere or of the high seas has the potential to becoming a *jus cogens* norm, even though it is not recognised as such today.[134] These obligations should in terms of their underlying cooperation problem (i.e. non-consumption due to the risk of extinction or destruction) rather be understood as CPR obligations, even though the mere enjoyment of a healthy environment also bears GPG characteristics. In sum, peremptory norms of general international law are determined on a case-by-case basis depending on their fundamental importance, universal applicability and deemed superiority in the hierarchy of international legal norms, while in economic terms, they relate in terms of their substance (at least as they are recognised today) to the provision of GPGs.

Another way to examine the degree of congruence between the concept of *jus cogens* norms and GPGs is to think about them as an abstract category of norms

---

[131] See Sect. 2.3.

[132] ARSIWA Commentaries, Part two, Chap. III, para. 7. See also the First Report of the Special Rapporteur Dire Tladi defining norms of *jus cogens* as protecting the fundamental values of the international community, being hierarchically superior to other norms of international law and being universally applicable. United Nations International Law Commission, *First Report on Jus Cogens by Special Rapporteur Dire Tladi*, Sixty-Eighth Session, 2016 (UN Doc. A/CN.4/693), p. 45, para. 74.

[133] Commentary to Article 19 of the Draft Articles, see United Nations International Law Commission, "Draft Articles on State Responsibility," in *Report of the Commission to the General Assembly on the Work of its Twenty-Eighth Session*, 1976 (UN Doc. A/31/10), in *Yearbook of the International Law Commission*, 1976, Volume II, Part Two (UN Doc. A/CN.4/SER.A/1976/Add.1 (Part 2)).

[134] United Nations International Law Commission, *Fourth Report on Peremptory Norms of General International Law (Jus Cogens) by Special Rapporteur Dire Tladi*, Seventy-First Session, 2019 (UN Doc. A/CN.4/727), pp. 61–62, para. 136. See in this regard also the demand to add "ecocide" beyond the context of an armed conflict to the list of international crimes falling in the remit of the Rome Statute of the International Criminal Court (concluded 17 July 1998, entered into force 1 July 2002) 2187 *UNTS* 3. See, in particular, Polly Higgins, *Eradicating Ecocide: Exposing the Corporate and Political Practices Destroying the Planet and Proposing the Laws Needed to Eradicate Ecocide* (London: Shepheard-Walwyn, 2010).

defined by their superior status entailing certain legal consequences. As discussed, Articles 53 and 64 VCLT foresee that treaties are void if they are in conflict with a peremptory norm and along the same lines Article 26 ARSIWA provides that states cannot invoke circumstances precluding wrongfulness in case of breach of a *jus cogens* obligation. According to the ARSIWA Commentaries, "peremptory norms of general international law focus on the scope and priority to be given to a certain number of fundamental obligations".[135] This suggests that one can understand the doctrinal consequence of *jus cogens* norms as a rule of conflict of norms, aiming to mitigate conflicts between competing interests and providing a degree of superiority to peremptory norms of general international law.[136] This demonstrates that the existence of *jus cogens* norms and the recognition of a distinct public dimension of international law are closely linked.[137] One can thus equate *jus cogens* norms due to their specific normative status with obligations aiming to protect GPGs, that is, as normative GPGs.[138] From an economic perspective, such difference in their normative status means that they are as non-use value GPGs of such fundamental importance to all states in the international community that a violation entails higher costs (in terms of the affected legal interest in compliance) than breach of a private goods or an "ordinary" GPG obligation. In this sense, *jus cogens* norms also overlap with *erga omnes* obligations, which will be discussed below.

Furthermore, Article 41 ARSIWA foresees—in addition to the "normal" consequences falling on the responsible state[139]—legal consequences notably for third states in case of breach of a *jus cogens* obligation in the sense of Article 40 ARSIWA. The first particular consequence for states facing a serious breach of a peremptory norm derives from Article 41 (1) ARSIWA, which provides that states are under a positive duty to cooperate—in an institutionalised or non-institutionalised form—in order to bring this breach to an end.[140] The ARSIWA state only that such cooperation must take place through "lawful means", but other than that, they are mute on what measures states—even if they are not individually affected—should take in order to end a serious breach of *jus cogens* norms.[141] At the time of adoption of the ARSIWA it was not clear to what extent international law foresees a positive duty of

[135] ARSIWA Commentaries, Part two, Chap. III, para. 7.

[136] On the balancing of competing interests and Article 26 ARSIWA as a conflict of norms rule favouring compliance with peremptory norms over flexibility, see Chap. 5.

[137] Frowein, "Ius Cogens," para. 3.

[138] See, for instance, Nollkaemper, defining *jus cogens* norms as "public goods at least in the normative sense." Nollkaemper, "International Adjudication of Global Public Goods: The Intersection of Substance and Procedure," 780.

[139] Article 41 (3) ARSIWA.

[140] ARSIWA Commentaries, Article 41, para. 2. On the genesis of this provision in the ILC, see further Nina H.B. Jørgensen, "The Obligation of Cooperation," in *The Law of International Responsibility*, ed. James Crawford, Alain Pellet, and Simon Olleson (Oxford: Oxford University Press, 2010), 695–701.

[141] ARSIWA Commentaries, Article 41, para. 3.

international cooperation in response to the gravest breaches of international law,[142] but at the very least, this provision seeks to strengthen existing mechanisms of cooperation, especially in the framework of international organisations such as the UN.[143] It can also relate to the formation of a group of states acting together, for instance, by entering into *ad hoc* cooperative arrangements.[144] On this basis, states are called upon to find an appropriate response to grave breaches of peremptory norms through a "joint and coordinated effort", which "is often the only way of providing an effective remedy".[145] Hence, this special obligation is neither creating a legal basis to excuse breach of other international obligations (e.g. humanitarian intervention and countermeasures) nor a primary obligation breach of which could entail international responsibility. It is rather a secondary obligation falling on third states (but without specific enforcement mechanism), which underpins the right of non-directly injured states to invoke state responsibility (Article 48 ARSIWA), to take "lawful" countermeasures (Article 54 ARSIWA), and—in the case of an armed attack—to act in collective self-defence (Article 21 ARSIWA).[146] The specifics of this obligation to cooperate to bring to an end a serious breach of peremptory norms correspond to public goods characteristics: it is a specific second-order cooperation problem following breach of a peremptory norm facing the collective action problem of free-riding on the cooperative efforts of other states. These characteristics also explain why the international community failed in the past to effectively end serious breaches of *jus cogens* norms (e.g. the Rwandan genocide) and why recourse to institutionalised forms may eventually be more promising than *ad hoc* cooperation between states (even though not necessarily effective either).

Two further consequences for states being confronted with a serious breach of a peremptory norm derive from Article 41 (2) ARSIWA in the form of duties of

[142] In favour of such third state obligations towards victim states, see Lea Brilmayer and Isaias Yemane Tesfalidet, "Third State Obligations and the Enforcement of International Law," *New York University Journal of International Law and Politics* 44, no. 1 (2011): 1–53.

[143] ARSIWA Commentaries, Article 41, para. 3. In that sense, the obligation to cooperate follows from the general duty to cooperate in international law, see, for instance, the fourth principle of United Nations General Assembly, Resolution 2625 (XXV), *Declaration on Principles of International Law Concerning Friendly Relations and Cooperation among States in Accordance with the Charter of the United Nations*, 24 October 1970 (UN Doc. A/8082). See also *Legal Consequences of the Construction of a Wall in the Occupied Palestinian Territory*, Advisory Opinion, p. 200, paras. 159–160. See also with reference to the right to self-determination as an obligation *erga omnes*, *Legal Consequences of the Separation of the Chagos Archipelago from Mauritius in 1965*, Advisory Opinion, 25 February 2019, ICJ Reports 2019, p. 95, p. 139, para. 180. ("The Court considers that, while it is for the General Assembly to pronounce on the modalities required to ensure the completion of the decolonization of Mauritius, all Member States must co-operate with the United Nations to put those modalities into effect.")

[144] United Nations International Law Commission, *Third Report on Peremptory Norms of General International Law (Jus Cogens) by Special Rapporteur Dire Tladi*, Seventieth Session, 2018 (UN Doc. A/CN.4/714), pp. 35–36, para. 91.

[145] ARSIWA Commentaries, Article 41, para. 3.

[146] Jørgensen, "The Obligation of Cooperation," in *The Law of International Responsibility*, ed. Crawford, Pellet, and Olleson, 697–698.

abstention: firstly, all states are obliged not to recognise as lawful situations created by serious breaches of peremptory norms and, secondly, not to render aid or assistance in maintaining that situation.[147] The first obligation—supported by international practice and case law—stipulates that the international community as a whole is under a collective obligation of non-recognition of the legality of situations resulting directly from breaches of *jus cogens* norms (e.g. acquisition of sovereignty over territory through the denial of the right of self-determination or the use of force).[148] Collective non-recognition constitutes the minimum response by states to such breaches (e.g. resolutions of the UN Security Council or General Assembly) and thus appears to be a prerequisite for any concerted community response to bring such breach to an end.[149] Since the breach of a peremptory norm by definition concerns the international community as a whole and thus all states have an interest in ensuring appropriate settlement and cessation of the breach, the illegality of such a situation is opposable *erga omnes* and it cannot be recognised as lawful even by states not members of the UN, nor by the responsible or the injured state.[150] The underlying cooperation problem is, however, equally to find a collective response of the international community to a given situation, thus exhibiting GPG characteristics, even if only mutual restraint and no active contribution is required.

The second obligation in Article 41 (2) ARSIWA consists in prohibiting states to render aid or assistance in maintaining a situation created by a serious breach of a peremptory norm. Although its introduction as a negative obligation in the framework of state responsibility contains a notion of progressive development, the obligation of non-assistance to responsible states is rooted in international practice.[151] This prohibition appears "as a logical extension of the duty of

[147] Even though no express reference was made to Article 41 ARISWA, the ICJ recognised both obligations in *Legal Consequences of the Construction of a Wall in the Occupied Palestinian Territory*, Advisory Opinion, p. 200, para. 159.

[148] ARSIWA Commentaries, Article 41, paras. 5–6. This obligation derives from the fifth principle of United Nations General Assembly, Resolution 2625 (XXV), *Declaration on Principles of International Law Concerning Friendly Relations and Cooperation among States in Accordance with the Charter of the United Nations*, 24 October 1970 (UN Doc. A/8082). See, in particular, *Legal Consequences for States of the Continued Presence of South Africa in Namibia (South West Africa) notwithstanding Security Council Resolution 276 (1970)*, Advisory Opinion, 21 June 1971, ICJ Reports 1971, p. 16, p. 56, para. 126.

[149] ARSIWA Commentaries, Article 41, para. 8. Martin Dawidowicz argues, firstly, that the obligation of non-recognition of an unlawful situation is practically limited to violations of *jus cogens* norms which result in a legal claim by the responsible state to a certain status or certain rights, and, secondly, that the exact content of the obligation remains unclear and difficult for states to identify. Martin Dawidowicz, "The Obligation of Non-Recognition of an Unlawful Situation," in *The Law of International Responsibility*, ed. James Crawford, Alain Pellet, and Simon Olleson (Oxford: Oxford University Press, 2010), 677–686.

[150] ARSIWA Commentaries, Article 41, paras. 9–10.

[151] See Jørgensen, "The Obligation of Non-Assistance to the Responsible State," in *The Law of International Responsibility*, ed. Crawford, Pellet, and Olleson, 687–693. This obligation also derives from the fifth principle of United Nations General Assembly, Resolution 2625 (XXV), *Declaration on Principles of International Law Concerning Friendly Relations and Cooperation*

non-recognition", but its focus lies on actions that go beyond implying recognition of the situation created by serious breaches of *jus cogens* norms.[152] It targets conduct after the commission of the serious breach which assists the responsible state in maintaining such a situation. It thus goes beyond the provisions dealing with aid or assistance in the commission of an internationally wrongful act covered by Article 16 ARSIWA.[153] Examples for such conduct constitute the sale and delivery of weapons which could be employed by the responsible state to maintain the repression of people on the acquired territory, and a collective response of non-assistance could, for instance, consist in an arms embargo (e.g. enshrined in UN Security Council resolution).[154] This obligation of non-assistance shares the GPG characteristics of the previous two obligations: it is a collective obligation applicable to all states requiring from them not to maintain a situation contrary to peremptory norms of international law, meaning that one or a few states can frustrate the effectiveness of the obligation. The analysis in this book will thus also address the question whether and under which conditions the legal consequences foreseen in the ARSIWA can work effectively, and whether it makes sense to limit them to a limited number of GPG obligations with a superior normative status.[155]

In terms of objectives of state responsibility, it can be concluded that the provisions relating to *jus cogens* norms do not have a punishment function (unlike international criminal law[156]) but aim to reinforce the objective of inducing compliance with community interest obligations with two different means: firstly, with a conflict of laws rule which aims to prevent breach of certain fundamental GPG obligations by excluding *ex ante* the applicability of flexibility provisions, and secondly, with a number of collective obligations (i.e. various duties to cooperate) placed on all states in the international community aiming to bring a situation arising from the breach of a *jus cogens* norm to an end.

---

among States in Accordance with the Charter of the United Nations, 24 October 1970 (UN Doc. A/8082). See, in particular, *Legal Consequences for States of the Continued Presence of South Africa in Namibia (South West Africa) notwithstanding Security Council Resolution 276 (1970)*, Advisory Opinion, p. 54, para. 119.

[152] ARSIWA Commentaries, Article 41, para. 12.

[153] ARSIWA Commentaries, Article 41, para. 11.

[154] See, for instance, United Nations Security Council, Resolution 418 (1977) on the Establishment of an Arms Ermbargo against South Africa, 4 November 1977 (UN Doc. S/RES/418(1977)).

[155] See Sect. 6.4 on the additional consequences on third states as second-order cooperation problems.

[156] See the preamble of the Rome Statute of the International Criminal Court.

3.3.3 Public Enforcement of International State Responsibility: Erga Omnes *and* Erga Omnes Partes *Obligations*

Objectives of state responsibility in the public dimension can also be derived from to the second doctrinal expression of the concept of community interests, namely obligations *erga omnes* and *erga omnes partes*,[157] to which references are made in two distinct parts of the ARSIWA, even if not explicitly. Article 48 ARSIWA, in complementarity to Article 42 ARSIWA on the invocation of state responsibility, provides that a state other than an injured state can invoke the responsibility of a state having breached an international obligation owed to a group of states established for the protection of a collective interest of the group (*erga omnes partes*) or owed to the international community as a whole (*erga omnes*).[158] Such third states (i.e. indirectly or non-directly injured states) may, individually or jointly,[159] claim from the responsible state cessation of the breach and assurances and guarantees of non-repetition as well as reparation, but only in the interest of the injured state or of the beneficiaries of the obligation breached.[160] While giving non-directly injured third states to a dispute the right to demand cessation of a wrongful act reflected previous practice,[161]

[157] For a discussion of the legal concept of international obligations *erga omnes*, see Maurizio Ragazzi, *The Concept of International Obligations Erga Omnes* (Oxford: Clarendon Press, 1997). For a general overview, extending beyond the context of state responsibility, see Karl Zemanek, "New Trends in the Enforcement of Erga Omnes Obligations," *Max Planck Yearbook of United Nations Law* 4 (2000): 1–52.

[158] Article 48 ARSIWA reads "1. Any State other than an injured State is entitled to invoke the responsibility of another State in accordance with paragraph 2 if:

(*a*) the obligation breached is owed to a group of States including that State, and is established for the protection of a collective interest of the group; or (*b*) the obligation breached is owed to the international community as a whole.

2. Any State entitled to invoke responsibility under paragraph 1 may claim from the responsible State:

(*a*) cessation of the internationally wrongful act, and assurances and guarantees of non-repetition in accordance with article 30; and (*b*) performance of the obligation of reparation in accordance with the preceding articles, in the interest of the injured State or of the beneficiaries of the obligation breached.

3. The requirements for the invocation of responsibility by an injured State under articles 43, 44 and 45 apply to an invocation of responsibility by a State entitled to do so under paragraph 1." See further, Gaja, "States Having an Interest in Compliance with the Obligation Breached," in *The Law of International Responsibility*, ed. Crawford, Pellet, and Olleson, 957–964.

[159] ARSIWA Commentaries, Article 48, para 4.

[160] The available remedies for interested third states are thus more limited than for injured states and the focus of the invocation will usually be on determining whether a breach has occurred and, if it is continuing, on demanding cessation of the wrongful act, thus returning to legality and protecting the international rule of law. See ARSIWA Commentaries, Article 48, para 11.

[161] For an historical example of a third party request for declaration of a wrongful act in addition to the claim for compensation by the injured party, see *S.S. "Wimbledon"*, Judgment, 17 August 1923, PCIJ Series A, No. 1, p. 15, p. 30.

introducing the right to claim compensation on behalf of affected individual beneficiaries was supposed to address notably the problem of enforcement of human rights obligations, in particular when the violation has a purely internal dimension, and thus contains as a general provision a notion of progressive development of international law, even though the possibility of inter-state claims in human rights matters is foreseen in certain human rights regimes, for instance, in the ECHR.[162] In addition, Article 54 ARSIWA foresees the possibility for third states within the meaning of Article 48 ARSIWA to take lawful measures against the responsible state to ensure cessation of the breach and reparation in the interest of the injured state or of the beneficiaries of the obligation.[163] This gives rise to the contentious question in the law of state responsibility whether a non-directly injured third state is entitled to take countermeasures against a responsible state or whether we need to live "with the negative consequence that the responsibility for breach of obligations towards the international community as a whole is for now restricted to a 'right of invocation' without any indication of the measures that the states invoking the responsibility may take in order to have this responsibility effectively implemented, if not always enforced".[164]

Among community interest norms, *erga omnes (partes)* obligations characterise collective obligations having a non-reciprocal compliance structure.[165] This means that performance of specific obligations protecting collective interests is, in the case of obligations arising from a multilateral treaty, owed *erga omnes partes* (Article 48 (1) lit. a ARSIWA) or, in the case of obligations owed to the international community as a whole, *erga omnes* (Article 48 (1) lit. b ARSIWA).[166]

Obligations owed to the international community as a whole (*erga omnes* norms) and peremptory norms of general international law (*jus cogens* norms) are both aspects of the basic idea of protecting community interests in international law, and there is indeed substantial overlap between them.[167] The examples which the ICJ has

[162] ARSIWA Commentaries, Article 48, para 12.

[163] Article 54 ARSIWA on measures taken by states other than an injured state reads: "This chapter does not prejudice the right of any State, entitled under article 48, paragraph 1, to invoke the responsibility of another State, to take lawful measures against that State to ensure cessation of the breach and reparation in the interest of the injured State or of the beneficiaries of the obligation breached."

[164] Pierre-Marie Dupuy, "Back to the Future of a Multilateral Dimension of the Law of State Responsibility for Breaches of 'Obligations Owed to the International Community as a Whole'," *European Journal of International Law* 23, no. 4 (2012): 1069. On third-party countermeasures, see Sect. 7.2.2.

[165] Feichtner, "Community Interest," paras. 43, 50.

[166] Ibid., paras. 43–44. See also, ARSIWA Commentaries, Article 48, para 5.

[167] ARSIWA Commentaries, Part two, Chap. III, para. 7. It has even been argued that both types of obligations coincide, see Antonio Cassese, "The Character of the Violated Obligation," in *The Law of International Responsibility*, ed. James Crawford, Alain Pellet, and Simon Olleson (Oxford: Oxford University Press, 2010), 415–420.

given of *erga omnes* obligations, notably in the *Barcelona Traction* case,[168] all concern obligations which have equally been accepted as *jus cogens* norms. Likewise, the examples of peremptory norms given by the ILC in its work on the law of treaties constitute also *erga omnes* obligations.[169] This can be easily explained with the scope of both types of obligations, as their application is extended to all states. Both concepts, however, differ, firstly, in their respective focus: the main characteristic of the limited number of *jus cogens* norms is their priority over less fundamental obligations, whereas the focus of *erga omnes* obligations lies on the legal interest of all states in compliance, as they are entitled to invoke the responsibility of any state in breach of these obligations.[170] While all states have an interest that states comply with norms that are of paramount importance and deemed superior in the hierarchy of international legal norms,[171] a universal interest in compliance does not induce that the respective norm is also peremptory in character. Hence, one can conclude that all obligations having been accorded *jus cogens* status are by definition also obligations owed to the international community as a whole. But their difference in focus explains why, *vice versa, erga omnes* obligations do not all have automatically *jus cogens* status.[172] This applies, for instance, to obligations which refer to the bilateral exchange of benefits between states, but which are at the same time considered to be of fundamental importance to the international community and therefore to be owed to all states, that is, *erga omnes*.[173] One example is the law of diplomatic and consular relations, which applies primarily in bilateral relations between states seeking to protect their mutual interests (or of their citizens abroad), but where grave breaches concern the international community as whole because functioning diplomatic and consular relations are of utmost importance to uphold international communication channels, especially in times of conflict.[174] Moreover, it is widely acknowledged that all states have a legal interest in the performance of certain community interest obligations that are not necessarily *jus cogens* norms, for instance, the protection of human rights within their jurisdiction or the reduction of

[168] *Barcelona Traction, Light and Power Company, Limited (Belgium v. Spain) (New Application: 1962)*, Judgment (Second Phase), p. 32, paras. 33–34.

[169] See Commentary to Article 50 of United Nations International Law Commission, "Draft Articles on the Law of Treaties with Commentaries," *in Report of the Commission to the General Assembly on the Work of its Eighteenth Session*, 1966 (UN Doc. A/21/9), in *Yearbook of the International Law Commission*, 1966, Volume II (UN Doc. A/CN.4/SER.A/1966/Add.1).

[170] ARSIWA Commentaries, Part two, Chap. III, para. 7.

[171] Jochen A. Frowein, "Obligations Erga Omnes," ed. Anne Peters and Rüdiger Wolfrum, *Max Planck Encyclopedia of Public International Law* (Oxford Public International Law: Oxford University Press, 2021), http://opil.ouplaw.com, Article last updated in December 2008, para. 3.

[172] See also United Nations International Law Commission, *Third Report on Peremptory Norms of General International Law (Jus Cogens) by Special Rapporteur Dire Tladi*, Seventieth Session, 2018 (UN Doc. A/CN.4/714), p. 42, para. 107.

[173] Feichtner, "Community Interest," para. 46.

[174] Along the same vein, albeit not using the term *erga omnes* obligations, *United States Diplomatic and Consular Staff in Tehran (United States of America v. Iran)*, Judgment, 24 May 1980, ICJ Reports 1980, p. 3, pp. 42–43, para. 92. See also Feichtner, "Community Interest," para. 46.

carbon dioxide emissions from their territories.[175] *Erga omnes* obligations derive their status uniquely from their specific non-reciprocal compliance structure, which is often linked to the importance of the interest protected by the respective obligation, and thus include but are not limited to obligations of paramount importance (*jus cogens* norms).[176]

Secondly, following their difference in focus, the concepts of *erga omnes* and *jus cogens* obligations differ with regard to their respective doctrinal consequences.[177] Peremptory norms of general international law, on the one hand, lead to the invalidity of treaties and the non-applicability of circumstances precluding wrongfulness.[178] Furthermore, serious breaches of obligations arising under peremptory norms, give rise to additional consequences for all other states (that is, in addition to the consequences for the responsible state towards the injured state, e.g. obligations of cessation/non-repetition and reparation), namely obligations of non-recognition, non-assistance, and cooperation to bring the situation to an end.[179] *Erga omnes* obligations, on the other hand, entitle all states to invoke responsibility for breaches of these obligations owed to the international community as a whole and thus create certain rights.[180] Such non-directly injured states may claim from the responsible state cessation of the breach and assurances and guarantees of non-repetition as well as reparation in the interest of the injured state or of the beneficiaries of the obligation breached. These third states having an interest in compliance may to a certain and debated extent also be permitted to have recourse to countermeasures.[181] Hence, while the doctrinal consequences of *erga omnes* obligations also apply to *jus cogens* norms, the same is not necessarily true the other way around: states can, in theory, conclude treaties contrary to *erga omnes* obligations not having *jus cogens* status or invoke circumstances precluding wrongfulness (for instance, in case of conflict between different *erga omnes* obligations—due to their relative but not absolute superiority). Furthermore, while all states have an interest in compliance with *erga omnes* obligations, they are, at least on a strict reading of the ARSIWA, not obliged to cooperate to bring to an end a breach of such non-peremptory obligations (only in case of serious breaches of *jus cogens* norms) or not to recognise as lawful a situation created by a breach of an *erga omnes* obligation.

Finally, *erga omnes* obligations need to be distinguished from *erga omnes partes* obligations. Obligations falling under Article 48 (1) lit. a ARSIWA must have two

[175] Feichtner, "Community Interest," para. 44. Another example are obligations relating to the preservation of the environment of the high seas and in the Area, see *Responsibilities and Obligations of States with Respect to Activities in the Area*, Advisory Opinion, 1 February 2011, ITLOS Reports 2011, p. 10, p. 59, para. 180.

[176] See also Feichtner, "Community Interest," para. 46.

[177] ARSIWA Commentary to Chap. III, part two, para. 7.

[178] Articles 53 and 64 VCLT, Article 26 ARSIWA.

[179] Articles 40, 41 ARSIWA.

[180] Article 48 ARSIWA.

[181] Article 54 ARSIWA.

characteristics: firstly, the obligation breached must have been owed to a group of states including the state invoking responsibility; and secondly, the obligation must have been established for the protection of a collective interest of that group. These *erga omnes partes* obligations thus share the characteristics of *erga omnes* norms—being collective obligations having a non-reciprocal compliance structure—with the difference that performance of these obligations is owed to all other parties of a multilateral treaty regime,[182] and not the international community as a whole. Examples can be found in multilateral treaty regimes establishing collective obligations concerning the environment or security of a region (e.g. a regional nuclear-free-zone treaty or a regional system for the protection of human rights).[183] However, *erga omnes partes* obligations are not limited to agreements established in the interest of the members of the group, but include also regimes established with a view to protect a broader common interest as long as the treaty regime extends beyond mere bilateral relations between state parties.[184] In other words, the principal purpose of *erga omnes partes* obligations is "to foster a common interest, over and above any interests of the [s]tates concerned individually", and thus includes norms protecting individuals.[185] Hence, like *erga omnes* obligations, *erga omnes partes* obligations derive their status from their specific non-reciprocal compliance structure, which is often linked to the importance of the interest protected by the respective obligation for the multilateral treaty regime (or beyond),[186] but their scope of application is limited to the parties thereof. Thus, *erga omnes* and *erga omnes partes* obligations may overlap in terms of their content, especially when a treaty regime creates obligations that benefit states and individuals beyond those participating in the arrangement (e.g. protection of human rights), but the number of states having an explicit right to compliance with these obligations in the interest of the collective is limited to the member states.

This leads to the question to what extent these two concepts, *erga omnes* and *erga omnes partes* obligations, are congruent with obligations dealing with different types of goods on the international level. While it is tempting on first sight to equate *erga omnes* obligations with GPGs (in the large sense) and *erga omnes partes* obligations to club goods (due to the restriction to members of a treaty regime), their interrelation is in fact more complex. Effective international law needs to clearly distinguish between different aspects of cooperation about a given issue, namely between the characteristics of the initial cooperation problem on the one hand, and the

---

[182] In theory, Article 48 (1) lit. a ARSIWA does not distinguish between different sources of international law and obligations protecting a collective group interest may derive from multilateral treaties or customary international law. In practice, however, *erga omnes partes* obligations will usually arise under treaties establishing particular regimes. ARSIWA Commentaries, Article 48, para. 6.

[183] ARSIWA Commentaries, Article 48, para. 7.

[184] Ibid.

[185] Ibid. The conditions are thus less strict than for injured states according to Article 42 lit. b (ii) ARSIWA.

[186] Feichtner, "Community Interest," para. 46.

second-order enforcement problem on the other hand. Regarding the first level, it is thus uniquely the underlying cooperation problem that determines the characterisation of the primary obligation in terms of different types of goods. This raises the question what obligations qualify as *erga omnes (partes)* obligations, bearing in mind that the condition is that they need to protect a collective interest of the international community or of the group. Against this background, community interest obligations relating to the provision of GPGs and the preservation of CPRs, thus generating non-excludable benefits, are always *erga omnes* obligations—or *erga omnes partes* obligations when they are established in the collective interest of a group. For instance, obligations with the objective to further international peace and security have either the additional status as *erga omnes* obligations when they are owed to the international community as a whole (usually because they are based on customary international law), or as *erga omnes partes* obligations when they are based on a multilateral treaty regime aiming to provide regional peace and security (i.e. a regional public good) or to facilitate the constitution of a *k-group* for the provision of international peace and security (i.e. a global public good). Equally, obligations having the objective to protect CPRs from consumption (e.g. protection of natural resources through reduction of carbon dioxide emissions) are either *erga omnes* obligations or *erga omnes partes* obligations. In addition, *erga omnes (partes)* obligations, as their scope is broader than for *jus cogens*, can also relate to scenarios of international economic relations or cross-border exercise of state authority, thus stemming rather from the private dimension of international law, if they protect also a collective interest of the international community or the group. A multilateral trade regime, for instance, is based on obligations granting the mutual exchange of benefits, but grave breaches of fundamental rules of the club (e.g. the WTO MFN and the NT clauses) can threaten the objective legal order and thus the survival of the cooperative arrangement, thus bearing public goods characteristics.[187] Compliance with these rules is thus in the collective interest, which accords them the status as *erga omnes partes* obligations. Furthermore, obligations regulating extraterritorial effects of state actions or of activities under state authority (e.g. the law of diplomatic and consular relations) can also have public goods characteristics, to the extent that abstention from serious breaches of fundamental obligations (in the sense of protecting objective community values) is in the common interest of the group or the international community as a whole, and thus constitute *erga omnes (partes)* obligations. The status as *erga omnes (partes)* obligations thus stems from the protection of a collective interest of the international community or the group and thus from (global or regional) public goods and common pool resource obligations.

With regard to the level of enforcement, *erga omnes (partes)* obligations create a corresponding right of performance for all states in the international community or

[187]Third parties can, for instance, intervene in WTO dispute resolution if they demonstrate a substantial interest, but they rarely do so in practice. See further, Chi Carmody, 'Of Substantial Interest: Third Parties under GATT," *Michigan Journal of International Law* 18, no. 4 (1997): 615–657.

for all group members. All (participating) states thus benefit from and have a legal interest in compliance with *erga omnes (partes)* obligations as they constitute an essential element of the international legal order (i.e. a global interest in compliance) or the objective legal order created by the multilateral treaty regime. From this non-reciprocal compliance structure derives that *erga omnes (partes)* obligations relate to goods that are non-excludable and non-rival in consumption. In terms of second-order enforcement problems, I equate therefore *erga omnes* obligations with GPGs obligations. *Erga omnes partes* obligations, however, as the right to performance is limited to the members of the group, cannot be characterised as GPGs, but rather—depending on the composition of its members—regional or transnational public goods. What needs to be borne in mind here, is that cooperative arrangements aiming to provide public goods (e.g. human rights protection) can use their underlying group structure to punish non-compliant behaviour with exclusion from certain benefits of the club.

In sum, when the first-order cooperation problem has public goods or common pool resource characteristics, state responsibility in the public dimension has the function of a multilateral enforcement mechanism. In addition to the enforcement mechanism for injured states, the doctrinal consequences of breach of *erga omnes (partes)* obligations offer the possibility to all states in the international community (or the respective group) to invoke the responsibility of the wrongdoing state and, eventually, to have recourse to countermeasures. Third-party countermeasures serve to induce compliance with, on the one hand, the obligation to cease and not to repeat the wrongful act (i.e. compliance with the primary obligation) and, on the other hand, the obligation to provide reparation for injury (e.g. compensation of damage) to the injured state. The cooperation problem for both *erga omnes* and *erga omnes partes* obligations lies in the implementation of these means: it is a second-order cooperation problem, where states face incentives to free-ride on the provision of the global or transnational public good of enforcement by other states, for instance, taking countermeasures, thus facing a sanctioners' dilemma.[188] The scarce practice of inter-state complaints, in particular in the field of international human rights law, illustrates this collective action problem.[189] They are an expression of the

---

[188] See also Nollkaemper, who points out that "creating a right of enforcement as such does not solve the problem of under-enforcement [of public goods], but just shifts the collective action problem to the realm of enforcement." Nollkaemper, "International Adjudication of Global Public Goods: The Intersection of Substance and Procedure," 777.

[189] However, a few noteworthy and promising exceptions exist. For an invocation of state responsibility for breach of the Torture Convention as an *erga omnes partes* obligation, see *Questions Relating to the Obligation to Prosecute or Extradite (Belgium v. Senegal)*, Judgment, p. 450, para. 69. For an invocation of state responsibility for breach of the Genocide Convention as an *erga omnes partes* obligation, see *Application of the Convention on the Prevention and Punishment of the Crime of Genocide (The Gambia v. Myanmar)*, Order (Provisional Measures), p. 17, paras. 41–42; *Application of the Convention on the Prevention and Punishment of the Crime of Genocide in the Gaza Strip (South Africa v. Israel)*, Order (Provisional Measures), p. 12, para. 33. On the exceptions in the context of the ECHR, see footnote 168 in Chap. 2. For another promising example in the context of the preservation of marine mammals and the marine environment, see *Whaling in the Antarctic (Australia v. Japan: New Zealand Intervening)*, Judgment, p. 246, paras. 40–41.

Doctrinal concept	First-order cooperation problem (underlying the primary obligation)	Second-order cooperation problem (compliance mechanism)
Jus cogens	**Global public goods** (case-by-case determination)	Collective obligations to cooperate: **global public goods**
Erga omnes	**Global public goods** or **common pool resources**	Collective rights of enforcement: **global public goods**
Erga omnes partes	**(Global) public goods** or **common pool resources**	Collective rights of enforcement: **regional or transnational public goods**

Fig. 3.1 Congruence of doctrinal concepts reflecting community interests with cooperation problems on the international level

decentralised international legal order that needs to rely in terms of enforcement mostly on unilateral efforts. An effective collective enforcement mechanism should then encourage those states that are willing to provide the public good to do so either unilaterally or, if this is not possible, through a viable *k-group*.[190] To what extent these doctrinal consequences of breach of *erga omnes (partes)* obligations are setting adequate incentives to provide this public good of enforcement in order to achieve compliance with fundamental international legal obligations will be discussed in Chap. 7 below on the implementation of state responsibility in international law. In terms of the objectives of state responsibility, it suffices to conclude for now that in the public dimension of international law, provisions on enforcement of state responsibility serve the defence of the objective international legal order *erga omnes (partes)* by providing the public good of collective enforcement, which ultimately aims to induce compliance with GPG and CPR obligations.[191]

Figure 3.1 summarises the extent to which the two doctrinal concepts reflecting community interests in the law of state responsibility, *jus cogens* and *erga omnes (partes)* norms, are congruent with the cooperation problems underlying GPGs and other types of goods on the international level.

Another explicit reference to the possibility for third states to invoke state responsibility and claim compensation (Article 48 ARSIWA) has been made by the Seabed Disputes Chamber of the International Tribunal for the Law of the Sea (ITLOS) with regard to the obligations relating to the preservation of the environment of the high seas and in the Area, see *Responsibilities and Obligations of States with Respect to Activities in the Area*, Advisory Opinion, p. 59, para. 180.

[190] See Barkin and Rashchupkina, "Public Goods, Common Pool Resources, and International Law," 386.

[191] Along the same vein, see Eric A. Posner, defining *erga omnes* norms as "facilitat[ing] collective enforcement of norms that create public goods, including the general rules of the international system, by making clear that certain aggressive acts that would otherwise appear to be violations of two-party norms are, in fact, permissible attempts to participate in collective action." Eric A. Posner, "Erga Omnes Norms, Institutionalization, and Constitutionalism in International Law," *Journal of Institutional and Theoretical Economics (JITE) / Zeitschrift für die gesamte Staatswissenschaft* 165, no. 1 (2009): 13.

Dimension	First-order cooperation problem (underlying the primary obligation)		Second-order cooperation problem (enforcement of secondary obligations)
Private	**Private goods**	Tort theory	Bilateral or first-party enforcement
	Club goods	Contract theory	
Public	**CPRs**	International law of GPGs and CPRs	Collective or third-party enforcement
	GPGs		

Fig. 3.2 Cooperation problems in the international law of state responsibility

3.4 Conclusion on the Objectives of State Responsibility in International Law

It follows from this overview that in order to determine the normative framework of state responsibility in international law it is helpful to distinguish between, on the one hand, the private and public dimensions of state responsibility and, on the other hand, between the first-order and second-order cooperation problems. To a certain extent, there exists a correlation, in that the private dimension relates to "private" first-order cooperation problems (that is, primary obligations related to private goods or club goods) and that the subsequent enforcement mechanisms of secondary obligations conducted by injured states is also "private" or bilateral. Similarly, the public dimension relates predominantly to "public" first-order cooperation problems (that is, primary obligations related to GPGs and CPRs) and the subsequent enforcement mechanisms conducted by non-directly injured third states are also "public" or collective. This correlation is illustrated in Fig. 3.2.

While the private or public nature of first-order and second-order enforcement problems usually corresponds, there is also a certain degree of overlap. For instance, the "private" enforcement of secondary obligations can also apply in the case of breach of a "public" obligation (GPG or CPR), either when a state is affected individually (that is, a private goods constellation where the affected state is injured in its property rights or entitlements beyond the legal interest in compliance with the GPG/CPR obligations) or when a GPG or CPR obligation has previously been transformed in a club goods mechanism to facilitate enforcement. Similarly, since one subject area can relate to different types of goods depending on the focus of cooperation (e.g. breach of diplomatic and consular obligations or an armed attack can have private goods and GPG characteristics), both first-party and third-party enforcement mechanisms can be combined with regard to the same obligation. Collective enforcement can in these scenarios play an additional role, but often bilateral enforcement will prove more effective as it is not facing the collective action problem of free-riding.

Along the same vein, the objectives of state responsibility sketched out in this chapter along the private and the public dimensions can overlap, depending on the elements under scrutiny (i.e. responsibility standards, exemptions, remedies, and enforcement). In sum, I therefore conclude that, from an economic perspective, state responsibility in international law pursues the following goals:

Compliance: state responsibility rules draw the line between legal and illegal state behaviour (in particular the concept of "objective responsibility" based on illegal behaviour and the *lex superior* rule in the case of *jus cogens* prohibiting the invocation of circumstances precluding wrongfulness) and set through specific consequences (in particular, the secondary obligations of cessation/non-repetition as well as restitution and satisfaction) incentives for returning to legality, thus protecting states from subjective legal injuries, but also the international legal order as such;

Flexibility: state responsibility rules allocate the risks associated with unforeseen circumstances, either through the varying degree of precision of primary obligations (or their responsibility standards), but in particular through the possibility of invoking circumstances precluding wrongfulness, which can exceptionally excuse or justify a breach of international obligations, for instance, in order to account for the materially impossibility of compliance (e.g. *force majeure*) or to avoid harm to an overriding private or community interest (i.e. private or public necessity);

Compensation: state responsibility rules (in particular the compensation requirement in the case of circumstances precluding wrongfulness and in the case of a damage caused by a wrongful act) allocate costs between the responsible state (or the state exempted from responsibility), the injured state and the international community as a whole, thus serving (i) to mitigate or repair harm (in the case of losses or material damage) and (ii) to prevent or deter (opportunistic) breach of international obligations and harmful outcomes by forcing states to anticipate and internalise the costs of their actions (thus, inducing compliance);[192]

Enforcement: state responsibility rules (in particular countermeasures) serve the defence of subjective rights of injured states as well as the defence of the objective international legal order by enforcing compliance with secondary obligations, that is (i) compensation for the injured state and (ii) return to compliance with the primary obligation in question (with a special emphasis on collective obligations to cooperate to end a situation in breach of *jus cogens*);

Cooperation: state responsibility rules by peacefully solving disputes (e.g. by restoring the *status quo ante*, cessation of the wrongful act, and reciprocal non-compliance) aim to secure future cooperation among states, and—like all

[192] As mentioned above, the international law of state responsibility does not follow the objective of penalising illegal behaviour (unlike international criminal law), even in the case of breaches of *jus cogens* norms. However, the objective of deterrence of breach (i.e. inducing compliance) may under certain conditions eventually justify recourse to punitive damages. See Sect. 6.3.2.2.

international law—need to set adequate incentives for addressing cooperative challenges, in particular those underlying GPGs and CPRs, that is inducing compliance with their underlying primary obligations, offering the possibility of breach of international obligations in order to protect such goods, providing adequate compensation in the case of harm, and for collectively taking enforcement measures as a non-directly injured third state.[193]

This summary shows that objectives of state responsibility are not only manifold but also competing. In fact, determining optimal rules of state responsibility requires to strike the right balance between different goals (for instance, between compliance and flexibility). This chapter served to demonstrate that the normative framework of state responsibility consists in essence in trade-offs between different aims to be decided against the background of the concrete underlying cooperative challenge.[194] This instrumental approach therefore addresses one of the main criticisms of international law and economics and the normative claims it sometimes produces, namely that international law should not be measured in terms of efficiency. This book demonstrates that an economic analysis of international law can take a different form than using the efficiency criterion in international law or, in other words, welfare maximisation in the global context as the overriding goal.[195] Admittedly, efficient cost allocation could be one objective in constellations of the private dimension of international law, for instance, where international law regulates pure economic relations between states.[196] But even in these scenarios the objective of state responsibility to protect the international legal order as such (i.e. the international rule of law as a global public good) plays a role and thus limits the transferability of the efficient breach concept to the international level. Efficiency as a normative guiding criterion is even less equipped in constellations of the public dimension, which need to take into account overarching values or interests of the

[193] In addition, as much as tortious liability in the domestic context should not over-deter socially desirable behaviour by inducing a sub-optimal activity level, state responsibility rules in international law should not deter cooperation of states, in particular in public good constellations. For an analysis of different rules of allocating state responsibility between multiple actors and their respective impact on the propensity to cooperate, see van Aaken, "Shared Responsibility in International Law: A Political Economy Analysis," in *Distribution of Responsibilities in International Law*, ed. Nollkaemper and Jacobs, 153–191.

[194] On trade-offs between different goals of state responsibility and the necessity to take them into account when assessing the effects of state responsibility rules, see ibid., 158–161. For a brief overview of the multiple purposes of state responsibility and tensions among them as the basis for a functional analysis of the law of state responsibility, noting the lack of reference to purposes commonly associated with criminal law, see also Creutz, *State Responsibility in the International Legal Order: A Critical Appraisal*, 4–6.

[195] Rejecting the efficiency criterion does not mean that, in turn, it is impossible to draw on the insights of economic analysis of tort and contract law as these insights also have a strong descriptive force.

[196] In particular Eric A. Posner and Alan O. Sykes transfer the argument of efficient breach of contract to the international level for the purpose of analysing remedies in the international law of state responsibility. Posner and Sykes, *Economic Foundations of International Law*, 127.

international community as a whole. The normative framework followed here for the economic analysis of the international law of state responsibility should thus make international law and economics as a scientific approach more acceptable and fruitful for international legal research. Nonetheless, this book does not claim to offer the only possible normative framework for international state responsibility. As much as for the assumptions of the research method of rational choice theory, the most important is to make the normative framework explicit at the outset since it will guide the subsequent analysis.

In the following chapters, this book will thus analyse the international law of state responsibility from an economic perspective, both in its private and public dimensions. It will test whether the different elements of state responsibility that are included to mirror the private or public dimension are setting adequate incentives to effectively achieve their objectives. This research design allows to demonstrate that the current rules of state responsibility are not setting optimal incentives in all constellations, especially in circumstances where the provision of GPGs is involved and enforcement of international law relies on collective action. It also allows for making theoretically founded suggestions about how the international law of state responsibility could better respond to global challenges.

Part II
Main Part

Chapter 4
Conditions for International State Responsibility: A Rational Choice Analysis of Responsibility Standards

This chapter analyses the conditions for state responsibility in international law. Apart from the question of attribution of conduct by non-state actors to the state, a controversial issue that is left aside in this book,[1] the only requirement for an internationally wrongful act, which triggers state responsibility,[2] is breach of an international obligation.[3] This definition has three important consequences. Firstly, responsibility of a state can only be engaged if the illegality of its behaviour has been established, thereby excluding compensation for harm caused by dangerous but not wrongful actions or omissions. As discussed below, these constellations are covered by the regime of international liability. Secondly, the requirement that illegality of behaviour is determined on the basis of whether it is compliant with an international obligation of that state excludes the applicability of the law of state responsibility in scenarios which are governed by soft law and not by "hard" international obligations.[4] Thirdly, state responsibility does not require damage as a condition for an act

[1] See Sect. 1.3. Individual conduct is assumed to be automatically attributed to the state, as the analysis in this book focuses on the interactions among states: the responsible state, the injured state who invokes responsibility on behalf of its citizens based on the principle of diplomatic protection, and third states that may under certain conditions be entitled to enforce state responsibility. For an economic analysis of the question of attribution using contract theory, see Posner and Sykes, "An Economic Analysis of State and Individual Responsibility under International Law", 72–134; Posner and Sykes, *Economic Foundations of International Law*, Chap. 8 .

[2] Article 1 ARSIWA reads: "Every internationally wrongful act of a State entails the international responsibility of that State".

[3] Article 2 ARSIWA on the elements of an internationally wrongful act of a state reads: "There is an internationally wrongful act of a State when conduct consisting of an action or omission:
(*a*) is attributable to the State under international law; and
(*b*) constitutes a breach of an international obligation of the State".

[4] On the distinction between hard and soft law, see Gregory Shaffer and Mark A. Pollack, "Hard and Soft Law", in *Interdisciplinary Perspectives on International Law and International Relations: The State of the Art*, ed. Jeffrey L. Dunoff and Mark A. Pollack (Cambridge: Cambridge University

J. Lemke, *The Protection of Community Interests in the International Law of State Responsibility*, International Law and Economics,
https://doi.org/10.1007/978-3-031-87927-2_4

of the state to be wrongful. The occurrence of damage only becomes relevant with regard to claims for reparation.[5] Legal injury is a sufficient criterion to engage the responsibility of a state in international law and can give rise to claims of cessation and assurances of non-repetition.[6] This is particularly relevant in the case of *erga omnes* obligations which protect the legal interests of all states in the international community. This is one reason why state responsibility has been characterised as objective in nature. The other reason relates to the fourth consequence, namely that state responsibility requires no element of fault, and thus contains no subjective dimension. This does not mean that notions of fault are absent in international law, because they exist, for instance, with regard to obligations of due diligence. Thus, while the law of state responsibility foresees as only requirement (besides attribution of conduct) breach of an international duty, the real "conditions" of state responsibility derive from the content of primary obligations which may include fault.

Economic analysis of liability rules in domestic law has approached the issue of conditions for liability from two different angles. With regard to tort law, as has been outlined in the previous chapter, the principal claim of economic analysts is that tort liability rules should set incentives for efficient levels of precaution and activity.[7] One essential aspect of the economic analysis of tort law was therefore the comparison of the incentive effects of strict liability and negligence rules, in particular whether and under which conditions these lead to efficient levels of precaution and activity.[8] These insights can, in principle, be transferred to the international level. Yet, the first caveat is that strict liability as it is understood in domestic tort law, namely as liability for damage caused irrespective of the fault of the tortfeasor, usually in the context of dangerous but beneficial activities, is the rare exception in international law. "Strict liability" is not recognised as a general principle in international law, and states have included such a rule only in very few treaty regimes which deal with the allocation of costs for transboundary damage from ultra-hazardous activities (e.g. damage caused by space objects).[9] An alternative approach in international law is the regime of "liability for lawful acts", as opposed to state responsibility based on illegality. Liability for lawful acts is essentially a "no-fault liability" regime with due diligence obligations of harm prevention and mitigation, in particular, of ensuring adequate compensation for victims through a system of

Press, 2013), 197–222. On the applicability of the concept of accountability covering non-binding commitments and norms established by non-state actors, see Sect. 1.1.

[5] Article 31 ARSIWA.

[6] Article 30 ARSIWA.

[7] This is because the purpose of tort law is to reduce the incidence of accidents at the lowest cost, or, in other words, to minimise the sum of the costs of accidents and the costs of avoiding them (i.e. optimal deterrence). Coleman, Hershovitz, and Mendlow, "Theories of the Common Law of Torts", section 2. See, in particular, Calabresi, *The Costs of Accidents: A Legal and Economic Analysis*. On economic theories of tort law, see Sect. 3.2.1.

[8] See, in particular, Shavell, "Strict Liability versus Negligence", 1–25.

[9] Article II of the Convention on International Liability for Damage Caused by Space Objects (concluded 29 March 1972, entered into force 1 September 1972) 961 *UNTS* 187.

civil liability of private actors under the state's jurisdiction and only *ultima ratio* through the state itself. Although the harm prevention rule and, to a certain degree, also the basic principles on loss allocation in the case of liability for lawful acts are widely recognised in international law, states have concluded liability regimes on a conventional basis only with regard to specific hazardous activities (e.g. transboundary harm caused by industrial accidents or cross-border movements of hazardous wastes).[10] Loss allocation rules in international law can thus take the form of strict liability or liability for lawful acts and exist predominantly in contexts of prevention and mitigation of transboundary harm (e.g. air or water pollution), and thus tort-like constellations. Katja Creutz also emphasises this point in her functional analysis of the law of state responsibility.[11] The rational choice analysis in this chapter adds to this discussion on how to best address tort-like constellations in international law by comparing the incentive effects of strict liability, liability for lawful acts, and state responsibility for breach of due diligence obligations, and outlining under which conditions they are equally effective. This is important in order to understand when state responsibility for breach of due diligence obligations can operate effectively as an alternative solution, in particular against the background that states are reluctant to agree on strict liability or "no-fault liability" as a general principle. This requires that primary due diligence obligations reflect the adequate level of care, which is inherently linked to the question of optimal design of international obligations (e.g. the use of substantive or procedural primary obligations).[12] This is even more so as the concept of due diligence is not identical to negligence in domestic tort law, because the relevant actor is the state as a corporate entity and the determination of the required level of care is also done based on objective criteria and not only the fault of the individual actor.

The second caveat to transferring insights from the economic analysis of tort law to the international level is that not all constellations of interstate relations are tort-like, in the sense that the primary objective of state responsibility or liability should be one of harm prevention and loss allocation. As discussed in the previous chapter,

[10] See, for example, Article 7 of the Convention on the Law of the Non-Navigational Uses of International Watercourses (concluded 21 May 1997, entered into force 17 August 2014) 2999 *UNTS* 120. Article 4 of the Basel Convention on the Control of Transboundary Movements of Hazardous Wastes and Their Disposal (Basel Convention) (concluded 22 March 1989, entered into force 5 May 1992) 1673 *UNTS* 57. Articles 2 and 3 of the Convention on the Protection and Use of Transboundary Watercourses and International Lakes (concluded 17 March 1992, entered into force 6 October 1996) 1936 *UNTS* 269. Articles 3 and 6 of the Convention on the Transboundary Effects of Industrial Accidents (concluded 17 March 1992, entered into force 19 April 2000) 2105 *UNTS* 457.

[11] Katja Creutz analyses the law of state responsibility with regard to the ability to influence the conduct of actors (social control), the ability to respond to different groups that are on the rise in international relations (collectivity), as well as the ability to indicate gradation of norms (signalling effect), and presents international liability and international criminal law as alternative constructions of responsibility for particular contexts. Creutz, *State Responsibility in the International Legal Order: A Critical Appraisal*, Chap. 4.

[12] On the rational design of international institutions and international law, see, in particular, Koremenos, Lipson, and Snidal, "The Rational Design of International Institutions", 761–799; Koremenos, *The Continent of International Law: Explaining Agreement Design*.

state responsibility rules also pursue other objectives, in particular in the public dimension, and thus need to set incentives in contexts where there is no transboundary harm. This is the case, for instance, when a state commits human rights violations against its own citizens, thus affecting other states in the international community only in their interest in compliance and respect of the international rule of law (i.e. international human rights as non-use value global public goods).[13] In other constellations, such as clubs with the objective to further free trade among members, breach of international obligations is rather equivalent to breach of mutual promises and thus similar to contract law.[14] In addition, not all international obligations contain elements of fault. Some are purely objective in the strict sense (e.g. determining a concrete level of permitted emissions). In that regard, state responsibility bears similarities with administrative law, where citizens, even without causing concrete harm, can be required by the state to comply with regulatory standards (e.g. regulation of water resources) and to pay fines, if they fail to do so. The task of standard setting and enforcement falls on the international level predominantly on states cooperating with each other. State responsibility based on illegality rather than injury thus also serves to uphold respect for the international legal order as such and to ensure that states can be held responsible for legal injuries to the international community (e.g. inducing compliance with GPG and CPR obligations), while acknowledging that international obligations are first and foremost negotiated and designed by states themselves. A rational choice analysis can therefore also draw on insights of economic contract theory in order to understand better the incentive effects of primary international obligations and how the design of primary international obligations impacts the different goals of state responsibility defined in the previous chapter: compliance, flexibility, compensation, enforcement, and cooperation.

To this end, this chapter is structured as follows: The first section analyses the concept of objective responsibility, marked by the absence of damage and fault as requirements and based on the notion of legal injury or breach of duty. As all the issues associated with establishing state responsibility have been shifted to the level of primary obligations, the design of primary obligations is relevant in order to determine whether they set optimal incentives. Variation in design (e.g. substance *versus* procedure, rules *versus* standards) may have an impact on the effectiveness of enforcement, which aims to ensure compensation and induce compliance, while keeping in mind the participation constraint of states and their willingness to preserve a certain degree of flexibility *ex ante*. These insights are needed to understand the incentive effects of primary international obligations which set out specific responsibility standards such as due diligence. The second section compares the incentive effects of these state responsibility rules (i.e. the consequences of breach of primary due diligence obligations) in tort-like situations with the incentive effects of liability rules (i.e. strict liability and liability for lawful acts as secondary due diligence obligations of loss remediation), which are marked by the mere

[13] See Sect. 3.2.2.

[14] On economic contract theory, see Sect. 3.2.2.

Table 4.1 Overview of different responsibility standards in international law

Responsibility standard	Requirements in primary obligations	Consequences as secondary obligations
Purely "objective" responsibility	Breach of a primary duty	Reparation for injury (including compensation for damage), cessation, and assurances of non-repetition
Subjective elements	Additional elements of fault (e.g. intent)	
Due diligence	Breach of a primary due diligence obligation	
Strict liability	Damage	Compensation
Liability for lawful acts	Damage (despite compliance with primary due diligence obligation)	Due diligence obligation of loss remediation

requirement of causation of damage. The last section concludes by outlining the conditions under which both concepts are comparable in terms of effectiveness and their relative advantages in different scenarios of international cooperation. Table 4.1 summarises the different responsibility standards which will be addressed in turn.

Thus, by taking an economic perspective on objective responsibility, this chapter aims to set the scene for the analysis of state responsibility based on illegality in subsequent chapters with regard to exemptions, remedies, and countermeasures as an enforcement tool.

4.1 Objective Responsibility in International Law: Breach of an International Obligation as the Core Element

In the law of state responsibility, breach of an international obligation through conduct attributed to a state is the essential requirement for an internationally wrongful act triggering state responsibility.[15] This means that responsibility of a state can only be engaged if the illegality of state behaviour, that is attributable conduct consisting of an action or omission, has been established. Even though the ARSIWA do not use that terminology, the element of breach of an international obligation is often described as "objective".[16] Any "subjective" requirements, such as fault, intention, negligence, or due diligence, derive only from the content of the primary international obligation in question and may thus vary from one context to

[15] Articles 1, 2 ARSIWA. See, for instance, *United States Diplomatic and Consular Staff in Tehran (United States of America v. Iran)*, Judgment, p. 29, para 56; *Military and Paramilitary Activities in and against Nicaragua (Nicaragua v. United States of America)*, Judgment (Merits), pp. 117–118, para. 226; *Gabčíkovo-Nagymaros Project (Hungary v. Slovakia)*, Judgment, p. 54, para. 78.

[16] ARSIWA Commentaries, Article 2, para. 3.

another.[17] Whether further elements, such as damage to another state, are required also depends on the content of primary obligations.[18] Thus, in order to determine whether conduct attributable to a state consists in a failure to comply with an international obligation, the focus will be on the primary obligation concerned.[19] In other words, "whether and when there has been a breach of an obligation depends on the precise terms of the obligation, its interpretation and application, taking into account its object and purpose and the facts of the case".[20]

Article 12 ARSIWA sets out a general provision specifying when it may be considered that there exists a breach of an international obligation: "There is a breach of an international obligation by a [s]tate when an act of that [s]tate is not in conformity with what is required of it by that obligation, regardless of its origin or character".[21] The formula "regardless of its origin" refers to all possible sources of international legal obligations of states, that is customary rules of international law, treaties, general principles, or unilateral acts, and to all possible subject matters.[22] It means that there is a single regime of state responsibility, which does not distinguish, as in domestic legal systems, between contractual and tortious responsibility.[23] Nor does it distinguish between civil and criminal responsibility, but covers both minor infringements and serious breaches of obligations under peremptory norms of general international law, and as such, the whole range from bilateral obligations to obligations owed to several states or the international community as a whole.[24]

---

[17] ARSIWA Commentaries, Article 2, paras. 3, 10. Certain primary obligations may explicitly foresee intention or knowledge of the state as a requirement. Regarding intent, see, for instance, Article II of the Convention on the Prevention and Punishment of the Crime of Genocide (Genocide Convention) (concluded 9 December 1948, entered into force 12 January 1951) 78 *UNTS* 277.

[18] ARSIWA Commentaries, Article 2, para 9.

[19] ARSIWA Commentaries, Part one, Chap. III, paras. 2–3.

[20] ARSIWA Commentaries, Article 12, para. 1.

[21] The remaining articles of Part one, Chap. III specify in more detail how the concept of breach of an international obligation applies to various situations: the question of the intertemporal law, that is the requirement that the obligation is in force for the state at the time of the breach (Article 13 ARSIWA), the question of continuing breaches (Article 14 ARSIWA), and the problem of determining whether and when there has been a breach of an obligation in the case of composite acts (Article 15 ARSIWA).

[22] ARSIWA Commentaries, Article 12, paras. 3, 9. See also *Difference between New Zealand and France Concerning the Interpretation or Application of two Agreements concluded on 9 July 1986 between the two States and Which Related to the Problems Arising from the Rainbow Warrior Affair*, Award, 30 April 1990, RIAA, Volume XX, p. 215, p. 251, para. 75; *Barcelona Traction, Light and Power Company, Limited (Belgium v. Spain) (New Application: 1962)*, Judgment (Second Phase), p. 46, para. 86; *Gabčíkovo-Nagymaros Project (Hungary v. Slovakia)*, Judgment, p. 38, para. 47.

[23] ARSIWA Commentaries, Article 12, para 5. See also *Difference between New Zealand and France Concerning the Interpretation or Application of two Agreements concluded on 9 July 1986 between the two States and Which Related to the Problems Arising from the Rainbow Warrior Affair*, Award, p. 251, para. 75.

[24] ARSIWA Commentaries, Article 12, paras. 5–7. Initially, the ILC acknowledged in its first project of Draft Articles that there was a need to distinguish in the law on state responsibility

"Regardless of its character" refers to the various classifications of international obligations, for instance, between obligations of conduct and obligations of result.[25] Thus, by building on the concept of breach of an international obligation, the regime of state responsibility is "comprehensive in scope, general in character and flexible in its application".[26] But it also means that key questions about the adequate responsibility standard have essentially been left open and are shifted to the level of primary obligations, thus offering room for an economic analysis which takes into account different scenarios of international cooperation.

Since "objective responsibility" means that the determination of non-compliant behaviour effectively depends on the content of primary obligations, this rational choice analysis of different responsibility standards can build on previous insights about the implications of the design of the primary obligations. Firstly, some primary international obligations contain no specific responsibility standard and are thus purely "objective". Thus, depending on their design (i.e. substance *versus* procedure) or degree of precision (i.e. rules *versus* standards), international obligations may allocate duties among states differently. This also means that they may accommodate competing objectives of state responsibility, namely compliance and flexibility, differently, which will have an impact on the probability of enforcement of remedies such as compensation for damage. Secondly, some primary international obligations require notions of fault and thus subjective elements as a precondition for state responsibility. A particular case is due diligence obligations, mostly known from the context of transboundary harm prevention, because they may combine elements of all of the above, precise rules and general standards, procedural and substantive requirements, and notions of fault of the individual actor and objective requirements such as failure to adopt certain legislation. This economic perspective on the design of primary obligations thus also serves to gain a better understanding of the incentive effects of due diligence obligations in international law. This facilitates the functional comparison in the second section of this chapter between "objective" state responsibility (in particular, the consequences of a primary due diligence obligation as a proxy for state negligence as a responsibility standard) and the concept of liability for lawful acts (i.e. both strict liability and secondary due diligence obligations of loss remediation), building on insights of the economic analysis of strict liability and negligence rules in domestic tort law.

---

between "international crimes of states" in contrast to all other internationally wrongful acts ("international delicts"). United Nations International Law Commission, "Draft Articles on State Responsibility", in *Report of the Commission to the General Assembly on the Work of its Twenty-Eighth Session*, 1976 (UN Doc. A/31/10), in *Yearbook of the International Law Commission*, 1976, Volume II, Part Two (UN Doc. A/CN.4/SER.A/1976/Add.1 (Part 2)), pp. 95–122. The ARSIWA in its current version do uphold this distinction with respect to the concept of an internationally wrongful act, but only address this issue with regard to the content of state responsibility by foreseeing specific consequences in the case of breach of peremptory norms of general international law. On the role of *jus cogens* obligations in the law of state responsibility, see Sect. 3.3.

[25] ARSIWA Commentaries, Article 12, para. 11.

[26] ARSIWA Commentaries, Article 12, para. 6.

4.1.1 Allocation of Duties and the Design of Primary Obligations

We have seen that the regime of state responsibility based on the concept of "objective responsibility" foresees basically only one condition: breach of an international obligation. Whether a state is responsible in international law for its actions thus depends on the content of primary international obligations and therefore on how international law allocates duties among states. Enquiring all international obligations regarding whether their content is apt to address international cooperation problems is beyond the scope of this book. But economic contract theory offers useful insights as it takes an analytical view, firstly, on why states chose certain rules (namely balancing *ex ante* precision against flexibility), and, secondly, on what the impact of different designs of rules is on compliance, which is one relevant factor for an analysis of state responsibility.[27] As the burden of proving the breach falls on the state invoking state responsibility (i.e. the plaintiff state), but information about the facts may be distributed asymmetrically among the parties to a dispute, whether breach of duty can be established depends on the observability and verifiability of the defendant state's behaviour. This may have different implications depending on the whether the obligation relies on first-party or third-party enforcement (i.e. the private or public dimension of international law).[28] The following sections therefore analyse different variations in the design of primary obligations: firstly, the difference between substantive and procedural obligations; secondly, the difference between rules and standards. The aim of this exercise is to draw conclusions on how their design matters to effectively address different underlying cooperation problems (in particular, for CPR and GPG obligations). Thirdly, as it lies in the nature of objective responsibility that different responsibility standards derive only from primary obligations, it is useful to transfer these insights to two examples: firstly, subjective elements of fault (e.g. intent), and, secondly, the concept of due diligence, as a proxy for state negligence.

Regarding the analytical framework on the allocation of responsibility and the design of primary obligations, this section draws on previous law and economics literature, in particular the most recent conclusions presented by Joel P. Trachtman.[29] He takes an economic perspective on the question of legality or illegality of a certain activity with transboundary effects by analysing how international legal responsibility is allocated among states, that is how it is shared between

---

[27] On economic contract theory, see Sect. 3.2.2.

[28] Whether breach of an international obligation can be clearly established influences, for instance, the level of political costs of countermeasures, which are then more likely to be supported by other states in the international community. See Sect. 7.2.1.4 on the incentives for injured states to take countermeasures.

[29] Trachtman, "Ex Ante and Ex Post Allocation of International Legal Responsibility", in *Distribution of Responsibilities in International Law*, ed. Nollkaemper and Jacobs, 87–119. For the theoretical background, see Trachtman, *The Economic Structure of International Law*.

the parties of a dispute.[30] Trachtman defines the relevant question as: "to what extent should principles of law be established to require acting states to internalise the beneficial or detrimental effects that they impose on one another?"[31] Furthermore, when states, as principal law-makers on the international level, negotiate legal rules, they aim to maximise the net benefits of internalisation of policy externalities (net of transaction costs), while taking into account the costs of reduced policy autonomy (i.e. the negative effect of international legal restriction of national regulatory measures).[32] International legal obligations are thus not only formulated in a way to cause internalisation of policy externalities but also to preserve maximum policy flexibility for the bound countries.[33] Furthermore, international legal rules are by definition incomplete contracts as it is impossible to define *ex ante* all possible states of the world, given that transaction costs become prohibitive.[34] When designing new rules, states thus need to choose between, on the one hand, substantive and procedural obligations, and, on the other hand, between *ex ante* specification by virtue of rules and *ex post* specification through application of standards. Both dichotomies are addressed in turn.

4.1.1.1 Substance *versus* Procedure

International norms can take the form of substantive or procedural obligations.[35] In their typology of positive duties that states might have with regard to other states or with respect to community interests, Benvenisti and Nolte distinguish between substantial and procedural duties, that is whether they call for a certain action to protect community interests (i.e. by legal definitions and norm prescription) or whether they require giving voice to affected persons (i.e. representation of other-

[30] Trachtman, "Ex Ante and Ex Post Allocation of International Legal Responsibility", in *Distribution of Responsibilities in International Law*, ed. Nollkaemper and Jacobs, 88.

[31] This question derives from the Coasean argument that under zero transaction costs, the parties to a dispute would negotiate the efficient solution. But when property rights are pre-assigned and transaction costs are positive, legal mechanisms of internalisation may be more efficient than a negotiated solution. The function of international law is then to bring national authorities to bear the external effects of national decisions, when it is reasonable to do so in terms of transaction costs. Ibid., 88–89.

[32] Ibid., 89.

[33] As Trachtman put it, "in theory they are designed to maximise the sum of the welfare benefits and detriments of (a) internalisation of externalities, (b) transaction costs, and (c) autonomy costs". Ibid., 94.

[34] Ibid., 103–104.

[35] This distinction needs to be differentiated from the more general debate about the concepts of form and substance in international law. Kal Raustiala, for instance, understands the form of international agreements, which is to be differentiated from their substantive obligations, as relating to, firstly, their legal bindingness, and, secondly, monitoring provisions. See Kal Raustiala, "Form and Substance in International Agreements", *American Journal of International Law* 99, no. 3 (2005): 581–614.

regarding interests in the decision-making process).[36] Procedure is thus understood here as a specific type of international obligations that states agree to respect, which is to be differentiated from the procedural law of international adjudication and its possible interaction with the substance of the underlying claim.[37] Beyond adjudication, the international legal norms that govern the relations between states can set different preconditions for state action or inaction either by prohibiting or permitting state action through substantive preconditions or by positing procedural requirements. This raises the question under which circumstances procedural obligations are preferable to substantive obligations and *vice versa*, but also, once we understand their comparative advantages and disadvantages, how both types of obligations can most effectively complement each other.

Trachtman takes an economic perspective on the distinction between procedural and substantial requirements and defines them as "procedure contingency" and "state contingency", respectively.[38] Based on contract theory, Trachtman understands international legal rules as state-contingent incomplete contracts when the legality of behaviour is not specifically determined in advance and their application thus depends on future states of the world, that is on the facts as they arise.[39] While in the case of state contingency, the preconditions for action are substantive and factual regarding the objective state of the world, they relate in the case of procedure contingency to the procedure to be followed by the acting state in order to determine the state of the world.[40] According to Trachtman, "procedure contingency, when it appears alone, can best be analogised to a conditional presumption to the effect that *if* the procedure followed by the respondent country conforms to legal requirements, then we will presume that the substantive act taken by the respondent country conforms to the relevant legal requirements".[41] Like state-contingent rules, procedure-contingent rules require states to internalise policy externalities, but they do that within the prescribed procedures, without that the acting state necessarily bears responsibility for adverse effects that may nevertheless arise.[42] Procedure contingency can also complement state contingency, which is the case when the resultant determination of the state of the world must additionally be determined to

---

[36] Benvenisti and Nolte, "Community Interests across International Law: Introduction", in *Community Interests across International Law*, ed. Benvenisti and Nolte, 7–8.

[37] See in this regard, Nollkaemper offering an in-depth analysis of the connections between the procedural law of international adjudication and the substantive law that protects public goods. Nollkaemper, "International Adjudication of Global Public Goods: The Intersection of Substance and Procedure", 769–791.

[38] Trachtman, "Ex Ante and Ex Post Allocation of International Legal Responsibility", in *Distribution of Responsibilities in International Law*, ed. Nollkaemper and Jacobs, 92.

[39] Ibid., 90.

[40] Ibid., 93.

[41] Ibid., 114.

[42] In that sense, procedure contingency implicates less autonomy costs as there is no determination whether the state acting was correct in its assessment of the existence of the relevant facts. Ibid., 91–92, 110.

be objectively correct.[43] Procedural rules are then ascribed some intrinsic value,[44] as following a specific procedure obliges states to take into account in their actions the concerns of other affected states.[45] In the end, both "[s]tate contingency and procedure contingency are ways of providing for the completion of incomplete contracts in international law"[46] and states can establish for the same action procedural and substantial preconditions or prescribe only one or the other.[47]

Both procedural and substantive obligations bear advantages, and the choice between one or the other (or their degree of complementarity) has important implications regarding the way non-compliance can be observed and verified by the actors applying the international legal norm.[48] This is foremost the acting state, which assesses the legality of its actions *ex ante*, but also states affected by a breach and third parties (other states or judicial institutions) need to determine *ex post* whether the international obligation in question has been violated before enforcing international law. The problem is that in a number of contexts, the factual conditions are becoming more complex, requiring greater information ("information problems") and expertise for their determination ("expertise problems"), whereas procedure contingency may implicate a lower level of information and expertise.[49] Trachtman argues that procedure contingency is advantageous compared to state contingency, when the factual conditions are easier for the acting state as the norm addressee and more difficult for other states or tribunals to observe.[50] This is important as the burden of proving a violation of an international legal obligation generally falls on the state invoking state responsibility.[51] When the acting state has better access to information and the resources to conduct expert analysis, it is inefficient that plaintiff states or other third parties replicate these analyses as this causes verification costs.[52]

---

[43] Ibid., 93.

[44] Ibid.

[45] Taking into account the interests of other states can consist in obligations for the acting state to demonstrate that other alternatives of action were considered, that a certain decision is based on scientific evidence, that other states or actors were consulted prior to action, that competing arguments were balanced, and that reasons are given for a certain decision. In that sense, procedure contingency overlaps with the concept of accountability in global administrative law and with procedural obligations known from the domestic administrative law context (e.g. the right to be heard, the obligation to give reasons). Ibid., 92, 112, 118.

[46] Ibid., 118.

[47] Ibid., 93.

[48] "[T]hat some states of the world are not verifiable to a court, even though they may be observable to both the parties", is one key problem of asymmetrical information in the context of contractual liability and enforcement of contracts. See Scott and Triantis, "Incomplete Contracts and the Theory of Contract Design", 191.

[49] Trachtman, "Ex Ante and Ex Post Allocation of International Legal Responsibility", in *Distribution of Responsibilities in International Law*, ed. Nollkaemper and Jacobs, 90–92.

[50] Ibid., 118.

[51] Ibid., 115.

[52] See also Eric L. Talley pointing out that in particular in a complex informational environment, "the burden [of proof] allocation may be the most influential in catalyzing information discovery,

In addition, the fulfilment of procedural obligations is for the plaintiff state often easier to observe and verify than the facts that underlie the substantive obligation.[53] However, it is questionable whether procedure contingency can adequately address cooperation problems.[54] Trachtman holds that "[p]rocedure contingency may be an appropriate substitute for state contingency where following the appropriate procedures is a close proxy for the existence of the desired conditions".[55] It is thus essential that the procedural requirements are almost perfectly correlated with the substantive conditions that ought to be achieved. When designing international legal norms, the costs of determining perfectly correlated procedural norms also need to be taken into account.[56]

Although we see procedural obligations predominantly, but not exclusively, in international environmental law, the choice between procedural and substantive rules is not one of the different subject areas. It is rather about addressing effectively underlying cooperation problems (i.e. information asymmetries and transaction costs), which may be differently pronounced depending on the private or public dimension of international law. In the private dimension of international law, the prime example of procedural obligations is norms aiming to prevent transboundary harm stemming from non-state actors under the author state's jurisdiction or control as one form of due diligence obligations.[57] In these private goods or tort-like scenarios, the focus lies on regulating legal, but dangerous activities by placing (in addition to substantive requirements) procedural harm prevention obligations on the state of origin, such as effective risk monitoring, creation of an authorisation regime, and notification requirements of affected states. Procedural obligations also exist in club goods constellations, similar to procedural due diligence obligations in domestic contract law. Examples can, for instance, be found in international trade law, such as provisions of risk assessment based on scientific evidence or of deferring the selection of the less trade-restrictive measure to the national regulator.[58] In the public dimension of international law, procedural obligations can serve to effectuate cooperation in GPG and CPR constellations. We have seen above that in the public dimension of international law, GPG and CPR obligations rely primarily on third-party enforcement, and thus on how effectively third states can observe

reducing verification costs, and ultimately contributing to overall welfare policy goals". Eric L. Talley, "Law, Economics, and the Burden(S) of Proof", in *Research Handbook on the Economics of Torts*, ed. Jennifer Arlen (Cheltenham, UK: Edward Elgar, 2013).

[53] With regard to the trade remedies, see Trachtman, "Ex Ante and Ex Post Allocation of International Legal Responsibility", in *Distribution of Responsibilities in International Law*, ed. Nollkaemper and Jacobs, 115.

[54] Ibid., 92.

[55] Ibid., 118.

[56] Ibid., 114–115, 118–119.

[57] On the definition, scope, and an economic perspective on due diligence obligations, see Sect. 4.1.2.2.

[58] See also Trachtman, "Ex Ante and Ex Post Allocation of International Legal Responsibility", in *Distribution of Responsibilities in International Law*, ed. Nollkaemper and Jacobs, 97–98.

and verify non-compliance, in particular in the absence of international judicial institutions.[59] When the probability of enforcement is lower, procedural obligations might be able to mitigate the observability and verifiability problem to a certain extent. Procedural obligations also have the advantage that it might be easier for states to agree on them, rather than on substantive commitments, in particular when they address collective action problems such as in the case of GPGs and CPRs. The problem is that in order to effectively protect GPGs or preserve CPRs, the procedural obligations need to correlate with what would be required from states in terms of substantive obligations. The more complex the underlying problem, the more difficult this correlation exercise becomes. Climate change mitigation might be the best illustration. Another challenge is to establish causation between the breach of a procedural obligation and the material damage,[60] but we have seen that under the concept of objective responsibility, this is not a precondition for establishing responsibility which can consist in a mere legal injury. In addition, it should not be neglected that when procedural obligations complement substantive obligations as preconditions, the emphasis will be on the added value of procedure, namely the requirement to take the interests of other states or the international community as a whole into account (e.g. the right to be heard as an administrative procedural law principle).

Benvenisti and Nolte rightly note that substantive and procedural aspects of community interest obligations are often interdependent, in particular in international environmental law.[61] Jutta Brunnée has enquired in more detail about the important role of procedural elements for the capacity of international environmental law to serve community interests.[62] Her findings confirm the theoretical conclusions outlined above. She finds that in the transboundary context, procedural obligations can strengthen the preventive aspects of the harm prevention rule and flesh out or even support the due diligence standard.[63] They can also reduce the difficulty for states and judges to deal with substantive arguments or establish causality of environmental harm as "[v]iolations of procedural obligations are more easily established and, by holding states to their procedural duties, they can sometimes be prompted to correct harmful conduct, or at least to take more effective preventive

[59] When non-compliance is easily observable and verifiable, this reduces the audience or political costs for states taking enforcement measures and thus lowers the risks for enforcing states to be perceived by the international community as opportunistic. See further in Sections 7.2.1.4 and 7.2.2 on the incentives for injured and non-directly injured third states to take countermeasures.

[60] An example would be the challenge to establish the link between China's alleged failure to communicate the outbreak of a new disease immediately to the World Health Organization as required by the International Health Regulations and the harm caused by the COVID-19 outbreak in other countries.

[61] Benvenisti and Nolte, "Community Interests across International Law: Introduction", in *Community Interests across International Law*, ed. Benvenisti and Nolte, 8.

[62] Brunnée, "International Environmental Law and Community Interests: Procedural Aspects", in *Community Interests across International Law*, ed. Benvenisti and Nolte, 151–175.

[63] Ibid., 174.

measures going forward".[64] With regard to the community interest dimension, however, she observes that the operation of procedural obligations is more difficult due to the lack of international practice and "the continued struggle with the substance of community obligations and the legal effects of *erga omnes* norms".[65] In general, treaty-based approaches have proven better suited to address community interests, for instance, by recognising particular environmental issues as common concerns, developing adequate responses, and placing a strong emphasis on procedural elements, thus allowing to overcome some of the constraints of general international law.[66] All this explains not only the increasing use of procedural obligations, in particular in GPG and CPR constellations, but also the importance of complementarity with substantive obligations.

4.1.1.2 Rules *versus* Standards

When states negotiate international norms, they can agree on substantial or procedural obligations with more or less precision.[67] From a contract theory perspective, international law can be structured to be more or less incomplete, depending on the degree of specificity, that is whether the conditions of an obligation are relatively well defined and whether their fulfilment is easily determinable.[68] International law, like all law, can therefore be characterised as consisting of "rules" and "standards".[69]

Taking an economic perspective on the issue, Louis Kaplow argues that "the only distinction between rules and standards is the extent to which efforts to give content to the law are undertaken before or after individuals act".[70] The relevant question is thus when a legal command is given content, that is *ex ante* or *ex post*, rather than

---

[64] Ibid.

[65] Ibid.

[66] Ibid., 174–175.

[67] *Precision* is also one of three components (alongside *obligation* and *delegation*) that characterise legalisation as a particular form of institutionalisation; see Kenneth W. Abbott et al., "The Concept of Legalization", *International Organization* 54, no. 3 (2000): 401.

[68] Trachtman, "Ex Ante and Ex Post Allocation of International Legal Responsibility", in *Distribution of Responsibilities in International Law*, ed. Nollkaemper and Jacobs, 92.

[69] For an early contribution to the legal debate on rules *versus* standards, see Pierre Schlag, "Rules and Standards," *UCLA Law Review* 33, no. 2 (1985): 379–430. Important contributions to the debate on why decision-makers choose one type of norm over the other and which type is preferable from a policy perspective in the domestic context, see Kaplow, "Rules versus Standards: An Economic Analysis", 557–629; Kathleen M. Sullivan, "Foreword: The Justices of Rules and Standards", *Harvard Law Review* 106, no. 1 (1992): 22–123; Gillian K. Hadfield, "Weighing the Value of Vagueness: An Economic Perspective on Precision in the Law", *California Law Review* 82, no. 3 (1994): 541–554; Cass R. Sunstein, "Problems with Rules", *California Law Review* 83, no. 4 (1995): 953–1026; Russell B. Korobkin, "Behavioral Analysis and Legal Form: Rules vs. Standards Revisited", *Oregon Law Review* 79, no. 1 (2000): 23–60.

[70] Kaplow, "Rules versus Standards: An Economic Analysis", 560. Emphasis in original omitted.

how much detail is used in differentiating cases.[71] It is difficult, however, to separate entirely the question of the moment of precision of legal norms from the question of their degree of precision. With regard to international law, Trachtman defines a law as a rule "*to the extent that* it is specified in advance of the conduct to which it is applied"[72] and as a standard "a law that is farther toward the more general end of the spectrum, in relative terms".[73] A standard "establishes general guidance to both the person governed and the person charged with applying the law, but does not specify in detail in advance the conduct required or prescribed".[74] Another dimension is who determines the content of a legal norm *ex post*, the parties themselves (i.e. auto-interpretation) or third parties who have been delegated interpretative powers (i.e. international courts and tribunals). Depending on whether international judicial institutions are mandated with interpretative powers, the decision of the parties between rules and standards is also one of how much scope for interpretation they want to delegate to third parties or to which degree they prefer to determine the content themselves. Ultimately, it is important to note that rules and standards constitute pure types at the extreme ends of a spectrum, although in practice legal obligations mix the two in varying degrees.[75]

While the rules *versus* standards literature aims to provide answers to the question to which extent legal commands should be promulgated as rules or standards,[76] thereby offering guidance for the design of international law,[77] the focus in the context of the analysis of the concept of objective responsibility is on the allocation of responsibility for state action. From this perspective, states may address the problem of internalisation of policy externalities by using very specific legal rules (*ex ante* allocation) or by using more general principles that require evaluation of the concrete circumstances of the state action or inaction in order to finally determine its

[71] Ibid., 559–560. According to Trachtman, "the distinction relates to how much work remains to be done to determine the applicability of the norm to a particular circumstance". Trachtman, *The Economic Structure of International Law*, 213.

[72] Trachtman, "Ex Ante and Ex Post Allocation of International Legal Responsibility", in *Distribution of Responsibilities in International Law*, ed. Nollkaemper and Jacobs, 106; Trachtman, *The Economic Structure of International Law*, 212.

[73] Trachtman, "Ex Ante and Ex Post Allocation of International Legal Responsibility", in *Distribution of Responsibilities in International Law*, ed. Nollkaemper and Jacobs, 107.

[74] Ibid.; Trachtman, *The Economic Structure of International Law*, 213. Sunstein notes that in the case of standards, "[t]o a considerable extent, we do not know what the law is until the particular cases arise". Sunstein, "Problems with Rules", 964.

[75] Kaplow, "Rules versus Standards: An Economic Analysis", 561.

[76] Ibid., 559. On an earlier economic analysis of the choice between rules and standards, see Isaac Ehrlich and Richard A. Posner, "An Economic Analysis of Legal Rulemaking", *Journal of Legal Studies* 3, no. 1 (1974): 257–286.

[77] On the rational design of international institutions and international law, see in particular, Koremenos, Lipson, and Snidal, "The Rational Design of International Institutions", 761–799; Koremenos, *The Continent of International Law: Explaining Agreement Design*.

legality (*ex post* allocation).[78] The relevant question here is thus not whether existing primary obligations are optimally designed to address their underlying cooperation problem, but what the impact of their design as rules or standards is on establishing and enforcing responsibility and thus ultimately on compliance. How the choice between rules and standards affects *ex ante* costs becomes relevant in a second step because they allow to explain why norms that would be preferable from a state responsibility point of view are not present in international law, at least not to a degree that would be desirable for the international community as a whole.

In terms of their impact on compliance, rules are preferable to standards.[79] Kaplow argues that the cost of learning the law is reduced and that the individual behaviour induced might be more in accordance with what the underlying norm requires.[80] *Ex ante* specification allows in effect for greater predictability or certainty. Rules enable, firstly, the persons subject to the law to plan and conform their conduct *ex ante*.[81] They thus reduce the costs of the person governed by the rule to determine the required behaviour, for instance, by seeking legal advice.[82] Secondly, after the relevant conduct has taken place, rules enable both parties to a dispute to better predict the outcome of dispute resolution.[83] Rules can thus reduce the costs that fall *ex post* on the persons charged with applying the law. Determination of breach is reduced to the establishment of the facts and comparison to the rule,[84] which involves less litigation costs both for the plaintiff and the defendant, including the costs for courts, provided that adjudication is available.[85] In the international

---

[78] Trachtman, "Ex Ante and Ex Post Allocation of International Legal Responsibility", in *Distribution of Responsibilities in International Law*, ed. Nollkaemper and Jacobs, 89–90.

[79] From a constructivist perspective, rules enjoy greater legitimacy and therefore exercise a greater "compliance pull" on states than standards. See Thomas M. Franck, *The Power of Legitimacy among Nations* (New York: Oxford University Press, 1990), 50–66. The "managerial approach" contends that non-compliance with international obligations is often the result of imprecise norms; see Abram Chayes and Antonia Handler Chayes, "On Compliance", *International Organization* 47, no. 2 (1993): 175–205; Abram Chayes and Antonia Handler Chayes, *The New Sovereignty: Compliance with International Regulatory Agreements* (Cambridge, MA: Harvard University Press, 1995).

[80] Kaplow, "Rules versus Standards: An Economic Analysis", 564.

[81] Trachtman, "Ex Ante and Ex Post Allocation of International Legal Responsibility", in *Distribution of Responsibilities in International Law*, ed. Nollkaemper and Jacobs, 108; Trachtman, *The Economic Structure of International Law*, 214.

[82] Trachtman, *The Economic Structure of International Law*, 215.

[83] Trachtman, "Ex Ante and Ex Post Allocation of International Legal Responsibility", in *Distribution of Responsibilities in International Law*, ed. Nollkaemper and Jacobs, 108; Trachtman, *The Economic Structure of International Law*, 214.

[84] On the subsumption technique following the rules of logic, see Robert Alexy, "On Balancing and Subsumption. A Structural Comparison", *Ratio Juris* 16, no. 4 (2003): 433–449.

[85] Trachtman, "Ex Ante and Ex Post Allocation of International Legal Responsibility", in *Distribution of Responsibilities in International Law*, ed. Nollkaemper and Jacobs, 108; Trachtman, *The Economic Structure of International Law*, 214–215. Russell B. Korobkin argues that the clarity of rules leads to more disputes being settled out of court, not requiring adjudication at all. Korobkin, "Behavioral Analysis and Legal Form: Rules vs. Standards Revisited", 32.

context, this means that precise rules make it easier for the acting state to calibrate its actions *ex ante* and for the plaintiff and third states to observe non-compliance *ex post*. This is particularly relevant if there is no international adjudicator involved, which could verify the existence of a breach, which is why precise rules might induce greater compliance than standards.[86] For instance, in the case of non-compliance with rules, the reputational costs might increase for the responsible state or states might be more willing to bear the costs associated with countermeasures in the light of lower audience costs.[87]

The problem is that "no international legal regime is ever completely specified in terms of rules".[88] In terms of *ex ante* costs, rules present the disadvantage that they are more costly to create than standards because rules involve advance determination of the law's content.[89] As Trachtman points out, "[r]ules are more expensive to develop than standards, *ex ante*, because rules entail specification costs, including drafting costs and negotiation costs, as well as the strategic costs involved in *ex ante* specification".[90] From a strategic perspective, Jason Scott Johnston suggests that "[...] bargaining may be more efficient under a blurry balancing test than under a certain rule".[91] Only when the relevant issue arises frequently, rules can provide economies of scale.[92] But when frequency is low, standards are relatively more efficient than rules. In particular, when the range of acts to be covered is too complex or may evolve over time, standards preserve more flexibility, while rules determined in advance bear the risk to be over- or under-inclusive.[93] The preference for incompleteness over specification can be explained by many factors: firstly, states may simply not have sufficient resources available to negotiate specific rules[94];

[86] Trachtman, "Ex Ante and Ex Post Allocation of International Legal Responsibility", in *Distribution of Responsibilities in International Law*, ed. Nollkaemper and Jacobs, 113.

[87] See Sects. 7.2.1.4 and 7.2.2 on the incentives for injured and non-directly injured third states to take countermeasures.

[88] Trachtman, "Ex Ante and Ex Post Allocation of International Legal Responsibility", in *Distribution of Responsibilities in International Law*, ed. Nollkaemper and Jacobs, 104.

[89] Kaplow, "Rules versus Standards: An Economic Analysis", 562–563.

[90] Trachtman, "Ex Ante and Ex Post Allocation of International Legal Responsibility", in *Distribution of Responsibilities in International Law*, ed. Nollkaemper and Jacobs, 107; Trachtman, *The Economic Structure of International Law*, 213–214.

[91] Jason Scott Johnston, "Bargaining under Rules versus Standards", *Journal of Law, Economics, & Organization* 11, no. 2 (1995): 257.

[92] Kaplow, "Rules versus Standards: An Economic Analysis", 563–564; Trachtman, "Ex Ante and Ex Post Allocation of International Legal Responsibility", in *Distribution of Responsibilities in International Law*, ed. Nollkaemper and Jacobs, 108, 118; Trachtman, *The Economic Structure of International Law*, 215.

[93] Daniel Bodansky, "Rules vs. Standards in International Environmental Law", *Proceedings of the Annual Meeting (American Society of International Law)* 98 (2004): 278. A rule is over-inclusive when it applies to a factual situation that should be excluded and under-inclusive when it does not cover facts to which it should apply.

[94] According to Daniel Bodansky, the presence of standards in early international environmental instruments can be explained with the lack of information, notably the scientific uncertainties about climate change at the time. Ibid., 277–278.

secondly, states may not be willing to reach an agreement at the negotiation stage, because concrete commitments can create costs in terms of public choice when governments face domestic opposition, and decide to defer the political hard decisions to *ex post* (judicial) interpretation; and thirdly, states may not want to pre-empt decisions that require balancing of competing interests.[95] Standards thus have the advantage that when adjudication is possible, they implicitly allocate authority to the tribunal responsible for rendering a decision on the legality of the state action or inaction.[96] But this also means that the *ex post* costs of content determination are greater both for the persons governed by the law due to the lack of predictability and for the persons involved in the enforcement of the law when applying the law, even more so when no adjudication is available.[97] All this explains why, in many instances, states have strong incentives to agree on standards instead of rules despite the negative impact on the compliance rate.[98]

What we see in practice is that rules and standards often complement each other. This can be explained in part by a temporal distinction. In the domestic context, where adjudication is more commonly available, the possibility exists that a standard is converted into a rule through the creation of precedent.[99] In other words, in the development of a field of law, standards may be used at an earlier stage by the legislature with the aim to establish more complete rules at a later point on the basis of jurisprudence developed by courts or of experience otherwise acquired.[100] This is similar in international law where we observe an evolutionary process from standards to rules as more knowledge and consensus emerge,[101] for example, as more unwritten norms of international law are codified.[102]

---

[95] Trachtman gives the example of states failing to decide how trade rules relate to other non-trade policies. Trachtman, "Ex Ante and Ex Post Allocation of International Legal Responsibility", in *Distribution of Responsibilities in International Law*, ed. Nollkaemper and Jacobs, 107; Trachtman, *The Economic Structure of International Law*, 213–214. Flexibility provisions in the form of exemptions from responsibility are another instrument to deal with the balancing of conflicting interests; see the discussion in Sect. 5.2.2.2 on the necessity excuse in international law.

[96] Trachtman, "Ex Ante and Ex Post Allocation of International Legal Responsibility", in *Distribution of Responsibilities in International Law*, ed. Nollkaemper and Jacobs, 118. See for a detailed law and economics perspective on international adjudication and the agency role of judges in particular, Trachtman, *The Economic Structure of International Law*, 208–271. Cass R. Sunstein also views the choice between rules and standards as a principal-agent problem, where the costs of standards might be acceptable if the legislature believes that the court or other interpreter is trustworthy. Sunstein, "Problems with Rules", 1012.

[97] Kaplow, "Rules versus Standards: An Economic Analysis", 562–563.

[98] From a strategic perspective, James D. Fearon argues that "though a long shadow of the future may make *enforcing* an international agreement easier, it can also give states an incentive to *bargain harder*, delaying agreement in hopes of getting a better deal". James D. Fearon, "Bargaining, Enforcement, and International Cooperation", *International Organization* 52, no. 2 (1998): 270.

[99] Kaplow, "Rules versus Standards: An Economic Analysis", 564.

[100] Trachtman, "Ex Ante and Ex Post Allocation of International Legal Responsibility", in *Distribution of Responsibilities in International Law*, ed. Nollkaemper and Jacobs, 108; Trachtman, *The Economic Structure of International Law*, 214–215.

[101] Bodansky, "Rules vs. Standards in International Environmental Law", 278.

[102] Examples include the Vienna Conventions on the Law of Treaties and on Diplomatic Relations, and important aspects of the UN Convention on the Law of the Sea; see Abbott et al., "The Concept

In international environmental law, for instance, we find many examples of the combination of rules and standards.[103] While Article 2(1) of the Vienna Convention for the Protection of the Ozone Layer requires states to "take appropriate measures [...] to protect human health and the environment against adverse effects resulting or likely to result from human activities which modify or are likely to modify the ozone layer",[104] the Montreal Protocol concluded two years later sets out precise phase-out targets for ozone-depleting substances. Climate change law follows a similar approach with a framework convention requiring states to adopt national programmes to combat climate change and a subsequent protocol or agreement setting concrete emission reduction targets.[105] Other environmental law conventions set out general obligations in the treaty text and precise specific obligations in Annexes.[106] The density of precise rules can also be explained by the fact that most international environmental regimes do not provide for third-party dispute settlement and that states prefer to apply the law themselves (i.e. auto-interpretation).[107]

International humanitarian law also builds on both rules and standards. States agreed with the Hague[108] and Geneva Conventions[109] on precise obligations

of Legalization", 414. For a theoretical analysis of general principles in international law, arguing they precede the articulation of legal regimes and norms, see Samantha Besson, "General Principles in International Law—Whose Principles?" in *Les Principes en Droit Européen - Principles in European Law*, ed. Samantha Besson and Pascal Pichonnaz (Geneva: Schulthess, 2011), 19–64.

[103] For a detailed analysis of the relative effectiveness of rules and standards and the reasons why states favour one over the other in the field of international environmental law, see Bodansky, "Rules vs. Standards in International Environmental Law", 275–280.

[104] Vienna Convention for the Protection of the Ozone Layer (concluded 22 March 1985, entered into force 22 September 1988) 1513 *UNTS* 293.

[105] United Nations Framework Convention on Climate Change (UNFCCC) (concluded 9 May 1992, entered into force 21 March 1994) 1771 *UNTS* 107; Kyoto Protocol to the United Nations Framework Convention on Climate Change (Kyoto Protocol) (concluded 11 December 1997, entered into force 16 February 2005) 2303 *UNTS* 162. For the period after 2020, the Kyoto Protocol has been updated and replaced with the Paris Agreement.

[106] See, for instance, the Convention on the Prevention of Marine Pollution by Dumping of Wastes and other Matter (concluded 29 December 1972, entered into force 30 August 1975) 1046 *UNTS* 120.

[107] Bodansky, "Rules vs. Standards in International Environmental Law", 279.

[108] Hague Convention Respecting the Laws and Customs of War on Land and its Annex: Regulations Concerning the Laws and Customs of War on Land (Hague Convention IV) (concluded 18 October 1907, entered into force 26 January 1910) International Peace Conference, The Hague, Official Record.

[109] Geneva Convention for the Amelioration of the Condition of the Wounded and Sick in Armed Forces in the Field (Geneva Convention I); Geneva Convention for the Amelioration of the Condition of the Wounded, Sick and Shipwrecked Members of the Armed Forces at Sea (Geneva Convention II) (concluded 12 August 1949, entered into force 21 October 1950) 75 *UNTS* 85; Geneva Convention Relative to the Treatment of Prisoners of War (Geneva Convention III) (concluded 12 August 1949, entered into force 21 October 1950) 75 *UNTS* 135; Geneva Convention Relative to the Protection of Civilian Persons in Time of War (Geneva Convention IV) (concluded 12 August 1949, entered into force 21 October 1950) 75 *UNTS* 287.

regarding the *jus in bello*, that is the methods of warfare and the treatment, for instance, of prisoners of war and medical personnel. It was in their mutual self-interest to give their military concrete guidelines on how to conduct warfare in a humane way.[110] The basic norms of international humanitarian law, however, take the form of broad standards rather than rules, for instance, the Martens Clause[111] or the principles of proportionality[112] and military necessity.[113] As the circumstances of warfare have evolved over time, judicial institutions have increasingly applied these humanitarian principles to account, for instance, for private actors involved in combats and new weapon systems.[114] This is also due to the increasing application of international human rights law to conflicts, as human rights tend to be based primarily on flexible standards aiming to reconcile competing interests.[115] This illustrates the advantage of standards, in particular in GPG constellations, to offer more flexibility to account for new circumstances, but also that states need to be willing to delegate interpretive powers to third-party adjudicators.

International trade law serves as another example of an area of international law where rules and standards complement each other. On the one hand, the foundational principles of WTO law, which aim to ensure equal competitive conditions between all members, are framed in general standards rather than rules, for instance, the most-favoured nation clause,[116] the national treatment clause,[117] or the inapplicability of general exceptions when measures constitute disguised restrictions on international trade.[118] On the other hand, the specific commitments made by individual member

---

[110] Amichai Cohen, "Rules and Standards in the Application of International Humanitarian Law", *Israel Law Review* 41, no. 1 & 2 (2008): 47–52.

[111] The Martens Clause, which first appeared in the preamble of the Hague conventions, recalls in different formulations that, in cases not covered by the international humanitarian law in force, the human person remains under the protection of the principles of humanity and the dictates of the public conscience. See further Vaios Koutroulis, "Martens Clause", ed. Anthony Carty, *Oxford Bibliographies in International Law* (Oxford Bibliographies Online: Oxford University Press, 2021), Article last modified on 24 July 2013, https://doi.org/10.1093/OBO/9780199796953-0101

[112] For instance, Article 51(5)(b) of the 1977 Additional Protocol I to the Geneva Conventions prohibits an attack which may be expected to cause incidental loss of civilian life, injury to civilians, damage to civilian objects, or a combination thereof, which would be excessive in relation to the concrete and direct military advantage anticipated. Protocol Additional to the Geneva Conventions of 12 August 1949, and Relating to the Protection of Victims of International Armed Conflicts (Protocol I) (concluded 8 June 1977, entered into force 7 December 1978) 1125 *UNTS* 3.

[113] For instance, Article 52(2) of the 1977 Additional Protocol I limits attacks strictly to military objectives.

[114] Cohen, "Rules and Standards in the Application of International Humanitarian Law", 52–53.

[115] Ibid., 55–56. However, human rights obligations can also be framed in more rule-like terms, notably when no derogations from them are permitted.

[116] Regarding the most-favoured nation clause, see, for instance, Article I of the GATT and Article II of the GATS.

[117] Regarding the national treatment clause, see, for instance, Article III of the GATT and Article XVII of the GATS.

[118] See, for instance, Article XX of the GATT.

states, which are listed in the schedules of concessions, can rather be understood as rule-like norms.[119] The WTO system is complemented with a dispute settlement mechanism tasked with the application of trade norms in individual cases.[120] Such adjudicative mechanism allows to complete incomplete contracts *ex post* and may thus minimise *ex ante* the costs of contracting, which explains the important role of standards in international trade law.[121] Yet, principal-agent theory can explain that the effectiveness of standards relies on whether states place sufficient trust in the dispute settlement mechanism to which they delegated authority; otherwise, they may wish to regain back control over the norms that constrain their actions more than they anticipated when agreeing to them.[122]

What lessons can we draw from these insights with regard to the distinction between obligations that relate to different types of economic goods and thus face different underlying cooperation problems? Since we observe rules and standards within single areas of international law, it is clear that there is no simple correlation between rules and standards on the one side and the private and public dimension of international obligations on the other side, but that the relation is more complex. From the pure perspective of compliance, rules evidently present many advantages as non-compliant state behaviour is easier to detect, thus facilitating the operation of the decentralised enforcement mechanisms like countermeasures, and thus the effectiveness of the remedies of cessation and reparation. In the public dimension of international law, GPG and CPR obligations rely essentially on third-party enforcement which is likely to be less effective than first-party enforcement. There is thus an even stronger case to favour precise rules over general standards in the regulation of CPRs and GPGs, in particular in order to increase the reputational costs of non-compliance and reduce barriers to third-party countermeasures. Greater *ex ante* specification thus constitutes a tool to render these obligations more effective. In addition, states may also prefer negotiating rules *ex ante* in GPG and CPR constellations because the precise definition of mutual requirements offers more assurance that other states will comply with their commitments, in particular in the

[119] These schedules of concessions reflect specific tariff concessions and other commitments that member states have given in the context of trade negotiations, such as the Uruguay Round; see https://www.wto.org/english/tratop_e/schedules_e/goods_schedules_e.htm

[120] Understanding on Rules and Procedures Governing the Settlement of Disputes (DSU), Annex 2 of the Agreement Establishing the World Trade Organization (WTO Agreement) (concluded at Marrakesh on 15 April 1994, entered into force 1 January 1995) 33 *ILM* 1226.

[121] Trachtman, "Ex Ante and Ex Post Allocation of International Legal Responsibility", in *Distribution of Responsibilities in International Law*, ed. Nollkaemper and Jacobs, 109–110. With reference to Henrik Horn, Giovanni Maggi and Robert W. Staiger, who propose a model of trade agreements in which contracting is costly, and as a consequence, the optimal agreement may be incomplete. Henrik Horn, Giovanni Maggi, and Robert W. Staiger, "Trade Agreements as Endogenously Incomplete Contracts", *The American Economic Review* 100, no. 1 (2010): 394–419.

[122] A recent example is the United States' blockade of nominations to the WTO Appellate Body, thus rendering the dispute settlement mechanism largely ineffective, which the EU and a number of trade partners seek to solve temporarily by setting up a multiparty interim appeal arbitration arrangement.

absence of international adjudication.[123] For standards to operate effectively to a similar degree, adjudication needs to play its facilitating role. We can observe this in particular in the field of international (or rather regional) human rights law regimes, where international courts are endowed with the authority to apply these GPG obligations usually designed as standard-like obligations balancing competing values.[124] The fact that we do not see GPG and CPR obligations exclusively in the form of rules can be explained with the fact that states when negotiating these rules take not only into account the benefits of inducing compliance of other states, but also the different *ex ante* costs of negotiation outlined above, namely to specify and agree in advance on all possible states of the world. Thus, in the case of GPGs and CPRs, states may also want to keep a certain degree of flexibility and agree only on broad standards. In particular in the absence of third-party adjudication, the disadvantage of standards of having a lower incentive effect on compliance might be offset with the advantage of broader participation in the treaty regime, which is particularly important in GPG and CPR constellations. The co-existence of rules and standards for both GPG and CPR obligations can thus be explained by the fact that the states agree first to general standards in order to increase the number of participating states and subsequently define them more precisely as the result of a learning process.

Thus, for the analysis of objective responsibility, this means that rules are preferable in order to ensure the effective operation of the responsibility regime, even more so in the case of GPG and CPR obligations. However, the benefits of better compliance do not always outweigh the costs of self-constraint associated with designing these rules. The state responsibility regime therefore also needs to account for the fact that international obligations are sometimes designed in general terms and ensure that the legal consequences, such as reparation of injury, can also take effect in these cases. The limitation of the conditions of responsibility to the element of breach of an international obligation thus accounts for the trade-off between two objectives of state responsibility, namely compliance and flexibility.

4.1.2 Responsibility Standards in International Obligations

As "objective responsibility" means that the determination of non-compliant behaviour depends on the content of primary obligations, an analysis of its effectiveness does not only require a closer look at the role of their design (i.e. substance *versus* procedure) or degree of precision (i.e. rules *versus* standards), but also at the degree

[123] Bodansky, "Rules vs. Standards in International Environmental Law", 279.

[124] The best example is the European Court of Human Rights (ECtHR), which adjudicates claims based on the European Convention for the Protection of Human Rights and Fundamental Freedoms (ECHR). See Nollkaemper, "International Adjudication of Global Public Goods: The Intersection of Substance and Procedure", 770.

to which primary international obligations reflect different standards of responsibility and thus allocate duties and costs among states. The ARSIWA Commentaries point out clearly that any "subjective" requirements, such as fault, intention, negligence, or due diligence, derive only from the content of the primary international obligation in question.[125] This section briefly outlines in a first step the role of subjective elements in the law of state responsibility, notably the notion of fault, not only in primary international obligations but also at different stages in the law of state responsibility. In a second step, the concept of due diligence is analysed, because it serves, on the one hand, as an illustrative example of the discussion in the previous section. On the spectrum between rules and standards, due diligence obligations may be placed rather towards the more general end. However, over time, the concept has been fleshed out increasingly with more concrete substantial and procedural obligations. On the other hand, due diligence is the most prominent reflection of the notion of fault in primary international obligations, as a proxy for state negligence, in particular in failing to prevent harmful activities of private actors under the state's jurisdiction. This section thus also serves to facilitate the functional comparison between "objective" state responsibility and the concept of state liability (in the form of strict liability and of liability for lawful acts) in tort-like constellations in international law, thus similar to the economic analysis of strict liability and negligence in domestic tort law.

4.1.2.1 The Notion of Fault in the Law of State Responsibility

Giuseppe Palmisano understands the notion of fault in a broad sense and defines it as "a set of blameworthy psychological attitudes of the [s]tate, resulting from a varying combination of factors", which "include the psychological attitudes of the organs involved in the commission of the wrongful act".[126] Thus, while the individual organs' fault plays a role in determining the blameworthiness of the state's behaviour, negligence or lack of diligence in preventing harm (for instance, to aliens on the state's territory) "is, rather, inferred from a different set of elements, including: inadequacy of the existing legislation of the [s]tate; insufficiency of governmental action, judicial and security policies included; inadequacy of the local security and administrative organization with respect to the peculiar situation of the territory concerned; lack of diligence, recklessness, bad faith, wilful neglect or intent on the part of the organ acting, or omitting to act, in the case in question".[127] In the context of state responsibility, fault is therefore to be understood as "an element to be referred to the [s]tate as an international person and subject of international law",

[125] ARSIWA Commentaries, Article 2, paras. 3, 10.

[126] Giuseppe Palmisano, "Fault", ed. Anne Peters and Rüdiger Wolfrum, *Max Planck Encyclopedia of Public International Law* (Oxford Public International Law: Oxford University Press, 2021), http://opil.ouplaw.com, Article last updated in September 2007, para. 45.

[127] Ibid., para. 28.

similar to other notions in international law which refer to other subjective elements of the state (e.g. consent).[128]

Despite being an important element for establishing state responsibility, fault on the part of the state is not a precondition for the existence of an internationally wrongful act.[129] Many primary international obligations are devoid of notions of fault, for instance, emission quotas or trade rules, and thus purely "objective" in nature. Other primary obligations, for instance, the prohibition of genocide, require intent as a subjective element.[130] Another group of primary obligations relating in particular to the prevention of harm to foreigners or in a transboundary context stemming from activities of private actors under the state's control contain a duty of due diligence (or vigilance or care), and thus, breach of these obligations builds upon the standard of state negligence.[131]

Notions of fault can, in addition, become relevant in relation to the consequences of a wrongful act.[132] Firstly, with regard to reparation for injury, the degree of blameworthiness of the responsible state's behaviour may not only have an impact on the level of compensation of the damage, either in the form of a higher level than full compensation of damage (i.e. punitive damages) or a lower level of compensation due to the victim's wilful or negligent contribution to the injury,[133] but also on the extent of satisfaction for moral damage as a remedy.[134] Secondly, notions of fault, in particular wilful intent, are reflected in the consequences for internationally wrongful acts of a certain gravity, namely serious breaches of peremptory norms of general international law.[135] Thirdly, countermeasures allow an injured state to

temporarily disregard international obligations owed to the state acting wrongfully

128 Ibid., para. 29. On state consent as a circumstance precluding wrongfulness, see Sect. 5.3.2.1.

129 Ibid., para. 45.

130 Article II of the Genocide Convention requires, amongst others, "intent to destroy, in whole or in part, a national, ethnical, racial or religious group, as such". Mental elements, such as wilful intent, special intent, recklessness, or culpable negligence, play also an important role in establishing individual criminal responsibility for international crimes. See further ibid., paras. 39–44, 47.

131 Ibid., para. 16.

132 Wrongful intent also plays a role with regard to state responsibility in connection with the act of another state, an aspect which will (as explained in Sect. 1.4) not be further discussed in this book. See further ibid., paras. 30–32, 46.

133 Both aspects will be discussed in Sect. 6.3.2. While punitive damages are not recognised in international law, contribution to injury is laid down in Article 39 ARSIWA: "In the determination of reparation, account shall be taken of the contribution to the injury by wilful or negligent action or omission of the injured State or any person or entity in relation to whom reparation is sought".

134 On satisfaction, see Sect. 6.3.3. On the role of fault with regard to the remedy of reparation and its different forms, see further Palmisano, "Fault", paras. 33–36, 46.

135 See further ibid., paras. 37–38, 46. For an economic theory of intentional torts in the domestic context, see William M. Landes and Richard A. Posner, "An Economic Theory of Intentional Torts", *International Review of Law and Economics* 1, no. 2 (1981): 127–154. Consequences of breaches of peremptory norms of general international law (*jus cogens*) will be discussed in Sect. 6.4. The focus in this chapter is on unintentional accidents with a cross-border dimension.

in the first place if they are taken for the purpose of inducing the target state to comply with its secondary obligations to cease the wrongful conduct (if it is continuing) and provide reparation.[136] Thus, while the purpose of breaching international obligations in the first place is not relevant, countermeasures represent a deviation from the principle of "objective responsibility" in the ARSIWA, because the reaction to such an internationally wrongful act requires a certain additional subjective element, namely a specific purpose.

The problem with additional subjective requirements for an internationally wrongful act is that they are more difficult to observe for other states and to verify by third-party adjudicators, if they are available. By definition, subjective elements are prone to information asymmetries. This bears consequences not only for victim states assessing whether they can prove the existence of a prior wrongful act, but also for responsible states assessing whether victim states contributed wilfully or negligently to the injury. It is also relevant for all other states in the international community assessing whether an injured (or non-directly injured third) state had recourse to countermeasures for the purpose of inducing compliance with the secondary obligations of cessation and reparation or whether such breach is the result of opportunistic behaviour under the disguise of countermeasures.[137] In international law, many of these difficulties also relate to the fact that the state is a corporate entity and subjective elements such as fault usually relate to individual actors. However, the international law of state responsibility deals with these difficulties in that fault of individual actors is only one element among many other factors, including objective elements such as the failure to adopt certain legislation in order to establish lack of diligence.

For the analysis in this chapter, it is important to note that fault is not a precondition for international state responsibility, and thus, it cannot be the distinctive feature between responsibility for wrongful acts and liability for lawful acts.[138] Yet, in order to compare the incentive effects of both concepts, due diligence obligations can serve as a proxy for primary obligations requiring fault in the form of negligence with breach of these primary due obligations entailing state responsibility.

[136] Article 49 ARSIWA. Federica I. Paddeu, "Countermeasures", ed. Anne Peters and Rüdiger Wolfrum, *Max Planck Encyclopedia of Public International Law* (Oxford Public International Law: Oxford University Press, 2021), http://opil.ouplaw.com, Article last updated in September 2015, paras. 15–16. See Sect. 7.1 on countermeasures in the international law of state responsibility.

[137] Thus, bearing the risk of increasing the political costs of countermeasures, see Sects. 7.2.1.4 and 7.2.2 on the incentives for injured and non-directly injured third states to take countermeasures.

[138] Palmisano, "Fault", paras. 20, 23.

4.1.2.2 An Economic Perspective on Due Diligence Obligations in International Law

Timo Koivurova defines the concept of due diligence as "an obligation of conduct on the part of a subject of law", which describes the blameworthiness for not acting as a responsible citizen or government, also termed as negligence.[139] The concept is to be distinguished from obligations of result, for instance, to compensate for harm caused, which is reflected in the concept of liability in international law and which will be discussed in the following section. Due diligence rather requires states to prevent harm by respecting a certain standard of due diligence; otherwise, they are responsible for the commission of an internationally wrongful act.[140]

In international law, the concept of due diligence as an expression of the "no-harm rule" constitutes a general principle of law.[141] However, more precise rules and standards have been developed over the years, setting out the requirements for due diligence in different contexts and areas of international relations.[142] With regard to

[139] Timo Koivurova, "Due Diligence", ed. Anne Peters and Rüdiger Wolfrum, *Max Planck Encyclopedia of Public International Law* (Oxford Public International Law: Oxford University Press, 2021), http://opil.ouplaw.com, Article last updated in February 2010, para. 1. See further Sarah Heathcote, "State Omissions and Due Diligence: Aspects of Fault, Damage and Contribution to Injury in the Law of State Responsibility", in *The ICJ and the Evolution of International Law: the Enduring Impact of the Corfu Channel Case*, ed. Karine Bannelier, Théodore Christakis, and Sarah Heathcote (London: Routledge, 2012), 295–314; International Law Association, *Due Diligence in International Law*, Second Report, Johannesburg Conference (2016), https://www.ila-hq.org/index.php/study-groups. For an overview of the historical evolution of the concept of due diligence in the law of state responsibility, see Riccardo Pisillo-Mazzeschi, "The Due Diligence Rule and the Nature of the International Responsibility of States", *German Yearbook of International Law* 35 (1992): 9–51; Jan Arno Hessbruegge, "The Historical Development of the Doctrines of Attribution and Due Diligence in International Law", *New York University Journal of International Law and Politics* 36 (2004): 265–306.

[140] Koivurova, "Due Diligence", para. 15.

[141] There exists in international law a general obligation for states to ensure that activities carried out on their sovereign territory or under their jurisdiction and control do not (i) cause damage to another state in the form of personal injury or property damage on its territory and (ii) respect the environment of others states and of areas beyond national control. This "no-harm rule" has been recognised under international law in diplomatic practice and a number of international judicial decisions. See in this regard, *Alabama (United States of America v. Great Britain)*, Award, 14 September 1872, RIAA, Volume XXIX, p. 125; *Trail Smelter (United States of America v. Canada)*, Award, 16 April 1938 and 11 March 1941, RIAA, Volume III, p. 1905; *Corfu Channel (United Kingdom of Great Britain and Northern Ireland v. Albania)*, Judgment (Merits), 9 April 1949, ICJ Reports 1949, p. 4, p. 22; *Lac Lanoux (Spain v. France)*, Award, 16 November 1957, RIAA, Volume XII, p. 281; *Legality of the Threat or Use of Nuclear Weapons*, Advisory Opinion, pp. 241–242, para. 29; *Pulp Mills on the River Uruguay (Argentina v. Uruguay)*, Judgment, 20 April 2010, ICJ Reports 2010, p. 14, p. 78, para. 193. See also Principle 21 of the Declaration of the United Nations Conference on the Human Environment, Stockholm, 16 June 1972 (UN Doc. A/CONF.48/14/Rev.1). See also Principle 2 of the Declaration of the United Nations Conference on Environment and Development, Rio de Janeiro, 14 June 1992 (UN Doc. A/CONF.151/26/Rev.1 (Vol. I)).

[142] Koivurova, "Due Diligence", paras. 2, 16.

state responsibility, due diligence historically plays an important role for the responsibility of states for failure to prevent breach of international obligations by private actors under their control or jurisdiction,[143] as it rests on the notion of territorial sovereignty.[144] Today, primary due diligence obligations can be observed in many fields of international law requiring states to take the necessary steps towards the desired result set out in the obligation, including but not limited to the prevention of harmful conduct by private actors under their control (e.g. diplomatic relations, protection of aliens, human rights protection,[145] international humanitarian law,[146] and the fight against terrorism).[147] Global public health can be cited as a more recent example with regard to due diligence obligations of states to prevent and halt the transmission of SARS-CoV-2 or to be better prepared for future pandemics.[148] In international environmental law, where due diligence obligations have mostly developed in the form of the harm prevention rule, they relate not only to the context of transboundary pollution, but also to the protection of the global commons.[149] Finally, the concept of due diligence has been operationalised with procedural obligations, mostly in the transboundary harm context.[150] Thus, due diligence is a general standard, but the concrete content often depends on the specific context and instrument, with the concept now being included in a large number of multilateral

[143] This is to account for the fact that acts of private actors cannot be directly attributed to the state.

[144] Koivurova, "Due Diligence", paras. 2, 31, 43–44. See, in particular, *United States Diplomatic and Consular Staff in Tehran (United States of America v. Iran)*, Judgment, p. 31, para. 63; *Military and Paramilitary Activities in and against Nicaragua (Nicaragua v. United States of America)*, Judgment (Merits), p. 85, para. 157.

[145] For instance, Article 2(1) International Covenant on Civil and Political Rights (concluded 16 December 1966, entered into force 23 March 1976) 999 *UNTS* 171. ("Each State Party to the present Covenant undertakes to respect and to ensure to all individuals within its territory and subject to its jurisdiction the rights recognized in the present Covenant, without distinction of any kind, such as race, colour, sex, language, religion, political or other opinion, national or social origin, property, birth or other status".)

[146] Common Article 1 of the Geneva Conventions I–IV and reiterated in the additional Protocols I–II. ("The High Contracting Parties undertake to respect and to ensure respect for the present Convention in all circumstances".)

[147] Koivurova, "Due Diligence", paras. 3, 45–46.

[148] Antonio Coco and Talita de Souza Dias, "Part I: Due Diligence and Covid-19: States' Duties to Prevent and Halt the Coronavirus Outbreak", *EJIL: Talk!* (Blog of the European Journal of International Law), 24 March 2020, https://www.ejiltalk.org/part-i-due-diligence-and-covid-19-states-duties-to-prevent-and-halt-the-coronavirus-outbreak/?utm_source=mailpoet&utm_medium=email&utm_campaign=ejil-talk-newsletter-post-title_2

[149] Koivurova, "Due Diligence", para. 3. See, for example, Article 194(2) United Nations Convention on the Law of the Sea (UNCLOS). ("States shall take all measures necessary to ensure that activities under their jurisdiction or control are so conducted as not to cause damage by pollution to other States and their environment, and that pollution arising from incidents or activities under their jurisdiction or control does not spread beyond the areas where they exercise sovereign rights in accordance with this Convention".)

[150] Koivurova, "Due Diligence", paras. 3, 21–22. See, in particular, *Pulp Mills on the River Uruguay (Argentina v. Uruguay)*, Judgment, pp. 83–84, para. 205. See also in Sect. 4.2.

treaties. For situations of risk of transboundary harm from hazardous activities, the concept of due diligence has been codified and partially progressively developed in the work of the ILC on preventive and liability rules,[151] which will both be discussed in the following section.

On the domestic level, in the economic analysis of tort law, negligence as a responsibility standard has been analysed with a view to understand how costs are allocated among the tortfeasor and the victim. To recall, the role of tort law is to minimise the social costs of accidents resulting from valuable, but risky activities.[152] Calabresi developed the claim that the aim of tort law should be to minimise the sum of the costs of accidents and the costs of avoiding them.[153] The expected costs of accidents (i.e. the magnitude of the losses times the probability of such accidents occurring) can be modelled as a function of precautionary care, and, thus, the focus of tort law is to align the incentives of potential injurers and potential victims, in particular with regard to optimal levels of precaution.[154]

This economic approach to tort law has also been reflected in the doctrinal understanding of negligence. Under a negligence standard, a tortfeasor is required to take reasonable care and to pay damages for harm caused if he fails to do so. This implies that some accident costs will have to be borne by the victim, namely when the injurer was not negligent.[155] In common law, reasonable care has been interpreted in terms of cost-effectiveness, as illustrated by the "Hand formula".[156] It determines the standard of care that a potential tortfeasor owes to potential victims as B, where B is the cost of precautionary care (i.e. the "burden"), p is the probability of an accident occurring, and L is the cost of such an accident (i.e. the accident "loss").[157] Assuming diminishing marginal effectiveness of precautions, the optimal level of precaution will be at the point where $B = p(L)$, thus placing accident costs upon injurers who exercised less care.[158] In other words, the tortfeasor is negligent if $B \leq p(L)$.[159] This formulation of negligence as efficient level of precautionary care has been widely accepted in the doctrinal law literature and the economic analysis of law.[160]

[151] Koivurova, "Due Diligence", para. 10.

[152] Posner and Parisi, *Law and Economics: Elgar Research Reviews in Economics*, section 7.

[153] Calabresi, *The Costs of Accidents: A Legal and Economic Analysis*.

[154] Posner and Parisi, *Law and Economics: Elgar Research Reviews in Economics*, section 7. For more formalised models of the tort problem, see, in particular, John Prather Brown, "Toward an Economic Theory of Liability", *The Journal of Legal Studies* 2, no. 2 (1973): 323–349; Peter A. Diamond, "Accident Law and Resource Allocation", *Bell Journal of Economics and Management Science* 5, no. 2 (1974): 366–405.

[155] Dnes, *Principles of Law and Economics*, 186.

[156] See the conclusions of Justice Learned Hand in *United States v. Carroll Towing Co.*, 159 F.2d 169 (2d Cir. 1947).

[157] Posner and Parisi, *Law and Economics: Elgar Research Reviews in Economics*, section 7.

[158] Ibid.

[159] Dnes, *Principles of Law and Economics*, 187.

[160] Posner and Parisi, *Law and Economics: Elgar Research Reviews in Economics*, section 7.

The incentive effects of a negligence rule can best be explained in comparison to the alternatives of "no liability" and "strict liability". In the absence of a liability rule, the costs of an accident are fully attributed to the victim, and, therefore, the potential victim is fully incentivised to take optimal precaution against being injured, whereas the potential tortfeasor has no incentives to take precautionary measures.[161] Under a strict liability rule, the injurer has to fully compensate the victim and thus fully bear the costs of the accident. A potential tortfeasor is thus fully incentivised to exercise optimal care against injuring anyone, whereas potential victims have no incentives to take precaution.[162] A negligence rule attributes the costs of an accident to the tortfeasor unless the tortfeasor failed to exercise an optimal level of care, thus setting incentives to both potential injurers and potential victims to take optimal precaution.[163] Hence, when simply comparing the incentive effects regarding the optimal levels of precaution of potential tortfeasors, strict liability and negligence are equivalent.[164] Steven Shavell examined why negligence is nonetheless the prevailing responsibility standard in most circumstances in tort law, both in the common and in the civil law traditions.[165] He analysed the effect of both responsibility standards on the level of activity, which can alongside the level of precaution influence the probability of an accident (e.g. driving less often).[166] He argued that under a strict liability rule, potential injurers, as they have to fully internalise the accident costs, are incentivised to take optimal precaution and engage in an optimal activity level, whereas potential victims face no incentives regarding the one or the other.[167] Under a negligence rule, by contrast, potential injurers are likely to engage in too high activity levels as these increase the personal benefits and are more difficult to be verified in court.[168] However, as potential victims bear the costs of accidents, when the injurer acted diligently, they are incentivised to not only take optimal precautionary care but also exercise an optimal level of activity.[169] Shavell came to the conclusion that while none of the two responsibility standards sets incentives for optimal precaution and the optimal level of activity for both parties (i.e. strict liability only for potential injurers and "no liability" only for potential victims), negligence sets incentives for the tortfeasor's and the victim's optimal precautionary care level and the victim's activity level.[170] In order for these

---

[161] Ibid.

[162] Ibid.

[163] Ibid.

[164] Ibid.

[165] Shavell, "Strict Liability versus Negligence", 1–25.

[166] Ibid., 1–3.

[167] Only under a strict liability rule with a defence of contributory negligence, victims would face incentives for exercising due care, but still not for engaging in an optimal level of activity. Ibid., 7, 19.

[168] Ibid., 6–7, 19, 22–23.

[169] Ibid., 6–7, 19.

[170] Ibid., 7, 19.

propositions to hold, it is important, however, that under a negligence rule the legal standard of care is set at the cost-effective level or equals efficient precautionary care.

These conclusions on the incentive effects of a negligence regime can, in principle, be transferred to the international level. It can thus be assumed that in constellations, where a balance needs to be struck between risky but economically beneficial activities (e.g. industrial production and international transportation) and potentially harmful cross-border effects or harm to the global commons, due diligence obligations can set optimal incentives for precautionary care of both potentially responsible and victim states, as well as for optimal activity levels of potential victim states. While this explains the prominence and widespread use of due diligence obligations in international law, it presupposes, however, that the respective primary obligations define the optimal level of precautionary care (i.e. the B). The adequate level of precaution thus varies, as outlined above, depending on the probability (p) and the severity of the harm (L), and thus on the specific context (e.g. diplomatic protection, environmental protection, global health). Due diligence obligations thus do not require the same measures in all constellations, as long as they coincide with what could be expected of a reasonable state (or government) in a given situation. Due diligence obligations thus offer a certain degree of flexibility and bear the advantage that as an expression of the "no-harm rule", they can cater for new global challenges, for instance, obligations for states to prevent harm to human beings or the global commons from climate change or future pandemics. They also allow to take into account, to a certain degree, different economic and technological capacities of states, in particular for developing states.[171] Yet, we have also seen in the previous section that with regard to subjective elements, such as fault, there exists a problem of observability of state negligence or lack of due diligence to the injured state due to information asymmetries and of verifiability by third-party adjudicators. However, fault does not require to prove the blameworthy psychological attitude of the organs involved in the commission of the wrongful act, but can also be established by building on a varying combination of factors, including objectively verifiable elements such as inadequate legislation. This is also true with regard to due diligence in international law, which reflects the idea of negligence as known from domestic law, but is determined differently as the state is considered the relevant person and subject of international law.

Whether primary due diligence obligations can set optimal incentives depends also on their design and thus reflects the same advantages and disadvantages discussed earlier in this chapter with regard to substance *versus* procedure and rules *versus* standards. Due diligence obligations can have a procedural and a substantial dimension, and they can be designed as broad standards or be specified

[171] The principle of common but differentiated responsibilities finds its limit, however, when international agreements specifically define the obligations falling on developing countries. Koivurova, "Due Diligence", para. 19. The idea of differential duties of care also exists in tort law. For instance, children or specific professions are not held to the normal standard of care. Dnes, *Principles of Law and Economics*, 188.

with concrete rules. From a compliance perspective, we have seen that procedural obligations and obligations which are specified *ex ante* present advantages. Designing due diligence obligations in such a way has an impact on the observability and verifiability of non-compliant behaviour, which is particularly relevant in GPG and CPR constellations. In these cases, third-party enforcement has the potential to become more effective, thus increasing the incentives for compliance. However, procedural obligations bear the risk of over- or under-inclusiveness compared to substantial obligations in the sense that they are not perfectly correlated to what a substantial obligation would require. Moreover, we have also seen that states are more likely to agree on due diligence obligations in the form of broad standards which are specified *ex post*, in particular in the context of GPG and CPR constellations. This explains why we observe across areas of international law as a first step usually broad standards which provide sufficient flexibility to adapt to new circumstances and which are subsequently fleshed out with more precise procedural and substantial obligations.[172] Another relevant factor is whether third-party adjudicators are available or whether the *ex post* determination of the optimal level of care depends on the parties themselves (i.e. auto-interpretation).

Due diligence obligations which are not fully aligned with the optimal level of precautionary care thus bear the risk that potential wrongdoing states take excessive or insufficient precaution. This means that the level of care is not cost-effective, as over-deterrence increases the costs of precaution for the potentially wrongdoing state beyond what is necessary, whereas under-deterrence shifts the costs to the victim state. Recourse to the comparison of the relative advantages of substantive *versus* procedural obligations and rules *versus* standards thus demonstrates how difficult it is to design optimal due diligence obligations and that complementarity of different design elements is often key to achieve optimal incentives in terms of precaution.

In sum, the trade-off between two objectives of state responsibility, namely compliance and flexibility, which is reflected in the concept of objective responsibility, applies also to due diligence obligations as a specific type of primary international obligations requiring a notion of fault. The consequence of a breach of a primary due diligence obligation is that it entails state responsibility and thus gives rise to the remedies (or secondary obligations) of cessation and reparation of injury in its different forms, including compensation for damage. This leads to the third function of state responsibility, which is cost allocation following an internationally wrongful act. Due diligence obligations shift the accident costs either to the responsible state, when it failed to exercise due care, or to the victim state, when it was diligent. In certain tort-like scenarios of international cooperation, notably the transboundary context where hazardous but economically beneficial activities emanating from one sovereign territory cause harm to individuals, property, or the environment within the jurisdiction of another state or to the global commons (i.e. private goods or CPR constellations), the state responsibility regime might be

[172] See, for example, the general obligation to protect and preserve the marine environment in Article 192 UNCLOS, which is subsequently specified in Article 194(2) UNCLOS.

complemented by different forms of state liability in international law. As outlined in detail in the following section, these are strict liability or liability for lawful acts as secondary due diligence obligations of loss remediation. In terms of objectives, the concept of state liability differs from the concept of state responsibility for wrongful acts, as the primary aim of liability regimes is to deal with harm prevention and the distribution of risks of hazardous activities as well as with the allocation of losses in the case transboundary harm occurs despite diligent state behaviour. These are either obligations of compensation or, at least, secondary due diligence obligations to mitigate harm by negotiating an adequate amount of compensation.[173]

4.2 The Concept of Liability in International Law

In order to understand in which constellations of international cooperation the different forms of "state liability" present advantages compared to state responsibility for breach of due diligence obligations, this section takes a closer look at their incentive effects. The first subsection examines from an economic perspective the concept of "strict liability" in international law. Strict liability can be defined as an absolute obligation of a state to pay full compensation for transboundary damage caused by a hazardous activity of that state (for instance, launching of space objects), independent of whether the state acted with or without due diligence. This corresponds to the definition of strict liability in domestic tort law. Thus, insights of the economic analysis in domestic tort law on the incentive effects on the level of precaution and the level of activity (in comparison to negligence) can be transferred to the international level. The second subsection analyses from an economic perspective the principles of loss allocation in the case of transboundary harm arising out of hazardous activities under the jurisdiction of a state and which are not prohibited by international law. Liability of lawful acts refers to secondary due diligence obligations falling on states despite compliance with all due diligence obligations of harm prevention. In such cases, states are nonetheless obliged to take appropriate measures to mitigate the costs of harm internally with regard to private actors (in particular, *via* a regime of civil liability) and only where appropriate, to negotiate compensation for damage. This corresponds to "no-fault" liability regimes in domestic tort law. Also in this regard, insights of the economic analysis of regimes of loss allocation in the absence of fault can be transferred to the international level to better understand the incentive effects.

[173] Palmisano, "Fault", para. 20. State responsibility then applies as a backup regime for liability, namely in case of breach of these obligations of compensation.

4.2.1 An Economic Perspective on Strict Liability in International Law

Some international agreements build on strict (or absolute) state liability as a standard in international law which consists in "the obligation to make full reparation upon the sheer occurrence of harm, irrespective of whether all due diligence measures have been adopted, only provided the causal link has been established between the dangerous activity of the [s]tate concerned and the transboundary damage".[174] Strict liability of states *stricto sensu* exists in international law only on an exceptional basis in very few treaty regimes which relate to transboundary damage from ultra-hazardous activities (e.g. damage caused by space objects[175]) and thus cannot be considered to apply under general international law.[176]

In domestic tort law, strict liability means that the tortfeasor needs to fully compensate the victim for an injury caused irrespective of the level of care.[177] Strict liability sets incentives for potential tortfeasors to take efficient level of precaution (and activity), but leads to suboptimal outcomes when potential victims can influence the probability of the accident.[178] A defence of contributory negligence can improve the incentives for potential victims to take cost-effective precautions.[179] A strict liability rule is superior to a negligence rule when it is important to lower the potential injurer's activity level.[180] In the domestic context, strict liability exists only for certain circumstances, such as hazardous activities, owner liability for harm caused by dangerous animals, or product liability. The reason is that the potential injurer is usually the least-cost avoider and potential victims are unlikely to take cost-effective preventive measures.[181]

---

[174] Attila Tanzi, "Liability for Lawful Acts", ed. Anne Peters and Rüdiger Wolfrum, *Max Planck Encyclopedia of Public International Law* (Oxford Public International Law: Oxford University Press, 2021), http://opil.ouplaw.com, Article last updated in January 2021, para. 16.

[175] Article II of the Convention on International Liability for Damage Caused by Space Objects. ("A launching [s]tate shall be absolutely liable to pay compensation for damage caused by its space object on the surface of the earth or to aircraft in flight".)

[176] Tanzi, "Liability for Lawful Acts", para. 16.

[177] Dnes, *Principles of Law and Economics*, 185.

[178] Ibid.

[179] Ibid. The defence of "contributory negligence" shifts the entire accident costs back to victims acting negligently, whereas the defence of "comparative negligence" divides the accident costs between both parties when the victim was also negligent (under both strict liability and negligence primary liability regimes). Posner and Parisi, *Law and Economics: Elgar Research Reviews in Economics*, section 7. A comparative negligence rule is also enshrined in the international law of state responsibility, as Article 39 ARSIWA foresees a lower level of compensation in the case of wilful or negligent contribution to the injury. See Sect. 4.1.2.1 on the notion of fault and Sect. 6.3.2 on compensation for damage.

[180] Dnes, *Principles of Law and Economics*, 188. See also Shavell, "Strict Liability versus Negligence", 7, 19.

[181] Dnes, *Principles of Law and Economics*, 185–186.

This rationale for a strict liability regime also holds with regard to interstate relations. Strict liability in international law is superior to responsibility for breach of due diligence obligations, when the focus needs to be on lowering the activity level of the potentially injuring state, which internalises the benefits of the activity. Under a strict liability rule, provided that compensation is granted in full, a potentially injuring state is incentivised to take optimal precautionary care and engage in an optimal level of activity. The launch of space objects by states is an illustrative example. Launching states can avoid damage caused by its space object on the surface of the earth or to aircraft in flight at the least cost by taking precautionary measures and by limiting their launching activities. In contrast, potential victim states (and global commons) are unlikely to influence the probability and the magnitude of the damage or, if at all, only at exorbitant costs. Setting incentives for potential injuring states to lower their activity level makes sense when the activity is extremely hazardous and when states are able to directly control the activity (for instance, activities in outer space which are carried out by state agencies and not private operators). This is why we see strict liability in international law only with regard to ultra-hazardous activities under direct state control and not with regard to "ordinary" hazardous activities carried out by private actors under the jurisdiction of the state (i.e. externalities emanating from the injuring state's territory), where the focus of state behaviour is on taking sufficient preventive measures internally. In these constellations, the focus will often not be on lowering the state's activity level of beneficial, but risky activities. It will rather lie on taking adequate care, which can also be achieved under a due diligence regime (provided that the legal standard of care is set at a cost-effective level). There is thus a strong rationale against a general strict liability rule in international law, but rather to let states predefine these specific ultra-hazardous activities on a conventional basis, as has been the case so far only with regard to state activities in outer space causing transboundary damage. This is in line with the approach taken in domestic tort law, where strict liability also has limited applicability as it usually relates only to situations specified *ex ante* where the abstract danger (e.g. driving a car) is strongest, independent of the individual culpability.

In sum, strict liability in international law can complement state responsibility for breach of primary due diligence obligations in constellations where the objective is to internalise negative externalities, that is transboundary damage caused by beneficial activities, to other states or the global commons (i.e. private goods and CPR scenarios). Here, a strict liability regime can be as effective as primary due diligence obligations regulating certain activities (provided these reflect the adequate level of precaution) in setting incentives for optimal precaution, but bears advantages when the focus lies on lowering the activity level, as is the case with specific ultra-hazardous activities.

4.2.2 An Economic Perspective on Liability for Lawful Acts in International Law

We have seen above that due diligence obligations shift the accident costs either to the responsible state, when it failed to exercise due care, or to the victim state, when the injuring state acted diligently. A strict liability regime, which is ignorant of the fault of the injuring state and which allocates the costs entirely to the injuring state, only provides an alternative in a limited number of constellations, where states engage in ultra-hazardous activities and the focus lies on setting incentives for an optimal level of activity. This raises the question of how losses should be allocated if transboundary damage (or damage to the global commons) is caused although the state under which authority the harmful activity took place exercised due care. The consequence under the law of state responsibility is that the costs are entirely shifted to the victim state, as the injuring state complied with the primary due diligence obligation and thus did not commit an internationally wrongful act ("no liability"). However, such an approach may not be appropriate in all constellations, in particular when one party contributed more to the risk and occurrence of damage and fully internalises the benefits of a potentially harmful activity, whereas the other party has only limited means to avoid the damage by calibrating its own level of precaution and activity. Thus, the question is whether there is a rationale for having a "no-fault liability" regime at the international level, and, if so, under which conditions.

On the domestic level, a consequence of the negligence rule in tort law is that the victim bears the costs of the accident if the injurer was not negligent. Calabresi pointed out that this all-or-nothing approach might be inappropriate when neither party was negligent, but could nonetheless have done something to avoid the loss.[182] With Jeffrey O. Cooper, he developed the idea of loss allocation in the absence of fault on both sides comparable to the splitting analysis under comparative negligence, thus a form of "comparative non-negligence".[183] Shared liability in case of non-negligence but based on relative causal contributions to the loss might not set optimal incentives for both parties, but it may, under certain conditions, create desirable incentives in terms of activity level and thus do better than primary liability rules such as negligence or strict liability.[184] No-fault compensation schemes are not unknown in domestic law, but are usually designed as insurance mechanisms.[185]

In international law, the idea of "no-fault liability" is reflected in the concept of international liability of states for injurious consequences arising out of acts not

---

[182] Guido Calabresi, "The Decision for Accidents: An Approach to Nonfault Allocation of Costs", *Harvard Law Review* 78, no. 4 (1965): 713–745. See also Guido Calabresi and Jeffrey O. Cooper, "New Directions in Tort Law", *Valparaiso University Law Review* 30, no. 3 (1996): 859–884.

[183] Calabresi and Cooper, "New Directions in Tort Law", 877.

[184] Posner and Parisi, *Law and Economics: Elgar Research Reviews in Economics*. Section 7. See, in particular, Francesco Parisi and Vincy Fon, "Comparative Causation", *American Law and Economics Review* 6, no. 2 (2004): 345–368.

[185] Dnes, *Principles of Law and Economics*, 196–197.

prohibited by international law (i.e. liability for lawful acts). This concept primarily focuses on the distribution of risks of hazardous activities and on the allocation of losses in the case transboundary harm occurs despite diligent state behaviour.[186] Liability of states in international law consists in the "duty to take reparatory and – somewhat surprisingly, also preventive – measures vis-à-vis other [s]tates for damage caused, or likely to be caused, by activities carried out under their jurisdiction, irrespective of the unlawfulness of the conduct by the origin [s]tate".[187] The damage, which needs to be transboundary in nature, is caused by activities (e.g. industrial or energy production) which are "usually lawful but hazardous and are carried out by private operators".[188] Examples stem mostly from international environmental law,[189] but can also be found in other contexts, where damage is caused although the state of origin took appropriate measures of prevention (e.g. damage to diplomatic or consular premises despite due diligence of the host state).[190]

The law of state responsibility as reflected in the ARSIWA contains secondary obligations, in particular to provide reparation for injury (e.g. full compensation for damage) in the case of an internationally wrongful act. In comparison, the law of state liability is wider in scope and relates to a set of rules (even though not in the form of absolute obligations) governing, on the one hand, the prevention, and, on the other hand, the consequences of the likely occurrence of harm, for instance, compensation for victims of transboundary damage.[191] Thus, state liability applies when the damage occurs despite compliance with the obligation of prevention. State responsibility residually applies *ex post* to situations where the state of origin took neither the appropriate preventive measures nor the appropriate compensatory measures to remediate the harm, thus setting additional incentives to comply with the liability regime.[192] In addition, although a given activity is potentially harmful, it is considered lawful for equity reasons because the payment of compensation can be negotiated between the states concerned prior to the actual occurrence of harm, which is a form of distributive negotiated justice.[193] In that sense, liability bears structural similarities with state consent to an internationally wrongful act, which is

---

[186] On the historical development of liability in the absence of an internationally wrongful act, see Alan Boyle, "Liability for Injurious Consequences of Acts not Prohibited by International Law", in *The Law of International Responsibility*, ed. James Crawford, Alain Pellet, and Simon Olleson (Oxford: Oxford University Press, 2010), 95–104.

[187] Tanzi, "Liability for Lawful Acts", para. 1.

[188] Ibid.

[189] See further Alena Douhan, "Liability for Environmental Damage", ed. Anne Peters and Rüdiger Wolfrum, *Max Planck Encyclopedia of Public International Law* (Oxford Public International Law: Oxford University Press, 2021), http://opil.ouplaw.com, Article last updated in March 2019.

[190] Tanzi, "Liability for Lawful Acts", para. 1.

[191] Ibid., paras. 2, 27.

[192] Ibid., para. 15.

[193] As compensation is negotiated *ex ante* between the parties involved based on the assessment of future transboundary harm, compensation might fall short of the full reparation available under the law of state responsibility. Ibid., paras. 2, 12.

usually combined with the *ex ante* negotiation of compensation.[194] More generally, the rationale of the liability regime corresponds to the compensation requirement for material loss caused by an act which is exempted from state responsibility due to the successful invocation of a circumstance precluding wrongfulness (Article 27 lit. b) ARSIWA).[195] When a state invokes an excuse (e.g. necessity or *force majeure*) or justification to be exempted from a breach of an international obligation, such an act, which may be considered lawful due to exceptional circumstances, may still entail financial consequences. But the compensation requirement relates only to any material loss caused by the excused or justified act, a concept which is narrower than the concept of damage in the case of reparation for injury caused by an internationally wrongful act.[196]

The liability regime derives from the principle of equitable utilisation of shared resources,[197] the no-harm rule,[198] and the "polluter pays" principle,[199] and contains essentially two types of due diligence obligations:[200] firstly, the due diligence obligation to take appropriate harm prevention measures, and, secondly, if the harm materialises nonetheless, to take appropriate measures to eliminate or mitigate the harm caused, for instance, by negotiating compensation.[201] The first type of obligations is those discussed above with regard to due diligence obligations in international law. As a reflection of the no-harm rule, they have, for instance, been outlined in the ILC Draft Articles on Prevention of Transboundary Harm from Hazardous Activities.[202] These Articles contain several due diligence obligations for the state of origin, most notably to take all appropriate measures to prevent

[194] On a rational choice analysis of consent as a justification for breach of international obligations, see Sect. 5.3.2.1.

[195] Tanzi, "Liability for Lawful Acts", para. 1. For a suggestion on how to allocate the costs following the invocation of the different circumstances precluding wrongfulness, see Sect. 5.4.

[196] ARSIWA Commentaries, Article 27, para. 4. See also Crawford, *State Responsibility: the General Part*, 318.

[197] See further Lilian del Castillo-Laborde, "Equitable Utilization of Shared Resources", ed. Anne Peters and Rüdiger Wolfrum, *Max Planck Encyclopedia of Public International Law* (Oxford Public International Law: Oxford University Press, 2021), http://opil.ouplaw.com, Article last updated in January 2010.

[198] See Sect. 4.1.2.2 on due diligence obligations.

[199] Instead of making states directly liable in international law, states are supposed to internalise the economic costs of pollution prevention by holding the polluter (i.e. the private operator at the origin of the hazardous activity) liable in national law. See further Alan Boyle, "Polluter Pays", ed. Anne Peters and Rüdiger Wolfrum, *Max Planck Encyclopedia of Public International Law* (Oxford Public International Law: Oxford University Press, 2021), http://opil.ouplaw.com, Article last updated in March 2009, para. 14.

[200] Tanzi, "Liability for Lawful Acts", paras. 2, 3.

[201] Ibid.

[202] United Nations International Law Commission, "Articles on the Prevention of Transboundary Harm from Hazardous Activities", in *Report of the Commission to the General Assembly on the Work of its Fifty-Third Session*, 2001 (UN Doc. A/56/10), in *Yearbook of the International Law Commission*, 2001, Volume II, Part Two (UN Doc. A/CN.4/SER.A/2001/Add.1 (Part 2)).

significant transboundary harm or at any event to minimise the risk thereof (Article 3), but also duties of cooperation (Article 4), implementation of monitoring mechanisms in domestic law (Article 5), establishment of an authorisation regime (Article 6) based on the assessment of risk, in particular the environmental impact (Article 7), notification and information of such risks to any affected state (Article 8), and consultation of the states concerned based on an equitable balance of interests (Articles 9 and 10).

The second type of obligations, which is the focus in this section, is specified in the ILC Draft Principles on the Allocation of Loss in the Case of Transboundary Harm Arising out of Hazardous Activities.[203] The purposes of these principles are (i) to ensure prompt and adequate compensation for victims of transboundary damage; and (ii) to preserve and protect the environment in the event of transboundary damage, especially with respect to mitigation of damage to the environment and its restoration or reinstatement (Principle 3). The obligation for the state under whose jurisdiction or control the harmful activity was carried out to ensure prompt and adequate compensation consists primarily in imposing civil liability on the operator, but also in requiring from the operator to establish and maintain financial security such as insurance, bonds, or other financial guarantees to cover claims of compensation, or even in requiring the establishment of industry-wide funds at the national level (Principle 4). Civil liability of the operator is thus the predominant characteristic of the liability regime, while the origin state's duty to make available additional financial resources is only the *ultima ratio*, in the event that the other measures are insufficient to provide adequate compensation (Principle 4 (5)).

Both texts have been commended by the UN General Assembly to the attention of governments, but no decision on the final format of the codification exercise, namely transformation into an international convention, has been taken so far.[204] Only with regard to transboundary effects of specific hazardous activities (e.g. utilisation of an international watercourse within state territory, use of transboundary watercourses, cross-border movements of hazardous wastes, and industrial accidents), states have concluded liability regimes on a conventional basis, including due diligence obligations to mitigate harm, for instance, by discussing the question of compensation.[205]

[203] United Nations International Law Commission, "Draft Principles on the Allocation of Loss in the Case of Transboundary Harm Arising out of Hazardous Activities", in *Report of the Commission to the General Assembly on the Work of its Fifty-Eighth Session*, 2006 (UN Doc. A/61/10), in *Yearbook of the International Law Commission*, 2006, Volume II, Part Two (UN Doc. A/CN.4/SER.A/2006/Add.1 (Part 2)).

[204] United Nations General Assembly, Resolution 62/68, *Consideration of Prevention of Transboundary Harm from Hazardous Activities and Allocation of Loss in the Case of Such Harm*, 6 December 2007 (UN Doc. A/RES/62/68). For the most recent decision on this issue, see United Nations General Assembly, Resolution 74/189, *Consideration of Prevention of Transboundary Harm from Hazardous Activities and Allocation of Loss in the Case of Such Harm*, 18 December 2019 (UN Doc. A/RES/74/189).

[205] See, respectively, Article 7 of the Convention on the Law of the Non-Navigational Uses of International Watercourses; Articles 2 and 3 of the Convention on the Protection and Use of

Moreover, the "polluter pays" principle, while being widely recognised in international environmental law, does not constitute an absolute obligation of loss allocation with the status of customary international law.[206]

Under the liability regime, the obligation to eliminate or mitigate the harm caused by the hazardous activity consists primarily in a due diligence obligation to ensure that an effective system of civil liability is in place in national law, under which individual victims can directly claim compensation from the operator (e.g. the operator of a nuclear power plant). As an expression of the "polluter pays" principle, liability is thus outsourced to private operators, while the state of origin only bears liability as a last resort. In terms of effectiveness, both types of compensation claims bear advantages and disadvantages. From a procedural perspective, claims directed against the operator give access to domestic courts and judgments enforceable in national law, but conflicts of laws can arise regarding the determination of the competent forum and the applicable law between those of the state of origin and the victim state.[207] Interstate liability claims are less confronted with fragmented application of international rules, but face the general enforcement problems of state responsibility, namely that invocation *via* diplomatic protection lies in the discretion of the state of the victim and that judicial assessment is neither compulsory nor enforceable by a central instance.[208] Yet, the fact that only few examples of interstate liability settlement in cases of transboundary harm are known[209] does not mean that states do not solve these disputes bilaterally and negotiate compensation. Regarding the question who ultimately bears the charges of compensation, civil liability has the advantage that it forces the private operator who profits from the activity to internalise the associated risks, but financial capacities may be limited to cover the compensation claim so that financial securities such as insurance or the establishment of an industry-wide fund are necessary.[210] It is necessary that the state of origin steps in as a last resort in the case of insolvency of the operator, even if that means that the costs of the compensatory payment are shifted away internally from the

---

Transboundary Watercourses and International Lakes; Article 4 of the Basel Convention on the Control of Transboundary Movements of Hazardous Wastes and Their Disposal (Basel Convention); and Articles 3 and 6 of the Convention on the Transboundary Effects of Industrial Accidents.

[206] Boyle, "Polluter Pays", paras. 2–6.

[207] Tanzi, "Liability for Lawful Acts", paras. 18–19, 21. Attempts have been made at the regional level to address the conflict of laws issue, but with limited success, see, for instance, Convention on Civil Liability for Damage Resulting from Activities Dangerous to the Environment (opened for signature 21 June 1993, not yet entered into force) Council of Europe Treaty No. 150; Protocol on Civil Liability and Compensation for Damage Caused by the Transboundary Effects of Industrial Accidents on Transboundary Waters (concluded on 21 May 2003, not yet entered into force) 44 *ILM* 258. A successful example of harmonisation of national legal regimes for civil liability regimes is the minimum standards relating to the financial protection against damage resulting from certain peaceful uses of nuclear energy in the Vienna Convention on Civil Liability for Nuclear Damage (concluded 21 May 1963, entered into force 12 November 1977) 1063 *UNTS* 265.

[208] Tanzi, "Liability for Lawful Acts", paras. 18, 21.

[209] Ibid., para. 17.

[210] Ibid., paras. 18, 20.

private operator to the taxpayer.[211] Civil liability and interstate liability for lawful acts in international law are thus complementary. An intermediary approach is international conventions that introduce directly a system of strict liability against private operators, for instance, with regard to shipowners in the case of oil pollution. This regime also provides for a claim settlement fund which is financed by contributions paid by entities that receive certain types of oil by sea transport, and normally not by states.[212]

"No-fault liability" of an injuring state is thus the means of last resort when transboundary harm is caused despite diligent state behaviour. The economic rationale of compensation in the case of lawful acts in international law is to avoid that the state at the origin of the hazardous activity of which it internalises the benefits shifts the externality costs caused by its actions entirely to an innocent victim state or the international community. "No-fault liability" thus complements state responsibility for breach of due diligence obligations when states are not responsible for breach of a primary due diligence obligation, but nonetheless contributed significantly to the transboundary harm and fully internalised the benefits of the activity. However, as the state of origin took appropriate preventive measures, thus explicitly acted lawfully, compensation can only serve to equitably allocate the losses depending on who benefitted from the activity and who contributed to the harm. Thus, the idea of the requirement to mitigate the harm, for instance, by negotiating adequate compensation, is not to set incentives for optimal precaution, but rather to have an impact on the level of activity of the injuring state, which may have contributed to the occurrence of the harm. When compensation is negotiated *ex post*, it can be granted in full or consist in cost-sharing, for instance, when the activity was also beneficial for the international community or when the victim state also contributed to the occurrence of harm. "No-fault liability" can in particular provide useful in constellations where harm is caused to the global commons (i.e. CPR scenarios), and, thus, injuring states should internalise at least partially the negative externalities stemming from their harmful activities. Michael G. Faure and André Nollkaemper argue along these lines in relation to liability for climate change, raising the question whether state liability could extent to compensation of costs incurred as a result of a risk of damage (e.g. adaptation measures).[213] In the particular case of climate change, the damage caused by greenhouse gas emissions is primarily to the common good which is the atmosphere, but the ultimate costs are borne by states most affected by climate change (e.g. by droughts, floods, or extreme weather phenomena). In addition, since there is no direct link between the amount of

---

[211] Ibid., para. 18.

[212] International Convention on Civil Liability for Oil Pollution Damage (concluded 29 November 1969, entered into force 19 June 1975) 973 *UNTS* 3. International Convention on the Establishment of an International Fund for Compensation for Oil Pollution Damage (concluded 18 December 1971, entered into force 16 October 1978) 1110 *UNTS* 57. Both instruments have been amended in 1992.

[213] Faure and Nollkaemper, "International Liability as an Instrument to Prevent and Compensate for Climate Change", 177.

greenhouse gas emissions and the damage caused to the atmosphere, Faure and Nollkaemper propose a rule of proportionate liability, that is depending on the probability of causation and different contributions to the climate change damage.[214] Another way to further develop "no-fault liability" at the international level is to envisage the creation of global funds as, for instance, in the case of compensation for oil pollution damage, but on the interstate level with the aim to mitigate harm from beneficial, but hazardous activities among states.[215] The underlying idea would be to allocate the losses stemming from lawful activities through *ex ante* financial contributions by states (not private operators) which engage in certain potentially harmful activities.

In sum, there is a rationale for having "no-fault liability" regimes at the international level, but only in cases of transboundary harm caused by hazardous activities, usually of private actors under the control or jurisdiction of the state of origin, despite compliance with necessary preventive measures. States have, however, concluded liability regimes, including due diligence obligations to mitigate harm, for instance, by discussing the question of compensation, on a conventional basis only with regard to transboundary effects of a limited number of hazardous activities (e.g. utilisation of an international watercourse within state territory, use of transboundary watercourses, cross-border movements of hazardous wastes, industrial accidents).[216] Although states managed to agree on the draft principles regarding the issue of loss allocation, these do not constitute principles of general international law (unlike the "no-harm rule"). Thus, once states have agreed to include a loss allocation mechanism for a limited number of activities *ex ante* on a conventional basis, they accept to negotiate the concrete measures of mitigating the harm *ex post*, either by outsourcing the risk to the operators *via* a system of civil liability or by negotiating the appropriate amount of compensation. This is in line with domestic tort law, where "no-fault liability" exists only in exceptional circumstances.

Despite their advantages, in particular in constellations of economically beneficial but hazardous activities with the potential to cause transboundary harm, strict liability and liability for lawful acts ("no-fault liability") are the exception in

---

[214] Ibid., 178.

[215] See, for example, the compensation fund for nuclear damage, to which contracting parties contribute by making available public funds in order to increase the amount of compensation compared to an established minimum national amount of compensation. Convention on Supplementary Compensation for Nuclear Damage (concluded 12 September 1997, entered into force 15 April 2015) 3038 *UNTS* 41. For an overview and evaluation of existing compensation funds in international law, see Chie Kojima, "Compensation Fund", ed. Anne Peters and Rüdiger Wolfrum, *Max Planck Encyclopedia of Public International Law* (Oxford Public International Law: Oxford University Press, 2021), http://opil.ouplaw.com, Article last updated in July 2019.

[216] See, respectively, Article 7 of the Convention on the Law of the Non-Navigational Uses of International Watercourses; Articles 2 and 3 of the Convention on the Protection and Use of Transboundary Watercourses and International Lakes; Article 4 of the Basel Convention on the Control of Transboundary Movements of Hazardous Wastes and Their Disposal (Basel Convention); and Articles 3 and 6 of the Convention on the Transboundary Effects of Industrial Accidents.

international law. This explains the importance of the general rule: the concept of objective responsibility, with or without the due diligence standard in primary obligations.

4.3 Conclusion on Responsibility Standards: An Economic Perspective on State Responsibility Based on Illegality

This chapter provided an overview of different responsibility standards in the international law of state responsibility and their incentive structures. The focus was on gaining a better understanding of objective responsibility, that is responsibility based on illegality, from an economic perspective.

It could be seen that the concept of objective responsibility bears, on the one hand, several advantages. Firstly, it is applicable to all constellations of international cooperation (i.e. private goods, club goods, and cooperation over CPRs and GPGs) and thus all types of underlying primary international obligations. That damage is not a requirement for state responsibility does not make a difference in the private law dimension of international law, because in tort-like and contract-like scenarios, reparation of damage is simply transferred to the level of remedies. State responsibility based on illegality rather offers the additional advantage that it also covers scenarios with a purely internal dimension (as often in the case of international human rights violations), and opens the door to other remedies than compensation (e.g. cessation, but also reparation in the forms of restitution or satisfaction) and enforcement by non-directly injured third parties.[217] In particular in GPG constellations, the focus of state responsibility for internationally wrongful acts lies on inducing compliance, because all states in the international community either derive value from the respect of international human rights obligations (i.e. non-use value global public goods) or the protection of the international legal order as such. In the case of *erga omnes* obligations which protect the legal interests of all states in the international community, the notion of legal injury matters above all for third-party enforcement facing itself cooperation problems of a GPG. Thus, there is an economic rationale in excluding damage from the necessary conditions of state responsibility in order to facilitate third-party enforcement. In addition, there is, from an economic perspective, no rationale to distinguish at the level of conditions between delictual and criminal liability, that is between breach of *jus cogens* norms and other international obligations. As outlined before, peremptory norms have a different normative status and can from an economic perspective be considered normative GPG obligations. The distinction is not reflected in the conditions of state

[217] Reparation for injury can be claimed by the injured state or by non-directly injured third states for the benefit of the former (Articles 31, 42, 48 (2) lit. b ARSIWA). Additionally, or in the absence of damage, injured and non-directly injured states can claim cessation and assurances of non-repetition (Articles 30, 42, 48 (2) lit. a ARSIWA).

responsibility and matters only when competing interests are at stake, as in the case of circumstances precluding wrongfulness, because violations of *jus cogens* obligations are considered socially undesirable. In addition, inducing compliance with peremptory norms of international law through a higher deterrence effect is a matter of the concrete design of the obligation, remedies (eventually punitive damages), and enforcement (in particular, effective third-party enforcement).

Secondly, objective state responsibility covers breach of international obligations which contain no element of fault, and are thus similar to non-compliance with regulatory standards in domestic law. This is in particular the case in the public dimension of international law (e.g. emission standards and human rights obligations). In addition, notions of fault may be accounted for with due diligence obligations, as a specific form of primary international obligations, notably referring to constellations where the internationally wrongful act of the state consists in a failure to prevent harmful activities by private actors under its jurisdiction or control. It could be seen that due diligence obligations can set incentives for optimal levels of precautionary care of both potentially responsible and victim states, as well as for optimal activity levels of potential victim states. However, whether primary due diligence obligations can set optimal incentives depends on whether they are fully aligned with the optimal level of precautionary care, thus bearing the risk that potential wrongdoing states take excessive or insufficient precaution. Recourse to the comparison of the relative advantages of substantive *versus* procedural obligations and rules *versus* standards thus demonstrated how difficult it is to design optimal due diligence obligations (as for all primary international obligations) and that complementarity of different design elements is often key to achieve optimal incentives in terms of precaution. The design of international obligations is extremely relevant as it has an impact on the effectiveness of enforcement, which may ensure compensation and thereby compliance in the first place.

On the other hand, in constellations, where a balance needs to be struck between risky but economically beneficial activities (e.g. industrial production, international transportation) and potentially transboundary harm or harm to the global commons, responsibility for breach of primary due diligence obligations should be complemented with liability rules. Firstly, a strict liability regime in international law can be as effective as primary due diligence obligations regulating certain activities (provided these reflect the adequate level of precaution) in setting incentives for optimal precaution, but bears advantages when the focus lies on lowering the activity level of potential injuring states. This is the case when the activity is extremely hazardous and when states are able to directly control the activity (for instance, activities in outer space which are carried out by state agencies and not private operators). There is thus a strong rationale against a general strict liability rule in international law, and states chose to predefine these specific ultra-hazardous activities on a conventional basis in very limited cases, namely strict liability for activities in outer space causing transboundary damage. Secondly, cost allocation under different responsibility rules does not always provide an equitable solution, for instance, when the accident costs are shifted entirely to the potentially injuring state (as under strict liability) or to the responsible state, when it failed to exercise due care (as under responsibility for breach of due diligence obligations), or to the victim state, when the injuring state acted diligently ("no liability"). Losses might have to be allocated differently if transboundary damage (or damage to the global commons) is caused although the state, under which authority the harmful activity took place, exercised due care. This is in particular the case when one party contributed more to the risk and occurrence of damage and fully internalises the benefits of a potentially harmful activity, whereas the other party has only limited means to avoid the damage by calibrating its own level of precaution and activity (especially, when harm occurs to CPRs). This chapter demonstrated that there is a rationale for having "no-fault liability" regimes at the international level, but only in cases of transboundary harm caused by hazardous activities, usually of private actors under the control or jurisdiction of the state of origin, despite compliance with necessary preventive measures. Loss allocation in the case of lawful acts is, however, not a general rule in international law (unlike the "no-harm rule"), and states have agreed to include a loss allocation mechanism only for a limited number of hazardous activities on a conventional basis. In exceptional and pre-defined circumstances, they accept to negotiate concrete measures of harm mitigation, either by outsourcing the risk to the operators *via* a system of civil liability or by negotiating an appropriate amount of compensation. International trust funds, which consist of contributions by certain industries or even public funds of states, are another way to address the issue of transboundary harm and harm to CPRs despite lawful state behaviour.

In sum, objective responsibility mirrors the trade-offs between different aims of state responsibility, namely compliance, flexibility, compensation, enforcement, and cooperation. There is an economic rationale for responsibility based on illegality as a general rule (with a comparative negligence rule as in Article 39 ARSIWA), as long as exceptions are possible which focus on calibrating the level of ultra-hazardous state activities (as under strict liability) or on the allocation of losses in the case of beneficial, but harmful activities under state control (as under liability for lawful acts).

Chapter 5
Exemptions of International State Responsibility: A Rational Choice Analysis of Justifications and Excuses in International Law

5.1 Introduction: An Economic Perspective on Circumstances Precluding Wrongfulness

This chapter analyses from a rational choice perspective the exemptions of state responsibility as laid down in Part one, Chapter V ARSIWA and the extent to which they integrate the protection of community interests.[1] Among the six circumstances precluding wrongfulness of state acts (or, in more general terms, defences) in customary international law exists a conceptual difference between justifications and excuses for breach of primary international obligations, even though no such distinction is mentioned in the ARSIWA.[2] While consent, self-defence, and countermeasures can be understood as justifications, *force majeure*, distress, and necessity may be seen as excuses.[3] One explanation of this categorisation rests on the idea that the former circumstances seemingly render an act lawful, at least as regards consent and self-defence.[4] In contrast, under the latter circumstances, the obligation

[1] For a comprehensive theoretical and doctrinal analysis of exceptions in customary international law and international treaty law, which encompass exemptions of state responsibility, see Lorand Bartels and Federica Paddeu, eds., *Exceptions in International Law* (Oxford: Oxford University Press, 2020).

[2] See, extensively, Federica Paddeu, *Justification and Excuse in International Law: Concept and Theory of General Defences* (Cambridge: Cambridge University Press, 2018). Specifically on the notion of circumstances precluding wrongfulness, see also Federica Paddeu, "Clarifying the Concept of Circumstances Precluding Wrongfulness (Justifications) in International Law," in *Exceptions in International Law*, ed. Lorand Bartels and Federica Paddeu (Oxford: Oxford University Press, 2020).

[3] Crawford, *State Responsibility: the General Part*, 278–279. With reference to United Nations International Law Commission, *Second Report on State Responsibility by Special Rapporteur James Crawford*, Fifty-First Session, 1999 (UN Doc. A/CN.4/498), p. 60, para. 231.

[4] United Nations International Law Commission, *Second Report on State Responsibility by Special Rapporteur James Crawford*, Fifty-First Session, 1999 (UN Doc. A/CN.4/498), p. 60, para. 230.

J. Lemke, *The Protection of Community Interests in the International Law of State Responsibility*, International Law and Economics,
https://doi.org/10.1007/978-3-031-87927-2_5

subsists and continues to exercise an influence on the situation, at least in the case of distress and necessity where one needs to determine whether a superior interest exists compared to the interest protected by the international obligation in question.[5] Another way to explain the difference between justifications and excuses is that in case of the former the defendant state's[6] action relates to some prior action of the plaintiff state[7] (e.g. an expression of consent, an act of aggression, or a wrongful act), and thus the justifying circumstances lie in the realm of the injured plaintiff state (i.e. internal circumstances), meaning that the subsequent breach of international law is rooted in reciprocal behaviour.[8] In contrast, in the case of the three excuses, wrongfulness of a breach of international law can be precluded in cases where a defendant state acts in order to protect a prevailing interest emanating from a source other than the plaintiff state (i.e. an external circumstance).[9] Thus, while both categories of circumstances entail the same consequence in that they preclude wrongfulness of state acts, they differ in their underlying problem constellation.

As regards the three justifications, in the case of consent,[10] the primary obligation continues to govern the relations between the plaintiff and the defendant state, but they have dispensed with it on the particular occasion or for the purpose of the conduct consented to.[11] Similarly, self-defence[12] as an inherent right of states justifies only lawful measures taken in conformity with Article 51 of the UN Charter (e.g. in response to a prior armed attack), which is why there is no breach of the prohibition of the threat or use of force as laid down in Article 2(4) UN Charter in the first place.[13] Countermeasures[14] are measures taken by the defendant state in respect

[5] Ibid.

[6] The defendant state is the state that is alleged of having a committed an international wrongful act and that invokes a circumstance precluding wrongfulness as a defence.

[7] The plaintiff state is the state that is affected by a breach of international law and therefore invokes the responsibility of the defendant state.

[8] ARSIWA Commentaries, Article 25, para. 2. Alan O. Sykes, "Economic "Necessity" in International Law," *American Journal of International Law* 109, no. 2 (2015): 298; Sarah Heathcote, "Circumstances Precluding Wrongfulness in the ILC Articles on State Responsibility: Necessity," in *The Law of International Responsibility*, ed. James Crawford, Alain Pellet, and Simon Olleson (Oxford: Oxford University Press, 2010), 496.

[9] ARSIWA Commentaries, Article 25, para. 2. Sykes, "Economic "Necessity" in International Law," 298; Heathcote, "Circumstances Precluding Wrongfulness in the ILC Articles on State Responsibility: Necessity," in *The Law of International Responsibility*, ed. Crawford, Pellet, and Olleson, 496.

[10] Article 20 ARSIWA.

[11] ARSIWA Commentaries, Article 20, para. 2. United Nations International Law Commission, *Second Report on State Responsibility by Special Rapporteur James Crawford*, Fifty-First Session, 1999 (UN Doc. A/CN.4/498), p. 60, para. 233. See also Crawford, *State Responsibility: the General Part*, 283.

[12] Article 21 ARSIWA.

[13] ARSIWA Commentaries, Article 21, para. 1. See also Crawford, *State Responsibility: the General Part*, 289–290.

[14] Article 22 ARSIWA.

of a prior internationally wrongful act of the plaintiff state and serve principally as a tool to implement state responsibility,[15] in particular to induce compliance with the secondary obligations of cessation and non-repetition of the wrongful act as well as reparation for the injury caused.[16] Since countermeasures are, at their core, an instrument to enforce compliance with international obligations,[17] this justification will be discussed in detail below in Chap. 7.

What unites the three excuses (i.e. *force majeure*, distress, and necessity) is that they all encompass situations where a state is confronted with some unforeseeable and extraordinary circumstances, which make them act in a way that is not in conformity with its international obligations.[18] The rationale behind these excuses is to avoid an overly rigid application of the law in circumstances where there are conflicting values, thus to allow for flexibility at the expense of legal stability.[19] In the case of *force majeure*,[20] a state is compelled to breach international law because its actions are due to circumstances beyond its control, meaning that the state (or its agent) is acting in a completely involuntary manner.[21] A classic example would be natural events such as extreme weather conditions that force an aircraft into foreign airspace. While *force majeure* thus covers situations of compulsion as well as material and absolute impossibility to comply with international law, distress and necessity refer to situations where non-compliance can be excused due to a voluntary choice of the defendant state to protect a higher interest (compared to the interests of the plaintiff state and to the interest of the international community in the respect of the international legal order).[22] In that sense, impossibility is relative as it results from the balancing of diverging interests, and subjective, since its application, which is necessarily unilateral, results from a deliberate choice.[23] Both characteristics (relativity and subjectivity) make necessity (but also distress) particularly interesting for an economic analysis which examines how states make decisions, for instance, between compliance or non-compliance with international law, thus the way

[15] The plaintiff state thus contests the lawfulness of the countermeasure taken by the defendant state.

[16] Article 49 (1) ARSIWA.

[17] See Sect. 2.4 on enforcement of international law and mechanisms of compliance.

[18] Crawford, *State Responsibility: the General Part*, 295.

[19] Heathcote, "Circumstances Precluding Wrongfulness in the ILC Articles on State Responsibility: Necessity," in *The Law of International Responsibility*, ed. Crawford, Pellet, and Olleson, 491.

[20] Article 23 ARSIWA.

[21] ARSIWA Commentaries, Article 25, para. 2. Attila Tanzi, "State of Necessity," ed. Anne Peters and Rüdiger Wolfrum, *Max Planck Encyclopedia of Public International Law* (Oxford Public International Law: Oxford University Press, 2021), http://opil.ouplaw.com, Article last updated in January 2021, para. 2.

[22] ARSIWA Commentaries, Article 25, para. 2. Heathcote, "Circumstances Precluding Wrongfulness in the ILC Articles on State Responsibility: Necessity," in *The Law of International Responsibility*, ed. Crawford, Pellet, and Olleson, 491, 495; Crawford, *State Responsibility: the General Part*, 295, 307.

[23] Heathcote, "Circumstances Precluding Wrongfulness in the ILC Articles on State Responsibility: Necessity," in *The Law of International Responsibility*, ed. Crawford, Pellet, and Olleson, 491, 495.

necessity (or distress) sets incentives for state behaviour. Distress,[24] on the one hand, excuses a specific type of act, which results from the moral choice of an individual state official to save his or her own life or the lives of other persons entrusted to his or her care.[25] Picking up the previous example, distress may be applicable in a situation where a case of emergency (e.g. a technical failure) causes a pilot to voluntarily change the course of an aircraft into foreign airspace to prevent a crash. Distress is limited to circumstances where human life is at stake and where there exists a direct relationship between the acting state organ and the person whose life is in peril.[26]

Necessity,[27] on the other hand, serves at protecting an essential interest of the state against a grave danger and thus covers emergency situations more generally, such as humanitarian situations.[28] An example for necessity is the protection of the environment, for instance, when a state bombs a foreign vessel to avert further oil pollution.[29] The necessity excuse appears particularly interesting for the purpose of this book as it deals predominantly with the issue of balancing competing interests, including community interests. Necessity as a flexibility provision needs to take into account the private and public dimensions of international law and set different incentives depending on the character of the international obligation in question as well as the nature of the essential interest protected in necessity. Rational choice theory can thus serve to analyse how the necessity excuse by allocating legal duties sets incentives to provide GPGs or protect CPRs.[30]

All six circumstances precluding wrongfulness entail the same exception in the case of breach of *jus cogens* norms (Article 26 ARSIWA) and the same consequences (Article 27 ARSIWA). The exception (or additional condition framed in negative terms) in Article 26 ARSIWA provides that no circumstance precluding wrongfulness can be invoked in the case of violations of *jus cogens* obligations, so that peremptory norms of general international law need to be complied with under all circumstances.[31] Hence, for some fundamental international norms, there is the

---

[24] Article 24 ARSIWA.

[25] ARSIWA Commentaries, Article 25, para. 2.

[26] Tanzi, "State of Necessity," para. 2.

[27] Article 25 ARSIWA.

[28] ARSIWA Commentaries, Article 25, para. 2. Tanzi, "State of Necessity," para. 2. Consequently, according to the ILC, a situation where the survival of a state's population is at stake is categorised as necessity and not distress. See Heathcote, "Circumstances Precluding Wrongfulness in the ILC Articles on State Responsibility: Necessity," in *The Law of International Responsibility*, ed. Crawford, Pellet, and Olleson, 495.

[29] Example taken from the British bombing of the Liberian-flagged oil tanker *Torrey Canyon* in 1967 which ran aground off the coast of Cornwall, spilling large amounts of oil towards the British coastline.

[30] Allocation of duties is to be understood in the sense that the necessity excuse constitutes an exemption from an international obligation. In a situation of necessity, a state is under no duty to comply with a primary obligation.

[31] On the definition of the concept of *jus cogens* norms, its role as a conflict of norms rule, and its congruence with the concept of global public goods, see Sect. 3.3.2.

presumption that the interest in upholding respect for the international legal order prevails over any unforeseeable and extraordinary circumstances.[32] This chapter assesses the underlying logic of this conflict of norms rule, notably whether there is an economic rationale to applying it in the case of all six circumstances precluding wrongfulness as well as to restricting it to *jus cogens* norms and not extending it to GPG and CPR obligations more generally.

Article 27 ARSIWA determines the consequences of invoking a circumstance precluding wrongfulness. First, the provision deals with the effect of invoking such an exceptional circumstance on the international obligation in question. Article 27 lit. a) ARSIWA provides that the obligation needs to be complied with if and to the extent that the circumstance no longer exists. Hence, such circumstance only defends against the obligation and justifies a state's non-performance for the duration and within the scope of the circumstance, but the obligation and the primary rule underlying it remain in place.[33] This is in line with the underlying rationale of flexibility provisions in international law, which allow non-compliance on an exceptional basis but have no effect on the validity of the primary international obligation in question and will thus not be further enquired here.

Second, Article 27 lit. b) ARSIWA provides as a consequence of invoking a circumstance precluding wrongfulness that compensation needs to be paid for any material loss caused by the act in question.[34] The rationale is that sometimes a state relying on a circumstance precluding wrongfulness may nonetheless be expected to make good any material loss suffered by a state affected by that act.[35] Hence, this provision determines that and how the costs incurred following the invocation of a circumstance precluding wrongfulness are allocated between the states involved.[36] This provision is different from the obligation to make full reparation for the injury caused by an internationally wrongful act.[37] Reparation includes compensation for

[32] On the work of the ILC on how to deal with conflicts of norms involving *jus cogens* obligations which ultimately led to the general provision in Article 26 ARSIWA, see Maja Ménard, "Circumstances Precluding Wrongfulness in the ILC Articles on State Responsibility: Compliance with Peremptory Norms," in *The Law of International Responsibility*, ed. James Crawford, Alain Pellet, and Simon Olleson (Oxford: Oxford University Press, 2010), 449–453.

[33] Heathcote, "Circumstances Precluding Wrongfulness in the ILC Articles on State Responsibility: Necessity," in *The Law of International Responsibility*, ed. Crawford, Pellet, and Olleson, 494; Crawford, *State Responsibility: the General Part*, 281.

[34] Article 27 lit. b) ARSIWA reads as follows: "The invocation of a circumstance precluding wrongfulness in accordance with this chapter is without prejudice to: [...] (b) the question of compensation for any material loss caused by the act in question." On this provision, see generally Mathias Forteau, "Reparation in the Event of a Circumstance Precluding Wrongfulness," in *The Law of International Responsibility*, ed. James Crawford, Alain Pellet, and Simon Olleson (Oxford: Oxford University Press, 2010), 887–893. See also, Paddeu, *Justification and Excuse in International Law: Concept and Theory of General Defences*, 77–94.

[35] ARSIWA Commentaries, Article 27, para. 4. See also Crawford, *State Responsibility: the General Part*, 318.

[36] ARSIWA Commentaries, Article 27, para. 4.

[37] Article 31 ARSIWA.

the damage caused by an internationally wrongful act, which is any financially assessable damage including loss of profits.[38] Even if this remedy is not applicable in the presence of circumstances precluding the wrongfulness of a state act, the invocation of such an exemption may still entail financial consequences. There is, in principle, a compensation requirement for any material loss caused by the excused or justified act, even if the concept of material loss is narrower than the one of damage, which can also encompass moral damage.[39]

When drafting the ARSIWA, there was no consensus among states on which circumstances precluding wrongfulness should induce an obligation to compensate the affected state for any material loss and whether this obligation also extends to innocent third states.[40] As a result, the compensation requirement in Article 27 lit. b) ARSIWA was framed in general terms as a without prejudice clause which does not specify when compensation is payable.[41] Thus, in practice, it is left to the states involved in a given dispute to agree with any affected states on "the possibility and extent of compensation payable".[42] Alternatively, international adjudicators will have to decide on the financial consequences of situations in which wrongfulness is precluded.[43] According to the ARSIWA Commentaries, the range of possible situations covered by the six circumstances precluding wrongfulness "is such that to lay down a detailed regime for compensation is not appropriate".[44] However, this chapter will demonstrate that taking an economic perspective on the six circumstances precluding wrongfulness allows one to sketch out constellations in which compensation can be considered appropriate.

The optimal allocation of duties and costs are classic law and economics questions because legal obligations and the consequences attached to their violation set incentives for the relevant actors. These two questions build the framework for the economic analysis of the six circumstances precluding wrongfulness as they constitute exemptions from international legal obligations and contain certain financial consequences following their invocation. This chapter will first analyse the necessity excuse because it is the broadest in scope and deals predominantly with the issue of balancing competing interests, including community interests. Insights from this

[38] Article 36 ARSIWA.

[39] ARSIWA Commentaries, Article 27, para. 4. See also Crawford, *State Responsibility: the General Part*, 318.

[40] Ibid., 319. See also United Nations International Law Commission, *Second Report on State Responsibility by Special Rapporteur James Crawford*, Fifty-First Session, 1999 (UN Doc. A/CN.4/498), pp. 84–85, paras. 340, 348.

[41] ARSIWA Commentaries, Article 27, paras. 1, 6. Forteau, "Reparation in the Event of a Circumstance Precluding Wrongfulness," in *The Law of International Responsibility*, ed. Crawford, Pellet, and Olleson, 892.

[42] ARSIWA Commentaries, Article 27, para. 6.

[43] Crawford, *State Responsibility: the General Part*, 320. See also United Nations International Law Commission, *Yearbook of the International Law Commission*, 1999, Volume I (UN Doc. A/CN.4/SER.A/1999), p. 176, para. 68.

[44] ARSIWA Commentaries, Article 27, para. 6.

rational choice analysis will then be transferred to the other five circumstances precluding wrongfulness in international law. The last section concludes notably by providing an overview on when the compensation requirement is economically justified.

5.2 A Rational Choice Analysis of the Necessity Excuse in International Law

Questions of necessity are very topical in the international legal discourse and have received particular attention in the field of international investment law in the context of the Argentinian economic crisis during the 1990s. In several arbitration cases, Argentina invoked necessity in order to justify breach of investor protection obligations deriving from a bilateral investment treaty with the United States.[45]

It is thus not surprising that scholars working in the law and economics tradition have focused in their research on necessity in the investment law context, on economic hardship as a circumstance invoked to defend violations thereof, and on the application of (economic) contract theory to explain the conditions and consequences of the necessity excuse.[46] The concept of necessity in customary international law as reflected in Article 25 ARSIWA,[47] however, is much broader as it constitutes a circumstance precluding wrongfulness of state acts that is part of the secondary law of state responsibility and as such applicable to all areas and kinds of

---

[45] See, in particular, *CMS Gas Transmission Company v. Argentine Republic*, Award, 12 May 2005, ICSID Case No. ARB/01/8; *CMS Gas Transmission Company v. Argentine Republic*, Decision on the application for annulment, 25 September 2007, ICSID Case No. ARB/01/8. On this case and the invocation of necessity in international investment law more generally, see Anne van Aaken, "Zwischen Scylla und Charybdis: Völkerrechtlicher Staatsnotstand und Internationaler Investitionsschutz. Eine Anmerkung zur ICSID-Entscheidung CMS Gas Transmission Company v. Argentinien, 12.5.2005 - ICSID Case No. Arb/01/8," *Zeitschrift für Vergleichende Rechtswissenschaft (ZVglRWiss), Archiv für Internationales Wirtschaftsrecht* 105, no. 4 (2006): 544–569.

[46] See, in particular, van Aaken, "International Investment Law between Commitment and Flexibility: A Contract Theory Analysis," 507–538; Sykes, "Economic "Necessity" in International Law," 296–323.

[47] Article 25 ARSIWA reads as follows:

"1. Necessity may not be invoked by a State as a ground for precluding the wrongfulness of an act not in conformity with an international obligation of that State unless the act:

(a) is the only way for the State to safeguard an essential interest against a grave and imminent peril; and

(b) does not seriously impair an essential interest of the State or States towards which the obligation exists, or of the international community as a whole.

2. In any case, necessity may not be invoked by a State as a ground for precluding wrongfulness if:

(a) the international obligation in question excludes the possibility of invoking necessity; or

(b) the State has contributed to the situation of necessity."

obligations in international law. Moreover, necessity can be invoked to protect other than mere economic interests, providing they pass the threshold of being essential, for instance, in order to protect the environment.[48] If "[a]pplying economic theory to the analysis of economic 'necessity' defenses in international law is highly desirable [...]",[49] then it is also the case for the analysis of other essential interests invoked in the name of necessity. It follows that an economic analysis of necessity in international law should draw on the functions of necessity in domestic liability law more generally, that is, contract and tort theory. It also requires taking into account the characteristics of the international legal order, which contains a private and a public dimension.[50]

This economic perspective on the necessity excuse is also what distinguishes this contribution from the legal literature on necessity in the international law of state responsibility. The work of legal scholars has predominantly focused on the historical genesis of the necessity excuse in international law, its abuse by states to defend against severe breaches of fundamental international legal norms, as well as its current understanding, its acceptance as a principle of customary international law, and its application to different areas of international law.[51] In contrast, this section consists of a positive analysis (in the social science sense) of how the current conditions of the necessity excuse (i.e. the allocation of duties) and the consequences of its invocation (i.e. the allocation of costs) are setting incentives for states. It also aims to make some normative suggestions for situations where the current allocation of duties and costs is not considered optimal.

This section on necessity is structured as follows: In a first step, it presents the normative framework used for the subsequent evaluation, namely the aims and problems of the necessity excuse in international law with reference to economic

[48] See, for instance, *Gabčíkovo-Nagymaros Project (Hungary v. Slovakia)*, Judgment.

[49] Anne van Aaken, "On the Necessity of Necessity Measures: A Response to Alan O. Sykes," *AJIL Unbound* 109 (2015): 181.

[50] See Chap. 3, in particular Sect. 3.1.

[51] The legal literature addressing the necessity excuse in international law includes, amongst others, Burleigh Cushing Rodick, *The Doctrine of Necessity in International Law* (New York: Columbia University Press, 1928); Julio Barboza, "Necessity (Revisited) in International Law," in *Essays in International Law in Honour of Judge Manfred Lachs / Études de Droit International en l'honneur du Juge Manfred Lachs*, ed. Jerzy Makarczyk (The Hague: Martinus Nijhoff Publishers, 1984), 27–43; Jean Salmon, "Faut-Il Codifier L'état de Nécessité en Droit International?," in *Essays in International Law in Honour of Judge Manfred Lachs / Études de Droit International en l'honneur du Juge Manfred Lachs*, ed. Jerzy Makarczyk (The Hague: Martinus Nijhoff Publishers, 1984), 235–270; Roman Boed, "State of Necessity as a Justification for Internationally Wrongful Conduct," *Yale Human Rights and Development Law Journal* 3 (2000): 1–44; Heathcote, "Circumstances Precluding Wrongfulness in the ILC Articles on State Responsibility: Necessity," in *The Law of International Responsibility*, ed. Crawford, Pellet, and Olleson, 491–501; Sarah Cassella, *La Nécessité en Droit International: de L'état de Nécessité aux Situations de Nécessité* (Leiden: Martinus Nijhoff Publishers, 2011); Robert D. Sloane, "On the Use and Abuse of Necessity in the Law of State Responsibility," *American Journal of International Law* 106, no. 3 (2012): 447–508; Crawford, *State Responsibility: the General Part*, 305–315; Paddeu, *Justification and Excuse in International Law: Concept and Theory of General Defences*, chap. 8.

theories of contracts, tort and public international law. In a second step, it analyses in detail the conditions of necessity, with a particular focus on what does and should constitute the essential interest to be protected in necessity and the conclusions to draw in case of competing essential interests protected by the international obligation in question. In a third step, it looks at the financial consequences of invoking necessity and determines the circumstances in which the compensation requirement is optimal. The section concludes with concrete suggestions on how to improve the necessity provision in order to set stronger incentives for the provision of GPGs and the protection of CPRs.

5.2.1 Aims and Problems of the Necessity Excuse in the Domestic and the International Legal Order

Whether and in which constellations the conditions and consequences of the necessity excuse are setting optimal incentives for states (i.e. whether the law is economically justified) depends on what one defines from a normative perspective as the rationale of the necessity excuse in the international legal order. Hence, it is important to clarify at the outset what the reasons for the necessity excuse are and which problems it creates that justify the compensation requirement.

In the legal literature, there are different modern explanations of why necessity should have a place in the international legal order.[52] On the one hand, rooted in the historical foundation of natural law, is the fairness argument, that is, the idea that the necessity principle is an expression of equity, which requires that legal rules may not be too rigidly applied in particular urgent circumstances in order to account for conflicting values.[53] On the other hand, necessity has been approached from a utilitarian angle, emphasising its link with the principles of proportionality and reasonableness.[54] Equally, the compensation requirement can be justified both with the argument of optimal cost allocation as well as fairness considerations.

---

[52] With reference to different historical schools of thought, see Heathcote, "Circumstances Precluding Wrongfulness in the ILC Articles on State Responsibility: Necessity," in *The Law of International Responsibility*, ed. Crawford, Pellet, and Olleson, 492. For an extensive historical overview of the concept of necessity in international law, see Cassella, *La Nécessité en Droit International: de L'état de Nécessité aux Situations de Nécessité.*

[53] This understanding is reflected in the expression *summum jus, summa injuria* ("extreme justice is extreme injustice"), attributed to Cicero. Heathcote, "Circumstances Precluding Wrongfulness in the ILC Articles on State Responsibility: Necessity," in *The Law of International Responsibility*, ed. Crawford, Pellet, and Olleson, 492–493. With reference to United Nations International Law Commission, *Addendum to the Eighth Report on State Responsibility by Special Rapporteur Roberto Ago*, Thirty-Second Session, 1980, in *Yearbook of the International Law Commission*, 1980, Volume II, Part One (UN Doc. A/CN.4/318/Add.5-7), p. 51, para. 80.

[54] Heathcote, "Circumstances Precluding Wrongfulness in the ILC Articles on State Responsibility: Necessity," in *The Law of International Responsibility*, ed. Crawford, Pellet, and Olleson, 493.

In order to determine the aims and problems of the necessity excuse in international law, this section draws on the economic rationale behind the concept of necessity in domestic liability law (i.e. economic theories of contracts and tort), distinguishing between private necessity and public necessity. It subsequently transfers these insights to the international legal order with its private and public dimensions. Other authors have already discussed the functions of necessity in international law from an economic perspective, following the same approach of building on the economic rationale of analogues defences in domestic law.[55] Therefore, this section only clarifies the normative framework that is used for the subsequent analysis.[56]

5.2.1.1 Aims and Problems of Private Necessity in Contract and Tort Law

In domestic liability law which regulates compensation claims among private persons, both contract and tort law know the concept of a private necessity excuse. From a legal perspective, the related doctrines might be termed differently, but from an economic perspective, they are based on similar considerations.[57]

Contract Theory: The Economics of Impossibility and Impracticability
In contractual relations, it is often exigent economic circumstances that create a situation that inhibits the debtor to comply with his or her contractual obligations.[58] Unless the necessity defence is explicitly provided for in the contract, the default rules contained in contract law apply.[59] These are the related doctrines of impossibility and impracticability, which are enshrined in the common and civil law traditions.[60] While the first concept relates to situations where compliance with contractual obligations becomes impossible, for instance, because the object to be sold was destroyed, the second covers situations where compliance becomes

---

[55] van Aaken, "International Investment Law between Commitment and Flexibility: A Contract Theory Analysis," 507–538; Sykes, "Economic "Necessity" in International Law," 296–323.

[56] For an overview of the objectives of the international law of state responsibility, see Chap. 3.

[57] Similarly, with regard to precaution, Cooter argues that there is unity in torts, contracts, and property, hence of the common law, at the simplest level of economic analysis. Robert Cooter, "Unity in Tort, Contract, and Property: The Model of Precaution," *California Law Review* 73, no. 1 (1985): 1–51.

[58] Sykes, "Economic "Necessity" in International Law," 300.

[59] Ibid. This is similar in international law, where we find necessity-like provisions in international treaties, such as international investment law, but there is also a default rule of necessity in the customary international law of state responsibility.

[60] See, for instance, § 261 of the Restatement (Second) of Contracts (1981). German contract law, for instance, provides that the performance claim is excluded insofar as performance is impossible and that the debtor may refuse performance to the extent that such performance would require an effort which would be grossly disproportionate to the creditor's interest in performance (§ 275 BGB).

inappropriately expensive and thus impracticable from a commercial point of view.[61] To put it more generally, performance excuses in contract law determine the rights and obligations of the contractual parties "in the event of various unspecified, often unanticipated, and sometimes exigent contingencies".[62]

From an economic perspective, the underlying rationale of these exceptions is to facilitate efficient deviation from contractual commitments because compliance has become extraordinarily costly.[63] This idea is rooted in the law and economics concept of efficient breach of contract.[64] In other words, in contracting, there is a trade-off between making a credible commitment and allowing for flexibility *ex post* in the presence of certain exigent circumstances.[65] Thus, as regards the conditions under which a performance excuse can be invoked, the question is always how to strike the right balance between these two goals, that is, in which circumstances, stability of the law should prevail over flexibility and *vice versa*.

However, the major problem with these performance excuses is that they can bring about adverse consequences. The possibility of being discharged from contractual obligations can diminish the incentive of the promisor to take precautions to avoid non-compliance, for instance, by gathering information about possible adverse events in order to protect against them or take out insurance.[66] In economic theory, this is commonly known as a moral hazard problem.[67] In other words contract law also needs to set incentives to counter *ex post* opportunistic behaviour of the debtor. This risk of opportunistic breach of contract inherent in necessity-like provisions is reinforced by the problem of information asymmetries. Because it is difficult for the creditor to determine whether the conditions for the performance excuse are fulfilled (i.e. the observability and verifiability problem), there is a risk of opportunistic breach of contractual obligations by the debtor.[68]

The crucial question is thus how the risks should be distributed between the contractual parties or which party should ultimately bear the losses in the presence of

[61] Jeffrey Lehman and Shirelle Phelps, eds., *West's Encyclopedia of American Law*, 2nd ed. (Detroit: Thomson/Gale, 2005), s.v. "impossibility". Retrieved from https://legal-dictionary.thefreedictionary.com/Impossibility (last accessed on 30 January 2022).

[62] Sykes, "Economic "Necessity" in International Law," 300.

[63] Ibid.

[64] The concept of efficient breach of contract, that is, the idea that a rational debtor will prefer breach of contract and the payment of damages over compliance, when the breach is efficient, can be traced back to Steven Shavell, who concluded that damage measures set incentives for parties to behave as they would have under a fully specified contract. Shavell, "Damage Measures for Breach of Contract," 466–490. See Sect. 3.2.2.

[65] van Aaken, "International Investment Law between Commitment and Flexibility: A Contract Theory Analysis," 11.

[66] Sykes, "Economic "Necessity" in International Law," 302. See also, Alan O. Sykes, "The Doctrine of Commercial Impracticability in a Second-Best World," *Journal of Legal Studies* 19, no. 1 (1990): 43–94.

[67] On moral hazard, see footnote 252 in Chap. 2.

[68] On the terms "observability" and "verifiability", see Sect. 4.1.1.

exigent circumstances. Richard A. Posner and Andrew M. Rosenfield have argued that "economic analysis suggests that the loss should be placed on the party who is the superior (that is, lower-cost) risk bearer".[69] In order to determine which party is the superior risk bearer, according to them, three factors are relevant: knowledge of the magnitude of the loss, knowledge of the probability that it will occur, and (other) insurance costs.[70] Contract law considers the superior risk bearer usually to be the promisor. Contract law rules force the debtor to internalise the adverse consequences of his or her actions, for instance, with the obligation to pay expectation damages, even in the presence of exigent circumstances, in order to uphold the deterrence effect of contractual liability rules.[71]

In sum, performance excuses in contract law have the advantage of inducing efficient contracting (i.e. preventing socially inefficient adherence to contractual obligations). Yet, they create the disadvantage of disincentivising debtors to take precautions against non-compliance (i.e. moral hazard problem), which explains the requirement to pay compensation in the case of impossibility or impracticability.

Tort Theory: The Economics of Private Necessity

In domestic tort law, the necessity defence has long been recognised as common law and is also part of statutory law in many states that follow a civil law tradition.[72] The necessity defence typically includes the following elements: "(1) the defendant acted to avoid a significant risk of harm; (2) no adequate lawful means could have been used to escape the harm; and (3) the harm avoided was greater than that caused by breaking the law".[73] The classic examples are cases that involve a trespass on property to save one's life or property.[74] This is the reason why this concept is generally referred to as "private necessity".[75]

---

[69] Posner and Rosenfield, "Impossibility and Related Doctrines in Contract Law: An Economic Analysis," 117.

[70] Ibid. It should be noted here that the possibility of insurance does not exist in classic inter-state relations. Thus, precaution is the only means to prevent a situation of impossibility or impracticability.

[71] Sykes, "Economic "Necessity" in International Law," 302. German contract law, for instance, provides that the debtor has to pay damages in case of impossibility (§§ 280 I, III, 283 in conjunction with § 275 BGB).

[72] See, for instance, §§ 196, 197 of the Restatement (Second) of Torts (1965), Article 7:101 of the Principles of European Tort Law. See generally, John Alan Cohan, "Private and Public Necessity and the Violation of Property Rights," *North Dakota Law Review* 83 (2007): 651–733.

[73] Lehman and Phelps, *West's Encyclopedia of American Law*, s.v. "necessity". Retrieved from https://legal-dictionary.thefreedictionary.com/necessity (last accessed on 30 January 2022).

[74] Bryan A. Garner, ed., *Black's Law Dictionary*, 8th ed. (St. Paul, MN: Thomson West, 2004), s.v. "private necessity". ("A necessity that involves only the defendant's personal interest and thus provides only a limited privilege. For example, if the defendant harms the plaintiff's dock by keeping a boat moored to the dock during a hurricane, the defendant can assert private necessity bust must compensate the plaintiff for the dock's damage.")

[75] The private necessity doctrine in United States common law dates back to *Vincent v. Lake Erie Transp. Co.*, 109 Minn. 456, 124 N.W. 221 (1910). See also, § 197 of the Restatement (Second) of Torts (1965).

Necessity in tort law differs from performance excuses in contract law in that, amongst others, (i) the underlying relationship between the parties is non-contractual, and (ii) typically threats of physical harm create a condition of necessity. Yet, the rationale behind the necessity defence is similar in that, in particular situations, a breach of the law is more advantageous to society than the consequence of strict adherence to the law.[76] From an economic perspective, "acts of necessity are efficient acts", because the purpose of the necessity defence is "to enable an actor to avoid a greater harm either by causing a lesser harm at the expense of the plaintiff or by violating an otherwise applicable legislative enactment".[77] Such necessity privilege, however, leads—as in contract law—to a moral hazard problem, because "actors will take risks that imperil them to an excessive degree if they can save themselves [from liability] by imposing costs on others".[78] Similar to contract law, this moral hazard problem is reinforced by the challenge of the plaintiff or the adjudicator to observe and verify *ex post* the information leading to the defendant's necessity privilege.[79]

Therefore, the private necessity doctrine provides that the defendant who acts out of necessity must pay for the actual harm caused to the plaintiff.[80] This compensation requirement eliminates the inefficiencies resulting from a liability exemption, since the defendant is forced to internalise the costs and benefits of his actions, including those preceding the act causing the harm to the plaintiff.[81] Another possibility to counter the moral hazard problem is that a tortfeasor loses the necessity privilege if imprudence contributed to the condition of necessity.[82]

In conclusion, private necessity in tort law prevents socially inefficient adherence to the law in situations where a defendant avoids a greater harm by causing a lesser harm at the expense of the plaintiff. However, it also has the downside of disincentivising actors to take precautions against non-compliance (i.e. moral hazard problem), which in turn explains the requirement to pay compensation in the case of private necessity.

---

[76] Lehman and Phelps, *West's Encyclopedia of American Law*, s.v. "necessity" Retrieved from https://legal-dictionary.thefreedictionary.com/necessity (last accessed on 30 January 2022).

[77] Sykes, "Economic "Necessity" in International Law," 298.

[78] Ibid., 299.

[79] Ibid.

[80] See *Vincent v. Lake Erie Transp. Co.*, 109. In German tort law, see, for instance, §§ 228 and 904 BGB.

[81] Sykes, "Economic "Necessity" in International Law," 299. For a justification based on fairness considerations, see Cohan, "Private and Public Necessity and the Violation of Property Rights," 732.

[82] Sykes, "Economic "Necessity" in International Law," 299.

5.2.1.2 Aims and Problems of Public Necessity in Tort Law

In domestic tort law, the scope of the necessity defence also depends on whether the actor is serving his or her own private interests or the interests of third parties.[83] If the defendant uses or destroys the plaintiff's property to prevent a greater harm to the community as a whole, thus acts in the public interest, he or she can invoke the defence of public necessity.[84] Examples are the destruction of a house to prevent the spread of a fire to the rest of the town or the destruction of a boat to avoid pollution of the coastal environment. The rationale underlying the public necessity doctrine in tort law is that the potential harm to society requires the destruction or use of private property for the greater good.[85]

The public necessity defence shields the defendant from liability, because efficient acts would be discouraged if he or she were required to compensate the plaintiff and thus to bear the costs of the act without recovering the benefits, which fall on the community at large.[86] Thus, without the public necessity defence, tort liability would inhibit socially beneficial decisions.[87] The underlying economic problem is the provision of public goods, and less—as in private necessity—the moral hazard problem, because actors theoretically have no personal interest in opportunistic non-compliance as they do not internalise the benefits of their actions (i.e. positive externalities).[88] When ultimately one private individual has to bear the costs of the incident, losses are allocated rather to the plaintiff than to the defendant acting for the benefit of the public at large.[89] Otherwise, the deterrence effect of liability would further aggravate the incentive problem which private actors face for the provision of public goods. Shifting the costs entirely to the plaintiff may, however, not be an equitable solution, as the costs should rather be borne by the community, which benefits from the provision of the public good. This is why exceptions exist, for instance, when the actor is a public official and compensation is provided by the state

[83] Ibid. Situations where a defendant caused harm to the plaintiff to safe someone else's life or property (i.e. third-party interest protection) are closer to private necessity than public necessity, which covers situations where a defendant causes harm to a plaintiff in order to protect the community as a whole.

[84] Garner, *Black's Law Dictionary*, s.v. "public necessity". ("A necessity that involves the public interest and thus completely excuses the defendant's liability. For example, if the defendant destroys the plaintiff's house to stop the spread of a fire that threatens the town, the defendant can assert public necessity.")

[85] The public necessity doctrine in United States common law dates back to *Surocco v. Geary*, 3 Cal. 69 (1853). See also, § 196 of the Restatement (Second) of Torts (1965).

[86] Sykes, "Economic "Necessity" in International Law," 299–300.

[87] Ibid., 300.

[88] Yet, if they contributed to the risk of harm to the community, the invocation of necessity should be excluded.

[89] For a justification based on fairness considerations, see Cohan, "Private and Public Necessity and the Violation of Property Rights," 733.

or when the law foresees other ways to transfer the losses borne by the victim to the community.[90]

5.2.1.3 Aims and Problems of Necessity in International Law

The preceding overview of necessity-like provisions in domestic law offers valuable insights for the aims and problems of the necessity excuse in the international legal order. Scholars that have discussed the functions of necessity in international law from an economic perspective also have built on the economic rationale of analogues defences in domestic liability law.[91] Yet, in this regard, they have focused only on the private dimension of the international legal order. In this private dimension, it is reasonable to draw on the economic rationale behind the concept of private necessity, which is similar in domestic contract and tort law.[92]

Hence, from economic theories of contracts and tort derives that the main function of private necessity on the international level is to mitigate the trade-off between, on the one hand, compliance with international obligations (i.e. credible commitments), and, on the other hand, flexibility in the presence of unforeseen or extraordinary circumstances.[93] The resulting moral hazard problem is then addressed with the requirement to pay compensation. Accordingly, Sarah Cassella argues that necessity in international law is about preventing or distributing excessive social costs which would derive from the strict application of the law.[94]

However, the international legal order shows also the characteristics of a public dimension,[95] where state responsibility rules follow the objective to induce compliance with community interest norms, that is international obligations regulating GPGs and CPRs. In the public dimension, it is reasonable to draw on the economic rationale behind the concept of public necessity in domestic tort law. According to this doctrine, a defendant is excused from liability in situations where he or she acted in order to protect a public interest and exempted from compensating the victim.[96]

---

[90] See ibid.

[91] van Aaken, "International Investment Law between Commitment and Flexibility: A Contract Theory Analysis," 507–538; Sykes, "Economic "Necessity" in International Law," 296–323.

[92] For more details on the analogy between contract and tort law and the private dimension of international law, see Sect. 3.2.

[93] See, in particular, van Aaken, "International Investment Law between Commitment and Flexibility: A Contract Theory Analysis," 11.

[94] Cassella, *La Nécessité en Droit International: de L'état de Nécessité aux Situations de Nécessité*, 515–519. Reviewed in: Federica I. Paddeu, "Book Review: Sarah Cassella, La Nécessité en Droit International: de L'état de Nécessité aux Situations de Nécessité (Leiden, Martinus Nijhoff Publishers, 2011)," *The British Yearbook of International Law* 82, no. 1 (2011): 505–508. Sarah Cassella borrows from law and economics to discuss the function of necessity in international law, yet without answering the question how the costs are and should be allocated, including in the public dimension of state responsibility in international law.

[95] On the objectives of state responsibility in the public dimension of international law, see Sect. 3.3.

[96] Alan O. Sykes refers to the concept of public necessity in tort law in his discussion of the functions of necessity in international law, but does not raise and answer the question how this concept could be integrated in the international law of state responsibility, focusing only on the

The underlying rationale is thus to not disincentivise an actor to protect a community interest by imposing a requirement to compensate any potential victim. On the international level, public necessity would relate to situations where a state breaches an international obligation in order to protect a community interest, which would usually take the form of a best-shot global public good.[97] Yet, the general rule in the law of state responsibility is that the state invoking the necessity defence is obliged to compensate the victim state for any material loss caused, independent of the character of the essential interest to be protected. Since international law should set incentives for states to provide GPGs and protect CPRs, the necessity excuse also needs to ensure that actions that are beneficial to the international community are not deterred. Thus, the conditions and consequences of the necessity excuse should at least not inhibit GPG provision.

In conclusion, an economic analysis of the necessity excuse needs to focus on how it reconciles multiple objectives alongside the two dimensions of the international legal order. Compliance with different types of international legal obligations (i.e. private good, club good, CPR or GPG obligations) needs to be balanced against flexibility in the presence of unforeseen circumstances (i.e. private or public necessity, depending on the objective of the breach). For instance, the necessity provision should deter opportunistic breach, but without discouraging the provision of GPGs. The conditions and consequences of the necessity excuse then need to be measured against all of these functions, thereby pointing out the trade-offs that are achieved in different constellations. The following analysis is therefore constructed around a twofold research question: in light of these conflicting aims, under which conditions should a state be excused from a breach of international law, and who should bear the costs of such exceptional circumstances? Or in other words, what is the optimal allocation of duties and costs in order to reconcile the aims of necessity in international law, and how should this allocation change depending on the underlying constellation?

5.2.2 *On the Allocation of Duties: Conditions of Private and Public Necessity in International Law*

Among the six circumstances precluding wrongfulness, the concept of necessity is not only the broadest in scope, it is also the most controversial.[98] Based on the

problem of 'regulatory chill' in the investment context, see Sykes, "Economic "Necessity" in International Law," 299–300, 315–316.

[97] Best-shot GPGs are those where the level of supply is determined by the largest contribution which is why a single large contribution may be sufficient to provide the good. See Sect. 2.2.

[98] For a brief overview of the controversies surrounding the concept of necessity, see Heathcote, "Circumstances Precluding Wrongfulness in the ILC Articles on State Responsibility: Necessity," in *The Law of International Responsibility*, ed. Crawford, Pellet, and Olleson, 492–494; Crawford, *State Responsibility: the General Part*, 305–306.

maxim "necessity knows no law", states have abused necessity to excuse all kinds of breaches of international law, culminating in justifying annexations of foreign territory.[99] The existence of necessity as a legal norm in (positive) international law (i.e. its normative status) and its limits have thus been subject of a long-standing debate.[100] As of today, no general conventional provision anchors the rule.[101] Following the majority of the doctrine, the ILC nonetheless included necessity in the ARSIWA, as it was a "notion [...] too deeply rooted in general legal thinking for silence on the subject to be" acceptable.[102] Despite the controversies, it is reasonable to assume that the concept of necessity now, in principle, forms part of customary international law.[103] Recent case law demonstrates that the necessity excuse, subjected to strict conditions, has been accepted in a growing number of cases, even though it has not been upheld on the facts in any of them.[104]

Moreover, many substantive rules in primary international law are based on or inspired by necessity, without necessarily using the term explicitly.[105] For instance, the law of armed conflict, both in the law regulating the use of force and in

---

[99] For instance, the German Reich occupied Denmark, Norway, the Netherlands, Belgium, and Luxemburg during the Second World War in the name of military necessity (i.e. the doctrine of *Kriegsraison*). ARSIWA Commentaries, Article 25, para. 2. Salmon, "Faut-Il Codifier L'état de Nécessité en Droit International?," in *Essays in International Law in Honour of Judge Manfred Lachs / Études de Droit International en l'honneur du Juge Manfred Lachs* ed. Makarczyk, 241–242.

[100] See on the different views in the literature over time, ARSIWA Commentaries, Article 25, para. 13.

[101] Heathcote, "Circumstances Precluding Wrongfulness in the ILC Articles on State Responsibility: Necessity," in *The Law of International Responsibility*, ed. Crawford, Pellet, and Olleson, 493.

[102] United Nations International Law Commission, *Yearbook of the International Law Commission*, 1980, Volume II, Part Two (UN Doc. A/CN.4/Ser. A/1980/Add. 1 (Part 2)), p. 49, para. 31. See also, Barboza, "Necessity (Revisited) in International Law," in *Essays in International Law in Honour of Judge Manfred Lachs / Études de Droit International en l'honneur du Juge Manfred Lachs*, ed. Makarczyk, 29.

[103] "Those conditions [set forth in Draft Article 33] reflect customary international law." *Gabčíkovo-Nagymaros Project (Hungary v. Slovakia)*, Judgment, p. 41, para. 52. See generally, ARSIWA Commentaries, Article 25, para. 3. Tanzi, "State of Necessity," para. 3.

[104] See, in particular, *Gabčíkovo-Nagymaros Project (Hungary v. Slovakia)*, Judgment; *Legal Consequences of the Construction of a Wall in the Occupied Palestinian Territory*, Advisory Opinion; *CMS Gas Transmission Company v. Argentine Republic*, Award; *CMS Gas Transmission Company v. Argentine Republic*, Decision on the application for annulment; *M/V "Saiga" (No. 2) (Saint Vincent and the Grenadines v. Guinea)*, Judgment, 1 July 1999, ITLOS Reports 1999, p. 10. For further cases, see Heathcote, "Circumstances Precluding Wrongfulness in the ILC Articles on State Responsibility: Necessity," in *The Law of International Responsibility*, ed. Crawford, Pellet, and Olleson, 493.

[105] "[N]ecessity might be considered a material source or extra-legal blueprint of all legal defences at the level of primary rules." Heathcote, "Circumstances Precluding Wrongfulness in the ILC Articles on State Responsibility: Necessity," in *The Law of International Responsibility*, ed. Crawford, Pellet, and Olleson, 496. For a general overview and discussion of necessity-based or necessity-inspired provisions in those diverse fields of international law, see Cassella, *La Nécessité en Droit International: de L'état de Nécessité aux Situations de Nécessité*. See also the different contributions to the special issue introduced by Tarcisio Gazzini, Wouter G. Werner, and Ige F. Dekker, "Necessity across International Law: An Introduction," *Netherlands Yearbook of International Law* 41 (2010): 3–10.

international humanitarian law, is conceived around the concept of military necessity.[106] International human rights law explicitly provides for necessity-like exceptions. *Prima facie* violations can be justified either by limitations in the norm itself or if a specific derogation applies (e.g. a state of emergency clause[107]). In case of such inherent limitations or derogations, there is no breach of international human rights law in the first place and the customary plea of necessity does not apply.[108] The concept of the necessity excuse is also contained in specific regimes of international economic law, for instance, in trade law (in particular, the general exceptions enumerated in Article XX GATT or the security exceptions in Article XXI GATT) and in many bilateral investment treaties.[109] The exact conditions and consequences of the necessity excuse might therefore be defined differently across different contexts.[110] Moreover, in these specialised or self-contained regimes, necessity provisions operate in a different institutional setting, which may include third-party adjudication, meaning that international courts or tribunals have the authority to verify *ex post* the legality of the unilateral invocation of necessity by the defendant state based on an subjective *ex ante* assessment of the conditions.[111] Differences in design and institutional framework have an impact on the way necessity provisions set incentives for states.[112]

Recourse to the general necessity rule in customary international law will thus be excluded *ex ante* in many instances. Firstly, the exclusion of the possibility to invoke necessity can be foreseen explicitly or implicitly by the international obligation in question, and thus by primary law (Article 25(2) lit. a) ARSIWA).[113] For instance, the invocation of military necessity finds its limits in international humanitarian law and the substantive rules of the law regulating the use of force.[114] The invocation of necessity to justify humanitarian interventions (e.g. entering a foreign territory in order to rescue national citizens) is only possible within the accepted exceptions to the prohibition of the use of force in Article 2(4) UN Charter. In other cases, the

---

[106] Gazzini, Werner, and Dekker, "Necessity across International Law: An Introduction," 9.

[107] See, for instance, Article 4 International Covenant on Civil and Political Rights. Article 15 European Convention for the Protection of Human Rights and Fundamental Freedoms (ECHR). In order to prevent abusive invocation of a state of emergency, derogations from protecting certain human rights obligations are only possible in exceptional circumstances and in a temporary and limited manner, combined with monitoring mechanisms under the respective human rights treaty.

[108] See further, Cedric Ryngaert, "State Responsibility, Necessity and Human Rights," *Netherlands Yearbook of International Law* 41 (2010): 79–98.

[109] Gazzini, Werner, and Dekker, "Necessity across International Law: An Introduction," 9.

[110] Sloane, "On the Use and Abuse of Necessity in the Law of State Responsibility," 507.

[111] Gazzini, Werner, and Dekker, "Necessity across International Law: An Introduction," 8–10.

[112] See Sect. 4.1.1 on the design of international norms and Sect. 2.4 on the facilitating role of international judicial institutions.

[113] ARSIWA Commentaries, Article 25, para. 19.

[114] ARSIWA Commentaries, Article 25, paras. 19, 21. In cases of military necessity violating the prohibition of the use of force and other rules of international humanitarian law there is thus a certain overlap to the exclusion of necessity based on Article 26 ARSIWA.

exclusion of the customary necessity plea derives implicitly from the object and the purpose of a rule of international humanitarian law applicable in situations of peril for an essential interest for the defendant state.[115] For example, the reliance on the necessity plea is excluded when international human rights obligations have inherent limitations. Secondly, as an expression of the *lex specialis* rule (Article 55 ARSIWA), necessity-like exceptions in primary international treaty regimes (e.g. an exhaustive list of situations governed by necessity) can exclude recourse to the general concept of necessity in customary international law. Examples can be found in international trade and investment law. Therefore, the customary necessity excuse as reflected in Article 25 ARSIWA applies residually either to fill gaps in specialised treaty regimes, in particular in international investment law (depending on the treaty in question), or in areas that are not governed by exceptions in primary international law, as in international environmental law.[116] The focus in this chapter lies on the economic rationale behind the necessity excuse as a basic principle which applies to all areas of international law to the extent that invocation is not explicitly or implicitly excluded by specific provisions in primary law.

As regards its scope, the concept of necessity in the law of state responsibility is narrowly defined and framed in negative terms by stating the strict cumulative conditions under which it can only exceptionally be invoked.[117] Article 25-(1) ARSIWA lists four constitutive elements of necessity: (i) an essential interest, (ii) threatened by a grave and imminent peril, (iii) the act in non-conformity with international law being the only means by which the state can safeguard the interest, and (iv) no serious impairment of an essential interest of the state or states towards which the obligation exists or of the international community as a whole. Hence, the interest protected by the international obligation, that is being disregarded, is of lesser value than that being safeguarded in necessity. In addition to the relative importance of the interest invoked in necessity, Article 25(2) ARSIWA states cases of absolute exclusion, namely (i) exclusion of necessity by the international obligation in question (as already discussed above), and (ii) contribution of the state to the situation of necessity.

---

[115] ARSIWA Commentaries, Article 25, para. 19.

[116] Gazzini, Werner, and Dekker, "Necessity across International Law: An Introduction," 7, 9. On the necessity plea in international investment law, see August Reinisch, "Necessity in Investment Arbitration," *Netherlands Yearbook of International Law* 41 (2010): 137–158; Jürgen Kurtz, "Adjudging the Exceptional at International Investment Law: Security, Public Order and Financial Crisis," *International and Comparative Law Quarterly* 59, no. 2 (2010): 325–371; Martins Paparinskis, "Circumstances Precluding Wrongfulness in International Investment Law," *ICSID Review – Foreign Investment Law Journal* 31, no. 2 (2016): 497–499. On the necessity excuse in international environmental law, see Malgosia Fitzmaurice, "Necessity in International Environmental Law," *Netherlands Yearbook of International Law* 41 (2010): 159–192.

[117] ARSIWA Commentaries, Article 25, para. 2. Heathcote, "Circumstances Precluding Wrongfulness in the ILC Articles on State Responsibility: Necessity," in *The Law of International Responsibility*, ed. Crawford, Pellet, and Olleson, 491; Crawford, *State Responsibility: the General Part*, 306.

This section analyses, first, the concept of an essential interest and other restrictive elements of necessity (i.e. the notion of a grave and imminent peril, the condition of non-contribution, and the "only way" requirement). It then enquires the balancing of conflicting interests between those protected by the international obligation in question and those safeguarded in necessity, including a discussion of the general provision in Article 26 ARSIWA, which excludes the invocation of necessity in the case of violations of *jus cogens* norms.

5.2.2.1 Safeguarding an Essential Interest

Regarding the conditions of necessity, the first controversial issue relates to the definition of the concept "essential interest", whose protection may excuse a breach of international law. Sarah Heathcote states that necessity in the ARSIWA is defined in abstract terms, and that "neither the ends to be safeguarded by an act in necessity, nor the means by which that act may be effected, are indicated by the rule, except to underline the relative importance of the values at stake".[118] The qualification as an "essential" interest points only to the fact that necessity does not excuse the protection of any interest, but that such interest needs to surpass a certain threshold worth of protection. However, according to the ILC, "[t]he extent to which a given interest is 'essential' depends on all the circumstances, and cannot be prejudged".[119] The ARSIWA Commentaries specify that necessity "[...] has been invoked to protect a wide variety of interests, including safeguarding the environment, preserving the very existence of the State and its people in time of public emergency, or ensuring the safety of a civilian population".[120] On a more systematic reading, one may derive from the ARSIWA Commentaries that the essential interest invoked can embrace two kinds of interests: (i) an individual interest of the state breaching international law or (ii) a collective interest of other states or the international community as a whole.[121] Nevertheless, the ARSIWA Commentaries do not explicitly mention a rationale for including collective interests in the notion of essential

[118] Heathcote, "Circumstances Precluding Wrongfulness in the ILC Articles on State Responsibility: Necessity," in *The Law of International Responsibility*, ed. Crawford, Pellet, and Olleson, 491.

[119] ARSIWA Commentaries, Article 25, para. 15.

[120] ARSIWA Commentaries, Article 25, para. 14. According to Attila Tanzi, necessity can be invoked "under a situation of danger for the State as a whole, or its population", so that "state of necessity applies to more general situations of emergencies, such as humanitarian situations, or cases in which the vital interests of the State are at stake, or its population is in danger." Tanzi, "State of Necessity," para. 2.

[121] ARSIWA Commentaries, Article 25, para. 15 ("It extends to particular interests of the State and its people, as well as of the international community as a whole."). Heathcote, "Circumstances Precluding Wrongfulness in the ILC Articles on State Responsibility: Necessity," in *The Law of International Responsibility*, ed. Crawford, Pellet, and Olleson, 497. ("According to article 25, the essential interest that is to be protected may belong to a plurality of States or even to the international community as a whole. This is implied in article 25(1)(a), and stated explicitly in the Commentary.")

interest protected in necessity.[122] The possibility to invoke the necessity defence to safeguard an essential interest of the international community as a whole was not included in draft Article 33 adopted by the ILC on first reading in 1996,[123] and might thus still be considered progressive development of international law, and not customary international law.[124] Hence, developing a sound economic rationale for extending the notion of essential interest to community interests may contribute to the progressive development of international law[125] and offer guidance for deciding what should constitute the "essential interest" safeguarded in necessity on a case-by-case basis.

We have seen above that domestic liability law distinguishes between private and public necessity, depending on the objective of the act in necessity, namely whether the interest safeguarded is that of the actor alone, a third party, or the community at large. Following rational choice theory at the international level, states always act in their individual self-interest, but their concrete actions can produce excludable and non-excludable benefits and thus relate to different types of goods. This section tries to categorise the possible "essential interests" to be protected in necessity along the lines of the private and public dimensions of international law based on economic theories of goods. It will illustrate these findings with essential interests invoked by states in international case law, independent of whether these existed on a factual basis and whether they prevailed over the interest protected by the international obligation in question, thus the necessity claim subsequently being successful.

Private Necessity in International Law

This section sheds light on private necessity in international law by building on the rationale which underlies the concept in domestic contractual liability and tort law. It relates to scenarios where the objective of the act in necessity is to protect an essential interest of the acting state alone, or in economic terms, the defence of its property rights. From an economic goods perspective, the defendant state's unilateral actions relate to the defence of private goods, thus creating benefits that are excludable with regard to other states.[126]

---

[122] It is only generally implied that the competing interests can be individual or collective, see ARSIWA Commentaries, Article 25, para. 17.

[123] United Nations International Law Commission, „Draft Articles on State Responsibility," in *Report of the Commission to the General Assembly on the Work of its Forty-Eighth Session*, 1996 (UN Doc. A/51/10), in *Yearbook of the International Law Commission*, 1996, Volume II, Part Two (UN Doc. A/CN.4/SER.A/1996/Add.1 (Part 2)). Cited hereinafter as 1996 Draft Articles on State Responsibility.

[124] Heathcote, "Circumstances Precluding Wrongfulness in the ILC Articles on State Responsibility: Necessity," in *The Law of International Responsibility*, ed. Crawford, Pellet, and Olleson, 495, 497.

[125] On the legal status of the ARSIWA, see Sect. 1.1.

[126] Rivalry in consumption as a characteristic does not play a role with regard to the essential interest invoked in necessity, which is why in this section only private goods at the extreme end of the spectrum in comparison to global public goods are considered.

First, private necessity can relate to the defence of the sovereign state's territory, its people, or even the "survival" of the state itself. In these cases, the essential interest being brought forward is rooted in national security. In the early case law, necessity was primarily discussed with regard to the notion of self-preservation, that is, situations that allegedly endangered the very existence of the state.[127] More recently, necessity has been invoked to justify humanitarian interventions (e.g. entering a foreign territory in order to rescue national citizens). Similarly, Israel argued in the *Wall* Advisory Opinion that the need to protect the life of its citizens justified the construction of a wall in the Occupied Palestinian Territory.[128] The notion of self-preservation is highly controversial, and there is still intense debate about whether a state should be able to invoke necessity to protect its territorial or military interests.[129] Yet, this can rather be considered an issue of the fulfilment of the other strict conditions of necessity rather than the qualification as an essential interest. There is consensus that necessity should not be understood as a subjective right to state survival, but that the necessity defence can only excuse temporary non-compliance with international legal obligations.[130] Such scenarios of territorial or military necessity thus mirror the doctrine of private necessity in tort law.

Second, private necessity describes situations where states are confronted with a severe domestic economic crisis that threatens the economic survival of the state.[131] These cases have in the literature been referred to as cases of "economic necessity".[132] Traditionally, they relate to situations where the state is no longer able to service its foreign debt and risks a sovereign default, which could have detrimental consequences for the defendant state's population.[133] An early example is the *Russian Indemnity* case, where the government of the Ottoman Empire tried to excuse its delay in debt payments to the Russian Government, amongst others, with its extremely difficult financial situation.[134] In *Société commerciale de*

---

[127] ARSIWA Commentaries, Article 25, paras. 4–5 (with further references).

[128] *Legal Consequences of the Construction of a Wall in the Occupied Palestinian Territory*, Advisory Opinion, p. 195, para. 141. The ICJ rejected this argument, because the measure was seriously impairing international humanitarian law and international human rights law as well as the essential interest of the Palestinian people to self-determination. Balancing of competing interests (Article 25(1) lit. b ARSIWA) and absolute grounds of exclusion (Article 26 ARSIWA) will be discussed in Sect. 5.2.2.2.

[129] Heathcote, "Circumstances Precluding Wrongfulness in the ILC Articles on State Responsibility: Necessity," in *The Law of International Responsibility*, ed. Crawford, Pellet, and Olleson, 497.

[130] Ibid., 496–497.

[131] On economic survival as one possible ground for necessity, see United Nations International Law Commission, *Addendum to the Eighth Report on State Responsibility by Special Rapporteur Roberto Ago*, Thirty-Second Session, 1980, in *Yearbook of the International Law Commission*, 1980, Volume II, Part One (UN Doc. A/CN.4/318/Add.5-7), p. 50, para. 78.

[132] See generally, Sykes, "Economic "Necessity" in International Law," 296–323; van Aaken, "On the Necessity of Necessity Measures: A Response to Alan O. Sykes," 181–186.

[133] On the possibility of obtaining payment on defaulted sovereign debt in ICSID arbitration, see Michael Waibel, "Opening Pandora's Box: Sovereign Bonds in International Arbitration," *American Journal of International Law* 101, no. 4 (2007): 711–759.

[134] *Affaire de L'indemnité Russe (Russie contre Turquie)*, Award, 11 November 1912, RIAA, Volume XI, p. 421, p. 443, para. 6. ARSIWA Commentaries Article 25, para. 7.

Belgique, the Greek government invoked necessity based on the country's serious budgetary and monetary situation in order to excuse the non-payment to a Belgian company owed under two arbitral awards.[135]

Economic necessity can also relate to situations where a state breaches other types of private or club good-type obligations, such as international trade or investment law, due to a domestic economic crisis, for instance, to generate in the short run financial resources in order to maintain its public services. Such actions can consist in raising tariffs or expropriating foreign investors, thus denying the reciprocal exchange of benefits as the associated costs have become inhibitive. In fact, "economic necessity" was the main argument brought forward by Argentina during its financial crisis in the 1990s in order to excuse measures to the detriment of foreign investors that were in breach of international obligations under several bilateral investment treaties.[136] These measures were the subject of several arbitration cases, albeit with differing conclusions about whether necessity was rightly invoked.[137] To a certain extent, scenarios of economic necessity, therefore mirror the doctrines of impossibility or impracticability in contractual liability law.

Even if the protection of territorial and economic interests exemplifies different scenarios of private necessity, the distinction between tort and contractual liability-like scenarios is in international law not always as clear as in domestic law. A national state of emergency type situation can, for instance, be due to an economic crisis, a military conflict or a natural disaster or all of them combined, and lead the defendant state to breach international obligations in order to protect the health and wealth of its population. From an economic perspective, it is therefore sufficient to distinguish clearly between scenarios of private and public necessity. This dividing line is more easily drawn as it requires a mere distinction whether the act in question produced excludable or non-excludable benefits, which has implications for the subsequent question of cost allocation. Private necessity on the international level thus relates to scenarios which have no cross-border dimension and where the benefits of the act in necessity fall on the defendant state alone.

However, in cases where the survival of the state's population is at stake, as in any kind of local humanitarian crisis, the protection of an essential state interest may

---

135 *Société Commerciale de Belgique*, Judgment, 15 June 1939, PCIJ Series A/B, No. 78, p. 160. ARSIWA Commentaries, Article 25, para. 8.

136 On the Argentinian case and adjudication of necessity as a defence in international investment arbitration, see Kurtz, "Adjudging the Exceptional at International Investment Law: Security, Public Order and Financial Crisis," 325–371.

137 See, for instance, *CMS Gas Transmission Company v. Argentine Republic*, Award; *CMS Gas Transmission Company v. Argentine Republic*, Decision on the application for annulment; *LG&E Energy Corp., LG&E Capital Corp., and LG&E International Inc. v. Argentine Republic*, Decision on Liability, 3 October 2006, ICSID Case No. ARB/02/1.

ultimately serve the protection of human rights and can, for instance, consist in maintaining the food supply of the population,[138] or protecting the health of endangered parts of the civilian population (e.g. spread of infectious diseases).[139] For example, in the *Suez* case, Argentina invoked the human right to water as an essential interest to justify its actions against foreign investors.[140] What these exemplary situations have in common is that a defendant state violates an international obligation, usually but not necessarily deriving from international trade or investment law, by taking regulatory emergency measures in order to ensure medical care or energy and food supply for the local population. When the benefits of protecting the own population are limited to the defendant state and create no positive externalities, they qualify as cases of private necessity. However, it might be difficult to determine in practice whether a concrete state action serves to protect an individual state or a community interest. Measures that aim to defend the economic survival of a state might in a global economy also benefit all other states (i.e. preventing a state's insolvency might be important for global financial stability). Actions in the name of public health can, in some cases, have a global dimension (e.g. placing a foreign national in quarantine in order to prevent a global pandemic), and, in other cases, only be in the interest of one individual state (e.g. protection of the own population from genetically modified agricultural products). Even when the defendant state acts in order to protect the human rights of its own population, this may have a cross-border dimension when other states derive value from such protection (i.e. human rights protection as non-use value public goods).[141] Whether a state acts in private or public necessity has to be decided on a case-by-case basis, depending on whether the benefits of the action are excludable or not. And when the protection of human rights is at stake, this points rather to public necessity due to the normative force of these obligations and the interest of all states in the international community in compliance (i.e. *erga omnes* obligations). This is relevant for all sorts of mixed goods, where the non-excludability of benefits needs to be the overriding characteristic in order to qualify as a reason for public necessity.

---

[138] Heathcote, "Circumstances Precluding Wrongfulness in the ILC Articles on State Responsibility: Necessity," in *The Law of International Responsibility*, ed. Crawford, Pellet, and Olleson, 496. On feeding of the population as a possible ground for necessity, see United Nations International Law Commission, *Addendum to the Eighth Report on State Responsibility by Special Rapporteur Roberto Ago*, Thirty-Second Session, 1980, in *Yearbook of the International Law Commission*, 1980, Volume II, Part One (UN Doc. A/CN.4/318/Add.5-7), p. 50, para. 78.

[139] The protection of social stability and the maintenance of essential services vital to the health and welfare of the population have been accepted as constituting 'essential interests' in investment treaty arbitration, see *National Grid Plc v. Argentine Republic*, Award, 3 November 2008, UNCITRAL arbitration case 1:09-cv-00248-RBW, para. 245.

[140] *Suez, Sociedad General de Aguas de Barcelona Sa and Vivendi Universal Sa v. Argentine Republic*, Decision on Liability, 30 July 2010, ICSID Case No ARB/03/19, para. 260. The necessity defence was, however, rejected because the measures taken by Argentina did not constitute the only means to protect its essential interests and because Argentina itself contributed to the emergency situation.

[141] See Sect. 2.3 on community interests and different types of goods across international law.

Public Necessity in International Law

Public necessity in international law builds on the rationale which underlies the concept in domestic tort law. It relates to scenarios where the objective of the act in necessity is to protect an essential interest of the community as a whole. From an economic perspective, the defendant state's unilateral actions are in its self-interest (as the share of total benefits of the action outweigh the costs), but they create benefits that are non-excludable with regard to other states. As both CPRs and GPGs have in common the characteristic of non-excludability of benefits, states face the same collective action problems underlying their provision (namely, the free-rider problematic).[142] As state actions in the name of public necessity are unilateral and exceptional in nature, they usually face the characteristic of a best-shot global public good, meaning that one single contribution may be sufficient to supply the good.

First, public necessity can relate to the preservation of CPRs. In these cases, the essential interest being brought forward consists, for instance, of the protection of natural resources or cultural heritage. State action in non-compliance with international law with the objective to protect the environment does not automatically qualify as public necessity, as natural resources can have been made excludable or pollution can take place in a mere transboundary context (e.g. river or coastal area). These scenarios, where a state acts in order to prevent serious harm stemming from negative externalities of foreign activities within its jurisdiction, should rather be understood as private necessity. In contrast, environmental protection in the name of public necessity can practically take on two forms: (i) the prevention of pollution of the global commons and (ii) the prevention of overfishing or -hunting in common waters (e.g. the conservation of fisheries). There can also be an overlap between the two categories. For instance, the pollution of an ocean can also lead to the extinction of a certain fish population. Scenarios where all states in the international community derive value from the preservation of the environment (e.g. enjoyment of a clean environment) should, however, rather be considered as GPGs and will be discussed further below.

These scenarios find examples in the existing international case law.[143] An often-cited example for the invocation of necessity for environmental reasons is the case where a state bombs a foreign vessel in order to prevent or avert pollution of the sea. For instance, when the Liberian-flagged oil tanker *Torrey Canyon* ran aground off the coast of Cornwall in 1967 and large amounts of spilling oil threatened the

---

[142] As for private necessity, rivalry in consumption as a characteristic does not play a role with regard to the essential interest invoked in necessity. Both categories of goods serve as example for public necessity, but the issue with regard to necessity is not consumption of the good, but its provision.

[143] On the protection of the ecological order as a possible ground for necessity, see United Nations International Law Commission, *Addendum to the Eighth Report on State Responsibility by Special Rapporteur Roberto Ago*, Thirty-Second Session, 1980, in *Yearbook of the International Law Commission*, 1980, Volume II, Part One (UN Doc. A/CN.4/318/Add.5-7), p. 50, para. 78.

English coastline, the British government ultimately decided to bomb the ship to burn the remaining oil.[144] Another example for the invocation of public necessity are concerns for the preservation of the global commons, which are threatened by overfishing or -hunting. For instance, in the *Russian Fur Seals* controversy of 1893, the Russian Government, facing the danger of extinction of a fur seal population by unrestricted hunting, issued a decree prohibiting sealing in an area of the high seas.[145] A similar issue arose in the *Fisheries Jurisdiction* case with regard to the measures taken by Canada to prevent the further destruction of straddling fish stocks.[146] In the *Gabčíkovo-Nagymaros Project* case, Hungary justified suspending and subsequently abandoning certain works on the dam project on the Danube river by relying essentially on a "state of ecological necessity".[147] The ICJ admitted that the concerns expressed by Hungary for its natural environment and the ecological equilibrium in the region affected by the project related to an essential interest of that state.[148] All these examples demonstrate that the qualification of an essential interest as private or public necessity depends on whether the peril (e.g. of pollution or extinction) concerns uniquely a state's territorial waters or the high seas, and thus whether the benefits of the act in necessity fall on the defendant state alone or the international community as a whole.

Second, public necessity can relate to the provision of GPGs. *Jus cogens* norms served for the ILC as the main justification to include the protection of community interests in the understanding of the notion of essential interest in Article 25(1) lit. a) ARSIWA, despite it being progressive development of international law.[149] All interests protected by peremptory norms of general international law are community interests, because they are considered as being of fundamental importance and

---

[144] ARSIWA Commentaries, Article 25, para. 9 (with further references). Subsequently, the International Convention relating to Intervention on the High Seas in Cases of Oil Pollution Casualties was concluded to cover future cases where intervention might prove necessary to avert serious oil pollution. International Convention Relating to Intervention on the High Seas in Cases of Oil Pollution Casualties (concluded 29 November 1969, entered into force 6 May 1975) 970 *UNTS* 211.

[145] ARSIWA Commentaries, Article 25, para. 6 (with further references).

[146] *Fisheries Jurisdiction (Spain v. Canada)*, Judgment (Jurisdiction of the Court), 4 December 1998, ICJ Reports 1998, p. 432. These questions are not addressed in the Agreement for the Implementation of the Provisions of the United Nations Convention on the Law of the Sea of 10 December 1982 Relating to the Conservation and Management of Straddling Fish Stocks and Highly Migratory Fish Stocks (concluded 4 August 1995, entered into force 11 December 2001) 2167 *UNTS* 3. ARSIWA Commentaries, Article 25, para. 12.

[147] *Gabčíkovo-Nagymaros Project (Hungary v. Slovakia)*, Judgment, p. 35, para. 40.

[148] Ibid., p. 41, para. 53. However, the ICJ rejected the invocation of necessity based on the absence of a grave and imminent peril and of proof that the measures taken by Hungary were the only possible response to it. Ibid., p. 45, para. 57.

[149] ARSIWA Commentaries, Article 25, paras. 15, 17–18. Heathcote, "Circumstances Precluding Wrongfulness in the ILC Articles on State Responsibility: Necessity," in *The Law of International Responsibility*, ed. Crawford, Pellet, and Olleson, 497. ("The feeling in the Commission was that this aspect of article 25 was progressive development, but was justified particularly in respect of *jus cogens* norms.")

universal reach.[150] Due to their higher status in the hierarchy of international norms, *jus cogens* obligations have been qualified as normative GPGs, but also in terms of substance the community interests covered by the currently accepted *jus cogens* norms can be considered GPGs.[151] Public necessity thus embraces fundamental interests protected by peremptory norms, which can by their very nature be considered essential.[152] This means that, theoretically, a state's motivation to act beyond its national security interests in order to prevent or avert genocide can invoke the public necessity excuse if this interest prevails any other interest protected by the international norm in question.[153] One could imagine as a concrete example a case where a state delivers humanitarian aid (without the use of force) against the will of the receiving state, but a breach of the obligation to respect the territorial integrity of the other state may be excused in order to protect fundamental rights of the civilian population.

It has been outlined above that the notion of community interests is larger than those protected by peremptory norms of international law.[154] Consequently, it has, in my opinion rightly, been argued that the concept of "essential interest" for the purposes of Article 25(1) lit. a) ARSIWA is broader than the concept of "fundamental interest" for the purposes of Article 40 ARSIWA, the latter being limited to peremptory norms.[155] While interests protected by *jus cogens* norms might from a legal perspective be different from other essential community interests in terms of hierarchy as well as regarding their specific consequences in case of breach, from an economic perspective, as an excuse of public necessity in international law, they function in the same way. Hence, public necessity covers also cases beyond the protection of "fundamental interests", as long as the essential interest protected belongs to a plurality of other states or the international community as a whole.[156] In economic terms, we can understand these as GPGs (and CPRs), as their provision creates positive externalities for every state that is part of the international community (or the plurality of states), including the state providing it, yet leading to the

[150]To recall, among the most commonly accepted peremptory norms are the right to self-determination, the basic rules of international humanitarian law in armed conflict as well as the prohibitions of aggression, genocide, slavery, apartheid and systematic racial discrimination, crimes against humanity, and torture.

[151]On a hierarchy of norms at the international level and congruence of the concept of *jus cogens* with different types of goods, in particular GPGs, see Sect. 3.3.2.

[152]Heathcote, "Circumstances Precluding Wrongfulness in the ILC Articles on State Responsibility: Necessity," in *The Law of International Responsibility*, ed. Crawford, Pellet, and Olleson, 497.

[153]One should bear in mind though that necessity will often not be applicable because the other strict conditions (e.g. grave and imminent peril, 'only way' requirement) are not fulfilled or its application is excluded by primary international law (i.e. the use of force). This is why military interventions conducted under the name of 'responsibility to protect' in order to shield people from mass atrocities can usually not be justified in necessity.

[154]See Sect. 2.1 on the concept of community interests in international law.

[155]Heathcote, "Circumstances Precluding Wrongfulness in the ILC Articles on State Responsibility: Necessity," in *The Law of International Responsibility*, ed. Crawford, Pellet, and Olleson, 497.

[156]Ibid. ARSIWA Commentaries, Article 25, paras. 2, 15.

problem that the benefits of provision are not fully internalised. This community-oriented aspect of necessity can, for instance, become relevant in a scenario of a regional humanitarian crises where the benefits of protecting the own population are not limited to the state, but create cross-border benefits. An example would be global public health as a GPG in a situation where a state invokes necessity for having quarantined a foreign national with a contagious disease in order to prevent a global pandemic. Essential interests such as health or economic stability can thus relate to both private and public necessity, depending on the excludability of benefits and thus the type of the underlying good protected, which will have to be determined on a case-by-case basis.

It is useful to add one last word on the scenario in which the defendant state acts in the interest of a third state. From an economic perspective, actions in the interest of a third state create a positive externality for the benefitting third state. To the extent that benefits are non-excludable beyond the third state, thus potentially benefitting all states in the international community, this constellation has GPG or CPR characteristics. However, to the extent that benefits do not concern the state acting in necessity and are exclusively falling on the third state, this constellation rather relates to a private goods scenario.

In sum, there is an economic rationale to allow a state acting in the interest of the international community to be excused from compliance with international obligations. Strict adherence to the law would disincentivise socially optimal behaviour as states would be obliged, for instance, to provide reparation for the damage caused by an internationally wrongful act. In cases of public necessity, where GPGs or CPRs are at stake, the necessity excuse allows for flexibility instead of compliance with the international obligation in question and seems economically justified. The difference between private and public necessity depends on whether in the concrete case the benefits of the act in necessity are excludable or not.

Observability and Verifiability of Private and Public Necessity

Successfully invoking necessity requires furthermore that the essential interest safeguarded is threatened by a grave and imminent peril and that the defendant state did not contribute to the situation of necessity. The act in question also needs to constitute the only way for the defendant state to safeguard that essential interest.

It derives from the general rule in international law that the party asserting a proposition must prove it (*actori incumbit probatio*).[157] Consequently, in an inter-state dispute the burden of establishing state responsibility (i.e. the commission of an internationally wrongful act) rests on the victim state as the plaintiff.[158] Yet, if the defendant state seeks to rely on a circumstance precluding wrongfulness, the burden of proof shifts to that state, because often only the defendant state knows the facts justifying the act.[159] Since the defendant state has more or better information about

[157] ARSIWA Commentaries, Part one, Chap. V, para. 8. Crawford, *State Responsibility: the General Part*, 320–321.

[158] See Chap. 4 on conditions for international state responsibility and different responsibility standards.

[159] ARSIWA Commentaries, Part one, Chap. V, para. 8. Crawford, *State Responsibility: the General Part*, 320–321.

its actions and the circumstances (i.e. information asymmetries), it will, on the one hand, be easier for that state to prove compliance with the conditions of necessity than for the plaintiff state to demonstrate the absence of a state of necessity. On the other hand, information asymmetries make it more difficult for the plaintiff state or third parties (i.e. other states or international judicial institutions) to observe and verify the defendant state's actions and intentions.[160]

It has been outlined earlier that the flexibility created by the necessity excuse in the presence of unforeseen circumstances serves to avoid excessive social costs that derive from the strict application of international law, but at the same time leads to a moral hazard problem. Having the possibility to invoke necessity sets adverse incentives for states not to take sufficient care in order to prevent situations of necessity from occurring in the first place. The problem of asymmetric information aggravates this risk for opportunistic breach of international obligations. This explains why the concept of necessity throughout history was susceptible to abuse.

To counter abuse or opportunistic breach, the necessity provision is formulated as an excuse that can only exceptionally be invoked if all conditions are cumulatively met. Additionally, each condition includes in itself a certain degree of strictness. We have seen, for instance, that the interest protected in necessity needs to be "essential", thus surpass a certain threshold worth of protection. Moreover, the essential interest needs to be threatened by a peril, which is "grave and imminent" and thus requires a certain degree of intensity and temporal proximity.[161] The notion of peril relates to the concept of risk as opposed to damage which relates to harm that has already materialised.[162] Necessity thus serves as a preventive mechanism,[163] which explains why the fulfilment of this condition is more difficult to determine than the occurrence of damage. It also obliges the defendant state to base its concrete actions on a subjective *ex ante* assessment of a given situation.[164] However, according to the ICJ, "the State concerned is not the sole judge of whether those conditions have been met".[165] This points to an objective *ex post* assessment of the conditions, by the plaintiff state or third parties (i.e. other states or international judicial institutions),

[160] See, in this regard, Sykes, "Economic "Necessity" in International Law," 297.

[161] ARSIWA Commentaries, Article 25, para. 15.

[162] ARSIWA Commentaries, Article 25, para. 16. Heathcote, "Circumstances Precluding Wrongfulness in the ILC Articles on State Responsibility: Necessity," in *The Law of International Responsibility*, ed. Crawford, Pellet, and Olleson, 497. See also *Gabčíkovo-Nagymaros Project (Hungary v. Slovakia)*, Judgment, pp. 41–42, para. 54.

[163] See Heathcote, "Circumstances Precluding Wrongfulness in the ILC Articles on State Responsibility: Necessity," in *The Law of International Responsibility*, ed. Crawford, Pellet, and Olleson, 497.

[164] Gazzini, Werner, and Dekker, "Necessity across International Law: An Introduction," 10.

[165] *Gabčíkovo-Nagymaros Project (Hungary v. Slovakia)*, Judgment, p. 40, para. 51.

thus limiting the subjective character of necessity.[166] With the benefit of hindsight, it will be much easier to assess whether a grave and imminent peril for an essential interest actually existed. At the same time, such an approach leads to the problem of hindsight bias, that is, the finding that the probability of an accident is perceived higher after the accident has occurred.[167] An objective *ex post* assessment of the situation may thus more likely lead to the conclusion that the peril to the essential interest was not sufficiently grave or imminent to justify non-compliance with an international obligation. Yet, a balanced judgement needs to take into account both perspectives, on the one hand, the rationale of necessity allowing for an exceptional breach of international law based on the defendant state's self-assessment of the gravity of the situation, and, on the other hand, the risk of opportunistic breach and thus the need to verify the existence of the conditions for necessity in the aftermath. An objective *ex post* assessment which takes into account the defendant state's *ex ante* view (e.g. the information available to the defendant state at the moment of the decision to act in necessity) seems to be the most adequate approach for the general necessity provision in the ARSIWA.[168] Specific necessity clauses in primary law, for instance, in some bilateral investment treaties and in international trade law, might give more discretion to the defendant state, but this needs to be seen against the background of the institutional context within which they operate.[169]

With regard to the second requirement that the defendant state should not have contributed to the situation of necessity, van Aaken argues in the same direction of an objective *ex post* assessment which takes into account the defendant state's *ex ante* view in order to limit the problem of hindsight bias.[170] Non-contribution to the state of necessity as a ground for excluding the invocation of the excuse also aims to counter opportunistic breach and thus to address the moral hazard problem. The

[166] Gazzini, Werner, and Dekker, "Necessity across International Law: An Introduction," 10. According to Heathcote, "compulsory jurisdiction at the international level [...] would 'objectivize' through impartial adjudication any invocation of the necessity plea." See Heathcote, "Circumstances Precluding Wrongfulness in the ILC Articles on State Responsibility: Necessity," in *The Law of International Responsibility*, ed. Crawford, Pellet, and Olleson, 494.

[167] See footnote 95 in Chap. 1.

[168] See, along the same lines, ARSIWA Commentaries, Article 25, para. 16. ("[...] a measure of uncertainty about the future does not necessarily disqualify a State from invoking necessity, if the peril is clearly established on the basis of the evidence reasonably available at the time.")

[169] For a qualification of necessity as self-judging in nature, see *Russia – Measures Concerning Traffic in Transit (Ukraine v Russian Federation)*, Panel Report, 5 April 2019, WT/DS512/R, p. 58. para. 7.146. The Panel considered with regard to the chapeau of Article XXI(b) of the GATT 1994 that it falls upon the invoking member to decide whether the contested action was necessary for the protection of its essential security interests. ("This being so, it is for Russia to determine the 'necessity' of the measures for the protection of its essential security interests. This conclusion follows by logical necessity if the adjectival clause 'which it considers' [in the chapeau of Article XXI(b)] is to be given legal effect.")

[170] van Aaken, "On the Necessity of Necessity Measures: A Response to Alan O. Sykes," 182. ("With hindsight, a tribunal will thus always find that the state contributed to the crisis, even though, to reach a fair judgment, an *ex ante* view should be taken.")

rationale is that states take into account this threat of exclusion of necessity and are thus disincentivised to deliberately create or negligently fail to prevent situations of necessity in the first place.[171] The notion of contribution is broader than the similar provisions regarding *force majeure* and distress,[172] which require that the situation "is due, either alone or in combination with other factors, to the conduct of the State invoking it", and thus seem to presuppose only a certain degree of causation. This more restrictive approach with regard to necessity is in line with the idea that necessity should only be invoked on an exceptional basis within strict limits.[173] However, the ARSIWA Commentaries also specify that "[...] the contribution to the situation of necessity must be sufficiently substantial and not merely incidental or peripheral".[174] There can be scenarios where the question of a substantial contribution is relatively easy to answer. This can, for instance, be the case when the defendant state evidently caused the situation of necessity and thus exclusively contributed to it (e.g. appropriation of foreign assets due to an internal armed conflict or egregious economic behaviour[175]). Another example would be a scenario where the defendant state did clearly not contribute to such a situation (e.g. pollution of its territorial waters by a foreign vessel, extinction of natural resources in the global commons unless the defendant state has also engaged in fishing or hunting in that area). In between these constellations, however, even with the qualification of substantiality, the determination of when a state contribution can be considered sufficiently significant to justify the exclusion of necessity is challenging as other contribution factors have to be considered. Independent of whether the source of the peril to the essential interest lies in the realm of the defendant state or beyond, there will be many instances where domestic policy choices contributed to the situation of necessity (e.g. in national state of emergency type situations where the health or wealth of the population is at stake), either by concrete action or by failure to prevent it, thus by omission. For instance, in the case of a severe economic crisis, where a state is in risk of sovereign default and unable to service its foreign debt, the situation of necessity may result from unsound public finances due, for example, to wrong public spending priorities and lack of fiscal discipline.[176] With regard to economic

[171] The ICJ held (with regard to Hungary) that a state contributed to the situation of necessity if it "helped, by act or omission to bring about" such situation. *Gabčíkovo-Nagymaros Project (Hungary v. Slovakia)*, Judgment, p. 46, para. 57.

[172] Article 23(2) lit. a) ARSIWA, Article 24(2) lit. a) ARSIWA.

[173] ARSIWA Commentaries, Article 25, para. 20. ("[...] necessity needs to be more narrowly confined.")

[174] Ibid. In favour of requiring a certain substantial degree of contribution to exclude the possibility to rely on the necessity excuse, see also Reinisch, "Necessity in Investment Arbitration," 154–155.

[175] van Aaken, "On the Necessity of Necessity Measures: A Response to Alan O. Sykes," 182. ("This assessment might make sense in many instances of necessity, but it is questionable if it makes sense for economic necessity except in cases of egregious economic behavior.")

[176] In *Impregilo v. Argentina*, the arbitral tribunal concluded that "Argentina's own economic policies over several years prior to the crisis rendered the economy of the country vulnerable to exogenous shocks and pressures, and impacted adversely the sustainability of its economic model on the national and local levels." *Impregilo S.P.A. v. Argentine Republic*, Award, 21 June 2011, ICSID Case No. ARB/07/17, para. 358.

necessity, van Aaken thus raises the question "how far arbitrators should scrutinize the economic policy measures taken by governments, and whether as legal experts they have the relevant economic expertise".[177] The problem is again that "with hindsight, we know much better what contributed to the crises. *Ex ante*, some policies are hard to judge".[178] This problem also exists in other policy areas as they relate to decisions of often democratically elected governments. If we take up again the example of an armed conflict, unless a state acting in necessity has been the mere victim of an armed attack by a third state, a state may also have contributed by national security policy choices to an ongoing territorial or military conflict, which would exclude acting in necessity (e.g. expropriation of assets belonging to the plaintiff state). Other examples relate to natural disasters, where the state may nonetheless have contributed to the situation of necessity by failing to provide an effective emergency response system (e.g. alert mechanisms, resilient infrastructure, and emergency medical care).[179] Thus, in cases where the defendant state failed to prevent a situation of necessity, for instance, by taking sufficient precaution against the risk of a peril to an essential interest, that state will almost always have contributed substantially to such situation.[180] Yet, as van Aaken put it, "a conditional requirement that must be answered always in the affirmative is not exactly conditional, and thus does not make much sense".[181] In the context of international investment law, some arbitral tribunals have therefore defined the standard of contribution to the situation of necessity in narrower terms, namely as requiring some degree of fault and a link of causality between the policy measure and the subsequent crisis.[182] It would, however, be even more appropriate to consider that governments having enacted policies in good faith did not contribute to the

[177] van Aaken, "On the Necessity of Necessity Measures: A Response to Alan O. Sykes," 181–182.

[178] Ibid., 182.

[179] It should be noted here that such lack of infrastructure can often, even if not exclusively, be explained by the lack of financial means, thus making the link to the problem that GPG provision depends, in particular in weakest-link scenarios, on the financial capabilities of a state.

[180] In *Impregilo v. Argentina*, the arbitral tribunal seemingly required a mere causal relationship between the adopted policies and the situation of necessity and held that "a State's contribution to its necessity situation need not be specifically intended or planned – it can be the consequence, *inter alia*, of well-intended but ill-conceived policies." *Impregilo S.P.A. v. Argentine Republic*, Award, para. 356.

[181] van Aaken, "On the Necessity of Necessity Measures: A Response to Alan O. Sykes," 182.

[182] In *Urbaser v. Argentina*, the arbitral tribunal stated that contribution to the state of necessity requires that "the Government's acts were such that they either were directed towards a crisis resulting in the emergency situation that the country experienced in early 2002, or at least of such a nature that the Government must have known that such crisis and emergency must have been the outcome of its economic and financial policy. [...] This also means that an allegation stating that the Argentine Government substantially contributed to these events requires a showing of a link of causality between such conduct of Argentine's economy and the outbreak of the crisis." *Urbaser S.A. And Consorcio de Aguas Bilbao Bizkaia, Bilbao Biskaia Ur Partzuergoa v. Argentine Republic*, Award, 8 December 2016, ICSID Case No. ARB/07/26, para. 711, 714.

emergency situation and may thus rely on the necessity plea.[183] In order to avoid that international judicial institutions fully scrutinise domestic policy measures, it seems adequate to make an objective *ex post* assessment which takes into account the defendant state's *ex ante* view based on a good faith test. This would sufficiently reduce the risk of moral hazard, while leaving enough room for flexibility in exceptional circumstances based on the defendant state's self-assessment.

In addition to the two strict conditions related to the situation of necessity, a successful invocation of the necessity requires that the act in question constitutes the "only way" for the defendant state to safeguard the essential interest against a grave and imminent peril. This condition thus relates to the specific act in question and whether that act constituted the only possible means at the disposal of the defendant state. According to the ARSIWA Commentaries, "[t]he plea [of necessity] is excluded if there are other (otherwise lawful) means available, even if they may be more costly or less convenient".[184] Furthermore, other available means do not only have to consist of unilateral acts, in particular when the objective is GPG provision. Alternative lawful means "may also comprise other forms of conduct available through cooperative action with other States or through international organizations (for example, conservation measures for a fishery taken through the competent regional fisheries agency [rather than seizing a foreign ship])".[185] This definition raises again the question about the degree to which international judicial institutions should scrutinise *ex post* policy choices of the defendant state, and whether they have sufficient expertise of doing so. This has notably been questioned for economic necessity in the investment law context.[186] The problem also exists in all other cases of necessity, where states have to make difficult policy choices in order to respond to an emergency situation.[187] In particular, the seizure of foreign assets in breach of

[183] On this basis, a state with unsound public finances leading to insufficient funding of the public health system. might not have contributed to the emergency situation of a pandemic such as the spread of the coronavirus, where drastic measures such as quarantines have to be taken in order to ensure adequate access to existing public healthcare services. Federica I. Paddeu and Freya Jephcott, "Covid-19 and Defences in the Law of State Responsibility: Part II," *EJIL: Talk!* (Blog of the European Journal of International Law), 17 March, 2020, https://www.ejiltalk.org/covid-19-and-defences-in-the-law-of-state-responsibility-part-ii/

[184] ARSIWA Commentaries, Article 25, para. 15.

[185] Ibid.

[186] Sykes, "Economic "Necessity" in International Law," 319. ("Even more to the point, how can an arbitral panel composed of experts on international economic law begin to assess the optimal policy instrument package for responding to a macroeconomic crisis?") van Aaken, "On the Necessity of Necessity Measures: A Response to Alan O. Sykes," 182. ("When full scrutiny is applied to the economic measures taken by governments, it is questionable whether arbitrators have enough economic expertise and should be second-guessing highly normative and politically laden policy choices. There are many ways of dealing with crises, many of them involving difficult distributive choices.")

[187] For instance, in the absence of an effective vaccine or targeted treatment, only a package of social distancing measures (taken together) might constitute the 'only way' to contain or mitigate the spread of a contagious disease such as COVID-19, but none of them individually (e.g. travel bans). Paddeu and Jephcott, "Covid-19 and Defences in the Law of State Responsibility: Part II".

international investment law, but potentially also other international obligations, may in hindsight only be one avenue among many ways to address an economic, military, political and/or humanitarian crisis. Judging whether a policy measure responded effectively to an emergency situation is not always a matter of the relevant expertise, it is generally an impossible task as "[a] tribunal would need to weigh all of the other (infinite) possibilities of crisis-mitigation measures and conclude that the measure taken was the only one possible to deal optimally with the necessity situation […]".[188] As much as a state almost always contributed to the state of necessity in a certain way, there will in hindsight almost always be alternative means available to the defendant state in order to safeguard an essential interest. Van Aaken proposes with regard to the customary international law norm reflected in Article 25 ARSIWA that arbitrators apply a good faith standard as an appropriate level of scrutiny of economic policy measures.[189] In order to find the right balance between full scrutiny by arbitrators and self-assessment by the state invoking necessity, van Aaken proposes "a 'purpose-restricted' necessity clause", according to which "[t]he tribunal is thus restricted to the full review of the purpose of the norm (necessity)".[190] With regard to the case of economic necessity, this means that a tribunal, once it "finds that this requirement is fulfilled, it should judge the measures taken by the state only on a good faith basis or not at all".[191] A similar approach has been taken in international trade law with regard to the security exception in Article XXI of the GATT.[192] This approach is, in my opinion, generalisable, if the purpose of the "only way" requirement is to limit abusive invocation (*mala fide*). International judicial institutions should thus fully review whether there is a grave and imminent peril to an essential interest and to which the state has not substantially contributed, based on an objective *ex post* assessment which takes into account the defendant state's *ex ante* view, while applying a *bona fide* test with regard to the concrete act in necessity.[193] In scenarios of public necessity, where states act in order to protect an

[188] van Aaken, "On the Necessity of Necessity Measures: A Response to Alan O. Sykes," 182.

[189] Ibid.

[190] Ibid., 183.

[191] Ibid. See along the same lines, suggesting a proportionality approach in assessing the appropriateness of the measures taken by a host state and determining whether they could be regarded as the 'only means' to counter a state of necessity, Reinisch, "Necessity in Investment Arbitration," 153–154. Martins Paparinskis proposes to relax the 'only available means' criterion to 'reasonable means'. Paparinskis, "The Once and Future Law of State Responsibility," 625.

[192] *Russia – Measures Concerning Traffic in Transit (Ukraine v Russian Federation)*, Panel Report, p. 57. para. 7.138. ("The obligation of good faith […] applies not only to the Member's definition of the essential security interests said to arise from the particular emergency in international relations, but also, and most importantly, to their connection with the measures at issue. Thus, as concerns the application of Article XXI(b)(iii), this obligation is crystallized in demanding that the measures at issue meet a minimum requirement of plausibility in relation to the proffered essential security interests, i.e. that they are not implausible as measures protective of these interests.")

[193] For a similarly critical view of the strict conditions of necessity and difficulties in their application, see Federica Paddeu and Michael Waibel, "Necessity 20 Years On: The Limits of Article 25 ARSIWA," *University of Cambridge Faculty of Law Research Paper*, no. 23 (2021), https://ssrn.com/abstract=3858530

essential interest of the international community, it might be all the more warranted to apply a less intensive level of scrutiny. When states act in necessity to protect a GPG or preserve a CPR, the problem is less about addressing the risk of moral hazard, but rather about overcoming the incentive problem of provision in the first place, and thus to allow for a certain degree of flexibility in exceptional circumstances.

It is important to bear in mind that there exist also other mechanisms to counter moral hazard and abusive invocation of necessity. This is, firstly, as will be discussed further below, the compensation requirement, which upholds the deterrence effect of reparation for injury and thus shifts the costs produced by the act in necessity to the defendant state invoking it. Secondly, self-enforcement mechanisms of international law serve not only to induce compliance with primary international obligations, they also aim to prevent abusive invocation of circumstances precluding wrongfulness, including necessity. Alan O. Sykes has argued with regard to the security exceptions in Article XXI of the GATT that "[o]pportunism is policed by the same self-enforcement mechanism that holds trade agreements together under ordinary circumstances; cheating is observable and is likely to carry a cost in the form of formal and informal retaliatory measures, and perhaps reputational sanctions".[194] The argument is similar for other costs of non-compliance, namely reciprocal non-compliance and outcasting (i.e. suspension of trading benefits).[195] Yet, this does not mean that one can simply rely on these self-enforcement mechanisms, which is why a certain degree of *ex post* scrutiny, ideally by international judicial institutions, is useful to avoid abuse of the necessity excuse. In fact, effective enforcement of international law is intrinsically linked to the issues of who judges whether the conditions of necessity are fulfilled (i.e. the defendant state, the plaintiff state, third states, or judicial institutions), from what perspective (i.e. *ex post* taking an *ex ante* view) and what standard of scrutiny will be applied for the assessment (notably, the *bona fide* test).

5.2.2.2 Balancing of Conflicting Interests

The restriction of the necessity clause to the full review of its purpose leads to the second essential condition of necessity outlined in Article 25(1) lit. b) ARSIWA, namely that the act in necessity does not seriously impair an essential interest of the state or states towards which the obligation exists, or of the international community as a whole. According to the ARSIWA Commentaries, "the interest relied on must outweigh all other considerations, not merely from the point of view of the acting

[194] Sykes, "Economic "Necessity" in International Law," 303. At least regarding the reputational effects mitigating the moral hazard problem, there is a difference in effectiveness of enforcement between international investment law and international trade law, with these reputational effects being less strong in the case of investment law as it involves mainly bilateral treaties. See van Aaken, "On the Necessity of Necessity Measures: A Response to Alan O. Sykes," 183.

[195] See Sect. 2.4 on enforcement of international law and mechanisms of compliance.

State but on a reasonable assessment of the competing interests, whether these are individual or collective".[196] Thus, the objective balancing test needs to lead to the conclusion that the essential interest protected by the international obligation, that is being disregarded, is of lesser value than the one being safeguarded in necessity.

Balancing competing interests is traditionally the tasks of lawyers. Yet, social science and economics can offer useful insights in this regard, as balancing of competing interests, although conducted on a case-by-case basis, is ultimately a rational procedure.[197] Robert Alexy introduces the Weight Formula, which builds on arithmetic rules and includes "judgments about degrees of interference [with competing principles], the importance of abstract weights and degrees of reliability".[198] The economic structure of balancing is actually close to cost-benefit analysis in decision theory, that is, the optimisation of a certain measure in the context of a defined system of goals and under consideration of constraints (e.g. legal constraints).[199] Transferred to the economic analysis of the necessity excuse, which assumes states as rational actors pursuing their self-interest, these essential interests can be understood as different objectives or purposes related to the protection or provision of different types of goods at the international level. The balancing of competing interests would then consist in comparing the expected costs of infringement of the relevant goods in order to determine which scenario creates minimum total social costs to the international community as a whole. This calculation consists of an objective *ex post* assessment which takes into account the information available to the state when considering whether to act in necessity or comply with the obligation in question (that is, the expected costs associated with each action alternative). The outcome of this calculation depends on the exact amount of the costs which will have to be determined in each individual case (and which depend, amongst others, on the gravity and imminence of the peril to the essential interest invoked and the severity of the harm to the interest protected by the obligation in question). Yet, such an economic reasoning offers guidance for deciding on a case-by-case basis whether the essential interest protected in necessity outweighs the essential interest protected by the international obligation in question.

We have seen that we can distinguish on the side of the defendant state between unilateral actions which relate to the defence of a private good (i.e. private necessity) and those that relate to the defence of a GPG or CPR (i.e. public necessity), depending on the excludability of benefits of the act in necessity with regard to other states. Similarly, the essential interest protected by the international obligation

[196] ARSIWA Commentaries, Article 25, para. 17.

[197] See, in particular, Alexy, "On Balancing and Subsumption. A Structural Comparison," 433–449.

[198] Ibid., 448.

[199] van Aaken, "Opportunities for and Limits to an Economic Analysis of International Law," 42. ("The optimal decision is the alternative that maximizes the net surplus, defined as benefits minus the costs of a measure. Benefits and costs are defined in legal terms and include the positive effects of the measure in question on all relevant "constitutional" principles as benefits and the negative effects as costs. To evaluate different decision alternatives, the proportionality principle of balancing is used.")

in question can be an individual state interest or a collective interest. It is therefore useful to distinguish according to the character of the international obligation affected by the breach. On the one hand, the international obligation may belong to the private dimension of international law (i.e. a private goods or club goods obligation) and thus be defined as a private law obligation. On the other hand, the international obligation may belong to the public dimension of international law (i.e. a CPR or GPG obligation) and thus be defined as a public law or community interest obligation. Each constellation will be addressed in turn: first, private and public necessity in the case of a private law obligation affected by the breach; second, private and public necessity in the case of an affected public law obligation.

Breach of a Private Law Obligation

The first scenario consists in comparing the expected costs in the case of compliance with a private law obligation and in the case of non-compliance excused in necessity. A situation of necessity is characterised, on the one side, by the fact that the expected costs of compliance for the defendant state have become excessive in the presence of unforeseen or extraordinary circumstances. These are the costs expected in the case of materialisation of the risk to the essential interest, which depend not only on the potential harm but also on the probability of that harm actually occurring. On the other side, in cases where a private law obligation is affected by a breach, the expected costs of non-compliance would fall entirely on the plaintiff state as the beneficiary of the private law obligation. As we will see below in more detail, these costs can be remediated by the requirement for the defendant state to compensate any material loss.[200] Thus, in the case of a successful invocation of necessity, the costs of non-compliance are offset and excessive compliance costs (that is, the difference between the expected costs of compliance in exigent circumstances and the compliance costs in "normal" circumstances) are avoided, thus leading to the minimum social costs for the international society as a whole. In terms of cost efficiency, it then makes sense to allow for flexibility in the form of necessity when a private law obligation is affected. This reasoning is reflected in the argument of efficient breach.[201] The problem is that every case of non-compliance with international obligations (although there is no breach *stricto sensu*, only an obligation affected) creates costs to the international community in that the integrity of the international rule of law, having itself global public good characteristics, is violated. Nonetheless, there is a difference in degree whether all states in the international community have an interest in compliance with the specific rule, as in the case of *erga omnes* obligations, or whether the obligation only creates benefits between the parties involved. These costs to the international community need to be factored in, but they are unlikely to shift the balance towards compliance, in cases where unforeseen or extraordinary circumstances create high expected compliance costs. The efficient breach argument, if at all, is therefore most likely to hold true in this constellation

[200] This statement is based on the assumption that first-party enforcement of compensation is given in the case of an affected private law obligation.

[201] On the concept of efficient breach, see Sects. 5.2.1.1 and 3.2.2.

where a private state interest is invoked to excuse temporary non-compliance with a private law obligation. According to the rationale which underlies the concept of private necessity in domestic contractual liability and tort law, it can make sense, in certain cases, to favour incentivising flexibility in the form of the necessity excuse over compliance with the private law obligation in question. And this is even the case when the objective of the act in necessity is to protect an essential interest of the acting state alone, or in economic terms, the defence of its property rights. Whether the essential interest protected in private necessity prevails over the essential interest protected by the private law obligation will, however, depend on the facts of the individual case.

This also applies in principle to public necessity, which builds on the rationale underlying the concept in domestic tort law as it relates to scenarios where the objective of the act in necessity is to protect an essential interest of the community as a whole. The problem is that "[...] balancing requires a value judgment for which economists have no special methodology. Economists' only contribution is in the evaluation of how high the opportunity costs will be if one value is chosen over the other (without denying valuation problems)".[202] It is therefore not possible to make a general normative statement about which type of interest always prevails, but a comparison of the respective expected costs points towards the conclusion that a community interest protected in public necessity usually prevails over another state's essential interest protected by a private law obligation.[203] When the objective of the act in necessity relates to the provision or protection of GPGs or CPRs at the international level, this will have to be taken into account in the concrete balancing of interest decision and plays a role in the relative weight of each interest.[204] Also, in terms of total social costs, successful invocation of public necessity is likely, given that, on the one side, the expected costs of compliance despite a grave and imminent peril to a GPG or CPR would fall on the international community (as the GPG/CPR is not protected). On the other side, the expected costs of non-compliance would fall entirely on the plaintiff state as the beneficiary of the private law obligation and can subsequently be offset by the requirement for the defendant state to compensate any material loss. Although, as noted above, even in the case of a private law obligation, certain costs to the international community are caused by non-compliance as the international community derives value from compliance in the sense that respect of the international legal order also constitutes a GPG. Yet, as the benefits of public necessity fall on the international community, the question arises whether all states profiting from the act should contribute in a certain way to the payment of compensation to the plaintiff state. Differentiating between private and public necessity will

[202] van Aaken, "Opportunities for and Limits to an Economic Analysis of International Law," 43.

[203] The specific case of human rights obligations will be further discussed in the following section on the breach of public law obligations.

[204] Alexy, "On Balancing and Subsumption. A Structural Comparison," 443–444.

thus be useful when enquiring about the financial consequences of an excused breach of a private law obligation.

Breach of a Public Law Obligation

The outcome of this reasoning changes in the case of a public law obligation affected by a breach, as, in practice, the expected costs of non-compliance will usually outweigh the benefits from protecting an essential "private" interest in extraordinary circumstances. GPG or CPR obligations are characterised by the fact that all states in the international community have an interest in compliance (i.e. *erga omnes* obligations).[205] The expected costs of non-compliance with a public law obligation thus fall not exclusively on the plaintiff state as in the case of non-compliance with a private law obligation. In addition to the concrete material losses borne by the directly affected plaintiff state, the costs falling on the international community lie in the violation of a legal interest of all other states (in compliance, but also in the provision or protection of the underlying GPG/CPR), in addition to the costs associated with an infringement of the international rule of law which lies in every violation of international law. Consequently, even if the expected compliance costs for a state acting in exceptional circumstances are excessive, the total social costs to the international community as a whole will usually remain lower in the case of compliance with an *erga omnes* obligation than in the case of non-compliance. Non-compliance with an *erga omnes* obligation also has long-term social costs, as states may consider a public law obligation, which can be easily disregarded in exceptional circumstances, less binding in the future. This is aggravated by the fact that the probability of enforcement of compliance with public law obligations is lower as in the case of a private law obligation. As demonstrated before, all states of the international community have an interest in compliance with GPG and CPR obligations, but face a sanctioners' dilemma when it comes to enforcement of compliance as public or third-party enforcement has itself GPG characteristics. If enforcement is less effective, the deterrence effect is lower, and thus the incentives for opportunistic breach or abusive invocation of necessity are higher. One possibility to counter this enforcement problem is to uphold the deterrence effect by increasing compensation. This might theoretically be a solution to overcome the enforcement problem in the case of reparation of damages caused by a wrongful act, but punitive damages are *de lege lata* not recognised in general international law.[206] This option is even less feasible in the case of compensation for material losses caused by situations of necessity as there is no breach and therefore no justification for punishment beyond the mere remediation of losses incurred by the plaintiff state. Thus, when other mechanisms to counter moral hazard are either not available (as with punitive damages) or very weak (as for third-party enforcement), breach of a public law obligation should not be too easily excused. The expected short and long-term social costs of non-compliance with a GPG or CPR obligation will

[205] On public enforcement of international state responsibility, in particular *erga omnes* and *erga omnes partes* obligations, see Sect. 3.3.3.

[206] On the rationale and possibility of punitive damages in international law, see Sect. 6.3.2.2.

therefore usually outweigh the compliance costs in exceptional circumstances. Exclusion of the invocation of private necessity qualifies the breach of the *erga omnes* obligation as an internationally wrongful act leading to the obligations of cessation and assurances of non-repetition (that is, return to compliance with the obligation in question) and reparation of damage incurred by the injured state. From an economic perspective, reliance on the customary necessity plea might therefore often be justified against a private law obligation, but not necessarily against a public law obligation.

To illustrate, it makes sense to enquire the example of international obligations protecting human rights.[207] We have seen that international human rights law has primarily an internal dimension, because it contains obligations relating to the treatment by the state of its own citizens. Yet, contrary to fundamental rights obligations under national constitutional law, they are not entirely a "private" matter of the state, but constitute promises towards other states. As the international community derives value from the knowledge that states protect the fundamental rights of their citizens in accordance with international standards, international human rights obligations can be considered community interest norms, and their protection, from an economic perspective, as a non-use value good or a normative global public good.[208] In a situation of crisis, a state may be inclined to disregard an international human rights obligation to the detriment of its own citizens by invoking necessity, for instance, national security or financial reasons (i.e. military or economic necessity). The internal dimension of the situation leads to the problem that no other state suffers a concrete material loss or injury, thus excluding compensation, and that third-party enforcement of such *erga omnes* obligation by states interested in compliance is difficult.[209] This reasoning does not change when necessity is invoked in a crisis situation in order to justify a breach of an international human rights law obligation caused by the exercise of state authority against foreign citizens within or outside its jurisdiction. In this cross-border dimension, an individual state may suffer concrete material losses or injury (i.e. a private good scenario due to infringement of "property rights"), and thus the compensation requirement and private enforcement can reduce incentives for abusive invocation of necessity. However, the underlying obligation also protects values and interest of the international community (i.e. a non-use value or normative GPG) and thus remains predominantly a public law obligation. Minimising the total social costs of

---

[207] To the extent that the customary plea of necessity is applicable and not excluded *ex ante* by the primary obligation in question or specific necessity-like exceptions in primary law.

[208] For human rights protection as a normative public good, see, for instance, Pinto de Albuquerque and van Aaken, "Punitive Damages in Strasbourg," in *The European Convention on Human Rights and General International Law*, ed. van Aaken and Motoc, 247.

[209] For individuals having suffered harm, there exist in international human rights law some individual complaint mechanisms against their own or foreign governments, e.g. the Council of Europe giving access to the European Court of Human Rights for complaints based on alleged infringements of the European Convention for the Protection of Human Rights and Fundamental Freedoms (ECHR).

non-compliance falling on the international community as a whole and upholding the deterrence effect of the *erga omnes* obligation in the future therefore justify the exclusion of the private necessity plea also in cross-border scenarios despite the high compliance costs for the defendant state. In parallel to the obligation to return to legality, losses of the injured state are then remediated by reparation of injury as the breach of the human rights law obligation constitutes an internationally wrongful act. In addition, non-directly injured third states can invoke cessation and assurances of non-repetition and reparation for the benefit of the injured state.

Public necessity differs from private necessity in that the act in necessity aims to protect a GPG or CPR and thus creates benefits which fall on the international community as a whole. Consequently, the costs of strict compliance with a public law obligation also fall on the international community and not exclusively on the state invoking necessity. The total social costs are thus comparable in the case of compliance and non-compliance with an *erga omnes* obligation. This economic reasoning mirrors the legal challenge to determine *ex ante* which community interest prevails over another.[210] In this constellation, more than in the others, the outcome of the balancing of interests or the comparison of expected costs will depend on the facts of the case, in particular the gravity of the impact on the respective good in question.[211] Taking up again the example of an international human rights law obligation, independent of whether the situation has a purely internal or a cross-border dimension, invocation of public necessity may be possible in some scenarios (e.g. temporary detention of foreigners in order to limit the global spread of a contagious disease), but not in others (e.g. bombing of a ship with passengers on board in order to prevent pollution of the high seas). It thus depends on the proportionality of the act in question. Another constellation are social dilemma situations where the protection of the lives of one group of individuals needs to be balanced against the lives of another group (e.g. shooting of an airplane highjacked by terrorists which threatens to attack a nuclear power station). Here, one factor usually shifts the balance towards favouring compliance with the public law obligation although the interests protected are both equally important, namely the overriding interest in the international rule of law. Exclusion of public necessity, even if the compliance costs are excessive for the international community, may be adequate in light of the long-term social costs that non-compliance with an *erga omnes* obligation creates, that is the reduced deterrence effect. In such a scenario, the

[210] No general statement can be made as to which community interest prevails over another, as this raises fundamental questions of legitimacy, see Besson, "Community Interests in International Law: Whose Interests Are They and How Should We Best Identify Them?," in *Community Interests across International Law*, ed. Benvenisti and Nolte, 37. ("As is the case regarding public interests in domestic law, community interests may therefore conflict, across international law regimes or within each of them, and their identification is likely, I will argue, to trigger reasonable disagreement, thereby raising difficult questions of legitimacy.")

[211] See above on the different elements of the Weight Formula. Alexy, "On Balancing and Subsumption. A Structural Comparison," 448.

public law obligation prevails over the community interest invoked in public necessity, because upholding compliance in the future is itself an overriding interest.[212]

With regard to certain international public law obligations, the ARSIWA even foresee the possibility to exclude the invocation of the necessity excuse even *ex ante*. According to Article 26 ARSIWA, the invocation of necessity (and all other circumstances precluding wrongfulness) is generally excluded for conduct in breach of peremptory norms of general international law (*jus cogens* obligations). Non-compliance with these international obligations protecting fundamental interests of the international community as a whole thus cannot be excused under any circumstances.[213] The balancing of competing interests thus shifts automatically in favour of the *jus cogens* obligation due to its normative status—similar to interests and values protected by national constitutions in necessity cases in the domestic context. The assessment made by the legislator thus replaces the weighing of interests in a given case. But even if the competing interests were being balanced in a concrete case, the result of the balancing exercise would almost certainly lead to the same result, namely that the invocation of necessity is excluded due to the relative weight of the community interest protected by the *jus cogens* norm compared to the essential interest invoked in necessity. The duties between states are thus clearly allocated in the sense that the defendant state—although acting with the objective to protect a private good or a GPG/CPR—is responsible for the commission of an internationally wrongful act and may, in the case of injury caused to the plaintiff state, be obliged to pay reparation and to cease the wrongful act. As outlined above, this provision secures the protection of certain GPGs (including fundamental human rights obligations such as prohibition of slavery or torture) which are considered *per se* a higher interest than the interest protected in necessity.[214] The distinction between these GPGs and other GPGs or CPRs protected by international community interest obligations derives only from their status as *jus cogens* obligations and is thus "only" normative. The economic rationale of differentiating between two types of public law obligations consists in replacing the assessment of the social costs in a given case with an assessment made *ex ante* proscribed by the law in Article 26 ARSIWA. The assessment of the minimum social costs in the case at hand would usually come to the same conclusion (given the importance goods protected by the *jus cogens* obligation), but an *ex ante* exclusion of the necessity plea in the case of peremptory norms of general international law is more likely to prevent

[212]The internationally wrongful act then leads to the application of secondary obligations. However, the probability of reputational sanctions for an act which aimed at protecting an essential community interest, but did not fulfil the conditions of public necessity due to an overriding public interest protected by the international obligation in question, would be limited or reduced to zero (provided that the state ceases the wrongful act as quickly as possible). This is because all states in the international community would be aware of the dilemma situation.

[213]Similarly, international human rights treaties that include the possibility for specific derogations (e.g. a state of emergency clause) exclude the invocation with regard to certain fundamental human rights obligations (e.g. the right to life). See footnote 107.

[214]On the definition of *jus cogens* obligations and the congruence with GPGs, see Sect. 3.3.2.

abusive invocation as it is clear from the outset that the invocation will not be successful.

This rationale of Article 26 ARSIWA is also reflected in the idea of considering certain international obligations as protecting inalienable entitlements [215] This concept dates back to theoretical framework underlying different forms of remedies developed by Guido Calabresi and A. Douglas Melamed from an economic theory perspective with regard to domestic property and tort law, defining an entitlement as "inalienable to the extent that its transfer is not permitted between a willing buyer and a willing seller".[216] Joost Pauwelyn transferred this idea to the international level, arguing that in certain circumstances a stronger protection of entitlements as inalienable is advisable, for instance, when the entitlement is of a higher value and cannot be monetised, as in the case of *jus cogens* norms.[217] This explains why necessity, even in the form of public necessity, cannot be invoked to excuse a breach of a *jus cogens* obligation and consequently not be remediated by the payment of compensation for material losses.

Figure 5.1 summarises the four different possible scenarios of necessity and the respective guidelines in terms of balancing of competing essential interests on a case-by-case basis.

In conclusion, this section demonstrated that including community interests in the conditions of the necessity excuse, as it was implied in Article 25(1) lit. a) ARSIWA and is considered a progressive development of international law, is economically justified and should be made explicit. While the remaining conditions of necessity are sufficiently strict to counter the moral hazard problem and the risk of opportunistic breach, the notion of essential interest should be interpreted broadly in order not to deter behaviour creating cross-border or global benefits. This is especially reasonable because the observability and verifiability problem is not so pertinent with regard to the nature of the interest invoked. In essence, the main conclusion of this section is that based on economic reasoning there is a need for a "public necessity rule" in international law, while giving guidance on how to apply the conditions of necessity in practice (in particular, the perspective in the assessment and the standard of proof for the defendant state invoking necessity). Moreover, an economic point of view offers guidelines on how to deal with the requirement of weighing competing essential interests.

---

[215] On the concepts of property, liability, and inalienable rules as well as the idea of variable protection which will be used in particular in the analysis of different remedies, see Sect. 6.1.

[216] Calabresi and Melamed, "Property Rules, Liability Rules, and Inalienability: One View of the Cathedral," 1092.

[217] Pauwelyn, *Optimal Protection of International Law: Navigating between European Absolutism and American Voluntarism*, 50–55.

	Breach of a private law obligation (Article 25 (1) lit. b) ARSIWA)	**Breach of a public law obligation (Articles 25 (1) lit. b), 26 ARSIWA)**
Invocation of private necessity (Article 25 (1) lit. a) ARSIWA)	Minimum social costs depend on the facts of the case	Private necessity more likely to be excluded in the case of a public law obligation (*ex ante* in the case of *jus cogens* norms)
Invocation of public necessity (Article 25 (1) lit. a) ARSIWA)	Public necessity more likely to prevail over the interest protected by the private law obligation	Minimum social costs depend on the facts of the case, but rule of law argument might shift balance toward excluding public necessity (*ex ante* in the case of *jus cogens* norms)

Fig. 5.1 Scenarios of necessity and guidelines for the balancing of interests

5.2.3 On the Allocation of Costs: Compensation as a Consequence of Necessity

Following the distinction between private and public necessity in international law, this section analyses the respective financial consequences. The question to be answered is how the costs following the invocation of the necessity excuse should be allocated. Or to answer the question raised, without answering, by Robert D. Sloane: "the real question is who—which state, states, or other international actors—should bear the cost occasioned by a violation defended as necessary".[218] The aim of the section is thus to determine the circumstances in which the compensation requirement is optimal.

The consequences of invoking the necessity excuse follow from Article 27 lit. b) ARSIWA, which provides that compensation needs to be paid for any material loss caused by the excused act.[219] According to the ARSIWA Commentaries, Article

[218] Sloane, "On the Use and Abuse of Necessity in the Law of State Responsibility," 506. See also van Aaken, "On the Necessity of Necessity Measures: A Response to Alan O. Sykes," 184. ("The relevant questions are, thus, who bears the costs of uncertainty and how are incentives affected by shifting these costs.")

[219] See also, *CMS Gas Transmission Company v. Argentine Republic*, Award, para. 390. ("The Tribunal is satisfied that article 27 establishes the appropriate rule of international law on this issue. The Respondent's argument is tantamount to the assertion that a Party to this kind of treaty, or its subjects, are supposed to bear entirely the cost of the plea of the essential interests of the other Party. This is, however, not the meaning of international law or the principles governing most domestic legal systems.") *Patrick Mitchell v. Democratic Republic of the Congo*, Decision on the Application for the Annulment of the Award, 1 November 2006, ICSID Case No. ARB/99/7, para. 57, note 30. ("bearing witness to the existence of a principle of international law in this regard")

27 lit. b) ARSIWA refers to the possibility of compensation in certain cases and is framed as a without prejudice clause because it is not possible to specify in general terms when compensation is payable.[220] The Commentaries state, in particular, that "[s]ubparagraph (b) does not attempt to specify in what circumstances compensation should be payable. Generally, the range of possible situations covered by chapter V [on circumstances precluding wrongfulness] is such that to lay down a detailed regime for compensation is not appropriate. It will be for the State invoking a circumstance precluding wrongfulness to agree with any affected States on the possibility and extent of compensation payable in a given case".[221] It might be true to a certain extent that it is difficult to determine *ex ante* in general terms the financial consequences of the invocation of all six circumstances precluding wrongfulness, since they are very different in kind. But this does not exclude the possibility to offer some guidance in abstract terms based on economic theory. For the necessity excuse, this section enquires about the different possible scenarios of its invocation (i.e. private and public necessity) and aims to offer guidelines on when and how compensation should be paid. As a refined interpretation of Article 27 lit. b) ARSIWA, these insights can serve as guidance for states negotiating the matter of compensation in a given dispute, or even more generally when negotiating treaties including flexibility provisions (i.e. guidelines for treaty design).

Whilst the conditions of necessity have been much discussed in the literature and case law, the consequences of invoking necessity are largely unexamined.[222] This is not surprising given that in most cases that dealt with necessity its invocation was rejected on a factual basis and international courts and tribunals thus did not get to the point of discussing the compensation requirement.[223] At first glance, the compensation requirement seems reasonable for the necessity excuse, because states make a voluntary choice to breach an international obligation that may cause material loss to another innocent state.[224] Thus, the original idea behind this compensation requirement in international law is to disincentivise a state to shift the costs of protecting its own interests to another state.[225] However, it is less evident whether

---

[220] ARSIWA Commentaries, Article 27, para. 1.

[221] ARSIWA Commentaries, Article 27, para. 6.

[222] For a discussion of compensation in the case of necessity in the context of international investment law, see Sergey Ripinsky, "State of Necessity: Effect on Compensation," *Transnational Dispute Management* 4, no. 6 (2007), www.transnational-dispute-management.com/article.asp?key=1177

[223] See, especially, *Gabčíkovo-Nagymaros Project (Hungary v. Slovakia)*, Judgment; *Legal Consequences of the Construction of a Wall in the Occupied Palestinian Territory*, Advisory Opinion. However, in *CMS Gas Transmission Company v. Argentina*, the ICSID tribunal awarded compensation on the basis of Article 27 ARSIWA despite having rejected the applicability of necessity on factual grounds. See *CMS Gas Transmission Company v. Argentine Republic*, Award, para. 356. This assessment was later criticised in the decision on application for annulment because the rejection of necessity on the level of conditions necessarily requires discussing the applicability of reparation as a remedy for an internationally wrongful act. See *CMS Gas Transmission Company v. Argentine Republic*, Decision on the application for annulment, paras. 144–149.

[224] Crawford, *State Responsibility: the General Part*, 319.

[225] Ibid., 318.

the compensation requirement should also be applicable (at all or to the full extent) when states act in order to protect a community interest. Coming back to the classic example of necessity, should a state that destroys a foreign vessel in order to avert oil pollution in the high seas, and thus severe environmental damage, compensate the other state or should the costs not be allocated differently?

This section examines how the compensation requirement in the case of necessity influences a state's decision to breach or comply with an international legal obligation in the first place. No differentiation is made here regarding the character of the obligation breached, because at this stage it has already been established that the interest invoked in necessity prevails over the interest protected by the international obligation in question. This will usually be a private law obligation, but as we have seen, this can also be a public law obligation in a scenario where a grave and imminent peril for a community interest prevails. Even in such a scenario, compensation is to be paid to the plaintiff state who incurred the losses, while all other states of the international community have a legal interest in that the defendant state returns quickly to legality and compensates the plaintiff state. However, the analysis follows the distinction between private and public necessity in order to determine whether the obligation to pay compensation sets optimal incentives in both scenarios.[226] Since compensation in both cases is the current default rule in international law, this section will demonstrate how shifting these costs affects the incentives for self-interested states to comply with international obligations or protect an essential interest of the state (i.e. private good) or of the international community (i.e. GPG or CPR) in necessity. Both scenarios will thus be addressed in turn: firstly, invocation of private necessity against an international obligation, and, secondly, invocation of public necessity against an international obligation.

5.2.3.1 Consequences of Private Necessity in International Law

The first scenario is the situation originally foreseen by the ILC and as it derives from the concept of private necessity in domestic contract and tort law. In this baseline scenario, a state invokes necessity in order to protect a private good prevailing over another state's interest protected by an international obligation. Before examining how the compensation requirement following the invocation of necessity influences a state's decision to breach or comply with an international obligation, it is useful to recall the cost-benefit calculation with regard to the compliance decision in international law generally.[227] A rational state complies with an international legal obligation if the benefits of compliance (e.g. long-term benefits of cooperation) outweigh the expected compliance costs. *Vice versa*, a rational state violates an international obligation if the benefits of this internationally wrongful act outweigh the total

[226] Even in domestic tort law, "the question of compensation has been somewhat case-specific." Cohan, "Private and Public Necessity and the Violation of Property Rights," 732.

[227] See Sect. 1.3.

expected costs of the breach, notably compensation, which equals the probability of damage to the plaintiff state.[228] The obligation to provide reparation, in particular compensation for damage, has a deterrence effect if the net benefits of compliance are higher than the net benefits of non-compliance. The compensation requirement in the case of the necessity excuse upholds this deterrence effect by allocating the costs of necessity to the state invoking it, thus forcing the state to internalise all the costs and benefits associated with the act in necessity. The absence of the compensation requirement would not only reduce the deterrence effect on the defendant state, it would also shift the costs of the act in necessity entirely to the injured plaintiff state.[229]

Hence, it can be assumed that a state will act in necessity if the expected benefits (B_N) for the state outweigh the associated costs of necessity (C_N). It will further be assumed, for simplicity reasons, that the expected costs of necessity (C_N) equal the material losses (L) incurred by the plaintiff state times the probability (p) of these losses occurring:[230]

$$B_N > C_N;\ \text{whereas}$$

$$C_N = p(L)$$

When the expected benefits of invoking necessity equal the associated costs, a state may prefer to rather comply with the international obligation in question due to the long-term reputational costs of non-compliance.[231] Reputation works at the margins of the cost-benefit calculation of states contemplating whether to breach or comply with an international legal obligation,[232] even though in the case of a successful invocation of the necessity excuse the reputational costs are limited as the state did not commit an internationally wrongful act *stricto sensu*.

However, it is questionable whether compensation in the case of private necessity is always the optimal solution. Some authors, while affirming the compensation requirement for necessity in principle, have criticised its adverse effects in the case of economic necessity. It has been argued that, when a domestic financial crisis is the reason to breach international obligations (for instance, in international investment law), the duty to pay compensation should be delayed or reduced.[233] This critique is,

---

[228] See Sect. 6.3.2 on compensation for damage in the law of state responsibility.

[229] ARSIWA Commentaries, Article 27, para. 5. ("Without the possibility of such recourse, the State whose conduct would otherwise be unlawful might seek to shift the burden of the defence of its own interests or concerns onto an innocent third State.")

[230] It will further be assumed, for simplicity reasons, that the probability (p) of having to pay compensation for the material loss is 1, both in the case of a private and a public law obligation. Variation in the probability of enforcement of compensation being effective depending on the type of the obligation will be discussed in Sect. 6.3.2.2 on punitive damages.

[231] On reputation as a compliance mechanism, see Sect. 2.4.

[232] Guzman, *How International Law Works: A Rational Choice Theory*, 117.

[233] Sykes, "Economic "Necessity" in International Law," 323; van Aaken, "On the Necessity of Necessity Measures: A Response to Alan O. Sykes," 185–186.

in my opinion, justified, at least as regards economic necessity. When a country is in economic distress, it is reasonable to reduce the financial pressure on public finances for the time being. It then makes sense to postpone payment to a time when the economic crisis is overcome. If the suspension of the obligation in question is only temporary, then the same is valid for the suspension of the compensation requirement for the duration of the crisis.[234] However, the need for postponement of a payment obligation is not evident for other than financial reasons. For instance, postponement of payment may not be granted in scenarios where a state acts out of national security concerns or to respond to a humanitarian crisis, where the challenges are rather of a logistical nature. Admittedly, there can also be exceptions in these cases (e.g. a humanitarian crisis leading to an economic crisis and a collapse of the state administration). The difference is that in the case of economic necessity the need for postponement of payment lies in the very nature of the reason for invoking necessity. Postponement of the compensation requirement should thus constitute an exception and always depend on the facts of the case.

In some cases of economic necessity, even a reduction of the amount of compensation to be paid might have to be considered, in particular when the situation of economic distress leads to devastating effects for the population, also discussed under the term "crippling compensation".[235] It suffices to say here, that the requirement to compensate material losses caused by an act in necessity is structurally more similar to "no-fault liability" (or liability for lawful acts) discussed in the previous chapter than to reparation for damage caused by an internationally wrongful act.[236] The function is to allocate the costs between the victim state and the state acting in necessity and, depending on the circumstances, these can be distributed in a different ratio. The economic rationale is to avoid moral hazard by shifting the burden of the necessity excuse, in principle, fully to the state invoking it, at least in cases where that state invokes the protection of a private good. However, in exceptional circumstances, the deterrence effect of reparation for injury can also be upheld with reduced

---

[234] *CMS Gas Transmission Company v. Argentine Republic*, Award, para. 392. ("The answer to this question by the Respondent's expert clarifies the issue from the point of view of both its temporary nature and the duty to provide compensation: while it is difficult to reach a determination as long as the crisis is unfolding, it is possible to envisage a situation in which the investor would have a claim against the government for the compliance with its obligations once the crisis was over; thereby concluding that any suspension of the right to compensation is strictly temporary, and that this right is not extinguished by the crisis events.") See also *Sempra Energy International v. Argentine Republic*, Award, 28 September 2007, ICSID Case No. ARB/02/16, para. 394. ("The Article thus does not exclude the possibility of an eventual compensation for past events.") For a different view stating that compensation is not due during the state of necessity, see *LG&E Energy Corp., LG&E Capital Corp., and LG&E International Inc. v. Argentine Republic*, Decision on Liability, para. 264. ("Article 27 of the International Law Commission's draft articles, as well as article XI of the Treaty, does not specify if any compensation is payable to the party affected by losses during the state of necessity. Nevertheless, ... this Tribunal has decided that the damages suffered during the state of necessity should be borne by the investor.")

[235] On crippling compensation, see the discussion in Sect. 6.3.2.1.

[236] See Sect. 4.2.2.

compensation, for instance, when the financial capacities of a state exiting a situation of economic distress are still limited. Even when an immediate economic crisis is over, full compensation of losses bears the risk of slowing down the economic recovery and would thus place a disproportionate burden on the state acting in necessity. Such reduction of the amount of compensation, however, needs to be the exception and to be decided on a case-by-case basis.

To sum up, the compensation requirement achieves optimal cost allocation in cases where states invoke the protection of a private good to excuse non-compliance with an international obligation (i.e. private necessity), as longs as there exists in exceptional cases the possibility to postpone the payment of compensation and reduce the amount (in particular, in situations of economic necessity).

5.2.3.2 Consequences of Public Necessity in International Law

In the second scenario, a state invokes necessity in order to protect a GPG or CPR prevailing over another state's or the international community's interest protected by an international obligation. While in domestic tort law, the plaintiff or the state, and thus the community, takes over the costs of the individual's act in public necessity, there is on the international level no central entity that could take over the payment. Hence, the costs of public necessity need to be allocated between the plaintiff state, the state acting in public necessity, and the international community benefitting from the act. Simply upholding the compensation requirement in this constellation would mean that a state acting in the interest of the international community would have to internalise the entire costs of its actions, without being able to fully internalise the benefits (i.e. positive externalities). In other words, for a state acting in public necessity, the costs—which remain the same compared to the private necessity scenario—would usually outweigh the immediate benefits of protecting a GPG or CPR (i.e. the benefits to the extent that the defendant state is part of the international community). Thus, while GPGs and CPRs already face the collective action problem of free-riding, shifting the costs of invoking the necessity excuse on the acting state would further disincentivise self-interested states to provide them, building on the assumption that states factor in all expected costs and benefits when making their decision to act. Hence, instead of acting in public necessity, a state, taking into account the compensation requirement, would rather comply with the international obligation in question, which is undesirable in terms of the total social costs (as the overall benefits of public necessity to the international community outweigh the losses to the victim state).

In contrast, without a requirement to pay compensation, a state is more likely to act in public necessity, and not comply with the international obligation in question, provided that the expected benefits of protecting the GPG or CPR outweigh the associated costs. Lifting the compensation requirement signifies that a state acting in the interest of the international community would partially internalise the benefits of its actions, without having to bear any additional costs to compensate for the losses which fall exclusively on the plaintiff state. It has to be kept in mind that the victim state also profits from the act in public necessity as a member of the international community (theoretically to the same degree as the defendant state). Shifting the costs of public necessity entirely to the plaintiff state can also be justified in constellations where the peril to the GPG or CPR stems from the sphere of that state (e.g. ownership of the vessel causing oil pollution in the high seas). In addition, the absence of the compensation requirement seems to be the preferable solution despite its reduction of the deterrence effect on the defendant state, given that the underlying problem in these constellations consists in GPG provision or CPR protection and less in avoiding moral hazard and opportunistic breach.

However, shifting the entire costs of public necessity to the plaintiff state might not always be the optimal solution. Cost-sharing between the defendant and the plaintiff state according to a certain ratio could be an alternative as long as the share falling on the defendant state is not too high as to disincentivise acting in public necessity. Or, as in the domestic context, where the costs of public necessity are sometimes borne by the community, one could think of alternative ways of cost allocation which include other states in the international community benefitting from the act in public necessity. The precondition is also here that these cost-sharing arrangements do not lead to the non-provision of the GPG by the defendant state, while providing that all states which derive benefits from the act contribute to the remediation of the losses incurred by the plaintiff state.

A first possibility, even if not foreseen in the ARSIWA, could be to share the costs proportionally between the defendant state and other benefitting third states.[237] The defendant state would remain obliged to compensate fully the plaintiff state for any material loss caused by the act in necessity, because the plaintiff state could only turn against and invoke the responsibility of the state taking the act excused in necessity, but not against third states that may have benefitted from the act in question. It is the defendant state that would then have to claim regress against third states profiting from the act in public necessity or to engage them in negotiations on how to jointly remediate the losses incurred by the victim state.[238] This idea builds on the rationale of "no-fault liability", that is on the concept of secondary due diligence obligations of loss remediation in the case of harm caused by lawful behaviour, even though this is not recognised as a general principle in international

[237] An analogy could be drawn here to Article 47 ARSIWA on the plurality of responsible states which reads as follows: "1. Where several States are responsible for the same internationally wrongful act, the responsibility of each State may be invoked in relation to that act. 2. Paragraph 1: (a) does not permit any injured State to recover, by way of compensation, more than the damage it has suffered; (b) is without prejudice to any right of recourse against the other responsible States."

[238] The reasoning is similar if the act in necessity creates benefits that are falling exclusively on a third state, thus creating a positive externality only for the benefitting third state. In this private goods scenario, the defendant state which does not profit from the act in private necessity would decide in favour of compliance with the international obligation in question if it has to bear the full costs of compensation to the plaintiff state. Facilitating private necessity in such a constellation would thus require that the defendant state can take full recourse (i.e. without an own contribution) against the third state, thus shifting the costs exclusively the third state. This is similar to domestic law where the costs of compensation are usually borne by the benefitting third party only.

law.[239] This approach of loss allocation thus relies on voluntary contributions from benefitting third states. Yet, the distribution of costs of public necessity among all states profiting from the act relates to the financing of GPG provision or CPR protection, which is a different public good than the provision of the good itself. While the act in public necessity has the characteristics of a best-shot GPG, achieving that all states benefitting from the act contribute proportionally to its financing has the characteristics of an aggregate-effort GPG. It is thus questionable whether the probability of successful regress is always 1 because third states might try to avoid a financial contribution. The probability will be higher when the number of states profiting directly from public necessity is limited and easily determined. This can, for instance, be the case of a regional or transnational public good: when one state bombs a foreign vessel polluting the high seas, it might be the nearest coastal states that seize the immediate benefits (even if potentially all states in the international community profit from the preservation of natural resources). In such a constellation with a limited and clearly identifiable number of states involved, the quota of compensation is easily determinable and traditional enforcement mechanisms of payment claims could apply (e.g. reputation). On the contrary, the probability of a successful regress will be lower when all states in the international community benefit from the act in public necessity, as in the case of GPGs. In such a constellation, the costs of compensation would need to be distributed between all states of the international community, thus rendering the share for each state very small and enforcement of the recourse claims by the defendant state difficult and expensive. When the chances of successful regress become limited, the state considering acting in public necessity faces the risk of bearing the full costs of compensation (while internalising only a very small share of the benefits), which is disadvantageous compared to shifting the costs to the plaintiff state.

Before having recourse to this *ultima ratio* solution, which shifts the costs to the victim state, a second possible cost-sharing arrangement can be thought of. It is also inspired by the solutions known from the context of liability for lawful acts ("no-fault liability"), namely claim settlement funds. While these are mostly financed by private operators engaging in certain hazardous activities (e.g. the International Compensation Fund for Marine Oil Pollution Damage),[240] others are created on an inter-state level with the aim to mitigate the harm stemming from hazardous activities with additional public funds (e.g. the Compensation Fund for Nuclear Damage). These funds facilitate, amongst others, compensation of the economic losses resulting from the contamination of the environment as well as costs incurred by clean-up operations or the reinstatement of the environment. The problem is that in some cases the losses stemming from acts in public necessity are not linked to a

[239] See Sect. 4.2.2.

[240] See also the similarly functioning Compensation Fund for Damages Caused by Transportation of Hazardous and Noxious Substances by Sea (HNS Fund) to be established under the International Convention on Liability and Compensation for Damage in Connection with the Carriage of Hazardous and Noxious Substances by Sea (concluded 1996, amended 2010, not yet entered into force) *International Maritime Organization*.

particular hazardous activity (covered by a particular convention) but consist in *prima facie* non-compliant behaviour in order to protect an overriding interest of the international community. The underlying rationale would nonetheless be to allocate the losses stemming from lawful activities excused in necessity through *ex ante* financial contributions by states (not private operators). An option could be to rely on trust funds established by multilateral treaty regimes with the objective to provide GPGs or preserve CPRs in primary law, in particular in the area of international environmental or climate change law (e.g. the Global Environment Facility,[241] the Green Climate Fund,[242] the Climate Investment Funds,[243] or the Fund for responding to Loss and Damage[244]). Paying compensation in the case of public necessity out of such trust funds could be an option, but an option which requires that states agree *ex ante* on such a purpose of the fund. The advantage of such a trust fund solution would be that states considering acting in public necessity know that they would not have to bear the costs and thus not be further disincentivised to provide a GPG or protect a CPR. This would not encourage opportunistic behaviour, as states are still confronted with the free-rider problematic and the risk that the measures do not fulfil the strict conditions of public necessity.

These findings are summarised in Fig. 5.2 which presents the conceivable scenarios of private and public necessity and the respective conclusions in terms of compensation.

In conclusion, the compensation requirement does not achieve optimal cost allocation in cases where states invoke the protection of GPG or CPR to excuse non-compliance with an international obligation. The preferable and *ultima ratio* solution is to shift the costs to the plaintiff state. Alternatively, costs could be shared between the defendant and the plaintiff state, as long as the share falling on the defendant state is not too large as to disincentivise acting in public necessity. Further alternative cost-sharing arrangements, which include other states in the international community benefitting from the act in public necessity (e.g. the possibility to claim regress or trust funds), are the optimal solution, but not readily available for this specific purpose in international law.

5.2.4 Conclusion on Necessity as an Excuse in International Law

This part of the chapter analysed the necessity excuse as a circumstance precluding wrongfulness of state acts in international law from an economic perspective. In terms of underlying theory, it relied on the economic analysis of private and public

[241] https://www.thegef.org

[242] https://www.greenclimate.fund

[243] https://www.climateinvestmentfunds.org

[244] https://unfccc.int/loss-and-damage-fund-joint-interim-secretariat

	Breach of a private or public law obligation (except *jus cogens*)
Invocation of private necessity	Compensation with possibility of postponement and reduction ('crippling compensation')
Invocation of public necessity	No compensation with possibility of cost-sharing between the parties involved or among benefitting states (e.g. possibility of regress or trust fund solutions)

Fig. 5.2 Compensation in the case of private and public necessity

necessity in domestic contract and tort law to capture the fact that the international legal order combines a private and a public dimension. It defined the objectives of the necessity excuse in international law as mitigating a trade-off between compliance with different types of international legal obligations (i.e. private good, club good, CPR or GPG obligations) and flexibility in the presence of unforeseen circumstances (i.e. private or public necessity, depending on the objective of the breach). For instance, the necessity provision should deter opportunistic breach, but without discouraging the provision of GPGs.

First, as regards the optimal allocation of duties, it has been argued in favour of a broad interpretation of what constitutes an essential interest that may be invoked by states breaching international law in order not to deter behaviour creating cross-border or global benefits. It is suggested to define the essential interest to be protected in necessity along the lines of different types of goods at the international level: private necessity relating to the protection of private goods and public necessity relating to the protection of GPGs or CPRs. The inclusion of community interests is in line with the current understanding of the necessity excuse, but an aspect that is still considered rather progressive development of international law.

Secondly, as regards the optimal allocation of costs, the analysis demonstrated the need to distinguish in terms of the financial consequences of invoking the necessity excuse depending on whether the essential interest protected relates to a private good or a GPG or CPR. It has been acknowledged that the compensation requirement sets optimal incentives in cases where states invoke private necessity, as it counters the moral hazard problem and the risk of opportunistic breach, as longs as there exists in exceptional cases the possibility to postpone payment of compensation and reduce its amount (in particular, in situations of economic necessity). In contrast, it is suggested to lift the compensation requirement and shift the costs to the plaintiff state as an *ultima ratio* solution, when states act in public necessity in order to protect a community interest. Nonetheless, a more fine-tuned approach may be preferable, which may consist of cost-sharing arrangements between the defendant and the plaintiff state or by including other states in the international community benefitting from the act in public necessity (e.g. the possibility to claim regress when the number of benefitting states is limited or trust funds in the case of GPGs and CPRs of global reach). Such alternative arrangements should, however, not lead to the non-provision of the GPG by the defendant state and bear the disadvantage that they are not readily available for this specific purpose in international law.

These findings offer a more nuanced theoretical understanding of the concept of necessity as an excuse in international law. These insights can be used as practical guidelines on cost allocation for solving inter-state disputes regarding necessity cases (i.e. through negotiation between the parties or, where available, international tribunals) or for drafting international agreements.[245]

In sum, the principal conclusion is that economic reasoning confirms the need for a "public necessity rule" in international law and offers guidance on how to apply the conditions of necessity in practice (in particular, the perspective in the assessment and the standard of proof for the defendant state invoking necessity as well as the weighing of competing essential interests). It also suggests differentiating further on the side of the financial consequences following the invocation of necessity. Thus, this section offered, based on rational choice theory, concrete suggestions on how the necessity excuse can set stronger incentives for the provision of GPGs and the protection of CPRs.

5.3 A Rational Choice Analysis of the Other Excuses and Justifications

The questions of optimal allocation of duties and costs are also pertinent regarding the other five circumstances precluding wrongfulness in international law. Drawing on the insights from the analysis of the necessity excuse, this section looks in the following, firstly, at the two other excuses, distress and *force majeure*. It has already been mentioned in the preface to this chapter that the three excuses bear similarities in their underlying problem constellation as they relate to situations where a defendant state acts in order to protect a prevailing interest emanating from a source other than the plaintiff state (i.e. an external circumstance) and is consequently for the time being dispensed from compliance with the international obligation in question.[246] In a second step, this section analyses the two justifications, consent and self-defence,

[245] See also, Paddeu, *Justification and Excuse in International Law: Concept and Theory of General Defences*, 92. ("In weighing the equities of the case, the parties may consider factors such as the legality of the conduct in question, the character of the interest protected (is it collective or individual?) and the interest impaired, and whether it is desirable to encourage (other) states to act in a similar way or whether they should be discouraged from so doing [...].")

[246] See Sect. 5.1.

while countermeasures will be dealt with at the level of implementation of state responsibility.[247] As already indicated, these justifications are conceptually different as the defendant state's action relates to some prior action of the plaintiff state (e.g. an expression of consent, an act of aggression, or a wrongful act).[248] Thus, the justifying circumstances lie in the realm of the injured plaintiff state (i.e. internal circumstances), and hence the subsequent breach of international law is rooted in reciprocal behaviour.[249] For both categories, the focus of the analysis will lie on the extent to which they integrate the protection of community interests by setting adequate incentives for the provision of GPGs and the protection of CPRs. In particular, it will question the adequacy of the general *jus cogens* exception and the compensation requirement, in particular with regard to innocent third states, depending on the underlying problem constellation.

5.3.1 Excuses

Like necessity, distress and *force majeure* aim to achieve a trade-off between conformity with international obligations and flexibility when values conflict in the presence of unforeseeable and extraordinary circumstances. Distress, which is discussed first, bears most similarities with necessity as both excuses relate to a deliberate subjective choice of the defendant state not to comply with an international obligation after balancing competing interests (i.e. relative impossibility).[250] It differs only in that it is limited to the moral choice of saving human life (in contrast to the broader notion of an endangered "essential interest") and requires, if it is not about the agent's own life, a direct relationship between the individual state official and the person whose life is in peril.[251] *Force majeure*, in contrast, covers situations where the state (or a state agent) is acting in a completely involuntary manner and is thus compelled to breach international law (i.e. material and absolute impossibility).[252] Even though the scope of both excuses is more limited than in the case of necessity, it is worthwhile to assess briefly how they counter moral hazard by allocating legal duties and the costs of acts in distress or *force majeure* while taking into account the private and public dimensions of international law.

[247] See Chap. 7.

[248] See Sect. 5.1.

[249] On this distinction between excuses and justifications, see ARSIWA Commentaries, Article 25, para. 2. Sykes, "Economic "Necessity" in International Law," 298; Heathcote, "Circumstances Precluding Wrongfulness in the ILC Articles on State Responsibility: Necessity," in *The Law of International Responsibility*, ed. Crawford, Pellet, and Olleson, 496.

[250] Heathcote, "Circumstances Precluding Wrongfulness in the ILC Articles on State Responsibility: Necessity," in *The Law of International Responsibility*, ed. Crawford, Pellet, and Olleson, 491, 495.

[251] ARSIWA Commentaries, Article 25, para. 2.

[252] ARSIWA Commentaries, Article 25, para. 2. Tanzi, "State of Necessity," para. 2.

5.3.1.1 Distress

The excuse of distress finds its basis in customary international law.[253] It has also been integrated in several international agreements, for instance, in the United Nations Convention on the Law of the Sea and in different international conventions on the prevention of maritime pollution.[254] As a concept of the law of state responsibility, it is laid down in Article 24 ARSIWA.[255] It precludes wrongfulness in scenarios where a state agent is in a situation of peril and there is "no other reasonable way" of saving his or her life or the life of persons under his or her care than by violating international obligations of the state.[256] The circumstances may be similar to a scenario of *force majeure* (e.g. severe weather conditions), but the individual situation of the agent is comparable to that of necessity (i.e. voluntary decision-making based on a balancing of competing interests).[257] Even if the choice of the agent is practically reduced to zero, he or she decides voluntarily (unlike in scenarios of *force majeure*, where impossibility is material and not due to the absence of other means) to protect the immediate interest of saving human lives to whom he or she has a special supervisory relationship (such as the passengers or crew of a ship or airplane), irrespective of their nationality.[258] The objective of this special relationship requirement was to exclude situations that depend on moral choice rather than compulsion.[259] In fact, the limitation to life-saving measures by an

---

[253] On the concept of distress, see Sandra Szurek, "Circumstances Precluding Wrongfulness in the ILC Articles on State Responsibility: Distress," in *The Law of International Responsibility*, ed. James Crawford, Alain Pellet, and Simon Olleson (Oxford: Oxford University Press, 2010), 481–489; Elena Fasoli, "Distress," ed. Anne Peters and Rüdiger Wolfrum, *Max Planck Encyclopedia of Public International Law* (Oxford Public International Law: Oxford University Press, 2021), http://opil.ouplaw.com, Article last updated in June 2013; Paddeu, *Justification and Excuse in International Law: Concept and Theory of General Defences*, chap. 9.

[254] Articles 18(2), 39(1)(c), 98 and 109 United Nations Convention on the Law of the Sea (UNCLOS). Article IV(1)(a) International Convention for the Prevention of Pollution of the Sea by Oil (concluded 12 May 1954, entered into force 26 July 1958) 327 *UNTS* 3. Article V (1) Convention on the Prevention of Marine Pollution by Dumping of Wastes and other Matter. For further examples, see ARSIWA Commentaries, Article 24, para. 5.

[255] Article 24 ARSIWA reads: "1. The wrongfulness of an act of a State not in conformity with an international obligation of that State is precluded if the author of the act in question has no other reasonable way, in a situation of distress, of saving the author's life or the lives of other persons entrusted to the author's care.

2. Paragraph 1 does not apply if:

(*a*) the situation of distress is due, either alone or in combination with other factors, to the conduct of the State invoking it; or

(*b*) the act in question is likely to create a comparable or greater peril."

[256] ARSIWA Commentaries, Article 24, para. 1.

[257] Szurek, "Circumstances Precluding Wrongfulness in the ILC Articles on State Responsibility: Distress," in *The Law of International Responsibility*, ed. Crawford, Pellet, and Olleson, 483.

[258] ARSIWA Commentaries, Article 24, paras. 1, 7. Crawford, *State Responsibility: the General Part*, 301.

[259] United Nations International Law Commission, *Yearbook of the International Law Commission*, 1999, Volume I (UN Doc. A/CN.4/SER.A/1999), p. 180, para. 40.

individual agent in distress is what distinguishes this excuse from necessity, which relates to the protection of legitimate state interests in more general cases of emergencies.[260] Classic examples of distress include aircrafts or ships entering foreign state territory by voluntarily changing the course under stress of weather or following mechanical or navigational failure.[261] Other examples relate to situations where aircrafts in distress discharge oil into the air or ships in distress discharge oil or wastes into the high seas or foreign territorial waters.[262] Article 24 ARSIWA precludes wrongfulness of such conduct only so far as it is necessary to avoid a life-threatening situation.[263] Thus, it can excuse breaches of obligations prohibiting passage through foreign territory, airspace or territorial waters or pollution of international or territorial waters, but does not exempt the state, for instance, from notification requirements related to the passage of foreign territory.[264]

If we compare the conditions of distress with those of necessity, we see that, firstly, the essential interest protected by the state agent (and therefore the state) relates only to the protection of human life.[265] However, in exceptional cases distress may extent to less than life-threatening situations. The tribunal in the *Rainbow Warrior* arbitration referred to the "existence of very exceptional circumstances of extreme urgency involving medical or other considerations of an elementary nature".[266] Thus, while a serious risk to the physical health of individuals may suffice, the challenge will be "to determine the threshold below which the situation is no longer one of distress",[267] which will often depend on the facts of the case. It is certain, however, that the concept of distress, as laid down in the ARSIWA and reflecting positive law, excludes humanitarian assistance in emergency situations of the state more generally, which fall, if any, under the necessity provision.[268] This derives from the additional requirement regarding the identity of the individuals in a life-threatening situation (other than the agent), namely the existence of a special

---

[260] ARSIWA Commentaries, Article 24, paras. 1, 7.

[261] Distress can also arise in situations where an agent violates a land frontier in order to save the life of a person in peril (e.g. on a river). ARSIWA Commentaries, Article 24, paras. 2, 4. Crawford, *State Responsibility: the General Part*, 301–302.

[262] See, for instance, the scenarios now regulated by the international conventions on the prevention of maritime pollution.

[263] ARSIWA Commentaries, Article 24, para. 8.

[264] ARSIWA Commentaries, Article 24, para. 8. See also Crawford, *State Responsibility: the General Part*, 304–305.

[265] ARSIWA Commentaries, Article 24, para. 6.

[266] *Difference between New Zealand and France Concerning the Interpretation or Application of two Agreements concluded on 9 July 1986 between the two States and Which Related to the Problems Arising from the Rainbow Warrior Affair*, Award, p. 255, para. 79.

[267] Szurek, "Circumstances Precluding Wrongfulness in the ILC Articles on State Responsibility: Distress," in *The Law of International Responsibility*, ed. Crawford, Pellet, and Olleson, 487.

[268] On the need to widen the relatively narrow conception of distress adopted by the ILC to elementary considerations of humanity (in particular, humanitarian assistance), see in particular ibid., 484–489.

supervisory relationship. Beyond the classic scenarios of ships or aircrafts in distress, this excuse may also apply to state interventions aiming at the unilateral removal of nationals in situations of serious unrest in the territory of another state,[269] at least if one interprets the special supervisory relationship requirement largely (e.g. the foreign minister in charge of his or her agents abroad).[270] In contrast, the distress does not cover the case of humanitarian interventions in other countries to protect parts of the populations against the government's will due to a lack of a special supervisory relationship; violation of the territorial sovereignty and interference in the internal affairs will thus not be excused.[271] From the perspective of economic theory of goods, we have seen before that life-saving measures can have two dimensions: on the one hand, they have private good characteristics to the extent that the state official protects his or her own life or that of other physical persons entrusted to his or her care (which is also in the interest of the agent's state). Whether these are nationals of the agent's state or of a third state matters only with regard to an eventual recourse against the benefitting third state in case the defendant state has to compensate the plaintiff state, as will be discussed further below. On the other hand, life-saving measures can also have GPG characteristics to the extent that all states in the international community derive value from the protection of human life as a fundamental human right. Distress can thus be understood as a very specific case of both private and public necessity (i.e. mixed good characteristics), bearing similarities to classic tort law scenarios in domestic law.

Secondly, given that the scope of distress with its focus on the protection of human life is more limited than necessity, the risk of opportunistic breach and moral hazard is potentially lower. In fact, it is "on the underlying facts of the situation that the positions of [s]tates often diverge, and not on the principle of distress as a circumstance precluding wrongfulness, which is only rarely contested by [s]tates".[272] Since distress relates to the concrete action of an individual state agent in an emergency situation (unlike a state taking a deliberate decision to protect a vital state interest), distress has a strong subjective dimension which relates to the agent's assessment of a situation of distress and available courses of action. If there is

---

[269] Ibid., 486.

[270] Federica I. Paddeu and Freya Jephcott argue that even if a general relationship between the state and its own population is not sufficient, "to some extent, the fate of the population is within the control of the central authorities," thus assuming that the special relationship criterion is met when states take measures of containment or mitigation of a contagious disease such as the coronavirus and concluding that such scenarios will most likely fall under distress. Paddeu and Jephcott, "Covid-19 and Defences in the Law of State Responsibility: Part II".

[271] Szurek, "Circumstances Precluding Wrongfulness in the ILC Articles on State Responsibility: Distress," in *The Law of International Responsibility*, ed. Crawford, Pellet, and Olleson, 487. A similar example consists in cases where a military ship rescues refugees from the territorial waters of a third state. This does not qualify as distress due to the lack of a special supervisory relationship, but it may constitute a case of necessity, provided there is no employment of force. However, if the ship with the rescued refugees on board finds itself in an emergency situation and seeks refuge in the harbour of another state, this may qualify as distress.

[272] Ibid., 485–486.

potential for abuse of the distress excuse, this is with regard to the intentions of the agent which are difficult to observe and verify.[273] For instance, it might be that, in hindsight, there existed in a given situation only a minor health risk to an individual in the agent's care, but at the time of action the agent did not have the time or the means to properly assess the situation and thus assumed a life-threatening situation. Sandra Szurek calls this the "psychological element" of distress which consists in the fact that "the author was reasonably justified in believing that there was no other means to save the lives in question but to breach international law".[274] Against the background of the problem of hindsight bias, I agree that distress cannot only be judged on the basis of the objective facts.[275] The "no other reasonable way" condition of distress, in my opinion, needs to foresee an objective *ex post* control taking into account the *ex ante* perspective of the agent, thus whether his or her assessment of the life-threatening situation and the chosen course of action to save the lives in peril was based on good faith.[276] This is in line with what has been argued above with relation to necessity and the assessment of the grave and imminent peril to an essential interest and the act in necessity constituting the "only way" to protect that interest.[277] Moreover, the notion of contribution to the situation of distress is narrower than in the case of necessity, and therefore the invocation of distress is less likely to be rendered inapplicable. Distress (and *force majeure*) are not applicable if the situation is due, either alone or in combination with other factors, to the conduct of the state invoking it,[278] and thus seem to presuppose a certain degree of causation. In fact, indirect or involuntary contribution to the situation of distress will often not suffice for the exclusion of its invocation, as the formulation in exceptional terms suggests that the state's role in the occurrence of distress must be substantial and that priority should be given to necessary life-saving measures done in good faith, even if, in hindsight, the state could have acted differently.[279] Hence, the conditions of distress and their way of assessment seem

[273] On the problem to observe and verify subjective elements in the law of state responsibility, see Sect. 4.1.2.1.

[274] Szurek, "Circumstances Precluding Wrongfulness in the ILC Articles on State Responsibility: Distress," in *The Law of International Responsibility*, ed. Crawford, Pellet, and Olleson, 482.

[275] This was argued during the deliberations in the ILC. United Nations International Law Commission, *Yearbook of the International Law Commission*, 1999, Volume I (UN Doc. A/CN.4/SER. A/1999), p. 179, para. 31. ("In other words, the State which was the author of the wrongful act should not be judged on its intentions, but on its acts.")

[276] See also United Nations International Law Commission, *Second Report on State Responsibility by Special Rapporteur James Crawford*, Fifty-First Session, 1999 (UN Doc. A/CN.4/498), p. 68, para. 273. ("For these reasons article 32 should be framed in terms of a reasonable belief in a life-threatening situation.")

[277] See Sect. 5.2.2.1. Thus, while the way of assessment of the respective conditions should be the same, the reasonableness criterion of distress provides more "flexibility regarding the choices of action by the agent in saving lives," as the necessity plea which requires that the measures taken constitute the 'only way' to respond to the emergency situation. ARSIWA Commentaries, Article 24, para. 6.

[278] Article 24(2) lit. a) ARSIWA, Article 23(2) lit. a) ARSIWA.

[279] ARSIWA Commentaries, Article 24, para. 9 with reference to Article 23, para. 9.

adequate to counter the risk of moral hazard while upholding the prevailing interest of saving human lives.

Thirdly, distress foresees, similar to necessity, a balancing of competing interests or a proportionality requirement. According to Article 24(2) lit. b) ARSIWA, distress does not cover conduct likely to create a comparable or greater peril than saving the lives of the persons entrusted to the agent's care. Distress can thus only preclude wrongfulness when the immediate interest in saving human lives clearly outweighs the other interests at stake in the given circumstance.[280] The ARSIWA Commentaries mention as examples cases where "a military aircraft carrying explosives might cause a disaster by making an emergency landing, or a nuclear submarine with a serious breakdown might cause radioactive contamination to a port in which it sought refuge".[281] In such scenarios, conduct of the state agent sought to be excused in distress might endanger more lives than it may save.[282] Thus, when assessing *ex post* the agent's decision of action, the balancing of competing interests needs to take into account the overall objective of the distress provision which is to save human lives.[283] The requirement to balance competing interests is specified in Article 26 ARSIWA, which excludes the application of circumstances precluding wrongfulness, including distress, in the case of breach of peremptory norms of general international law.[284] This is logical in the case of distress given that all peremptory norms recognised so far relate directly or indirectly to the protection of human life or legal rights of comparable importance,[285] and thus breach of *jus cogens* obligations automatically entails that there was substantial harm to human life. Hence, the invocation of distress is excluded *ex ante* in cases where specific GPG obligations are concerned (i.e. *jus cogens* norms). Beyond this general exception, it will depend on the facts of the case, whether the interest protected by the obligation in question is higher or comparable to saving lives in distress. It does not necessarily extend to all public law obligations (that is, protecting GPGs and CPRs), but can probably be affirmed when the act in distress causes serious harm to common resources endangering, at least indirectly, the health and the lives of a large number of people in the affected region. An example would a nuclear submarine in failure causing radioactive contamination in the high seas. Thus, the typical scenarios where distress can be invoked are against private law obligations (relating to private goods), that is obligations prohibiting passage through or pollution of foreign territory, airspace, or territorial waters.[286] Yet, the excuse of distress is only

[280] ARSIWA Commentaries, Article 24, para. 10.

[281] Ibid.

[282] Ibid.

[283] Ibid. See also Crawford, *State Responsibility: the General Part*, 305.

[284] Ibid., 315, 317.

[285] To recall, among the most commonly accepted peremptory norms are the right to self-determination, the basic rules of international humanitarian law in armed conflict as well as the prohibitions of aggression, genocide, slavery, apartheid and systematic racial discrimination, crimes against humanity, and torture. See further Sect. 3.3.2.

[286] This is similar to domestic tort law where a situation of distress is usually invoked to excuse breach of an obligation protecting the property of the plaintiff.

applicable insofar as the conduct is necessary to avoid a life-threatening situation, and so the state is not exempted, for instance, from notification requirements related to the passage of foreign territory.[287] Hence, no general statement can be made as to which abstract type of obligation excludes the invocation of distress, as the provision is not about the protection of mere legal interests, with the exception of *jus cogens* obligations as normative GPGs. As Szurek rightly points out, "no domestic legal system requires of any of its subjects" to "sacrifice [...] lives for the respect of the law".[288] The balancing of interests concerns rather a comparative risk assessment between, on the one hand, the concrete threat to life, and, on the other hand, the similar or greater risk of harm to a comparable legal right (usually human life) protected by the obligation in question, and thus depends on the facts of the case at hand. It is the essence of the concept of distress that violations of mere legal interests can temporarily be excused, even more so when there is no concrete risk of physical harm (e.g. simple passage through foreign territory).

Finally, if we look at the legal consequences of distress, compensation (Article 27 lit. b) ARSIWA) seems justified, as for necessity, since both excuses relate to choices voluntarily made by a state which may cause material loss to another state.[289] Moreover, in situations of necessity and distress, the circumstance precluding wrongfulness is not the fault of the victim state,[290] a state (or its agent) acting in distress shall thus not be tempted to shift the burden of protecting its own interests on to another state.[291] Due to the similarities with necessity, James Crawford proposed in the Second Report of the ILC to limit the possibility of compensation to the cases of necessity and distress, the idea being that "an innocent third [s]tate is not expected to bear alone any actual losses arising from the invocation of distress or necessity".[292] For instance, it seems appropriate that the state whose leaking vessel causes oil pollution in a situation of distress will pay for the actual clean-up costs.[293] Szurek confirms that "distress does not necessarily preclude an obligation to pay compensation to the [s]tate to which the obligation was due" and that "it can be conceived

[287] Another example, similar to the ones outlined above with regard to necessity, is the excused breach of the fair and equitable treatment obligation deriving from international investment treaties by ordering severe quarantine measures which risk to delay foreign investment projects or of bilateral aviation agreements by ordering travel bans. See Federica I. Paddeu and Freya Jephcott, "Covid-19 and Defences in the Law of State Responsibility: Part I," *EJIL: Talk!* (Blog of the European Journal of International Law), 17 March 2020, https://www.ejiltalk.org/covid-19-and-defences-in-the-law-of-state-responsibility-part-i/

[288] Szurek, "Circumstances Precluding Wrongfulness in the ILC Articles on State Responsibility: Distress," in *The Law of International Responsibility*, ed. Crawford, Pellet, and Olleson, 483.

[289] Crawford, *State Responsibility: the General Part*, 319.

[290] Forteau, "Reparation in the Event of a Circumstance Precluding Wrongfulness," in *The Law of International Responsibility*, ed. Crawford, Pellet, and Olleson, 893.

[291] ARSIWA Commentaries, Article 27, para. 5.

[292] United Nations International Law Commission, *Second Report on State Responsibility by Special Rapporteur James Crawford*, Fifty-First Session, 1999 (UN Doc. A/CN.4/498), p. 85, paras. 346, 349.

[293] Crawford, *State Responsibility: the General Part*, 318.

that for equitable reasons or to prevent the third innocent [s]tate bearing the unjust burden compensation may possibly be due".[294]

It is useful to examine whether these arguments for the compensation requirement in the case of distress are confirmed from an economic perspective. As regards the rationale of compensation, it serves the same objective than necessity, which is to counter moral hazard by upholding the deterrence effect of reparation and thus inducing actors to factor in the costs of the action in distress.[295] Taking a look at the different scenarios, we have seen that distress serves to protect individual human life and thus predominantly a private good of the defendant state (if the life of the agent or its nationals is concerned) or a third state (if the life of other nationals in a special supervisory relationship with the acting state agent is concerned). Thus, while there is also a GPG dimension, as all states derive value from the life-saving measures, the benefitting states will always be easily identified. The compensation requirement thus falls, in principle, fully on the state whose agent acted in distress, but with the possibility of partial recourse (if in addition to the agent or own nationals, citizens of third states are rescued) or full recourse against third states (if exclusively citizens of those states are rescued). Compensation should even be upheld in a scenario where not a private law obligation is affected (e.g. obligations prohibiting passage through or pollution of foreign territory, airspace, or territorial waters), but a public law obligation (e.g. pollution of the high seas as a CPR). If the risk of harm to individuals is not prevailing over the interest in life-saving measures (having also GPG characteristics), the act in distress can be excused, but any clean-up costs falling on any voluntary state (that is, restoration of common resources as another public good) should be compensated. However, in some constellations, exceptions from the compensation requirement may be warranted. Federica Paddeu argues that the compensation requirement might not be adequate for equity reasons, for instance, when "the captain of a public vessel of a developing country carrying refugees rescued at sea takes shelter from a storm in the military port of a developed state without the latter's consent [and causing damage when entering the port]".[296] In her opinion, payment of compensation may not be a fair solution in light of the financial capacities of the developing state and in order not to discourage the life-saving measures excused in distress.[297] This reasoning reflects, on the one hand, the

[294] Szurek, "Circumstances Precluding Wrongfulness in the ILC Articles on State Responsibility: Distress," in *The Law of International Responsibility*, ed. Crawford, Pellet, and Olleson, 483–484.

[295] Crawford argues that the compensation requirement "may facilitate reliance on distress as a basis for saving lives, which must be in the general interest." United Nations International Law Commission, *Second Report on State Responsibility by Special Rapporteur James Crawford*, Fifty-First Session, 1999 (UN Doc. A/CN.4/498), p. 85, para. 346. This reasoning is, however, not persuasive, as the compensation requirement in itself cannot justify the concept of distress, but the compensation requirement may increase the acceptance of the distress excuse as a principle of law since it can effectively counter cases of moral hazard and opportunistic breach.

[296] Paddeu, *Justification and Excuse in International Law: Concept and Theory of General Defences*, 85.

[297] Ibid.

concept of "crippling compensation", and, on the other hand, the problem of disincentivising acts in distress which are in the interest of the international community. In exceptional cases, in particular, when the costs cannot be borne by the state acting in distress or cannot be shared with the states benefitting from the act (as in the case of refugees), the costs may be shifted fully or partially to the victim state. It should, however, be noted that, unlike in the case of necessity, the agent in a situation of distress has no real choice other than to break the law. The margin of appreciation in favour of live-saving measures will usually be reduced to zero.[298] Hence, there is little risk that the compensation requirement *ex ante* discourages live-saving measures in a situation of distress (as the benefits of the action usually outweigh the costs of non-compliance including compensation for losses), but on the contrary it can deter opportunistic breach and behaviour that may have contributed to the situation of distress. Nonetheless, the compensation requirement plays a strong role as a tool of *ex post* cost allocation (like *force majeure*, as we will see in the following section), which allows taking into account equity considerations.

5.3.1.2 *Force Majeure*

Force majeure, as laid down in Article 23 ARSIWA,[299] derives from a general principle of international law accepted by international tribunals and has been incorporated as a primary rule in several international agreements, for instance, related to the innocent passage of ships (e.g. Article 18(2) UNCLOS).[300] It relates

---

[298] Fasoli, "Distress," para. 7. ("The agent, conscious of behaving in violation of international law and theoretically in a position to avoid the wrongful conduct, nonetheless chooses to violate the rule, since compliance with international law would almost certainly cause his or her death or that of the persons entrusted to his care.")

[299] Article 23 ARSIWA reads: "1. The wrongfulness of an act of a State not in conformity with an international obligation of that State is precluded if the act is due to force majeure, that is the occurrence of an irresistible force or of an unforeseen event, beyond the control of the State, making it materially impossible in the circumstances to perform the obligation.

2. Paragraph 1 does not apply if:

(*a*) the situation of force majeure is due, either alone or in combination with other factors, to the conduct of the State invoking it; or

(*b*) the State has assumed the risk of that situation occurring."

[300] ARSIWA Commentaries, Article 23, paras. 6–7. On the genesis of *force majeure* in international law, emphasising that analogous doctrines exist in domestic legal systems, see Federica I. Paddeu, "A Genealogy of Force Majeure in International Law," *The British Yearbook of International Law* 82, no. 1 (2011): 381–494. For an overview of the concept of *force majeure* in international law, see also Szurek, "Circumstances Precluding Wrongfulness in the ILC Articles on State Responsibility: Force Majeure," in *The Law of International Responsibility*, ed. Crawford, Pellet, and Olleson, 475–480; Simon Hentrei and Ximena Soley, "Force Majeure," ed. Anne Peters and Rüdiger Wolfrum, *Max Planck Encyclopedia of Public International Law* (Oxford Public International Law: Oxford University Press, 2021), http://opil.ouplaw.com, Article last updated in April 2011; Paddeu, *Justification and Excuse in International Law: Concept and Theory of General Defences*, chap. 7.

to situations where a state is compelled to act in a manner not in conformity with its international obligations (e.g. prohibition of passage through foreign territory, airspace, or territorial waters, pollution of international or territorial waters, duty to protect aliens and foreign property from harm).[301] Such a situation requires: (1) the occurrence of an irresistible force (i.e. a constraint which the state was unable to avoid or oppose by its own means) or an unforeseen event (i.e. neither foreseen nor easily foreseeable), also called the "triggering event";[302] (2) which is beyond the control of the state concerned; and (3) which makes it materially impossible in the circumstances to perform the obligation.[303] Material impossibility of performance may be due to a natural or physical event (e.g. weather conditions, earthquakes, floods, or droughts) or to human intervention (e.g. loss of control over a portion of the state's territory as a result of an insurrection or devastation of an area by military operations carried out by a third state), or some combination of the two.[304] It does thus not cover circumstances in which the performance of an obligation has merely become more difficult, for example due to some political or economic crisis.[305] A classic example of *force majeure* is the case of a state aircraft which may be diverted without prior authorisation into foreign airspace due to damage or loss of control of the aircraft owing to extreme weather conditions.[306]

---

301 ARSIWA Commentaries, Article 23, para. 1.

302 See Paddeu and Jephcott arguing that although the spread of SARS-CoV-2 was neither unforeseen nor unforeseeable once the outbreak was known, the event may have been irresistible as states could not have avoided the virus reaching its territory or spreading within, but dismissing *force majeure* on the grounds that performance was not materially impossible since the state behaviour potentially in breach of international law is voluntary. Paddeu and Jephcott, "Covid-19 and Defences in the Law of State Responsibility: Part I".

303 ARSIWA Commentaries, Article 23, para. 2.

304 ARSIWA Commentaries, Article 23, para. 3. See also Crawford, *State Responsibility: the General Part*, 297–298; Szurek, "Circumstances Precluding Wrongfulness in the ILC Articles on State Responsibility: Force Majeure," in *The Law of International Responsibility*, ed. Crawford, Pellet, and Olleson, 477.

305 ARSIWA Commentaries, Article 23, paras. 3–4, 7. See, for instance, *Difference between New Zealand and France Concerning the Interpretation or Application of two Agreements concluded on 9 July 1986 between the two States and Which Related to the Problems Arising from the Rainbow Warrior Affair*, Award, pp. 252–253, para. 77. The degree of difficulty associated with *force majeure* as a circumstance precluding wrongfulness, though considerable, is less than is required by Article 61 VCLT for termination of a treaty on grounds of supervening impossibility, see *Gabčíkovo-Nagymaros Project (Hungary v. Slovakia)*, Judgment, p. 63, para. 102. For instance, the impossibility to repay a loan is often rejected as a case of *force majeure* on the facts of the case, see, for instance, *Serbian Loans*, Judgment, 12 July 1929, PCIJ Series A, No. 20, p. 5, pp. 39–40; *Brazilian Loans*, Judgment, 12 July 1929, PCIJ Series A, No. 21, p. 93, p. 120. On the notion of 'economic impossibility' of performance, see further Szurek, "Circumstances Precluding Wrongfulness in the ILC Articles on State Responsibility: Force Majeure," in *The Law of International Responsibility*, ed. Crawford, Pellet, and Olleson, 479–480. See also the discussion above on the necessity excuse, in particular in Sect. 5.2.2.1 on private necessity.

306 ARSIWA Commentaries, Article 23, paras. 3, 5.

Although the circumstances may be similar to a scenario of distress, *force majeure* differs from a situation of distress (and necessity), firstly, in that the conduct of the state which would otherwise be internationally wrongful is involuntary or at least involves no element of free choice.[307] Secondly, it differs in that the state invoking *force majeure* does not act in order to protect a prevailing interest as there is precisely no conscious balancing of competing interests at all. Whether a certain situation qualifies as *force majeure* cannot be stated in general terms as, according to Szurek, "[a]ll depends on the exceptional character of the event, on the [s]tate obligations in question, and the means at the disposal of the [s]tate".[308] Furthermore, material impossibility of performance is to be assessed rigorously.[309] There needs to be a causal link between the *force majeure* event and the resulting material impossibility to perform the obligation, in that the conduct of the state relying on *force majeure* must be adequate to the exigencies of the situation.[310] In addition, the longer a situation of *force majeure* continues, the more will the state relying on the excuse be required to have taken steps to overcome the event, to be assessed on a case-by-case basis.[311] In order to address the problem of hindsight bias, it is suggested to use the same standard of control (i.e. an *ex post* assessment taking into account the *ex ante* perspective of the defendant state). Thirdly, as for distress, the plea of *force majeure* is not admitted when such situation is due, either alone or in combination with other factors, to the conduct of the state invoking it (Article 23(2) lit. a) ARSIWA).[312] Fourthly, another exception relates to situations where the state has assumed the risk of the occurrence of a situation of *force majeure* (Article 23(2) lit. b) ARSIWA). This exception reflects the principle that *force majeure* should not excuse the performance of international obligations if the state has accepted the responsibility for a particular risk and has made a commitment to prevent the situation arising.[313] States may assume in advance the risk of a particular *force majeure* event in terms of the obligation itself, by its conduct, by virtue of some unilateral act, or by agreement, and thereby renounce the right to rely on *force majeure*.[314] Thus, the relatively confined conditions of *force majeure* reduce the

---

[307] ARSIWA Commentaries, Article 23, para. 1. See also Crawford, *State Responsibility: the General Part*, 295. Impossibility in the sense of *force majeure* thus needs not only to be material (i.e. physical inability of performance) but also absolute. *Difference between New Zealand and France Concerning the Interpretation or Application of two Agreements concluded on 9 July 1986 between the two States and Which Related to the Problems Arising from the Rainbow Warrior Affair*, Award, pp. 252–253, para. 77.

[308] Szurek, "Circumstances Precluding Wrongfulness in the ILC Articles on State Responsibility: Force Majeure," in *The Law of International Responsibility*, ed. Crawford, Pellet, and Olleson, 477.

[309] Ibid., 478.

[310] Ibid.

[311] Ibid., 478–479.

[312] The exact formulation has been retained for distress and *force majeure*, see comments in the previous section on Article 24(2) lit. a) ARSIWA. See also the analogous exception in the provision for material impossibility as a ground for termination of a treaty in Article 61 VCLT.

[313] ARSIWA Commentaries, Article 23, para. 10.

[314] Ibid.

problem of observability and verifiability and thus of opportunistic breach. It offers flexibility in exceptional circumstances, while avoiding moral hazard, for instance, by excluding its invocation when the state has contributed to the situation arising.

Force majeure as a provision serves primarily to allocate the risk of such an external event between the states involved. The risk can be allocated *ex ante* either to the defendant state or to the plaintiff state, depending on whether breach of an international obligation can be excused. Since *force majeure* implies that conduct is involuntary and requires no conscious balancing of competing interests, it is indifferent to the character of the obligation breached and the kind of interests it protects. Thus, *force majeure* can, in principle, also excuse breach of public law obligations relating to the protection of GPGs and CPRs, depending on the facts of the case. Accidents in situations of *force majeure* can, for instance, excuse actions which led to the loss of lives of individuals, as in an airplane crash due to extreme weather conditions, or the pollution of the high seas, as in an oil tanker accident. However, as mentioned above, whether in a given case an exceptional situation qualifies as *force majeure* also depends on the obligation in question. Certain public law obligations require that the violation is carried out in a deliberate or systematic way, such as genocide, torture, apartheid, crimes against humanity or acts of aggression. Involuntary behaviour in such scenarios means that there will usually not be a *prima facie* breach of the obligation in question. These are thus not the typical scenarios of *force majeure*. Hence, due to the absence of free choice and a balancing of conflicting interest, there is no clear economic rationale for a general *ex ante* exclusion of *force majeure* in the case of *jus cogens* norms (Article 26 ARSIWA). To the contrary, an *ex post* case-by-case assessment of the situation in question, which takes into account the requirements of the primary obligation breached, is needed.

The ARSIWA also allocate *ex post* the costs of the invocation of *force majeure*. As for the other two excuses, the circumstance precluding wrongfulness is no fault of the victim state. In principle, compensation according to Article 27 lit. b) ARSIWA seems therefore justified.[315] However, it differs from necessity and distress in that it relates to the involuntary action of the state invoking it. Crawford considers the compensation requirement in the case of *force majeure* as problematic.[316] He argues that the state invoking it has not contributed to the situation either (nor assumed the risk of the occurrence of damage as this would have excluded the invocation of *force majeure* from the outset), and is thus no more responsible for the material loss than the state suffering it.[317] Mathias Forteau argues that in the case of *force majeure* "a division of the reparation must be imposed, since neither of the two [s]tates is responsible for the damage".[318] Regarding the consequences of invoking *force*

---

[315] Forteau, "Reparation in the Event of a Circumstance Precluding Wrongfulness," in *The Law of International Responsibility*, ed. Crawford, Pellet, and Olleson, 893.

[316] Crawford, *State Responsibility: the General Part*, 319.

[317] Ibid. See also United Nations International Law Commission, *Second Report on State Responsibility by Special Rapporteur James Crawford*, Fifty-First Session, 1999 (UN Doc. A/CN.4/498), p. 85, para. 345.

[318] Forteau, "Reparation in the Event of a Circumstance Precluding Wrongfulness," in *The Law of International Responsibility*, ed. Crawford, Pellet, and Olleson, 893.

majeure, that is whether compensation should be paid to the state suffering material loss or not, it is useful to have a look at the rationale of the exclusion of compensation in domestic law. In domestic contract law, the contractual parties usually exclude *ex ante* liability for breach of contract in cases of *force majeure* and exempt the party invoking it from having to pay damages. The invocation of *force majeure* leads to a temporary suspension of contractual obligations, the risks between the contractual parties being allocated such that each party has to bear the detrimental consequences of the disruption of the contract and mutual claims on compensating the losses following the materialisation of the risk of *force majeure* do not exist.[319] This is similar to international commercial contracts.[320] In domestic tort law, where it is not possible to assume the risk of a *force majeure* event *ex ante* in the absence of a contractual relationship, strict liability for damages is usually excluded since neither the plaintiff nor the defendant is responsible for the accident in a situation of *force majeure*.[321] Louis T. Visscher argues from an economic point of view that "[t]he costs of applying a care level that even could have avoided the losses in a situation of force majeure are excessively high" and that "[i]t is not desirable that actors base their care decisions on these exceptional situations".[322] Hence, in the domestic context, the costs of an accident even in the case of *force majeure* remain on the plaintiff state and are not shifted *ex post* to the injurer with an obligation to provide compensation.

For the international level, it is nonetheless suggested that the costs of a *force majeure* event are shared among the parties to the dispute. Full compensation is not justified as the losses caused by the defendant state's act due to the external event could not have been avoided at all or only at exorbitant costs. But no compensation is not justified either as the plaintiff state is as innocent as the defendant state. It has also been argued before that the invocation of an excuse without having to pay compensation increases the risk of moral hazard, and states should not be encouraged to assume the risk of the occurrence of a situation of *force majeure*. For precisely that reason, the conditions of *force majeure* are much stricter than for distress or necessity where the compensation requirement upholds the deterrence

---

[319] However, German contract law foresees that liability is not excluded in the exceptional case where *force majeure* occurs in a situation where the debtor is in delay with his contractual performance (§ 287 BGB).

[320] In addition to its application in inter-state cases as a matter of public international law, *force majeure* plays an important role in the field of international commercial arbitration (i.e. private international law). See ARSIWA Commentaries, Article 23, para 8. See, for instance, Article 79 of the United Nations Convention on Contracts for the International Sale of Goods (concluded 11 April 1980, entered into force 1 January 1988) 1489 *UNTS* 3.

[321] See, for instance, § 7(2) StVG for the exclusion of strict liability in German law regarding accidents in street traffic.

[322] Louis T. Visscher, "Justifications and Excuses in the Economic Analysis of Tort Law," *Rotterdam Institute of Law and Economics (RILE) Working Paper*, no. 3 (2008): 9, https://ssrn.com/abstract=1111547

effect of ordinary remedies, including reparation of injury.[323] Hence, a cost-sharing solution seems more appropriate and the costs thus fall partially on the state acting in the case of *force majeure* and on the plaintiff state or states.

5.3.2 Justifications

In contrast to the excuses presented in the previous sections, all three justifications share the characteristic of reciprocity in that the circumstance precluding the wrongfulness of the defendant state's action emanates from some prior action of the plaintiff state. In addition, the justifying circumstances—at least consent and self-defence—seemingly render an act lawful (instead of the obligation subsisting by exercising an influence on the situation that requires a balancing of competing interests).[324] Finally, the underlying economic rationale of consent, self-defence, and countermeasures differs not only from the excuses (i.e. trade-off between compliance and flexibility in the presence of unforeseeable and extraordinary circumstances, while avoiding moral hazard), but also among the three justifications. They will therefore be analysed subsequently with regard to how they allocate legal duties and costs of otherwise wrongful acts in the case of consent or self-defence while taking into account the private and public dimensions of international law. Since countermeasures are, at their core, an instrument to enforce compliance with international obligations,[325] this justification will be discussed in detail below in Chap. 7.[326]

---

[323] United Nations International Law Commission, *Second Report on State Responsibility by Special Rapporteur James Crawford*, Fifty-First Session, 1999 (UN Doc. A/CN.4/498), pp. 65–66, para. 258. ("Thus the [*Rainbow Warrior*] decision adds to the many cited in the commentary and in the Secretariat survey which accept the principle that wrongfulness is precluded in international law, as well as in many systems of national law, by force majeure, while at the same time attaching stringent conditions to its application.") Szurek, "Circumstances Precluding Wrongfulness in the ILC Articles on State Responsibility: Force Majeure," in *The Law of International Responsibility*, ed. Crawford, Pellet, and Olleson, 476. ("The meaning retained by the ILC responds to a traditional and strict conception of *force majeure* both in respect of its characteristics and its consequences.")

[324] United Nations International Law Commission, *Second Report on State Responsibility by Special Rapporteur James Crawford*, Fifty-First Session, 1999 (UN Doc. A/CN.4/498), p. 60, para. 230.

[325] See Sect. 2.4 on enforcement of international law and mechanisms of compliance.

[326] On the role of countermeasures for the implementation of state responsibility, see Chap. 7.

5.3.2.1 Consent

In the case of consent (Article 20 ARSIWA),[327] the primary obligation continues to govern the relations between the two affected states, but they have dispensed with it on the particular occasion or for the purpose of the conduct consented to.[328] It is rooted in the maxim *volenti non fit injuria* ("to a willing person injury is not done").[329] Classic examples would be a state's consent to a foreign aircraft to transit its airspace, to a foreign vessel to transit its territorial waters, or to foreign forces to transit its territory, for instance, in order to provide humanitarian relief or to establish a military base.[330] In such cases, a state decides to "allow" for a specific occasion and purpose a breach of primary international obligations such as the prohibition of the threat or use of force against the territorial integrity of another state, of the exercise of jurisdiction on its territory or of intervention in its internal affairs.[331] Thus, consent essentially makes the primary obligation inapplicable in the first place, especially when the concept is directly integrated into particular primary obligations (i.e. certain activities are only prohibited without the other state's consent).[332] This makes it difficult to distinguish between consent as an element of the definition of the primary obligation and consent as a circumstance precluding the wrongfulness of the non-performance of the obligation.[333] According to Crawford, consent could have been deleted from the ARSIWA,[334] but most states ultimately preferred to retain the

[327] Article 20 ARSIWA reads: „Valid consent by a State to the commission of a given act by another State precludes the wrongfulness of that act in relation to the former State to the extent that the act remains within the limits of that consent." For on overview of consent as a justification for breach of international obligations, see Affef Ben Mansour, "Circumstances Precluding Wrongfulness in the ILC Articles on State Responsibility: Consent," in *The Law of International Responsibility*, ed. James Crawford, Alain Pellet, and Simon Olleson (Oxford: Oxford University Press, 2010), 439–447; Paddeu, *Justification and Excuse in International Law: Concept and Theory of General Defences*, chap. 4.

[328] ARSIWA Commentaries, Article 20, para. 2. United Nations International Law Commission, *Second Report on State Responsibility by Special Rapporteur James Crawford*, Fifty-First Session, 1999 (UN Doc. A/CN.4/498), p. 60, para. 233. See also Crawford, *State Responsibility: the General Part*, 283.

[329] United Nations International Law Commission, *Yearbook of the International Law Commission*, 1999, Volume II, Part Two (UN Doc. A/CN.4/SER.A/1999/Add.1 (Part 2)), p. 75. para. 303.

[330] ARSIWA Commentaries, Article 20, para. 2. Crawford, *State Responsibility: the General Part*, 284.

[331] See in particular the obligations stemming from the United Nations General Assembly, Resolution 2625 (XXV), *Declaration on Principles of International Law Concerning Friendly Relations and Cooperation among States in Accordance with the Charter of the United Nations*, 24 October 1970 (UN Doc. A/8082). See also in relation to consent, United Nations International Law Commission, *Second Report on State Responsibility by Special Rapporteur James Crawford*, Fifty-First Session, 1999 (UN Doc. A/CN.4/498), p. 62, para. 240. See also Crawford, *State Responsibility: the General Part*, 288.

[332] Crawford, *State Responsibility: the General Part*, 288.

[333] Ibid. This does, however, not diminish the usefulness to analyse the economic rationale and the allocation of duties and costs of consent as a circumstance precluding wrongfulness.

[334] United Nations International Law Commission, *Second Report on State Responsibility by Special Rapporteur James Crawford*, Fifty-First Session, 1999 (UN Doc. A/CN.4/498), p. 62, para. 241.

provision as discarding it "could be interpreted as the abrogation of an important principle".[335]

When taking an economic perspective on the rationale of consent, it is useful to draw on the economic analysis of the concept of permission in tort law. The reasoning of the "victim" is such that he or she derives more benefits from the commission of the tort, taking into account the associated costs that come along with the infringement of his or her rights, than from the situation without the tort. Visscher explains that when a "victim" allows the "injurer" to commit the tort, "[t]he parties involved have made a weighing of interests that differs from the weighing made by the legislator, or the weighing that resulted in the subjective right that was invaded".[336] He argues further that permission is an application of the Coase theorem:[337] "if transaction costs are absent or at least low enough to enable parties to negotiate and to reach an agreement which allocates rights to the person valuing them the most, law should not deviate from those agreements".[338] This reasoning is, however, based on several assumptions. It presupposes, firstly, that parties know their own interests best.[339] This will probably be the case regarding the use of property or minor bodily injuries (e.g. sports like boxing), but less with regard to severe injuries or harm to life, as bodily integrity and life are goods whose protection lies in the interest of the community. Domestic tort law usually excludes consent in these cases, where individuals cannot dispose of certain goods valued by the community, although exceptions exist (e.g. euthanasia). In the case of inalienable entitlements, the social costs of allowing permission as a justification are prohibitively high.[340] Secondly, the permission needs to be freely given and not under duress in order to protect the "weaker" party from actions that are against his or her will.[341] Thirdly, asymmetric information can have an impact on the validity of the expression of consent, as for a "victim" which gave its permission under incomplete information (for instance, about the risks of the tort), the act does not necessarily bring him or her into a better position than without the commission of the tort.[342] Lastly, if the act permitted by the "victim" causes negative externalities, it might be socially desirable not to allow the act after all (thus, to exclude consent), and to allow

[335]United Nations International Law Commission, *Yearbook of the International Law Commission*, 1999, Volume II, Part Two (UN Doc. A/CN.4/SER.A/1999/Add.1 (Part 2)), p. 75. para. 305; Crawford, *State Responsibility: the General Part*, 288–289. See also Ben Mansour, "Circumstances Precluding Wrongfulness in the ILC Articles on State Responsibility: Consent," in *The Law of International Responsibility*, ed. Crawford, Pellet, and Olleson, 440–441, 447.

[336]Visscher, "Justifications and Excuses in the Economic Analysis of Tort Law," 12–13.

[337]Coase, "The Problem of Social Cost," 1–44.

[338]Visscher, "Justifications and Excuses in the Economic Analysis of Tort Law," 13.

[339]Ibid.

[340]The concept of inalienability dates back to Calabresi and Melamed, "Property Rules, Liability Rules, and Inalienability: One View of the Cathedral," 1089–1128. See Sect. 5.2.2.2 with regard to necessity and Sect. 6.1 with regard to different remedies.

[341]Visscher, "Justifications and Excuses in the Economic Analysis of Tort Law," 13.

[342]Ibid.

affected third parties to claim compensation from the injurer.[343] The economic rationale of permission applies in principle also to contract law. It is the underlying logic of a contractual agreement that it allocates the rights to the party valuing them the most. The parties to a contract thus negotiate and agree *ex ante*, for instance, on the transfer of property, and that such consent is compensated by the payment of a certain price.[344] Consent can also play a role *ex post* at a later stage of the contractual relation, for instance, when the buyer accepts an incomplete delivery or the seller accepts a lower payment. Thus, also in contract law it is assumed that the parties know their interests best, while the same caveats apply (i.e. no violation of a higher interest, voluntary decision-making, complete information, and no negative externalities).

Consent in international law builds on the same economic rationale than in domestic tort and contract law. From the perspective of the consenting state, it is only reasonable to consent to the commission of an act in breach of an international obligation if the benefits of that act, taking into account the associated costs, would outweigh the benefits of compliance with the obligation in question. To give one example, a state may invite another state to establish a military base on its territory. The deployment of foreign troops can be beneficial for the receiving state, for instance, when these help in an armed conflict or create opportunities of employment for the local civilian population. And this may even be the case when taking into account any associated costs (e.g. the provision of certain infrastructure, or the internal political costs of an infringement of the territorial integrity). Consent to the deployment of troops is thus likely to outweigh the benefits of compliance with the prohibition of the exercise of jurisdiction on its territory or of intervention in its internal affairs. Thus, the weighing of interests in the given case (i.e. military and economic advantages *versus* respect of borders) differs from the weighing of interests that international law provides by the rule of mutual respect of territorial integrity of sovereign states. From the perspective of the international community, international law should not prohibit such arrangements. As in domestic law, this reasoning rests, however, on the assumption that consent is valid and that the act remains within the limits of that consent. The validity requirement concerns questions such as whether consent was clearly expressed (can be tacit or implicit), whether the consenting person or group was authorised to do so on the state's behalf (e.g. a regional authority, depending on the content of the primary obligation), and whether consent was freely given (i.e. without coercion, error, fraud, or corruption).[345] The issue of the scope regards the material and temporal dimension of consent, for instance, in the case of consent to the stationing of foreign troops,

---

[343] Ibid.

[344] This is the rationale underlying the concept of property rules, which dates back to Calabresi and Melamed, "Property Rules, Liability Rules, and Inalienability: One View of the Cathedral," 1089–1128. See Sect. 6.1 with regard to different remedies.

[345] ARSIWA Commentaries, Article 20, paras. 4–6. Crawford, *State Responsibility: the General Part*, 284–286.

questions such as what kind of military presence, within which territorial limits, for which duration and with which objective.[346] Any harm caused in the exercise of these functions outside the material and temporal scope of the consent thus gives rise to the obligation to provide reparation for the commission of an internationally wrongful act. The problem of information asymmetries should, in my opinion, also be addressed. Thus, when assessing the validity and the scope of consent, it is important to verify whether the consenting state disposed of sufficient information to assess the costs and benefits of the expression of consent in order to protect "weaker" states from giving permission to more powerful states based on an erroneous assessment.

While all these issues can be highly controversial in a given international dispute, two aspects however deserve particular attention. Firstly, as in domestic tort law, there exist cases in which consent may not be validly given at all.[347] This relates to Article 26 ARSIWA, which excludes the application of circumstances precluding wrongfulness, thus including consent, in the case of peremptory norms of general international law. That consent has no effect in respect of *jus cogens* norms can be explained by their very nature, since, by definition, no derogation from these peremptory norms is permitted.[348] From a legal perspective, the problem with this provision lies in the identification of *jus cogens* norms and especially in the application of consent to the principle of prohibition of the use of force (Article 2(4) UN Charter), a norm widely to considered to be peremptory in character.[349] Unlike for other peremptory norms such as genocide or torture, states may consent to the military intervention of another state (or international organisation) on its territory.[350] Crawford argues that "although a state cannot dispense with a peremptory obligation itself, some such obligations incorporate an intrinsic element of consent".[351] In these cases, there may be no breach of the peremptory norm in the first place and therefore no conflict with Article 26 ARSIWA.[352] Thus, the determination of the exact scope of consent with relation to peremptory norms remains unclear.[353] The Commentaries to the ARSIWA refer to other rules of international

[346] ARSIWA Commentaries, Article 20, para. 9. Ibid., 286–287.

[347] ARSIWA Commentaries, Article 20, para. 7.

[348] Ben Mansour, "Circumstances Precluding Wrongfulness in the ILC Articles on State Responsibility: Consent," in *The Law of International Responsibility*, ed. Crawford, Pellet, and Olleson, 446. On the concept of *jus cogens*, its doctrinal consequences and congruence with economic categories of goods, see Sect. 3.3.2.

[349] Ibid.

[350] ARSIWA Commentaries, Article 26, para. 6. Ibid., 447. See also Crawford, *State Responsibility: the General Part*, 317.

[351] See also Crawford, *State Responsibility: the General Part*, 317.

[352] Ibid.

[353] See also United Nations International Law Commission, *Third Report on Peremptory Norms of General International Law (Jus Cogens) by Special Rapporteur Dire Tladi*, Seventieth Session, 2018 (UN Doc. A/CN.4/714), p. 31, para. 81.

law in order to determine in which circumstances consent has been validly given.[354] If one looks at the *jus cogens* exception from an economic goods perspective, thus translating it into their underlying GPG obligations, it may become clearer why consent is applicable in certain scenarios, but not in others where negative externalities are created. Generally, the justifying circumstance of consent covers only the bilateral relations between the two states in question.[355] Thus, states have the right to dispense with the performance of an obligation owed to them individually, but consent by a state to a particular conduct by another state cannot preclude the wrongfulness of that act in relation to other than the consenting state.[356] In particular, in circumstances where an obligation is owed to multiple states and thus the consent of several states is required, the consent of one state will not preclude wrongfulness in relation to another.[357] In the case of *jus cogens* norms, however, wrongfulness is not even precluded in relation to the consenting state. We have seen that multilateral obligations can be translated into all four economic categories of goods. In relation to private or club good obligations (e.g. international investment or trade law), a state can naturally consent to non-compliant behaviour in its bilateral relations, but not on behalf of a third state. This is different in relation to GPG and CPR obligations (including *jus cogens* norms as normative GPGs), which are characterised by the non-excludability of their benefits (e.g. in the form of non-use value goods). In these scenarios, a state should not be able to dispense another state from the performance even in the relation to the consenting state itself. This logic allows to explain also the relation between consent and the prohibition of the use of force. As previously outlined, certain obligations have two dimensions, private goods and global public goods, depending on the excludability of benefits (i.e. mixed goods characteristics). The prohibition of the use of force can thus relate to the protection of national sovereignty and territory and/or to the protection of international peace and security. While consent may be validly expressed in the former case (e.g. invitation of foreign forces to establish a military base), it may be excluded in the latter (e.g. invitation to occupy parts of the national territory to suppress a minority population). From an economic goods perspective, it makes thus little sense to attach different consequences to *jus cogens* norms in comparison to GPG or CPR obligations more generally. It also helps to overcome the issue whether the absence of consent is an

[354] ARSIWA Commentaries, Article 26, para. 6. On the concept of consent in international law, see Jutta Brunnée, "Consent," ed. Anne Peters and Rüdiger Wolfrum, *Max Planck Encyclopedia of Public International Law* (Oxford Public International Law: Oxford University Press, 2021), http://opil.ouplaw.com, Article last updated in October 2010.

[355] ARSIWA Commentaries, Article 20, para. 9.

[356] ARSIWA Commentaries, Article 20, paras. 1–2.

[357] ARSIWA Commentaries, Article 20, para. 9. Crawford, *State Responsibility: the General Part*, 283. United Nations International Law Commission, *Second Report on State Responsibility by Special Rapporteur James Crawford*, Fifty-First Session, 1999 (UN Doc. A/CN.4/498), pp. 60–61, para. 233.

intrinsic element of certain negative obligations, thus avoiding the doctrinal question whether there was no breach in the first place or whether breach is only justified.[358] Moreover, extending the scope of obligations to which consent cannot be validly expressed to GPG and CPR obligations (that is, *erga omnes* norms) leads to an internationally wrongful act, which entails, amongst others, the requirement to cease that act, and gives rise to third-party enforcement mechanisms. In sum, the exception in Article 26 ARSIWA in relation to consent excludes that the individual weighing of interests of the parties involved supersedes the balancing of interests prescribed by international law as the consenting state does not have the authority or ownership to dispense another state from compliance with GPG and CPR obligations,[359] and the total social costs to the international community as a whole are thus minimised.[360]

A second issue that deserves attention is the question of compensation in the case of consent to a breach of an international obligation (Article 27 lit. b) ARSIWA). As discussed previously, the rationale of this provision is that sometimes a state relying on a circumstance precluding wrongfulness may nonetheless be expected to make good any material loss suffered by a state affected by that act, and thus to adjust *ex post* the losses following from the act.[361] Yet, in the case of consent, it seems not clear why a state acting with the consent of another state should be obliged to compensate the latter given that the act in question depends on a prior voluntary decision of the consenting state.[362] As mentioned before, a rational state would only give its consent to an act in breach of international law if that act provides more benefits than compliance with the obligation. Compensation can nonetheless play a role in the decision-making of the consenting state. To give an example, a state may grant permission to another state to install a military base on its territory and deploy troops, for instance, to launch air strikes towards a neighbouring country. If the consenting state is not directly involved in the conflict, the benefits of such permission are less evident. However, the cost associated with the stationing of foreign troops could be offset with compensatory payments. Consent thus leaves room for negotiating compensation, but typically before a state expresses consent to a certain

---

[358] On why consent must be recast as a defence (and is not part of the definition of the prohibition of force), thus considering consent as a justification for the use of force, see Federica I. Paddeu, "Military Assistance on Request and General Reasons against Force: Consent as a Defence to the Prohibition of Force," *Journal on the Use of Force and International Law* 7, no. 2 (2020): 227–269.

[359] See also Besson, "Community Interests in International Law: Whose Interests Are They and How Should We Best Identify Them?," in *Community Interests across International Law*, ed. Benvenisti and Nolte, 49.

[360] In other words, in the case of *jus cogens* norms a stronger protection of entitlements as inalienable is advisable, for instance when the entitlement is of a higher value and cannot be monetised. Pauwelyn, *Optimal Protection of International Law: Navigating between European Absolutism and American Voluntarism*, 50–55.

[361] ARSIWA Commentaries, Article 27, para. 4. See also Crawford, *State Responsibility: the General Part*, 318.

[362] See United Nations International Law Commission, *Second Report on State Responsibility by Special Rapporteur James Crawford*, Fifty-First Session, 1999 (UN Doc. A/CN.4/498), p. 84, para. 344.

activity.[363] Compensation in the case of consent thus relates more to the content to initial agreement and would usually be negotiated *ex ante*, rather than to questions of state responsibility and *ex post* cost allocation.[364] *Ex ante* negotiation of compensation is also acceptable since consent can only be expressed with regard to obligations relating to private goods and club goods (thus, scenarios similar to tort and contract law, relating to "property rights" of states).[365] As consent covers only the relation to the consenting state and does not dispense another state from respecting its obligations with regard to third states, negative externalities of consent are excluded from the outset, and there is no room for an obligation of compensation of innocent third states for any material loss caused. These scenarios give directly rise to claims of reparation following a breach of international obligations.

5.3.2.2 Self-Defence

This section turns to another justification, that is self-defence (Article 21 ARSIWA).[366] This circumstance precluding wrongfulness echoes Article 51 of the UN Charter which reflects the inherent right of states to act in individual or collective self-defence despite the prohibition of the threat or use of force as laid down in Article 2(4) UN Charter.[367] Self-defence in the law of state responsibility specifically justifies only lawful measures, thus measures taken in conformity with

---

[363] Crawford, *State Responsibility: the General Part*, 319. See also United Nations International Law Commission, *Second Report on State Responsibility by Special Rapporteur James Crawford*, Fifty-First Session, 1999 (UN Doc. A/CN.4/498), p. 84, para. 344.

[364] Crawford, *State Responsibility: the General Part*, 319. Forteau concludes that "[r]eparation would thus not be the consequence of an act of [s]tate, but would arise from the creation of a primary norm." Forteau, "Reparation in the Event of a Circumstance Precluding Wrongfulness," in *The Law of International Responsibility*, ed. Crawford, Pellet, and Olleson, 892.

[365] Consent combined with *ex ante* compensation can thus be considered a property rule in international law. On the concepts of property, liability, and inalienable rules as well as the idea of variable protection which will be used in particular in the analysis of different remedies, see Sect. 6.1.

[366] Article 21 ARSIWA reads: "The wrongfulness of an act of a State is precluded if the act constitutes a lawful measure of self-defence taken in conformity with the Charter of the United Nations." For an overview of self-defence as a circumstance precluding wrongfulness, see Jean-Marc Thouvenin, "Circumstances Precluding Wrongfulness in the ILC Articles on State Responsibility: Self-Defence," in *The Law of International Responsibility*, ed. James Crawford, Alain Pellet, and Simon Olleson (Oxford: Oxford University Press, 2010), 455–467; Christopher Greenwood, "Self-Defence," ed. Anne Peters and Rüdiger Wolfrum, *Max Planck Encyclopedia of Public International Law* (Oxford Public International Law: Oxford University Press, 2021), http://opil.ouplaw.com, Article last updated in April 2011; Paddeu, *Justification and Excuse in International Law: Concept and Theory of General Defences*, chap. 5.

[367] *Legality of the Threat or Use of Nuclear Weapons*, Advisory Opinion, p. 244, para. 38, p. 263, para. 96. ARSIWA Commentaries, Article 21, para. 1. Article 51 UN Charter can be considered an expression of the rules of general international law on the right to self-defence. See also Greenwood, "Self-Defence," para. 3; Crawford, *State Responsibility: the General Part*, 289.

the primary rules under the UN Charter on when and to what extent self-defence is permitted (in particular, the condition of a prior armed attack[368] as well as the necessity and proportionality requirements).[369] Thus, similarly to consent, self-defence renders an act lawful instead of excluding its wrongfulness as the inherent right to act in self-defence is part of the primary obligation itself, which is why there is no breach of the prohibition of the use of force in the first place.[370] However, self-defence can also justify the non-performance of other international obligations than Article 2(4) UN Charter if it is related to an action of threat or use of force in self-defence.[371] For instance, a state acting in self-defence may trespass on to the aggressor state's territory, interfere in its internal affairs or disrupt its external trade contrary to the provisions of international trade agreements.[372] Self-defence can therefore be considered at the same time a right and a circumstance precluding wrongfulness.[373]

Self-defence is a justification well known from criminal law, where it excludes criminal charges of the initial victim acting in necessary self-defence against an attacker, as well as from tort law, where it excludes liability of the victim for losses inflicted on the assailant.[374] Necessary self-defence, even if it implies the use of deadly force or the infliction of serious bodily harm, constitutes an exception to the rule that "crimes cause (large) negative externalities and are therefore socially undesirable".[375] If the act in self-defence is both necessary and proportional, the response of the initial victim, that is sued in a tort case, becomes socially

[368] From a legal perspective, controversial issues surrounding self-defence concern the questions of what constitutes an armed attack (in terms of nature, scale, source, and target), when it begins, and whether a state may take action in the face of an imminent armed attack (i.e. anticipatory self-defence). See Greenwood, "Self-Defence," para. 52.

[369] *Military and Paramilitary Activities in and against Nicaragua (Nicaragua v. United States of America)*, Judgment (Merits), p. 94, para. 176. ARSIWA Commentaries, Article 21, para. 6. Crawford, *State Responsibility: the General Part*, 289. Thouvenin, "Circumstances Precluding Wrongfulness in the ILC Articles on State Responsibility: Self-Defence," in *The Law of International Responsibility*, ed. Crawford, Pellet, and Olleson, 461–464.

[370] ARSIWA Commentaries, Article 21, para. 1. See also Crawford, *State Responsibility: the General Part*, 290.

[371] ARSIWA Commentaries, Article 21, para. 2. Ibid., 290–291.

[372] United Nations International Law Commission, *Second Report on State Responsibility by Special Rapporteur James Crawford*, Fifty-First Session, 1999 (UN Doc. A/CN.4/498), pp. 74–75, para. 299. See also Crawford, *State Responsibility: the General Part*, 290.

[373] Thouvenin, "Circumstances Precluding Wrongfulness in the ILC Articles on State Responsibility: Self-Defence," in *The Law of International Responsibility*, ed. Crawford, Pellet, and Olleson, 459–461. On the function of self-defence as a secondary rule compared to the right of self-defence as an exception to the prohibition of force in primary international law, see further Federica I. Paddeu, "Self-Defence as a Circumstance Precluding Wrongfulness: Understanding Article 21 of the Articles on State Responsibility," *British Yearbook of International Law* 85, no. 1 (2015): 90–132.

[374] In German law, for instance, the principle of self-defence is reflected in § 32 StGB (exclusion of criminal liability) and § 227 BGB (exclusion of liability for damages).

[375] Visscher, "Justifications and Excuses in the Economic Analysis of Tort Law," 11.

desirable.[376] The economic rationale of self-defence has three aspects: first, the initial assailant is usually the cheapest cost avoider because losses are avoided if there is no attack on the victim in the first place.[377] If the initial attacker knows that he or she ultimately has to bear his or her own losses stemming from an act in necessary self-defence, he or she might be deterred from proceeding with the attack in the first place.[378] Self-defence thus primarily has a deterrence function. Second, self-defence might reduce the expected losses as it can avoid more losses than it causes.[379] An act in self-defence puts an end to an attack and consequently the losses caused to the victim are lower than they would have been if the attack had been brought to an end. Cost allocation is efficient if the losses caused to the initial assailant to end the attack are lower than the losses that were avoided with the act in self-defence. But due to the deterrent effect, self-defence is also accepted when the former losses exceed the losses that the attacker could have caused to the initial victim as the assailant is the cheapest cost avoider.[380] This is also linked to the third aspect: that the deterrent effect on the initial victim is rather limited. Even if the attacked person were liable for the losses caused to the assailant, this would not lead to a change in behaviour.[381] Under normal circumstances, the initial victim would not have caused any losses, but in the case of an attack, he or she is placed in an unusual situation where there was no real choice left than to act in self-defence.[382] Thus, imposing liability on the victim of an attack would not set any incentives for prevention but would only shift the losses (which could have been prevented by the assailant), thereby creating administrative costs (i.e. tertiary costs).[383]

This economic rationale is easily transferrable to the international level. Allowing for the justification of self-defence can minimise the expected social costs to the extent that the act in self-defence can avoid more losses than it causes to the attacking state. In addition, self-defence by one state against the armed attack of another state has primarily a deterrence function, in the sense that it aims to prevent the initial attack rather than the act in self-defence. From this perspective, self-defence is a specific enforcement tool as it aims to induce compliance with one

---

[376] Domestic law usually distinguishes between necessary self-defence which serves as a justification and self-defence with excessive force which might be excusable depending on the facts of the individual case. See ibid., 11, 20.

[377] Ibid., 11.

[378] Ibid. With reference to Landes and Posner, *The Economic Structure of Tort Law*, 152, 172–173.

[379] Visscher, "Justifications and Excuses in the Economic Analysis of Tort Law," 11.

[380] Ibid.

[381] Ibid.

[382] Ibid.

[383] Ibid. Tertiary costs are the costs of administering the treatment accidents. See Calabresi, *The Costs of Accidents: A Legal and Economic Analysis*, 28.

specific international obligation which is the prohibition of the use of force.[384] It creates incentives for compliance by placing the cost burden on the attacking state as the cheapest cost avoider and by not shifting the losses to the initial victim state, thus avoiding administrative costs. As discussed further below, unlike for necessity or other excuses, the victim state should not be obliged to pay compensation for material loss caused to the attacking state. This requires, however, that the conditions for an act to be justified in self-defence need to be sufficiently strict, namely that the act in self-defence was necessary and proportionate. For instance, the use of excessive force excludes the invocation of self-defence and thus obliges the initial victim state to pay reparation for damage caused to the initial attacking state, although the amount may be adjusted to the extent that the latter contributed to the injury (Article 39 ARSIWA). The obligation to provide reparation in case of an internationally wrongful act reduces the risk of abuse of the justification as it limits the act in self-defence to what is necessary and proportionate to stop the attack. As for all circumstances precluding wrongfulness, the burden of proof lies on the state invoking the justifying circumstance and should follow a similar assessment: an objective *ex post* assessment which takes into account the perspective of the victim state regarding the necessary and proportionate means to end the attack.

In addition, when considering the lawfulness of actions taken in self-defence, in particular the necessity and proportionality test, conflicting interests play a role.[385] For instance, in its advisory opinion *Legality of the Threat or Use of Nuclear Weapons* the ICJ held that "[s]tates must take environmental considerations into account when assessing what is necessary and proportionate in the pursuit of legitimate military objectives".[386] Thus, the interest protected by the obligation affected by the act in self-defence will have to be taken into account in the necessity and proportionality assessment. Self-defence as a right to have recourse to the threat or use of force against an aggressor state constitutes a typical scenario of bilateral inter-state relations where both states act to defend their national interest and territory. The obligations affected by the act in self-defence, such as trespass on the aggressor state's territory or interference in its internal affairs, usually relate to private goods, although club good obligations might be violated as a side effect depending on the circumstances, for instance, international trade obligations following the disruption of external trade. Self-defence finds its limits in Article 26 ARSIWA, thus its actions cannot justify non-compliance with peremptory norms of general international law.[387] Yet, as for consent, a state using force in self-defence in accordance with the primary rules would not be in breach of this *jus*

---

[384] Countermeasures, which will be discussed further below in Chap. 7, primarily pursue the objective to induce compliance with specific secondary obligations in the law of state responsibility (that is, reparation for injury and cessation of the wrongful act, if it is continuing), but as an implementation tool incidentally play a role in inducing compliance with all types of international obligations.

[385] ARSIWA Commentaries, Article 21, para. 6. Crawford, *State Responsibility: the General Part*, 291.

[386] *Legality of the Threat or Use of Nuclear Weapons*, Advisory Opinion, p. 242, para. 30. ARSIWA Commentaries, Article 21, para. 4.

[387] ARSIWA Commentaries, Article 26, para. 4.

cogens norm in the first place.[388] The invocation of self-defence is, however, excluded in relation to intransgressible norms of international humanitarian law[389] and fundamental international human rights obligations, since actions of self-defence are considered unlawful whenever they violate obligations of total restraint applicable in international armed conflicts.[390] Beyond the general exception for *jus cogens* norms in Article 26 ARSIWA, states need to take into account community interests in their decision to act in self-defence. This is what the ICJ held, for instance, with regard to environmental considerations.[391] To put it more broadly, when assessing the necessity and proportionality of actions in self-defence, obligations protecting GPGs or CPRs have to be taken into account as limiting factors, as the effects are non-excludable beyond the boundaries of the aggressor state. Moreover, all issues related to the effects of actions in self-defence on third states have been left open in the Articles on State Responsibility.[392] These controversial matters are dealt with in the primary rules on self-defence.[393] While it is possible that a state acting in self-defence has certain belligerent rights even against neutral states,[394] it is held here that the effects of actions in self-defence not only on obligations protecting GPGs and CPRs, but also on obligations protecting the rights of innocent third states (i.e. private good or club good obligations) need to be taken into account when assessing the lawfulness. Unlike consent, self-defence is thus not generally excluded

388 ARSIWA Commentaries, Article 26, para. 6. Crawford, *State Responsibility: the General Part*, 318; United Nations International Law Commission, *Third Report on Peremptory Norms of General International Law (Jus Cogens) by Special Rapporteur Dire Tladi*, Seventieth Session, 2018 (UN Doc. A/CN.4/714), p. 31, para. 81.

389 It is the essence of international humanitarian law that even if the use of force is legitimate in times of war (*jus ad bellum*), measures of warfare must respect certain humanitarian standards (*ius in bello*). See Greenwood, "Self-Defence," para. 4.

390 ARSIWA Commentaries, Article 21, paras. 3, 6. The ILC agreed that 'lawful' as a prerequisite for self-defence would be understood to cover compliance with intransgressible rules of international humanitarian law (*ius in bello*). See United Nations International Law Commission, *Yearbook of the International Law Commission*, 1999, Volume II, Part Two (UN Doc. A/CN.4/SER.A/1999/Add.1 (Part 2)), pp. 77–78, paras. 325–331. When international human rights treaties foresee that certain rights cannot be derogated from in times of emergency, one can also argue that such actions taken in self-defence are not lawful in the first place and thus a conflict of laws addressed by Article 26 ARSIWA does not even arise. Crawford, *State Responsibility: the General Part*, 291–292. See also Thouvenin, "Circumstances Precluding Wrongfulness in the ILC Articles on State Responsibility: Self-Defence," in *The Law of International Responsibility*, ed. Crawford, Pellet, and Olleson, 465–466.

391 *Legality of the Threat or Use of Nuclear Weapons*, Advisory Opinion, p. 242, para. 30.

392 ARSIWA Commentaries, Article 21, para. 5.

393 Thouvenin, "Circumstances Precluding Wrongfulness in the ILC Articles on State Responsibility: Self-Defence," in *The Law of International Responsibility*, ed. Crawford, Pellet, and Olleson, 464–465.

394 United Nations International Law Commission, *Second Report on State Responsibility by Special Rapporteur James Crawford*, Fifty-First Session, 1999 (UN Doc. A/CN.4/498), pp. 75–76, para. 302; Crawford, *State Responsibility: the General Part*, 292.

with regard to third states, but any harm (i.e. externalities) should be mitigated through compensation.

Regarding the compensation requirement in Article 27 lit. b) ARSIWA, self-defence shares the logic of consent in that it seems difficult to justify compensation for losses since the circumstance precluding wrongfulness emanates reciprocally from a prior action of the injured state, in this case with an armed attack even a prior wrongful act to which self-defence constitutes an appropriate response.[395] This is line with the economic rationale of self-defence outlined above and according to which the cost burden is placed on the attacking state as the cheapest cost avoider in order to set incentives for compliance. However, compensation may be warranted with regard to innocent third states suffering loss from acts of self-defence.[396] This seems appropriate given that these states are not the authors of the original wrongful act.[397] Such a compensation requirement would also induce a state acting in self-defence to price in the associated costs on innocent third states and the international community and ultimately to better target the action taken in self-defence to the author of the original armed attack. However, these costs should be shifted partially to the author of the armed attack as the cheapest cost avoider. The focus of the compensation requirement thus lies on how to deal with adverse effects on innocent third states and the international community as well as on setting incentives to internalise the costs of excessive actions in self-defence.

Finally, under certain conditions, third states have the right to engage in actions of collective self-defence for the benefit of the state victim of an armed attack.[398] The ICJ identified in the *Nicaragua* case three requirements: firstly, at least one state needs to be entitled to take action by way of individual self-defence; secondly, this state has to declare itself victim of an armed attack; thirdly, the victim state has to request assistance to another state to resort to force by way of collective self-

---

[395] Crawford, *State Responsibility: the General Part*, 319. Consequently, self-defence (and countermeasures) were explicitly excluded from compensation in draft Article 35 adopted by the ILC on first reading in 1996. Forteau, "Reparation in the Event of a Circumstance Precluding Wrongfulness," in *The Law of International Responsibility*, ed. Crawford, Pellet, and Olleson, 892. See also United Nations International Law Commission, *Second Report on State Responsibility by Special Rapporteur James Crawford*, Fifty-First Session, 1999 (UN Doc. A/CN.4/498), pp. 83–84, paras. 338, 344.

[396] Crawford, *State Responsibility: the General Part*, 319–320; Forteau, "Reparation in the Event of a Circumstance Precluding Wrongfulness," in *The Law of International Responsibility*, ed. Crawford, Pellet, and Olleson, 893. See also United Nations International Law Commission, *Yearbook of the International Law Commission*, 1999, Volume II, Part Two (UN Doc. A/CN.4/SER.A/1999/Add.1 (Part 2)), p. 85, para. 407. See also United Nations International Law Commission, *Yearbook of the International Law Commission*, 1999, Volume I (UN Doc. A/CN.4/SER.A/1999), pp. 174–176.

[397] In that regard, self-defence differs from consent which cannot dispense another state from compliance vis-à-vis third states, leading to an internationally wrongful act in their regard giving rise to reparation.

[398] Thouvenin, "Circumstances Precluding Wrongfulness in the ILC Articles on State Responsibility: Self-Defence," in *The Law of International Responsibility*, ed. Crawford, Pellet, and Olleson, 462–463.

defence.[399] Collective self-defence has to be clearly distinguished from different forms of collective security, in which case the legality of the use of force is dependent upon the authorisation of the Security Council under Chapter VII or Chapter VIII UN Charter,[400] requiring in particular a threat to international peace and security.[401] In practice, military alliances may contain elements of both collective self-defence and collective security measures (e.g. the NATO as a standing alliance has also assumed responsibilities in the implementation of Security Council collective security decisions).[402] However, collective self-defence is not only following the objective of maintaining international peace and security, but also a manifestation of the law regulating the use of force between individual sovereign nation states. The underlying cooperation problem is thus mixed. It consists in the provision of international peace and security as a global public good and in assisting each other in the defence of national state interests, notably the interest in survival (that is, private goods). In this regard, collective self-defence differs also from third-party countermeasures which serve predominantly as a tool to enforce compliance with community interest obligations.[403] Nonetheless, collective self-defence renders the deterrence function of self-defence more effective as the existence of this possibility sends a clear signal to a potential aggressor state that the victim of the attack will have sufficient means at his disposal to bring the armed attack to an end. However, increasing the deterrent effect requires that the promise for mutual assistance is credible, as there exists a collective action problem in getting states to participate in measures of collective self-defence. For instance, the collective self-defence guarantee of the NATO member states is comparable to providing a regional public good (i.e. peace and security, in particular in Europe), which is subject to free-riding in particular regarding the respective financial contributions.[404] Whether effective or not, collective self-defence also pursues the objective to enforce compliance with the obligation of the prohibition of the threat or use of force. Like individual self-defence, collective self-defence needs to remain within the authorised limits. That means it can only serve to reverse the effects of the armed attack (i.e. to halt and repel that attack and to recover territory occupied during the attack),[405] in line with the necessity and proportionality requirement.[406] This requires also taking

399 *Military and Paramilitary Activities in and against Nicaragua (Nicaragua v. United States of America)*, Judgment (Merits), p. 105, para. 199. See also Greenwood, "Self-Defence," paras. 35–39.

400 Greenwood, "Self-Defence," para. 40. Chapter VIII UN Charter relates to regional arrangements dealing with the maintenance of international peace and security.

401 On the relation between self-defence and collective security, sustaining a primacy in international law of the collective security system over the right of self-defence, which can be substantially limited by the UN Security Council, see Nico Krisch, *Selbstverteidigung und Kollektive Sicherheit* (Berlin: Springer, 2001).

402 Greenwood, "Self-Defence," para. 40.

403 See Chap. 7.

404 See the topical debate on defence spending among NATO alliance members.

405 See Greenwood, "Self-Defence," paras. 26–28.

406 The measure taken in collective self-defence is thus assessed in terms of whether the degree of force used was necessary to respond to the armed attack and proportionate to the threat posed by that attack.

into account the interests protected by the obligation in question, notably whether they relate to GPGs or CPRs and *jus cogens* obligations in particular (Article 26 ARSIWA). The compensation requirement would also apply to states acting in collective self-defence with regard to costs falling on innocent third states and the international community. After being shifted partially to the author of the armed attack as the cheapest cost avoider, the costs of compensation would probably need to be allocated among the states acting in collective self-defence by way of regress. States participating in collective self-defence can however not be considered innocent third states in relation to each other, and thus may not claim compensation from each other in case of material losses.

5.4 Conclusion on the Economic Analysis of Circumstances Precluding Wrongfulness

This chapter examined how duties and costs are allocated along the six circumstances precluding wrongfulness, and thus how exemptions from international legal obligations and the financial consequences of their invocation set incentives either for the plaintiff state alleging the commission of an internationally wrongful act or the defendant state invoking a justification or excuse.

It could be seen that all excuses and justifications apply to exceptional circumstances where the behaviour of the state in breach of international law was socially desirable and is thus exempted from responsibility which would under normal circumstances apply. Without going into detail again, the economic rationale (that is, the reason why the particular action in a given case was socially desirable) differs not just between excuses and justifications, but between all six circumstances precluding wrongfulness: the protection of an essential interest caused less losses to the international community than compliance with an international obligation would have caused (private necessity, or, when the defendant state acted to protect a prevailing community interest, public necessity), an individual state agent acted to save human life (distress), the losses caused by the defendant state's act could not have been avoided or only at exorbitant costs (*force majeure*), the plaintiff state authorised the otherwise wrongful act and accepted the losses (consent), the defendant state's act reduced the losses from an armed attack and deterred states from launching an armed attack in the future (self-defence) or the defendant state's act aimed to induce compliance with secondary obligations and incidentally with international obligations more generally (countermeasures).[407] Thus, some provisions (those that rely on reciprocal behaviour) serve to induce a change in behaviour of the state author of the initial act (i.e. self-defence, countermeasures, and, to a lesser extent, consent). Other provisions, notably the excuses, aim to set incentives

[407] On the role of countermeasures as a compliance instrument in the international law of state responsibility, see Sect. 7.1.

for the state relying on a circumstance precluding wrongfulness (i.e. necessity and, to a lesser extent, distress) or focus predominantly on *ex post* cost allocation (i.e. distress and *force majeure*). What they all have in common is that they allow for flexibility in exceptional circumstances and thus for non-compliance with the international obligation in question, while trying to avoid abusive invocation by setting relatively strict conditions for invocation (e.g. limitation of the means at choice, non-contribution to the situation, validity and scope of the expression of consent on the basis of sufficient information, necessity and proportionality of the act in self-defence). The exceptionality of these circumstances is also reflected in the reversal of the burden of proof. That the fulfilment of the conditions needs to be proven by the state invoking them makes sense from an economic perspective "because the probability that such circumstances exist is much smaller than the probability that they do not exist".[408] The defendant state will often be the only state who knows the facts justifying the act.[409] Such information asymmetries make it easier for the defendant state, who has more or better information about its actions and the circumstances, to prove compliance with the conditions of the justification or excuse invoked in a given case. However, it will be more difficult for the plaintiff state or third parties (i.e. other states or international judicial institutions) to observe and verify the defendant state's unilateral actions and intentions. As discussed throughout the chapter, there are good arguments (in particular, the problem of hindsight bias) that speak for an objective *ex post* assessment of the conditions taking into account the perspective of the state relying on a circumstance precluding wrongfulness, notably the information available at the time of the act in question and whether the state acted in good faith. This is particularly relevant with regard to the choice of available means and the non-contribution requirement, which both depend heavily on prior policy choices with the consequence that invocation of the relevant excuses would otherwise almost always be excluded.[410] In fact, this good faith standard of assessment allows for an adequate balance between *ex post* control of the stringent conditions and the possibility of invoking justifications and excuses in extraordinary circumstances. Limiting that possibility to zero would be against the economic rationale underlying their existence.

Before turning to the financial consequences of invoking the different circumstances precluding wrongfulness, one word on the common provision of Article

[408] See with regard to excuses in domestic tort law, Visscher, "Justifications and Excuses in the Economic Analysis of Tort Law," 22.

[409] ARSIWA Commentaries, Part one, Chap. V, para. 8. Crawford, *State Responsibility: the General Part*, 320–321.

[410] Paddeu and Jephcott make this argument with regard to global emergencies such as the coronavirus pandemic which is due to complex causes, not just natural events, but also man-made factors such as ecological and societal trends or political choices, and that are thus not easily covered by the circumstances precluding wrongfulness in the ARSIWA that were drafted on the basis of old state practice (in particular, natural disasters as a classic source of emergency). They claim that "[a] new balance between the needs for compliance and flexibility built into these rules may need to be struck" and that "[s]tates should not unjustifiably breach obligations owed to other international actors, but at the same time they should have sufficient flexibility to address these disasters—especially when the lives of individuals, both within their jurisdictions and beyond, are at stake." Paddeu and Jephcott, "Covid-19 and Defences in the Law of State Responsibility: Part II".

26 ARSIWA, which excludes their invocation with regard to *jus cogens* norms.[411] The legal rationale of this conflict of norms rule is that for some fundamental norms of international law there is the presumption that the interest in upholding the respect for the international legal order prevails over any unforeseeable and extraordinary circumstances. This provision thus amounts to a balancing of competing interests where the result is pre-determined by the law. From an economic point of view, it is not socially desirable to replace this assessment with a weighing of interests in an individual case given that the costs to the international community of a breach of peremptory norms are prohibitive (i.e. *jus cogens* obligations as normative GPGs). However, not all six circumstances precluding wrongfulness build on the rationale of balancing conflicting interests. This is the case for *force majeure*, which contains no element of free choice (thus usually excluding intentional and systematic breach of fundamental community norms), and for self-defence, which constitutes in itself a right to the use force. In such scenarios, there is from a legal perspective no *prima facie* breach of a peremptory norm. Article 26 ARSIWA does, however, not exclude that, in a given case, other community interests protected by an international obligation in question prevail and thus exclude the reliance on a circumstance precluding wrongfulness. From an economic point of view, these are obligations relating to the protection of GPGs or the preservation of CPRs and where the costs of a breach to the international community will usually outweigh the interests protected by the non-compliant act.

In addition, this chapter served to provide an overview on when the compensation requirement in Article 27 lit. b) ARSIWA is economically justified. The question of compensation had been deliberatively left open when the ARSIWA were finalised, although it was already clear at that time that compensation for material losses was not appropriate for all six circumstances precluding wrongfulness. Whether compensation is adequate depends on the underlying economic rationale of each justification or excuse. As regards necessity, compensation of material losses is indeed justified as a general rule because it upholds the deterrent effect of reparation for injury (being the classic remedy in the case of a wrongful act). It thus serves to avoid moral hazard by inducing states to take sufficient care or hedge against the risk of peril for an essential interest, thereby limiting opportunistic breach of international obligations. However, a postponement of the payment of compensation and a reduction of the amount should be possible in the case of severe economic distress causing devastating effects for the population ("crippling compensation"). I have also argued that deviations from this principle of compensation may be justified, when states act in public necessity, that is, to protect a prevailing essential interest of the international community as a whole. In order to set incentives for GPG provision or CPR protection, losses should as an *ultima ratio* remain with the plaintiff state, unless there are mechanisms available to share the costs among the parties involved, ideally including those states that benefitted from the act in public necessity

[411] On the exclusion of countermeasures when they consist in a violation of *jus cogens* norms, see Sect. 7.2.1.2.

(e.g. compensation with possibility of regress in case of a limited number of beneficiaries or trust fund solutions in primary law). In the case of distress, which differs in that an individual state agent acted to save human life, the compensation requirement derives from the same rationale and should also provide the possibility of partial or full recourse against other states benefitting from the act in distress. However, in some constellations, exceptions from the compensation requirement may be warranted, in particular, when the costs cannot be borne by the state acting in distress (i.e. reduction of the amount in the case of "crippling compensation") or cannot be shared with other states benefitting from the act (i.e. full or partial shift to the victim state). As regards *force majeure*, full compensation is not justified as the losses caused by the defendant state's act due to the external event could not have been avoided at all or only at exorbitant costs. A cost-sharing solution seems more appropriate and the costs thus fall partially also on the plaintiff state which is not more innocent than the defendant state. In the case of consent, where the plaintiff state authorised the otherwise wrongful act and accepted the losses following breach of a private and club goods obligation, these are usually remediated to the extent negotiated *ex ante* with compensatory payments. However, any material losses that are caused to innocent third states will have to be remediated *ex post* by way of reparation for injury as these acts are not covered by the consent (private and club goods obligations relating to third states or GPG and CPR obligations) and thus constitute internationally wrongful acts. Self-defence (also in the form of collective self-defence) should not give rise to an obligation to provide compensation for material losses as the purpose of the justification is to deter other states from causing damage with an armed attack. An exception relates to material losses incurred by innocent third states as in this scenario the compensation requirement can induce the state acting in self-defence to respect the legal limits of the justification. Here, the costs should nonetheless be shifted partially to the author of the armed attack as the cheapest cost avoider, and in the case of collective self-defence to other benefitting states by way of regress. Finally, with regard to countermeasures,[412] the general compensation requirement for material loss inflicted upon the target state does not set the right incentives, as the author of the prior wrongful act is the cheapest cost avoider. However, an exception to this cost allocation has to be made for material losses incurred by innocent third states. In this scenario, the compensation requirement can induce the state taking countermeasures to internalise any harmful side-effects (i.e. externalities) and thus to better target the countermeasure. Yet, in order not to deter multiple directly or indirectly injured states further from taking countermeasures due to the sanctioners' dilemma, cost-sharing arrangements for the financial consequences are necessary. Costs should be shared primarily with the target state being the author of the prior wrongful act, and, secondly, with other injured states profiting from the countermeasures by way of recourse or with a trust fund solution among indirectly injured states. When non-directly injured states take third-party countermeasures for the protection of a GPG or CPR, the *ultima ratio*

[412] On the financial consequences of countermeasures, see Sect. 7.3.

could even be to envisage an exemption from the requirement to compensate innocent third states benefitting *pro rata*, unless non-compensation would in a concrete case create a disproportionate burden for the innocent state.

In sum, this chapter demonstrated from an economic point of view that and how the general compensation requirement in Article 27 lit. b) ARSIWA needs to be further refined across and within the different excuses and justifications. These findings are summarised in Fig. 5.3.

	Compensation for material losses (Article 27 lit. b) ARSIWA)
Necessity	Private necessity: compensation with possibility of postponement and reduction ('crippling compensation') Public necessity: no compensation with possibility of cost-sharing between the parties involved or among benefitting states (e.g. possibility of regress or trust fund solutions)
Distress	Compensation with possibility of full or partial regress, exceptionally reduction or cost-sharing between the parties
Force majeure	Cost-sharing with the plaintiff state (as both states are innocent)
Consent	Compensation subject to *ex ante* negotiation (only private and club good obligations); reparation for injury for innocent third states (as outside the scope of consent)
(Collective) self-defence	No compensation for the author of the armed attack (cheapest cost avoider), but compensation for innocent third states possible (incl. cost-sharing with the target state, possibility of regress from other benefitting states in the case of collective self-defence)
Countermeasures	No compensation for the author of the internationally wrongful act (cheapest cost avoider), but compensation for innocent third states possible (incl. cost-sharing with the target state, possibility of regress from other injured states, trust fund solution among non-directly injured states)

Fig. 5.3 The compensation requirement across all circumstances precluding wrongfulness

Chapter 6
Consequences of International State Responsibility: A Rational Choice Analysis of Remedies in International Law

The international responsibility of a state, which is entailed by an internationally wrongful act, engages certain legal consequences, which are outlined in the second part of the ARSIWA dealing with the so-called content of the international responsibility of a state.[1] These legal consequences consist in different secondary obligations[2] which fall on the responsible state and in turn provide remedies for the state or states to whom the international obligation is owed, thus creating a new legal relationship between them.[3] Absent any specific provisions in a given treaty regime,[4] the core obligations are cessation of the wrongful conduct (Article 30 ARSIWA) and reparation for the injury caused by the wrongful act (Articles 31, 34–39 ARSIWA).[5] These remedial duties are deeply rooted in customary international law and

[1] See the introductory Article 28 ARSIWA: "The international responsibility of a State which is entailed by an internationally wrongful act in accordance with the provisions of part one involves legal consequences as set out in this part."

[2] In essence, secondary obligations are those that follow the breach of a primary international obligation. They differ in their content, but the enforcement mechanisms are assumed to be the same. On the dichotomy between primary and secondary rules, see Sect. 1.3 on the research objective.

[3] ARSIWA Commentaries, Part two, para. 1. Article 33 (2) ARSIWA clarifies that the legal consequences are "without prejudice to any right, arising from the international responsibility of a [s]tate, which may accrue directly to any person or entity other than a [s]tate", as for instance in the case of human rights violations where the primary beneficiaries of the obligations breached are individuals.

[4] Article 55 ARSIWA reaffirms the *lex specialis* principle in relation to state responsibility. See also, ARSIWA Commentaries, Part two, para. 2.

[5] Article 29 ARSIWA states the principle that these legal consequences of an internationally wrongful act do not affect the continued duty of the responsible state to perform the obligation breached. The pre-existing legal relationship established by the primary obligation thus remains in place, notwithstanding a breach. See ARSIWA Commentaries, Article 29, para. 2.

J. Lemke, *The Protection of Community Interests in the International Law of State Responsibility*, International Law and Economics,
https://doi.org/10.1007/978-3-031-87927-2_6

recognised as such by international courts and tribunals.[6] In addition, Article 41 ARSIWA provides for certain consequences in the case of a serious breach of an obligation arising under a *jus cogens* norm in the form of additional obligations falling on all states in the international community. The objective of this chapter is to examine how these different remedies operate on the international level depending on the underlying cooperation problem, thus in particular when violations of community interest norms are at stake.

Eric A. Posner and Alan O. Sykes describe the topic of remedies as "one of the most undeveloped areas of international law".[7] It is certainly true that research on how international rules on remedies (that is, secondary obligations operating as restrictions) set incentives for states, in particular the impact they have on the compliance decision, is scarce.[8] In their analysis, Posner and Sykes take an economic contract theory perspective on remedies in general international law.[9] They use the concept of efficient breach, thus pointing out instances where the costs of compliance exceed the associated benefits, with the consequence that their analysis is much broader in scope and encompasses also circumstances precluding wrongfulness (especially, the necessity excuse) and countermeasures. Beyond this extensive scope, an analytical framework building on the concept of efficient breach and rooted in contract theory fails to account for constellations in international law that are more similar to tort law or for cooperation problems underlying the provision of GPGs. In his book on the optimal protection of international law, Pauwelyn also analyses remedies in general international law, including circumstances precluding wrongfulness and countermeasures alongside the classic secondary obligations, but

[6]With regard to cessation, see, for instance, *United States Diplomatic and Consular Staff in Tehran (United States of America v. Iran)*, Judgment, p. 44, para. 95; *Military and Paramilitary Activities in and against Nicaragua (Nicaragua v. United States of America)*, Judgment (Merits), pp. 146–149, para. 292; *Legal Consequences of the Construction of a Wall in the Occupied Palestinian Territory*, Advisory Opinion, p. 197, para. 150. With regard to reparation, see, in particular, *Factory at Chorzów (Germany v. Poland)*, Judgment (Merits), 13 September 1928, PCIJ Series A, No. 17, p. 4, p. 29.

[7]Posner and Sykes, *Economic Foundations of International Law*, 126.

[8]There is, however, vast legal literature on the subject. See, in particular, F. A. Mann, "The Consequences of an International Wrong in International and National Law," *British Yearbook of International Law* 48, no. 1 (1977): 1–65; Christine D. Gray, *Judicial Remedies in International Law* (Oxford: Clarendon, 1990); Dinah Shelton, *Remedies in International Human Rights Law*, 3rd ed. (Oxford: Oxford University Press, 2015); Francesca Capone, "Remedies," ed. Anne Peters and Rüdiger Wolfrum, *Max Planck Encyclopedia of Public International Law* (Oxford Public International Law: Oxford University Press, 2021), http://opil.ouplaw.com, Article last updated in October 2020. The topic of remedies has also been discussed extensively in the existing law and economics research on remedies in contract and tort law.

[9]Posner and Sykes, *Economic Foundations of International Law*, Chap. 9. Along the same vein, see also John K. Setear, "Responses to Breach of a Treaty and Rationalist International Relations Theory: The Rules of Release and Remediation in the Law of Treaties and the Law of State Responsibility," *Virginia Law Review* 83, no. 1 (1997): 1–126.

from a more holistic perspective than Posner and Sykes.[10] He tries to accommodate the realist approach (termed 'American voluntarism') with the other extreme of legal formalism (termed 'European absolutism').[11] His analysis builds on the seminal paper by Calabresi and Melamed which presents an integrated economic approach to analyse legal problems in the domestic context, namely property and torts, by articulating a concept of entitlements, which are protected by property rules or liability rules or considered inalienable.[12] This is indeed a useful approach to achieve a better understanding of the functioning of remedies in the international legal order. This chapter therefore uses the framework of variable protection developed by Pauwelyn, arguing for different levels of protection in different contexts, for the analysis of secondary obligations in the ARSIWA. Yet, it goes further in that it endeavours to gain a more systematic understanding of how the secondary obligations set incentives for states with regard to their compliance decision depending on the underlying problem structures and, in particular, the level of compensation. In this regard, this chapter also takes into account previous analyses of remedies from a social science perspective in different issue areas of international law. This includes the literature on the functioning of remedies in international trade law, in particular within the WTO and its dispute settlement mechanism.[13] Further insights on the functioning of remedies exist with regard to international investment law[14] and international human rights law (with regard to punitive damages).[15]

In line with the overall objective of this book, the focus of the analysis in this chapter lies on the extent to which the different legal and financial consequences of an internationally wrongful act take into account the protection of community interests in international law.[16] From an economic or rationalist perspective the question is how the different remedies (e.g. the rights to compensation or to return to compliance) set incentives for the injured state affected by a breach of an international obligation and, by backward induction, what impact these secondary

---

[10] Pauwelyn, *Optimal Protection of International Law: Navigating between European Absolutism and American Voluntarism.*

[11] See, in particular, ibid., 16–25.

[12] Calabresi and Melamed, "Property Rules, Liability Rules, and Inalienability: One View of the Cathedral," 1089–1128.

[13] See, amongst others, John H. Jackson, "The WTO Dispute Settlement Understanding - Misunderstandings on the Nature of Legal Obligation," *American Journal of International Law* 91, no. 1 (1997): 60–64; John H. Jackson, "International Law Status of WTO Dispute Settlement Reports: Obligation to Comply or Option to "Buy Out"?," *American Journal of International Law* 98, no. 1 (2004): 109–125; Schwartz and Sykes, "The Economic Structure of Renegotiation and Dispute Resolution in the World Trade Organization," S179–S204.

[14] van Aaken, "Primary and Secondary Remedies in Investment Arbitration and State Liability: A Functional and Comparative View," in *International Investment Law and Comparative Public Law*, ed. Schill, 721–754.

[15] Pinto de Albuquerque and van Aaken, "Punitive Damages in Strasbourg," in *The European Convention on Human Rights and General International Law*, ed. van Aaken and Motoc, 230–247.

[16] On the congruence between the legal concept of community interests and the economic concept of global public goods and common pool resources, see Sect. 2.3.

obligations (as legal constraints or cost factors) have on the compliance decision of the potentially wrongdoing state. The objective here is thus to analyse how the incentive structures vary between the private and public dimensions of international law, that is the extent to which remedies are likely to work differently depending on whether the obligation breached relates to the protection of private goods compared to the provision of a GPG or preservation of a CPR. In this regard, the private and public enforcement dimensions (notably countermeasures) also play a role because potentially wrongdoing states will not only take into account the expected costs of their decision but also the probability by which a secondary obligation is likely to be enforced, and this may vary equally depending on the underlying problem constellation.[17] By doing so, this chapter seeks to contribute from a rationalist perspective to the existing debates on the optimal form and level of reparation for injury (depending on the underlying cooperation problem) as well as on the most adequate ways to deal with breaches of peremptory norms of international law (i.e. additional obligations on the international community *versus* punitive damages).

To this end, after briefly setting out the aims and problems of remedies in the international law of state responsibility from a normative perspective (Sect. 6.1), this chapter analyses, in a first step, the obligations of cessation and assurances or guarantees of non-repetition (Sect. 6.2) and, in a second step, the obligation of reparation for injury (Sect. 6.3) by focusing in particular on the optimal level of compensation. The following section examines the consequences of violations of *jus cogens* norms and their ability to induce compliance with peremptory norms of international law (Sect. 6.4). Section 6.5 concludes.

6.1 Aims and Problems of Remedies in the International Law of State Responsibility

This section outlines the normative framework that will guide the subsequent economic analysis of the different remedies in the ARSIWA. Whether and in which constellations the different secondary obligations are setting optimal incentives for states (i.e. whether the law is economically justified) depends on what one defines from a normative perspective as their rationale in the international legal order. Therefore, it is important to clarify at the outset what the reasons for having the different remedies are and which problems they face depending on the underlying cooperation problems.

From the economic perspective followed throughout this book, the rationale of remedies is less one of fairness considerations, in the sense that any injuries caused to victim states should be repaired as an expression of equity, but rather a matter of allocating the costs or secondary duties following the breach of an international

[17] On private and public enforcement of international state responsibility, see Chap. 3. On countermeasures in particular, see Chap. 7.

obligation.[18] Costs can still be allocated fairly or efficiently, but from a functional perspective, this should be done by reconciling different competing objectives in the most optimal way.[19] In order to determine the aims and problems of remedies in international law, this section draws on the economic rationale of remedies in domestic liability law, that is economic theories of contracts and tort. It transfers these insights to the international legal order, which shows the characteristics of a private and a public dimension, both with regard to the substance of primary obligations and with regard to decentralised enforcement.[20] This section builds on the normative framework outlined in Chap. 3 and only clarifies the functions of remedies in international law from an economic perspective to the extent necessary for the subsequent analysis.[21]

The first function of remedies in international law derives from the obligations of cessation of an ongoing violation of an international obligation and assurances of non-repetition. It can be determined as ensuring compliance with international legal obligations.[22] That a wrongdoing state ceases ongoing wrongful behaviour, returns to a state of compliance at the earliest convenience, and reaffirms its commitment to comply in the future, is both in the interest of the victim state (as a remedy) and of the international community as a whole (as protection of the international legal order). The quest for compliance is comparable to the obligation of specific performance in contract law, injunctions in tort law, and to the rationale of administrative law being to return to legality. Compliance as an objective of remedies is therefore particularly relevant in the public law dimension of international law, when there is breach of GPG or CPR obligations, in particular in the case of *jus cogens* norms.

In addition, with regard to the victim state, the main objective of remedies is, as the name suggests, to remediate any harm caused to the injured state by way of reparation. This principle is deeply rooted in domestic contract and tort law and has with regard to the international legal order been recognised in the *Factory at Chorzów* decision of the Permanent Court of International Justice (PCIJ), stating "that it is a principle of international law, and even a general conception of law, that any breach of an engagement involves an obligation to make reparation".[23]

[18] On the allocation of duties and the design of primary obligations, including different responsibility standards in international law, see Sect. 4.1.

[19] Pauwelyn frames this as the quest for optimal protection of entitlements in international law. See Pauwelyn, *Optimal Protection of International Law: Navigating between European Absolutism and American Voluntarism.*

[20] Nollkaemper and Jacobs, "Shared Responsibility in International Law: A Conceptual Framework," 400–403.

[21] For more details on the normative framework and objectives of state responsibility in both the private and public dimension of international law, see Chap. 3.

[22] See also ARSIWA Commentaries, Part two, Chap. I, para. 1. ("But over and above the gravity or effects of individual cases, the rules and institutions of State responsibility are significant for the maintenance of respect for international law and for the achievement of goals which States advance through law-making at the international level.")

[23] *Factory at Chorzów (Germany v. Poland)*, Judgment (Merits), p. 29.

Reparation for injury is, however, not just an aim in itself, it may also serve other purposes, depending also on the concrete form, that is restitution (Article 35 ARSIWA), compensation for damage (Article 36 ARSIWA), or satisfaction (Article 37 ARSIWA).

Another possible objective of remedies is flexibility for the potentially wrongdoing state, a notion rooted in economic contract theory. Posner and Sykes, for instance, transfer the idea of efficient breach of contract, namely that "[t]he right to pay damages rather than perform permits the promisor to avoid inefficient performance",[24] to the international level. They argue that states, in the absence of punitive damages in international law, may prefer to pay compensatory damages rather than comply with an international legal obligation, in particular when withdrawing from the treaty regime as a whole would be inefficient and the transaction costs for obtaining consent for a breach (including negotiating *ex ante* compensation) would be too high due to holdup problems, especially in multi-issue bilateral treaties or multilateral treaties such as the WTO.[25] Understanding the obligation to pay compensation for damages caused by an internationally wrongful act as a flexibility provision bears similarities to the rationale of circumstances precluding wrongfulness, in particular the necessity excuse.[26] The rationale of necessity lies in permitting non-performance in the presence of unforeseen and extraordinary circumstances while deterring opportunistic breach with the requirement to pay compensation for material losses. Yet, the flexibility rationale is less evident with regard to reparation for injury in the case of an internationally wrongful act, as there is precisely no prevailing interest except cost efficiency for the wrongdoing state (and thus the protection of a 'private' interest in nature). In contrast to the compensation requirement following the invocation of the necessity excuse, the obligation to provide reparation for injury in the case of breach of an international obligation can thus, in principle, not be understood as a 'right to (efficient) non-performance'. In particular, there is always a third-party effect in terms of violating the integrity of the international legal order, not only with regard to obligations protecting GPGs or CPRs (i.e. *erga omnes* obligations), but also to the international rule of law as a GPG.[27] However, there may be instances where breaches of international law occur without intention or opportunistic behaviour, but simply due to uncertainties of the

---

[24] Posner and Sykes, *Economic Foundations of International Law*, 127. With reference to Shavell, "Damage Measures for Breach of Contract," 466–490. On the concept of efficient breach in contract theory, see Sect. 3.2.2.

[25] Posner and Sykes, *Economic Foundations of International Law*, 126–129. With reference to Setear, "Responses to Breach of a Treaty and Rationalist International Relations Theory: The Rules of Release and Remediation in the Law of Treaties and the Law of State Responsibility," 1–126; Trachtman, *The Economic Structure of International Law*, 142–144.

[26] See, in particular, Sect. 5.2.1 on the aims and problems of the necessity excuse in the domestic and the international legal order.

[27] On this argument see in particular Sect. 5.2.2.2 on breach of a private law obligation in the case of necessity. See also Pauwelyn, *Optimal Protection of International Law: Navigating between European Absolutism and American Voluntarism*, 16–25.

applicable law and the facts of the case.[28] Immediate return to legality and payment of compensation can in these cases signal interest in ongoing cooperation and may help building a reputation for compliance (with second-order obligations), in particular within the same treaty regime.[29] Hence, unlike for exemptions of state responsibility, remedies in general international law are not considered to pursue the objective of flexibility, but rather to secure cooperation in the future.

Another objective of remedies is to avoid opportunistic breaches in the first place, that is, their deterrence function. This relates to the question which incentives the reparation requirement (in the form of restitution or compensation) is setting *ex ante* for any potentially wrongdoing state in the international community. From this perspective, the objective of remedies, at least of reparation, is to induce states to internalise the costs of the internationally wrongful act, and thus to limit the risk of abuse.[30] This function is particularly important with regard to the public dimension of international law where the international community has an interest that violations of GPG or CPR obligations, in particular in the case of *jus cogens* norms, do not occur in the first place. However, as reparation has, in principle, only a compensatory function,[31] punishment is not an objective envisioned by the drafters of the ARSIWA,[32] not even for peremptory norms of international law.[33] Any costs exceeding full reparation of injury (e.g. punitive damages) would amount to retaliatory actions and thus the enforcement dimension of international law.[34] Excessive penalties as a secondary enforcement rule bear the risk of undermining the long-term stability of the cooperative regime.[35] The limitation to compensatory damages

[28] In contract theory, contracts are usually incomplete as the parties could not (or only at exorbitant costs) foresee every possible state of the world at the time of conclusion. In addition, there may be opposing views on whether breach of contract has occurred, depending on the distribution of information between the parties. On insights from the economic analysis of contract law, see Sect. 3.2.2.

[29] This argument appears in the international law and international relations literature. See, for instance, Brewster, "Pricing Compliance: When Formal Remedies Displace Reputational Sanctions," 259–314.

[30] The deterrence function underlies also the obligation of compensation in the economic analysis of tort law, as it is setting incentives for potential tortfeasors to internalise the externality costs of accidents. See Sect. 3.2.

[31] On the principle of full reparation, see Sect. 6.3.

[32] ARSIWA Commentaries, Article 36, para. 4. ("Compensation corresponds to the financially assessable damage suffered by the injured State or its nationals. It is not concerned to punish the responsible State, nor does compensation have an expressive or exemplary character.")

[33] ARSIWA Commentaries, Part two, Chap. III, para. 5. ("There has been, however, no development of penal consequences for States of breaches of these fundamental norms. For example, the award of punitive damages is not recognized in international law even in relation to serious breaches of obligations arising under peremptory norms. In accordance with article 34, the function of damages is essentially compensatory.")

[34] In certain integrated treaty regimes, the payment of fines can be imposed by courts, often in the case of non-compliance with judicial decisions, for example in the EU.

[35] Hathaway and Shapiro, "Outcasting: Enforcement in Domestic and International Law," 323–324. In their work on outcasting, Hathaway and Shapiro think of legal rules as forming 'enforcement chains', that is, a link between a conduct rule being enforced by subsequent enforcement rules, namely a first rule which imposes duties on those who violate the initial conduct rule (e.g. to pay a

therefore means that the aim of deterrence is not absolute, in the sense that it may not be sufficient to deter a breach of international law (but may uphold cooperation in the long-run) and that in order to effectively deter wrongful acts, the obligation to provide reparation has to be backed up with enforcement measures, such as countermeasures.[36]

In sum, an economic analysis of remedies in international law needs to focus on how each one reconciles best the multiple objectives alongside the private and public dimensions of the international legal order: compliance with different types of international legal obligations (i.e. private good, club good, CPR or GPG obligations), reparation of injury, long-term cooperation, and deterrence of internationally wrongful acts in the future. For instance, compensation needs to remediate the harm suffered by a victim state and at the same time credibly deter future opportunistic breaches. Hence, the different remedies need to be measured against all of these functions, thereby pointing out the trade-offs that are achieved in different problem constellations. The following analysis is therefore seeking to answer the following research question: depending on the underlying cooperation problem, how do the remedies in general international law as set out in the ARSIWA allocate the costs of a breach of international law (between the injured state, the responsible state, and third states in the international community) and can this cost allocation with its underlying incentive structures be considered optimal in light of the different conflicting aims of remedies in international law?

Pauwelyn tries to answer this question, albeit framed in more general terms as the quest for the optimal protection of entitlements in international law, by differentiating between liability rules, property protection, and inalienable entitlements.[37] This theoretical framework underlying different forms of remedies has first been developed by Calabresi and Melamed from an economic theory perspective with regard to domestic property and tort law, defining them as follows: "An entitlement is protected by a property rule to the extent that someone who wishes to remove the entitlement from its holder must buy it from him in a voluntary transaction in which the value of the entitlement is agreed upon by the seller. [...] Whenever someone may destroy the initial entitlement if he is willing to pay an objectively determined value for it, an entitlement is protected by a liability rule. [...] An entitlement is inalienable to the extent that its transfer is not permitted between a willing buyer and a willing seller".[38] They point out that property rules require the least amount of state intervention, as the value of the entitlement is determined freely between the parties,

fine) and a secondary rule that enforces the prior rule (and transitively the initial conduct rule). In addition, primary enforcement rules are often backed by multiple secondary enforcement rules or enforcement chains may be split into sub-chains. Ibid., 271–272. Against this background, remedies in international law can be understood as primary enforcement rules and countermeasures as a secondary enforcement rule.

[36] See Chap. 7 on countermeasures in international law as an enforcement tool.

[37] Pauwelyn, *Optimal Protection of International Law: Navigating between European Absolutism and American Voluntarism*, 5–15.

[38] Calabresi and Melamed, "Property Rules, Liability Rules, and Inalienability: One View of the Cathedral," 1092.

whereas under a liability rule the objective value of the entitlement is decided by some organ of the state.[39] Additionally, "most entitlements to most goods are mixed" and may be protected by a property rule, a liability rule, and by a rule of inalienability depending on the situation.[40] In their view, the relevant criteria to determine the optimal rule for a specific situation, using the example of pollution, is transaction costs: if transaction costs are low, property rules are best suited, whereas a liability rule is preferable when transaction costs are high (e.g. uncertainty about the cheapest cost avoider).[41] Pauwelyn transfers this integrated approach to the protection of entitlements on the international level by examining when inalienability should be imposed or when international law should be protected by a property or liability rule. He argues that a property rule is in place when an agreement on exchange is necessary, whereas a liability rule is chosen if no consent but compensation is required.[42] He also acknowledges "that entitlements can be protected by hybrid regimes, such as combinations of property and liability protection, and that all three rules of protection come in different degrees".[43] Any attempt to determine the optimal level of protection of entitlements, he argues, "must be made in context" by taking into account the preceding allocation of entitlements (i.e. the participation problems) and the subsequent level of "non-centralized back-up enforcement", that is the response of international law "when entitlements are taken against the rules".[44] This ties in with my line of argument throughout this book, namely that rules of state responsibility, and in this chapter remedies, may differ depending on the first-order cooperation problem and the probability of effective enforcement (which in turn may also vary depending on the private or public dimension). From a normative viewpoint, Pauwelyn then argues that property protection ought to be the default rule in international law, because "the consent-based nature of allocation of entitlements under traditional international law [...] offers the prototype background for a market-based system of property protection".[45] In addition, as property protection requires the least amount of outside intervention, it is best suited in an international legal order that relies on decentralised law-making and enforcement and can thus

[39] Ibid.

[40] Ibid., 1093.

[41] Ibid., 1119. In particular with regard to accidents, negotiations with the holder of the entitlement are difficult, thus pointing towards a liability rule, as in tort law. This is the same for takings in the domestic context, but due to hold-out problems. Property rules point towards the consent-based exchange of goods in the market negotiated *ex ante* against compensation. For such a presentation of the framework developed by Calabresi and Melamed, see van Aaken, "Primary and Secondary Remedies in Investment Arbitration and State Liability: A Functional and Comparative View," in *International Investment Law and Comparative Public Law*, ed. Schill, 744–745.

[42] Pauwelyn, *Optimal Protection of International Law: Navigating between European Absolutism and American Voluntarism*, 33–34. This is why consent coupled with *ex ante* compensation has been described as a property rule. See Sect. 5.3.2.1.

[43] Ibid., 34.

[44] Ibid., 39–40.

[45] Ibid., 49.

easier be achieved than the prohibition of transfers (i.e. inalienability) or the objective valuation of entitlements that were unilaterally taken (i.e. liability protection).[46] However, in certain circumstances deviation from the default rule of property protection towards a stronger or higher protection of entitlements as inalienable is advisable. He summarises them, following the explanations of Calabresi and Melamed, as significant externalities where transfer would necessarily be inefficient (e.g. large-scale cross-border pollution), moralisms and incommensurability (i.e. the entitlement cannot be monetised, for instance, in the case of *jus cogens* norms), and paternalism.[47] The first two grounds can be translated into economic categories of goods at the international level, namely common pool resources and non-use value global public goods. As outlined in Chap. 5, the concept of inalienability underlies the provision excluding the invocation of circumstances precluding wrongfulness in the case of *jus cogens* norms (Article 26 ARSIWA). Not all CPR or GPG entitlements are inalienable (e.g. not all CPR or GPG obligations have *jus cogens* status) as inalienability may come at different levels, but property protection may still be preferable to a liability rule.[48] Pauwelyn also presents, in line with the framework offered by Calabresi and Melamed, three arguments that favour deviation towards weaker or lower protection of entitlements under a liability rule, namely certain market failures that require social intervention: (i) strategic hold-out problems (i.e. holders of entitlements refusing to sell, as in takings in the domestic context), (ii) free-riding behaviour of potential buyers of entitlements, and (iii) high transaction costs making forced transfer of entitlements with objective valuation more efficient (e.g. in the case of a high number of stakeholders).[49] By offering more flexibility, liability rules have the advantage that they facilitate participation in treaty regimes and help to deal with uncertainty which may require incomplete contracting (e.g. vague rules and exceptions).[50] At the same time, liability rules require a more institutionalised setting with strong third-party dispute settlement mechanisms (for collective *ex post* valuation) and effective back-up enforcement in order to enable credible commitments.[51] They are nonetheless confronted with the risk of errors of collective valuation (problems of under- or over-compensation).[52]

---

[46] Ibid., 49–50.

[47] Ibid., 50–55.

[48] Ibid., 41–43.

[49] Ibid., 55–66.

[50] Ibid., 66–75. This is the rationale underlying, for instance, the customary necessity excuse in the law of state responsibility, including the requirement to provide compensation for material loss.

[51] Ibid., 77–90.

[52] Ibid. Rachel Brewster questions whether a liability rule is the preferable approach in international law, arguing *inter alia* that a property rule may be preferable in bilateral and regional treaty regimes due to lower transaction costs and less hold-out problems, see Rachel Brewster, "Posner and Sykes Book Symposium: Comment by Rachel Brewster," *OpinioJuris* (Blog), 26 March, 2013, http://opiniojuris.org/2013/03/26/posner-and-sykes-book-symposium-comment-by-rachel-brewster/

The concepts of property, liability, and inalienable rules as well as the idea of variable protection will also guide the analysis in the following sections with regard to the different remedies in the ARSIWA and their adequacy in different problem constellations: firstly, the obligations of cessation and assurances or guarantees of non-repetition; secondly, the obligation of reparation for injury in its different forms; and, thirdly, the consequences of violations of *jus cogens* norms.[53]

6.2 Cessation and Assurances of Non-repetition of the Wrongful Act

The first type of remedies, cessation and assurances of non-repetition, needs to be understood in relation with Article 29 ARSIWA.[54] This provision reaffirms the principle that the responsible state is under the continued duty to perform the primary obligation breached.[55] It clarifies that the conduct of the responsible state has no effect on the obligation that has previously been breached.[56] Article 30 ARSIWA provides that the responsible state is under two distinct but linked obligations, namely (a) to cease the internationally wrongful act, if it is continuing, and (b) to offer appropriate assurances and guarantees of non-repetition, if circumstances so require. That the underlying primary obligation remains in force is thus a necessary precondition for both obligations, because otherwise the question of cessation does not arise and assurances or guarantees of non-repetition in the future become irrelevant.[57] Both obligations aim to restore the pre-existing legal relation between

[53] Another type of remedy, in particular in international human rights law, is the exhaustion of local remedies, which can be classified as a primary remedy, as it is the precondition for bringing claims on the international level, unless the national procedures amount to 'denial of justice'. Exhaustion of local remedies is also the general principle in international law and in the law of state responsibility based on the principle of diplomatic protection. Article 44 lit. b) ARSIWA on the admissibility of claims reads: "The responsibility of a State may not be invoked if: [...] the claim is one to which the rule of exhaustion of local remedies applies and any available and effective local remedy has not been exhausted." Exhaustion of local remedies will not be discussed here as a self-standing remedy, but the focus will be on the remedies applicable on the international level outlined in the second part in the ARSIWA. On the exhaustion of local remedies as primary remedy, and the role in international investment law in particular, see van Aaken, "Primary and Secondary Remedies in Investment Arbitration and State Liability: A Functional and Comparative View," in *International Investment Law and Comparative Public Law*, ed. Schill, 732–743.

[54] For an overview of both forms, see respectively Olivier Corten, "The Obligation of Cessation," in *The Law of International Responsibility*, ed. James Crawford, Alain Pellet, and Simon Olleson (Oxford: Oxford University Press, 2010), 545–549; Sandrine Barbier, "Assurances and Guarantees of Non-Repetition," in *The Law of International Responsibility*, ed. James Crawford, Alain Pellet, and Simon Olleson (Oxford: Oxford University Press, 2010), 551–561.

[55] Article 29 ARSIWA on the continued duty of performance reads: "The legal consequences of an internationally wrongful act under this part do not affect the continued duty of the responsible State to perform the obligation breached."

[56] See ARSIWA Commentaries, Article 29, para. 1.

[57] ARSIWA Commentaries, Article 30, para. 1.

the responsible state and the state or states to whom the violated obligation was owed, with cessation putting an emphasis on ending an ongoing wrongful conduct and assurances or guarantees on preventing future wrongful conduct.[58]

For the obligation of cessation to arise, the wrongful conduct needs to have a 'continuing character'.[59] Cessation of a wrongful act as a remedy is thus excluded, when the breach of an international obligation occurs only at the moment when the act is performed, even if its effects continue.[60] According to the ARSIWA Commentaries, "[t]he function of cessation is to put an end to a violation of international law and to safeguard the continuing validity and effectiveness of the underlying primary rule. The responsible [s]tate's obligation of cessation thus protects both the interests of the injured [s]tate or [s]tates and the interests of the international community as a whole in the preservation of, and reliance on, the rule of law".[61]

Injured states may seek appropriate assurances or guarantees of non-repetition when the mere return to compliance by ending an ongoing violation does not suffice to be adequately protected from future potential breaches of the international obligation in question, for instance, threats to diplomatic premises or personnel or insufficient consular protection of its citizens.[62] Assurances of non-repetition may consist in some verbal expression, whereas guarantees may involve a stronger commitment, for instance, preventive measures designed to inhibit repetition of the wrongful act (e.g. repeal of legislature which allowed for the breach to occur).[63] There is broad international practice of states seeking different forms of assurances and guarantees of non-repetition as a remedy following a breach of an international obligation.[64] Assurances and guarantees of non-repetition, by focusing on compliance in the future, have essentially a preventive function and aim to repair

---

[58] Ibid.

[59] In the *Rainbow Warrior* arbitration, the tribunal referred explicitly to this requirement, thus distinguishing cessation from the remedy of restitution as a form of reparation, but also to the linked condition "that the violated rule is still in force at the time in which the order is issued", which is now reflected in Article 29 ARSIWA. *Difference between New Zealand and France Concerning the Interpretation or Application of two Agreements concluded on 9 July 1986 between the two States and Which Related to the Problems Arising from the Rainbow Warrior Affair*, Award, p. 270, para. 114. These requirements have previously also been affirmed by the ICJ. See *United States Diplomatic and Consular Staff in Tehran (United States of America v. Iran)*, Judgment, p. 44, para. 95; *Military and Paramilitary Activities in and against Nicaragua (Nicaragua v. United States of America)*, Judgment (Merits), pp. 146–149, para. 292.

[60] Article 14 (1) ARSIWA. On the characteristics of a continuing wrongful act, see Article 14 (2) and (3) ARSIWA and the related Commentaries.

[61] ARSIWA Commentaries, Article 30, para. 5.

[62] ARSIWA Commentaries, Article 30, para. 9.

[63] ARSIWA Commentaries, Article 30, paras. 11–12.

[64] See, in particular, the examples cited in the ARSIWA Commentaries, Article 30, paras. 10–13. In the *LaGrand* case, the ICJ responded to Germany's request for a general assurance of non-repetition, without discussing its legal basis, but also affirmed that there are various ways to respond to such obligation. *LaGrand (Germany v. United States of America)*, Judgment, 27 June 2001, ICJ Reports 2001, p. 466, pp. 513–514, para. 125.

and reinforce the continuing legal relationship between the responsible state and the state or states affected by the breach (including non-directly injured states).[65] Whether assurances or guarantees of non-repetition may consist in the adoption of specific measures or only in a general restatement by the responsible state to protect the rights of the injured state in the future will depend on the circumstances of the case, including the nature of the obligation and the breach in question.[66] As indicated in Article 30 lit. b) ARSIWA, the remedy of appropriate assurances and guarantees of non-repetition is only pertinent if circumstances so require. Such assurances and guarantees are thus much more flexible than cessation, but will also not be appropriate in all cases.[67] In order to prevent abusive and excessive claims, assurances and guarantees of non-repetition are exceptional in character.[68]

The remedies of cessation and appropriate assurances or guarantees of non-repetition with their focus on future compliance are thus conceptually different from the remedy of reparation of injury, focusing on remediating harm caused by the wrongful act in the past. Due to their different functions, cessation and assurances of non-repetition, on the one hand, and reparation, on the other hand, are alternative remedies which are not mutually exclusive. Affected states thus do not need to choose between future compliance and reparation for past injuries. Still, one remedy may be more effective than the other, depending on the underlying problem constellation. Hence, both types of remedies complement each other and can also operate independently of one another, in cases where one or the other is not applicable (e.g. absence of an ongoing violation or an injury). There is also no hierarchy between them, in the sense that one is the primary and the other the secondary remedy, unlike for the different forms of reparation which are characterised by their subsidiarity.[69] However, cessation will often be the central issue in inter-state disputes regarding state responsibility, despite the importance the obligation of reparation may have in many cases.[70]

Taking up the framework on property and liability rules sketched out in the previous section, both remedies, cessation and assurances or guarantees of non-repetition, aim for specific performance (i.e. ongoing and future compliance with the primary obligation in question). They can therefore be characterised as property rules concerning the prospective protection of initial entitlements.[71] Both

[65] ARSIWA Commentaries, Article 30, para. 11.

[66] ARSIWA Commentaries, Article 30, para. 13.

[67] ARSIWA Commentaries, Article 30, para. 9.

[68] ARSIWA Commentaries, Article 30, para. 13.

[69] See Sect. 6.3 on reparation for injury.

[70] ARSIWA Commentaries, Article 30, para. 4.

[71] This conclusion is also drawn by Pauwelyn, specifying that responsible states cannot buy their way out of future performance, with circumstances precluding wrongfulness (including consent) being the only exception from the obligation of cessation, thus sustaining the argument that international law is by default protected by a property rule, not a liability rule. Pauwelyn, *Optimal Protection of International Law: Navigating between European Absolutism and American Voluntarism*, 113–114.

remedies do not require objective determination of the value of the entitlement and thus rely on self-enforcement by the states concerned.[72] International courts and tribunals can nonetheless facilitate decentralised enforcement by affirming the illegality of the act, in particular when there is high uncertainty regarding the applicable law and the facts of the case, and by determining the content of specific performance (e.g. order to repeal a certain administrative act or law).[73] Unlike with liability rules, valuation of the entitlement is not an issue here. The problem from an incentive point of view is that both secondary obligations (cessation and assurances/guarantees of non-repetition) are not providing additional incentives to comply with the primary obligation in the first place, as they simply restate that the responsible state remains under the obligation to perform the obligation in the presence and in the future. In order to have a deterrent effect on the compliance decision by backward induction, these obligations would need to play a role in the cost–benefit calculation of the state considering to breach or comply with the primary obligation in question. Yet, both remedies can only play a role for the decision of the responsible state to comply in the future, that is to stop an ongoing violation or not breach the obligation again, and thus rely heavily on the self-enforcement mechanisms outlined earlier in this book.[74] Cessation and assurances/guarantees of non-repetition depend for their effectiveness on negative or positive back-up enforcement mechanisms, such as countermeasures which increase the costs of non-compliance or even rewarding mechanisms which consist in offering the payment of a reward for future compliance. The aim of these enforcement mechanisms must be to shift the cost-benefit calculation of the responsible state such that future compliance becomes less costly compared to the benefits it derives from an ongoing violation. The injured state would seek cessation and non-repetition of the wrongful act, if it has an interest in continued performance of the obligation (and the treaty regime as a whole); otherwise, it could also terminate the treaty according to the rules and procedures in the VCLT.[75] The responsible state is expected to return to or give assurances for future compliance if the costs of non-compliance (e.g. threat of reciprocal non-compliance) exceed the associated benefits or, *vice versa*, if the long-term benefits from cooperation outweigh the costs of compliance. In this regard, assurances and guarantees of non-repetition can play a crucial role in signalling the responsible state's long-term interest in cooperation and thus be an attempt to restore a reputation for compliance. There is thus an economic rationale for having them in the toolbox of remedies.

In order to examine in which problem constellations these remedies are effective, it is useful to distinguish the private and public law dimensions. As mentioned earlier, cessation (and assurances/guarantees of non-repetition) can be requested in addition to claims for reparation, when the wrongful act has caused harm to the

[72] Ibid., 49–50.

[73] On the facilitating role of international judicial institutions, see Sect. 2.4.

[74] See Sect. 2.4 on the compliance mechanisms in international law.

[75] Article 60 VCLT.

injured state, or independently. In tort-like private goods situations like cross-border pollution, infringement of the victim state's integrity of the territory or its citizens, full reparation of a causal injury will play a crucial role. Yet, cessation of an ongoing violation or assurances/guarantees of non-repetition in the future can constitute a complementary remedy for an injured state requiring adequate protection from continuing and future breaches of the international obligation in question. In this regard, there is a certain overlap with restitution and satisfaction as forms of reparation (e.g. repeal of certain legislation in order to re-establish the *status quo ante* or to ensure non-repetition of the wrongful act in the future), as will be discussed in the next section. In more contract law like private goods constellations, where states cooperate to further their economic gains (e.g. by eliminating trade restrictions), remediation of harm is of lesser significance than the restoration and long-term functioning of the cooperative relationship. One example are the specific provisions on remedies in international trade law, as the focus of the WTO dispute settlement mechanism is on cessation rather than reparation.[76] Article 3 (7) of the Understanding on Rules and Procedures Governing the Settlement of Disputes (DSU)[77] clearly points out that "the first objective of the dispute settlement mechanism is usually to secure the withdrawal of the measures concerned if these are found to be inconsistent with the provisions of any of the covered agreements. The provision of compensation should be resorted to only if the immediate withdrawal of the measure is impracticable and as a temporary measure pending the withdrawal of the measure which is inconsistent with a covered agreement. The last resort which this Understanding provides to the Member invoking the dispute settlement procedures is the possibility of suspending the application of concessions or other obligations under the covered agreements on a discriminatory basis vis-à-vis the other Member, subject to authorization by the [Dispute Settlement Body, DSB] of such measures". In practice, however, compensatory damages remain the exception, notably because they are granted only on a voluntary basis.[78] By contrast, withdrawal of the measures concerned is usually enforced with the suspension of the application of concessions or other obligations under the covered agreements subject to the authorisation of the DSB.[79] Thus, the primary remedy in WTO law can be

[76] ARSIWA Commentaries, Article 30, para. 4, note 431.

[77] Understanding on Rules and Procedures Governing the Settlement of Disputes (DSU), Annex 2 of the Agreement Establishing the World Trade Organization (WTO Agreement).

[78] Article 22 (1) DSU. See also, van Aaken, "Primary and Secondary Remedies in Investment Arbitration and State Liability: A Functional and Comparative View," in *International Investment Law and Comparative Public Law*, ed. Schill, 732. In favour of introducing financial compensation in the context of the WTO due to the costs of retaliatory restrictions, see Marco Bronckers and Naboth van den Broek, "Financial Compensation in the WTO: Improving the Remedies of WTO Dispute Settlement," *Journal of International Economic Law* 8, no. 1 (2005): 101–126.

[79] Article 22 (2) and (3) DSU.

considered as cessation of the wrongful act backed-up with authorised retaliatory countermeasures or cross-countermeasures.[80]

In the public law dimension, the remedies of cessation and assurances or guarantees of non-repetition play a particularly important role. Article 33 (1) ARSIWA clarifies that the scope of the secondary obligations of the responsible state "may be owed to another [s]tate, to several [s]tates, or to the international community as a whole, depending in particular on the character and content of the international obligation and on the circumstances of the breach".[81] According to Article 48 (2) ARSIWA, also non-directly injured states can in the case of breach of *erga omnes* or *erga omnes partes* obligations, in addition to the injured state, claim from the responsible state (a) cessation of the internationally wrongful act and assurances or guarantees of non-repetition and (b) reparation in the interest of the injured state or of the beneficiaries of the obligation breached.[82] Thus, states who have not suffered an injury but whose legal interest in compliance is infringed can request specific performance in the form of cessation of the wrongful act and assurances of non-repetition in the future, but reparation of an injury only for the injured state (or the direct beneficiaries of the international obligation in question). In the public law dimension, the focus of cooperation is on the provision of GPGs and the preservation of CPRs, requiring foremost compliance with the underlying obligation. Hence, in these constellations, there is a strong rationale for opening the possibility to claim cessation and assurances/guarantees of non-repetition also to non-directly injured states, which can then have recourse to a wide variety of enforcement mechanisms, including positive incentives such as rewards.

The remedies of cessation and assurances or guarantees of non-repetition can also operate independently from claims for reparation, for instance, when no injury

[80] Van Aaken and Pauwelyn also conclude that the predominant remedy in international trade law is a property rule. See, van Aaken, "Primary and Secondary Remedies in Investment Arbitration and State Liability: A Functional and Comparative View," in *International Investment Law and Comparative Public Law*, ed. Schill, 732, 745; Pauwelyn, *Optimal Protection of International Law: Navigating between European Absolutism and American Voluntarism*, 134–145. Whether dispute settlement in the WTO amounts to a property rule or a liability rule has, however, been fiercely debated. For a property rule and preference for an obligation to perform (and compensation or retaliation only as a fallback in the case of non-compliance), see, amongst others, Jackson, "The WTO Dispute Settlement Understanding - Misunderstandings on the Nature of Legal Obligation," 60–64; Jackson, "International Law Status of WTO Dispute Settlement Reports: Obligation to Comply or Option to "Buy Out"?," 109–125. For a liability rule permitting efficient breach by paying compensation or suffering equivalent trade restrictions, see, amongst others, Schwartz and Sykes, "The Economic Structure of Renegotiation and Dispute Resolution in the World Trade Organization," S179-S204.

[81] See also Article 42 ARSIWA on the definition of the injured state or states.

[82] According to Article 48 (1) ARSIWA, any State other than an injured State is entitled to invoke the responsibility of another State in accordance with paragraph 2 if: (*a*) the obligation breached is owed to a group of States including that State, and is established for the protection of a collective interest of the group; or (*b*) the obligation breached is owed to the international community as a whole. For more details, see Sect. 3.3.3 on public enforcement of international state responsibility and the notion of *erga omnes* and *erga omnes partes* obligations.

occurred, determination of the damage is difficult, or causation of harm by the wrongful act in question cannot be established. The key issue about these two secondary obligations is that they serve to uphold the rule of law in the interest of the concerned treaty parties or the international community as a whole, and thus focus on the positive third-party effects of compliance with international legal obligations. As regards GPG obligations, this can, for instance, be illustrated with the example of violations of diplomatic or consular obligations (e.g. the protection of diplomatic premises or consular personnel). Here, all states have an interest in the continuous functioning of the diplomatic communication channels and may thus request cessation of the wrongful act, notwithstanding any request for reparation of the state directly affected by the breach. But also with regard to breaches of international human rights obligations, cessation can remediate the effects on interested third parties deriving value from ongoing and future human rights protection, also in addition to any requests for reparation made by the injured state or individual beneficiaries.[83] Since it is difficult to determine how much other states in the international community value the protection of a certain GPG (e.g. human rights), cessation as a remedy provides clear advantages to reparation (at least in relation to third states). Cessation is, in fact, frequently demanded by states in the event of serious breaches of international law.[84] In particular, with regard to international human rights law, international courts and tribunals not only predominantly issue declaratory judgments (and award pecuniary damages) but also order specific performance in the form of cessation (e.g. the release of prisoners).[85] The argument is similar with regard to obligations protecting common pool resources, where all states in the international community derive value from the protection of the environment or from stopping large-scale cross-border pollution. Here, cessation and assurances or guarantees of non-repetition will often be the only available remedy, when causality between the wrongful act and the harm cannot be established. Cessation and assurances or guarantees of non-repetition are also the only remedy when the wrongful act does not cause any harm, but the international obligation consisted in taking the necessary precautions to prevent the harm.[86] While the two remedies are thus particularly relevant in the public law dimension of international law, when there is breach of GPG or CPR obligations, in particular in the case of *jus cogens* norms, their effectiveness depends on the probability of being actually implemented and thus third-party enforcement being effective. Third-party

---

[83] On the classification of human rights protection as a non-use value global public good, see Sect. 2.3.

[84] ARSIWA Commentaries, Article 30, para. 4.

[85] See, for instance, with references to case law, van Aaken, "Primary and Secondary Remedies in Investment Arbitration and State Liability: A Functional and Comparative View," in *International Investment Law and Comparative Public Law*, ed. Schill, 732. The different types of remedies in international human rights law will be discussed in the following section on the different forms of reparation. As mentioned earlier, there is a certain overlap between cessation and restitution as well as assurances of non-repetition and satisfaction.

[86] See Sect. 4.1.2.2 on due diligence obligations in international law.

countermeasures might be one possibility to enforce the obligation of cessation,[87] but also other positive inducements may play a role here. Yet, states will face collective action problems regarding their provision due to the public good characteristics.

6.3 Reparation for Injury

The second type of remedies in the law of state responsibility is reparation for injury.[88] The obligation for the responsible state to make full reparation for the injury caused by the internationally wrongful act is included in Article 31 (1) ARSIWA. This fundamental principle of the consequences of the breach of an international legal obligation has been stated by the PCIJ in the *Factory at Chorzów* case regarding jurisdiction and the question whether Poland owed reparations to Germany following the seizure of a German factory.[89] It has also been reaffirmed in many decisions of the ICJ.[90] In the *Factory at Chorzów* case, the PCIJ defined further, firstly, the function of reparation as the reestablishment of the situation which would have existed without the breach, secondly, the principle of full reparation as the adequate level, and, thirdly, the different forms of reparation (i.e. restitution in kind, compensation for the value, or damages for loss sustained).[91]

---

[87] On countermeasures, in particular third-party countermeasures in accordance with Article 54 ARSIWA, see Chap. 7.

[88] For an overview, see Brigitte Stern, "The Obligation to Make Reparation," in *The Law of International Responsibility*, ed. James Crawford, Alain Pellet, and Simon Olleson (Oxford: Oxford University Press, 2010), 563–571.

[89] *Factory at Chorzów (Germany v. Poland)*, Judgment (Jurisdiction), 26 July 1927, PCIJ Series A, No. 9, p. 4, p. 21. ("It is a principle of international law that the breach of an engagement involves an obligation to make reparation in an adequate form.") *Factory at Chorzów (Germany v. Poland)*, Judgment (Merits), p. 29. ("[...] it is a principle of international law, and even a general conception of law, that any breach of an engagement involves an obligation to make reparation.")

[90] *United States Diplomatic and Consular Staff in Tehran (United States of America v. Iran)*, Judgment, pp. 44–45, para. 95; *Military and Paramilitary Activities in and against Nicaragua (Nicaragua v. United States of America)*, Judgment (Merits), pp. 146–149, para. 292; *Avena and Other Mexican Nationals (Mexico v. United States of America)*, Judgment, 31 March 2004, ICJ Reports 2004, p. 12, pp. 70–72, para. 153; *Legal Consequences of the Construction of a Wall in the Occupied Palestinian Territory*, Advisory Opinion, pp. 201–202, para. 163.

[91] *Factory at Chorzów (Germany v. Poland)*, Judgment (Merits), p. 47. ("The essential principle contained in the actual notion of an illegal act – a principle which seems to be established by international practice and in particular by the decisions of arbitral tribunals – is that reparation must, as far as possible, wipe out all the consequences of the illegal act and re-establish the situation which would, in all probability, have existed if that act had not been committed. Restitution in kind, or, if this is not possible, payment of a sum corresponding to the value which a restitution in kind would bear; the award, if need be, of damages for loss sustained which would not be covered by restitution in kind or payment in place of it – such are the principles which should serve to determine the amount of compensation due for an act contrary to international law.")

The purpose of reparation which underlies the *Factory at Chorzów* decision, but also the subsequent jurisprudence, is "to rectify the wrong done to an injured party and correct injustice by restoring the *status quo ante* [...]".[92] The costs of the breach are thus shifted to the wrongdoing state, with the consequence that reparation from an economic point of view also has a deterrence function and the challenge is to determine the appropriate level of costs.[93] From both a legal and economic perspective, reparation thus differs due to its different functions from the obligations of cessation and assurances or guarantees of non-repetition of the wrongful act, focusing on restoring the legal relationship and inducing compliant behaviour in the future. Reparation is complementary to the remedy of cessation and assurances/ guarantees of non-repetition and does also not replace the continued duty of performance.[94] The obligation of reparation even remains in place even when a treaty is terminated and continued duty of performance (and cessation of the wrongful act) is no longer required.[95] Reparation can also operate independently when the wrongful act is no longer ongoing and assurances or guarantees of non-repetition are not required in the particular circumstances.

The obligation of reparation for the responsible state requires that an injury has been caused by the internationally wrongful act. According to Article 31 (2) ARSIWA, injury includes any damage, whether material or moral. The ARSIWA Commentaries outline that "[t]his formulation is intended both as inclusive, covering both material and moral damage broadly understood, and as limitative, excluding merely abstract concerns or general interests of a [s]tate which is individually unaffected by the breach".[96] Article 31 ARSIWA thus leaves it to the primary obligation in question to specify what is required in a given case.[97] Regarding the notions of material and moral damage, the ARSIWA Commentaries define them respectively as "damage to property or other interests of the [s]tate and its nationals which is assessable in financial terms" and "damage [which] includes such items as individual pain and suffering, loss of loved ones or personal affront associated with an intrusion on one's home or private life".[98] Material damage and pecuniary loss are thus not a precondition for reparation as the damage can also relate to non-material interests such as the honour, dignity, and prestige of the victim state,[99] an issue which will become relevant as regards the appropriate form of

---

[92] Dinah Shelton, "Reparations," ed. Anne Peters and Rüdiger Wolfrum, *Max Planck Encyclopedia of Public International Law* (Oxford Public International Law: Oxford University Press, 2021), http://opil.ouplaw.com, Article last updated in August 2015, para. 3.

[93] Ibid.

[94] ARSIWA Commentaries, Part two, Chap. I, para. 2.

[95] ARSIWA Commentaries, Article 29, para. 3.

[96] ARSIWA Commentaries, Article 31, para. 5.

[97] ARSIWA Commentaries, Article 31, paras. 6, 8.

[98] ARSIWA Commentaries, Article 31, para. 5.

[99] *Difference between New Zealand and France Concerning the Interpretation or Application of two Agreements concluded on 9 July 1986 between the two States and Which Related to the Problems Arising from the Rainbow Warrior Affair*, Award, p. 267, paras. 109–110.

reparation, namely satisfaction. Another issue is the necessary and sufficient causal link between the internationally wrongful act and the injury in order to limit reparation to effects that directly result from the wrongful act and to exclude coverage of consequences that are too indirect or remote.[100] A consequence of this causal link between the wrongful act and the injury is that in line with Article 42 ARSIWA only injured states (broadly speaking, states which are directly affected by the breach) can invoke responsibility and thus claim reparation. According to Article 48 (2) ARSIWA, non-directly injured states may in the case of breach of *erga omnes* or *erga omnes partes* obligations request from the responsible state—in addition to their own legal interest in cessation of the internationally wrongful act and assurances or guarantees of non-repetition—reparation only in the interest of the injured state or of the beneficiaries of the obligation breached.[101] If multiple states are injured by the same internationally wrongful act, each injured state may separately invoke the responsibility of the state having committed the wrongful act, and thus claim reparation (and cessation).[102]

The second principle outlined in the *Factory at Chorzów* decision was the level of reparation. The principle of full reparation is also reflected in the ARSIWA, notably in Article 31 (1) ARSIWA, but also in Article 34 ARSIWA, which outlines the different forms of reparation.[103] Since the underlying rationale of reparation, as reflected in the ARSIWA, is to place the injured state in the same position as if no wrongful act had occurred, the relevant determinant for the level of reparation is the size of the injury (e.g. the material damage) without taking into account any possible consequences for the responsible state.[104] The principle of proportionality is not an aspect of the obligation to make full reparation, as notions of proportionality are only included with regard to restitution and satisfaction, but not in the context of compensation,[105] an issue which will be discussed in the relevant sections below. The only general exception to full reparation provided in the ARSIWA is the reduction of reparation in cases of contributory fault (Article 39 ARSIWA).[106] A

[100] ARSIWA Commentaries, Article 31, paras. 9–10.

[101] On the distinction between injured states and non-directly injured states see Chap. 3 in the respective sections on private and public enforcement of international state responsibility.

[102] Article 46 ARSIWA on the plurality of injured states reads as follows: "Where several States are injured by the same internationally wrongful act, each injured State may separately invoke the responsibility of the State which has committed the internationally wrongful act."

[103] Article 34 ARSIWA on forms of reparation reads as follows: "Full reparation for the injury caused by the internationally wrongful act shall take the form of restitution, compensation and satisfaction, either singly or in combination, in accordance with the provisions of this chapter."

[104] Shelton, "Reparations," para. 3.

[105] See ARSIWA Commentaries, Article 34, para. 5.

[106] Article 39 ARSIWA on contribution to the injury reads as follows: "In the determination of reparation, account shall be taken of the contribution to the injury by wilful or negligent action or omission of the injured State or any person or entity in relation to whom reparation is sought." See also Sect. 4.1.2.1 on notions of fault in the law of state responsibility.

failure of the injured state to mitigate the damage may preclude reparation to the extent that the damage could have been avoided.[107] The economic rationale of this cost allocation rule between the injured and the responsible state is to address moral hazard, that is to incentivise the injured state to avoid wilful or take precautions against a negligent aggravation of the injury.[108] There is, by contrast, no deviation from the principle of full reparation in the case of serious breaches of *jus cogens* or other fundamental international norms, as punitive damages are not recognised under general international law.[109] Determining the adequate level of reparation, in particular the sum of compensation, is crucial in order to calibrate the incentives for optimal deterrence of future breaches of international law, as any downward or upward deviation would lead to under- or over-deterrence. In their compliance decision, states will factor in the expected costs of reparation and the probability with which they are likely to be enforced.

The determination of the appropriate level of reparation is linked to the different forms of reparation and the analysis of their incentive structures will be the key aspect in this chapter. Article 34 ARSIWA outlines that "[f]ull reparation for the injury caused by the internationally wrongful act shall take the form of restitution, compensation and satisfaction, either singly or in combination [...]".[110] Depending on the type and extent of the injury, the three different forms of reparation, restitution (Article 35 ARSIWA), compensation (Article 36 ARSIWA), and satisfaction (Article 37 ARSIWA), may have to complement each other, while following a certain order of subsidiarity.[111] For instance, reestablishment of the situation which would have been existed without the breach may not be sufficient to wipe out all the consequences, for instance, because the seizure of property can also cause pecuniary damages due to the loss of the possibility to use it over a certain period of time.[112] The different remedies have therefore been regarded as primary and secondary remedies, with primary remedies relating to property rules (in particular, restitution of the *status quo ante*, for instance, withdrawal of an illegal legislative or administrative act) and secondary remedies relating to liability rules (in particular, payment

[107] ARSIWA Commentaries, Article 31, para. 11. With reference to *Gabčíkovo-Nagymaros Project (Hungary v. Slovakia)*, Judgment, p. 55, para. 80.

[108] The underlying rationale of this comparative negligence defence is to improve incentives for potential victim states to choose an optimal level of precaution. See Sect. 4.2.1.

[109] The consequences of violations of *jus cogens* obligations will also be discussed in Sect. 6.4.

[110] In the *Factory at Chorzów* case, the court only dealt with restitution and compensation as the injury was only a material one. *Factory at Chorzów (Germany v. Poland)*, Judgment (Merits), p. 47.

[111] Compensation is only applicable, insofar as the injury cannot be made good with restitution, and satisfaction is only applicable, insofar as the injury cannot be made good with restitution and/or compensation.

[112] ARSIWA Commentaries, Article 34, para. 2.

of compensation for financially assessable damages).[113] An injured state may choose which form reparation should take (as well as the conduct the responsible state should take in order to cease an ongoing wrongful act) and may, depending on the circumstances, request compensation rather than restitution.[114] Assuming they have jurisdiction over a given case, international courts or tribunals may also have to determine the appropriate form (and level) of reparation as well as any specific conduct required of the responsible state. The analysis in the following sections therefore seeks to offer guidance regarding the question in which constellations a property rule or a liability rule might be more appropriate, or in other words in which constellations objective valuation of the entitlement is preferable to specific performance and *vice versa*. It will in particular examine the impact of different forms of reparation on the compliance decision, both in the private and public dimensions in international law (private good *versus* GPG/CPR obligations), taking into account the problem of enforcement.

6.3.1 Restitution

Restitution is the first form of reparation of the consequences of an internationally wrongful act and is outlined in Article 35 ARSIWA.[115] It offers injured states the possibility to claim "the re-establishment as far as possible of the situation which existed prior to the commission of the internationally wrongful act, to the extent that any changes that have occurred in that situation may be traced to that act".[116] The

[113]On restitution (and cessation) as a property rule and compensation as a liability rule, see Pauwelyn, *Optimal Protection of International Law: Navigating between European Absolutism and American Voluntarism*, 112–114. On the equation of property rules with primary remedies being preventive or restorative and liability rules with secondary remedies being pecuniary damage claims, granted *ex post*, see van Aaken, "Primary and Secondary Remedies in Investment Arbitration and State Liability: A Functional and Comparative View," in *International Investment Law and Comparative Public Law*, ed. Schill, 722, 745.

[114]See Article 43 (2) ARSIWA on the notice of a claim by the injured state.

[115]Article 35 ARSIWA reads as follows: "A State responsible for an internationally wrongful act is under an obligation to make restitution, that is, to re-establish the situation which existed before the wrongful act was committed, provided and to the extent that restitution:

(*a*) is not materially impossible;

(*b*) does not involve a burden out of all proportion to the benefit deriving from restitution instead of compensation." See further Christine Gray, "The Different Forms of Reparation: Restitution," in *The Law of International Responsibility*, ed. James Crawford, Alain Pellet, and Simon Olleson (Oxford: Oxford University Press, 2010), 589–597; Attila Tanzi, "Restitution," ed. Anne Peters and Rüdiger Wolfrum, *Max Planck Encyclopedia of Public International Law* (Oxford Public International Law: Oxford University Press, 2021), http://opil.ouplaw.com, Article last updated in January 2021.

[116]ARSIWA Commentaries, Article 35, para. 1.

focus is thus, at least in the understanding which underlines the ARSIWA, on the factual reestablishment of the *status quo ante*.[117] Restitution encompasses any action necessary to restore the situation prior to the wrongful act and can, in practice, take the form of material restoration or the return of occupied territory, seized property or the release of detained individuals, but it can also require more complex measures, such as the reversal of a legislative provision or the reconsideration of an administrative or judicial act, or some combination thereof.[118] However, the obligation to provide restitution also has limits and may according to Article 35 ARSIWA be partially excluded to the extent that restitution is either materially impossible or involves a burden out of all proportion to the benefit deriving from restitution instead of compensation. Material impossibility relates, for instance, to seized property being lost, destroyed or deteriorated, or more complex situations such as rights of third states acting in good faith which preclude restitution.[119] Disproportionality refers to the relation between the benefit to be expected from restitution and the cost burden for the responsible state which needs to be grave compared to compensation.[120] The fact that injured states may choose compensation over restitution or international tribunals may use their discretion to favour compensation over restitution in the alleged interest of the parties does not diminish the primacy of restitution over compensation.[121] In practice, states have often insisted on their request for restitution being an important element of rectifying non-compliant behaviour with certain international obligations, notably those protecting peremptory norms.[122]

Restitution amounts to an obligation of specific performance requiring certain conduct from the responsible state, supporting the argument that "[i]nternational law is, by default, protected by a property rule".[123] Property rules or primary remedies, such as restitution, offer "a stronger protection of an entitlement than a liability rule. Furthermore, they induce the state to reconsider its decision".[124] As mentioned before, this is particularly the case when the order of restitution consists in reversing a legislative provision or reconsidering an administrative or judicial act.

[117] Restitution does not require the establishment of the hypothetical situation that would have existed if the wrongful act had not been committed, but such damages, in particular pecuniary damages, can be remediated with the obligation of compensation. ARSIWA Commentaries, Article 35, para. 2.

[118] ARSIWA Commentaries, Article 35, paras. 1, 5 with numerous references to examples in international case law.

[119] However, mere political or administrative difficulties will not be sufficient. ARSIWA Commentaries, Article 35, paras. 8–10.

[120] ARSIWA Commentaries, Article 35, para. 11.

[121] ARSIWA Commentaries, Article 35, paras. 3–4. Subsidiarity of compensation is also affirmed in *Factory at Chorzów (Germany v. Poland)*, Judgment (Merits), p. 47. On the distinction between restitution and compensation, see also Christine Gray, "The Choice between Restitution and Compensation," *European Journal of International Law* 10, no. 2 (1999): 413–423.

[122] ARSIWA Commentaries, Article 35, para. 3.

[123] Pauwelyn, *Optimal Protection of International Law: Navigating between European Absolutism and American Voluntarism*, 111–113.

[124] van Aaken, "Primary and Secondary Remedies in Investment Arbitration and State Liability: A Functional and Comparative View," in *International Investment Law and Comparative Public Law*, ed. Schill, 745.

Administrative or judicial review bears the advantage of reconsidering the actions of the responsible state (or its organs) while protecting the due process rights and requirements of the injured state (or the beneficiary of the international obligation breached, for instance, the individual deprived from its consular protection).[125] The ICJ has been carefully considering the sovereignty concerns of responsible states and refrained from overstepping its competences by conditioning too strictly the exercise of the substantive powers of state organs and leaving the choice of means to review and reconsider wrongful actions taken (e.g. criminal convictions and prison sentences) to the national governments.[126] Property rules, and restitution in particular, also favour reaching a consensual agreement first before ordering the payment of compensation in the second step.[127] Primary remedies, such as specific performance, are therefore a common remedy in international law, at least in state-to-state disputes.[128]

There is also an economic rationale for favouring restitution over compensation, depending on the problem constellation underling the primary obligation in question. Restitution as a primary rule or property rule offers strong protection when it relates to the protection of property rights. This is the case, when restitution seeks to make good the injury resulting from breach of international obligations prohibiting, for instance, the occupation of foreign territory, the seizure of foreign property (in particular, diplomatic premises) or the violation of consular obligations (e.g. by wrongfully detaining foreign nationals). Thus, in the private dimension of the law of state responsibility, restitution plays an important role in tort-like situations where the wrongful act causes injury to private goods protected by international law. Since private goods are rival in consumption and their benefits are excludable, restitution is preferable to compensation, when the entitlement holder values the restitution of the good or entitlement more than being compensated, unless restitution is materially impossible or wholly disproportionate. This is based on the assumption that reparation of the injury would be granted in full (e.g. the return of occupied territory, seized property or the release of prisoners or hostages). In terms of the result and the specific measures to be taken by the responsible state, restitution albeit focusing on repairing the harmful effects of the wrongful act in the past can thus overlap with cessation as another remedy of specific performance, provided that the international obligation breached is of continuing character and the violation ongoing (e.g. the repeal of a legislative or administrative act).[129] Both remedies differ, however, to the

---

[125] Ibid.

[126] Ibid., 732. See, in particular, *Avena and Other Mexican Nationals (Mexico v. United States of America)*, Judgment, p. 72, para. 153. See also, albeit with respect to assurances and guarantees of non-repetition, *LaGrand (Germany v. United States of America)*, Judgment, p. 516, para. 128. See also, ARSIWA Commentaries, Article 34, para. 3.

[127] van Aaken, "Primary and Secondary Remedies in Investment Arbitration and State Liability: A Functional and Comparative View," in *International Investment Law and Comparative Public Law*, ed. Schill, 745.

[128] Ibid., 731–732.

[129] See ARSIWA Commentaries, Article 35, para. 6.

extent that cessation is not limited to proportionality, but "may give rise to a continuing obligation, even when literal return to the *status quo ante* is excluded or can only be achieved in an approximate way".[130] Cessation also provides added value in cases where no injury has occurred and where the focus of cooperation is the mutual exchange of benefits to further economic gains (e.g. trade law) and not the protection of property rights.

Posner and Sykes even propose that "[p]erhaps restitution will be or should be limited to property right-like violations (the seizure of land, ships, equipment, and so forth), where the return of the property approximates compensatory damages (minus, of course, any lost 'rental value')".[131] This restrictive understanding of restitution derives from their economic analysis of remedies on the basis of the idea of efficient breach. Yet, restitution can also play a crucial role in the public dimension of international law, in particular with regard to peremptory norms of general international law.[132] Restitution can generate positive spillovers for third states, for instance, the clean-up after pollution of the seas or the restoration of natural resources, reestablishment of human rights protection (e.g. release of detained persons), and return to the rule of law more generally. In contrast, monetary compensation usually benefits only the injured state and/or the ultimate beneficiary of the obligation breached. The argument here is that GPGs and CPRs are non-use value public goods, meaning that all states in the international community derive value from their protection or preservation and therefore have an interest not only in ongoing compliance (as induced with cessation), but also in the restoration of compliant behaviour in the form of the *status quo ante* (as induced with restitution *in integrum*). Compared to compensation, restitution thus places the focus on the provision of the public good and the preservation of the common resource. Also in the public dimension the specific conduct required by the responsible state (e.g. withdrawal of occupying forces, annulment of a decree of annexation of foreign territory, the return of persons detained, or property seized in the course of a military invasion) may be considered either cessation or restitution.[133] Another advantage of cessation in GPG or CPR constellations is that it can be claimed not only by injured states, but also by non-directly injured states, whereas restitution can only be requested by the latter in the interest of the injured state or of the beneficiaries of the obligation breached.[134] Hence, under the condition that the wrongful act is still ongoing and/or restitution is not materially impossible, restitution and cessation can in many tort-like situations and in those with a GPG/CPR dimension be used interchangeably, with a preference for cessation, and exhibit many benefits over compensation.

---

[130] ARSIWA Commentaries, Article 30, para. 7.

[131] Posner and Sykes, *Economic Foundations of International Law*, 134.

[132] See ARSIWA Commentaries, Article 35, para. 6.

[133] Ibid.

[134] Article 48 (2) ARSIWA.

Apart from the reparation objective, restitution has also a deterrence function. The idea is that restitution wipes out all the consequences of the wrongful act so that the responsible state does not derive benefits from the act and cannot simply buy itself out from compliance.[135] A state knowing that restitution will have to be provided for a wrongful act may decide to rather not breach the international obligation in question. This requires, however, that restitution covers the whole injury and that the probability of enforcement is sufficiently high. Regarding the former, states may still derive short-term benefits from the breach, for instance, the temporary occupation of territory or seizure of property, and there will also be (pecuniary or other) damages that cannot be made good with restitution. Compensation thus plays a complementary role in capturing the whole dimension of the injury, notwithstanding its usefulness in cases where restitution is not materially possible. Regarding the probability of enforcement, compliance with the obligation of restitution (as with cessation) depends on effective back-up enforcement by injured states and other states in the international community and might fail in many instances, for instance, occupied territory not being returned (e.g. in the case of Crimea).

6.3.2 Compensation for Damage

The second form of reparation is compensation for the damage caused.[136] It is outlined in Article 36 ARSIWA[137] and a well-established and probably the most often claimed principle in international law.[138] Compensation plays a subsidiary role, as expressed by the half-sentence in Article 36 (1) ARSIWA, which reads

[135] Posner and Sykes, *Economic Foundations of International Law*, 134. ("If a state must make restitution, then it may not obtain any benefit from the breach.")

[136] For an overview, see Stephan Wittich, "Compensation," ed. Anne Peters and Rüdiger Wolfrum, *Max Planck Encyclopedia of Public International Law* (Oxford Public International Law: Oxford University Press, 2021), http://opil.ouplaw.com, Article last updated in May 2008; John Barker, "The Different Forms of Reparation: Compensation," in *The Law of International Responsibility*, ed. James Crawford, Alain Pellet, and Simon Olleson (Oxford: Oxford University Press, 2010), 599–611.

[137] Article 36 ARSIWA reads as follows: "1. The State responsible for an internationally wrongful act is under an obligation to compensate for the damage caused thereby, insofar as such damage is not made good by restitution.

2. The compensation shall cover any financially assessable damage including loss of profits insofar as it is established."

[138] *Factory at Chorzów (Germany v. Poland)*, Judgment (Merits), pp. 27–28. ("It is a principle of international law that the reparation of a wrong may consist in an indemnity corresponding to the damage which the nationals of the injured State have suffered as a result of the act which is contrary to international law. This is even the most usual form of reparation [...].") See also, *Gabčíkovo-Nagymaros Project (Hungary v. Slovakia)*, Judgment, p. 81, para. 152. ("It is a well-established rule of international law that an injured State is entitled to obtain compensation from the State which has committed an internationally wrongful act for the damage caused by it.") The principle of compensation for damage has subsequently been applied and further refined by other international courts and arbitral tribunals, on the basis of the general law of state responsibility or specific treaty provisions, including in the areas of the international law of the sea, international human rights, and international investment law.

"insofar as such damage is not made good by restitution". Restitution may frequently be impossible or inappropriate (either fully or partially) or injured states may opt for compensation for some other reason. The role of compensation is thus to complement restitution, when the latter cannot achieve full reparation of the injury suffered.[139] This is the reason why compensation is considered a secondary remedy.[140] Compared to restitution with its focus on specific performance, compensation can be regarded a liability rule, because it allows other states to take or destroy the entitlement of another state against the payment of an objectively determined price.[141]

Article 36 (2) ARSIWA further develops the notion of damage, defined in Article 31 (2) ARSIWA as material or moral damage, and specifies that "compensation shall cover any financially assessable damage including loss of profits insofar as it is established". Compensation, usually in the form of monetary payments, serves the function "to address the actual losses incurred as a result of the internationally wrongful act".[142] Thus, with its focus on 'financially assessable' damage it is to be distinguished from satisfaction, which deals with moral damage.[143] Satisfaction, which may also come in the form of monetary payments, addresses non-material injury resulting from the wrongful act, in particular non-material damage incurred by the injured state itself, "on which a monetary value can be put only in a highly approximate and notional way".[144] Satisfaction is therefore a subsidiary form of compensation, because it covers a type of damage (i.e. moral damage) that cannot be accounted for with the monetary payment of compensation for 'financially assessable' damage.

The term 'financially assessable' delimits the scope of the obligation to provide compensation to "any damage which is capable of being evaluated in financial terms" and which "encompasses both damage suffered by the [s]tate itself (to its property or personnel or in respect of expenditures reasonably incurred to remedy or mitigate damage flowing from an internationally wrongful act) as well as damage suffered by nationals, whether persons or companies, on whose behalf the [s]tate is claiming within the framework of diplomatic protection".[145] The burden of proving the occurrence of damage thereby falls on the injured state as also indicated by the half-sentence at the end of Article 36 (2) ARSIWA, namely that compensation shall

---

[139] ARSIWA Commentaries, Article 36, para. 3. See also, *Factory at Chorzów (Germany v. Poland)*, Judgment (Merits), p. 47.

[140] van Aaken, "Primary and Secondary Remedies in Investment Arbitration and State Liability: A Functional and Comparative View," in *International Investment Law and Comparative Public Law*, ed. Schill, 722, 731.

[141] On the definition of liability rules, see Sect. 6.1.

[142] ARSIWA Commentaries, Article 36, para. 4.

[143] ARSIWA Commentaries, Article 36, para. 1.

[144] ARSIWA Commentaries, Article 36, para. 4. Non-material or moral damage suffered by individuals is, however, financially assessable and compensation thereof may be claimed by injured states within the framework of diplomatic protection. Ibid., para. 16.

[145] ARSIWA Commentaries, Article 36, para. 5.

cover any financially assessable damage including loss of profits "insofar as it is established".

The possible types of compensable damage and the methods of quantification will depend on "the content of particular primary obligations, an evaluation of the respective behaviour of the parties and, more generally, a concern to reach an equitable and acceptable outcome".[146] Compensation requires that the appropriate types of damages in a given case and the quantification thereof are objectively assessed, which is the key characteristic of a liability rule. In practice, compensation claims are either decided upon by international courts and tribunals or are settled by mutual agreement between the responsible and the injured state, normally on a without prejudice basis.[147] Yet, if compensation is the result of negotiations between the parties to the dispute, it would not qualify as a liability rule (rather as a property rule), because a monetary payment to the injured state without acknowledging the breach of an international obligation would be outside the scope of the law of state responsibility.[148] An objective *ex post* valuation of the damage requires therefore the intervention of a third-party, ideally a strong, institutionalised dispute settlement mechanism.[149] The key challenge for the court is to determine the sum of damages that amounts to full reparation. This is not only important from an *ex post* perspective focusing on reparation and equitable outcomes, but also from an incentive point of view, and thus the deterrence function of compensation. Optimal incentives for compliance, however, do not only depend on the appropriate level of compensation, but also on the probability of enforcement of these costs,[150] with international courts and tribunals only playing a facilitating role. The probability of enforcement depends in turn on the underlying problem constellations, broadly speaking the private and public dimensions of international law. Due to its complementary nature, compensation can apply to all constellations, including CPR and GPG scenarios, but only to the benefit of injured states (e.g. the injured state incurring losses for the restoration of polluted waters) or the immediate beneficiaries of the international obligation in question (e.g. an innocent prisoner).

This section will analyse the incentives of the compensation requirement in different constellations in order to demonstrate how full compensation operates and what the consequences of an inappropriate level of compensation are for the compliance decision of states. The following analysis builds on the assumption that a

---

[146] ARSIWA Commentaries, Article 36, para. 7. In addition, Article 38 ARSIWA foresees that interest on any principal sum due shall be payable when necessary in order to ensure full reparation. The evaluation of the respective behaviour of the parties includes an assessment on whether the injured state contributed to the injury. See Article 39 ARSIWA and the discussion in the introduction of this Sect. 6.3.

[147] ARSIWA Commentaries, Article 36, para. 6.

[148] Another property rule would be consent to the breach of an international obligation (entitlement) with the *ex ante* negotiation of compensation. See Sect. 5.3.2.1.

[149] See also Pauwelyn, *Optimal Protection of International Law: Navigating between European Absolutism and American Voluntarism*, 77–90.

[150] For the domestic context, see Polinsky and Shavell, "The Optimal Tradeoff between the Probability and Magnitude of Fines," 880–891.

state will violate an international obligation if the expected benefits of the act (B_V)[151] for the wrongdoing state outweigh the associated costs of non-compliance (C_V).[152] It will further be assumed, for simplicity reasons, that the expected (material) costs of the violation of an international obligation (C_V) equal the sum of compensation to be paid to the injured state (i.e. the cost previously imposed on the victim state), which equals the amount of damages (D) times the probability (p) of being held responsible, that is enforcement of compensation for damages being effective:

$$B_V > C_V; \text{whereas}$$
$$C_V = p(D)$$

When the expected benefits of non-compliance equal the associated costs, a state may be rather inclined to comply with the international obligation in question due to the long-term reputational costs of non-compliance.[153] Reputation thus works at the margins of the cost-benefit calculation of states contemplating whether to breach or comply with an international legal obligation.[154]

In the baseline scenario, a state considers breaching a private goods obligation potentially causing injury to another state and thus will have to take a binary decision between compliance or non-compliance, weighing the payoffs associated with each option against another. Before committing the wrongful act, a state will compare the expected benefits of the wrongful act (B_V) with the expected costs (C_V).[155] The rationale behind the requirement to provide 'full' reparation for the injury, in this case a monetary payment equivalent to damage to the injured state (D), is to induce the wrongdoing state to internalise the costs to the same extent as they would otherwise have to be borne by the injured state. This is the rationale underlying

---

[151] The expected benefits of non-compliance (B_V) are assumed to be immediate or short-term benefits, as long-term benefits from non-compliance would lead to the breakdown of the cooperative regime (e.g. withdrawal from the treaty regime).

[152] In accordance with the research method explained in Sect. 1.3, state preferences are assumed to consist in the quest for maximising absolute gains (i.e. being better or at least not worse off than before) and to be given and fixed. This means that in the following analysis, states are assumed to have neither an inherent preference for compliance nor for enforcement. When a state has a strong preference for compliance (i.e. a high preference intensity), this needs to be reflected in the expected benefits resulting from compliance with an international obligation. The benefits of compliance (e.g. building a reputation for compliance) can also be increased with positive inducements such as rewards.

[153] On reputation as a compliance mechanism, see Sect. 2.4.

[154] Guzman, *How International Law Works: A Rational Choice Theory*, 117.

[155] Accordingly, the payoffs of compliance are the result from the comparison between, on the one hand, the costs of compliance, and, on the other hand, the benefits of compliance, including the forfeited expected costs of compensation. Thus, a state would breach an international obligation when the costs of compliance exceed the benefits of compliance.

the efficient breach argument, namely that the compensation requirement can deter inefficient breach of international obligations.[156] Yet, other states may nonetheless have an interest in the respect of the rule of law in private goods constellations,[157] but this would rather have to be addressed with requests for cessation or other property rules than with variations in the level of reparation. Compliance is not an absolute goal of international state responsibility so that monetary damages beyond full reparation do not seem appropriate, at least, when the internationally wrongful act concerns a private goods obligation.

By backward induction, deviations from the level of full compensation will have an impact on the compliance decisions of states. If compensation is set at a lower level, for instance, because the size of the damage is difficult to observe and verify by the injured state and an international adjudicator, this may lead to under-deterrence; if it is set at a higher level, it includes a retaliatory component which is costly and may cause cooperation to fail. Hence, in order to set optimal incentives for the potentially wrongdoing state, the level of compensation has to be set objectively by a third party so as to correspond to the actual damage. This ties in with the problem of proving the damage, as the burden of proof falls on the injured state. Two possible exceptions from this general rule of full compensation are discussed in the following sub-sections.

6.3.2.1 Crippling Compensation

Unlike for restitution and satisfaction, notions of proportionality are not part of the concept of compensation which underlies the ARSIWA, with full reparation of the injury remaining the guiding principle and proportionality being "addressed in the context of each form of reparation, taking into account its specific character".[158] Restitution contains in Article 35 lit. b) ARSIWA an exception of disproportionality referring to the relation between the benefit to be expected from restitution for the injured state and the cost burden for the responsible state which needs to be grave compared to compensation as alternative form of reparation.[159] Satisfaction must "not be out of proportion to the injury and may not take a form humiliating to the responsible state".[160] Compensation is only restricted by the requirement of a causal link between the internationally wrongful act and the injury and thus "excludes damage which is indirect or remote",[161] but this requirement applies to all three forms of reparation and is not specific to compensation or an expression of the principle of proportionality. The ARSIWA Commentaries mention that "[c]oncerns

[156] As defended, in particular, by Posner and Sykes, *Economic Foundations of International Law*, 130. See also ibid., p. 134. ("[…] states have an implicit option to perform or pay reparations, just as contract parties under domestic law have an implicit option to perform or pay expectation damages.")

[157] See Sect. 6.1 on the aims and problems of remedies.

[158] See ARSIWA Commentaries, Article 34, para. 5.

[159] ARSIWA Commentaries, Article 35, para. 11.

[160] Article 37 (3) ARSIWA.

[161] See ARSIWA Commentaries, Article 34, para. 5.

have sometimes been expressed that the principle of full reparation may lead to disproportionate and even crippling requirements so far as the responsible [s]tate is concerned" and that "[t]he issue is whether the principle of proportionality should be articulated as an aspect of the obligation to make full reparation".[162] This debate has been taken up recently with regard to concerns about crippling compensation in the international law of state responsibility.[163]

Martins Paparinskis endeavours to make the case against the permissibility of crippling compensation, considering from a doctrinal perspective whether the customary principle of full compensation traditionally underpinned by the bilateralist idea of corrective justice has "evolved in a more communitarian direction or can be changed in line with the broader structural shifts in modern international law".[164] By pointing out a tendency of international courts and tribunals to grant huge compensation awards, in particular in investment arbitration, but also very occasionally in human rights law when property rights are concerned, he argues that the capacity of the responsible state to fulfil the obligation to pay full compensation is a legally relevant factor and that the likely effects of compensation awards on the responsible state and its people need to be taken into account when determining the content of state responsibility.[165] He concludes that "an exception to the principle of full compensation"[166] seems adequate to account for the protection of community interests when compensation is crippling and seeks to give guidance for weaker

[162] Ibid. The 1996 Draft Articles on State Responsibility contained a general rule against crippling reparation in Article 42 (3), stating that "[i]n no case shall reparation result in depriving the population of a State of its own means of subsistence," with the respective commentary in para. 8 explaining that "[t]here may be other equitable considerations that might be taken into account in providing full reparation, particularly in cases involving an author State with limited financial resources, but only to the extent that such considerations can be reconciled with the principle of the equality of all States before the law and the corresponding equality of the legal obligations of all States." This provision and the respective commentary was not maintained in the 2001 ARSIWA adopted on second reading on the grounds, amongst others, that the issue of indeterminate liability has not arisen in practice, states could establish limitations of liability regimes in particular fields of ultrahazardous activity (e.g. oil pollution, nuclear accidents), and the issue could be dealt with by delaying the payment on the grounds of necessity as a circumstance precluding wrongfulness or rescheduling the payment claim alongside with other sovereign debt. See United Nations International Law Commission, *Third Report on State Responsibility by Special Rapporteur James Crawford*, Fifty-Second Session, 2000 (UN Doc. A/CN.4/507), pp. 161–164, paras. 38–42.

[163] Martins Paparinskis, "A Case against Crippling Compensation in International Law of State Responsibility," *The Modern Law Review* 83, no. 6 (2020): 1246–1286; Martins Paparinskis, "Crippling Compensation in the Law of State Responsibility," *EJIL: Talk!* (Blog of the European Journal of International Law), 17 May, 2021, https://www.ejiltalk.org/crippling-compensation-in-the-law-of-state-responsibility/. For a deviation from the principle of full reparation, see also Benoît Mayer, "Less-Than-Full Reparations in International Law," *Indian Journal of International Law* 56, no. 3 (2016): 463–502.

[164] Paparinskis, "A Case against Crippling Compensation in International Law of State Responsibility," 1252–1253.

[165] Ibid., 1247–1251.

[166] Ibid., 1251.

states, hesitant to raise such defensive arguments in the past, to change this fundamental rule in the future international legal process.[167]

From a normative perspective, this attempt to integrate the protection of community interests in the law of state responsibility is certainly to welcome and in line with the objective of this book. A devastating economic situation of a state can have an impact on the well-being of the population, as resources, for instance, for the domestic health or social security system are limited. Where human rights are affected, all states in the international community derive value from their protection (i.e. human rights as non-use value GPGs). This is not diminished by the fact that the state facing a situation of unsustainable debt has itself been the author of an internationally wrongful act, as the financial consequences are borne by the population. However, an incentive-based analysis would come to a more nuanced conclusion than suggesting a general exception to the principle of full compensation in the case of crippling compensation.

Less-than-full compensation deviates from the rationale of compensation in the international law of state responsibility, which follows notions of tort and contractual liability law with its focus on the occurrence of actual damage. The principle in tort and contract law is full reparation of the harm independent from the financial situation of the tortfeasor or debtor. It is true that notions of adapting compensation claims to the level of income are not unknown in national law, as in criminal law or administrative law, where the determination of the level of fines takes into account the ability to pay the fine in order to calibrate incentives for optimal deterrence. This argument can also be made for states at the international level, in the sense that less-than-full compensation would still have a deterrent effect on poorer states. Taking into account the financial capability of the responsible state when determining the amount of compensation for damage would thus ensure optimal incentives for both poorer and richer states. Yet, the difference in international law is that even in the public law dimension compensation is not paid to a central entity (unlike fines in the domestic context which are paid to the state), but to the victim state. Hence, the determination of the optimal level of compensation also needs to take into account the effects on the injured state and its population. Equity concerns play a role in the determination of the sum of compensation, but the financial situation of the responsible state is neither the sole nor the determinant factor, as measurement of the damage will also depend on the content of the primary obligation in question and the respective behaviour of the injured and the responsible state.[168] Equity concerns need to be reconciled with the principle of the equality of all states before the law and corresponding international legal obligations.[169] Crippling compensation awards in international economic law might be less problematic, because an exception from the principle of full compensation would shift the costs partially to investors affected in

---

[167] Ibid., 1253.

[168] ARSIWA Commentaries, Article 36, para. 7.

[169] See commentary to the 1996 Draft Article on State Responsibility 42 (3).

their economic interests or states which are only affected in their 'private' interests. However, the case is different when the international legal obligation breached has GPG or CPR characteristics. Here, the international community also derives value from full compensation of the beneficiaries of the obligations (e.g. individuals suffering from serious human rights violations) or states directly affected by the breach of a public law obligation (e.g. the occupation of its territory and the destruction of state infrastructure). Therefore, a general exception in the secondary law of state responsibility from the principle of full compensation in the case of crippling compensation seems not an adequate solution, but differentiation should be possible when determining the appropriate amount depending on the type of obligation breached. In addition, there are other legal and political ways to deal with the issue of crippling compensation, when public law obligations are breached, which are, in my view, not too "optimistic".[170]

First, deviation from the principle of full compensation in certain cases means taking into account that the wrongdoing state is facing extraordinary circumstances and that a 'full' payment obligation would have disproportionate effects due to the difficult economic situation and different financial capacities. This is the rationale of the necessity excuse as a circumstance precluding wrongfulness and as such part of the general law of state responsibility (Article 25 ARSIWA).[171] Wrongdoing states can invoke economic hardship (either as private necessity or, if it has already devastating effects on the population, as public necessity) in order to temporarily excuse non-performance of a monetary payment obligation owed to another state (e.g. sovereign loans), including compensation claims. Compensation entitlements are monetary payment obligations to injured states, even if they still have to be seen in connection with the private or public characteristics of the international obligation underlying the wrongful act. The law of state responsibility provides also principles as to how to allocate the costs following the invocation of circumstances precluding wrongfulness, and suggestions on the interpretation of the compensation requirement in Article 27 lit. b) ARSIWA have been made in the respective section above.[172] An additional compensation requirement seems inadequate in constellations of economic hardship, but since necessity allows to temporarily defect from an international obligation which remains in place, the monetary payment obligation (here: compensation for the damage resulting from a wrongful act) can be postponed. One can make the procedural argument that circumstances precluding wrongfulness offering the possibility to delay payment, such as necessity, "may be available in principle, but the record of their successful invocation in the last 20 years is not particularly impressive".[173] But that does not provide a convincing argument why one should generally deviate from a customary principle of state responsibility, as

[170] Paparinskis, "A Case against Crippling Compensation in International Law of State Responsibility," 1252.

[171] See extensively, Sect. 5.2.

[172] See Sect. 5.2.3.

[173] Paparinskis, "Crippling Compensation in the Law of State Responsibility".

full compensation is, rather than to further develop others, such as necessity and the relating financial consequences. If a responsible state cannot comply with an obligation to provide reparation in the form of compensation due to economic hardship, it can invoke necessity as a performance excuse either in the ongoing proceedings or wait until it is counter-sued in international courts or national courts, as with ICSID awards.

The second alternative legal solution is that budgetary concerns of responsible states can be addressed by using property rules,[174] such as cessation, if the wrongful act is still ongoing, restitution, or if this is materially impossible, with satisfaction. Property rules bear advantages when the breach concerns a public law obligation (i.e. relating to GPGs or CPRs) as they focus on the good to be provided or preserved. For instance, objective valuation of the damage can be difficult in the case of mass atrocities (e.g. genocide).[175] Property rules also seem a more adequate tool to address concerns about crippling compensation than a deviation from the general principle of full reparation, since at least the obligations of restitution and satisfaction contain a proportionality requirement. Crippling compensation lowers the probability of the compensation obligation being complied with, and thus injured states may choose to favour in their request property rules over compensation as a liability rule. In addition, responsible states in economic distress may be more inclined to agree to a remedy consisting in a property rule than a liability rule. From an institutional perspective, even international courts and tribunals may take into account the probability of remedies being complied with, thus favouring in the case of crippling compensation, property over liability rules. Even in specialised treaty regimes, like international investment law, traditionally favouring liability rules (or secondary remedies), there are strong arguments to make more use of property rules (or primary remedies) allowing for the reconsideration of the regulatory action taken by the responsible state.[176]

Third, it has been argued before that liability rules require an objective *ex post* valuation by an institutionalised third-party dispute settlement mechanism in order to be effective. Primary treaty regimes which foresee standing for the immediate beneficiaries of the international obligations, as in regional human rights treaty regimes, like the ECtHR, or in international investment law, help to effectuate these compensation claims even further. These are also the issue areas where compensation awards of huge sums have been most observed following claims for economic injuries suffered by non-state actors.[177] Variances regarding the level of

---

[174] van Aaken, "Primary and Secondary Remedies in Investment Arbitration and State Liability: A Functional and Comparative View," in *International Investment Law and Comparative Public Law*, ed. Schill, 745.

[175] For a recent illustration of this challenge, while reaffirming the principle of full reparation, see *Armed Activities on the Territory of the Congo (Democratic Republic of the Congo v. Uganda)*, Judgment (Reparations), 9 February 2022, ICJ Reports 2022, p. 1.

[176] van Aaken, "Primary and Secondary Remedies in Investment Arbitration and State Liability: A Functional and Comparative View," in *International Investment Law and Comparative Public Law*, ed. Schill, 752–754.

[177] Paparinskis, "Crippling Compensation in the Law of State Responsibility".

compensation can make sense in primary international treaty regimes based on the *lex specials* rule[178] and should be addressed in this context, if deemed appropriate.[179] Not only the appropriate type of remedy but also the measurement of the damage depends inherently on the purpose of a specialised treaty regime and the design of the primary obligations. Bilateral or regional investment protection agreements, for instance, can legitimately deviate from the idea of corrective justice underlying the principle of full reparation in the law of state responsibility either by foreseeing higher amounts of compensation than expected under the law of state responsibility, due to the quantification of economic damages of private investors, or by admitting an exception in the case of crippling compensation in the form of caps. In addition, private investors can be expected to bear the risk that crippling compensation awards are not enforceable, if they invest in a country which already finds itself in a difficult economic situation.

Lastly, the issue of crippling compensation can be addressed at the enforcement level. In theory, injured states cannot enforce the compensation award with retaliatory countermeasures if compensation is crippling for the responsible state, because that would violate basic human rights in the responsible state, as outlined in Article 50 (1) lit. b) ARSIWA.[180] Also in primary treaty regimes or rules of procedures can exceptions be integrated to temporarily halt enforcement proceedings for the duration of a severe economic crisis.

In addition to these legal solutions, there are also political ways to deal with crippling compensation. Any reduction of payment obligations could be negotiated and settled bilaterally in the aftermath of the compensation award, as also suggested by Paparinskis.[181] A rescheduling of the payment could also be facilitated in an appropriate multilateral framework alongside other sovereign debt to states or private investors.[182] For heavily indebted countries this could provide an avenue out of the poverty circle. Another policy option could consist, at least for injured states, in 'enforcing' the payment obligation by accompanying it with positive inducements, such as rewards in the form of economic aid or access to trading benefits, which serve to remediate the economic hardship at the origin of crippling compensation.[183]

---

[178] Article 55 ARSIWA.

[179] Another avenue to address the problem of crippling compensation in primary rules would be in international treaties governing liability for ultrahazardous activities not prohibited in international law. These are also the areas where crippling compensation would lead to over-deterrence of activities which are accepted in international law. See Sect. 4.2.

[180] See Sect. 7.2.1.2 on possible scenarios for injured states taking countermeasures.

[181] Paparinskis, "Crippling Compensation in the Law of State Responsibility".

[182] See, for instance, the G20 Debt Service Suspension Initiative (DSSI) and the G20 Common Framework for Debt Treatments beyond the DSSI as multilateral initiative to address debt vulnerabilities due to the economic crisis following the COVID-19 pandemic.

[183] For example, German war reparations after World War II were not crippling in order to avoid the mistakes from World War I, but consisted to a large extent also in primary remedies (e.g. satisfaction offered in the form of admission of guilt and apologies) and were accompanied with a huge economic aid programme, the Marshall Plan, to rebuild the economy after the war.

Thus, there is a strong economic rationale for the principle of full compensation in the international law of state responsibility, but deviation should be possible in the case of private law obligations and in primary law.

6.3.2.2 Punitive Damages

That compensation has to be awarded in full and that its function in the law of state responsibility is to remediate the actual losses caused by the wrongful act means that "[i]t is not concerned to punish the responsible [s]tate, nor does compensation have an expressive or exemplary character".[184] Thus, even in constellations of serious breaches of *jus cogens* or other fundamental international norms, there is no deviation from the principle of full reparation foreseen, as punitive damages are not recognised under general international law.[185] Punitive damages in international law are legally disputed for many theoretical and practical reasons, such as the principle of sovereign equality of states, the need for third-party adjudication and compulsory jurisdiction, as well as scarcity of state practice.[186] However, as Stephan Wittich argues, "the real problem with punitive damages in international law is that the various approaches to the concept are incoherent".[187] This raises the question whether there is an economic rationale against punitive damages, at least in the secondary law of international state responsibility.

An analogy to domestic tort law would suggest that the responsible state should pay punitive damages.[188] The economic rationale of punitive damages in the domestic context is twofold: enhancing the function of compensatory damages to deter the defendant and other potential tortfeasors by adding a punitive component to the sum of damages, and punishing the tortfeasor for especially outrageous behaviour.[189]

[184] ARSIWA Commentaries, Article 36, para. 4.

[185] On punitive damages in international law, see Nina H.B. Jørgensen, "A Reappraisal of Punitive Damages in International Law," *British Yearbook of International Law* 68, no. 1 (1998): 247–266; Stephan Wittich, "Punitive Damages," in *The Law of International Responsibility*, ed. James Crawford, Alain Pellet, and Simon Olleson (Oxford: Oxford University Press, 2010), 667–675.

[186] Wittich, "Punitive Damages," in *The Law of International Responsibility*, ed. Crawford, Pellet, and Olleson, 668.

[187] Ibid.

[188] This has also been noted by Posner and Sykes, *Economic Foundations of International Law*, 137–138. On the economic analysis of punitive damages in tort law, see, in particular, Dorsey D. Ellis Jr., "Fairness and Efficiency in the Law of Punitive Damages," *Southern California Law Review* 56, no. 1 (1982): 1–78; Robert Cooter, "Punitive Damages for Deterence: When and How Much?," *Alabama Law Review* 40, no. 3 (1989): 1143–1196; Polinsky and Shavell, "Punitive Damages: An Economic Analysis," 869–962. For an overview, see Catherine M. Sharkey, "Economic Analysis of Punitive Damages: Theory, Empirics, and Doctrine," in *Research Handbook on the Economics of Torts*, ed. Jennifer Arlen (Cheltenham, UK: Edward Elgar, 2013), 486–510.

[189] Pinto de Albuquerque and van Aaken, "Punitive Damages in Strasbourg," in *The European Convention on Human Rights and General International Law*, ed. van Aaken and Motoc, 241. See further, Shelton, *Remedies in International Human Rights Law*, 402–408.

First, as regards the deterrence function, punitive damages in tort law can serve to uphold the deterrent effect when the probability of being held liable is less than 1 (for instance, when there is a problem of 'rational apathy'), mitigate the problem of underestimation of harm (in particular, immaterial losses), correct socially unaccepted costs of the victim or benefits of the tortfeasor, or set incentives for potential tortfeasors to favour a voluntary exchange with the victim rather than to commit the tort.[190] Second, the goal of punishment refers to the condemnation of reprehensible behaviour (e.g. intentional torts), the role of the defendant's wealth level, the question whether insurance against punitive damages should be allowed and the question whether the relevant parameter to determine damages the harm to the victim or the gains of the tortfeasor.[191] Most of these multiple objectives of punitive damages can, in principle, be transferred to the international level.

As demonstrated earlier, in their decision to comply or not with an international obligation, states will not only take into account the amount of the compensatory damages (D), but also the probability (p) with which the entitlement to compensation is successfully enforced. Thus, the level of compensation and the probability of enforcement are inherently linked in the determination of the costs (C_V) of a breach of an international obligation. For an optimal deterrent effect of full compensation, the probability of enforcement would need to be 100 per cent. If the probability of enforcement is 1 or close to 1, higher damages would lead to overdeterrence. However, in international law, there are different scenarios in which the probability of enforcement falls below 1. First, it might be difficult for the victim state to prove the breach of duty and causation of damage by the wrongdoing state.[192] This can be related to information asymmetries or because no clear link between the action (or actions by multiple actors), the breach, and the harm can be established, as in the case of damage resulting from climate change (e.g. a flood or drought due to the long-term effects of climate change caused by multiple states failing to meet their emission targets). Second, when a wrongdoing state intentionally caused damage, it might take steps to avoid detection and thus profit from the asymmetrical distribution of information about its actions and intentions.[193] Third, in scenarios where losses are distributed over multiple injured states, but total losses for the international community are substantial (e.g. in the case of GPGs or CPRs, such as mass atrocities, large-scale pollution, or overfishing in the high seas), holding the wrongdoing state responsible would overall be beneficial, but individual victim states might find it too expensive to sue the wrongdoing state for their share of the damage (i.e. the problem of "rational apathy").[194] This is because injured states will have to enforce the

[190] Louis T. Visscher, "Economic Analysis of Punitive Damages," in *Punitive Damages: Common Law and Civil Law Perspectives*, ed. Helmut Koziol and Vanessa Wilcox (Wien: Springer, 2009), 236.

[191] Ibid.

[192] With regard to tort law, see ibid., 222.

[193] With regard to tort law, see ibid., 223. With reference to Landes and Posner, *The Economic Structure of Tort Law*, 160.

[194] With regard to tort law, see Visscher, "Economic Analysis of Punitive Damages," in *Punitive Damages: Common Law and Civil Law Perspectives*, ed. Koziol and Wilcox, 223.

monetary payment of damages, for instance, with first-party countermeasures.[195] Since reciprocal non-compliance does not work to enforce payment obligations, enforcement consists in retaliatory countermeasures which are, by definition, costly to the injured state. Multiple injured states considering to take retaliatory countermeasures then face a sanctioners' dilemma,[196] which is aggravated the more the losses are diffused over multiple injured states. Examples could be large-scale pollution affecting multiple costal states or an armed attack to multiple neighbouring countries. According to Article 46 ARSIWA, all states can independently claim reparation for their respective injuries. However, even though all injured states would fully internalise the benefits of their request for damages, enforcing such claims is expensive and states face a collective action problem as they all are inclined to wait for others to bear the or a significant part of the enforcement costs.[197] Thus, in particular, but not exclusively in the public dimension of international law, the probability of enforcement can be lower than 100 per cent. In such scenarios of under-enforcement, punitive damages could serve to uphold the deterrence function of compensation for injury, because the additional damages would outweigh the lower probability of enforcement, holding the expected costs of the violation (C_V) constant. In other words, the factor with which compensatory damages (D) should be multiplied (m) is the reciprocal of the probability of being held liable (p).[198] For example, if the probability of being held liable is 50 per cent, compensatory damages should be doubled to provide the optimal incentives.[199] Polinsky and Shavell refer to this reciprocal (m) as the 'punitive damages multiplier'.[200] This reasoning can be illustrated with the following formula:

$$C_V = p\,(D \times m); \text{ whereas}$$

$$m = \frac{1}{p}$$

[195] See Sect. 7.2.1.4. The analysis here builds on countermeasures as the enforcement tool contained in the law of state responsibility, but certainly the payment of compensation can also be enforced with other compliance mechanisms discussed in Sect. 2.4.

[196] Thompson, "The Rational Enforcement of International Law: Solving the Sanctioners' Dilemma," 307–321.

[197] On the decreasing probability of recourse to countermeasures, depending on the number of injured states, see in detail Sect. 7.2.1.4. On the argument in favour of punitive damages in order to overcome "rational apathy" in cases of widespread violations which are not too grave so that victims may wait for others to bring a claim, in particular when a judgment can have a *de facto* inter omnes effect, see Pinto de Albuquerque and van Aaken, "Punitive Damages in Strasbourg," in *The European Convention on Human Rights and General International Law*, ed. van Aaken and Motoc, 242–243.

[198] Visscher, "Economic Analysis of Punitive Damages," in *Punitive Damages: Common Law and Civil Law Perspectives*, ed. Koziol and Wilcox, 223.

[199] Ibid.

[200] Polinsky and Shavell, "Punitive Damages: An Economic Analysis," 898.

Punitive damages are then the difference between total damages and the compensatory damages[201] and can also be termed a 'punitive surplus'. Adding this factor to the equation thus not only has the advantage that it sets correct incentives for the potentially wrongdoing state, but also that it helps to overcome the problem of 'rational apathy', as victim states can obtain higher damages when holding the wrongdoing state responsible. This is particularly, but not exclusively, important in GPG and CPR constellations, when the losses are spread over a large number of countries.

Remedies in international law could also build on other rationales of punitive damages in tort law. First, punitive damages are used in the domestic context to mitigate the problem of underestimation or harm. When losses are difficult to quantify, for instance, in the case of immaterial losses, or when the subjective valuation of the harm is difficult to determine, compensatory damages fall short of remediating the actual losses and incentives for potential wrongdoing states are set below the optimal level.[202] However, measurement and valuation problems are not limited to compensatory damages and it is not clear how punitive damages facing the same problems could help to overcome them.[203] On the international level, these problems consist, for instance, with regard to the moral damage suffered by injured states. Property rules, such as satisfaction, might be more appropriate than elevating the level of damages.

Second, they can serve to condemn reprehensible behaviour.[204] The equivalence on the international level are wrongful acts consisting in grave violations of fundamental norms of the international community (i.e. *jus cogens* obligations). With regard to such inalienable entitlements, additional damages could serve to punish reproachable behaviour (similar to the payment of a fine) and have an expressive character. Yet, this objective is explicitly excluded in general international law.[205] When states intentionally commit serious breaches of fundamental duties (e.g. genocide), additional damages could nonetheless reinforce their deterrence

---

[201] Visscher, "Economic Analysis of Punitive Damages," in *Punitive Damages: Common Law and Civil Law Perspectives*, ed. Koziol and Wilcox, 223.

[202] Ibid., 225.

[203] Polinsky and Shavell, "Punitive Damages: An Economic Analysis," 939–941.

[204] Visscher, "Economic Analysis of Punitive Damages," in *Punitive Damages: Common Law and Civil Law Perspectives*, ed. Koziol and Wilcox, 232–233.

[205] On an equally cautious approach towards punitive damages as general principle in international law, arguing that property rules are the default rule, see Pauwelyn, *Optimal Protection of International Law: Navigating between European Absolutism and American Voluntarism*, 151–157.

function and be justified because the gains for the responsible state are socially unacceptable and outweighed by the enormous costs to the international community.[206]

Third, punitive damages allow to take into account the wealth level of the injurer.[207] They should not go beyond compensatory damages multiplied with the factor offsetting the lower probability of being held liable, as this would lead to overdeterrence.[208] Yet, the poorer the injurer, the lower the award of punitive damages can be, while still being able to offset the lower probability of being held liable.[209] It has already been argued above with regard to crippling compensation, that lower compensation could uphold the deterrent effect for poorer states, but that the effects on the injured state also need to be taken into account and that a general deviation from the principle of full compensation of damage is not adequate, in particular, when the breach relates to a public law obligation. However, taking into account the financial capability of the responsible state when determining the amount of additional compensation for damage could ensure optimal incentives for both poorer and richer states. In fact, such differentiation would ensure equality before the law, in particular against the background that often only powerful and rich states have the capacity to bring up the associated material enforcement costs in the case of GPG/CPR violations.[210] Hence, financial capacity considerations should relate to the size of the punitive surplus in order to calibrate incentives for optimal deterrence, while compensatory damages, in principle, still cover the full losses in the case of breach of a GPG or CPR obligation.

In sum, the fact that punitive damages are legally disputed as a generally accepted remedy in the international law of state responsibility does not mean they are excluded as a specific remedy.[211] The deterrence function of damages provides a strong economic rationale for more-than-full compensation in constellations where the probability of enforcement is low. This is particularly the case when the losses are spread over a large number of injured states and thus a heightened level of responsibility could help to overcome the problem of 'rational apathy' and set optimal incentives for potentially wrongdoing states. Hence, the main argument for an elevated level of compensation is not rooted in the punishment function and thus needs not to be limited to breach of *jus cogens* norms. Additional damages can

[206]Visscher, "Economic Analysis of Punitive Damages," in *Punitive Damages: Common Law and Civil Law Perspectives*, ed. Koziol and Wilcox, 226–227, 232. On the argument in favour of punitive damages in cases where outrageous violations were committed intentionally, see also Pinto de Albuquerque and van Aaken, "Punitive Damages in Strasbourg," in *The European Convention on Human Rights and General International Law*, ed. van Aaken and Motoc, 242–243.

[207]Visscher, "Economic Analysis of Punitive Damages," in *Punitive Damages: Common Law and Civil Law Perspectives*, ed. Koziol and Wilcox, 233.

[208]Ibid.

[209]Ibid. With reference to Polinsky and Shavell, "Punitive Damages: An Economic Analysis," 913.

[210]For more details, see also Sect. 7.2.1.4.

[211]Wittich, "Punitive Damages," in *The Law of International Responsibility*, ed. Crawford, Pellet, and Olleson, 674.

be considered adequate when the breach concerned multiple injured states (in their private goods) or related to a public law obligation with underlying GPG or CPR characteristics.

This does not mean that a higher level of compensation as such will always be sufficient to overcome the sanctioners' dilemma, as the cost of sanctioning might still be prohibitively high. Yet, that damages beyond full compensation can be employed has been shown implicitly in the context of international/regional human rights law.[212] These integrated treaty regimes bear the advantage that they include a third-party adjudicatory mechanism[213] and individual complaint mechanisms, at least in the major regional human rights treaties. In cases with a purely internal dimension marked by the absence of an injured state able to claim reparation, punitive damages rely on an authoritative judgment by an international court in the legal interest of all other states in the treaty regime.[214] Here, punitive damages can play an important role, when states commit systematic and grave human rights violations against their own citizens, deliberately fail to comply with judgments of the adjudicatory body or curtail access to courts as a primary remedy.[215] In these contexts, punitive damages can serve to effectuate *inter omnes* obligations of states, such as human rights as GPG obligations.[216] In inter-state relations, not only adjudicatory mechanisms are needed (as for the award of compensatory damages), but whether the additional damages can shift the potentially wrongdoing state's cost-benefit calculation towards compliance will depend on whether there is at least a minimum degree of probability that decentralised enforcement mechanisms, in particular in GPG and CPR constellations, for instance, with cross-countermeasures, are effective. Property rules can also serve as a back-up solution. Satisfaction constitutes an important tool to remedy the effects of international disputes, including those stemming from serious breaches of international law, and if the wrongful act is ongoing, cessation can also play an important complementary role (reinforced with the specific additional obligations in Article 41 ARSIWA). Both remedies will be discussed in turn in the following sections.

---

[212] See Pinto de Albuquerque and van Aaken, "Punitive Damages in Strasbourg," in *The European Convention on Human Rights and General International Law*, ed. van Aaken and Motoc, 246. ("Whereas, between sovereign nations, the question of the power to impose penalties is political rather than legal in nature, if there is no court adjudicating the case, the conclusion is different between nations bound by a human rights treaty, such as the [European] Convention [on Human Rights], which confers rights on natural and legal persons and imposes negative and positive obligations on the Contracting Parties enforceable by an international court through binding judgments.")

[213] On the necessity of a court as an adjudicatory body to impose punitive damages, see ibid.

[214] In such a framework, sanctions by one state against another state are not needed, see ibid.

[215] Ibid., 245.

[216] Ibid., 247.

6.3.3 Satisfaction

The third form of reparation is to give satisfaction for the injury caused, as outlined in Article 37 ARSIWA.[217] It is also a well-established remedy in international law, as stated in the *Rainbow Warrior* arbitration,[218] and a common tool to remediate disputes in diplomatic state practice.[219] As Article 37 (1) ARSIWA indicates, satisfaction is exceptional in character, in the sense that it may only be claimed if restitution or compensation cannot provide full reparation of the injury.[220] In its subsidiarity to restitution, satisfaction is similar to compensation, because it becomes relevant when restitution is fully or partially impossible or inappropriate, or because injured states prefer satisfaction for some other reason. Satisfaction differs from compensation in that it addresses a type of damage, that is moral or non-material damage to the injured state itself, which cannot be accounted for with the monetary payment of compensation for damages which are 'financially assessable'. These non-material injuries consist in an affront to the state and "are frequently of a symbolic character, arising from the very fact of the breach of the obligation, irrespective of its material consequences for the [s]tate concerned".[221] Satisfaction may also take the form of a monetary payment, but the difference from compensation is that the moral damage to the injured state can only be expressed in terms of a monetary value "in a highly approximate and notional way".[222] A strict reading of the ARSIWA on the three respective forms of reparation might suggest to classify satisfaction as a 'tertiary' remedy. However, as it covers explicitly a type of damage, which is not financially assessable, satisfaction can be considered a property rule and not as a liability rule. And since satisfaction, at least in the form of declaratory judgments, is always possible and may even be the only available or requested

[217] Article 37 ARSIWA reads as follows: "1. The State responsible for an internationally wrongful act is under an obligation to give satisfaction for the injury caused by that act insofar as it cannot be made good by restitution or compensation.

2. Satisfaction may consist in an acknowledgement of the breach, an expression of regret, a formal apology or another appropriate modality.

3. Satisfaction shall not be out of proportion to the injury and may not take a form humiliating to the responsible State." For an overview, see Eric Wyler and Alain Papaux, "The Different Forms of Reparation: Satisfaction," in *The Law of International Responsibility*, ed. James Crawford, Alain Pellet, and Simon Olleson (Oxford: Oxford University Press, 2010), 623–637.

[218] *Difference between New Zealand and France Concerning the Interpretation or Application of two Agreements concluded on 9 July 1986 between the two States and Which Related to the Problems Arising from the Rainbow Warrior Affair*, Award, pp. 272–273, para. 122. ("There is a long established practice of States and international Courts and Tribunals of using satisfaction as a remedy or form of reparation (in the wide sense) for the breach of an international obligation. This practice relates particularly to the case of moral or legal damage done directly to the State, especially as opposed to the case of damage to persons involving international responsibilities.")

[219] ARSIWA Commentaries, Article 37, para. 4.

[220] ARSIWA Commentaries, Article 37, para. 1.

[221] ARSIWA Commentaries, Article 37, para. 3.

[222] ARSIWA Commentaries, Article 36, para. 4.

remedy,[223] I consider satisfaction as a primary remedy (in contrast to compensation as a secondary remedy).[224] Moreover, satisfaction also has the function of restoring the cooperative relation between the responsible and the injured state, at least to the extent that assurances or guarantees of non-repetition as remedies aiming to prevent future violations overlap with satisfaction in terms of the concrete measure taken (e.g. apologies for threats to diplomatic premises or personnel and repeal of the legislative act which allowed the breach to occur).[225]

The ARSIWA Commentaries outlines several historic examples for moral damages that may give rise to the remedy of satisfaction: insults to symbols of the state (e.g. national flags), violations of sovereignty or territorial integrity, attacks on state property (e.g. ships and aircrafts), ill-treatment of heads of state or government or other diplomatic or consular representatives, and violations of the premises of embassies or consulates.[226] Article 37 (2) ARSIWA describes in a non-exhaustive and non-hierarchical way some forms of satisfaction, namely "acknowledgement of the breach, an expression of regret, a formal apology or another appropriate modality", but the appropriate form will depend on the circumstances of the case and can consist, for instance, in an inquiry into the causes of an accident, disciplinary or penal action against the individuals who caused the wrongful act, a trust fund to manage compensation payments to the individual beneficiaries, or the award of symbolic damages.[227] Expressions of regret or apologies by an organ of the responsible state are a common form of satisfaction and are frequently requested or offered in diplomatic practice, but they may not always suffice to resolve a dispute, especially when the injured state needs further reinsurances that the wrongful act will not be repeated in the future.[228]

Another modality explicitly mentioned in the ARSIWA is acknowledgement of the breach by the responsible party. That this is a strong remedy for the benefit of the injured state can be derived from the fact that wrongdoing states often prefer to settle cases outside the law of state responsibility and to negotiate *ex gratia* payments.

---

[223] This has to be seen in line with the well-established principle that an international court or tribunal having jurisdiction over a claim of state responsibility has the authority not only to determine the wrongfulness of the conduct but also to decide upon the adequate remedy. See, in particular, *Factory at Chorzów (Germany v. Poland)*, Judgment (Jurisdiction), p. 21. ("Reparation therefore is the indispensable complement of a failure to apply a convention and there is no necessity for this to be stated in the convention itself. Differences relating to reparations, which may be due by reason of failure to apply a convention, are consequently differences relating to its application.")

[224] For the classification of declaratory decisions rather as primary remedies, alongside specific performance and injunctions, compared to pecuniary damages, see also van Aaken, "Primary and Secondary Remedies in Investment Arbitration and State Liability: A Functional and Comparative View," in *International Investment Law and Comparative Public Law*, ed. Schill, 731.

[225] ARSIWA Commentaries, Article 30, para. 11 and Article 37, para. 5.

[226] ARSIWA Commentaries, Article 37, para. 4.

[227] ARSIWA Commentaries, Article 37, para. 5.

[228] ARSIWA Commentaries, Article 37, para. 7.

These are payments without recognising the breach of an international obligation. Thus states accept the material costs of a payment while avoiding other consequences that recognition of a wrongful act could entail, for instance, other remedies or a reputation for non-compliance (in relation to the injured state but also to other states in the international community). Another common modality of satisfaction, not listed explicitly in Article 37 (2) ARSIWA, is declaratory relief, that is "a declaration of the wrongfulness of the act by a competent court or tribunal".[229] Such declaratory judgment can either be the only remedy requested by the injured state or be the prerequisite for any other form of reparation or the claim for cessation, but it requires, unlike other modalities of satisfaction, necessarily the implication of a competent third-party dispute settlement institution.[230] Declaratory judgments are a common remedy in international law, at least in inter-state disputes, but also used in international human rights law.[231]

Lastly, Article 37 (3) ARSIWA places a limitation on the obligation to give satisfaction, as any measures "shall not be out of proportion to the injury and may not take a form humiliating to the responsible State". Like restitution, and unlike compensation, satisfaction thus contains a proportionality requirement relating to the level and to the form of satisfaction. While there are certain modalities of satisfaction, such as declaratory judgments, which remain by definition within these limits,[232] this provision was introduced to prevent abusive invocation as excessive demands or requests for unreasonable forms had sometimes been made in the past.[233] The exact scope of this provision remains, however, unclear. The ARSIWA Commentaries simply clarify that „satisfaction is not intended to be punitive in character, nor does it include punitive damages".[234] With regard to the level of satisfaction, the rationale is certainly that, for instance, symbolic damages do not exceed full reparation of the injury. The restriction to non-humiliating forms bears similarities with the discussion on crippling compensation, namely the idea to take into account the specific situation of the responsible state.

In sum, satisfaction can constitute an effective tool to remedy the effects of international disputes, especially when these cannot be monetised. This is not only the case in the private dimension, to which most historical examples cited above relate, namely moral damage in scenarios where property rights (private goods) of the injured state are affected (e.g. violation of territorial sovereignty or attacks on state property). But satisfaction is also extremely valuable in the public dimension,

---

[229] ARSIWA Commentaries, Article 37, para. 6. See, for instance, *Corfu Channel (United Kingdom of Great Britain and Northern Ireland v. Albania)*, Judgment (Merits), pp. 35–36.

[230] ARSIWA Commentaries, Article 37, para. 6.

[231] Although in international human rights law the award of pecuniary damages and orders of specific performance are also increasingly used. Van Aaken, "Primary and Secondary Remedies in Investment Arbitration and State Liability: A Functional and Comparative View," in *International Investment Law and Comparative Public Law*, ed. Schill, 731–732.

[232] ARSIWA Commentaries, Article 37, para. 6.

[233] ARSIWA Commentaries, Article 37, paras. 2, 8.

[234] ARSIWA Commentaries, Article 37, para. 8.

when all states in the international community derive value from reparation of the moral damage, for instance, when GPG obligations are concerned, as in serious human rights violations. The argument is thus similar to what has been said earlier with regard cessation and restitution, namely that GPGs are non-use value public goods and therefore all states in the international community not only have an interest in ongoing compliance (as induced with cessation), restoration of compliant behaviour in the form of the *status quo ante* (as induced with restitution *in integrum*), but also reparation of the future cooperative relation if it deals with the protection of GPG (as induced with satisfaction, for instance, payments in the form of symbolic damages or contributions to trust fund). Satisfaction has, however, the disadvantage that it may not be sufficient in scenarios where harm concerns a rival good, in particular in CPR constellations, as the problem lies in depletion or pollution of the resource. Here, preference may be given to restitution in the form of restoration of the resource or compensation for restorative measures of the environment taken by injured states as ultimate cost bearer (e.g. regeneration of fish stocks or cleansing of oil pollution). But satisfaction by establishing a trust fund can also be an alternative, provided that it contains sufficient means to restore the resource and restoration is possible. Otherwise it reinforces the argument for higher-than-compensatory damages to uphold the deterrence effect. Another disadvantage of satisfaction is that interested non-directly injured third states can only claim it only to the benefit of the injured state or the immediate beneficiaries, whereas cessation and assurances or guarantees of non-repetition (as a form of satisfaction) can also be sought in their own name.[235]

6.4 Consequences of Violations of *Jus Cogens* Obligations

It has been pointed out in the previous section on the reparation for injury that the law of state responsibility, in contrast to the international criminal liability of individuals, does note pursue the aim of punishing states for the commission of serious breaches of peremptory norms. Despite attempts in the ILC to develop a veritable regime of aggravated responsibility which differentiates between international 'delicts' (as 'normal' wrongful acts) and 'crimes', agreement could finally only be reached on certain additional obligations which fall, in the case of serious breaches of *jus cogens* obligations, on all states in the international community, in

[235] Article 48 ARSIWA. See also, ARSIWA Commentaries, Article 30, para. 11.

addition to the 'normal' obligations falling on the responsible state outlined above.[236] The concept of *jus cogens* norms, the definition of serious breaches of peremptory norms of general international law enshrined in Article 40 ARSIWA and the particular legal consequences that derive from these violations as set out in Article 41 ARSIWA have been outlined in detail in Sect. 3.3.2.[237] The emphasis was, firstly, on the degree of congruence of *jus cogens* norms with the concept of global public goods, and I have defined them above as normative global public goods which relate to a limited number of GPG obligations. Secondly, I have briefly explained the cooperation challenges underlying these exceptional legal consequences and pointed out that all three collective obligations (i.e. obligations of non-recognition, non-assistance, and cooperation to end the serious breach of a *jus cogens* norm) have global public goods characteristics. Against the background that these secondary obligations, despite having roots in general international law,[238] contain a notion of progressive development of international law in the context of state responsibility, this section will address the question whether and under which conditions the legal consequences foreseen in the ARSIWA can work effectively, and whether it makes sense to limit them to a limited number of GPG obligations with a superior normative status.

What all three collective obligations have in common is that they face second-order cooperation problems and share GPG characteristics. They all require to find a collective response of the international community to a situation caused by the serious breach of a peremptory norm and thus constitute additional property rules aiming to protect inalienable entitlements. A conceptual differences exists, however, between, on the one hand, the obligation not to recognise as lawful situations created by serious breaches of peremptory norms as well as the obligation not to render aid or assistance in maintaining such situations (Article 41 (2) ARSIWA), which are negative obligations or duties of abstention, and, on the other hand, the positive obligation to cooperate in order to bring such a breach to an end (Article

---

[236] ARSIWA Commentaries, Part two, Chap. III, para. 7.

[237] Article 40 ARSIWA on the application of Part two, Chap. III reads: "1. This chapter applies to the international responsibility which is entailed by a serious breach by a State of an obligation arising under a peremptory norm of general international law. 2. A breach of such an obligation is serious if it involves a gross or systematic failure by the responsible State to fulfil the obligation." Article 41 ARSIWA on the particular consequences of a serious breach of an obligation under this chapter reads: "1. States shall cooperate to bring to an end through lawful means any serious breach within the meaning of article 40. 2. No State shall recognize as lawful a situation created by a serious breach within the meaning of article 40, nor render aid or assistance in maintaining that situation. 3. This article is without prejudice to the other consequences referred to in this part and to such further consequences that a breach to which this chapter applies may entail under international law."

[238] In particular, United Nations General Assembly, Resolution 2625 (XXV), *Declaration on Principles of International Law Concerning Friendly Relations and Cooperation among States in Accordance with the Charter of the United Nations*, 24 October 1970 (UN Doc. A/8082).

41 (1) ARSIWA).[239] Both groups of obligations also differ in their objective, as the focus of the former lies on collective obligations in relation to the responsible state, namely on the prohibition of actions lending support to the responsible state which could further manifest the illegal situation, and the latter concerns an obligation towards the international community as a whole, namely to end the situation contrary to peremptory norms and to return to legality. Thus, while the obligations of non-recognition and non-assistance require mutual restraint in order to provide the global public good, the obligation of cooperation to end the breach of a peremptory norm requires active state contributions.[240]

To be more precise, the obligations of non-recognition and non-assistance both bear characteristics of a weakest link GPG, in the sense that the good can only be effectively provided if all states in the international community participate.[241] In legal terms, universal participation means that the illegality of a situation created by a breach of a peremptory norm is opposable *erga omnes* and cannot be recognised as lawful even by states not members of the United Nations, nor by the responsible or the injured state.[242] In principle, the costs of providing the good through abstention are relatively low, provided that all other states participate as well, so that states will only have to coordinate their efforts. When it is not entirely clear what actions are to be avoided by states in a given case (in particular, actions that go beyond implying recognition of the situation created by a *jus cogens* violation), international institutions can help to reduce uncertainty about the contributions of other states (e.g. UN Security Council resolutions requiring an arms embargo).[243] The biggest challenge for effective provision is, however, to include the weakest link, and with regard to the obligations of non-recognition and non-assistance the problem will typically not be the lack of capacities. The problem is that successful provision can be deliberately frustrated by one or few other states which have more to gain from non-cooperation, for instance, from recognising the acquisition of foreign territory or selling weapons. If one or few states thereby succeed in maintaining the illegality of the situation caused by the breach of the peremptory norm, they can effectively undermine the

---

[239] Even if no explicit reference was made to Article 41 ARSIWA, these obligations were confirmed in principle in *Legal Consequences of the Construction of a Wall in the Occupied Palestinian Territory*, Advisory Opinion, p. 200, paras. 159–160.

[240] See also United Nations International Law Commission, *Third Report on Peremptory Norms of General International Law (Jus Cogens) by Special Rapporteur Dire Tladi*, Seventieth Session, 2018 (UN Doc. A/CN.4/714), p. 40, para. 101. ("While the duty to cooperate to bring to an end situations created by a breach requires positive concerted, perhaps onerous, action, the duty to not to recognize, aid or assist, merely requires State to abstain from conduct. It is thus understandable that the threshold in the case law is not as high as with respect to the duty to cooperate to bring to an end the situation created by a breach.")

[241] On different types of global public goods in terms of their provision, see Sect. 2.2.

[242] ARSIWA Commentaries, Article 41, paras. 9–10.

[243] This would even apply to the obligation of non-recognition, which among the three obligations is probably the easiest GPG to be provided, as "there remains uncertainty as to the precise content of the obligation." Dawidowicz, "The Obligation of Non-Recognition of an Unlawful Situation," in *The Law of International Responsibility*, ed. Crawford, Pellet, and Olleson, 686.

collective efforts of all other states. This leads to the question of how a breach of these collective secondary obligations can be credibly enforced in order to induce compliance in the first place, and thus to a third-order enforcement problem. Extending sanctions to the non-cooperating state or providing side-payments may be options, but both exhibit GPG characteristics with free-riding as the dominant strategy and may not suffice to convince a single hold-out country to change its behaviour. Thus, the collective obligations of non-recognition and non-assistance are useful instruments in the framework of state responsibility, but may only be effective under certain circumstances, in particular when states achieve to provide more clarity about the required behaviour through an international institution and when all countries have more to gain from participation than from the active frustration of these efforts.[244] These impediments need to be kept in mind, as they relate to collective obligations which constitute the minimum requirement for further community action in response to a breach of *jus cogens* norms, namely the third obligation falling on all states to cooperate to bring such breach to an end.[245]

In contrast, the obligation to cooperate to bring to an end a serious breach of peremptory norms requires positive collective action of the international community of states and rather bears characteristics of an aggregate-effort GPG, in the sense that the benefits of the good (here, breach of a *jus cogens* norm coming to an end) only materialise once the cooperative efforts of states exceed some threshold level. This is reflected in the obligation of cooperation being framed rather as an obligation of means (i.e. to coordinate a collective response) and not as an obligation of result, that is to actually end the breach of the peremptory norm, which ultimately depends on whether the cumulative cooperate efforts succeed in changing the behaviour of the responsible state. The obligation of cooperation then differs from the previous two obligations of non-recognition and non-assistance in that effective provision does not depend on universal participation (even though the obligation of cooperation applies to all states in the international community) to the same extent, but on how much each state contributes to the ultimate goal of ending the serious breach of a *jus cogens* norm and this result can also be achieved by a coalition of states if they succeed in coordinating their respective contribution levels. One might assume that when the stakes are high enough, cooperation to end the breach will be successful, but examples such as the Rwandan genocide and the inaction of the international community show that this is not automatically the case. The obligation of cooperation abides by a prisoner's dilemma with free-riding on the collaborative efforts of others being the dominant strategy (similar to the sanctioners' dilemma). This does

---

[244]The UN Security Council resolutions under Chapter VII of the UN Charter condemning apartheid in South Africa or the invasion of Iraq in Kuwait are successful examples in this regard. Frustration of collective efforts can, however, also consist in blocking an institutionalised response, for instance by vetoing resolutions in the Security Council, as it was the case by Russia with regard to the situation in Kosovo or by China with regard to the situation in Darfur.

[245]ARSIWA Commentaries, Article 41, para. 8. See also, Jørgensen, "The Obligation of Non-Assistance to the Responsible State," in *The Law of International Responsibility*, ed. Crawford, Pellet, and Olleson, 693.

not mean that the negative prognosis for successful cooperation cannot be overcome. As much as for the obligations of non-recognition and non-assistance, international institutions can facilitate coordination of state actions by reducing uncertainty about the concrete action being required and the cooperative intent of other states. Even if universal participation is not necessary, but certainly helpful, partial cooperation by a group of states also faces the risk that non-cooperative states either have not the (financial) capacities to participate or have more to gain from undermining the collaborative efforts of the group. In the case of the former, financial support might help to overcome the collective action problem of achieving the necessary threshold level of participation, bearing in mind that financing also bears GPG characteristics. In the case of states deliberately frustrating that the serious breach of a *jus cogens* norms ends, for instance, because they are forming an alliance with the responsible state, this third-order enforcement problem is likely to be impossible to solve.

In sum, integrating the obligation for non-directly injured third states to cooperate to end a serious breach of a *jus cogens* norm in the regime of state responsibility is generally to be welcomed, because it provides some clarity to third states that they can act outside the framework of international institutions to form an *ad hoc* minimal-sized coalition, as long as they stay within the limits of international law.[246] It thus strengthens existing mechanisms within the law of state responsibility, which can, for instance, consist in 'lawful' countermeasures or—in the case of an armed attack—in collective self-defence.[247] Under which conditions non-directly injured states might have recourse to "unlawful" countermeasures and their probability of effectiveness will be discussed in the following Chap. 7, which analyses in detail the incentive structures and the cost-benefit calculation of states considering taking countermeasures. It suffices to say here that the prognosis of the obligation of cooperation to effectively induce the responsible state to cease the wrongful act consisting in the breach of a peremptory norm is rather negative, and will depend on

[246] United Nations International Law Commission, *Third Report on Peremptory Norms of General International Law (Jus Cogens) by Special Rapporteur Dire Tladi*, Seventieth Session, 2018 (UN Doc. A/CN.4/714), pp. 35–36, para. 91. See in this regard, albeit in the context of the obligation of non-assistance, Jørgensen, "The Obligation of Non-Assistance to the Responsible State," in *The Law of International Responsibility*, ed. Crawford, Pellet, and Olleson, 692.

[247] See Jørgensen, "The Obligation of Cooperation," in *The Law of International Responsibility*, ed. Crawford, Pellet, and Olleson, 697–698.

the concrete cooperative measures taken.[248] Yet, due to the lack of clarity about what kind of measures third states should take and how these would increase the costs for the responsible state in maintaining such a situation in breach of *jus cogens* obligations combined with the low probability of enforcement, this specific consequence of a serious breach of *jus cogens* norms can in its general form not be considered an effective tool to deter wrongful acts of such kind and gravity in the first place. Thus, entitlements that are considered inalienable are insufficiently protected in international law.[249] Nonetheless, at the very least, the obligation of cooperation seeks to require as a minimum that states use existing mechanisms, especially in the framework of international organisations, and such an institutionalised response (e.g. UN Security Council resolutions) can in turn help to overcome the free-rider problem, for instance, by authorising countermeasures, and thus providing more clarity about the existence of a prior wrongful act and the appropriate measures.

One issue discussed in the legal literature is whether these three collective obligations currently restricted to respond to serious breaches of *jus cogens* norms could be extended to apply also to grave violations of *erga omnes (partes)* obligations.[250] This would extend the scope of applicability, for instance, to serious

---

[248] Similarly, Posner and Sykes, *Economic Foundations of International Law*, 138. Eric A. Posner further argues that an obligation on third states to punish violations of *jus cogens* norms does not further reduce the collective action problem underlying the right of third states to punish violations of *erga omnes* norms, as "a rule that states cannot free ride does not solve the free-riding problem," while acknowledging that states may be more willing to cooperate to end a breach of *jus cogens* norms, as the violation is more serious and thus the stakes are higher. Posner, "Erga Omnes Norms, Institutionalization, and Constitutionalism in International Law," 14–15.

[249] Along the same vein, see Pauwelyn, *Optimal Protection of International Law: Navigating between European Absolutism and American Voluntarism*, 188–189. ("Moreover, it is not just that community obligations are, notwithstanding their higher goal, backed up by more or less the *same* instruments as entitlements protected as property. The situation is worse than that. There is a genuine risk that back-up enforcement for *jus cogens* and collective obligations turns out to be *weaker* than the general rule.")

[250] In this regard, see, for instance, Crawford, "International Crimes of States," in *The Law of International Responsibility*, ed. Crawford, Pellet, and Olleson, 411. ("No doubt it is true that other breaches of international law may have particularly serious consequences, depending on the circumstances. The notion of serious breaches of peremptory norms is without prejudice to this possibility, and to that extent the consequences referred to in article 41 are indicative and non-exclusive.") See also, Frowein, "Obligations Erga Omnes," para. 11. ("Where a widely acknowledged grave breach of an erga omnes obligation occurs, all the States to which the obligation is owed shall endeavour to bring the breach to an end through lawful means in accordance with the Charter of the United Nations. They shall not recognize as lawful a situation created by the breach, and are entitled to take non-forcible countermeasures under conditions analogous to those applying to a State specially affected by the breach.") With reference to Institut de Droit International, *Obligations Erga Omnes in International Law*, Resolution, Krakow Session (2005), Article 5. Antonio Cassese also argues that serious breaches of *jus cogens* and *erga omnes* obligations entail in principle the same legal consequences, but this derives from his understanding that both types of obligations coincide in substance. Cassese, "The Character of the Violated Obligation," in *The Law of International Responsibility*, ed. Crawford, Pellet, and Olleson, 415–420.

breaches of international obligations protecting the environment as a common resource.[251] From an economic perspective, there a good arguments not to limit the aggravated consequences to a limited number of GPG obligations with a superior normative status. While the superior status of *jus cogens* obligations in the hierarchy of international norms is properly reflected in the inalienability provision Article 26 ARSIWA, which excludes *ex ante* the invocation of circumstances precluding wrongfulness and thus any exemptions from breaches of peremptory norms, it does not provide a convincing rationale to restrict compliance-enhancing measures to serious breaches of peremptory norms. As the primary objective of the three collective obligations is not punishment or deterrence, but to avoid the further manifestation of a situation caused by the breach of a peremptory norm and to return to legality by inducing the responsible state collectively to cease the wrongful act, they can rather be derived from the non-reciprocal compliance structure of *erga omnes* norms. This seems to be what the ICJ suggested in its advisory opinions on these collective obligations, even though it needs to be noted that the obligations breached (i.e. international humanitarian law and the right to self-determination) also have *jus cogens* status.[252] As non-directly injured states have under certain conditions the right to take at least 'lawful' countermeasures in the case of breach of *erga omnes* obligations, placing on them obligations of non-recognition, non-assistance, and cooperation might not create further incentives for collective action due to the underlying third-order enforcement problem, but it may at least not deter action beneficial for the international community. It is thus suggested here not to restrict these cooperative obligations derived from general international law to situations stemming from the breach of *jus cogens* norms as normative GPGs, but to apply them also to violations of other GPG and CPR obligations, as their protection is an important objective of the law of state responsibility.[253]

Another issue is the question whether there is any rationale to restrict these collective obligations to 'serious' breaches of peremptory norms and not to apply them to the breach of all peremptory norms.[254] It is certainly true that some *jus cogens* norms (e.g. prohibitions of aggression and genocide) already require by

---

[251] See, for instance, *Responsibilities and Obligations of States with Respect to Activities in the Area*, Advisory Opinion, p. 59, para. 180. ("Each State Party may also be entitled to claim compensation in light of the *erga omnes* character of the obligations relating to preservation of the environment of the high seas and in the Area.")

[252] See with regard to all three collective obligations in the case of breach of international humanitarian law containing obligations *erga omnes*, *Legal Consequences of the Construction of a Wall in the Occupied Palestinian Territory*, Advisory Opinion, p. 200, paras. 157–160. See also with regard to the obligation of cooperation in the case of breach of the right to self-determination as an obligation *erga omnes*, *Legal Consequences of the Separation of the Chagos Archipelago from Mauritius in 1965*, Advisory Opinion, p. 139, para. 180.

[253] See also Posner and Sykes, *Economic Foundations of International Law*, 138.

[254] In this regard, see Jørgensen, "The Obligation of Non-Assistance to the Responsible State," in *The Law of International Responsibility*, ed. Crawford, Pellet, and Olleson, 692–693. Similarly, Gaeta, "The Character of the Breach," in *The Law of International Responsibility*, ed. Crawford, Pellet, and Olleson, 421–426.

definition an intentional violation on a large scale and thus fulfil the requirement of a gross or systematic failure by the responsible state to comply with the obligation.[255] But even more generally, it is hard to imagine what kind of breach of these limited number of peremptory norms would not be serious (for instance, the prohibition of apartheid, the basic rules of international humanitarian law or the right to self-determination), and why the international community in these cases should not be obliged to take collective action. The notion of 'seriousness', which is not part of the provision on *jus cogens* in Article 26 ARSIWA, can rather be explained with the origin of these collective obligations in the ILC, namely with the objective to include aggravated consequences for international 'crimes'. The question is then rather, if the collective obligations of non-recognition, non-assistance, and cooperation are extended to apply also to violations of *erga omnes (partes)* obligations, whether these breaches would need to be serious. It is suggested here that introducing such a restriction is not necessary.[256] This is because these obligations do not create a corresponding right for non-directly injured third states to take 'unlawful' countermeasures, thus excusing breach of an international obligation, but merely reflect obligations rooted in general international law to engage in lawful cooperative efforts. Depending on the gravity of the breach of the GPG or CPR obligation, a milder institutionalised or non-institutionalised cooperative response may be sufficient (e.g. a press release condemning a human rights violation or pollution of the high seas). Third-party 'lawful' countermeasures may be one possible instrument, and whether the right to take 'unlawful' countermeasures requires a serious breach of an *erga omnes (partes)* obligation will be discussed below in further detail.[257]

6.5 Conclusion on Remedies in the Law of State Responsibility

This chapter analysed the extent to which the different consequences of an internationally wrongful act in the law of state responsibility take into account in their allocation of duties and costs the protection of community interests in international law.

At the outset, several objectives of remedies in general international law have been identified: compliance with different types of international legal obligations (i.e. private good, club good, CPR or GPG obligations), reparation of injury, deterrence of internationally wrongful acts in the future, and securing long-term cooperation. Against this background, the chapter examined how the different types

[255] See ARSIWA Commentaries, Article 40, para. 8.

[256] Posner and Sykes also suggest to extend the collective obligations to not-serious violations of *erga omnes* norms, especially when victim states are too weak to retaliate with their own means, see Posner and Sykes, *Economic Foundations of International Law*, 138.

[257] See Sect. 7.2.2.

of remedies set incentives for the injured state in the case of breach of an international obligation. By backward induction it then assessed the impact of these secondary obligations (as legal constraints or cost factors) and their probability of enforcement in the private and public dimension of international law on the compliance decision of the potentially wrongdoing state. This approach helps to better understand in which problem constellations (i.e. protection of private goods, provision of GPGs, or preservation of CPRs) which type of remedy, broadly distinguished between property rules and liability rules, is most adequate. The main findings of the different sections are summarised in Table 6.1.

Three main conclusions can be drawn from this analysis. Firstly, in contrast to what some earlier economic analyses on remedies in international law suggest by putting reparation of injury and the concept of efficient breach at the centre stage, there is a strong rationale for property rules as primary remedies in the law of state responsibility as reflected in the ARSIWA. The return to compliance and the restoration of the cooperative relationship are key concerns as expressed with cessation and assurances or guarantees of non-repetition, in particular in constellations less concerned with the reparation of past harm but the functioning of the future exchange of benefits (e.g. trade law). Nonetheless, most disputes need to be rather thought of as relating to the protection of entitlements (i.e. property rights or private goods), bearing similarities to tort law in the domestic context (e.g. infringement of the territorial integrity or foreign property, cross-border pollution). Specific performance is the common remedy in state practice aiming not only to return to compliance but also to eradicate the consequences of the wrongful act with restitution, thus deterring breach in the first place as states cannot buy themselves out of non-compliance. This is particularly relevant with regard to environmental damage (i.e. common resources as rival goods). The focus on compliance, establishing the

Table 6.1 Functioning of different remedies in the law of state responsibility

	Function	Requirements	Type of rule
Cessation	Return to compliance	Ongoing wrongful act	Property rule (specific performance)
Assurances or guarantees of non-repetition	Future compliance	"if circumstances so require"	Property rule (specific performance)
Restitution	Reparation of injury/ deterrence	Status quo ante	Property rule (specific performance)
Compensation	Reparation of injury/ deterrence	Financially assessable damage	Liability rule
Satisfaction	Reparation of injury/ deterrence	Moral damage	Property rule (apology, declaratory judgment, symbolic damages, and trust fund)
Article 41 on *jus cogens* norms	Return to compliance (GPG)	Ongoing *jus cogens* violation	Property rule

status quo ante, and satisfactory remedies such as declaratory judgments, apologies and symbolic damages are also extremely valuable in GPG scenarios (e.g. serious harm to diplomatic personnel). Here, not only the interests of the injured state and its nationals as beneficiaries of the international obligation are concerned, but all states in the international community derive value from compliance.

Secondly, compensation as a liability rule constitutes the secondary remedy in the law of state responsibility, as it exhibits fundamental advantages when other remedies reach their limits, for instance, when restitution is materially impossible or highly inappropriate, or specific performance is perceived as too sovereignty infringing. The downside of compensation is that the measurement of the injury and thus the determination of the appropriate sum of damages requires a third-party adjudicator which could exercise the objective valuation. This creates the risk of error costs which may lead to over- or underdeterrence. Full compensation as the optimal level of compensation should therefore remain the guiding principle in the law of state responsibility. However, when compensation would be crippling, a deviation to the bottom should be possible in the case of private law obligations and in primary law. In addition, a deviation from the principle of compensatory damages to the top (i.e. "punitive damages multiplier") can serve to uphold the deterrent effect when the probability of being held liable is less than 1. This occurs particularly, but not exclusively, in GPG and CPR constellations, when the losses are spread over a large number of countries and/or causation between the wrongful act and the damage is difficult to establish. Adding an additional factor to total sum of damages thus not only has the advantage that it sets correct incentives for the potentially wrongdoing state, but also that it helps to overcome the problem of 'rational apathy', as victim states can obtain higher damages when holding the wrongdoing state responsible.

Lastly, remedies cannot be thought of independently but they hinge on enforcement which varies depending on the underlying problem constellation. Thus, remedies need to take into account that, in particular in the public dimension and with regard to the most serious violations of fundamental norms, the probability of enforcement may be too low so that they cannot successfully deter such wrongful acts. The ARSIWA attempt to address this issue with the somewhat rudimentary additional obligations on third states not to recognise a situation caused by a breach of *jus cogens* norms, not to render aid or assistance and to cooperate to bring such situation to an end. In a way, these obligations simply reinforce what has been stated above, namely that the primary remedy in the law of state responsibility are property rules, the primacy of compliance, even in the face of the gravest violations of international law. The advantage of this approach is that they open the door to a wide variety of enforcement tools that exist in international law. This is the reason why they should also apply to violations of other GPG and CPR obligations (i.e. breach of *erga omnes* obligations) and without the qualification of seriousness of the breach. Specific performance does not necessarily rely on countermeasures for enforcement, but other mechanisms such as outcasting (in primary treaty regimes) or positive inducements such as technical assistance or rewards in other issue areas can also play a role here, in particular in order to overcome the inherent weaknesses of enforcement in the public dimension. The ARSIWA placed countermeasures, and thus retaliation, at the forefront of enforcement of state responsibility, in particular for compensation. This approach relies heavily on the mutual imposition of costs, contrary to what has been mentioned above, namely that a key function of state responsibility is also to restore the cooperative relationship. The opportunities and limits of countermeasures as an implementation tool of state responsibility will therefore be discussed in the following chapter.

Chapter 7
Implementation of International State Responsibility: A Rational Choice Analysis of Countermeasures in International Law

This chapter analyses from a rational choice perspective countermeasures in international law, in particular their role in implementing state responsibility.[1] Countermeasures can be defined as "pacific unilateral reactions which are intrinsically unlawful, which are adopted by one or more states against another state, when the former consider that the latter has committed an internationally wrongful act which could justify such reaction".[2] In the international law of state responsibility, countermeasures are relevant at two stages: firstly, and primarily, as a justified means to implement state responsibility against a state in breach of an international obligation (Part three, Chapter II ARSIWA), and, secondly, with regard to circumstances precluding the wrongfulness of such an act as a state taking countermeasures is exempted from its own international responsibility (Article 22 ARSIWA).[3] According to Article 49 (1) ARSIWA,[4] countermeasures are intended to induce compliance with secondary obligations, notably reparation for injury and cessation of the internationally wrongful act, if it is continuing.[5] Even if countermeasures as a specific decentralised enforcement instrument primarily aim to induce compliance with the obligations to provide compensation or to return to legality by cessation of

---

[1] For an overview of the legal concept of countermeasures in international law, see Paddeu, *Justification and Excuse in International Law: Concept and Theory of General Defences*, chap. 6.

[2] Denis Alland, "The Definition of Countermeasures," in *The Law of International Responsibility*, ed. James Crawford, Alain Pellet, and Simon Olleson (Oxford: Oxford University Press, 2010), 1135.

[3] Article 22 ARSIWA reads: "The wrongfulness of an act of a State not in conformity with an international obligation towards another State is precluded if and to the extent that the act constitutes a countermeasure taken against the latter State in accordance with chapter II of part three."

[4] Article 49 (1) ARSIWA reads: "An injured State may only take countermeasures against a State which is responsible for an internationally wrongful act in order to induce that State to comply with its obligations under part two."

[5] Articles 30 and 31 ARSIWA. On these secondary obligations, see Chap. 6.

J. Lemke, *The Protection of Community Interests in the International Law of State Responsibility*, International Law and Economics,
https://doi.org/10.1007/978-3-031-87927-2_7

the wrongful act, the underlying theoretical compliance mechanisms are the same as those negative compliance mechanisms aiming to induce compliance with primary obligations more generally.[6] Depending on the concrete measure, countermeasures therefore either consist in reciprocal non-compliance or, to the extent that they are costly to the retaliating state, constitute retaliatory actions.[7]

Against the background that countermeasures have been designed for a "private" international order, this analysis focuses, in line with the overall objective of this book, on the extent to which the different provisions governing countermeasures, namely the conditions and consequences (in particular, the compensation requirement), take into account the protection of community interests in international law. This relates, firstly, to the question of whether countermeasures by an injured state can effectively induce compliance with global public good (GPG) and common pool resource (CPR) obligations.[8] Secondly, this chapter examines whether and under what conditions other states than the injured first party can have recourse to countermeasures (that is, third states providing the public good of international law enforcement as a second-order cooperation problem).[9] The intention here is to contribute from a rationalist perspective to the doctrinal debate about whether non-directly injured third states can only take "lawful measures" as suggested in Article 54 ARSIWA.

To this end, this chapter begins by briefly presenting the conditions and legal consequences of countermeasures in the international law of state responsibility and the role of countermeasures as a compliance instrument from an economic perspective (Sect. 7.1). It then analyses, in a first step, the conditions for first-party and third-party countermeasures by presenting the incentive structures for directly and non-directly injured states to take countermeasures (Sect. 7.2). In a second step, it discusses the financial consequences of countermeasures, that is the compensation requirement when countermeasures have effects on innocent third parties (Sect. 7.3). The last section concludes, notably by presenting avenues for improving the protection of community interests in the different provisions governing countermeasures (Sect. 7.4).

---

[6] See Sect. 2.4 on enforcement of international law and mechanisms of compliance.

[7] Guzman, *How International Law Works: A Rational Choice Theory*, 47–48.

[8] On the congruence between the legal concept of community interests and the economic concept of global public goods and common pool resources, see Sect. 2.3.

[9] On private and public enforcement of international state responsibility, see Chap. 3 on the normative framework.

7.1 Countermeasures as a Specific Compliance Instrument in the International Law of State Responsibility

Countermeasures are not defined in the ARSIWA, but based on their characteristics they can be understood as pacific unilateral and intrinsically unlawful measures adopted by one or more states (the "injured" state or states) in response to an internationally wrongful act of another state (the "wrongdoing" or "target" state) that are aimed at inducing the target state by affecting its rights to provide cessation or reparation to the injured state.[10] Although countermeasures have been known as an instrument of self-help in international law for a long time, even if formerly under the notion of "reprisals",[11] the term countermeasures is relatively recent, starting with the *Air Service Agreement* tribunal award in the late 1970s,[12] references by the ICJ in several landmark cases,[13] and the ultimate inclusion of the concept by the ILC in the ARSIWA in 2001.[14] Since countermeasures are now understood as pacific measures, they differ from reprisals, that were historically linked to the use of force and in their current meaning are "now used exclusively to refer to belligerent reprisals in the field of international humanitarian law".[15] Countermeasures can conceptually also be distinguished from other related self-help measures in the law of treaties, namely the "exception of non-performance" (i e. reciprocal non-performance of synallagmatic obligations with the aim to reestablish the

[10] Paddeu, "Countermeasures," para. 1; Alland, "The Definition of Countermeasures," in *The Law of International Responsibility*, ed. Crawford, Pellet, and Olleson, 1135.

[11] The *Naulilaa Arbitration* award articulated the conditions of the then 'law of reprisals', such as requirements of a prior wrong and proportionality. *Responsibilité de l'Allemagne à raison des dommages causés dans les colonies portugaises du Sud de l'Afrique (sentence sur le principe de la responsabilité) (Portugal contre Allemagne)*, Award, 31 July 1928, RIAA, Volume II, p. 1011, pp. 1025–1028.

[12] *Air Service Agreement of 27 March 1946 between the United States of America and France*, Award, 9 December 1978, RIAA, Volume XVIII, p. 417, p. 443, para. 81. ("If a situation arises which, in one State's view, results in the violation of an international obligation by another State, the first State is entitled, within the limits set by the general rules of international law pertaining to the use of armed force, to affirm its rights through 'counter-measures'.")

[13] *United States Diplomatic and Consular Staff in Tehran (United States of America v. Iran)*, Judgment, pp. 27–28, para. 53; *Military and Paramilitary Activities in and against Nicaragua (Nicaragua v. United States of America)*, Judgment (Merits), p. 127, paras. 248–249; *Gabčíkovo-Nagymaros Project (Hungary v. Slovakia)*, Judgment, pp. 55–57, paras. 82–87.

[14] Paddeu, "Countermeasures," paras. 2–3; Alland, "The Definition of Countermeasures," in *The Law of International Responsibility*, ed. Crawford, Pellet, and Olleson, 1127–1128.

[15] Paddeu, "Countermeasures," para. 2. See also Alland, "The Definition of Countermeasures," in *The Law of International Responsibility*, ed. Crawford, Pellet, and Olleson, 1130; Matthias Ruffert, "Reprisals," ed. Anne Peters and Rüdiger Wolfrum, *Max Planck Encyclopedia of Public International Law* (Oxford Public International Law: Oxford University Press, 2021), http://opil.ouplaw.com, Article last updated in January 2021.

contractual balance between the parties) and the treaty-law concept of "suspension or termination of treaties due to material breach" (Article 60 VCLT).[16] There is, however, in practice a certain overlap between the two reciprocal mechanisms resulting from the law of treaties and countermeasures resulting from the law of state responsibility. In addition, invocation of the former does not exclude the invocation of countermeasures as they are broader in scope and can also consist in reactions to non-substantial breaches of treaty obligations, to breaches of non-conventional obligations, and to breaches of non-synallagmatic or unrelated obligations (e.g. stemming from a different treaty regime).[17] Countermeasures are also "intrinsically unlawful measures"[18] as they consist in the non-performance of an obligation owed by the injured state to the target state in reaction to a prior internationally wrongful act and thus need to be distinguished from another type of self-help measures, that is "retorsions" (i.e. unfriendly but lawful measures).[19]

The ARSIWA regime be on countermeasures in the international law of state responsibility can be seen as the authoritative statement of the law of countermeasures, although it combines principles from customary international law and progressive developments of international law.[20] From a doctrinal legal perspective, countermeasures have two characteristics or fulfil a dual function in international law: as a means for the implementation of state responsibility, and, incidentally, of precluding the wrongfulness of the breach of an obligation owed to the target state.[21]

As regards the first function of countermeasures, that is implementation of international state responsibility, their objective is to induce another state that is acting wrongfully to comply with its international obligations under part two of the ARSIWA, in particular to cease the wrongful conduct (if it is continuing) and provide reparation. Article 49 ARSIWA on the object and limits of countermeasures reads as follows:

---

[16] Paddeu, "Countermeasures," para. 3.

[17] Alland, "The Definition of Countermeasures," in *The Law of International Responsibility*, ed. Crawford, Pellet, and Olleson, 1132–1134.

[18] Ibid., 1132.

[19] Paddeu, "Countermeasures," paras. 3, 12.

[20] Ibid., para. 10. *Cargill, Incorporated v. United Mexican States*, Award, 18 September 2009, ICSID Case No. ARB(AF)/05/2, para. 381. ("The ILC *Articles on State Responsibility* in part are a codification of custom and in part manifest a progressive development of international law. It is not always apparent whether a particular article should be viewed as the codification of custom or the progressive development of it.")

[21] Hubert Lesaffre, "Circumstances Precluding Wrongfulness in the ILC Articles on State Responsibility: Countermeasures," in *The Law of International Responsibility*, ed. James Crawford, Alain Pellet, and Simon Olleson (Oxford: Oxford University Press, 2010), 469–470; Paddeu, "Countermeasures," para. 11. See also Alland, "The Definition of Countermeasures," in *The Law of International Responsibility*, ed. Crawford, Pellet, and Olleson, 1131.

1. An injured State may only take countermeasures against a State which is responsible for an internationally wrongful act in order to induce that State to comply with its obligations under part two.
2. Countermeasures are limited to the non-performance for the time being of international obligations of the State taking the measures towards the responsible State.
3. Countermeasures shall, as far as possible, be taken in such a way as to permit the resumption of performance of the obligations in question.

Countermeasures thus allow an injured state to temporarily disregard international obligations owed to the state acting wrongfully in the first place if they are taken for the purpose of inducing the target state to comply with its obligations.[22] The notion of injury as defined in Article 42 ARSIWA thus limits the right to take countermeasures to a certain category of states.[23] Certain further conditions outlined in Part three, Chapter II ARSIWA need to be fulfilled in order for an injured state to be allowed to resort to countermeasures. Article 50 ARSIWA lists several obligations that restrict the range of countermeasures, notably obligations under peremptory norms of general international law (*jus cogens* norms), including the prohibition of the use of force, fundamental human rights obligations and obligations of international humanitarian law prohibiting reprisals.[24] In addition, Article 51 ARSIWA imposes a proportionality requirement, namely that countermeasures must be commensurate with the injury suffered, taking into account the gravity of the internationally wrongful act and the rights in question.[25] Procedural requirements for

[22] Paddeu, "Countermeasures," paras. 15–16. While the purpose of breaching international obligations in the first place is not relevant, countermeasures thus represent a deviation from the principle of 'objective responsibility' in the ARSIWA, because the reaction to such an internationally wrongful act requires a certain additional subjective element, namely a specific purpose. See Sect. 4.1.2.1 on the notion of fault in the law of state responsibility.

[23] For a presentation of the notion of injury and its implications for the invocation of state responsibility and the recourse to countermeasures, see Sect. 3.2.3.

[24] Article 50 ARSIWA reads: "1. Countermeasures shall not affect:

(a) the obligation to refrain from the threat or use of force as embodied in the Charter of the United Nations;
(b) obligations for the protection of fundamental human rights;
(c) obligations of a humanitarian character prohibiting reprisals;
(d) other obligations under peremptory norms of general international law.

2. A State taking countermeasures is not relieved from fulfilling its obligations:

(a) under any dispute settlement procedure applicable between it and the responsible State;
(b) to respect the inviolability of diplomatic or consular agents, premises, archives and documents."

[25] See also Roger O'Keefe, "Proportionality," in *The Law of International Responsibility*, ed. James Crawford, Alain Pellet, and Simon Olleson (Oxford: Oxford University Press, 2010), 1157–1168.

taking countermeasures are laid down in Article 52 ARSIWA[26] and Article 53 ARSIWA regarding the temporal limits of countermeasures.[27]

Regarding the second function, countermeasures taken in accordance with the previously cited provisions are (albeit being intrinsically unlawful) not wrongful acts engaging the responsibility of the injured state as their wrongfulness is precluded due to the fact that they constitute a reaction to a prior wrongful act of the target state. This principle is well established in state practice, endorsed by international tribunals,[28] and ultimately laid down in Article 22 ARSIWA:

> The wrongfulness of an act of a State not in conformity with an international obligation towards another State is precluded if and to the extent that the act constitutes a countermeasure taken against the latter State in accordance with chapter II of part three.

Countermeasures bear similarities with consent and self-defence as circumstances precluding wrongfulness as the defendant state's action relates to some prior action of the plaintiff state and can thus be characterised as a justification in international law.[29]

---

[26] Article 52 ARSIWA reads: "1. Before taking countermeasures, an injured State shall:

(a) call upon the responsible State, in accordance with article 43, to fulfil its obligations under part two;
(b) notify the responsible State of any decision to take countermeasures and offer to negotiate with that State.

2. Notwithstanding paragraph 1 (*b*), the injured State may take such urgent countermeasures as are necessary to preserve its rights.

3. Countermeasures may not be taken, and if already taken must be suspended without undue delay if:

(a) the internationally wrongful act has ceased; and
(b) the dispute is pending before a court or tribunal which has the authority to make decisions binding on the parties.

4. Paragraph 3 does not apply if the responsible State fails to implement the dispute settlement procedures in good faith." See also Yuji Iwasawa and Naoki Iwatsuki, "Procedural Conditions," in *The Law of International Responsibility*, ed. James Crawford, Alain Pellet, and Simon Olleson (Oxford: Oxford University Press, 2010), 1149–1155.

[27] Article 53 ARSIWA reads: "Countermeasures shall be terminated as soon as the responsible State has complied with its obligations under part two in relation to the internationally wrongful act." See also Maurice Kamto, "The Time Factor in the Application of Countermeasures," in *The Law of International Responsibility*, ed. James Crawford, Alain Pellet, and Simon Olleson (Oxford: Oxford University Press, 2010), 1169–1176.

[28] *Air Service Agreement of 27 March 1946 between the United States of America and France*, Award, pp. 441–446; *Gabčíkovo-Nagymaros Project (Hungary v. Slovakia)*, Judgment, p. 55, para. 83.

[29] Alland, "The Definition of Countermeasures," in *The Law of International Responsibility*, ed. Crawford, Pellet, and Olleson, 1132. See Chap. 5 for a comprehensive analysis of all five other circumstances precluding wrongfulness, including the common provisions Articles 26 and 27 ARSIWA.

The ARSWIA contain a specific provision for measures taken by states other than an injured state. According to Article 54 ARSIWA:

> This chapter does not prejudice the right of any State, entitled under article 48, paragraph 1, to invoke the responsibility of another State, to take lawful measures against that State to ensure cessation of the breach and reparation in the interest of the injured State or of the beneficiaries of the obligation breached.[30]

Hence, a non-directly injured state which is entitled to invoke the responsibility of another state in case of breach of an *erga omnes* or *erga omnes partes* obligation (i.e. an obligation owed to the international community as a whole or established for the protection of a collective interest of a group of states)[31] may take "lawful measures" against the target state to ensure cessation of the breach and reparation in the interest of the injured state or of the beneficiaries of the obligation breached. Thus, a strict reading of the provision suggests that measures of a non-directly injured state acting to protect community interests are limited to lawful measures, with the consequence that they cannot take countermeasures in the sense of the ARSIWA. Since lawful measures can, by definition, not engage the responsibility of the state adopting them,[32] the exemption from state responsibility for intrinsically unlawful countermeasures laid down as a justifying circumstance precluding wrongfulness in Article 22 ARSIWA does not apply. The exception for indirectly injured third states in Article 54 ARSIWA is, however, highly controversial in the international legal literature. The following sections contribute, amongst others, to this debate by offering an economic perspective on the issue, in particular by analysing the incentives the current provisions are setting for states to take countermeasures in order to induce compliance with international law.

An economic perspective on countermeasures shifts the focus of the analysis on whether the conditions and legal consequences are designed in a way to effectively achieve their purposes by setting adequate incentives for states. The predominant objective of countermeasures in the decentralised international legal order is to induce compliance. From an economic perspective, the "dual function" of countermeasures of implementing state responsibility and precluding wrongfulness of the act does therefore not so much exist, as these are rather doctrinal categories dealt with at different places in the ARSIWA. A rationalist approach would classify the justification of wrongful behaviour rather as a legal consequence of countermeasures injured states take into account when deciding whether to have recourse to

[30] Article 48(1) ARSIWA reads: "Any State other than an injured State is entitled to invoke the responsibility of another State in accordance with paragraph 2 if:

(a) the obligation breached is owed to a group of States including that State, and is established for the protection of a collective interest of the group; or
(b) the obligation breached is owed to the international community as a whole."

[31] On the concepts of *erga omnes* and *erga omnes partes* obligations and the public enforcement of international state responsibility, see Sect. 3.3.3.

[32] Alland, "The Definition of Countermeasures," in *The Law of International Responsibility*, ed. Crawford, Pellet, and Olleson, 1131.

countermeasures (i.e. whether to breach an international obligation owed to the target state). The economic rationale of countermeasures can rather be described as twofold in a different sense. Firstly, countermeasures pursue the objective to induce compliance with specific secondary obligations in the law of state responsibility, that is, reparation for injury and cessation of the wrongful act, if it is continuing.[33] Cessation of the wrongful act basically means compliance with the primary obligation in question (and may overlap with restitution as a form of reparation requiring the return to the *status quo ante*). Countermeasures can also have the objective of achieving compliance with the obligation to provide compensation in the form of a monetary payment. In that sense, countermeasures are limited in their duration to achieve a concrete purpose. Secondly, countermeasures as an implementation tool, incidentally, play a role in inducing compliance with international obligations more generally, even if their commensurate character indicates that they do "not seek to achieve absolute or maximal deterrence of violations".[34] Based on the assumption that states interact in repeated games, countermeasures can have an impact on future compliance decisions of the target state and even a deterrence effect on other countries. From this perspective, countermeasures differ from other circumstances precluding wrongfulness, in particular necessity, which has a self-standing function as a flexibility mechanism allowing non-compliance as the result of a balancing of competing interests in the case of unforeseeable or extraordinary circumstances.

Countermeasures as a specific compliance instrument in the international law of state responsibility draw on two general compliance mechanisms in international law: reciprocity and retaliation. Depending on the concrete measure, countermeasures either consist in reciprocal non-compliance, which would usually be allowed under the VCLT, or, to the extent that they are costly to the retaliating state, constitute retaliatory actions. Countermeasures rely on reciprocity to the extent that they are enacted by the parties to an international agreement themselves, concern obligations that are similar in-kind to the obligation violated in the first place, and not already allowed under the VCLT. Countermeasures operating outside the base treaty are retaliatory actions as they create material and political costs for the sanctioning state. Thus, insights on how these two mechanisms operate, in particular under which conditions they effectively induce compliance, can be used for the economic analysis of countermeasures.[35]

Briefly summarised, reciprocity is a powerful self-enforcing compliance mechanism between parties of a reciprocal agreement, provided that non-compliance imposes costs on the wrongdoing state and both parties have more to gain from ongoing cooperation than from immediate defection.[36] In non-reciprocal treaties,

---

[33] ARSIWA Commentaries, Article 49, para. 1. ("Countermeasures are not intended as a form of punishment for wrongful conduct, but as an instrument for achieving compliance with the obligations of the responsible State under Part Two.")

[34] Posner and Sykes, *Economic Foundations of International Law*, 133.

[35] See Sect. 2.4 for an overview of the different compliance mechanisms in international law.

[36] See, for instance, Guzman, *How International Law Works: A Rational Choice Theory*, 42–43.

especially in GPG constellations (e.g. arms control, human rights, or environmental treaties), reciprocal non-compliance is ineffective, because the wrongdoing state continues to enjoy the benefits of the agreement at no significant costs.[37] Issue linkage at the compliance stage with other reciprocal treaties constitutes one possibility to use reciprocity as an enforcement mechanism to ensure compliance in GPG and CPR constellations,[38] for example by unilaterally withdrawing benefits from trade agreements. In this regard, reciprocity overlaps with retaliation[39] operating outside the treaty regime.[40]

Retaliation is most effective in bilateral relations, where it is more likely that retaliating states immediately affected by a breach of international law accept the associated enforcement costs when the benefits of sanctioning the breach prevail, for instance, if the sanctions succeed in forcing the wrongdoing state to cease an ongoing wrongful act.[41] In contrast, the costs of retaliatory actions often become prohibitively high in multilateral settings,[42] where multiple states are involved in providing enforcement, because each state has incentives to free-ride on the enforcement efforts of other states (i.e. the "sanctioners' dilemma").[43] Enforcement, as a global public good, will eventually be provided by a single powerful state (or group of states, a *k-group*), when the share of the benefits it can obtain (including the long-term benefits supplied by the relevant treaty regime) exceeds the material and political costs of providing the good.[44]

Rooted in both compliance mechanisms, countermeasures can function effectively under certain conditions, in particular in the private law dimension. However, their unilateral character also leads to problems, which become particularly to the

---

[37] See, for instance, Thompson, "The Rational Enforcement of International Law: Solving the Sanctioners' Dilemma," 309; von Stein, "The Engines of Compliance," in *Interdisciplinary Perspectives on International Law and International Relations: The State of the Art*, ed. Dunoff and Pollack, 481.

[38] van Aaken, "Die Befolgung des Völkerrechts zwischen Rationalismus, Konstruktivismus und Verhaltensökonomik," in *Warum befolgen wir Recht? Rechtsverbindlichkeit und Rechtsbefolgung in interdisziplinärer Perspektive*, ed. Hilbert and Rauber, 143.

[39] Some authors consider issue linkage rather as a retaliatory mechanism, because reciprocity is about responding to a certain behaviour with the same behaviour. von Stein, "The Engines of Compliance," in *Interdisciplinary Perspectives on International Law and International Relations: The State of the Art*, ed. Dunoff and Pollack, 479.

[40] van Aaken and Simsek, "Rewarding in International Law," 204.

[41] See, for instance, Guzman, *How International Law Works: A Rational Choice Theory*, 32, 34, 46–48; van Aaken, "Die Befolgung des Völkerrechts zwischen Rationalismus, Konstruktivismus und Verhaltensökonomik," in *Warum befolgen wir Recht? Rechtsverbindlichkeit und Rechtsbefolgung in interdisziplinärer Perspektive*, ed. Hilbert and Rauber, 141.

[42] Guzman, *How International Law Works: A Rational Choice Theory*, 66–68, 138.

[43] Thompson, "The Rational Enforcement of International Law: Solving the Sanctioners' Dilemma," 307–321.

[44] The political costs of sanctioning can expected to be lower when the retaliatory measure receives wide international support, which is more likely if the breach of international law by the target state is egregious and obvious. Ibid., 315, 317.

forefront in the public law dimension. Firstly, as a mechanism of general international law, countermeasures exist independently of any particular provision specifically allowing a state to have recourse to countermeasures and they can be triggered without previous authorisation by an external authority, except in self-contained compliance regimes.[45] For instance, in the context of the WTO, specific rules and procedures on the settlement of disputes do not permit, at least initially, to have recourse to the general compliance instrument of countermeasures. The withdrawal of trade concessions by the injured state requires prior approval by an authoritative decision-making body, namely a finding of wrongdoing and an *ex ante* authorisation of the proposed "countermeasure" by the WTO's Dispute Settlement Body.[46] As outlined previously, international judicial institutions can play an important role in facilitating unilateral and collective enforcement of international law, in particular as information-disseminating devices to facilitate third-party enforcement in GPGs constellations.[47]

Secondly, and relatedly, in the absence of prior authorisation of countermeasures, their legality needs to be assessed by states themselves, in particular whether the prior act of the target state was actually wrongful.[48] Self-interpretation bears the risk that states take prejudicial measures on the basis of subjective claims about alleged violations of international law.[49] This risk is amplified if information about the circumstances are asymmetrically distributed among the states involved, including the international community as an audience. If there is uncertainty about the existence of a breach of an international obligation, reciprocal non-compliance bears the risk to set off "spirals of non-compliance", even in bilateral constellations.[50] The conditions and consequences for countermeasures thus need to strike the appropriate balance between, on the one hand, countering abusive invocation of countermeasures and, on the other hand, allowing countermeasures to play out their role as an effective compliance mechanism, at least in constellations where they can successfully induce compliant behaviour.

The focus of this rational choice analysis will be on the incentive structures in both the private and public dimensions of international law: firstly, on the incentives

[45] Article 55 ARSIWA contains a *lex specialis* rule. ARSIWA Commentaries, Article 50, para. 10. Alland, "The Definition of Countermeasures," in *The Law of International Responsibility*, ed. Crawford, Pellet, and Olleson, 1129.

[46] Only if the treaty mechanism fails (e.g. the dispute resolution mechanism not being operational due to a hold-out on the nomination of judges), recourse to countermeasures as an instrument of general international law may be possible. Other international treaty regimes with their own dispute settlement procedures (e.g. EU treaties) also exclude recourse to countermeasures between its members.

[47] On the facilitating role of international judicial institutions, see Sect. 2.4.

[48] Alland, "The Definition of Countermeasures," in *The Law of International Responsibility*, ed. Crawford, Pellet, and Olleson, 1129.

[49] Ibid.

[50] von Stein, "The Engines of Compliance," in *Interdisciplinary Perspectives on International Law and International Relations: The State of the Art*, ed. Dunoff and Pollack, 480–481.

for injured states to take countermeasures (i.e. first-party enforcement), in particular when the prior wrongful act consists in the breach of a GPG or CPR obligation, and, secondly, on the incentives for non-directly injured states (i.e. third-party enforcement). When analysing from an economic perspective the decision of states considering to have recourse to countermeasures (i.e. decision of non-compliance with another international obligation owed to the target state) two issues play a role. The first sub-section focuses on the conditions of countermeasures and inquires how duties are allocated between the target state and the state or states taking countermeasures: for instance, obligations which may not be impaired by countermeasures, the proportionality requirement, or the controversial issue of whether countermeasures protecting community interests by non-directly injured third states are limited to lawful measures. The second sub-section focuses on the possible financial consequences of countermeasures (i.e. the compensation requirement in Article 27 lit. b) ARSIWA) and analyses how costs following the invocation of countermeasures are allocated, in particular when these have detrimental effects on innocent third parties.

7.2 The Conditions of Countermeasures: First-party and Third-party Countermeasures

This sub-section analyses in a first step the conditions for countermeasures as laid down in Articles 49 to 53 ARSIWA in the so-called baseline scenario, that is countermeasures taken by the injured state (i.e. first-party enforcement). The focus will be on the incentives for injured states to take countermeasures when the prior wrongful act consists in the breach of a GPG or CPR obligation. In a second step, it analyses the incentives for non-directly injured states acting only in order to protect community interests (i.e. third-party enforcement), in particular whether there is an economic rationale to allow them to have recourse to countermeasures within the meaning of the ARSIWA or only to lawful measures (i.e. retorsions).

7.2.1 First-party Countermeasures: Conditions for Injured States

The crucial question when analysing how duties are allocated between the target state and the injured state is whether the conditions strike the appropriate balance between countering abusive invocation of countermeasures and allowing countermeasures to play out their role as an effective compliance mechanism. In the logic of circumstances precluding wrongfulness, the burden of proof for invoking countermeasures as a justification for an otherwise illegal act falls for all conditions on the injured state resorting to countermeasures.

7.2.1.1 Characteristics of the Prior Wrongful Act

The most important precondition of countermeasures is the existence of an internationally wrongful act (Article 49 (1) ARSIWA).[51] While it falls, in the absence of an authoritative decision-making body involved prior to the countermeasure, on the injured state alone to assess whether this condition is fulfilled, believing in good faith that a prior wrongful act existed will be insufficient.[52] The existence of a prior wrongful act by the target state is an objective standard, subject to an *ex post* control.[53] The risk associated with an asymmetric distribution of information and the ultimate determination whether a countermeasure was actually justified thus falls on the injured state.[54] Compared to other circumstances precluding wrongfulness, in particular necessity, this is a relatively high burden of proof. This can be explained by the function of countermeasures being predominantly an implementation tool of state responsibility and less a flexibility mechanism allowing non-compliance as the result of a balancing of competing interests in the case of unforeseeable or extraordinary circumstances. A high threshold for legally invoking countermeasures is justified to counter the risk that states violate international commitments based on subjective claims about being the victim of an allegedly wrongful act and, ultimately, setting of "spirals of non-compliance".

The prior wrongful act can consist in a violation of a primary international obligation independent of its object, which is in economic terms the underlying first-order cooperation problem in the private or public dimension of international law.[55] This means that injured states can take countermeasures in case of a violation of either a private law or public law (or community interest) obligation.[56] Hence, the prior wrongful act can relate, in theory, not only to private or club goods (e.g. aiming to mitigate externalities or to further economic gains) but also to the protection of GPGs or CPRs.

However, in order to take first-party countermeasures the state needs to be "injured" by that wrongful act.[57] A state is qualified as injured for the purpose of invoking state responsibility if the obligation breached is owed to that state individually. According to Article 42 ARSIWA, it can also be owed to a group of states including that state or the international community as a whole, under the condition

[51] See also *Gabčíkovo-Nagymaros Project (Hungary v. Slovakia)*, Judgment, p. 55, para. 83.

[52] Paddeu, "Countermeasures," para. 18.

[53] See ibid.

[54] ARSIWA Commentaries, Article 49, para. 3. ("A State taking countermeasures acts at its peril, if its view of the question of wrongfulness turns out not to be well founded. A State which resorts to countermeasures based on its unilateral assessment of the situation does so at its own risk and may incur responsibility for its own wrongful conduct in the event of an incorrect assessment.")

[55] On the congruence between community interest and different types of goods in international law, see Sect. 2.3.

[56] On the notions of private law and public law obligation in the international context, see Sect. 5.2.2.2 on balancing of conflicting interests in the case of necessity.

[57] On private enforcement of international state responsibility, see Sect. 3.2.3.

that the breach of the obligation either specifically affects that state or radically changes the position of all other states with respect to the further performance of the obligation.[58] In private good constellations, injury can easily be assumed when the obligation breached is owed to the injured state individually, in particular where a parallel to tort liability can be drawn (e.g. pollution of territorial waters, non-extradition of a foreign citizen, and destruction of diplomatic premises).[59] Club good constellations, where non-compliance bears similarities with contractual liability, can also be envisaged, but in particular trade relations are covered by the WTO as a self-contained regime with specific rules on remedies and enforcement in the case of a wrongful act (e.g. export subsidies).

For GPG and CPR constellations, establishing an individual injury is less evident, because free-riding in the form of non-compliance principally affects all (participating) states to a certain extent. Injury thus needs to require more than a mere legal interest in compliance. Briefly summarised, in GPG and CPR constellations, a state can be considered injured, if that state is either specifically affected by a breach (that is, when the wrongful act has particular adverse effects on that state, even in cases where the legal effects of that act extend by implication to the whole group of states bound by the obligation or to the international community as a whole) or when the breach of a collective obligation affects *per se* every other State to which the obligation is owed (that is, treaties with interdependent obligations such as disarmament treaties where each party's performance is effectively conditioned upon and requires the performance of each of the others).[60] Therefore, first-party countermeasures in CPR and GPG constellations require a certain private goods dimension, as they do not serve to ensure compliance generally, but rather to defend the subjective rights of injured states (usually their own demand for compensation or restitution).[61] This means as a consequence that there can also be a plurality of injured states having the right to separately take first-party countermeasures, for instance, if the damage caused by the breach of a GPG or CPR obligation falls on multiple states.[62]

---

[58] Article 42 ARSIWA reads as follows: "A State is entitled as an injured State to invoke the responsibility of another State if the obligation breached is owed to:

(a) that State individually; or
(b) a group of States including that State, or the international community as a whole, and the breach of the obligation:
    (i) specially affects that State; or
    (ii) is of such a character as radically to change the position of all the other States to which the obligation is owed with respect to the further performance of the obligation."

[59] Article 42 lit. a) ARSIWA. See further, ARSIWA Commentaries, Article 42, paras. 6–10.

[60] Article 42 lit. b) ARSIWA. See further, ARSIWA Commentaries, Article 42, paras. 11–15.

[61] Material damage is, however, not a precondition for an injury in the sense of the ARSIWA, see Gaja, "The Concept of an Injured State," in *The Law of International Responsibility*, ed. Crawford, Pellet, and Olleson, 942.

[62] See Article 46 ARSIWA, which reads as follows: "Where several States are injured by the same internationally wrongful act, each injured State may separately invoke the responsibility of the State which has committed the internationally wrongful act."

This scenario is therefore to be distinguished from third-party countermeasures which may eventually be taken by non-directly injured interested states, as will be discussed further below.[63]

7.2.1.2 Limitation of Countermeasures to Breach of Private Law Obligations

Article 49 (2) ARSIWA indicates that countermeasures can consist, in principle, in temporary non-performance of international obligations, independent of their object.[64] However, Article 50 (1) ARSIWA lists several obligations that may not be impaired by countermeasures.[65] These are the obligation to refrain from the threat or use of force (as embodied in the UN Charter), obligations for the protection of fundamental human rights, obligations of a humanitarian character prohibiting reprisals, and other obligations under peremptory norms of general international law.[66] Thus, in brief, countermeasures are excluded when they consist in a violation of *jus cogens* norms,[67] that is certain obligations in international law that have been accorded a distinctive normative status. These are determined on a case-by-case basis depending on their fundamental importance and deemed superiority in the hierarchy of international legal norms and relate, as of today, in terms of their underlying first-order cooperation problems, almost exclusively to GPG constellations (without excluding the theoretical possibility to relate also to the protection of

---

[63] See Sect. 7.2.2.

[64] Article 49 (2) ARSIWA reads: "Countermeasures are limited to the non-performance for the time being of international obligations of the State taking the measures towards the responsible State."

[65] Article 50 (1) ARSIWA reads: "Countermeasures shall not affect:

(a) the obligation to refrain from the threat or use of force as embodied in the Charter of the United Nations;
(b) obligations for the protection of fundamental human rights;
(c) obligations of a humanitarian character prohibiting reprisals;
(d) other obligations under peremptory norms of general international law."

[66] See ARSIWA Commentaries, Article 50, paras. 3–9. See further Silvia Borelli and Simon Olleson, "Obligations Relating to Human Rights and Humanitarian Law," in *The Law of International Responsibility*, ed. James Crawford, Alain Pellet, and Simon Olleson (Oxford: Oxford University Press, 2010), 1177–1196; Charles Leben, "Obligations Relating to the Use of Force and Arising from Peremptory Norms of International Law," in *The Law of International Responsibility*, ed. James Crawford, Alain Pellet, and Simon Olleson (Oxford: Oxford University Press, 2010), 1197–1204; Laurence Boisson de Chazournes, "Other Non-Derogable Obligations," in *The Law of International Responsibility*, ed. James Crawford, Alain Pellet, and Simon Olleson (Oxford: Oxford University Press, 2010), 1205–1214.

[67] The prohibition of the use of force, fundamental human rights obligations and obligations of international humanitarian law prohibiting reprisals are specific *jus cogens* norms, but the general exclusion in lit. d) clarifies that countermeasures cannot consist in a violation of any 'other' obligation under peremptory norms of general international law. See ARSIWA Commentaries, Article 50, para. 9.

CPRs).[68] With regard to the objectives of state responsibility in the public dimension of international law, the provisions relating to *jus cogens* norms in the law of state responsibility have essentially the function to induce compliance with certain fundamental community interest obligations (i.e. normative GPGs) with two different means. These are, firstly, a conflict of laws rule which aims to prevent breach by excluding the application of flexibility provisions (Article 26 ARSIWA), and, secondly, collective obligations of cooperation placed on the international community aiming to bring such situation to an end (Article 41 ARSIWA). The specific grounds for exclusion of countermeasures in Article 50 (1) ARSIWA thus reiterate for this context the general provision in Article 26 ARSIWA, excluding the invocation of circumstances precluding wrongfulness in the case of breach of *jus cogens* obligations.[69] The legal rationale of this conflict of norms rule is that for some fundamental norms of international law there is the presumption that the interest in upholding the respect for the international legal order prevails over any unforeseeable and extraordinary circumstances. This provision thus amounts to a balancing of competing interests where the result is pre-determined by the law. From an economic point of view, it is not socially desirable to replace this assessment with a weighing of interests in an individual case given that the costs to the international community of a breach of peremptory norms are prohibitive.[70] The economic rationale to exclude *jus cogens* obligations from the remit of countermeasures, and thus rendering them illegal, differs slightly as it mainly lies in the reciprocal nature of countermeasures as an implementation tool. Reciprocal non-compliance is ineffective in non-reciprocal treaties, especially in GPG constellations, because the target state continues to enjoy the benefits of the agreement at no significant costs of the non-compliant behaviour, falling rather on other parties to the agreement or the international community at large (and in the case of *jus cogens* norms are prohibitive).[71] For instance, it would not be credible if the injured state responded to a violation of human rights obligations by seriously breaching fundamental human rights obligations against its own citizens.[72] Similarly, even though recourse to the use of force or reprisals increase the costs of non-compliance for the target state, as serious violations of fundamental norms of international law they would be out of proportion[73] and create significant costs not only for the injured state taking them, especially in the form of reputational costs towards the international audience, but

[68] On the role of *jus cogens* obligations in the hierarchy of international norms, see Sect. 3.3.2.

[69] ARSIWA Commentaries, Article 50, para. 9.

[70] See Sect. 5.4 concluding the economic analysis of circumstances precluding wrongfulness.

[71] See, for instance, Thompson, "The Rational Enforcement of International Law: Solving the Sanctioners' Dilemma," 309; von Stein, "The Engines of Compliance," in *Interdisciplinary Perspectives on International Law and International Relations: The State of the Art* ed. Dunoff and Pollack, 481.

[72] See Guzman, *How International Law Works: A Rational Choice Theory*, 45.

[73] The use of force can only be justified as self-defence if it is used in response to an armed attack, see Sect. 5.3.2.2 on self-defence. However, Posner and Sykes argue with regard to the NATO military intervention in Kosovo which aimed to stop Serbian forces from committing further human rights violations that sometimes "the only available retaliation may entail substantial collateral costs, yet may be preferable to inaction" and "may thus have been justified as an 'efficient breach' of the usual remedial rules." Posner and Sykes, *Economic Foundations of International Law*, 133.

also to the international community. Recourse to forcible countermeasures also bears the risk to set off "spirals of non-compliance" leading to the breakdown of cooperation over *jus cogens* obligations which should not be breached under any circumstances in the first place. The use of force is thus counterproductive as a tool designed primarily to induce compliance with secondary obligations of cessation and reparation. The underlying economic rationale thus suggests to refrain from countermeasures whenever they impair GPG and CPR obligations generally, and not only those that have been accorded the normative status as *jus cogens* norms, rendering countermeasures expressly illegal by law. This differs slightly with what has been argued above with regards to the general conflict of laws rule in Article 26 ARSIWA. For instance, in the case of necessity, community interests protected by an international obligation (i.e. "ordinary" obligations relating to the protection of GPGs or the preservation of CPRs) will most likely prevail the (community) interests protected by the act in necessity and thus exclude the reliance on a circumstance precluding wrongfulness. However, except for *jus cogens* norms, this depends always on the balancing of the competing interests in the given case at hand. Countermeasures do not follow the logic of weighing competing interest but are a first-party compliance mechanism rooted in reciprocity. Hence, there is no scenario conceivable where countermeasures may consist in the violation of an obligation relating to the protection of GPGs or the preservation of CPRs, in particular due to the external costs falling on the international community and not the target state. This demonstrates that countermeasures affecting GPG or CPR obligations are inadequate to induce the target state to comply with its secondary obligations of reparation and cessation, which in turn is a necessary requirement for countermeasures to be justified as laid down in Article 49 (1) ARSIWA. It is therefore suggested here to understand Article 50 (1) ARSIWA as a general prohibition of countermeasures affecting GPG or CPR obligations, independent of the normative status of the interest protected (i.e. *jus cogens* norms).

This argument is also valid with regard to the second group of obligations contained in Article 50 (2) ARSIWA and which may not be impaired by countermeasures.[74] These include, firstly, obligations under dispute settlement procedures applicable between the responsible state and the injured state, and, secondly, obligations to respect the inviolability of diplomatic or consular agents, premises, archives and documents. The underlying rationale of these exclusions is that they serve to maintain the channels of communication between the parties of the dispute that gave rise to the threat or use of countermeasures.[75] On first sight, these

---

[74] Article 50 (2) ARSIWA reads: "A State taking countermeasures is not relieved from fulfilling its obligations:

(a) under any dispute settlement procedure applicable between it and the responsible State;
(b) to respect the inviolability of diplomatic or consular agents, premises, archives and documents."

[75] ARSIWA Commentaries, Article 50, para. 2. Paddeu, "Countermeasures," para. 21.

obligations seem to impose only procedural requirements on the involved parties, but their function to work towards amicable dispute resolution and to uphold international communication speaks for a certain GPG dimension. It has been outlined earlier that both peaceful dispute settlement and international communication *via* diplomatic and consular relations are GPGs in their own right.[76] This does not exclude that countermeasures violating, for instance, certain diplomatic and consular obligations (e.g. search of embassy premises) affect also private goods of the target state, but the main purpose here is to uphold channels of communication to resolve the dispute. This is also in the interest of the international community, and thus relates to the GPG dimension. Therefore, this second set of obligations which are excluded from the scope of countermeasures confirms the proposition made above, namely that countermeasures shall not consist in the violation of an obligation relating to the protection of GPGs or the preservation of CPRs. At the time of their adoption, the list of obligations in Article 50 ARSIWA was criticised "for its apparent arbitrariness resulting from the lack of a common underlying principle".[77] It is argued here that the common underlying principle is that of the concepts of GPGs and CPRs, because countermeasures affecting these types of obligations by definition impose costs on the international community and therefore miss their aim to induce compliance with secondary obligations, independent of whether the prior wrongful act consisted in the breach of a private or public law obligation.

This argument is supported by the fact that issue linkage with other reciprocal obligations outside the treaty regime in question constitutes a more effective enforcement mechanism to ensure compliance in GPG and CPR constellations.[78] An example constitutes the unilateral withdrawal of benefits from trade agreements (i.e. club goods). Retaliatory countermeasures are most effective in bilateral relations, where it is more likely that retaliating states immediately affected by a breach of international law accept the associated enforcement costs when the benefits of sanctioning the breach prevail, for instance, if the sanctions succeed in forcing the target state to cease an ongoing wrongful act.[79] The most effective way to use countermeasures is certainly in scenarios where the wrongful act consists in a breach of a private goods obligation and the countermeasure affects a synallagmatic or another private goods obligation. Therefore, the understanding followed throughout

[76] On *erga omnes* obligations, see above Sect. 3.3.3.

[77] Paddeu, "Countermeasures," para. 19.

[78] van Aaken, "Die Befolgung des Völkerrechts zwischen Rationalismus, Konstruktivismus und Verhaltensökonomik," in *Warum befolgen wir Recht? Rechtsverbindlichkeit und Rechtsbefolgung in interdisziplinärer Perspektive*, ed. Hilbert and Rauber, 143. When GPG and CPR regimes are previously transformed into clubs in order to be able to rely on first-party cross-countermeasures within the same treaty regime, the compliance mechanism is outcasting (see Sect. 2.4).

[79] See, for instance, Guzman, *How International Law Works: A Rational Choice Theory*, 32, 34, 46–48; van Aaken, "Die Befolgung des Völkerrechts zwischen Rationalismus, Konstruktivismus und Verhaltensökonomik," in *Warum befolgen wir Recht? Rechtsverbindlichkeit und Rechtsbefolgung in interdisziplinärer Perspektive*, ed. Hilbert and Rauber, 141.

<table>
<tr><th></th><th>Countermeasure affecting a private law obligation</th><th>Countermeasure affecting a public law obligation</th></tr>
<tr><td>Prior wrongful act relating to a private good</td><td>Reciprocal or retaliatory in-kind countermeasure</td><td rowspan="2">Exclusion of countermeasures</td></tr>
<tr><td>Prior wrongful act relating to a GPG or CPR obligation</td><td>Cross- or non-in-kind countermeasure</td></tr>
</table>

Fig. 7.1 Possible scenarios for injured states taking countermeasures

this chapter is that countermeasures are limited to justify breaches of private law obligations.

The different possible scenarios for injured states taking countermeasures are summarised in Fig. 7.1. The left-hand row relates to the object of the obligation breached by the target state triggering the right to first-party countermeasures (Article 49 (1) ARSIWA). This prior wrongful act can be either private or public in nature, that is relating to private goods (and theoretically club goods) obligations or GPG/CPR obligations. Breach of the latter requires, however, a certain private goods dimension (i.e. mixed good characteristics) for states to qualify as "injured" by the prior wrongful act in the sense of Article 42 ARSIWA. The right-hand column relates to character of the obligation temporarily disregarded by the injured state taking countermeasures (Article 49 (2) ARSIWA). I argue that in this baseline scenario, first-party countermeasures should be possible where a private law obligation is affected, but be excluded where they impair a GPG or CPR obligation, even those without *jus cogens* status. That countermeasures affecting public law or community interest obligations are excluded can, in my opinion, be derived from Articles 50 and 26 ARSIWA (i.e. the concept of GPGs/CPRs as an underlying economic rationale) and from Article 49 (1) ARSIWA because of their inadequacy to induce compliance. Thus, first-party countermeasures are limited to justify breaches of private law obligations, that is reciprocal or retaliatory in-kind countermeasures in the case of a prior "private" wrongful act and cross- or non-in-kind countermeasures in the case of a prior "public" wrongful act.

Interpreting the relevant ARSIWA provisions regarding countermeasures from an economic perspective allows for a better understanding of the scenarios where countermeasures should be possible and where they should be excluded. This limitation of countermeasures to breach of private law obligations also explains why we observe in practice countermeasures mostly in the form of economic sanctions, such as the seizure of assets, import/export restrictions, or the withdrawal of overfly rights.

7.2.1.3 Other Substantive and Procedural Conditions, Notably the Proportionality Requirement

The exclusion of countermeasures affecting GPG and CPR obligations, and in particular the prohibition of the use of force, reduces already significantly the risk of abuse, as the scope of application is limited. The ARSIWA include further provisions which aim to strike the appropriate balance between countering abusive invocation of countermeasures and allowing countermeasures to play out their role as an effective tool to implement state responsibility.

A first limitation to countermeasures is the necessity requirement. According to Article 49 (1) ARSIWA, countermeasures only allow an injured state to temporarily disregard international obligations owed to the state acting wrongfully in the first place if they are taken for the purpose of inducing the target state to comply with its secondary obligations. In order to be justified, countermeasures thus require a specific purpose, in the sense that they must be necessary to induce compliance with the obligations of cessation and reparation.[80] The necessity requirement relates, for instance, to the question to which extent injured states need to engage in negotiations with the target state or in dispute settlement procedures before resorting to countermeasures.[81] This relationship between countermeasures and dispute settlement mechanisms is far from resolved, with the ARSIWA containing only very few provisions in this regard.[82] However, even if the countermeasure was necessary to achieve compliance, it must be proportionate.[83]

Article 51 ARSIWA imposes such a proportionality requirement as a second limitation, stating that "[c]ountermeasures must be commensurate with the injury suffered, taking into account the gravity of the internationally wrongful act and the rights in question".[84] This limitation of the right to take countermeasures is well established in international law.[85] The proportionality principle requires a comparison between, on the one hand, the effects of the countermeasure on the target state,

---

[80] O'Keefe, "Proportionality," in *The Law of International Responsibility*, ed. Crawford, Pellet, and Olleson, 1157–1158.

[81] Iwasawa and Iwatsuki, "Procedural Conditions," in *The Law of International Responsibility*, ed. Crawford, Pellet, and Olleson, 1153–1154.

[82] On this debate, see, for instance, Paddeu, "Countermeasures," paras. 35–38.

[83] Ibid., para. 25. See also, ARSIWA Commentaries, Article 51, para. 7.

[84] For further details, see Enzo Cannizzaro, "The Role of Proportionality in the Law of International Countermeasures," *European Journal of International Law* 12, no. 5 (2001): 889–916; O'Keefe, "Proportionality," in *The Law of International Responsibility*, ed. Crawford, Pellet, and Olleson, 1157–1168.

[85] ARISWA Commentaries, Article 51, para. 2. See, for instance, *Responsibilité de l'Allemagne à raison des dommages causés dans les colonies portugaises du Sud de l'Afrique (sentence sur le principe de la responsabilité) (Portugal contre Allemagne)*, Award, p. 1028; *Air Service Agreement of 27 March 1946 between the United States of America and France*, Award, pp. 443–444, para. 83; *Gabčíkovo-Nagymaros Project (Hungary v. Slovakia)*, Judgment, p. 56, para. 85.

and, on the other hand, the injury previously suffered by the state taking the countermeasure, while taking into account the interests protected by each of the obligations infringed.[86] In that sense, "proportionality establishes a functional connection between the ends and the means of countermeasures".[87] Although countermeasures are primarily a first-party compliance mechanism rooted in reciprocity, and thus do not follow the logic of weighing competing interest like other circumstances precluding wrongfulness, in particular necessity,[88] balancing of conflicting interests becomes nonetheless relevant under the proportionality requirement. The injured state needs to self-assess whether the envisaged countermeasure is proportionate, subject to an *ex post* control with the burden of proof (as for all other conditions of countermeasures) falling on the injured state. Thus, the injured state bears the risk that the countermeasure actually was not proportionate and thus it is reasonable to take into account the *ex ante* perspective of the injured state in the *ex post* assessment of proportionality to address the problem of hindsight bias. This risk is likely to be smaller when the countermeasure consists in the breach of a reciprocal obligation, especially in the case of breach of a synallagmatic obligation, because proportionality is easier to observe and to objectively verify. Paddeu argues that "[w]hile there is no requirement of reciprocity, countermeasures affecting the same or closely related obligation are more likely to be deemed proportionate".[89] With regard to cross-countermeasures, that is, when the prior wrongful act consisted in a violation of a GPG or CPR obligation, the community interest protected by these obligations is likely to prevail the private state interest affected by the countermeasure (e.g. trade sanctions). Yet, in the case of unrelated breaches it will be more difficult to establish and to objectively verify whether the cross-countermeasure was proportionate. As the risk of the countermeasure ultimately being disproportionate falls on the injured state, this may be one reason why injured states are less likely to take retaliatory cross-countermeasures compared to purely reciprocal countermeasures.

Procedural requirements and temporal limits for taking countermeasures are laid down in Article 52 ARSIWA and Article 53 ARSIWA. According to Article 52 (1) ARSIWA, the injured state must, firstly, call on the target state to fulfil its secondary obligations of reparation and cessation of the wrongful act, if it is

[86] Paddeu, "Countermeasures," para. 23.

[87] Ibid., para. 24.

[88] On the economic structure of balancing competing interests in the case of necessity, see Sect. 5.2.2.2.

[89] Paddeu, "Countermeasures," para. 24.

continuing,[90] and, secondly, notify the target state of its intention to take countermeasures and make an offer to negotiate.[91] These procedural conditions intend to give the target state an opportunity to reconsider its previous actions, either by complying with the obligation in question and, where appropriate, providing reparation for injury, or by justifying its conduct, and thus introduce a certain temporal delay.[92] From a rational choice perspective, these procedural conditions serve to slow down the process of first-party enforcement, in particular due to the absence of authoritative decision-making bodies involved prior to the recourse to countermeasures. Offering the target state the opportunity to rectify or justify its conduct may pre-empt misunderstandings and ultimately avoid "spirals of non-compliance".[93] However, even if a reasonable delay may be necessary between the *sommation* and the offer to negotiate and the recourse to the countermeasure,[94] under exceptional circumstances, urgent countermeasures may be taken immediately upon commission of the wrongful act if this is necessary to preserve the rights of the injured state (Article 52 (2) ARSIWA). In addition, countermeasures may not be taken or must be suspended if the wrongful act has ceased, the dispute is pending before a court or tribunal which has the authority to make decisions binding on the parties, and the wrongdoing state implements the dispute settlement procedures in good faith (Article 52 (3) and (4) ARSIWA). Hence, there is no obligation in the ARSIWA to engage in dispute settlement procedures before resorting to countermeasures,[95] but once a dispute settlement mechanism has been activated in good faith, countermeasures shall not be taken or be suspended. As a mechanism of general international law, countermeasures can be triggered without prior authorisation by an external authority to the states involved,[96] but international judicial institutions can play an important role in facilitating unilateral and collective enforcement of international law.[97] It is therefore reasonable to suspend recourse to countermeasures as long as

[90]This condition, derived from the French term *sommation*, is well-established in customary international law. *Responsibilité de l'Allemagne à raison des dommages causés dans les colonies portugaises du Sud de l'Afrique (sentence sur le principe de la responsabilité) (Portugal contre Allemagne)*, Award, p. 1026; *Air Service Agreement of 27 March 1946 between the United States of America and France*, Award, p. 444, paras. 84–87; *Gabčíkovo-Nagymaros Project (Hungary v. Slovakia)*, Judgment, p. 56, para. 84.

[91]While an injured state does not need to specify the measures it intends to take, a detailed explanation of the countermeasures envisaged can be helpful in inducing the target state to cease the wrongful act. Iwasawa and Iwatsuki, "Procedural Conditions," in *The Law of International Responsibility*, ed. Crawford, Pellet, and Olleson, 1151–1152.

[92]Paddeu, "Countermeasures," paras. 26, 29.

[93]See also, Posner and Sykes, *Economic Foundations of International Law*, 133–134.

[94]See also, Kamto, "The Time Factor in the Application of Countermeasures," in *The Law of International Responsibility*, ed. Crawford, Pellet, and Olleson, 1171.

[95]This does not exclude the existence of other obligations in international law to solve disputes peacefully, for instance in Articles 2 (3) and 33 of the UN Charter.

[96]See ARSIWA Commentaries, Article 50 ARSIWA, para. 10. Alland, "The Definition of Countermeasures," in *The Law of International Responsibility*, ed. Crawford, Pellet, and Olleson, 1129.

[97]On the facilitating role of international judicial institutions, in particular as information-disseminating devices to facilitate third-party enforcement in GPG constellations, see Sect. 2.4.

dispute settlement procedures are ongoing, in particular when the potential outcome is to explicitly authorise these countermeasures.[98]

Article 53 ARSIWA provides that the injured state must terminate the countermeasure as soon as the target state has complied with its obligations of cessation and/or reparation. This temporary character also derives from Article 49 (2) ARSIWA, providing that countermeasures are "limited to the non-performance for the time being", and Article 27 lit. a) ARSIWA, providing with regard to all circumstances precluding wrongfulness that the obligation needs to be complied with if and to the extent that the circumstance no longer exists. The temporary character of countermeasures implicates that "countermeasures must be reversible".[99] Article 49 (3) ARSIWA states explicitly that "[c]ountermeasures shall, as far as possible, be taken in such a way as to permit the resumption of performance of the obligations in question". This requirement is line with the purpose of countermeasures to induce compliance with secondary obligations and thus as a remedial instrument without any punitive component.

In conclusion, the conditions for countermeasures contain many safeguards that aim to prevent abusive recourse to countermeasures. These are the limited scope (i.e. limitation to countermeasures affecting private law obligations), the requirements of necessity and proportionality, as well as the procedural and temporal restrictions. These emphasise that countermeasures need to be strictly limited to their function to induce compliance with the secondary obligations of reparation and, if the wrongful act is ongoing, cessation. These conditions also allow for sufficient flexibility, for instance, in choosing the type, timing, or intensity of the countermeasure, in order to allow them to play out their role as an effective compliance mechanism.

7.2.1.4 Incentives for Injured States to Take Countermeasures

Whether first-party countermeasures can operate effectively depends notably on whether a state is injured by the prior wrongful act.[100] This can be one single state or multiple states. Multiple states can, for instance, each be separately affected by the breach of the same wrongful act concerning private goods obligations, but still face collective action problems as to which state is willing to move first and bear the costs of bringing the claim to court or enforcing compliance.[101] Other examples for multiple states being injured following the breach of GPG or CPR obligations are large-scale pollution affecting multiple coastal states or attacks on embassies of

[98] See Sect. 7.1 on the role of international judicial institutions in facilitating enforcement in the decentralised international legal order, notably by prior authorisation of countermeasures.

[99] Paddeu, "Countermeasures," para. 32.

[100] See Sect. 7.2.1.1 on the characteristics of the prior wrongful act and, more extensively, Sect. 3. 2.3 on private enforcement of international state responsibility.

[101] See Sect. 6.3.2.2 on the problem of 'rational apathy' and the discussion of punitive damages.

several countries. Another example are treaty regimes, which contain interdependent GPG or CPR obligations breach of which affects all other parties to the agreement (e.g. arms control treaties). This section will focus on the incentives for injured states to resort to countermeasures and conclude by summarising the conditions under which they are likely take countermeasures.

The following analysis builds on the general assumption that a state will have recourse to a countermeasure (CM) if the expected benefits (B_{CM}) for the sanctioning state outweigh the associated costs of the countermeasure (C_{CM}).[102] It will further be assumed, for simplicity reasons, that the expected benefits (B_{CM}) equal the probability (p) of the countermeasure being effective (E_{CM})[103] and that the associated costs (C_{CM}) equal the sum of the material costs (C_m) and the political costs (C_p)[104] as well as compensation to innocent third states, which equals the probability (p) of material losses (L)[105]:

$$B_{CM} \geq C_{CM}; \text{ whereas}$$
$$B_{CM} = p(E_{CM}),$$
$$C_{CM} = C_m + C_p + p(L)$$

When the expected costs equal the immediate expected benefits of the countermeasure, a state may still be inclined to take the countermeasure due to the long-term benefits. A successful and justified countermeasure enhances the sanctioning state's reputation as one that legitimately sanctions wrongful behaviour and thus can deter future breaches of international obligations by the target state and third states in the international community.[106] Like reputation as a compliance mechanism, reputation for sanctioning can work at the margins of the cost-benefit calculation of states contemplating whether to take countermeasures.

The first scenario to be analysed is that of a single injured state contemplating about whether to take a countermeasure against a target state which previously breached a private goods obligation. The injured state will take a binary decision

---

[102] In accordance with the research method explained above, state preferences are assumed to consist in the quest for maximising absolute gains (i.e. being better or at least not worse off than before) and to be given and fixed. This means that in the following cost-benefit analysis, states are assumed to have neither an inherent preference for compliance nor for enforcement. See Sect. 1.3. When a state has a strong preference for sanctioning (i.e. a high preference intensity), this needs to be reflected in the expected benefits resulting from taking a countermeasure.

[103] The countermeasure is effective, if it achieves a change in behaviour of the target state, that is cessation of the wrongful act, and in the case of an injury, provision of reparation.

[104] On the distinction between material and political costs and why it is important to consider both in the cost-benefit calculation of sanctioning, see Thompson, "The Rational Enforcement of International Law: Solving the Sanctioners' Dilemma," 311–312.

[105] The compensation requirement and how this variable influences the outcome of the equation will be discussed in Sect. 7.3. For now, p(L) will be assumed to be zero.

[106] With regard to retaliation as a compliance mechanism, see Guzman, *How International Law Works: A Rational Choice Theory*, 46–48.

between accepting the wrongful act or taking a countermeasure, and thus weigh the payoffs associated with each option against another. Before having recourse to a countermeasure an injured state will compare, on the one hand, the expected benefits resulting from the probability of the countermeasure to successfully induce the target state to cease the wrongful act, if it is continuing, and provide reparation for the injury, and, on the other hand, the material and political costs of the countermeasure.[107] Between parties of a reciprocal agreement, the probability of an in-kind countermeasure being effective is relatively high, provided that the withdrawal of benefits is costly to the target state and the "shadow of the future" is sufficiently long. In repeated interactions, the credible threat of non-performance can be enough to induce compliance by the target state, as long as both parties have more to gain from ongoing cooperation than from immediate defection.[108] The potential material costs of a reciprocal countermeasure consist in the risk of losing the long-term cooperative benefits from the agreement. If the target state perceives the countermeasure as unjustified, this may set off "spirals of non-compliance", thus shortening the "shadow of the future", that is the costs of the entire treaty regime breaking down.[109] This can be the case when there is disagreement about whether the prior act was in breach of an international obligation and whether the countermeasure can be interpreted as proportionate. Yet, as mentioned in the previous section, proportionality will be relatively easy to observe and verify when the countermeasure consists in the breach of a reciprocal obligation, especially in the case of breach of a synallagmatic obligation. The procedural conditions (e.g. *sommation* and negotiation) and temporal safeguards enshrined in the conditions of countermeasure serve to further reduce the risk of breakdown of cooperation and thus to lower the material costs. The potential political costs of the countermeasure consist in the risk that other states in the international community (beyond the target state) perceive the countermeasure as opportunistic behaviour and not as a form of sincere enforcement in defence of international legal rules (i.e. negative reputation).[110] However, political costs of reciprocal countermeasures are rather low, because they are more likely to be perceived as proportionate and legitimate by the target state (and then probably also by international community). Thus, for a single injured state, the expected benefits of a countermeasure are likely to exceed the associated material and political costs provided that it consists in an in-kind countermeasure within the framework of

[107] Accordingly, the payoffs for accepting the wrongful are the result from the comparison between, on the one hand, the costs of non-compliance of the wrongdoing state (i.e. an ongoing wrongful act and the injury), which correspond to the forfeited expected benefits of a countermeasure, and the benefits of avoiding the material and political costs of the countermeasure.

[108] See, for instance, Guzman, *How International Law Works: A Rational Choice Theory*, 42–43.

[109] Behavioural insights also suggest that reciprocal non-compliance (i.e. negative reciprocity) may lead to counter-threats and the escalation of conflicts. See van Aaken and Simsek, "Rewarding in International Law," 232, 235.

[110] Thompson, "The Rational Enforcement of International Law: Solving the Sanctioners' Dilemma," 311–312.

a reciprocal agreement, where both states continue to profit from the benefits of ongoing cooperation.

Within the same scenario of a single injured state contemplating about whether to take a countermeasure against a target state which previously breached a private goods obligation, the payoffs change when the countermeasure relates to a private law obligation outside the reciprocal base treaty (e.g. economic sanctions). The retaliatory component of such "external" countermeasures (as opposed to "internal" countermeasures operating within reciprocal base treaty regime) increases primarily the associated material costs. For instance, the freezing of foreign assets and import/export restrictions targeting the foreign industry may also have negative effects on the domestic economy.[111] Retaliatory countermeasures may also diminish the prospects of future cooperation, in particular when they are perceived by the target state as being out of proportion compared to the prior wrongful act.[112] In addition, the political costs might be higher than for "internal" reciprocal countermeasures when the existence of a prior wrongful act is not clearly determined or deemed by the international community as a minor infringement of a private goods obligation, increasing the risk that the countermeasure will be judged as opportunistic and excessive. The problem is that the threat of retaliatory countermeasures is only credible if the sanctioning state succeeds in demonstrating a willingness to impose further costly sanctions in order to end an ongoing violation of international law.[113] The substantial short-term and long-term material costs of the retaliatory countermeasures explain why they often lack credibility and are often ineffective in inducing a change in the target state's behaviour.[114] That states have recourse to costly retaliatory countermeasures despite a lower probability of effectiveness requires reducing significantly the material costs, which is usually the case when the sanctioner is much more powerful and richer than the target state.[115] Theoretically, countermeasures "are the only means equally available (at least formally) to all [s] tates to pursue reparation for injuries suffered".[116] However, only powerful and rich states have the available means to sustain costly sanctions over a longer period of

[111] See also, Posner and Sykes, *Economic Foundations of International Law*, 130.

[112] Behavioural insights also suggest that external retaliatory penalties may be perceived as stigmatising, unfair or illegitimate, and may generate negative emotions such as feelings of hostility, which can result in the aggravation of conflicts. See van Aaken and Simsek, "Rewarding in International Law," 230–232. With reference, amongst others, to Hofer, "The Efficacy of Targeted Sanctions in Enforcing Compliance with International Law," 163–168. On how excessive retaliation may escalate a conflict, therefore arguing that countermeasures need to be well calibrated in order to ensure that defection is efficient and avoid instability of the broader treaty regime, see also Posner and Sykes, *Economic Foundations of International Law*, 131–132.

[113] Guzman, *How International Law Works: A Rational Choice Theory*, 47.

[114] See also, Posner and Sykes, *Economic Foundations of International Law*, 133. With reference to Gary Clyde Hufbauer et al., *Economic Sanctions Reconsidered*, 3rd ed. (Washington, DC: Peterson Institute for International Economics, 2007).

[115] Thompson, "The Rational Enforcement of International Law: Solving the Sanctioners' Dilemma," 317.

[116] Paddeu, "Countermeasures," para. 11.

time, thus rendering the threat of the countermeasure more credible and increasing the probability of the countermeasure being effective.[117] The advantage in the constellation of an injured state taking a retaliatory countermeasure against the author of prior wrongful act concerning a private goods obligation is that it internalises all the expected immediate benefits of the successful countermeasure, namely those deriving from cessation of the ongoing wrongful act and reparation for the injury. Thus, for a single injured state, the expected benefits of an "external" countermeasures are likely to exceed the associated material and political costs, if the prior wrongful act consisting in the violation of a private goods obligation is still ongoing (and reparation yet to be provided) and the sanctioning state has the power and financial means to sufficiently reduce the material costs of the in-kind countermeasure.

The second scenario to be analysed is that of a single injured state considering whether to take countermeasures against a target state which previously breached a GPG or CPR obligation. Examples are constellations of non-compliance with multilateral environmental obligations, where the immediate harm occurs, for instance, in the territorial waters of only one state, or with international human rights obligations causing physical harm to persons under the jurisdiction of only one particular state.[118] This scenario differs in that the possible countermeasures are not in-kind, as they can only affect private law obligations (e.g. unilateral withdrawal of trade benefits), and have therefore previously been described as cross-countermeasures. Compared to the "external" (retaliatory) in-kind countermeasures discussed before, the payoffs change such that recourse to countermeasures becomes less likely. While material costs remain high (and thus countermeasures only available for states with the necessary financial means and power), they are likely to increase even further due to the risk that non-in-kind countermeasures are not perceived as proportionate by the target state. At the same time, the potential political costs are lower as the international community might value the countermeasure as necessary and sincere enforcement of international legal obligations in the public dimension due to their own interest in compliance with the obligation violated by the target state, especially when the obligation protected fundamental interests of the international community (i.e. *jus cogens* norms) and the violation was egregious.[119] What shifts the payoffs towards a more pessimistic prognosis about countermeasures taken in the case of breach of a GPG or CPR obligation is that the probability of effectiveness of the countermeasure is lower as an injured state only partially internalises the immediate expected benefits of the measure, namely reparation of injury, whereas cessation of the wrongful act is beneficial for all states in the

[117]This is also because the countermeasure increases the costs of sustained non-compliance for the target state, in addition to the costs of reparation for injury ultimately to be paid to the sanctioning state.

[118]See Article 42 lit. b) (i) ARSIWA.

[119]Thompson, "The Rational Enforcement of International Law: Solving the Sanctioners' Dilemma," 317.

international community without contributing to the countermeasure and thus limiting the credibility of the threat. Hence, incentives for a single injured state to take cross-countermeasures in the case of breach of a GPG or CPR obligation are limited and these are only expected to be taken if the prior wrongful act is still ongoing (and reparation yet to be provided) and the sanctioning state has the power and financial means to sufficiently reduce the material costs of the countermeasure

The incentives for cross-countermeasures differ significantly when multiple states are injured by the breach of a GPG or CPR obligation, in particular when these are interdependent obligations breach of which affects all other parties to the agreement (e.g. arms control treaties).[120] The decision of an injured state to have recourse to countermeasures is no longer a binary one, but a strategic interaction with all other injured states affected by the prior wrongful act. All injured states can individually invoke the responsibility of the wrongdoing state and claim reparation for their respective injury, so that no joint action is needed (i.e. provision of an aggregate GPG). Yet, since each injured state internalises at least the benefits of cessation of the wrongful act (and future compliance), they face incentives to free-ride on the enforcement efforts of other injured states willing to accept the costs of taking a cross-countermeasure. This constellation is the previously described sanctioners' dilemma, which is a second-order prisoner's dilemma.[121] It is aggravated the more states are directly affected by a breach of a GPG or CPR obligation, for instance, in the case of pollution or destruction of CPRs a large number of states are injured *pro ratio*. Hence, there is, in principle, no incentive for injured states to take countermeasures, as the probability of the countermeasure being effective is extremely low and the associated material and political costs often become prohibitively high,[122] thus most likely exceeding the expected benefits.[123] Nonetheless, cross-countermeasures in the case of breach of a GPG or CPR obligation can be expected to be taken on an exceptional basis, if the prior wrongful act is still ongoing (and reparation yet to be provided) and the sanctioning state has the power and financial means to sufficiently reduce the material costs of the countermeasure. This will be either a single injured state or a group of injured states (a *k-group*), when the share of the expected benefits (including the long-term benefits supplied by the relevant treaty regime) exceeds the material and political costs of providing enforcement as a global public good (i.e. best-effort or best-shot GPG).[124] Further reduction of the material and political costs (that is, beyond a powerful and rich state volunteering to take the countermeasure, and high international support especially in case of serious

---

[120] See Article 42 lit. b) (ii) ARSIWA.

[121] Thompson, "The Rational Enforcement of International Law: Solving the Sanctioners' Dilemma," 311. On retaliation as an enforcement mechanism in international law, see also Sect. 2.4.

[122] There is no variation in the material and political costs compared to the scenario where a single injured state is considering whether to take a countermeasure against a target state which previously breached a GPG or CPR obligation.

[123] Guzman, *How International Law Works: A Rational Choice Theory*, 66–68, 138.

[124] On different types of global public goods in terms of their provision, see Sect. 2.2.

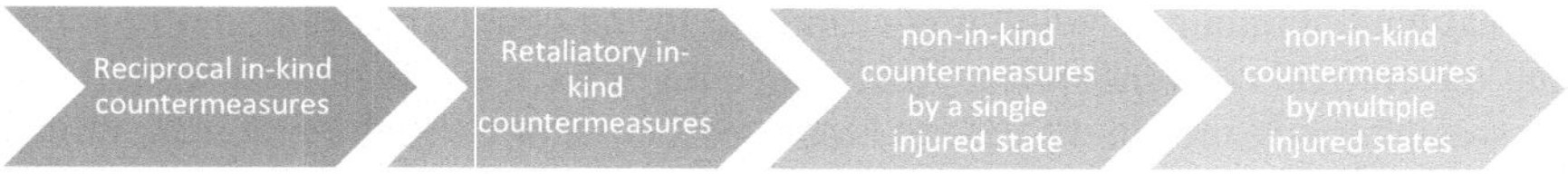

Fig. 7.2 Incentives for injured states to take countermeasures

violations of *jus cogens* norms) would require a facilitating role of international institutions which would authorise the countermeasure beforehand, and thereby facilitate cost-sharing between the injured states taking the countermeasures and increase acceptance by the international community.[125] It is also important that the effectiveness of countermeasures requires the absence of a weakest-link deliberately frustrating, for instance, a trade embargo.

Another option, especially in scenarios where only few states are directly affected by the breach of a GPG or CPR obligation, but the international community has an interest in compliance (e.g. human rights or environmental treaties), could be to authorise also interested third states to take countermeasures against the state that committed the prior wrongful act. This could increase the effectiveness of enforcement especially when the rich and powerful state or states capable of providing the public good are not directly injured. This will be analysed in the following section.

Figure 7.2 summarises the main findings of this section and presents the different scenarios in which states might contemplate about whether to take countermeasures and how the incentives to do so decrease with each variation (from left to right). Incentives for first-party countermeasures vary in particular depending on whether the countermeasures are internal (i.e. reciprocal) or external (i.e. retaliatory) to the base treaty, whether the initial wrongful act concerned a private goods obligation (i.e. in-kind countermeasures) or a GPG/CPR obligation (i.e. non-in-kind countermeasures), and whether one or multiple injured states consider taking countermeasures.

7.2.2 *Third-party Countermeasures: Conditions for Non-directly Injured States Protecting Community Interests*

We have seen that first-party countermeasures are less likely to be effective when the prior wrongful act consists in the breach of a GPG or CPR obligation because multiple injured states need to cooperate to overcome the sanctioners' dilemma. This section will analyse the incentives in GPG/CPR constellations for non-directly injured third states defending community interests, and thus cooperating to provide the GPG of law enforcement.

[125] Thompson, "The Rational Enforcement of International Law: Solving the Sanctioners' Dilemma," 309, 317–318.

Non-directly injured states are defined in Article 48(1) ARSIWA as states that are entitled to invoke the responsibility of another state in case of breach of an *erga omnes* or *erga omnes partes* obligation (i.e. obligation owed to the international community as a whole or established for the protection of a collective interest of a group of states). The doctrinal concepts of *erga omnes* and *erga omnes partes* obligations and the extent to which they are congruent with cooperation problems on the international level have been analysed in detail in Chap. 3.[126] In short, they relate to specific second-order cooperation problems in constellations where the first-order cooperation problem underlying the primary obligation that has been breached by the wrongdoing state has (global) public goods or common pool resource characteristics. Obligations that are owed to the international community as a whole (i.e. *erga omnes*) or established for the protection of a collective interest of a group of states (i.e. *erga omnes partes*) create a corresponding right of performance for all states in the international community or for all group members. All—participating—states thus benefit from and have a legal interest in compliance with *erga omnes (partes)* obligations as they constitute an essential element of the international legal order (i.e. a global interest in compliance) or the objective legal order created by the multilateral treaty regime. From this non-reciprocal compliance structure derives that *erga omnes (partes)* obligations relate to goods that are non-excludable and non-rival in consumption. In terms of second-order enforcement problems, *erga omnes* obligations can be equated with GPG obligations. *Erga omnes partes* obligations, however, as the right to performance is limited to the members of the group, cannot be characterised GPGs, but rather—depending on the composition of its members—regional or mere transnational public goods. *Erga omnes partes* obligations can also have club goods characteristics, if the treaty regime has been established, amongst others, with the objective to further the provision of public goods, while providing the possibility to enforce compliance with the threat of outcasting from other benefits of the club (e.g. trading benefits).

According to Article 54 ARSIWA, a non-directly injured state may take "lawful" measures against the responsible state to ensure cessation of the breach and reparation in the interest of the injured state or of the beneficiaries of the obligation breached.[127] Thus, a strict reading of the provision suggests that measures of an indirectly injured state acting in the interest of the international community are limited to retorsions. Hence, non-directly injured states cannot take countermeasures in the sense of the ARSIWA, but only unfriendly lawful measures. These can consist, for instance, in the reduction or discontinuation of diplomatic relations (e.g. expulsion of diplomatic staff and temporary embassy closure), exclusion of foreign nationals from international sport events, or economic sanctions provided

[126] On public enforcement of international state responsibility, see Sect. 3.3.3.

[127] Article 54 ARSIWA reads: "This chapter does not prejudice the right of any State, entitled under article 48, paragraph 1, to invoke the responsibility of another State, to take lawful measures against that State to ensure cessation of the breach and reparation in the interest of the injured State or of the beneficiaries of the obligation breached."

they are as unilateral sanctions not violating trade agreements or as collective sanctions have been authorised by the UN Security Council under Chapter VII of the UN Charter.[128] The limitation to "lawful" measures means that the exemption from state responsibility for intrinsically unlawful countermeasures laid down as a justifying circumstance precluding wrongfulness in Article 22 ARSIWA does not apply.[129]

Whether states other than a directly injured state have the right to take third-party countermeasures is, however, highly controversial.[130] There had been strong differences of opinion in the ILC and among UN member states in the Sixth Committee (i.e. the legal committee of the General Assembly).[131] At the time of the adoption of the ARSIWA, practice of unilateral measures, taken individually or collectively with other interested non-directly injured states outside institutional frameworks, was considered "limited and rather embryonic".[132] Other sources of controversy were, firstly, the large number of states which might potentially be entitled to take countermeasures without setting sufficiently clear conditions, in particular a certain threshold of gravity of the breach, and, secondly, uncertainties regarding the subsidiarity of third-party countermeasures to the institutional framework of the UN Security Council allowing for sanctions under Chapter VII UN Charter to maintain international peace and security.[133] All this explains why the ILC finally opted for

---

[128] On sanctions, in particular, see Alain Pellet and Alina Miron, "Sanctions," ed. Anne Peters and Rüdiger Wolfrum, *Max Planck Encyclopedia of Public International Law* (Oxford Public International Law: Oxford University Press, 2021), http://opil.ouplaw.com, Article last updated in August 2013.

[129] At the same time, Article 22 ARSIWA does not exclude the possibility of countermeasures by a non-directly injured state. ARSIWA Commentaries, Article 22, para. 6.

[130] Crawford, *State Responsibility: the General Part*, 703. Crawford uses the term 'collective countermeasures' to discuss countermeasures by non-directly injured states acting in the public interest, but also countermeasures by a plurality of injured states. United Nations International Law Commission, *Third Report on State Responsibility by Special Rapporteur James Crawford*, Fifty-Second Session, 2000 (UN Doc. A/CN.4/507), pp. 101–102, para. 386. In order to clearly distinguish these two constellations, the term third-party countermeasures will be used to describe "peaceful unilateral coercive measures adopted by a non-directly injured State in defence of the public interest and not otherwise justified under international law." Martin Dawidowicz, "Public Law Enforcement without Public Law Safeguards? An Analysis of State Practice on Third-Party Countermeasures and Their Relationship to the UN Security Council," *British Yearbook of International Law* 77, no. 1 (2007): 333.

[131] Paddeu, "Countermeasures," para. 39. See also United Nations International Law Commission, Fourth Report on State Responsibility by Special Rapporteur James Crawford, Fifty-Third Session, 2001 (UN Doc. A/CN.4/517), p. 18, para. 72. ("The thrust of Government comments is that article 54, and especially paragraph 2, has no basis in international law and would be destabilizing. This is stressed both by those Governments which are generally worried about the 'subjectivity' and risks of abuse inherent in the taking of countermeasures, and by those who are more supportive of countermeasures as a vehicle for resolving disputes about responsibility.")

[132] ARSIWA Commentary, Article 54, paras. 2–3.

[133] Linos-Alexander Sicilianos, "Countermeasures in Response to Grave Violations of Obligations Owed to the International Community," in *The Law of International Responsibility*, ed. James Crawford, Alain Pellet, and Simon Olleson (Oxford: Oxford University Press, 2010), 1138–1142.

the introduction of a saving clause in Article 54 ARSIWA.[134] This clause essentially says that the provisions in the ARSIWA do not prejudice the right of interested third states to take lawful measures.[135] The question whether and under which conditions non-directly injured states can take countermeasures remains highly relevant, in particular when collective enforcement by the UN Security Council fails.[136] It has been argued in the literature that there actually exists a widespread practice of countermeasures adopted by indirectly injured states in the interest of the international community and that a right of third states to take countermeasures in the case of serious violations of obligations *erga omnes* should be recognised.[137] Other authors have pointed to the risk of abuse of such a right to third-party countermeasures[138] or underlined the problem of power asymmetries between states (i.e. the fear of smaller states that more powerful states will engage in excessive self-help despite being only indirectly affected).[139] The key question is thus which safeguards are needed to prevent the misuse of third-party countermeasures. Yet, until today the issue of legality of third-party countermeasures remains open,[140] in particular due to the continued resistance of several states (e.g. China, Russia, and Iran).[141]

From an economic perspective, the analysis focuses on why and under which conditions one can expect non-directly injured states to take countermeasures given

---

[134] ARSIWA Commentary, Article 54, para. 6.

[135] ARSIWA Commentary, Article 54, para. 7.

[136] Feichtner, "Community Interest," para. 55.

[137] Sicilianos, "Countermeasures in Response to Grave Violations of Obligations Owed to the International Community," in *The Law of International Responsibility*, ed. Crawford, Pellet, and Olleson, 1145–1148. See further, in particular, Tams, *Enforcing Obligations Erga Omnes in International Law*; Katselli Proukaki, *The Problem of Enforcement in International Law: Countermeasures, the Non-Injured State and the Idea of International Community*; Martin Dawidowicz, *Third-Party Countermeasures in International Law* (Cambridge: Cambridge University Press, 2017). See also, Frowein, "Obligations Erga Omnes," para. 11. ("Where a widely acknowledged grave breach of an erga omnes obligation occurs, all the States to which the obligation is owed shall endeavour to bring the breach to an end through lawful means in accordance with the Charter of the United Nations. They shall not recognize as lawful a situation created by the breach, and are entitled to take non-forcible countermeasures under conditions analogous to those applying to a State specially affected by the breach.") With reference to Institut de Droit International, *Obligations Erga Omnes in International Law*, Resolution, Krakow Session (2005), Article 5. See also, Dupuy, "Back to the Future of a Multilateral Dimension of the Law of State Responsibility for Breaches of 'Obligations Owed to the International Community as a Whole'," 1059–1069. See also, Posner and Sykes, *Economic Foundations of International Law*, 138. ("But the rule that authorizes such intervention may have sound justification when the conduct in question is clearly undesirable [...].")

[138] The risk of abuse is mentioned as an objection, for instance, by Feichtner, "Community Interest," para. 55.

[139] Pauwelyn, *Optimal Protection of International Law: Navigating between European Absolutism and American Voluntarism*, 191–193.

[140] Paddeu, "Countermeasures," para. 40.

[141] See, with further references, Paparinskis, "The Once and Future Law of State Responsibility," 624.

that already multiple injured states face a sanctioners' dilemma, while taking into account the difference between "lawful" measures and *prima facie* "unlawful" countermeasures in the cost-benefit calculation of states.

Compared to injured states (i.e. those directly affected by a breach of a GPG or CPR obligation), non-directly injured states expect benefits not in the form of reparation of the injury (which can only be claimed in the interest of the injured state or of the beneficiaries of the obligation breached), but only in the form of cessation of the wrongful act. Since *erga omnes (partes)* obligations constitute an essential element of the international legal order (i.e. a global interest in compliance) or the objective legal order created by the multilateral treaty regime, all—participating—states have a strong legal interest in compliance. They certainly derive more benefits from compliance with such an obligation than with private law obligations between an injured state and the target state. The problem here is that these benefits of upholding the international legal order or the stability of the treaty regime are shared among all states of the international community (or the treaty regime in question) due to the global or transnational public goods characteristics. Hence, each non-directly injured third state has incentives to free-ride on the efforts of other non-directly injured states taking a cross-countermeasure in the community interest by accepting the associated costs. Like injured states directly affected by the breach of the GPG or CPR obligation, third states in the international community thus face a sanctioners' dilemma, which reduces the credibility of the threat and thus renders the probability of effectiveness of countermeasures very low. However, extending to indirectly injured states the right to take *prima facie* "unlawful" measures to induce compliance with a GPG/CPR obligation (and not only "lawful" measures) should have an impact on the deterrent effect. A rationalist approach would see the difference between retorsions and cross-countermeasures in the different extent to which they can impose higher costs on the target state (and thus increase the probability of being effective).

At the same time, interested third states taking a countermeasure have to fully internalise the associated costs. As with regard to previously analysed scenarios, material and political costs of cross-countermeasures are high and likely to increase further if the existence of a prior wrongful act is disputed and the countermeasure is perceived as disproportionate by the target state. Compared to unfriendly lawful measures (i.e. retorsions), the legal possibility to take countermeasures (i.e. justified violations of international private law obligations), might have a higher deterrent effect for the target state, but they also come with higher material and political costs for the indirectly injured state, due to the risk to set off "spirals of non-compliance" potentially leading to the breakdown of other cooperative regimes. These risks are for the moment aggravated by the uncertainty which results from the unresolved issue about the legality of third-party countermeasures.

The question is therefore under which conditions we would expect third-party countermeasures to take place despite the sanctioners' dilemma, that is, under which conditions the material and political costs are sufficiently low. Firstly, this can depend on the underlying scenario. On the one hand, there is the relatively uncontroversial scenario where an injured state (e.g. the victim on an armed attack or of a human rights violation of nationals by a foreign state) requests assistance by other non-directly injured states in taking countermeasures against the target state.[142] Here, an analogy can be drawn to collective self-defence, suggesting that non-forcible countermeasures by other members of the international community should be possible if requested by an injured state in addition to the cross-countermeasures taken by the injured state itself.[143] Otherwise, according to Crawford, the state being victim of a breach of a multilateral obligation will be left alone in seeking redress at the level of implementation.[144] A consequence of power asymmetries is that retaliatory countermeasures will often be only taken by powerful and rich states. Weaker or poorer injured states may not have sufficient financial means to afford the necessary material costs and thus to credibly maintain the threat of sustaining countermeasures over a longer period of time. Hence, serious breaches of *erga omnes* norms may be left without redress, if weaker states could not request support by other interested indirectly injured states in the international community.[145] In this scenario, it is relatively likely that one or few like-minded states or members of the same alliance are willing to bear the material costs of the third-party countermeasures and achieve to increase their effectiveness by acting collectively in a coordinated manner (e.g. the Russian aggression against Ukraine). This argument can be extended to CPR constellations, where injured states (e.g. a coastal state particularly affected by oil pollution in the high seas and small island states affected by rising sea levels due to climate change) request assistance by other indirectly injured states. On the other hand, there are scenarios where no state is injured in the sense of being directly affected by the breach.[146] These can be GPG constellations where serious human rights violations have a purely internal dimension, as in the case of torture against own citizens or genocide against a minority of the population of that state. Here, all states of the international community are only indirectly

[142] Crawford, *State Responsibility: the General Part*, 704.

[143] Ibid. However, as much as collective self-defence is excluded without the consent of the victim state, according to Crawford, it does not seem appropriate that a third state can take countermeasures irrespective of the wishes of the victim state. United Nations International Law Commission, *Third Report on State Responsibility by Special Rapporteur James Crawford*, Fifty-Second Session, 2000 (UN Doc. A/CN.4/507), p. 105, para. 400.

[144] Crawford, *State Responsibility: the General Part*, 704. United Nations International Law Commission, *Third Report on State Responsibility by Special Rapporteur James Crawford*, Fifty-Second Session, 2000 (UN Doc. A/CN.4/507), p. 105, para. 400.

[145] Dawidowicz, "Public Law Enforcement without Public Law Safeguards? An Analysis of State Practice on Third-Party Countermeasures and Their Relationship to the UN Security Council," 336–337.

[146] Ibid., 336.

injured in their compliance interest with human rights obligations (i.e. non-use value GPGs).[147] Other scenarios relate to the preservation of CPRs as in serious violations of obligations stemming from international environmental law, for instance, large-scale pollution of the high seas or excessive overfishing. Here, all states in the international community are indirectly affected in their compliance interest similar to GPG constellations because they value the preservation of the common resource.[148] Alternatively, due to the characteristic of rivalry in consumption, all states could even be considered injured *pro rata*. It could be seen with regard to remedies, that the spread of the damage over a large number of victim states can lead to a problem of "rational apathy". Considering all states in the international community as partially injured states would at least open the possibly to obtain reparation for damage and thus increase incentives to invoke responsibility and, eventually, take countermeasures individually or collectively. Otherwise, in the absence of an injured state, provision of the public good of law enforcement by recourse to third-party countermeasures in the interest of individual beneficiaries in other states or for the mere interest of compliance will be difficult to achieve, both in CPR and GPG constellations. Thus, breaching *erga omnes* obligations implicates for the responsible state a certain additional cost, if non-directly injured states could also take countermeasures (without or in addition to the injured states), provided that there is a state or coalition of states willing to bear the associated material costs.[149]

Secondly, third-party countermeasures require that the potential political costs are sufficiently low, otherwise we cannot expect powerful and richer states to bear the material costs of enforcing compliance in the collective interest and reparation in the interest of a "weak" injured state or individual beneficiaries. For the sanctioning state, it is important that countermeasures receive wide support from the international community in order to build a reputation as a sincere enforcer of international

[147] For an invocation of state responsibility for breach of the Torture Convention as an *erga omnes partes* obligation, see *Questions Relating to the Obligation to Prosecute or Extradite (Belgium v. Senegal)*, Judgment, p. 450, para. 69. For an invocation of state responsibility for breach of the Genocide Convention as an *erga omnes partes* obligation, see *Application of the Convention on the Prevention and Punishment of the Crime of Genocide (The Gambia v. Myanmar)*, Order (Provisional Measures), p. 17, paras. 41–42; *Application of the Convention on the Prevention and Punishment of the Crime of Genocide in the Gaza Strip (South Africa v. Israel)*, Order (Provisional Measures), p. 12, para. 33.

[148] For an example in the context of the preservation of marine mammals and the marine environment, see *Whaling in the Antarctic (Australia v. Japan: New Zealand Intervening)*, Judgment, p. 246, paras. 40–41. With regard to obligations relating to the preservation of the environment of the high seas and in the Area, see also *Responsibilities and Obligations of States with Respect to Activities in the Area*, Advisory Opinion, p. 59, para. 180.

[149] See also Eric A. Posner, defining *erga omnes* norms as "facilitat[ing] collective enforcement of norms that create public goods [...] by making clear that certain aggressive acts that would otherwise appear to be violations of two-party norms are, in fact, permissible attempts to participate in collective action" and thus arguing that "by giving states a right to punish states that violate erga omnes norms, international law reduces, or at least avoids exacerbating, the problem of free riding when the violation of a norm injures many states rather than just one." Posner, "Erga Omnes Norms, Institutionalization, and Constitutionalism in International Law," 13–14.

legal obligations in the public dimension and to avoid the negative perception of being an opportunistic state pursuing selfish goals under the disguise of countermeasures.[150] Indirectly injured states will face a higher scrutiny than directly injured states and may thus limit their interventions to cases of serious breaches of *erga omnes* obligations, where gathering sufficient support from the international audience is more likely.[151] Limiting third-party countermeasures to serious breaches of GPG and CPR violations (e.g. of a gross and systematic nature) is also a means to prevent abusive invocation. Similarly to the argument made with regard to the collective obligations in Article 41 ARSIWA, it is suggested here not to restrict third-party countermeasures to situations stemming from the breach of *jus cogens* norms as normative GPGs, but to apply them also to violations of other GPG and CPR obligations (in particular, international environmental law), as their protection is an important objective of the law of state responsibility.[152] However, since third-party countermeasures give a right to take *prima facie* unlawful measures, a limitation to breaches of a certain gravity is justified. The consequence is that in the case of non-serious breaches of GPG and CPR obligations the political costs for third-party countermeasures are likely to be too high, so that indirectly injured states may limit their enforcement efforts to "lawful" measures.

Finally, the question remains which safeguards exist to prevent the misuse of third-party countermeasures. As could be seen, the problem of third-party countermeasures is primarily to overcome the sanctioners' dilemma, and thus to prevent inaction of the international community in the face of mass atrocities, but since this instrument is factually only available to powerful states, safeguards are needed to avoid abuse. In addition to the limitation to serious breaches of *erga omnes* obligations, third-party countermeasures need to respect a number of conditions outlined above, namely prohibition of the use of force, exclusion of breach of GPG and CPR obligations, requirement of proportionality, procedural and temporal conditions.[153] These are subject to an *ex post* control with the burden of proof falling on the interested state taking third-party countermeasures. The most effective way is to require a prior authorisation of countermeasures by an international institution, because this helps to reduce uncertainty regarding the legality of the measure, to build a positive reputation of sincere enforcement and, eventually, facilitate cost-sharing among participating states. This is the rationale underlying the collective sanctions regime in Chapter VII of the UN Charter, requiring prior authorisation of the UN Security Council. However, there will be instances where the UN Security Council is paralysed by a veto power, for instance, when one of the veto powers is

[150] Guzman, *How International Law Works: A Rational Choice Theory*, 46–47.

[151] Thompson, "The Rational Enforcement of International Law: Solving the Sanctioners' Dilemma," 317. This is also in line with the proportionality requirement (Article 51 ARSIWA) which provides that countermeasures must be commensurate with the injury suffered, taking into account the gravity of the internationally wrongful act and the rights in question.

[152] See Sect. 6.4.

[153] See also Dawidowicz, *Third-Party Countermeasures in International Law*, chap. 6.

directly involved in the conflict (e.g. Russian aggression against Ukraine). In light of these limitations, third-party countermeasures should remain possible as a subsidiary option to the institutional response foreseen in the UN Charter. One possibility to reduce abuse could be to ask for a UN General Assembly Resolution with a majority of states voting in favour, along the lines of the Uniting for Peace Resolution.[154] This could facilitate collective action in the form of a coalition of the willing, that is states cooperating on an *ad hoc* basis or within informal institutions (e.g. the G7). A coordinated response creates higher transaction costs, but might still be preferable to indirectly injured states acting unilaterally. In many instances, in particular economic sanctions, unilateral countermeasures will not be sufficient to effectively induce a change in the target state's behaviour as there are many possibilities to circumvent the sanctions. In the end, a trade-off needs to be made between restricting third-party actions to lawful measures, that is retorsions, in order to avoid abuse or allowing unilateral countermeasures in exceptional circumstances, namely serious breaches of *erga omnes* obligations and inaction of the UN Security Council. An alternative means to reduce the residual risk of abuse is the third cost variable in the equation above: the requirement to compensate any material losses (L) that result from countermeasures.[155]

7.3 The Financial Consequences of Countermeasures: The Compensation Requirement and Third-party Effects of Countermeasures

Article 27 lit. b) ARSIWA provides as a financial consequence of invoking a circumstance precluding wrongfulness that compensation needs to be paid for any material loss caused by the act in question. The rationale and genesis of this general compensation requirement in the ARSIWA have been presented in detail in Chap. 5 above with regard to the other circumstances precluding wrongfulness, in particular the necessity excuse.[156] In brief, the rationale of this provision is that sometimes a state relying on a circumstance precluding wrongfulness may nonetheless be expected to make good any material loss suffered by a state affected by that act.[157] Hence, this provision determines that and how the cost incurred following the invocation of a circumstance precluding wrongfulness are allocated between the states involved (i.e. the adjustment of losses).[158] However, in the absence of

[154] United Nations General Assembly, Resolution 377 (V), Uniting for Peace, 3 November 1950 (UN Doc. A/RES/377(V)).

[155] See Sect. 7.2.1.4.

[156] See, in particular, Sect. 5.2.3 on the allocation of costs following the invocation of necessity.

[157] ARSIWA Commentaries, Article 27, para. 4. See also Crawford, *State Responsibility: the General Part*, 318.

[158] ARSIWA Commentaries, Article 27, para. 4.

consensus in the ILC about which circumstances precluding wrongfulness should induce an obligation to compensate the affected state for any material loss, and whether this obligation also extends to innocent third states,[159] these questions had been deliberatively left open when the ARSIWA were finalised, with the compensation requirement in Article 27 lit. b) ARSIWA being framed in general terms as a without prejudice clause.[160] Yet, it was already clear at that time that compensation for material losses was not appropriate for all six circumstances precluding wrongfulness. By taking an economic perspective on the six circumstances precluding wrongfulness, Chapter 5 sketched out constellations in which compensation can be considered appropriate.[161] Whether the compensation requirement in Article 27 lit. b) ARSIWA is economically justified depends effectively on the underlying economic rationale of each justification or excuse. This section thus aims to offer some guidance in abstract terms based on economic theory on when and how compensation should be paid in scenarios where directly or indirectly injured states have recourse to countermeasures. As a refined interpretation of Article 27 lit. b) ARSIWA, these insights can serve as guidance for states negotiating the matter of compensation in a given dispute, or even more generally when negotiating treaties including countermeasures as a compliance mechanism (i.e. guidelines for treaty design).

Regarding the compensation requirement, countermeasures share the logic of consent and self-defence in that it seems difficult to justify compensation for losses since the circumstance precluding wrongfulness emanates reciprocally from a prior action of the target state, in this case a prior wrongful act.[162] Like for self-defence, the economic rationale of countermeasures is that the cost burden is placed on the target state as the cheapest cost avoider in order to set incentives for compliance. Compensating the author of the prior wrongful act would contradict the function of countermeasures as a unilateral implementation tool. Unlike for necessity or other excuses, the injured state should thus not be obliged to pay compensation for material loss caused to the target state which violated an international obligation in the first place. This requires, however, that the conditions for an act to be justified as a countermeasure need to be sufficiently strict. As outlined above, countermeasures

---

159 Crawford, *State Responsibility: the General Part*, 319. See also United Nations International Law Commission, *Second Report on State Responsibility by Special Rapporteur James Crawford*, Fifty-First Session, 1999 (UN Doc. A/CN.4/498), pp. 84–85, paras. 340, 348.

160 ARSIWA Commentaries, Article 27, paras. 1, 6. Forteau, "Reparation in the Event of a Circumstance Precluding Wrongfulness," in *The Law of International Responsibility*, ed. Crawford, Pellet, and Olleson, 892.

161 See above Sect. 5.4 concluding the economic analysis of the five other circumstances precluding wrongfulness.

162 Crawford, *State Responsibility: the General Part*, 319. Consequently, countermeasures (and self-defence) were explicitly excluded from compensation in the Draft Article 35 adopted on first reading, see Forteau, "Reparation in the Event of a Circumstance Precluding Wrongfulness," in *The Law of International Responsibility*, ed. Crawford, Pellet, and Olleson, 892. See also United Nations International Law Commission, *Second Report on State Responsibility by Special Rapporteur James Crawford*, Fifty-First Session, 1999 (UN Doc. A/CN.4/498), pp. 83–84, paras. 338, 344.

are excluded when they impair GPG and CPR obligations, they need to be necessary and proportionate and respect certain procedural requirements and temporal limits. A countermeasure not respecting these limits, for instance, because it consists in recourse to the use of force, is not justified and engages the responsibility of the state injured by the initial wrongful act. The possible consequence is an obligation to pay reparation for damage caused to the state author of the prior wrongful act, although the amount may be adjusted to the extent that the latter contributed to the injury (Article 39 ARSIWA). The obligation to provide reparation in case of an internationally wrongful act reduces the risk of abuse of the justification as it limits the countermeasure to what is necessary and proportionate to induce compliance with the secondary obligations of cessation and reparation.

The costs of countermeasures may, however, be allocated differently when they have collateral effects on innocent third parties (that is, third states or entities or persons within these states). In such a scenario, compensation may be warranted with regard to innocent third states suffering loss from countermeasures directed against the target state.[163] In fact, mitigating collateral damage seems appropriate given that these third states are not the author of the original wrongful act. Article 49 (1) ARSIWA states specifically that an injured state may only take countermeasures against a state which is responsible for an internationally wrongful act. Similar to consent, countermeasures can thus not excuse breach of international obligations owed to other states than the author of the wrongful act.[164] A violation of third-party rights constitutes an internationally wrongful act engaging the responsibility of the state injured by the prior wrongful act, and thus leading, amongst others, to the obligation to provide reparation to the affected state (Article 31 ARSIWA). In addition, I have argued above that countermeasures affecting GPG and CPR obligations are excluded,[165] precisely because they infringe rights of third states in the international community, and are thus not an adequate tool to implement state responsibility and induce compliance of the target state. Third-party effects of countermeasures falling under the compensation requirement in Article 27 lit. b) ARSIWA are thus those which fall below the threshold of breaching an international private law obligation owed the third state and consist rather in an impairment of interests (not rights) of these third states.[166] The countermeasure is only a justified breach of a private law obligation owed to the target state, but any harm (or material

[163] See, in particular, Crawford, *State Responsibility: the General Part*, 319–320; Forteau, "Reparation in the Event of a Circumstance Precluding Wrongfulness," in *The Law of International Responsibility*, ed. Crawford, Pellet, and Olleson, 893.

[164] This is different from self-defence which is not generally excluded with regard to third states, but the effects of actions in self-defence on obligations protecting the rights of innocent third states (i.e. private good or club good obligations) need to be taken into account when assessing the lawfulness. See above Sect. 5.3.2.2.

[165] In addition to the fundamental obligations in international law enumerated explicitly in Article 50 ARSIWA and *jus cogens* obligations as derived from Article 26 ARSIWA.

[166] Paddeu, "Countermeasures," para. 41. ARSIWA Commentaries, Article 22, paras. 4–5, Article 49, paras. 4–5.

losses) which might occur as a side-effect to innocent third states, that is as negative externalities, should be mitigated through compensation. Examples could be negative side-effects of economic sanctions which impact third countries that also have economic ties with the target state (e.g. supply chain disruptions and increases in food or energy prices) or an overflight ban which *de facto* also cuts an innocent neighbouring country from air traffic with the target state. Following the same logic as self-defence, such a compensation requirement would induce a state taking countermeasures to price in the associated costs on innocent by-standers and ultimately to better target the measure to the author of the prior wrongful act. The focus of the compensation requirement thus lies on how to deal with adverse effects on innocent third states and on setting incentives to internalise these external costs of countermeasures.

The remaining question is how much compensation can be considered optimal. While compensation has the advantage of setting incentives for states taking countermeasures to internalise negative externality costs on innocent third parties and thus to better target the measure, it may also deter the injured state from taking countermeasures in the first place, because the costs of retaliatory action become prohibitive. Full compensation also increases the sanctioners' dilemma when multiple states are injured by a prior breach of a GPG or CPR obligation and may thus shift the cost-benefit calculation towards not taking the countermeasure. Shifting the costs of compensation partially to the author of the prior wrongful act as the cheapest cost avoider would be an economically justified solution. The remaining costs could then be shared voluntarily among the injured states profiting from the countermeasure taken by other injured states. Injured states free-riding on the countermeasures of other injured states should, however, not be considered innocent third states in relation to each other, and thus may not claim compensation in case of material losses. Cost-sharing between injured states would mean in practice that the state taking countermeasures and having to pay compensation to an innocent third state should have the possibility to claim regress against other benefitting injured states, assuming that they are easily identifiable.

The underlying economic rationale against compensating the target state and in favour of sharing the costs resulting from the compensation of innocent third states with the target state as the cheapest cost avoider does not change in the case of third-party countermeasures by non-directly injured states acting in the collective interest. Yet, especially in this scenario, even partial compensation may increase the costs for the sanctioning state such that they become prohibitive and third-party countermeasures are not taken at all. In addition, cost allocation between the large number of indirectly injured states profiting from the countermeasure in response to a prior serious breach of an *erga omnes* obligation (i.e. an underlying GPG or CPR constellation) may create high administrative costs with the risk that they will, in practice, have to be born entirely by the indirectly injured state taking the countermeasure in the collective interest. An alternative means to remediate this problem could be to operate with international trust funds.[167] When non-directly injured

[167] See the discussion in Sect. 5.2.3.2 on compensation in the case of public necessity.

states take third-party countermeasures for the protection of a GPG or CPR, the *ultima ratio* could be to envisage an exemption from the requirement to compensate innocent states benefitting *pro rata*, unless non-compensation would in a concrete case create a disproportionate burden for the innocent state.

In conclusion, first-party and third-party countermeasures should not give rise to an obligation to provide compensation for material losses towards the target state. This is because the purpose of the justification is to implement state responsibility of the target state being the author of the prior wrongful act, and thus the cheapest cost avoider, and to induce compliance with secondary obligations and in the future. An exception to this cost allocation relates to material losses incurred by innocent third states. In this scenario, the compensation requirement can induce the state taking countermeasures to internalise any harmful side-effects (i.e. externalities) and thus to better target the measure. However, in order not to deter multiple directly or indirectly injured states further from taking countermeasures due to the sanctioners' dilemma, cost-sharing arrangements for the financial consequences are necessary. Costs could be shared, on the one hand, with the target state being the author of the prior wrongful act, and, on the other hand, with other injured states profiting from the countermeasures by way of recourse or with a trust fund solution among indirectly injured states. An exemption from the compensation requirement in the case of third-party countermeasures, because innocent states benefit *pro rata*, can only be an *ultima ratio* solution, under the condition that in a concrete case it does not create a disproportionate burden for the innocent state. Therefore, regarding the financial consequences of countermeasures laid down in Article 27 lit. b) ARSIWA more differentiation is needed to account for the rationale, the side-effects and the costs associated with first-party and third-party countermeasures involving multiple states.

7.4 Conclusion on Countermeasures in International Law

This chapter analysed the incentive structures in the law of state responsibility with regard to the decision to have recourse to countermeasures in response to an internationally wrongful act. Against the objective of countermeasures to induce compliance with the obligations of cessation of the wrongful act, if it is continuing, and reparation for injury, as well as future compliance, it examined the incentives in both the private and public dimensions of international law, notably the extent to which first-party and third-party countermeasures are expected to induce compliance with GPG and CPR obligations.

The findings show, firstly, that an economic perspective on the conditions of state responsibility, in particular economic theory of goods, allows for a better understanding of the scenarios where countermeasures should be possible and where they should be excluded. While the prior wrongful act triggering the right to countermeasures can consist in a breach of an international obligation independent of its character, countermeasures should only be possible where a private law obligation is affected, but be excluded where they impair a GPG or CPR obligation. The analysis in this chapter thus provided an economic rationale for Article 50 ARSIWA excluding countermeasures affecting certain fundamental community interest obligations and proposes to broaden the scope of the provision to cover more systematically GPG and CPR obligations.

Secondly, the findings on the incentive structures demonstrate that incentives vary significantly depending on the underlying scenario. Reciprocal countermeasures by a single injured state, that is breach of an international obligation that is similar in-kind to the international obligation underlying the prior wrongful act (i.e. both relating to private goods) and stemming from the same base treaty, can be very effective in inducing compliance. This presupposes that both states continue to gain more from ongoing cooperation than from immediate defection and uncertainty about whether the prior act was wrongful and the countermeasure proportionate is low (thus, the risk to set off "spirals of non-compliance" is limited). The incentives to take countermeasures become increasingly limited the more they are costly for the sanctioning state, that is with an increasing retaliatory component (e.g. in-kind countermeasures outside the base treaty), thus limiting their usefulness to the sanctioning of ongoing violations. The incentives for countermeasures become even weaker when the probability of their effectiveness, that is inducing compliance with the secondary obligations of cessation and reparation, decreases. This is the case when the prior wrongful act consists in the breach of a GPG or CPR obligation and the cross-countermeasure affects a private law obligation (i.e. non-in-kind), in particular when multiple states are injured but face incentives to free-ride on the willingness of other injured states to take countermeasures (i.e. sanctioners' dilemma). In these scenarios, the potential material and political costs will become prohibitive, with the exception that only powerful and rich states will have the financial means to afford countermeasures in light of serious violations GPG and CPR obligations where they can expect to receive the support of the international community. Non-directly injured third states face the additional problem that they internalise only the benefits of cessation of the prior wrongful act, so that their incentives to respond to a breach of a GPG or CPR obligation are even further limited. There is thus no economic rationale to prohibit third-party countermeasures in GPG and CPR constellations (or restrict them to lawful measures, that is retorsions, as suggested in Article 54 ARSIWA), but rather to allow them in exceptional circumstances (i.e. serious breaches of *erga omnes* obligations and inaction of the UN Security Council), provided that abusive invocation can be avoided (e.g. exclusion of the use of force, proportionality requirement, and procedural and temporal conditions).

Thirdly, the general compensation requirement for material loss inflicted upon the target state in Article 27 lit. b) ARSIWA does not set the right incentives with regard to first-party and third-party countermeasures, as the author of the prior wrongful act is the cheapest cost avoider. However, an exception to this cost allocation has to be made for material losses incurred by innocent third states. Here, the compensation requirement can induce the state taking countermeasures to internalise any harmful side-effects (i.e. externalities) and thus to better target the countermeasure. Yet, in order not to deter multiple directly or indirectly injured states further from taking countermeasures due to the sanctioners' dilemma, cost-sharing arrangements for the financial consequences are necessary. Costs should be shared primarily with the target state being the author of the prior wrongful act, and, secondly, with other injured states profiting from the countermeasures by way of recourse or with a trust fund solution among indirectly injured states. The *ultima ratio* solution would be an exemption from the compensation requirement in the case of third-party countermeasures, because innocent states benefit *pro rata*.

However, even with the suggested improvements regarding the protection of community interests in the different provisions governing countermeasures, these face substantial limits as an enforcement tool in the international law of state responsibility. Enforcement of state responsibility with countermeasures is, apart from reciprocal non-compliance, essentially left to a few powerful and rich states, in particular when the prior wrongful act consisted in the breach of a GPG or CPR obligation. From a legal perspective, this may appear incompatible with the principle of state equality as a key structural feature of international law.[168] Yet, acknowledging that power asymmetries among states lead to the fact that countermeasures in certain constellations are only available to the most powerful and rich is the consequence of integrating realist accounts in an economic analysis which follows the institutionalist tradition.[169] From an economic viewpoint, power asymmetries are a factor to be integrated in the model with the result that they can have advantages if they help to achieve certain aims (here, compliance with GPG and CPR obligations) and if sufficient safeguards exist against abuse (here, exclusion of the use of force, proportionality requirement etc.).

A more equitable access to countermeasures as an instrument to induce compliance with GPG and CPR obligations can only be facilitated by an institutional framework.[170] Prior authorisation of a countermeasure by a centralised institution (e.g. WTO Dispute Settlement Body and UN Security Council) can reduce uncertainties about the wrongfulness of the prior act and the legality of the countermeasure, thus reducing the risk to incur a negative reputation for opportunistic enforcement, and facilitate negotiations about a possible cost-sharing arrangement (thereby reducing the potential political and material costs of countermeasures).

Ultimately, other enforcement mechanisms in international law need to step in when countermeasures as an external penalty reach their limits in inducing

[168] Besson, "Community Interests in International Law: Whose Interests Are They and How Should We Best Identify Them?," in *Community Interests across International Law*, ed. Benvenisti and Nolte, 48. ("Third and last, *state equality* is another structural feature of international law that is sometimes considered incompatible with the protection of community interests. This is what has been observed in particular with respect to the hindrances set by state equality in the decentralized enforcement of community interests in practice.")

[169] See Sect. 1.3.

[170] Similarly, on the facilitating role of international judicial institutions (e.g. by clarifying legal norms and reducing ambiguity about non-compliant behaviour), even though more cautious about their ability to solve collective action problems, see Posner, "Erga Omnes Norms, Institutionalization, and Constitutionalism in International Law," 15–18.

compliance, notably with GPG and CPR obligations, and ideally complement each other. On the one hand, there is outcasting, which builds on a similar rationale as cross-countermeasures, with the difference that it operates within the base treaty, that is a club with the objective of providing a GPG or preserving a CPR.[171] The sanction for the target state in the case of violations of treaty commitments, including remedies, consists then in the penalty of exclusion from the club and the loss of the associated benefits, usually trading benefits. Cross-countermeasures, in contrast, only lead to the withdrawal of certain bilateral benefits protected by a private law obligation, threatening the stability of other treaty regimes. Outcasting can thus be more effective and cheaper for the sanctioning states than countermeasures, because they keep the benefits from cooperation among each other. Certainly, outcasting mechanisms also have their limits, for instance, when it comes to excluding powerful players, as there is the risk that the cooperative regime breaks down as a whole. Outcasting is also a powerful tool when it builds on market mechanisms by involving the private sector and civil society actors, a component that is difficult to combine with countermeasures as a self-standing and *ad hoc* implementation tool. On the other hand, rewarding can as a positive inducement mechanism outbalance many of the negative connotations of retaliatory countermeasures (and outcasting), as it considers ways to increase the benefits of compliance for the target state, including compliance with secondary obligations.[172] Rewards can, for instance, play a role when retaliatory countermeasures are unlikely to induce compliance because the prior wrongful act is the result of incapacity (e.g. lack of financial, administrative, or technological resources) and reciprocal countermeasures and complete outcasting are undesirable in GPG/CPR constellations. However, rewards in the form of side-payments may be counterproductive to enforce the monetary payment of compensation. Rewarding may also be costly for the rewarding state (even if it does not require as many resources as retaliatory countermeasures), thereby creating incentives to free-ride on the contributions of others to the reward (i.e. the rewarders' dilemma having public good characteristics) and cause moral hazard at the compliance stage because states may want to present themselves in need of assistance in order to receive a reward. There are ways to address these limitations, for example, through generating a positive reputation for rewarding at the enforcement level or burden sharing (e.g. co-financed programmes). Yet, serious breaches of peremptory norms of international law as deliberate violations of *jus cogens* obligations will usually not be the result of incapacity, so that, absent an institutionalised framework, countermeasures, in particular by indirectly injured third parties, may be the only instrument left to enforce compliance and bring ongoing violations of *erga omnes* obligations to an end.

[171] See Sect. 2.4 on outcasting as a compliance mechanism in international law and, in particular, Hathaway and Shapiro, "Outcasting: Enforcement in Domestic and International Law," 252–349.

[172] See Sect. 2.4 on rewarding as a compliance mechanism in international law and, in particular, van Aaken and Simsek, "Rewarding in International Law," 195–241.

In sum, these compliance mechanisms are likely to work best when they complement each other, for instance, outcasting combined with subsequent readmission, and retaliatory countermeasures with subsequent rewards (i.e. redemption). The law of state responsibility thus needs to rely on other enforcement mechanisms, in particular when sanctioning states do not have the power or financial means to effectively induce compliance with GPG and CPR obligations.

Part III
Concluding Part

Chapter 8
Conclusion

8.1 The Protection of Community Interests in the International Law of State Responsibility

More than 20 years after the adoption of the ARSIWA, the international legal order has evolved further away from the traditional bilateralist model to a multilateral one, centred around the notion of community interest protection and the quest to address global challenges. The law of state responsibility, as reflected in the ARSIWA, already mirrors these developments. It contains not only fundamental principles of bilateral dispute resolution deeply enshrined in customary international law, broadly understood as the private dimension of international state responsibility. It also attempts to contribute progressively to the further development of international law, in particular with regard to the so-called public dimension of international law. This book sought to contribute to a better theoretical understanding of how community interests are protected in the international law of state responsibility by using a social science approach, namely the economic analysis of (international) law and, more specifically, rational choice theory. It aimed to clarify the extent to which the different rules on international state responsibility, that is the ARSIWA, set adequate incentives for states as unitary rational actors to respond to the underlying cooperation challenges.

That states can be modelled as unitary rational actors maximising gains in absolute terms has extensively been justified in Chap. 1. Firstly, the assumption that states are unitary actors and the principal actor in international relations (i.e. states are acting themselves, according to their own preferences, and in interaction only with other states) has been defended against the objections of methodological individualism as well as public choice theory and liberalism. The unitary actor assumption is used both in the institutionalist and the realist tradition and considered to be the most promising tool for generating strong predictions about state behaviour. This is particularly the case with regard to the international law of

J. Lemke, *The Protection of Community Interests in the International Law of State Responsibility*, International Law and Economics,
https://doi.org/10.1007/978-3-031-87927-2_8

state responsibility, characterised by the determination of states as the relevant legal personality (or unit of analysis) with the ability to incur responsibility for wrongful behaviour and invoke responsibility of others in inter-state relations. Secondly, I have countered the objection of "bounded rationality" and the constructivist critique and defended the assumption of states being rational actors. The state's self-interest is assumed to be a function of given and fixed preferences (i.e. state preferences being exogenous and remaining stable in the short run), while leaving out aspects regarding the formation and change of preferences. As a starting point, the rationality assumption persuades by its simplicity in predicting and explaining behaviour in complex settings and by deriving testable hypotheses about the effectiveness of certain international legal rules. These can subsequently be contrasted with actual state behaviour. This simplicity is especially attractive with regard to the law of state responsibility, because it is, from an economic perspective, a relatively unexplored area of international law. Thirdly, in order to keep the model workable to explain how state responsibility rules set incentives for states, no commitment is made to any particular assumption about the exact content of state interests. Following the institutionalist tradition, the only assumption is that states seek to maximise absolute gains (i.e. being better or at least not worse off than before). That does not mean, however, that some aspects in the law of state responsibility cannot be better explained with the realist tradition focusing on relative gains among states. The relative power of states (i.e. their functional inequality), for instance, plays a role with regard to the enforcement of international law with costly retaliatory countermeasures.

Chapter 2 translated the concept of community interest protection, as used in the international law literature, into economic terms. It analysed the extent to which the concept is congruent with different types of goods, in particular the concept of global public goods (GPGs), which is used in international relations theory and the economic analysis of international law in order to explain the collective action problems underlying many global challenges of our time. Examples for private goods, club goods, common pool resources (CPRs) and GPGs can be found throughout international law, each pointing towards different cooperative challenges. International law can address these challenges, for instance, by protecting entitlements (e.g. territorial integrity), facilitating the mutual exchange of benefits, prohibiting the destruction of common resources and safeguarding fundamental values of the international community. Unlike national law, international law is, however, confronted with the inherent problem that it operates in a decentralised legal order and thus states themselves need to agree on commitments on a consensual basis and subsequently self-enforce compliance with their own rules. Rational choice theory in international law has offered strong explanations under which conditions we can expect states to comply with international law and five distinct compliance mechanisms have been presented in this chapter, namely retaliation, reciprocity, reputation, outcasting, and rewarding. It also pointed out that international judicial institutions in a context of self-enforcement by states can only play a facilitating role, but a role which is certainly not to be neglected in matters of state responsibility, for instance, when it comes to the award of compensatory damages. What we learn from these general theories about the functioning of international law is that in bilateral constellations compliance with international obligations can usually be enforced more effectively than in multilateral contexts, because states internalise the benefits of their enforcement efforts and are thus willing to bear the associated costs. In contrast, enforcement in the public dimension of international law exhibits GPG characteristics and states have incentives to free-ride on the enforcement efforts of others.

These findings constituted the basis for the normative framework developed for the analysis of state responsibility in international law in Chap. 3. In order to define the multiple objectives of state responsibility, this chapter builds upon the current research on the law of state responsibility proposing to distinguish between a private and public dimension. Against this background, I distinguished, first, on the level of problem constellations between, on the one hand, scenarios that relate more to tort or contractual liability-like situations discussed in the economic analysis of domestic law, and, on the other hand, scenarios relating to the protection of GPGs and the preservation of CPRs (including international obligations with *jus cogens* status). Second, a distinction was made with regard to the level of enforcement, namely whether state responsibility can be enforced by the injured state itself or whether there is the possibility for third-party enforcement, such as in the case of *erga omnes* and *erga omnes partes* obligations. The different objectives of state responsibility can overlap between the private and the public dimension, as they depend on the elements under scrutiny (i.e. responsibility standards, excuses and justifications, remedies as well as countermeasures). From an economic perspective, they can briefly be summarised as: compliance, flexibility, compensation, enforcement, and cooperation.

Chapter 4 marked the beginning of the rational choice analysis and started with the conditions for international state responsibility. It provided an overview of different responsibility standards and their incentive structures. The focus was on gaining a better understanding of the concept of objective responsibility, that is responsibility based on illegality, from an economic perspective. The concept is marked by the absence of damage and fault as requirements and based on the notion of legal injury or breach of duty. It is applicable to all constellations of international cooperation and underlying types of primary obligations and there is thus a good economic rationale for turning towards it. That damage is not a requirement for state responsibility does not make a difference in the private dimension of international law, because in tort-like and contract-like scenarios reparation of damage is simply transferred to the level of remedies. In addition, objective responsibility bears advantages in the public dimension of international law as it covers scenarios with a purely internal dimension (as often in the case of international human rights violations). It also opens the way to other remedies than compensation (i.e. cessation, restitution, and satisfaction) and enforcement by non-directly injured third parties in CPR and GPG constellations, thus emphasising the compliance objective of the law of state responsibility. In addition, notions of fault may be accounted for with due diligence obligations, as a specific form of primary international obligations, notably referring to constellations where the internationally wrongful act of the state consists in a failure to prevent harmful activities by private actors under its jurisdiction or control. It could be seen that due diligence obligations can set incentives for optimal levels of precautionary care of both potentially responsible and victim states as well as for optimal activity levels of potential victim states. However, whether primary due diligence obligations can set optimal incentives depends on whether they are fully aligned with the optimal level of precautionary care thus bearing the risk that potential wrongdoing states take excessive or insufficient precaution. Recourse to the comparison of the relative advantages of substantive versus procedural obligations and rules versus standards demonstrated how difficult it is to design optimal due diligence obligations and that complementarity of different design elements is often key to achieve optimal incentives in terms of precaution. In general, the design of international obligations is extremely relevant, as the degree to which compliance with international obligations is observable for the states involved in a given dispute or verifiable by third parties (i.e. states and international adjudicators, if available) determines how effectively remedies in case of non-compliance can be enforced. In essence, the analysis thus confirmed the importance of responsibility based on illegality as a general rule (combined with a comparative negligence rule as in Article 39 ARSIWA). However, it also outlined that in constellations, where a balance needs to be struck between risky but economically beneficial activities (e.g. industrial production and international transportation) and potentially transboundary harm or harm to the global commons, responsibility for breach of primary due diligence obligations should be complemented with liability rules. Conventional strict liability regimes offer an alternative when the focus lies on calibrating the level of certain ultra-hazardous state activities. Treaty regimes with provisions on liability for lawful acts ("no-fault liability") are a useful tool to allocate the losses if transboundary damage (or damage to the global commons) is caused although the state under which jurisdiction or control the harmful activity by a private operator took place exercised due care. In exceptional and pre-defined circumstances, states accept to negotiate concrete measures of harm mitigation, either by outsourcing the risk to the operators via a system of civil liability or by negotiating *ex post* an appropriate amount of compensation. International trust funds consisting of contributions by certain industries or even public funds of states have been identified as another way to address the issue of transboundary harm and harm to CPRs despite lawful state behaviour.

Chapter 5 constituted the cornerstone of the rational choice analysis with its focus on exemptions of state responsibility, namely the justifications and excuses in international law. The key issue here was not only the allocation of duties, thus the conditions for invoking the different circumstances precluding wrongfulness of state acts, but foremost the question of cost allocation following such invocation. Cost allocation had deliberatively been left open in the ARSIWA, with Article 27 lit. b) foreseeing only a general compensation requirement for material loss to be applied "depending on the circumstances". Whether compensation is economically justified depends on the underlying economic rationale of each justification or excuse, which differs between all six circumstances precluding wrongfulness: protection of an essential interest causing less losses to the international community than compliance with an international obligation would have caused (private necessity, or when the defendant state protected a prevailing community interest, public necessity), an individual state agent acted to save human life (distress), the losses caused by the defendant state's act could not have been avoided or only at exorbitant costs (*force majeure*), the plaintiff state authorised the otherwise wrongful act and accepted the losses (consent), the defendant state's act reduced the losses from an armed attack and aimed to deter states from launching an armed attack in the future (self-defence) or the defendant state's act aimed to induce compliance with secondary obligations and incidentally with international obligations more generally (countermeasures, discussed in Chap. 7). What all justifications and excuses have in common is that they allow for flexibility in exceptional circumstances and thus for non-compliance with the international obligation in question, while trying to avoid abusive invocation by setting relatively strict conditions for invocation (e.g. limitation of the means at choice, non-contribution to the situation, validity and scope of the expression of consent on the basis of sufficient information, necessity and proportionality of the act in self-defence, exclusion in the case of *jus cogens* norms according to common Article 26 ARSIWA). As regards necessity, compensation of material losses is indeed justified as a general rule because it upholds the deterrent effect of reparation for injury (being the classic remedy in the case of a wrongful act). It thus serves to avoid moral hazard by inducing states to take sufficient care or hedge against the risk of peril for an essential interest, thereby limiting opportunistic breach of international obligations. However, a postponement of the payment of compensation and a reduction of the amount should be possible in the case of severe economic distress causing devastating effects for the population ("crippling compensation"). I have also argued that deviations from this principle of compensation may be justified, when states act in public necessity, that is, to protect a prevailing essential interest of the international community as a whole. In order to set incentives for GPG provision or CPR protection, losses should as an ultima ratio remain with the plaintiff state, unless there are mechanisms available to share the costs among the parties involved, ideally including those states that benefitted from the act in public necessity (e.g. compensation with possibility of regress in case of a limited number of beneficiaries or trust fund solutions in primary law). In the case of distress, which differs in that an individual state agent acted to save human life, the compensation requirement derives from the same rationale and should also provide the possibility of partial or full recourse against other states benefitting from the act in distress. However, in some constellations, exceptions from the compensation requirement may be warranted, in particular, when the costs cannot be borne by the state invoking distress (i.e. reduction of the amount in the case of "crippling compensation") or cannot be shared with other states benefitting from the act (i.e. full or partial shift to the victim state). As regards *force majeure*, full compensation is not justified as the losses caused by the defendant state's act due to the external event could not have been avoided at all or only at exorbitant costs. A cost-sharing solution seems more appropriate and the costs thus fall partially also on the plaintiff state which is not more innocent than the defendant state. In the case of consent, where the plaintiff state authorised the otherwise wrongful act and accepted the losses following breach of a private and club goods obligation, these are usually remediated to the extent negotiated *ex ante* with compensatory payments. However, any material losses that are caused to innocent third states will have to be remediated *ex post* by way of reparation for injury as these acts are not covered by the consent (private and club goods obligations relating to third states or GPG and CPR obligations) and thus constitute internationally wrongful acts. Self-defence (also in the form of collective self-defence) should not give rise to an obligation to provide compensation for material losses as the purpose of the justification is to deter other states from causing damage with an armed attack. An exception relates to material losses incurred by innocent third states as in this scenario the compensation requirement can induce the state acting in self-defence to respect the legal limits of the justification. Here, the costs should nonetheless be shifted partially to the author of the armed attack as the cheapest cost avoider, and in the case of collective self-defence to other benefitting states by way of regress. Chapter 5 thus demonstrated from an economic point of view that and how the general compensation requirement in Article 27 lit. b) ARSIWA needs to be further refined across and within the different excuses and justifications.

Chapter 6 dealt with the consequences of a breach of an international obligation, in other words the *ex post* allocation of duties and costs, and analysed the impact the different secondary obligations (as legal constraints or cost factors) have on the compliance decision of the potentially wrongdoing state. A key issue here was that the effectiveness of remedies hinges on self-enforcement which varies depending on the underlying problem constellation, the probability of successful enforcement being lower in the public dimension. This chapter demonstrated that there is a strong rationale for "property rules" as primary remedies in the law of state responsibility. Specific performance is the common remedy in state practice. It aims not only to induce the return to compliance and restore the cooperative relationship. This relates to cessation and assurances or guarantees of non-repetition, in particular in constellations which are less concerned with the reparation of past harm but with the functioning of the future exchange of benefits, as in trade law. Specific performance also pursues the objective to eradicate the consequences of the wrongful act with restitution (or satisfaction), as in tort-like scenarios where entitlements (or property rights or private goods) have been infringed (e.g. territorial integrity, foreign property, or cross-border pollution). It helps to deter breach of international obligations in the first place as states cannot buy themselves out of non-compliance. The focus on compliance, reestablishment of the *status quo ante*, and satisfactory remedies such as declaratory judgments, apologies and symbolic damages are also extremely valuable in GPG scenarios in the sense that beyond the interests of the injured state all states in the international community derive value from compliance (e.g. armed attack on foreign territory and detention of diplomatic personnel). By contrast, compensation as a "liability rule", not be confounded with the concept of "liability of lawful acts", constitutes the secondary remedy in the law of state responsibility. It exhibits fundamental advantages when other remedies reach their limit, for instance, when restitution is materially impossible or highly inappropriate, or specific performance perceived as too sovereignty infringing. The downside of compensation is that the measurement of the damage and thus the determination of the appropriate sum of damages requires a third-party adjudicator to conduct the objective valuation, but faces nonetheless the risk of error costs which may lead to over- or underdeterrence. Full compensation as the optimal level of compensation should therefore remain the guiding principle in the law of state responsibility. However, when compensation would be crippling, a deviation to the bottom should be possible in the case of private law obligations and in primary law. In addition, a deviation from the principle of compensatory damages to the top (i.e. "punitive damages multiplier") can serve to uphold the deterrent effect when the probability of being held liable is less than 1. This occurs particularly, but not exclusively, in GPG and CPR constellations, when the losses are spread over a large number of countries and/or causation between the wrongful act and the damage is difficult to establish. Adding an additional factor to the total sum of damages thus not only has the advantage that it sets correct incentives for the potentially wrongdoing state, but also that it helps to overcome the problem of "rational apathy", as victim states can obtain higher damages when holding the wrongdoing state responsible (in particular, in the case of environmental harm). Lastly, the ARSIWA attempt to address the issue of enforcement in the public dimension with regard to the most serious violations of fundamental norms with the somewhat rudimentary additional obligations on third states not to recognise a situation caused by a breach of *jus cogens* norms, not to render aid or assistance and to cooperate to bring such situation to an end. In a way, these obligations simply reinforce that the primary remedy in the law of state responsibility are property rules, the primacy of compliance, even in the face of the gravest violations of international law. The advantage of this approach is that these additional obligations open the door to a wide variety of enforcement tools that exist in international law. Specific performance does not necessarily rely on countermeasures for enforcement, but other mechanisms such as outcasting (in primary treaty regimes) or positive inducements such as technical assistance or rewards in other issue areas can also play a role here. This is the reason why these additional requirements should also apply to violations of other GPG and CPR obligations (i.e. breach of *erga omnes* obligations) and without the qualification of seriousness of the breach.

Chapter 7 concluded the main part with a rational choice analysis of countermeasures in the international law of state responsibility and thus the level of implementation of the remedies of cessation and reparation and the role of countermeasures as an enforcement tool to induce compliance in the future. The analysis in this chapter provided, firstly, an economic rationale of the provision in Article 50 ARSIWA, which excludes countermeasures when they would affect certain fundamental community interest obligations, and proposes to broaden the scope of the provision to cover GPG and CPR obligations more generally. Secondly, the findings on the incentive structures demonstrated that incentives vary significantly depending on the underlying scenario. Reciprocal countermeasures by a single injured state, that is breach of an international obligation that is similar in-kind to the international obligation underlying the prior wrongful act (i.e. both relating to private goods) and stemming from the same base treaty, can be very effective in inducing compliance, provided that both states continue to gain more from ongoing cooperation than from immediate defection and uncertainty about whether the prior act was wrongful and the countermeasure proportionate is low (thus, the risk to set off "spirals of non-compliance" is limited). The incentives to take countermeasures become increasingly limited the more they are costly for the sanctioning state, that is with an increasing retaliatory component (e.g. in-kind countermeasures outside the base treaty), thus limiting their usefulness to the sanctioning of ongoing violations. The incentives for countermeasures become even weaker when the probability of their effectiveness, that is inducing compliance with the secondary obligations of cessation and reparation, decreases. This is the case when the prior wrongful act consists in the breach of a GPG or CPR obligation and the cross-countermeasure is affecting a private goods obligation (i.e. non-in-kind), in particular when multiple states are injured but face incentives to free-ride on the willingness of other injured states to take countermeasures (i.e. sanctioners' dilemma). In these scenarios, the potential material and political costs will become prohibitive, with the exception that only powerful and rich states will have the financial means to afford countermeasures in light of serious violations of GPG and CPR obligations where they can expect to receive the support of the international community. Non-directly injured third states face the additional problem that they internalise only the benefits of cessation of the prior wrongful act, so that their incentives to respond to a breach of a GPG or CPR obligation are even further limited. There is thus no economic rationale to prohibit third-party countermeasures in GPG and CPR constellations (or restrict them to lawful measures, that is retorsions, as suggested in Article 54 ARSIWA), but rather to allow them in exceptional circumstances (i.e. serious breaches of *erga omnes* obligations and inaction of the UN Security Council), provided that abusive invocation can be avoided (e.g. exclusion of the use of force, proportionality requirement, and procedural and temporal conditions). Thirdly, the general compensation requirement for material loss inflicted upon the target state in Article 27 lit. b) ARSIWA does not set the right incentives with regard to first-party and third-party countermeasures, as the author of the prior wrongful act is the cheapest cost avoider. However, an exception to this cost allocation has to be made for material losses incurred by innocent third states. Here, the compensation requirement can induce the state taking countermeasures to internalise any harmful side-effects (i.e. externalities) and thus to better target the countermeasure. Yet, in order not to deter multiple directly or non-directly injured states further from taking countermeasures due to the sanctioners' dilemma, cost-sharing arrangements for the financial consequences are necessary. Costs should be shared primarily with the target state being the author of the prior wrongful act, and, secondly, with other injured states profiting from the countermeasures by way of recourse or with a trust fund solution among indirectly injured states. The ultima ratio solution would be an exemption from the compensation requirement in the case of third-party countermeasures, because innocent states benefit pro rata.

My overall conclusion of the rational choice analysis on the protection of community interests in the international law of state responsibility is threefold. Firstly, shifting the perspective of the analysis from a mere "internal" doctrinal view to an "external" analysis of the incentive structures of the ARSIWA within the broader context of the functioning of the international legal order, in particular the mechanisms of self-enforcement, allows to underpin fundamental principles of the law of state responsibility with an economic rationale. It also allows to make normative suggestions both for the interpretation of provisions, which are unclear or incomplete, as well as for the further development of the ARSIWA in order to better account for the protection of community interests. The analysis in this book demonstrated that there is a strong rationale for well-established principles in the law of state responsibility, which are, at least partially, deeply rooted customary international law. This relates, for instance, to the principle of objective responsibility, which is indifferent to the type of primary obligation and thus includes due diligence obligations and opens the way for third-party enforcement in the absence of injury. It also relates to the necessity excuse which applies equally to prevailing interests of either the defendant state (private necessity) or the international community (public necessity). Other examples are the toolbox of remedies with the primacy of property rules and the principle of full reparation of injury, but also countermeasures with their limitation to infringements of private law obligations and a strong rationale, in particular when employed on a reciprocal, non-retaliatory basis.

This book also made normative suggestions regarding provisions in the ARSIWA that were formulated in vague terms or even deliberately left open in order to effectuate GPG and CPR protection. This concerns, for instance, the economic arguments in favour of complementing the general rule of responsibility based on illegality with conventional rules on strict liability (when the focus lies on calibrating the level of ultra-hazardous state activities) or "liability for lawful acts" (when the focus is on loss allocation in the case of beneficial, but harmful activities under state control), in particular in the environmental context. Another example for normative proposals is the issue of cost allocation following the invocation of necessity, where further refinement is clearly needed, as well as with regard to the other five circumstances precluding wrongfulness, which are each based on different economic rationales and imposing a compensation requirement indiscriminately on all of them can be counterproductive. A further example are possible deviations from the principle of full compensation, when compensation would be crippling or when a "punitive damages multiplier" can serve to uphold the deterrent effect when the probability of being held liable is less than 1 and when victim states face the problem of "rational apathy" (e.g. in CPR constellations where losses are widespread). A last example is the contribution to the legal debate about whether countermeasures by non-directly injured states should be restricted to "lawful" measures.

Secondly, the law of state responsibility reaches its limits with regard to enforcement, in particular in the public dimension and with regard to the most serious violations of fundamental norms, where the probability of enforcement may be too low to successfully deter such wrongful acts, even if the sum of monetary damages is increased infinitively. The ARSIWA attempt to address this issue, on the one hand, with the somewhat rudimentary additional obligations on third states not to recognise a situation caused by a breach of a *jus cogens* norms and to cooperate to bring such situation to an end. On the other hand, the ARSIWA place the right to countermeasures, and thus retaliation by directly and indirectly injured states, at the forefront of enforcement of state responsibility, in particular for compensation. Hence, they take an approach that relies heavily on the mutual imposition of costs, contrary to another key function of state responsibility, namely to restore the cooperative relationship and ensure compliance. The primacy of compliance is also reflected in the choice of property rules as the primary remedy in the law of state responsibility, even in the face of the gravest violations of international law. The advantage of this approach is that it opens the door to a wide variety of enforcement tools that exist in international law. Specific performance (but also compensation) does not necessarily rely on countermeasures for enforcement, but other enforcement mechanisms in international law such as outcasting (in primary treaty regimes) or positive inducements such as technical assistance or rewards in other issue areas can also play a role. This is in particular the case when countermeasures as an external penalty reach their limits in inducing compliance, notably with GPG and CPR obligations. Taking into account that also outcasting and rewarding present advantages and disadvantages, these compliance mechanisms are likely to work best when they complement each other, for instance, outcasting combined with subsequent readmission, and retaliatory countermeasures with subsequent rewards (i.e. redemption). In sum, the law of state responsibility was conceived as a system which builds on countermeasures for the enforcement of its remedies, but this need not be so. It should also rely on other enforcement mechanisms, in particular when sanctioning states do not have the power or financial means to effectively induce compliance with GPG and CPR obligations.

Thirdly, the law of state responsibility will be most effective if international judicial institutions are involved in their application, provided that states have accepted their jurisdiction. Third-party adjudicatory bodies can then play an important role in facilitating enforcement, for instance, by deciding on the wrongfulness of state acts and on the applicability of exemptions, thus reducing the uncertainty about the existence of an internationally wrongful act. International courts and tribunals are also key for determining the appropriate remedy, including the appropriate level of compensation. They are also crucial for the prior authorisation of countermeasures, in particular in GPG/CPR constellations and with regard to third-party countermeasures by non-directly injured states, thereby reducing the potential political and material costs of countermeasures.

In sum, the lessons learned from the analysis in this book are meant to provide guidance from a social-scientific perspective for the interpretation and application of the ARSIWA on a case-by-case basis, in state negotiations or judicial proceedings, as well as for treaty design, because state responsibility rules play a crucial role in effectuating treaty objectives. The remaining question is how these guidelines can be further developed and refined in the future. The first avenue for further research is certainly to broaden the analysis to other aspects of international responsibility that were excluded in this book. For instance, they could be complemented with insights gained elsewhere, including from an economic perspective, on the attribution of conduct to the state or questions of shared responsibility, that is including multiple responsible actors, in particular in the context of climate change. Another field of research is issues of the responsibility of international organisations, which would require necessarily an adaptation of the research method to analyse organisational behaviour which may be different from states (e.g. budgetary constraints and principal-agent problems). The second avenue would be to refine the insights and suggestions of this book with future developments at the intersection of international law, international relations and economic analysis of international law on the enforcement of international obligations as well as on the functioning of treaty regimes. The third avenue regards the research method. As discussed extensively in the first chapter, the rational choice approach needs to be understood as a starting point. The suggestions offered here can be further tested by including in the model systematically the role of relative power in state interactions (i.e. realism). Another possibility is to break up the "black box" of the state by integrating either the cost-benefit calculations of individual state agents towards state responsibility rules (i.e. methodological individualism) or including domestic policy considerations based on a two-level approach (i.e. public choice or liberalism). A last refinement would be to question the rationality assumption of states by either including the aspects regarding the formation and change of state preference (i.e. constructivism) or insights from behavioural (international) law and economics. This last approach can, in particular, enrich our understanding of how states react to punishments and retaliatory sanctions.

More than 20 years after the adoption of the ARSIWA, we can conclude that the need to integrate concerns of community interest protection in the law of state responsibility has been well anticipated at the time of drafting, but the rules as they stand also offer room for further development in order to put the articulation of the private and public dimensions on a more systematic footing. The rational choice analysis presented here intends to launch this debate.

References

Bibliography

Abbott, Kenneth W. "Modern International Relations Theory: A Prospectus for International Lawyers." *Yale Journal of International Law* 14, no. 2 (1989): 335-411.

Abbott, Kenneth W., Robert O. Keohane, Andrew Moravcsik, Anne-Marie Slaughter, and Duncan Snidal. "The Concept of Legalization." *International Organization* 54, no. 3 (2000): 401-419.

Abbott, Kenneth W., and Duncan Snidal. "Values and Interests: International Legalization in the Fight against Corruption." *Journal of Legal Studies* 31, no. S1 (2002): S141-S177.

———. "Law, Legalization, and Politics: An Agenda for the Next Generation of IL/IR Scholars." In *Interdisciplinary Perspectives on International Law and International Relations: The State of the Art*, edited by Jeffrey L. Dunoff and Mark A. Pollack, 33-56. Cambridge: Cambridge University Press, 2013.

Adler, Emanuel. "Constructivism in International Relations: Sources, Contributions, and Debates." In *Handbook of International Relations*, edited by Walter Carlsnaes, Thomas Risse and Beth A. Simmons. 2nd ed., 112-145. London: SAGE, 2013.

Alexy, Robert. "On Balancing and Subsumption. A Structural Comparison." *Ratio Juris* 16, no. 4 (2003): 433-449.

Alland, Denis. "The Definition of Countermeasures." In *The Law of International Responsibility*, edited by James Crawford, Alain Pellet and Simon Olleson, 1127-1136. Oxford: Oxford University Press, 2010.

Alston, Carmen M. "Adverse Selection." In *Encyclopaedia Britannica*. https://www.britannica.com/topic/expected-utility. Article last modified on 20 May 2016.

Alter, Karen J. "Do International Courts Enhance Compliance with International Law?". *Review of Asian and Pacific Studies* 25 (2003): 51-78.

———. "Agents or Trustees? International Courts in Their Political Context." *European Journal of International Relations* 14, no. 1 (2008): 33-63.

Arce M., Daniel G., and Todd Sandler. "Transnational Public Goods: Strategies and Institutions." *European Journal of Political Economy* 17, no. 3 (2001): 493–516.

Arlen, Jennifer, ed. *Research Handbook on the Economics of Torts*. Cheltenham, UK: Edward Elgar, 2013.

Arrow, Kenneth J. *Social Choice and Individual Values*. 2nd ed. New Haven: Yale University Press, 1970.

J. Lemke, *The Protection of Community Interests in the International Law of State*

Axelrod, Robert. *The Evolution of Cooperation.* New York: Basic Books, 1984.
Axelrod, Robert, and Robert O. Keohane. "Achieving Cooperation under Anarchy: Strategies and Institutions." *World Politics* 38, no. 1 (1985): 226-254.
Bækkeskov, Erik. "Market Failure." In *Encyclopaedia Britannica.* https://www.britannica.com/topic/market-failure. Article last modified on 1 October 2019.
Baird, Douglas G., ed. *Economics of Contract Law.* Cheltenham, UK: Edward Elgar, 2007.
Baldwin, David A. "The Power of Positive Sanctions." *World Politics* 24, no. 1 (1971): 19-38.
Baldwin, Robert, Martin Cave, and Martin Lodge. *Understanding Regulation: Theory, Strategy, and Practice.* 2nd ed. Oxford: Oxford University Press, 2012.
Barbier, Sandrine. "Assurances and Guarantees of Non-Repetition." In *The Law of International Responsibility*, edited by James Crawford, Alain Pellet and Simon Olleson, 551-561. Oxford: Oxford University Press, 2010.
Barboza, Julio. "Necessity (Revisited) in International Law." In *Essays in International Law in Honour of Judge Manfred Lachs/Études de Droit International en l'honneur du Juge Manfred Lachs*, edited by Jerzy Makarczyk, 27-43. The Hague: Martinus Nijhoff Publishers, 1984.
Barker, John. "The Different Forms of Reparation: Compensation." In *The Law of International Responsibility*, edited by James Crawford, Alain Pellet and Simon Olleson, 599-611. Oxford: Oxford University Press, 2010.
Barkin, J. Samuel, and Yuliya Rashchupkina. "Public Goods, Common Pool Resources, and International Law." *American Journal of International Law* 111, no. 2 (2017): 376-394.
Barrett, Scott. *Why Cooperate? The Incentive to Supply Global Public Goods.* Oxford: Oxford University Press, 2007.
Bartels, Lorand, and Federica Paddeu, eds. *Exceptions in International Law.* Oxford: Oxford University Press, 2020.
Ben Mansour, Affef. "Circumstances Precluding Wrongfulness in the ILC Articles on State Responsibility: Consent." In *The Law of International Responsibility*, edited by James Crawford, Alain Pellet and Simon Olleson, 439-447. Oxford: Oxford University Press, 2010a.
Benedek, Wolfgang, Koen De Feyter, Matthias C. Kettemann, and Christina Voigt, eds. *The Common Interest in International Law.* Cambridge, UK: Intersentia, 2014.
Benvenisti, Eyal. "Sovereigns as Trustees of Humanity: On the Accountability of States to Foreign Stakeholders." *American Journal of International Law* 107, no. 2 (2013): 295-333.
———. "Community Interests in International Adjudication." In *Community Interests across International Law*, edited by Eyal Benvenisti and Georg Nolte, 70-85. Oxford: Oxford University Press, 2018.
Benvenisti, Eyal, and Georg Nolte, eds. *Community Interests across International Law.* Oxford: Oxford University Press, 2018a.
———, eds. "Community Interests across International Law: Introduction." In *Community Interests across International Law*, edited by Eyal Benvenisti and Georg Nolte, 3-16. Oxford: Oxford University Press, 2018b.
Benzing, Markus. "Community Interests in the Procedure of International Courts and Tribunals." *Law and Practice of International Courts and Tribunals* 5, no. 3 (2006): 369–408.
Besson, Samantha. "General Principles in International Law – Whose Principles?". In *Les Principes en Droit Européen - Principles in European Law*, edited by Samantha Besson and Pascal Pichonnaz, 19-64. Geneva: Schulthess, 2011.
———. "Community Interests in International Law: Whose Interests Are They and How Should We Best Identify Them?". In *Community Interests across International Law*, edited by Eyal Benvenisti and Georg Nolte, 36-49. Oxford: Oxford University Press, 2018.
Bix, Brian. *A Dictionary of Legal Theory.* Oxford: Oxford University Press, 2004.
Blau, Peter M. *Exchange and Power in Social Life.* New York: Wiley, 1964.
Bodansky, Daniel. "Rules vs. Standards in International Environmental Law." *Proceedings of the Annual Meeting (American Society of International Law)* 98 (2004): 275-280.
Boed, Roman. "State of Necessity as a Justification for Internationally Wrongful Conduct." *Yale Human Rights and Development Law Journal* 3 (2000): 1-44.

Boisson de Chazournes, Laurence. "Other Non-Derogable Obligations." In *The Law of International Responsibility*, edited by James Crawford, Alain Pellet and Simon Olleson, 1205-1214. Oxford: Oxford University Press, 2010.

Bolton, Patrick, and M. Dewatripont. *Contract Theory*. Cambridge, MA: MIT Press, 2005.

Bordin, Fernando Lusa. "Reflections of Customary International Law: the Authority of Codification Conventions and ILC Draft Articles in International Law." *International and Comparative Law Quarterly* 63, no. 3 (2014): 535-567.

Borelli, Silvia, and Simon Olleson. "Obligations Relating to Human Rights and Humanitarian Law." In *The Law of International Responsibility*, edited by James Crawford, Alain Pellet and Simon Olleson, 1177-1196. Oxford: Oxford University Press, 2010.

Boyle, Alan. "Liability for Injurious Consequences of Acts not Prohibited by International Law." In *The Law of International Responsibility*, edited by James Crawford, Alain Pellet and Simon Olleson, 95-104. Oxford: Oxford University Press, 2010.

———. "Polluter Pays." In *Max Planck Encyclopedia of Public International Law*, edited by Anne Peters and Rüdiger Wolfrum. Oxford Public International Law: Oxford University Press, 2021. http://opil.ouplaw.com. Article last updated in March 2009.

Bradford, Anu, and Omri Ben-Shahar. "Efficient Enforcement in International Law." *Chicago Journal of International Law* 12, no. 2 (2012): 375-431.

Brewster, Rachel. "Unpacking the State's Reputation." *Harvard International Law Journal* 50, no. 2 (2009): 231-269.

———, "Posner and Sykes Book Symposium: Comment by Rachel Brewster," *OpinioJuris* (Blog), 26 March, 2013a, http://opiniojuris.org/2013/03/26/posner-and-sykes-book-symposium-comment-by-rachel-brewster/.

———. "Pricing Compliance: When Formal Remedies Displace Reputational Sanctions." *Harvard International Law Journal* 54, no. 2 (2013b): 259-314.

———. "Reputation in International Relations and International Law Theory." In *Interdisciplinary Perspectives on International Law and International Relations: The State of the Art*, edited by Jeffrey L. Dunoff and Mark A. Pollack, 524-543. Cambridge: Cambridge University Press, 2013c.

Brilmayer, Lea, and Isaias Yemane Tesfalidet. "Third State Obligations and the Enforcement of International Law." *New York University Journal of International Law and Politics* 44, no. 1 (2011): 1-53.

Bronckers, Marco, and Naboth van den Broek. "Financial Compensation in the WTO: Improving the Remedies of WTO Dispute Settlement." *Journal of International Economic Law* 8, no. 1 (2005): 101-126.

Broude, Tomer. "Behavioral International Law." *University of Pennsylvania Law Review* 163, no. 4 (2015): 1099-1157.

Brousseau, Eric, Tom Dedeurwaerdere, and Bernd Siebenhüner, eds. *Reflexive Governance for Global Public Goods*. Cambridge, MA: MIT Press, 2012.

Brown, John Prather. "Toward an Economic Theory of Liability." *The Journal of Legal Studies* 2, no. 2 (1973): 323-349.

Brunnée, Jutta. "International Legal Accountability through the Lens of the Law of State Responsibility." *Netherlands Yearbook of International Law* 36 (2005): 21-56.

———. "International Environmental Law and Community Interests: Procedural Aspects." In *Community Interests across International Law*, edited by Eyal Benvenisti and Georg Nolte, 151-175. Oxford: Oxford University Press, 2018.

———. "Consent." In *Max Planck Encyclopedia of Public International Law*, edited by Anne Peters and Rüdiger Wolfrum. Oxford Public International Law: Oxford University Press, 2021. http://opil.ouplaw.com. Article last updated in October 2010.

Brunnée, Jutta, and Stephen J. Toope. "Constructivism and International Law." In *Interdisciplinary Perspectives on International Law and International Relations: The State of the Art*, edited by Jeffrey L. Dunoff and Mark A. Pollack, 119-145. Cambridge: Cambridge University Press, 2013.

Buchanan, James M. "An Economic Theory of Clubs." *Economica* 32, no. 125 (1965): 1-14.

———. *The Demand and Supply of Public Goods.* Chicago: Rand McNally, 1968.

Bueno de Mesquita, Bruce. *The War Trap.* New Haven: Yale University Press, 1981.

Calabresi, Guido. "The Decision for Accidents: An Approach to Nonfault Allocation of Costs." *Harvard Law Review* 78, no. 4 (1965): 713-745.

———. *The Costs of Accidents: A Legal and Economic Analysis.* New Haven: Yale University Press, 1970.

Calabresi, Guido, and Jeffrey O. Cooper. "New Directions in Tort Law." *Valparaiso University Law Review* 30, no. 3 (1996): 859–884.

Calabresi, Guido, and A. Douglas Melamed. "Property Rules, Liability Rules, and Inalienability: One View of the Cathedral." *Harvard Law Review* 85, no. 6 (1972): 1089-1128.

Cannizzaro, Enzo. "The Role of Proportionality in the Law of International Countermeasures." *European Journal of International Law* 12, no. 5 (2001): 889–916.

———. "Common Interests of Humankind and the International Regulation of the Use of Force." In *Community Interests across International Law*, edited by Eyal Benvenisti and Georg Nolte, 417-429. Oxford: Oxford University Press, 2018.

Capone, Francesca. "Remedies." In *Max Planck Encyclopedia of Public International Law,* edited by Anne Peters and Rüdiger Wolfrum. Oxford Public International Law: Oxford University Press, 2021. http://opil.ouplaw.com. Article last updated in October 2020.

Carmody, Chi. "Of Substantial Interest: Third Parties under GATT." *Michigan Journal of International Law* 18, no. 4 (1997): 615-657.

Caron, David D. "The ILC Articles on State Responsibility: The Paradoxical Relationship between Form and Authority." *American Journal of International Law* 96, no. 4 (2002): 857-873.

Carraro, Carlo, and Domenico Siniscalco, eds. *New Directions in the Economic Theory of the Environment.* New York: Cambridge University Press, 1997.

Casini, Lorenzo. "Cultural Sites between Nationhood and Mankind." In *Community Interests across International Law*, edited by Eyal Benvenisti and Georg Nolte, 176-187. Oxford: Oxford University Press, 2018.

Cassella, Sarah. *La Nécessité en Droit International: de L'état de Nécessité aux Situations de Nécessité.* Leiden: Martinus Nijhoff Publishers, 2011.

Cassese, Antonio. "The Character of the Violated Obligation." In *The Law of International Responsibility*, edited by James Crawford, Alain Pellet and Simon Olleson, 415-420. Oxford: Oxford University Press, 2010.

Chayes, Abram, and Antonia Handler Chayes. "On Compliance." *International Organization* 47, no. 2 (1993): 175-205.

———. *The New Sovereignty: Compliance with International Regulatory Agreements.* Cambridge, MA: Harvard University Press, 1995.

Coase, R. H. "The Problem of Social Cost." *Journal of Law and Economics* 3 (1960): 1-44.

Coco, Antonio, and Talita de Souza Dias, "Part I: Due Diligence and Covid-19: States' Duties to Prevent and Halt the Coronavirus Outbreak," *EJIL: Talk!* (Blog of the European Journal of International Law), 24 March, 2020, https://www.ejiltalk.org/part-i-due-diligence-and-covid-19-states-duties-to-prevent-and-halt-the-coronavirus-outbreak/?utm_source=mailpoet&utm_medium=email&utm_campaign=ejil-talk-newsletter-post-title_2.

Cohan, John Alan. "Private and Public Necessity and the Violation of Property Rights." *North Dakota Law Review* 83 (2007): 651-733.

Cohen, Amichai. "Rules and Standards in the Application of International Humanitarian Law." *Israel Law Review* 41, no. 1 & 2 (2008): 41-67.

Coleman, Jules, Scott Hershovitz, and Gabriel Mendlow. "Theories of the Common Law of Torts." In *The Stanford Encyclopedia of Philosophy,* edited by Edward N. Zalta. http://plato.stanford.edu/archives/fall2010/entries/tort-theories/. Article last revised on 17 December 2015.

Cooter, Robert. "Unity in Tort, Contract, and Property: The Model of Precaution." *California Law Review* 73, no. 1 (1985): 1-51.

———. "Punitive Damages for Deterence: When and How Much?". *Alabama Law Review* 40, no. 3 (1989): 1143-1196.

Cooter, Robert, and Thomas Ulen. *Law & Economics.* 6th international ed. Boston, MA: Pearson, 2012.

Cornes, Richard, and Todd Sandler. *The Theory of Externalities, Public Goods and Club Goods.* Cambridge: Cambridge University Press, 1986.

Corten, Olivier. "The Obligation of Cessation." In *The Law of International Responsibility*, edited by James Crawford, Alain Pellet and Simon Olleson, 545-549. Oxford: Oxford University Press, 2010.

Crawford, James. *The International Law Commission's Articles on State Responsibility: Introduction, Text, and Commentaries.* Cambridge: Cambridge University Press, 2002.

———. "International Crimes of States." In *The Law of International Responsibility*, edited by James Crawford, Alain Pellet and Simon Olleson, 405-414. Oxford: Oxford University Press, 2010.

———. *State Responsibility: the General Part.* 1st paperback ed. Cambridge: Cambridge University Press, 2014.

Crawford, James, Alain Pellet, and Simon Olleson, eds. *The Law of International Responsibility.* Oxford: Oxford University Press, 2010b.

Crawford, James R. "Responsibility to the International Community as a Whole." *Indiana Journal of Global Legal Studies* 8, no. 2 (2001): 303-322.

Crawford, James, and Jeremy Watkins. "International Responsibility." In *The Philosophy of International Law*, edited by Samantha Besson and John Tasioulas, 283-298. Oxford: Oxford University Press, 2010.

Creutz, Katja. *State Responsibility in the International Legal Order: A Critical Appraisal.* Cambridge: Cambridge University Press, 2020.

Cristol, Jonathan. "Realism." In *Oxford Bibliographies in International Relations,* edited by Patrick James. Oxford Bibliographies Online: Oxford University Press, 2021. Article last modified on 27 June 2017. https://doi.org/10.1093/OBO/9780199743292-0042.

Curtin, Deirdre, and André Nollkaemper. "Conceptualizing Accountability in International and European Law." *Netherlands Yearbook of International Law* 36 (2005): 3-20.

Dasgupta, Partha, Karl-Göran Mäler, and Alessandro Vercelli, eds. *The Economics of Transnational Commons.* Oxford: Oxford University Press, 1997.

David, Eric. "Primary and Secondary Rules." In *The Law of International Responsibility*, edited by James Crawford, Alain Pellet and Simon Olleson, 27-33. Oxford: Oxford University Press, 2010.

Davis, James W. *Psychology, Strategy and Conflict: Perceptions of Insecurity in International Relations.* London: Routledge, 2013.

Davis, James W., and Rose McDermott. "The Past, Present, and Future of Behavioral IR." *International Organization* 75, no. 1 (2021): 147-177.

Dawidowicz, Martin. "Public Law Enforcement without Public Law Safeguards? An Analysis of State Practice on Third-Party Countermeasures and Their Relationship to the UN Security Council." *British Yearbook of International Law* 77, no. 1 (2007): 333-418.

———. "The Obligation of Non-Recognition of an Unlawful Situation." In *The Law of International Responsibility*, edited by James Crawford, Alain Pellet and Simon Olleson, 677-686. Oxford: Oxford University Press, 2010.

———. *Third-Party Countermeasures in International Law.* Cambridge: Cambridge University Press, 2017.

De Geest, Gerrit, ed. *Encyclopedia of Law and Economics.* 2nd ed. 12 vols. Cheltenham, UK: Edward Elgar, 2012.

del Castillo-Laborde, Lilian. "Equitable Utilization of Shared Resources." In *Max Planck Encyclopedia of Public International Law,* edited by Anne Peters and Rüdiger Wolfrum. Oxford Public International Law: Oxford University Press, 2021. http://opil.ouplaw.com. Article last updated in January 2010.

Diamond, Peter A. "Accident Law and Resource Allocation." *Bell Journal of Economics and Management Science* 5, no. 2 (1974): 366–405.

Dill, Janina. "'The Rights and Obligations of Parties to International Armed Conflicts': From Bilateralism but Not Towards Community Interest?". In *Community Interests across International Law*, edited by Eyal Benvenisti and Georg Nolte, 430-447. Oxford: Oxford University Press, 2018.

Dnes, Anthony W. *Principles of Law and Economics.* 3rd ed. Cheltenham, UK: Edward Elgar, 2018.

Douhan, Alena. "Liability for Environmental Damage." In *Max Planck Encyclopedia of Public International Law,* edited by Anne Peters and Rüdiger Wolfrum. Oxford Public International Law: Oxford University Press, 2021. http://opil.ouplaw.com. Article last updated in March 2019.

Downs, George W., and Michael A. Jones. "Reputation, Compliance, and International Law." *Journal of Legal Studies* 31, no. S1 (2002): 95-114.

Dunoff, Jeffrey L., and Joel P. Trachtman. "Economic Analysis of International Law." *Yale Journal of International Law* 24, no. 1 (1999): 1-59.

Dupuy, Pierre-Marie. "Back to the Future of a Multilateral Dimension of the Law of State Responsibility for Breaches of 'Obligations Owed to the International Community as a Whole'." *European Journal of International Law* 23, no. 4 (2012): 1059-1069.

Dutta, Prajit K. *Strategies and Games: Theory and Practice.* Cambridge, MA: MIT Press, 1999.

Ehrlich, Isaac, and Richard A. Posner. "An Economic Analysis of Legal Rulemaking." *Journal of Legal Studies* 3, no. 1 (1974): 257-286.

Ellis, Dorsey D., Jr. "Fairness and Efficiency in the Law of Punitive Damages." *Southern California Law Review* 56, no. 1 (1982): 1-78.

Fasoli, Elena. "Distress." In *Max Planck Encyclopedia of Public International Law,* edited by Anne Peters and Rüdiger Wolfrum. Oxford Public International Law: Oxford University Press, 2021. http://opil.ouplaw.com. Article last updated in June 2013.

Fastenrath, Ulrich, Rudolf Geiger, Daniel-Erasmus Khan, Andreas Paulus, Sabine von Schorlemer, and Christoph Vedder, eds. *From Bilateralism to Community Interest: Essays in Honour of Bruno Simma.* Oxford: Oxford University Press, 2011.

Faure, Michael G., and André Nollkaemper. "International Liability as an Instrument to Prevent and Compensate for Climate Change." *Stanford Journal of International Law* 43 A (2007): 123-179.

Fearon, James D. "Bargaining, Enforcement, and International Cooperation." *International Organization* 52, no. 2 (1998): 269-305.

Fearon, James D., and Alexander Wendt. "Rationalism v. Constructivism: A Skeptical View." In *Handbook of International Relations*, edited by Walter Carlsnaes, Thomas Risse and Beth A. Simmons, 52-72. London: SAGE, 2002.

Feichtner, Isabel. "Community Interest." In *Max Planck Encyclopedia of Public International Law,* edited by Anne Peters and Rüdiger Wolfrum. Oxford Public International Law: Oxford University Press, 2021. http://opil.ouplaw.com. Article last updated in February 2007.

Ferroni, Marco, and Ashoka Mody, eds. *International Public Goods: Incentives, Measurement, and Financing*. Boston, MA: Springer, 2002.

Finnemore, Martha, and Kathryn Sikkink. "International Norm Dynamics and Political Change." *International Organization* 52, no. 4 (1998): 887-917.

Fisher, Roger. *Improving Compliance with International Law.* Charlottesville: University Press of Virginia, 1981.

Fitzmaurice, Malgosia. "Necessity in International Environmental Law." *Netherlands Yearbook of International Law* 41 (2010): 159-192.

Fletcher, George P. "Fairness and Utility in Tort Theory." *Harvard Law Review* 85, no. 3 (1972): 537-573.

Forteau, Mathias. "Reparation in the Event of a Circumstance Precluding Wrongfulness." In *The Law of International Responsibility*, edited by James Crawford, Alain Pellet and Simon Olleson, 887-893. Oxford: Oxford University Press, 2010.

Francioni, Francesco. "Public and Private in the International Protection of Global Cultural Goods." *European Journal of International Law* 23, no. 3 (2012): 719-730.

Franck, Thomas M. *The Power of Legitimacy among Nations*. New York: Oxford University Press, 1990.

Frowein, Jochen A. "Obligations Erga Omnes." In *Max Planck Encyclopedia of Public International Law,* edited by Anne Peters and Rüdiger Wolfrum. Oxford Public International Law: Oxford University Press, 2021a. http://opil.ouplaw.com. Article last updated in December 2008.

———. "Ius Cogens." In *Max Planck Encyclopedia of Public International Law,* edited by Anne Peters and Rüdiger Wolfrum. Oxford Public International Law: Oxford University Press, 2021b. http://opil.ouplaw.com. Article last updated in March 2013.

Gaeta, Paola. "The Character of the Breach." In *The Law of International Responsibility*, edited by James Crawford, Alain Pellet and Simon Olleson, 421-426. Oxford: Oxford University Press, 2010.

Gaja, Giorgio. "The Concept of an Injured State." In *The Law of International Responsibility*, edited by James Crawford, Alain Pellet and Simon Olleson, 941-947. Oxford: Oxford University Press, 2010a.

———. "States Having an Interest in Compliance with the Obligation Breached." In *The Law of International Responsibility*, edited by James Crawford, Alain Pellet and Simon Olleson, 957-964. Oxford: Oxford University Press, 2010b.

———. "The Protection of General Interests in the International Community." *Collected Courses of the Hague Academy of International Law* 364, no. 1 (2012): 9-185.

Garner, Bryan A., ed. *Black's Law Dictionary*. 8th ed. St. Paul, MN: Thomson West, 2004.

Gazzini, Tarcisio, Wouter G. Werner, and Ige F. Dekker. "Necessity across International Law: An Introduction." *Netherlands Yearbook of International Law* 41 (2010): 3-10.

Gerring, John. *Social Science Methodology: A Unified Framework*. 2nd ed. Cambridge: Cambridge University Press, 2012.

Goetz, Charles J., and Robert E. Scott. "Enforcing Promises: An Examination of the Basis of Contract." *Yale Law Journal* 89, no. 7 (1980): 1261-1322.

Goldsmith, Jack L., and Eric A. Posner. *The Limits of International Law*. Oxford: Oxford University Press, 2005.

Goldsmith, Jack, and Daryl Levinson. "Law for States: International Law, Constitutional Law, Public Law." *Harvard Law Review* 122, no. 7 (2009): 1791-1868.

Gray, Christine. "The Choice between Restitution and Compensation." *European Journal of International Law* 10, no. 2 (1999): 413-423.

———. "The Different Forms of Reparation: Restitution." In *The Law of International Responsibility*, edited by James Crawford, Alain Pellet and Simon Olleson, 589-597. Oxford: Oxford University Press, 2010.

Gray, Christine D. *Judicial Remedies in International Law*. Oxford: Clarendon, 1990.

Greenwood, Christopher. "Self-Defence." In *Max Planck Encyclopedia of Public International Law,* edited by Anne Peters and Rüdiger Wolfrum. Oxford Public International Law: Oxford University Press, 2021. http://opil.ouplaw.com. Article last updated in April 2011.

Guzman, Andrew T. "A Compliance-Based Theory of International Law." *California Law Review* 90, no. 6 (2002): 1823-1887.

———. *How International Law Works: A Rational Choice Theory*. Oxford: Oxford University Press, 2008a.

———. "International Tribunals: A Rational Choice Analysis." *University of Pennsylvania Law Review* 157, no. 1 (2008b): 171-235.

———. "Against Consent." *Virginia Journal of International Law* 52, no. 4 (2012): 747-790.

Hadfield, Gillian K. "Weighing the Value of Vagueness: An Economic Perspective on Precision in the Law." *California Law Review* 82, no. 3 (1994): 541-554.

Hafner-Burton, Emilie M. "Trading Human Rights: How Preferential Trade Agreements Influence Government Repression." *International Organization* 59, no. 3 (2005): 593-629.

———. "Sticks and Stones: Naming and Shaming the Human Rights Enforcement Problem." *International Organization* 62, no. 4 (2008): 689-716.

———. *Forced to Be Good: Why Trade Agreements Boost Human Rights.* Ithaca, NY: Cornell University Press, 2009.

Hardin, Garrett. "The Tragedy of the Commons." *Science* 162, no. 3859 (1968): 1243-1248.

Hart, Oliver, and John Moore. "Foundations of Incomplete Contracts." *Review of Economic Studies* 66, no. 1 (1999): 115-138.

Hathaway, Oona A. "Do Human Rights Treaties Make a Difference?". *The Yale Law Journal* 111, no. 8 (2002): 1935-2042.

———. "The Cost of Commitment." *Stanford Law Review* 55, no. 5 (2003): 1821-1862.

———. "Why Do Countries Commit to Human Rights Treaties?". *The Journal of Conflict Resolution* 51, no. 4 (2007): 588-621.

Hathaway, Oona, and Scott J. Shapiro. "Outcasting: Enforcement in Domestic and International Law." *The Yale Law Journal* 121, no. 2 (2011): 252-349.

Heathcote, Sarah. "Circumstances Precluding Wrongfulness in the ILC Articles on State Responsibility: Necessity." In *The Law of International Responsibility*, edited by James Crawford, Alain Pellet and Simon Olleson, 491-501. Oxford: Oxford University Press, 2010.

———. "State Omissions and Due Diligence: Aspects of Fault, Damage and Contribution to Injury in the Law of State Responsibility." In *The ICJ and the Evolution of International Law: the Enduring Impact of the Corfu Channel Case*, edited by Karine Bannelier, Théodore Christakis and Sarah Heathcote, 295-314. London: Routledge, 2012.

Hentrei, Simon, and Ximena Soley. "Force Majeure." In *Max Planck Encyclopedia of Public International Law,* edited by Anne Peters and Rüdiger Wolfrum. Oxford Public International Law: Oxford University Press, 2021. http://opil.ouplaw.com. Article last updated in April 2011.

Hessbruegge, Jan Arno. "The Historical Development of the Doctrines of Attribution and Due Diligence in International Law." *New York University Journal of International Law and Politics* 36 (2004): 265-306.

Higgins, Polly. *Eradicating Ecocide: Exposing the Corporate and Political Practices Destroying the Planet and Proposing the Laws Needed to Eradicate Ecocide.* London: Shepheard-Walwyn, 2010.

Hirshleifer, Jack. "From Weakest-Link to Best-Shot: The Voluntary Provision of Public Goods." *Public Choice* 41, no. 3 (1983): 371-386.

Hofer, Alexandra. "The Efficacy of Targeted Sanctions in Enforcing Compliance with International Law." *AJIL Unbound* 113 (2019): 163-168.

Horn, Henrik, Giovanni Maggi, and Robert W. Staiger. "Trade Agreements as Endogenously Incomplete Contracts." *The American Economic Review* 100, no. 1 (2010): 394-419.

Hufbauer, Gary Clyde, Jeffrey J. Schott, Kimberly Ann Elliott, and Barbara Oegg. *Economic Sanctions Reconsidered.* 3rd ed. Washington, DC: Peterson Institute for International Economics, 2007.

Ingham, Sean. "Pareto-Optimality." In *Encyclopaedia Britannica.* https://www.britannica.com/topic/Pareto-optimality. Article last modified on 28 November 2019.

Iovane, Massimo, Fulvio M. Palombino, Daniele Amoroso, and Giovanni Zarra, eds. *The Protection of General Interests in Contemporary International Law: A Theoretical and Empirical Inquiry*. Oxford: Oxford University Press, 2021.

Iwasawa, Yuji, and Naoki Iwatsuki. "Procedural Conditions." In *The Law of International Responsibility*, edited by James Crawford, Alain Pellet and Simon Olleson, 1149-1155. Oxford: Oxford University Press, 2010.

Jackson, John H. "The WTO Dispute Settlement Understanding - Misunderstandings on the Nature of Legal Obligation." *American Journal of International Law* 91, no. 1 (1997): 60-64.

———. "International Law Status of WTO Dispute Settlement Reports: Obligation to Comply or Option to "Buy Out"?". *American Journal of International Law* 98, no. 1 (2004): 109-125.
Johnston, Alastair Iain. "Treating International Institutions as Social Environments." *International Studies Quarterly* 45, no. 4 (2001): 487-515.
Johnston, Jason Scott. "Bargaining under Rules versus Standards." *Journal of Law, Economics, & Organization* 11, no. 2 (1995): 256-281.
Johnstone, Ian. "Status as a Reward." *AJIL Unbound* 115 (2021): 226-231.
Jørgensen, Nina H.B. "A Reappraisal of Punitive Damages in International Law." *British Yearbook of International Law* 68, no. 1 (1998): 247-266.
———. *The Responsibility of States for International Crimes.* Oxford: Oxford University Press, 2000.
———. "The Obligation of Cooperation." In *The Law of International Responsibility*, edited by James Crawford, Alain Pellet and Simon Olleson, 695-701. Oxford: Oxford University Press, 2010a.
———. "The Obligation of Non-Assistance to the Responsible State." In *The Law of International Responsibility*, edited by James Crawford, Alain Pellet and Simon Olleson, 687-693. Oxford: Oxford University Press, 2010b.
Kahneman, Daniel, and Amos Tversky. "Prospect Theory: An Analysis of Decision under Risk." *Econometrica* 47, no. 2 (1979): 263-291.
Kamto, Maurice. "The Time Factor in the Application of Countermeasures." In *The Law of International Responsibility*, edited by James Crawford, Alain Pellet and Simon Olleson, 1169-1176. Oxford: Oxford University Press, 2010.
Kaplow, Louis. "Rules versus Standards: An Economic Analysis." *Duke Law Journal* 42, no. 3 (1992): 557-629.
Kaplow, Louis, and Steven Shavell. "Property Rules versus Liability Rules: An Economic Analysis." *Harvard Law Review* 109, no. 4 (1996): 713-790.
———. *Fairness versus Welfare.* Cambridge, MA: Harvard University Press, 2002.
Katselli Proukaki, Elena. *The Problem of Enforcement in International Law: Countermeasures, the Non-Injured State and the Idea of International Community.* London: Routledge, 2010.
Katz, Avery Wiener, ed. *Foundations of the Economic Approach to Law.* New York: Oxford University Press, 1998.
Kaul, Inge. "Global Public Goods: Explaining Their Underprovision." *Journal of International Economic Law* 15, no. 3 (2012): 729-750.
———, ed. *Global Public Goods.* Cheltenham, UK: Edward Elgar, 2016.
Kaul, Inge, Donald Blondin, and Neva Nahtigal. "Understanding Global Public Goods: Where We Are and Where to Next." In *Global Public Goods*, edited by Inge Kaul, xiii-xcii. Cheltenham, UK: Edward Elgar, 2016.
Kaul, Inge, and Pedro Conceição, eds. *The New Public Finance: Responding to Global Challenges.* New York: Oxford University Press, 2006.
Kaul, Inge, Pedro Conceição, Katell Le Goulven, and Ronald U. Mendoza, eds. *Providing Global Public Goods: Managing Globalization.* New York: Oxford University Press, 2003.
Kaul, Inge, Isabelle Grunberg, and Marc A. Stern. "Defining Global Public Goods." In *Global Public Goods: International Cooperation in the 21st Century*, edited by Inge Kaul, Isabelle Grunberg and Marc A. Stern, 2-19. New York: Oxford University Press, 1999a.
———, eds. *Global Public Goods: International Cooperation in the 21st Century.* New York: Oxford University Press, 1999b.
Keohane, Robert O. *After Hegemony: Cooperation and Discord in the World Political Economy.* Princeton: Princeton University Press, 1984.
———. "Reciprocity in International Relations." *International Organization* 40, no. 1 (1986): 1-27.
———. "International Relations and International Law: Two Optics." *Harvard International Law Journal* 38, no. 2 (1997): 487-502.

———. "Rational Choice Theory and International Law: Insights and Limitations." *Journal of Legal Studies* 31, no. S1 (2002): S307-S319.

Khaitan, Bulbul. "Alternative to the Existing Rule of Attribution for Use of Force by Non-State Actors in an Armed Conflict." *Journal of Conflict and Security Law* 26, no. 1 (2020): 41-78.

Kingsbury, Benedict. "The Concept of Compliance as a Function of Competing Conceptions of International Law." *Michigan Journal of International Law* 19, no. 2 (1998): 345-372.

Koivurova, Timo. "Due Diligence." In *Max Planck Encyclopedia of Public International Law,* edited by Anne Peters and Rüdiger Wolfrum. Oxford Public International Law: Oxford University Press, 2021. http://opil.ouplaw.com. Article last updated in February 2010.

Kojima, Chie. "Compensation Fund." In *Max Planck Encyclopedia of Public International Law,* edited by Anne Peters and Rüdiger Wolfrum. Oxford Public International Law: Oxford University Press, 2021. http://opil.ouplaw.com. Article last updated in July 2019.

Koremenos, Barbara. "Institutionalism and International Law." In *Interdisciplinary Perspectives on International Law and International Relations: The State of the Art*, edited by Jeffrey L. Dunoff and Mark A. Pollack, 59-82. Cambridge: Cambridge University Press, 2013.

———. *The Continent of International Law: Explaining Agreement Design.* Cambridge: Cambridge University Press, 2016.

Koremenos, Barbara, Charles Lipson, and Duncan Snidal. "The Rational Design of International Institutions." *International Organization* 55, no. 4 (2001): 761-799.

Kornhauser, Lewis A. "Incentives, Compensation, and Irreparable Harm." In *Distribution of Responsibilities in International Law*, edited by André Nollkaemper and Dov Jacobs, 120-152. Cambridge: Cambridge University Press, 2015.

Korobkin, Russell B. "Behavioral Analysis and Legal Form: Rules vs. Standards Revisited." *Oregon Law Review* 79, no. 1 (2000): 23-60.

Koskenniemi, Martti. "Doctrines of State Responsibility." In *The Law of International Responsibility*, edited by James Crawford, Alain Pellet and Simon Olleson, 45-51. Oxford: Oxford University Press, 2010.

Koutroulis, Vaios. "Martens Clause." In *Oxford Bibliographies in International Law* edited by Anthony Carty. Oxford Bibliographies Online: Oxford University Press, 2021. Article last modified on 24 July 2013. doi:https://doi.org/10.1093/OBO/9780199796953-0101.

Krasner, Stephen D. "Structural Causes and Regime Consequences: Regimes as Intervening Variables." In *International Regimes*, edited by Stephen D. Krasner, 1-22. Ithaca, NY: Cornell University Press, 1983.

Kratochwil, Friedrich V. *Rules, Norms, and Decisions: On the Conditions of Practical and Legal Reasoning in International Relations and Domestic Affairs.* Cambridge: Cambridge University Press, 1989.

Krieger, Heike. "Rights and Obligations of Third Parties in Armed Conflicts." In *Community Interests across International Law*, edited by Eyal Benvenisti and Georg Nolte, 448-467. Oxford: Oxford University Press, 2018.

Krisch, Nico. *Selbstverteidigung und Kollektive Sicherheit.* Berlin: Springer, 2001.

———. "The Decay of Consent: International Law in an Age of Global Public Goods." *American Journal of International Law* 108, no. 1 (2014): 1-40.

Kritsiotis, Dino. "Imagining the International Community." *European Journal of International Law* 13, no. 4 (2002): 961-992.

Kurtz, Jürgen. "Adjudging the Exceptional at International Investment Law: Security, Public Order and Financial Crisis." *International and Comparative Law Quarterly* 59, no. 2 (2010): 325-371.

Kydd, Andrew H. "Methodological Individualism and Rational Choice." In *The Oxford Handbook of International Relations*, edited by Christian Reus-Smit and Duncan Snidal, 425-443. Oxford: Oxford University Press, 2008.

Laffont, J. J. "Externalities." In *The New Palgrave Dictionary of Economics*. London: Palgrave Macmillan. Article last modified on 13 March 2017. doi:https://doi.org/10.1057/978-1-349-95121-5_126-2.

Landes, William M., and Richard A. Posner. "An Economic Theory of Intentional Torts." *International Review of Law and Economics* 1, no. 2 (1981): 127-154.

———. *The Economic Structure of Tort Law*. Cambridge, MA: Harvard University Press, 1987.

Leben, Charles. "Obligations Relating to the Use of Force and Arising from Peremptory Norms of International Law." In *The Law of International Responsibility*, edited by James Crawford, Alain Pellet and Simon Olleson, 1197-1204. Oxford: Oxford University Press, 2010.

Lehman, Jeffrey, and Shirelle Phelps, eds. *West's Encyclopedia of American Law*. 2nd ed. Detroit: Thomson/Gale, 2005.

Lesaffre, Hubert. "Circumstances Precluding Wrongfulness in the ILC Articles on State Responsibility: Countermeasures." In *The Law of International Responsibility*, edited by James Crawford, Alain Pellet and Simon Olleson, 469-473. Oxford: Oxford University Press, 2010.

Loomis, John B. "How Large Is the Extent of the Market for Public Goods: Evidence from a Nationwide Contingent Valuation Survey." *Applied Economics* 28, no. 7 (1996): 779-782.

Lutz, Ellen L., and Kathryn Sikkink. "International Human Rights Law and Practice in Latin America." *International Organization* 54, no. 3 (2000): 633-659.

Mahoney, Paul G. "Contract Remedies: General." In *Encyclopedia of Law and Economics*, edited by Boudewijn Bouckaert and Gerrit de Geest, 117-140. Cheltenham, UK: Edward Elgar, 2000.

Mann, F. A. "The Consequences of an International Wrong in International and National Law." *British Yearbook of International Law* 48, no. 1 (1977): 1-65.

Mayer, Benoît. "Less-Than-Full Reparations in International Law." *Indian Journal of International Law* 56, no. 3 (2016): 463-502.

McDermott, Rose. *Risk-Taking in International Politics: Prospect Theory in American Foreign Policy*. Ann Arbor: University of Michigan Press, 1998.

———. *Political Psychology in International Relations*. Ann Arbor: University of Michigan Press, 2004.

Mearsheimer, John J. *The Tragedy of Great Power Politics*. New York: Norton, 2001.

Ménard, Maja. "Circumstances Precluding Wrongfulness in the ILC Articles on State Responsibility: Compliance with Peremptory Norms." In *The Law of International Responsibility*, edited by James Crawford, Alain Pellet and Simon Olleson, 449-453. Oxford: Oxford University Press, 2010.

Mercer, Jonathan. *Reputation and International Politics*. Ithaca, NY: Cornell University Press, 1996.

Moravcsik, Andrew. "Taking Preferences Seriously: A Liberal Theory of International Politics." *International Organization* 51, no. 4 (1997): 513-553.

———. "Liberal Theories of International Law." In *Interdisciplinary Perspectives on International Law and International Relations: The State of the Art*, edited by Jeffrey L. Dunoff and Mark A. Pollack, 83-118. Cambridge: Cambridge University Press, 2013.

Morgenthau, Hans J. *Politics among Nations: The Struggle for Power and Peace*. New York: Alfred A. Knopf, 1948.

Morrow, James D. *Game Theory for Political Scientists*. Princeton: Princeton University Press, 1994.

Murphy, Liam. "International Responsibility." In *The Philosophy of International Law*, edited by Samantha Besson and John Tasioulas, 299-315. Oxford: Oxford University Press, 2010.

Musgrave, Richard A. *The Theory of Public Finance: A Study in Public Economy*. New York: McGraw-Hill, 1959.

Musgrave, Richard A., and Alan T. Peacock, eds. *Classics in the Theory of Public Finance*. London: Macmillan, 1958.

Nollkaemper, André. "Constitutionalization and the Unity of the Law of International Responsibility." *Indiana Journal of Global Legal Studies* 16, no. 2 (2009): 535-563.

———. "International Adjudication of Global Public Goods: The Intersection of Substance and Procedure." *European Journal of International Law* 23, no. 3 (2012): 769-791.

Nollkaemper, André. "Responsibility." In *Concepts for International Law: Contributions to Disciplinary Thought*, edited by Jean d'Aspremont and Sahib Singh, 760-772. Cheltenham, UK: Edward Elgar, 2019.

Nollkaemper, André, Jean d'Aspremont, Christiane Ahlborn, Berenice Boutin, Nataša Nedeski, Ilias Plakokefalos, and Dov Jacobs. "Guiding Principles on Shared Responsibility in International Law." *European Journal of International Law* 31, no. 1 (2020): 15-72.

Nollkaemper, André, and Dov Jacobs. "Shared Responsibility in International Law: A Conceptual Framework." *Michigan Journal of International Law* 34, no. 2 (2013): 359-438.

———, eds. *Distribution of Responsibilities in International Law*. Cambridge: Cambridge University Press, 2015.

Nollkaemper, André, and Ilias Plakokefalos, eds. *Principles of Shared Responsibility in International Law: An Appraisal of the State of the Art*. Cambridge: Cambridge University Press, 2014.

———, eds. *The Practice of Shared Responsibility in International Law*. Cambridge: Cambridge University Press, 2017.

Nolte, Georg. "From Dionisio Anzilotti to Roberto Ago: The Classical International Law of State Responsibility and the Traditional Primacy of a Bilateral Conception of Inter-State Relations." *European Journal of International Law* 13, no. 5 (2002): 1083–1098.

———. "The International Law Commission and Community Interests." In *Community Interests across International Law*, edited by Eyal Benvenisti and Georg Nolte, 101-117. Oxford: Oxford University Press, 2018.

Norman, George, and Joel P. Trachtman. "The Customary International Law Game." *American Journal of International Law* 99, no. 3 (2005): 541-580.

O'Keefe, Roger. "Proportionality." In *The Law of International Responsibility*, edited by James Crawford, Alain Pellet and Simon Olleson, 1157-1168. Oxford: Oxford University Press, 2010.

Olson, Mancur. *The Logic of Collective Action: Public Goods and the Theory of Groups*. Cambridge, MA: Harvard University Press, 1965.

Orakhelashvili, Alexander. *Peremptory Norms in International Law*. Oxford: Oxford University Press, 2006.

Oye, Kenneth A. "Explaining Cooperation under Anarchy: Hypotheses and Strategies." In *Cooperation under Anarchy*, edited by Kenneth A. Oye, 1-24. Princeton: Princeton University Press, 1986.

Paddeu, Federica. *Justification and Excuse in International Law: Concept and Theory of General Defences*. Cambridge: Cambridge University Press, 2018.

———. "Clarifying the Concept of Circumstances Precluding Wrongfulness (Justifications) in International Law." In *Exceptions in International Law*, edited by Lorand Bartels and Federica Paddeu, 203-224. Oxford: Oxford University Press, 2020a.

Paddeu, Federica I. "Book Review: Sarah Cassella, La Nécessité en Droit International: de L'état de Nécessité aux Situations de Nécessité (Leiden, Martinus Nijhoff Publishers, 2011)." *The British Yearbook of International Law* 82, no. 1 (2011a): 505-508.

———. "A Genealogy of Force Majeure in International Law." *The British Yearbook of International Law* 82, no. 1 (2011b): 381-494.

———. "Self-Defence as a Circumstance Precluding Wrongfulness: Understanding Article 21 of the Articles on State Responsibility." *British Yearbook of International Law* 85, no. 1 (2015): 90-132.

———. "Military Assistance on Request and General Reasons against Force: Consent as a Defence to the Prohibition of Force." *Journal on the Use of Force and International Law* 7, no. 2 (2020b): 227-269.

———. "Countermeasures." In *Max Planck Encyclopedia of Public International Law*, edited by Anne Peters and Rüdiger Wolfrum. Oxford Public International Law: Oxford University Press, 2021. http://opil.ouplaw.com. Article last updated in September 2015.

Paddeu, Federica I., and Freya Jephcott, "Covid-19 and Defences in the Law of State Responsibility: Part I," *EJIL: Talk!* (Blog of the European Journal of International Law), 17 March, 2020, https://www.ejiltalk.org/covid-19-and-defences-in-the-law-of-state-responsibility-part-i/.

———, "Covid-19 and Defences in the Law of State Responsibility: Part II," *EJIL: Talk!* (Blog of the European Journal of International Law), 17 March, 2020c, https://www.ejiltalk.org/covid-19-and-defences-in-the-law-of-state-responsibility-part-ii/.

Paddeu, Federica I., and Christian J. Tams, "Dithering, Trickling down, and Encoding: Concluding Thoughts on the 'ILC Articles at 20' Symposium," *EJIL: Talk!* (Blog of the European Journal of International Law), 9 August, 2021, https://www.ejiltalk.org/dithering-trickling-down-and-encoding-concluding-thoughts-on-the-ilc-articles-at-20-symposium/.

———, "The ILC Articles at 20: Introduction to the Symposium," *EJIL: Talk!* (Blog of the European Journal of International Law), 2 August, 2021b, https://www.ejiltalk.org/the-ilc-articles-at-20-introduction-to-the-symposium/.

Paddeu, Federica, and Michael Waibel. "Necessity 20 Years On: The Limits of Article 25 ARSIWA." *University of Cambridge Faculty of Law Research Paper*, no. 23 (2021). https://ssrn.com/abstract=3858530.

Paine, Joshua. "International Adjudication as a Global Public Good?". *European Journal of International Law* 29, no. 4 (2019): 1223-1249.

Palmer, Daniel E. "Expected Utility." In *Encyclopaedia Britannica*. https://www.britannica.com/topic/expected-utility. Article last modified on 18 May 2016.

Palmisano, Giuseppe. "Fault." In *Max Planck Encyclopedia of Public International Law*, edited by Anne Peters and Rüdiger Wolfrum. Oxford Public International Law: Oxford University Press, 2021. http://opil.ouplaw.com. Article last updated in September 2007.

Paparinskis, Martins. "Circumstances Precluding Wrongfulness in International Investment Law." *ICSID Review - Foreign Investment Law Journal* 31, no. 2 (2016): 484-503.

———. "A Case against Crippling Compensation in International Law of State Responsibility." *The Modern Law Review* 83, no. 6 (2020a): 1246-1286.

———. "The Once and Future Law of State Responsibility." *American Journal of International Law* 114, no. 4 (2020b): 618-626.

———, "Crippling Compensation in the Law of State Responsibility," *EJIL: Talk!* (Blog of the European Journal of International Law), 17 May, 2021, https://www.ejiltalk.org/crippling-compensation-in-the-law-of-state-responsibility/.

Parisi, Francesco, and Vincy Fon. "Comparative Causation." *American Law and Economics Review* 6, no. 2 (2004): 345-368.

Parisi, Francesco, and Nita Ghei. "The Role of Reciprocity in International Law." *Cornell International Law Journal* 36, no. 1 (2003-2004): 93-124.

Pauwelyn, Joost. *Optimal Protection of International Law: Navigating between European Absolutism and American Voluntarism*. Cambridge: Cambridge University Press, 2008.

Pellet, Alain. "The Definition of Responsibility in International Law." In *The Law of International Responsibility*, edited by James Crawford, Alain Pellet and Simon Olleson, 3-16. Oxford: Oxford University Press, 2010a.

———. "The ILC's Articles on State Responsibility for Internationally Wrongful Acts and Related Texts." In *The Law of International Responsibility*, edited by James Crawford, Alain Pellet and Simon Olleson, 75-94. Oxford: Oxford University Press, 2010b.

Pellet, Alain, and Alina Miron. "Sanctions." In *Max Planck Encyclopedia of Public International Law*, edited by Anne Peters and Rüdiger Wolfrum. Oxford Public International Law: Oxford University Press, 2021. http://opil.ouplaw.com. Article last updated in August 2013.

Peterson, Martin. *An Introduction to Decision Theory*. Cambridge: Cambridge University Press, 2009.

Petrova, Margarita H. "Naming and Praising in Humanitarian Norm Development." *World Politics* 71, no. 3 (2019): 586-630.

Pindyck, Robert S., and Daniel L. Rubinfeld. *Microeconomics*. 9th global ed. Harlow, UK: Pearson, 2018.

Pinto de Albuquerque, Paulo, and Anne van Aaken. "Punitive Damages in Strasbourg." In *The European Convention on Human Rights and General International Law*, edited by Anne van Aaken and Iulia Motoc, 230-247. Oxford: Oxford University Press, 2018.

Pisillo-Mazzeschi, Riccardo. "The Due Diligence Rule and the Nature of the International Responsibility of States." *German Yearbook of International Law* 35 (1992): 9-51.

Polinsky, A. Mitchell. "Private versus Public Enforcement of Fines." *Journal of Legal Studies* 9, no. 1 (1980): 105-127.

———. *An Introduction to Law and Economics*. 5th ed. New York: Wolters Kluwer, 2019.

Polinsky, A. Mitchell, and Steven Shavell. "The Optimal Tradeoff between the Probability and Magnitude of Fines." *American Economic Review* 69, no. 5 (1979): 880-891.

———. "Punitive Damages: An Economic Analysis." *Harvard Law Review* 111, no. 4 (1998): 869-962.

———, eds. *Handbook of Law and Economics*. 2 vols. Amsterdam: North-Holland, 2007.

Posner, Eric A. "Contract Theory." In *The Blackwell Guide to the Philosophy of Law and Legal Theory*, edited by Martin P. Golding and William A. Edmundson, 138-147. Malden, MA: Blackwell, 2005.

———. "Erga Omnes Norms, Institutionalization, and Constitutionalism in International Law." *Journal of Institutional and Theoretical Economics (JITE)/Zeitschrift für die gesamte Staatswissenschaft* 165, no. 1 (2009): 5-23.

———., ed. *Economics of Public International Law*. Cheltenham, UK: Edward Elgar, 2010.

Posner, Eric A., and Alan O. Sykes. "An Economic Analysis of State and Individual Responsibility under International Law." *American Law and Economics Review* 9, no. 1 (2007): 72-134.

———. *Economic Foundations of International Law*. Cambridge, MA: Belknap Press of Harvard University Press, 2013.

Posner, Richard A. *Economic Analysis of Law*. 9th ed. New York: Wolters Kluwer, 2014.

Posner, Richard A., and Francesco Parisi. *Law and Economics: Elgar Research Reviews in Economics*. Elgaronline: Edward Elgar, 2016.

Posner, Richard A., and Andrew M. Rosenfield. "Impossibility and Related Doctrines in Contract Law: An Economic Analysis." *Journal of Legal Studies* 6, no. 1 (1977): 83-118.

Putnam, Robert D. "Diplomacy and Domestic Politics: The Logic of Two-Level Games." *International Organization* 42, no. 3 (1988): 427-460.

Ragazzi, Maurizio. *The Concept of International Obligations Erga Omnes*. Oxford: Clarendon Press, 1997.

Ranganathan, Surabhi. "The Law of the Sea and Natural Resources." In *Community Interests across International Law*, edited by Eyal Benvenisti and Georg Nolte, 121-135. Oxford: Oxford University Press, 2018.

Raustiala, Kal. "Form and Substance in International Agreements." *American Journal of International Law* 99, no. 3 (2005): 581-614.

Reinisch, August. "Necessity in Investment Arbitration." *Netherlands Yearbook of International Law* 41 (2010): 137-158.

Ripinsky, Sergey. "State of Necessity: Effect on Compensation." *Transnational Dispute Management* 4, no. 6 (2007). www.transnational-dispute-management.com/article.asp?key=1177.

Roberts, Anthea. "Comparative International Law? The Role of National Courts in Creating and Enforcing International Law." *International and Comparative Law Quarterly* 60, no. 1 (2011): 57-92.

Rodick, Burleigh Cushing. *The Doctrine of Necessity in International Law*. New York: Columbia University Press, 1928.

Ruffert, Matthias. "Reprisals." In *Max Planck Encyclopedia of Public International Law*, edited by Anne Peters and Rüdiger Wolfrum. Oxford Public International Law: Oxford University Press, 2021. http://opil.ouplaw.com. Article last updated in January 2021.

Ryngaert, Cedric. "State Responsibility, Necessity and Human Rights." *Netherlands Yearbook of International Law* 41 (2010): 79-98.

Salmon, Jean. "Faut-Il Codifier L'état de Nécessité en Droit International?". In *Essays in International Law in Honour of Judge Manfred Lachs/Études de Droit International en l'honneur du Juge Manfred Lachs*, edited by Jerzy Makarczyk, 235-270. The Hague: Martinus Nijhoff Publishers, 1984.
Samuelson, Paul A. "The Pure Theory of Public Expenditure." *Review of Economics and Statistics* 36, no. 4 (1954): 387-389.
Sandler, Todd. *Collective Action: Theory and Applications*. Ann Arbor: University of Michigan Press, 1992.
———. *Global Challenges: An Approach to Environmental, Political, and Economic Problems*. Cambridge: Cambridge University Press, 1997.
———. *Global Collective Action*. Cambridge: Cambridge University Press, 2004.
———. "Overcoming Global and Regional Collective Action Impediments." *Global Policy* 1, no. 1 (2010): 40-50.
———. "Strategic Aspects of Difficult Global Challenges." *Global Policy* 7, Supplement 1 (2016): 33–44.
Sarvarian, Arman. "The Ossified Debate on a UN Convention on State Responsibility." *International and Comparative Law Quarterly* 70, no. 3 (2021): 769-798.
Schachter, Oscar. *International Law in Theory and Practice*. Dordrecht: Martinus Nijhoff Publishers, 1991.
Schäfer, Hans-Bernd, and Claus Ott. *The Economic Analysis of Civil Law*. Cheltenham, UK: Edward Elgar, 2004.
Schill, Stephan, and Vladislav Djanic. "International Investment Law and Community Interests." In *Community Interests across International Law*, edited by Eyal Benvenisti and Georg Nolte, 221-248. Oxford: Oxford University Press, 2018.
Schill, Stephan W. *The Multilateralization of International Investment Law*. Cambridge: Cambridge University Press, 2009.
———. "MFN Clauses as Bilateral Commitments to Multilateralism: A Reply to Simon Batifort and J. Benton Heath." *American Journal of International Law* 111, no. 4 (2017): 914-935.
Schlag, Pierre. "Rules and Standards." *UCLA Law Review* 33, no. 2 (1985): 379-430.
Schlager, Edella, and Elinor Ostrom. "Property-Rights Regimes and Natural Resources: A Conceptual Analysis." *Land Economics* 68, no. 3 (1992): 249-262.
Schwartz, Alan. "The Case for Specific Performance." *Yale Law Journal* 89, no. 2 (1979): 271-306.
Schwartz, Warren F., and Alan O. Sykes. "The Economic Structure of Renegotiation and Dispute Resolution in the World Trade Organization." *Journal of Legal Studies* 31, no. S1 (2002): S179-S204.
Scott, Robert E. "The Law and Economics of Incomplete Contracts." *Annual Review of Law and Social Science* 2, no. 1 (2006): 279-297.
Scott, Robert E., and Paul B. Stephan. *The Limits of Leviathan: Contract Theory and the Enforcement of International Law*. Cambridge: Cambridge University Press, 2006.
Scott, Robert E., and George G. Triantis. "Incomplete Contracts and the Theory of Contract Design." *Case Western Reserve Law Review* 56, no. 1 (2005): 187-201.
Setear, John K. "Responses to Breach of a Treaty and Rationalist International Relations Theory: The Rules of Release and Remediation in the Law of Treaties and the Law of State Responsibility." *Virginia Law Review* 83, no. 1 (1997): 1-126.
Shaffer, Gregory, and Mark A. Pollack. "Hard and Soft Law." In *Interdisciplinary Perspectives on International Law and International Relations: The State of the Art*, edited by Jeffrey L. Dunoff and Mark A. Pollack, 197-222. Cambridge: Cambridge University Press, 2013.
Shany, Yuval. *Assessing the Effectiveness of International Courts*. Oxford: Oxford University Press, 2014.
Sharkey, Catherine M. "Economic Analysis of Punitive Damages: Theory, Empirics, and Doctrine." In *Research Handbook on the Economics of Torts*, edited by Jennifer Arlen, 486-510. Cheltenham, UK: Edward Elgar, 2013.

Shavell, Steven. "Damage Measures for Breach of Contract." *Bell Journal of Economics* 11, no. 2 (1980a): 466-490.

———. "Strict Liability versus Negligence." *Journal of Legal Studies* 9, no. 1 (1980b): 1-25.

———. "Liability for Harm versus Regulation of Safety." *Journal of Legal Studies* 13, no. 2 (1984): 357-374.

———. *Economic Analysis of Accident Law*. Cambridge, MA: Harvard University Press, 1987.

———. *Foundations of Economic Analysis of Law*. Cambridge, MA: Belknap Press of Harvard University Press, 2004.

Shaw, Malcolm N. *International Law*. 7th ed. Cambridge: Cambridge University Press, 2014.

Shelton, Dinah. *Remedies in International Human Rights Law*. 3rd ed. Oxford: Oxford University Press, 2015.

———. "Reparations." In *Max Planck Encyclopedia of Public International Law*, edited by Anne Peters and Rüdiger Wolfrum. Oxford Public International Law: Oxford University Press, 2021. http://opil.ouplaw.com. Article last updated in August 2015.

Sicilianos, Linos-Alexander. "Countermeasures in Response to Grave Violations of Obligations Owed to the International Community." In *The Law of International Responsibility*, edited by James Crawford, Alain Pellet and Simon Olleson, 1137-1148. Oxford: Oxford University Press, 2010.

Simma, Bruno. "From Bilateralism to Community Interest in International Law." *Collected Courses of the Hague Academy of International Law* 250, no. 2 (1994): 217-384.

———. "Reciprocity." In *Max Planck Encyclopedia of Public International Law*, edited by Anne Peters and Rüdiger Wolfrum. Oxford Public International Law: Oxford University Press, 2021. http://opil.ouplaw.com. Article last updated in April 2008.

Simma, Bruno, and Andreas L. Paulus. "The 'International Community': Facing the Challenge of Globalization." *European Journal of International Law* 9, no. 2 (1998): 266-277.

Simma, Bruno, and Dirk Pulkowski. "*Leges Speciales* and Self-Contained Regimes." In *The Law of International Responsibility*, edited by James Crawford, Alain Pellet and Simon Olleson, 139-163. Oxford: Oxford University Press, 2010.

Simmons, Beth A. "Compliance with International Agreements." *Annual Review of Political Science* 1, no. 1 (1998): 75-93.

———. "International Law and State Behavior: Commitment and Compliance in International Monetary Affairs." *American Political Science Review* 94, no. 4 (2000): 819-835.

———. "Treaty Compliance and Violation." *Annual Review of Political Science* 13, no. 1 (2010): 273-296.

Slaughter, Anne-Marie. "International Law and International Relations." *Collected Courses of the Hague Academy of International Law* 285, no. 1 (2000): 9-249.

———. *A New World Order*. Princeton: Princeton University Press, 2004.

———. "Remarks, The Big Picture: Beyond Hot Spots & Crises in Our Interconnected World." *Penn State Journal of Law & International Affairs* 1, no. 2 (2012): 286-302.

Slaughter, Anne-Marie, Andrew S. Tulumello, and Stepan Wood. "International Law and International Relations Theory: A New Generation of Interdisciplinary Scholarship." *American Journal of International Law* 92, no. 3 (1998): 367-397.

Sloane, Robert D. "On the Use and Abuse of Necessity in the Law of State Responsibility." *American Journal of International Law* 106, no. 3 (2012): 447-508.

Snidal, Duncan. "The Limits of Hegemonic Stability Theory." *International Organization* 39, no. 4 (1985): 579-614.

———. "Rational Choice and International Relations." In *Handbook of International Relations*, edited by Walter Carlsnaes, Thomas Risse and Beth A. Simmons. 2nd ed., 85-112. London: SAGE, 2013.

Steinberg, Richard H. "Wanted - Dead or Alive: Realism in International Law." In *Interdisciplinary Perspectives on International Law and International Relations: The State of the Art*, edited by Jeffrey L. Dunoff and Mark A. Pollack, 146-172. Cambridge: Cambridge University Press, 2013.

Stern, Brigitte. "The Obligation to Make Reparation." In *The Law of International Responsibility*, edited by James Crawford, Alain Pellet and Simon Olleson, 563-571. Oxford: Oxford University Press, 2010.

Sullivan, Kathleen M. "Foreword: The Justices of Rules and Standards." *Harvard Law Review* 106, no. 1 (1992): 22-123.

Sunstein, Cass R. "Problems with Rules." *California Law Review* 83, no. 4 (1995): 953-1026.

Sykes, Alan O. "The Doctrine of Commercial Impracticability in a Second-Best World." *Journal of Legal Studies* 19, no. 1 (1990): 43-94.

———. "The Economics of Public International Law." *John M. Olin Program in Law and Economics Working Paper*, no. 216 (2004). https://chicagounbound.uchicago.edu/law_and_economics/515/.

———. "Public versus Private Enforcement of International Economic Law: Standing and Remedy." *Journal of Legal Studies* 34, no. 2 (2005): 631-666.

———., ed. *Economics of Tort Law*. 2 vols. Cheltenham, UK: Edward Elgar, 2007.

———. "Economic "Necessity" in International Law." *American Journal of International Law* 109, no. 2 (2015): 296-323.

Szurek, Sandra. "Circumstances Precluding Wrongfulness in the ILC Articles on State Responsibility: Distress." In *The Law of International Responsibility*, edited by James Crawford, Alain Pellet and Simon Olleson, 481-489. Oxford: Oxford University Press, 2010a.

———. "Circumstances Precluding Wrongfulness in the ILC Articles on State Responsibility: Force Majeure." In *The Law of International Responsibility*, edited by James Crawford, Alain Pellet and Simon Olleson, 475-480. Oxford: Oxford University Press, 2010b.

Talley, Eric L. "Law, Economics, and the Burden(S) of Proof." In *Research Handbook on the Economics of Torts*, edited by Jennifer Arlen, 305-329. Cheltenham, UK: Edward Elgar, 2013.

Tams, Christian J. *Enforcing Obligations Erga Omnes in International Law*. Cambridge: Cambridge University Press, 2005.

Tanzi, Attila. "Liability for Lawful Acts." In *Max Planck Encyclopedia of Public International Law*, edited by Anne Peters and Rüdiger Wolfrum. Oxford Public International Law: Oxford University Press, 2021a. http://opil.ouplaw.com. Article last updated in January 2021.

———. "Restitution." In *Max Planck Encyclopedia of Public International Law*, edited by Anne Peters and Rüdiger Wolfrum. Oxford Public International Law: Oxford University Press, 2021b. http://opil.ouplaw.com. Article last updated in January 2021.

———. "State of Necessity." In *Max Planck Encyclopedia of Public International Law*, edited by Anne Peters and Rüdiger Wolfrum. Oxford Public International Law: Oxford University Press, 2021c. http://opil.ouplaw.com. Article last updated in January 2021.

Thompson, Alexander. "The Rational Enforcement of International Law: Solving the Sanctioners' Dilemma." *International Theory* 1, no. 2 (2009): 307-321.

———. "Coercive Enforcement of International Law." In *Interdisciplinary Perspectives on International Law and International Relations: The State of the Art*, edited by Jeffrey L. Dunoff and Mark A. Pollack, 502-523. Cambridge: Cambridge University Press, 2013.

Thouvenin, Jean-Marc. "Circumstances Precluding Wrongfulness in the ILC Articles on State Responsibility: Self-Defence." In *The Law of International Responsibility*, edited by James Crawford, Alain Pellet and Simon Olleson, 455-467. Oxford: Oxford University Press, 2010.

Tietje, Christian, and Andrej Lang. "Community Interests in World Trade Law." *Beiträge zum Transnationalen Wirtschaftsrecht* Heft 141 (Dezember 2016).

———. "Community Interests in World Trade Law." In *Community Interests across International Law*, edited by Eyal Benvenisti and Georg Nolte, 191-220. Oxford: Oxford University Press, 2018.

Tirole, Jean. "Incomplete Contracts: Where Do We Stand?". *Econometrica* 67, no. 4 (1999): 741-781.

Trachtman, Joel P. *The Economic Structure of International Law*. Cambridge, MA: Harvard University Press, 2008.

———. "International Law and Domestic Political Coalitions: The Grand Theory of Compliance with International Law." *Chicago Journal of International Law* 11, no. 1 (2010): 127-158.

———. "Open Economy Law." In *Interdisciplinary Perspectives on International Law and International Relations: The State of the Art*, edited by Jeffrey L. Dunoff and Mark A. Pollack, 544-567. Cambridge: Cambridge University Press, 2013.

———. "Ex Ante and Ex Post Allocation of International Legal Responsibility." In *Distribution of Responsibilities in International Law*, edited by André Nollkaemper and Dov Jacobs, 87-119. Cambridge: Cambridge University Press, 2015.

van Aaken, Anne. *"Rational Choice" in der Rechtswissenschaft: Zum Stellenwert der ökonomischen Theorie im Recht.* Baden-Baden: Nomos, 2003.

———. "To Do Away with International Law? Some Limits to 'The Limits of International Law'." *European Journal of International Law* 17, no. 1 (2006a): 289-308.

———. "Zwischen Scylla und Charybdis: Völkerrechtlicher Staatsnotstand und Internationaler Investitionsschutz. Eine Anmerkung zur ICSID-Entscheidung CMS Gas Transmission Company v. Argentinien, 12.5.2005 - ICSID Case No. Arb/01/8." *Zeitschrift für Vergleichende Rechtswissenschaft (ZVglRWiss), Archiv für Internationales Wirtschaftsrecht* 105, no. 4 (2006b): 544-569.

———. "Effectuating Public International Law through Market Mechanisms?". *Journal of Institutional and Theoretical Economics (JITE)/Zeitschrift für die gesamte Staatswissenschaft* 165, no. 1 (2009a): 33-57.

———. "International Investment Law between Commitment and Flexibility: A Contract Theory Analysis." *Journal of International Economic Law* 12, no. 2 (2009b): 507-538.

———. "Primary and Secondary Remedies in Investment Arbitration and State Liability: A Functional and Comparative View." In *International Investment Law and Comparative Public Law*, edited by Stephan Schill, 721-754. Oxford: Oxford University Press 2010a.

———. "Trust, Verify, or Incentivize? Effectuating Public International Law Regulating Public Goods through Market Mechanisms." *Proceedings of the Annual Meeting (American Society of International Law)* 104 (2010b): 153-156.

———. "Opportunities for and Limits to an Economic Analysis of International Law." *Transnational Corporations Review* 3, no. 1 (2011): 27-46.

———. "Behavioral International Law and Economics." *Harvard International Law Journal* 55, no. 2 (2014): 421-481.

———. "On the Necessity of Necessity Measures: A Response to Alan O. Sykes." *AJIL Unbound* 109 (2015a): 181-186.

———. "Shared Responsibility in International Law: A Political Economy Analysis." In *Distribution of Responsibilities in International Law*, edited by André Nollkaemper and Dov Jacobs, 153-191. Cambridge: Cambridge University Press, 2015b.

———. "Is International Law Conducive to Preventing Looming Disasters?". *Global Policy* 7, Supplement 1 (2016): 81-96.

———. "Behavioral Aspects of the International Law of Global Public Goods and Common Pool Resources." *American Journal of International Law* 112, no. 1 (2018): 67-79.

———. "Die Befolgung des Völkerrechts zwischen Rationalismus, Konstruktivismus und Verhaltensökonomik." In *Warum befolgen wir Recht? Rechtsverbindlichkeit und Rechtsbefolgung in interdisziplinärer Perspektive*, edited by Patrick Hilbert and Jochen Rauber, 135-160. Tübingen: Mohr Siebeck, 2019.

———. "Rational Choice Theory." In *Oxford Bibliographies in International Law* edited by Anthony Carty. Oxford Bibliographies Online: Oxford University Press, 2021. Article last modified on 30 November 2015. doi:https://doi.org/10.1093/OBO/9780199796953-0051.

van Aaken, Anne, and Tomer Broude. "The Psychology of International Law: An Introduction." *European Journal of International Law* 30, no. 4 (2019): 1225-1236.

van Aaken, Anne, and Betül Simsek. "Rewarding in International Law." *American Journal of International Law* 115, no. 2 (2021): 195-241.

van Aaken, Anne, and Joel P. Trachtman. "Political Economy of International Law: Towards a Holistic Model of State Behavior." In *The Political Economy of International Law: A European Perspective*, edited by Alberta Fabbricotti, 9-43. Cheltenham, UK: Edward Elgar, 2016.

Vicary, Simon. "Transfers and the Weakest-Link: An Extension of Hirshleifer's Analysis." *Journal of Public Economics* 43, no. 3 (1990): 375–394.

Vicary, Simon, and Todd Sandler. "Weakest-Link Public Goods: Giving in-Kind or Transferring Money." *European Economic Review* 46, no. 8 (2002): 1501–1520.

Villalpando, Santiago. *L'émergence de la communauté internationale dans la responsabilité des Etats*. Paris: Presses universitaires de France, 2005.

———. "The Legal Dimension of the International Community: How Community Interests Are Protected in International Law." *European Journal of International Law* 21, no. 2 (2010): 387-419.

———. "Codification Light: A New Trend in the Codification of International Law at the United Nations." *VIII Anuário Brasileiro de Direito Internacional* 2, no. 15 (2013): 117-155.

Visscher, Louis T. "Justifications and Excuses in the Economic Analysis of Tort Law." *Rotterdam Institute of Law and Economics (RILE) Working Paper*, no. 3 (2008). https://ssrn.com/abstract=1111547.

———. "Economic Analysis of Punitive Damages." In *Punitive Damages: Common Law and Civil Law Perspectives*, edited by Helmut Koziol and Vanessa Wilcox, 219-236. Wien: Springer, 2009.

von Stein, Jana. "The Engines of Compliance." In *Interdisciplinary Perspectives on International Law and International Relations: The State of the Art*, edited by Jeffrey L. Dunoff and Mark A. Pollack, 477-501. Cambridge: Cambridge University Press, 2013.

Waibel, Michael. "Opening Pandora's Box: Sovereign Bonds in International Arbitration." *American Journal of International Law* 101, no. 4 (2007): 711-759.

Waltz, Kenneth N. *Theory of International Politics*. New York: McGraw-Hill, 1979.

Weber, Max. *Economy and Society: An Outline of Interpretive Sociology*. Edited by Guenther Roth and Claus Wittich. Berkeley: University of California Press, 1968. Reprint, 1978.

Wendt, Alexander. *Social Theory of International Politics*. Cambridge: Cambridge University Press, 1999.

Wijkman, Per Magnus. "Managing the Global Commons." *International Organization* 36, no. 3 (1982): 511-535.

Wilde, Ralph. "Socioeconomic Rights, Extraterritorially." In *Community Interests across International Law*, edited by Eyal Benvenisti and Georg Nolte, 381-395. Oxford: Oxford University Press, 2018.

Wittich, Stephan. "Punitive Damages." In *The Law of International Responsibility*, edited by James Crawford, Alain Pellet and Simon Olleson, 667-675. Oxford: Oxford University Press, 2010.

———. "Compensation." In *Max Planck Encyclopedia of Public International Law*, edited by Anne Peters and Rüdiger Wolfrum. Oxford Public International Law: Oxford University Press, 2021. http://opil.ouplaw.com. Article last updated in May 2008.

Wuerth, Ingrid. "Compliance." In *Concepts for International Law: Contributions to Disciplinary Thought*, edited by Jean d'Aspremont and Sahib Singh, 117-126. Cheltenham, UK: Edward Elgar, 2019.

Wyler, Eric. "From 'State Crime' to Responsibility for 'Serious Breaches of Obligations under Peremptory Norms of General International Law'." *European Journal of International Law* 13, no. 5 (2002): 1147-1160.

Wyler, Eric, and Alain Papaux. "The Different Forms of Reparation: Satisfaction." In *The Law of International Responsibility*, edited by James Crawford, Alain Pellet and Simon Olleson, 623-637. Oxford: Oxford University Press, 2010.

Zamir, Eyal, and Doron Teichman. *Behavioral Law and Economics*. New York: Oxford University Press, 2018.

Zemanek, Karl. "New Trends in the Enforcement of Erga Omnes Obligations." *Max Planck Yearbook of United Nations Law* 4 (2000): 1-52.

Table of Cases

Accordance with International Law of the Unilateral Declaration of Independence in Respect of Kosovo, Advisory Opinion, 22 July 2010, ICJ Reports 2010, p. 403.

Affaire de L'indemnité Russe (Russie contre Turquie), Award, 11 November 1912, RIAA, Volume XI, p. 421.

Air Service Agreement of 27 March 1946 between the United States of America and France, Award, 9 December 1978, RIAA, Volume XVIII, p. 417.

Alabama (United States of America v. Great Britain), Award, 14 September 1872, RIAA, Volume XXIX, p. 125.

Application of the Convention on the Prevention and Punishment of the Crime of Genocide (Bosnia and Herzegovina v. Serbia and Montenegro), Judgment, 26 February 2007, ICJ Reports 2007, p. 43.

Application of the Convention on the Prevention and Punishment of the Crime of Genocide (Bosnia and Herzegovina v. Yugoslavia), Order (Counter-Claims), 17 December 1997, ICJ Reports 1997, p. 243.

Application of the Convention on the Prevention and Punishment of the Crime of Genocide (Bosnia and Herzegovina v. Yugoslavia (Serbia and Montenegro)), Order (Provisional Measures), 13 September 1993, ICJ Reports 1993, p. 325.

Application of the Convention on the Prevention and Punishment of the Crime of Genocide (Bosnia and Herzegovina v. Yugoslavia), Judgment (Preliminary Objections), 11 July 1996, ICJ Reports 1996, p. 595.

Application of the Convention on the Prevention and Punishment of the Crime of Genocide (Croatia v. Serbia), Judgment, 3 February 2015, ICJ Reports 2015, p. 3.

Application of the Convention on the Prevention and Punishment of the Crime of Genocide (The Gambia v. Myanmar), Order (Provisional Measures), 23 January 2020, ICJ Reports 2020, p. 3.

Application of the Convention on the Prevention and Punishment of the Crime of Genocide in the Gaza Strip (South Africa v. Israel), Order (Provisional Measures), 26 January 2024, ICJ Reports 2024, p. 1.

Armed Activities on the Territory of the Congo (Democratic Republic of the Congo v. Rwanda) (New Application: 2002) Judgment (Jurisdiction of the Court and Admissibility of the Application), 3 February 2006, ICJ Reports 2006, p. 6.

Armed Activities on the Territory of the Congo (Democratic Republic of the Congo v. Uganda), Judgment (Reparations), 9 February 2022, ICJ Reports 2022, p. 1.

Austria v. Italy, Decision on admissibility, 11 January 1961, European Commission of Human Rights (Application No. 788/60).

Avena and Other Mexican Nationals (Mexico v. United States of America), Judgment, 31 March 2004, ICJ Reports 2004, p. 12.

Barcelona Traction, Light and Power Company, Limited (Belgium v. Spain) (New Application: 1962), Judgment (Second Phase), 5 February 1970, ICJ Reports 1970, p. 3.

Brazilian Loans, Judgment, 12 July 1929, PCIJ Series A, No. 21, p. 93.

Cargill, Incorporated v. United Mexican States, Award, 18 September 2009, ICSID Case No. ARB (AF)/05/2.

CMS Gas Transmission Company v. Argentine Republic, Award, 12 May 2005, ICSID Case No. ARB/01/8.

CMS Gas Transmission Company v. Argentine Republic, Decision on the application for annulment, 25 September 2007, ICSID Case No. ARB/01/8.

Corfu Channel (United Kingdom of Great Britain and Northern Ireland v. Albania), Judgment (Merits), 9 April 1949, ICJ Reports 1949, p. 4.

Difference between New Zealand and France Concerning the Interpretation or Application of two Agreements concluded on 9 July 1986 between the two States and Which Related to the Problems Arising from the Rainbow Warrior Affair, Award, 30 April 1990, RIAA, Volume XX, p. 215.

East Timor (Portugal v. Australia), Judgment, 30 June 1995, ICJ Reports 1995, p. 90.
Factory at Chorzów (Germany v. Poland), Judgment (Jurisdiction), 26 July 1927, PCIJ Series A, No. 9, p. 4.
Factory at Chorzów (Germany v. Poland), Judgment (Merits), 13 September 1928, PCIJ Series A, No. 17, p. 4.
Fisheries Jurisdiction (Spain v. Canada), Judgment (Jurisdiction of the Court), 4 December 1998, ICJ Reports 1998, p. 432.
Gabčíkovo-Nagymaros Project (Hungary v. Slovakia), Judgment, 25 September 1997, ICJ Reports 1997, p. 7.
Impregilo S.P.A. v. Argentine Republic, Award, 21 June 2011, ICSID Case No. ARB/07/17.
Jurisdictional Immunities of the State (Germany v. Italy: Greece Intervening), Judgment, 3 February 2012, ICJ Reports 2012, p. 99.
Lac Lanoux (Spain v. France), Award, 16 November 1957, RIAA, Volume XII, p. 281.
LaGrand (Germany v. United States of America), Judgment, 27 June 2001, ICJ Reports 2001, p. 466.
Legal Consequences for States of the Continued Presence of South Africa in Namibia (South West Africa) notwithstanding Security Council Resolution 276 (1970), Advisory Opinion, 21 June 1971, ICJ Reports 1971, p. 16.
Legal Consequences of the Construction of a Wall in the Occupied Palestinian Territory, Advisory Opinion, 9 July 2004, ICJ Reports 2004, p. 136.
Legal Consequences of the Separation of the Chagos Archipelago from Mauritius in 1965, Advisory Opinion, 25 February 2019, ICJ Reports 2019, p. 95.
Legality of the Threat or Use of Nuclear Weapons, Advisory Opinion, 8 July 1996, ICJ Reports 1996, p. 226.
LG&E Energy Corp., LG&E Capital Corp., and LG&E International Inc. v. Argentine Republic, Decision on Liability, 3 October 2006, ICSID Case No. ARB/02/1.
M/V "Saiga" (No. 2) (Saint Vincent and the Grenadines v. Guinea), Judgment, 1 July 1999, ITLOS Reports 1999, p. 10.
Military and Paramilitary Activities in and against Nicaragua (Nicaragua v. United States of America), Judgment (Merits), 27 June 1986, ICJ Reports 1986, p. 14.
National Grid Plc v. Argentine Republic, Award, 3 November 2008, UNCITRAL arbitration case 1: 09-cv-00248-RBW.
Patrick Mitchell v. Democratic Republic of the Congo, Decision on the Application for the Annulment of the Award, 1 November 2006, ICSID Case No. ARB/99/7.
Pulp Mills on the River Uruguay (Argentina v. Uruguay), Judgment, 20 April 2010, ICJ Reports 2010, p. 14.
Questions Relating to the Obligation to Prosecute or Extradite (Belgium v. Senegal), Judgment, 20 July 2012, ICJ Reports 2012, p. 422.
Responsibilité de l'Allemagne à raison des dommages causés dans les colonies portugaises du Sud de l'Afrique (sentence sur le principe de la responsabilité) (Portugal contre Allemagne), Award, 31 July 1928, RIAA, Volume II, p. 1011.
Responsibilities and Obligations of States with Respect to Activities in the Area, Advisory Opinion, 1 February 2011, ITLOS Reports 2011, p. 10.
Russia – Measures Concerning Traffic in Transit (Ukraine v Russian Federation), Panel Report, 5 April 2019, WT/DS512/R.
S.S. "Wimbledon", Judgment, 17 August 1923, PCIJ Series A, No. 1, p. 15.
Sempra Energy International v. Argentine Republic, Award, 28 September 2007, ICSID Case No. ARB/02/16.
Serbian Loans, Judgment, 12 July 1929, PCIJ Series A, No. 20, p. 5.
Société Commerciale de Belgique, Judgment, 15 June 1939, PCIJ Series A/B, No. 78, p. 160.
Suez, Sociedad General de Aguas de Barcelona Sa and Vivendi Universal Sa v. Argentine Republic, Decision on Liability, 30 July 2010, ICSID Case No ARB/03/19.

Trail Smelter (United States of America v. Canada), Award, 16 April 1938 and 11 March 1941, RIAA, Volume III, p. 1905.
United States Diplomatic and Consular Staff in Tehran (United States of America v. Iran), Judgment, 24 May 1980, ICJ Reports 1980, p. 3.
Urbaser S.A. And Consorcio de Aguas Bilbao Bizkaia, Bilbao Biskaia Ur Partzuergoa v. Argentine Republic, Award, 8 December 2016, ICSID Case No. ARB/07/26.
Whaling in the Antarctic (Australia v. Japan: New Zealand Intervening), Judgment, 31 March 2014, ICJ Reports 2014, p. 226.

Table of Treaties

Agreement Establishing the World Trade Organization (WTO Agreement) (concluded at Marrakesh on 15 April 1994, entered into force 1 January 1995) 33 *ILM* 1144.

Agreement for the Implementation of the Provisions of the United Nations Convention on the Law of the Sea of 10 December 1982 Relating to the Conservation and Management of Straddling Fish Stocks and Highly Migratory Fish Stocks (concluded 4 August 1995, entered into force 11 December 2001) 2167 *UNTS* 3.

Agreement on Trade-Related Aspects of Intellectual Property Rights, Annex 1C of the Agreement Establishing the World Trade Organization (WTO Agreement) (concluded at Marrakesh on 15 April 1994, entered into force 1 January 1995) 33 *ILM* 1197.

Basel Convention on the Control of Transboundary Movements of Hazardous Wastes and Their Disposal (Basel Convention) (concluded 22 March 1989, entered into force 5 May 1992) 1673 *UNTS* 57.

Charter of the United Nations (UN Charter) (concluded 26 June 1945, entered into force 24 October 1945, as amended 24 September 1973) 892 *UNTS* 119.

Convention against Torture and other Cruel, Inhuman or Degrading Treatment or Punishment (Torture Convention) (concluded 10 December 1984, entered into force 26 June 1987) 1465 *UNTS* 85.

Convention on Civil Liability for Damage Resulting from Activities Dangerous to the Environment (opened for signature 21 June 1993, not yet entered into force) Council of Europe Treaty No. 150.

Convention on International Liability for Damage Caused by Space Objects (concluded 29 March 1972, entered into force 1 September 1972) 961 *UNTS* 187.

Convention on International Trade in Endangered Species of Wild Fauna and Flora (CITES) (concluded 3 March 1973, entered into force 1 July 1975) 993 *UNTS* 243.

Convention on Supplementary Compensation for Nuclear Damage (concluded 12 September 1997, entered into force 15 April 2015) 3038 *UNTS* 41.

Convention on the Law of the Non-Navigational Uses of International Watercourses (concluded 21 May 1997, entered into force 17 August 2014) 2999 *UNTS* 120.

Convention on the Prevention and Punishment of the Crime of Genocide (Genocide Convention) (concluded 9 December 1948, entered into force 12 January 1951) 78 *UNTS* 277.

Convention on the Prevention of Marine Pollution by Dumping of Wastes and other Matter (concluded 29 December 1972, entered into force 30 August 1975) 1046 *UNTS* 120.

Convention on the Protection and Use of Transboundary Watercourses and International Lakes (concluded 17 March 1992, entered into force 6 October 1996) 1936 *UNTS* 269.

Convention on the Transboundary Effects of Industrial Accidents (concluded 17 March 1992, entered into force 19 April 2000) 2105 *UNTS* 457.

Convention on Wetlands of International Importance Especially as Waterfowl Habitat (Ramsar Convention) (concluded 2 February 1971, entered into force 21 December 1975) 996 *UNTS* 245.

European Convention for the Protection of Human Rights and Fundamental Freedoms (ECHR) (concluded 4 November 1950, entered into force 3 September 1953) 213 *UNTS* 221.

General Agreement on Trade in Services (GATS), Annex 1B of the Agreement Establishing the World Trade Organization (WTO Agreement) (concluded at Marrakesh on 15 April 1994, entered into force 1 January 1995) 33 *ILM* 1168.

Geneva Convention for the Amelioration of the Condition of the Wounded and Sick in Armed Forces in the Field (Geneva Convention I) (concluded 12 August 1949, entered into force 21 October 1950) 75 *UNTS* 31.

Geneva Convention for the Amelioration of the Condition of the Wounded, Sick and Shipwrecked Members of the Armed Forces at Sea (Geneva Convention II) (concluded 12 August 1949, entered into force 21 October 1950) 75 *UNTS* 85.

Geneva Convention Relative to the Protection of Civilian Persons in Time of War (Geneva Convention IV) (concluded 12 August 1949, entered into force 21 October 1950) 75 *UNTS* 287.

Geneva Convention Relative to the Treatment of Prisoners of War (Geneva Convention III) (concluded 12 August 1949, entered into force 21 October 1950) 75 *UNTS* 135.

Hague Convention Respecting the Laws and Customs of War on Land and its Annex: Regulations Concerning the Laws and Customs of War on Land (Hague Convention IV) (concluded 18 October 1907, entered into force 26 January 1910) International Peace Conference, The Hague, Official Record.

International Convention for the Prevention of Pollution of the Sea by Oil (concluded 12 May 1954, entered into force 26 July 1958) 327 *UNTS* 3.

International Convention on Civil Liability for Oil Pollution Damage (concluded 29 November 1969, entered into force 19 June 1975) 973 *UNTS* 3.

International Convention on Liability and Compensation for Damage in Connection with the Carriage of Hazardous and Noxious Substances by Sea (concluded 1996, amended 2010, not yet entered into force) *International Maritime Organization.*

International Convention on the Establishment of an International Fund for Compensation for Oil Pollution Damage (concluded 18 December 1971, entered into force 16 October 1978) 1110 *UNTS* 57.

International Convention Relating to Intervention on the High Seas in Cases of Oil Pollution Casualties (concluded 29 November 1969, entered into force 6 May 1975) 970 *UNTS* 211.

International Covenant on Civil and Political Rights (concluded 16 December 1966, entered into force 23 March 1976) 999 *UNTS* 171.

Kyoto Protocol to the United Nations Framework Convention on Climate Change (Kyoto Protocol) (concluded 11 December 1997, entered into force 16 February 2005) 2303 *UNTS* 162.

Montreal Protocol on Substances that Deplete the Ozone Layer (Montreal Protocol) (concluded 16 September 1987, entered into force 1 January 1989) 1522 *UNTS* 28.

Multilateral Agreements on Trade in Goods, General Agreement on Tariffs and Trade (GATT), Annex 1A of the Agreement Establishing the World Trade Organization (WTO Agreement) (concluded at Marrakesh on 15 April 1994, entered into force 1 January 1995) 33 *ILM* 1154.

Paris Agreement (concluded 12 December 2015, entered into force 4 November 2016) 55 *ILM* 743.

Protocol Additional to the Geneva Conventions of 12 August 1949, and Relating to the Protection of Victims of International Armed Conflicts (Protocol I) (concluded 8 June 1977, entered into force 7 December 1978) 1125 *UNTS* 3.

Protocol on Civil Liability and Compensation for Damage Caused by the Transboundary Effects of Industrial Accidents on Transboundary Waters (concluded on 21 May 2003, not yet entered into force) 44 *ILM* 258.

Rome Statute of the International Criminal Court (concluded 17 July 1998, entered into force 1 July 2002) 2187 *UNTS* 3.

Statute of the International Court of Justice (ICJ Statute) (concluded 26 June 1945, entered into force 24 October 1945) 15 *UNCIO* 355.

Understanding on Rules and Procedures Governing the Settlement of Disputes (DSU), Annex 2 of the Agreement Establishing the World Trade Organization (WTO Agreement) (concluded at Marrakesh on 15 April 1994, entered into force 1 January 1995) 33 *ILM* 1226.

UNESCO Convention for the Protection of the World Cultural and Natural Heritage (concluded 16 November 1972, entered into force 7 December 1975) 1037 *UNTS* 151.

United Nations Convention on Contracts for the International Sale of Goods (concluded 11 April 1980, entered into force 1 January 1988) 1489 *UNTS* 3.

United Nations Convention on the Law of the Sea (UNCLOS) (concluded 10 December 1982, entered into force 16 November 1994) 1833 *UNTS* 397.

United Nations Framework Convention on Climate Change (UNFCCC) (concluded 9 May 1992, entered into force 21 March 1994) 1771 *UNTS* 107.

Vienna Convention for the Protection of the Ozone Layer (concluded 22 March 1985, entered into force 22 September 1988) 1513 *UNTS* 293.

Vienna Convention on Civil Liability for Nuclear Damage (concluded 21 May 1963, entered into force 12 November 1977) 1063 *UNTS* 265.
Vienna Convention on Consular Relations (concluded 24 April 1963, entered into force 19 March 1967) 596 *UNTS* 261.
Vienna Convention on Diplomatic Relations (concluded 18 April 1961, entered into force 24 April 1964) 500 *UNTS* 95.
Vienna Convention on the Law of Treaties (VCLT) (concluded 23 May 1969, entered into force 27 January 1980) 1155 *UNTS* 331.

Table of International Documents

Declaration of the United Nations Conference on Environment and Development, Rio de Janeiro, 14 June 1992 (UN Doc. A/CONF.151/26/Rev.1 (Vol. I)).
Declaration of the United Nations Conference on the Human Environment, Stockholm, 16 June 1972 (UN Doc. A/CONF.48/14/Rev.1).
Institut de Droit International, *Obligations Erga Omnes in International Law*, Resolution, Krakow Session (2005).
International Law Association, *Due Diligence in International Law*, Second Report, Johannesburg Conference (2016), https://www.ila-hq.org/index.php/study-groups.
International Task Force on Global Public Goods, *Meeting Global Challenges: International Cooperation in the National Interest*, Final Report, Stockholm, Sweden (2006), https://ycsg.yale.edu/sites/default/files/files/meeting_global_challenges_global_public_goods.pdf.
United Nations General Assembly, Resolution 56/83, *Responsibility of States for Internationally Wrongful Acts*, 12 December 2001 (UN Doc. A/RES/56/83).
United Nations General Assembly, Resolution 62/68, *Consideration of Prevention of Transboundary Harm from Hazardous Activities and Allocation of Loss in the Case of Such Harm*, 6 December 2007 (UN Doc. A/RES/62/68).
United Nations General Assembly, Resolution 74/189, *Consideration of Prevention of Transboundary Harm from Hazardous Activities and Allocation of Loss in the Case of Such Harm*, 18 December 2019 (UN Doc. A/RES/74/189).
United Nations General Assembly, Resolution 377 (V), Uniting for Peace, 3 November 1950 (UN Doc. A/RES/377(V)).
United Nations General Assembly, Resolution 2625 (XXV), *Declaration on Principles of International Law Concerning Friendly Relations and Cooperation among States in Accordance with the Charter of the United Nations*, 24 October 1970 (UN Doc. A/8082).
United Nations International Law Commission, "Articles on the Prevention of Transboundary Harm from Hazardous Activites," in *Report of the Commission to the General Assembly on the Work of its Fifty-Third Session*, 2001 (UN Doc. A/56/10), in *Yearbook of the International Law Commission*, 2001, Volume II, Part Two (UN Doc. A/CN.4/SER.A/2001/Add.1 (Part 2)).
United Nations International Law Commission, "Commentaries to the Draft Articles on Responsibility of States for Internationally Wrongful Acts," in *Report of the Commission to the General Assembly on the Work of its Fifty-Third Session*, 2001 (UN Doc. A/56/10), in *Yearbook of the International Law Commission*, 2001, Volume II, Part Two (UN Doc. A/CN.4/SER.A/2001/Add.1 (Part 2)).
United Nations International Law Commission, "Draft Articles on Diplomatic Protection," in *Report of the Commission to the General Assembly on the Work of its Fifty-Eighth Session*, 2006 (UN Doc. A/61/10).
United Nations International Law Commission, "Draft Articles on Responsibility of States for Internationally Wrongful Acts," in *Report of the Commission to the General Assembly on the Work of its Fifty-Third Session*, 2001 (UN Doc. A/56/10), in *Yearbook of the International Law Commission*, 2001, Volume II, Part Two (UN Doc. A/CN.4/SER.A/2001/Add.1 (Part 2)).
United Nations International Law Commission, "Draft Articles on State Responsibility," in *Report of the Commission to the General Assembly on the Work of its Forty-Eighth Session*, 1996 (UN Doc. A/51/10), in *Yearbook of the International Law Commission*, 1996, Volume II, Part Two (UN Doc. A/CN.4/SER.A/1996/Add.1 (Part 2)).
United Nations International Law Commission, "Draft Articles on State Responsibility," in *Report of the Commission to the General Assembly on the Work of its Twenty-Eighth Session*, 1976 (UN Doc. A/31/10), in *Yearbook of the International Law Commission*, 1976, Volume II, Part Two (UN Doc. A/CN.4/SER.A/1976/Add.1 (Part 2)).
———, "Draft Articles on the Law of Treaties with Commentaries," *in Report of the Commission to the General Assembly on the Work of its Eighteenth Session*, 1966 (UN Doc. A/21/9), in

Yearbook of the International Law Commission, 1966, Volume II (UN Doc. A/CN.4/SER.A/1966/Add.1).
United Nations International Law Commission, "Draft Principles on the Allocation of Loss in the Case of Transboundary Harm Arising out of Hazardous Activities," in *Report of the Commission to the General Assembly on the Work of its Fifty-Eighth Session*, 2006 (UN Doc. A/61/10), in *Yearbook of the International Law Commission*, 2006, Volume II, Part Two (UN Doc. A/CN.4/SER.A/2006/Add.1 (Part 2).
United Nations International Law Commission, *Addendum to the Eighth Report on State Responsibility by Special Rapporteur Roberto Ago*, Thirty-Second Session, 1980, in *Yearbook of the International Law Commission*, 1980, Volume II, Part One (UN Doc. A/CN.4/318/Add.5-7).
United Nations International Law Commission, *First Report on Jus Cogens by Special Rapporteur Dire Tladi*, Sixty-Eighth Session, 2016 (UN Doc. A/CN.4/693).
United Nations International Law Commission, *Fourth Report on Peremptory Norms of General International Law (Jus Cogens) by Special Rapporteur Dire Tladi*, Seventy-First Session, 2019 (UN Doc. A/CN.4/727).
United Nations International Law Commission, Fourth Report on State Responsibility by Special Rapporteur James Crawford, Fifty-Third Session, 2001 (UN Doc. A/CN.4/517).
United Nations International Law Commission, *Second Report on Jus Cogens by Special Rapporteur Dire Tladi*, Sixty-Ninth Session, 2017 (UN Doc. A/CN.4/706).
United Nations International Law Commission, *Second Report on State Responsibility by Special Rapporteur James Crawford*, Fifty-First Session, 1999 (UN Doc. A/CN.4/498).
United Nations International Law Commission, *Third Report on Peremptory Norms of General International Law (Jus Cogens) by Special Rapporteur Dire Tladi*, Seventieth Session, 2018 (UN Doc. A/CN.4/714).
United Nations International Law Commission, *Third Report on State Responsibility by Special Rapporteur James Crawford*, Fifty-Second Session, 2000 (UN Doc. A/CN.4/507).
United Nations International Law Commission, *Yearbook of the International Law Commission*, 1980, Volume II, Part Two (UN Doc. A/CN.4/Ser. A/1980/Add. 1 (Part 2)).
United Nations International Law Commission, *Yearbook of the International Law Commission*, 1999, Volume I (UN Doc. A/CN.4/SER.A/1999).
United Nations International Law Commission, *Yearbook of the International Law Commission*, 1999, Volume II, Part Two (UN Doc. A/CN.4/SER.A/1999/Add.1 (Part 2)).
United Nations Secretary-General, "Responsibility of States for Internationally Wrongful Acts: Compilation of Decisions of International Courts, Tribunals and other Bodies," in *Reports to the General Assembly*, Sixty-Second Session, 2007 (UN Doc. A/62/62 and A/62/62/Add.1), Sixty-Fifth Session, 2010 (UN Doc. A/65/76), Sixty-Eighth Session, 2013 (UN Doc. A/68/72), Seventy-First Session, 2016 (UN Doc. A/71/80), Seventy-Fourth Session, 2019 (UN Doc. A/74/83), and Seventy-Seventh Session, 2022 (UN Doc. A/77/74).
United Nations Security Council, Resolution 418 (1977) on the Establishment of an Arms Embargo against South Africa, 4 November 1977 (UN Doc. S/RES/418(1977)).

The manufacturer's authorised representative in the EU is Springer Nature Customer Service Centre GmbH, Europaplatz 3, 69115 Heidelberg, Germany. If you have any concerns regarding our products, please contact ProductSafety@springernature.com

Printed and bound by CPI Group (UK) Ltd, Croydon, CR0 4YY
01/10/2026
02225950-0016